THE PERFECT LION

The Perfect Lion

The Life and Death of Confederate Artillerist John Pelham

Jerry H. Maxwell

THE UNIVERSITY OF ALABAMA PRESS

Tuscaloosa

Typeface: AGarmond

∞

The paper on which this book is printed meets the minimum requirements of
American National Standard for Information Sciences-Permanence of Paper for
Printed Library Materials, ANSI Z39.48-1984.

Library of Congress Cataloging-in-Publication Data

Maxwell, Jerry H. (Jerry Hollis), 1942–
The perfect lion : the life and death of Confederate artillerist John Pelham / Jerry
H. Maxwell.
p. cm.
Includes bibliographical references and index.
ISBN 978-0-8173-1735-5 (cloth : alk. paper) — ISBN 978-0-8173-8548-4
(electronic) 1. Pelham, John, 1838–1863. 2. Soldiers—Confederate States of
America—Biography. 3. Confederate States of America. Army—Biography.
4. United States—History—Civil War, 1861–1865—Artillery operations. I. Title.
E467.1.P36M39 2011
973.7′42092—dc22
[B]

2010045693

Front cover: John Pelham 1861. John Pelham Association Archives,
Jacksonville, Alabama, Public Library.

This book is dedicated to my grandchildren, Will and Sofia.
May they someday realize their legacy within these pages.

Contents

Preface

In twenty-seven years of teaching Civil War history my earliest hero, who remains so to this day, was Stonewall Jackson. Gradually, I took on a second idol, Jeb Stuart. My extended readings on these two brought my attention to an artillerist in his mid-twenties: John Pelham. I found that Pelham and Stuart were so completely intertwined during the Civil War that they seemed inseparable. Furthermore, the normally reticent Jackson, who praised his God first after every victory, was quick to acknowledge Pelham's heroics in glowing terms. Who else could have sparked the comment: "With a Pelham on each flank, I believe I could whip the world"? In my readings I found that Pelham possibly came as near to being the "perfect soldier" as any who fought in the war. Moreover, not only were his military techniques highly praised, he was considered by Northern and Southern contemporaries alike as a gentleman of the truest nineteenth-century ideals. Fellow West Pointers, all Northerners, extolled Pelham's virtues: "a discourteous act was wholly foreign to [Pelham's] nature," "Nature was in a fine mood when she moulded his clay," "He was . . . the kind of man whom you felt instinctively, 'Here is a friend.'" George Armstrong Custer supposedly sent Pelham a congratulatory note following the Battle of Fredericksburg: "I rejoice, dear Pelham, in your success." His roommate, Texan Tom Rosser, flatly stated, "[Pelham] was the mildest, gentlest man out of a fight and the fiercest man in a fight I ever knew." Numerous officers and countless common soldiers named their own children after Pelham. Quite naturally this youthful, modest warrior appealed to me as well as my students.

I continued to pursue Pelham's exploits, reading about Antietam where his placement and movement of his cannons helped the Confederates stave off defeat in the morning hours at the Miller cornfield and at Fredericksburg where he held off more than a division of men for an hour with a lone cannon. I wondered how could this have happened; was it simply Southern myth? In 1972 I joined a Civil War Round Table group. I later became a member of the John Pelham Historical Association. For the past thirty-five years I have given thirty to fifty talks per year to other Round Table groups, historical societies, universities, high schools, and middle schools on a wide variety of Civil War topics. And always in the back of my mind I could not forget the passion that Pelham generated from his contemporaries.

My frustration came in the lack of solid biographies of Pelham. I was troubled that the three major books on his life (published in 1929, 1959, and 1960) all contained deficiencies: lack of footnoting, glowing errors in content, omissions, and conflicting information, as well as brief bibliographies. Although each biography included excellent foundational material, something seemed to be missing in all of them. Pelham's mortal wounding and death, as well publicized as they were, remained shrouded in mystery. How could so many who were there have such varied opinions on those circumstances? Even his love life has often been misrepresented. Did three women actually put on black mourning clothes for his funeral? And what were the facts of his relationship with Sallie Dandridge and Bessie Shackelford? As I told every Civil War class I taught, "Someday I am going to write a worthwhile biography on Pelham" with the intention of eliminating these failures. In my book I have liberally employed footnotes, many of them lengthy, to explain further information and include differing contemporary accounts before stating with a certain amount of reason why I came to various conclusions. I hope readers will find the endnotes useful and fulfilling.

As my research progressed over the years, I wondered if even half of the glowing accounts of Pelham's heroics were true. Was he lionized because of his age, good looks, and early death? Was he a legitimate Confederate icon or simply cherished by the "lost cause" to symbolize the Confederacy's ultimate defeat? Certainly he was immortalized in romantic post–Civil War poetry and the near tearful accounts of his military deeds and the sadness of his tragic early death. But had his adventures been overblown to excite a younger generation? Other questions, some of them conjectural, kept cropping up. What more would he have accomplished had he lived? Did he die at the "right time," just as the Confederacy began to decline in military prowess? What might he have accomplished at Gettysburg had he been there? Was he destined to suffer defeats, as did his Confederate counterparts, when the Union army improved in leadership, cavalry, and artillery techniques? Had he survived the war, it is entirely possible that his legacy might have been tainted in comparison to the near sainthood many bestow on him today.

Confederate artillerists received fewer promotions than those in other branches of military service, and Pelham's elevations in rank often came equally as slow. Readers must keep in mind that at the time of his death, Pelham was twenty-four and looked even younger. Yet, numerous contemporaries stated that without question he should have been awarded the rank of general. "Had he been spared," penned Jeb Stuart's astute adjutant, Channing Price, "another great battle would have made him a general." Stuart himself maintained, "No field grade is too high for [Pelham's] merit and capacity." Even Europeans read of Pelham, as the *London Times* editorialized, "No one of an equal age in either army has won an equal reputation." It is certainly possible that had Pelham been promoted to general, he might have lost his autonomy on the battlefield, where he was often given discretionary orders or simply acted swiftly to the sound of battle. Instead, he might have been restricted to a behind-the-scenes posture, thus removing one of his greatest assets as a horse artillerist.

Included in this work are various accounts that have not yet been published. One brief tale informs readers of a fistfight between Pelham, a cadet of only two weeks at West Point, and a senior from New York of much larger stature. Another tells of Pelham's embarrassment at his inability to enforce military discipline on local militia when he first returned home from the academy.

I believe this work will correct most mistakes and clear up discrepancies from earlier biographies and will appeal to those who are familiar with John Pelham's military deeds. It should also attract an audience that is mildly acquainted with or totally new to him. As many accolades as he has received, I think he has not been given his just due. I hope my fascination for the subject, who in reality was a mere speck on the battlefield, will carry over to readers and that they will recognize him for what he was, "The Perfect Lion."

Acknowledgments

Perhaps the most gratifying phase in the completion of writing a book is the author's chance to thank those who in some fashion assisted or inspired the endeavors in that work. I am indebted to so many scholars, associates, and historians, as well as a variety of institutions where help was always available. Friends and family were ever present, persistently inquiring about the book's status. To all of them I submit my sincerest expression of gratitude.

Numerous libraries, depositories, and private collections provided a great variety of material, and staff members offered kindness and professionalism. I wish to thank the Jacksonville Public Library, where I started my quest on John Pelham. Former chief librarian Kathryn Childress (now retired) and her staff were gracious and generous. Current librarian assistant Stephanie Surrett has willingly helped me, even answering a few of my inane questions. The "Alabama Room" staff, Dianne Betts and Tom Mullins of the Anniston-Calhoun County Public Library, was exemplary. I won't soon forget their eager assistance as they hauled out boxes of Pelham material and simply said, "Help yourself." Archivist Jim Baggett of the Birmingham Public Library willingly allowed me the use of the Fred Martin newspaper clipping collection, which benefited my research greatly. Diane Santia of the Commerce Township Public Library in Michigan patiently assisted me by finding sources through the interlibrary lending program.

The United States Military Academy staff at West Point answered all of my questions and sent material, and I wish to thank archivist Charlyn Richardson and manuscripts curator Susan Lintelman for their efforts. Paul Harrison of the National Archives assisted me in finding leads from the vast file of source material there, and Kevin D. Moriarty from the Library of Congress willingly offered his help and patiently answered all of the questions I posed to him.

The Alabama Department of Archives and History in Montgomery presented a treasure trove of John Pelham material, and I am indebted to chief curator Robert Bradley and senior archivist Nancy Dupree for their considerable kindness in allowing me to handle and photograph some of Pelham's personal effects. Staff members Frazine Taylor, Rickie Brunner, and Norwood Kerr were also mighty helpful and tolerant in working with me.

I also wish to thank E. Lee Shepard, the director of manuscripts and archives at the Virginia Historical Society in Richmond, Virginia, as well as Frances Pollard for their diligence and professionalism. Research services librarian, Janie C. Morris, from Duke University's Rare Books, Manuscript and Special Collections Library in Durham, North Carolina, provided me with a copy of the highly treasured Pelham note written from Evelynton Heights. Susan M. Collins, the curator of the Jefferson County Museum in Charles Town, West Virginia, graciously allowed me the use of George W. Shreve's "Reminiscences" from the Roger Preston Chew Papers. Reference archivist Susan Boone of Smith College in Northampton, Massachusetts, deserves thanks for allowing me to use a little-known Pelham letter from the Garrison Family Papers, Sophia Smith Collection. Meg Hughes and Meghan Holder of the Valentine History Center in Richmond, Virginia, were extraordinarily helpful and patient with my incessant questions. I also wish to thank Robert Brett Bradshaw, the acting president of the John Pelham Historical Association, for allowing me permission to publish photographs of John Pelham and Sallie Dandridge from the Pelham Association Archives in the Jacksonville Public Library. I appreciated his kind words and suggestions.

I am much obliged to archivist Terry Barkley of the Baer Memorial Library, Marion Military Institute, in Marion, Alabama, who deserves special recognition for reading the entire manuscript and offering suggestions to improve the work. Richmond National Battlefield Park historian Robert E. L. Krick critiqued the chapters on the Seven Days Battles and Antietam, and I am greatly indebted to him for his advice in altering the text. I have been an admirer of the writings and research of Robert Trout, and I appreciate the thick packet of material he sent me as well as his encouraging words. Historian Dennis Frye helped me comprehend the importance of the terrain at Antietam Battlefield. Frank O'Reilly, historian, scholar, and friend, was, as always, helpful, especially regarding Pelham's heroic role at Fredericksburg Battlefield. I am also appreciative of Dr. L. J. Dragovic, the chief medical examiner of Oakland County, Michigan, for taking time from his busy schedule to answer my questions on Pelham's mortal wound. A special thank you must be given to Wallace Johnston Jamerman for her kind permission in allowing me the use of John Pelham's unpublished letter to her great-grandfather, artillerist Philip Preston Johnston. I greatly appreciate the positive efforts of my copyeditor, Jenn Backer. Her patience and expertise were invaluable.

Longtime friends Ken Baumann and Ron Cleveland deserve mention. Ken's expertise on artillery helped me better understand cannons and projectiles. Ron owns an authentic 3-inch ordnance rifle (#194) that was captured by the Confederates and was most likely used by Pelham's battery. It was recaptured by George Custer at the battle of Tom's Brook on October 9, 1864. Talking to Ron and seeing this cannon immediately made me want to join the horse artillery.

Tom Nanzig merits praise as an author, researcher, and scholar, and I am grateful to him for his encouragement and help. His unselfishness and research acumen went a long way in helping me finish this project. I also thank Tom's neighbor and friend, Fred Olsen, a graphic artist, for the excellent maps he rendered for this work.

I do not have enough kind words for my mentor and good friend Dr. Weldon Petz, a nationally known Abraham Lincoln scholar. Weldon has always provided sage wisdom and advice. He has taught me the value of thorough research and attention to detail, and I look upon him as my second father. I am also indebted to the thousands of students in my Civil War classes at North Farmington High School who over the years encouraged me to write this book.

Lastly, my family has had much to do with finalizing this book. My daughter, Holly, and her fiancé, Chris, have patiently listened to my stories on Pelham and the Civil War, and I thank them for their indulgence. My son, Brent, a true Civil War scholar himself, read the book chapter by chapter and offered suggestions for improvement on the historical aspects of the characters and battles. His wife, Janet, proved to be an intuitive listener who never doubted that I would finish this work. Lastly, my wife, Carlene, cannot be thanked enough. From proofreading to researching to traveling from one battlefield or museum to another, she never wavered or complained. Her companionship, encouragement, and love never ceased in this journey.

THE PERFECT LION

Introduction

Fannie Lewis Gwathmey, a young girl of nearly fifteen years of age, resided at Hay-field, a beautiful colonial plantation home approximately ten miles below Fred-ericksburg, Virginia, on the south side of the Rappahannock River. Fannie lived with her widowed mother and her older sister Bessie. On numerous occasions the family was visited by some of the Confederacy's most illustrious military personnel. On one such visit during a cold winter day in early 1863, Generals Robert E. Lee, Stonewall Jackson, William Pendleton, and Jeb Stuart, along with his ever-present friend, Major John Pelham, stopped by for warmth and a bite to eat. The men were herded into the dining room at Hayfield.

Presently, General Lee glanced over at Pelham, who was sitting unobtrusively by a window. Lee smiled and said rather matter-of-factly, "There sits Major Pel-ham looking today as if butter wouldn't melt in his mouth, but in battle he is a per-fect lion. The reason he looks so modest today is he has on a borrowed overcoat." Fannie later described Pelham's reaction to this glorious accolade: "With that the blood mounted in Major Pelham's face up to his forehead, and when he got up to leave the overcoat almost touched the floor. He walked so close to the wall so it wouldn't be noticed."[1]

The camaraderie and wartime enthusiasm of three of this book's most outstand-ing warriors is expressed in the following seldom acknowledged tale by Val C. Giles, a member of Fourth Texas Infantry. Unfortunately, Giles ascribes no date to his recollection:

On a glorious Sunday morning in the Shenandoah Valley General Stonewall Jackson rode to a small country church with his friend and pastor, Dr. Robert Lewis Dabney. The church was already packed with soldiers awaiting Dr. Dabney's sermon when the two riders arrived. As Jackson and Dabney en-tered the church, General Jeb Stuart and Major John Pelham rode up "their horses covered with sweat." After doffing his hat Stuart excitedly informed Jackson that the Yankees were "crossing the river two miles below here, and they are not coming to hear Dr. Dabney preach." Stuart then posed the question: "General Jackson, what are you going to do first, fight or pray?" Jackson's reply was terse: "Well . . . that being the case, we'll fight now and pray later. Go back and punish those fellows, and I will support you with infantry." Stuart shouted his good-bye and he and his young artillerist, John Pelham, galloped off. Jackson then poked his head inside the church and stated: "Soldiers, join your regiments at once. There will be services here at eight o'clock tonight." Obeying to a fault, Jackson's soldiers "rushed out the door, jumped through the windows, and went double-quick in every direction."

Along the way to the fight, Giles "heard 'Pelham's Mountain Bull Dogs' barking and baying at the enemy. . . . Cavalry carbines were popping and singing down in the valley and all over the hills. Bugles sounded, regiments and brigades formed in the ranks of war, and marched to the front, but Stuart with his cavalry and Pelham with his artillery checked the vanguard and drove the enemy back."

"That same night," Giles remembered, "I saw General Jackson, General Stuart, and Major Pelham sitting together in the little church. When Dr. Dabney gave out the hymn, 'Rock of Ages, Cleft for Me,' they joined in with the soldiers and made that old tune hum."[2]

I
"The Most Adventuresome Member of That Adventurous Group"

Those wild Pelham boys. . . . Some day they're all gonna hang.

—Jacob Forney, neighbor

John Pelham was the third son born to Dr. Atkinson and Martha McGehee Pelham on Tuesday, September 7, 1838, in Benton County (now Calhoun County), Alabama.[1] Ultimately, the household numbered seven sons and a daughter, although one of the boys lived but three days. The lineage of the Pelham family established its military bearing well, as all six of the Pelham brothers would serve in the Confederate forces.

The name Pelham is said to have originated from the Old English words "pale hame," meaning paled (or picketed) home. One of the earliest known ancestors, Peter Pelham, a gifted portrait painter and copper engraver, born about 1690, hailed from Chichester, Sussex. In 1726 Peter sailed to America, the first Pelham to do so, and settled in fashionable Boston, again taking up his marketable trades. He died in December 1751, leaving two sons, Peter Jr. and Charles. Son Peter settled in Williamsburg, Virginia, as a noted citizen and talented musician who also moonlighted as the town jailer. His son Charles (John's grandfather), born in 1748, nobly served in the American Revolution as a major of the First Virginia Regiment, ultimately under the command of the Marquis de Lafayette. Charles's reputation as an officer grew with his participation in the battles of White Plains, New York, Brandywine, Germantown, and Monmouth. One tale that was obviously passed down through the generations of Pelhams concerned Charles giving his only pair of shoes to an unshod soldier suffering the bitter winter at Valley Forge. Ultimately captured by the British, Charles remained a prisoner of war in Charleston, South Carolina, for the duration of the war.

Following the war Charles married Isabelle Atkinson and fathered eleven children, the eighth of whom was Atkinson, John's father, born on November 21, 1797. Shortly after the Revolutionary War, taking advantage of a land grant for his military services, Charles settled with his constantly growing family in Mason County near Maysville, Kentucky. Here he hacked out a home, Cotton Bush, in the wilderness. When the Marquis de Lafayette returned to the United States for a triumphant tour in 1824, Charles, now in his mid-seventies, reportedly welcomed his old French officer and friend to the town of Maysville. Grandpa Charles succumbed to illness in 1829 at about the age of eighty-one.[2]

The military attracted numerous other relatives. One of John Pelham's great-uncles, General Henry Atkinson, fought in the War of 1812 and supposedly captured the noted Indian chief Black Hawk during the Black Hawk War of the early 1830s. Uncle Peter Pelham served as a captain in the War of 1812 and was wounded and captured by the British. Following the war, he continued in the service and died in camp near Tampa, Florida, about 1829. Another uncle, Charles Hollis Pelham, fought in the War of 1812 as a private and served in the Mexican War. Uncle William, reportedly a general, battled in the War for Texas Independence. John Burrell Pelham Jr., a distant cousin of Atkinson, served in an Arkansas regiment during the Mexican War; word of his death reached the Pelham family following the Battle of Buena Vista. One of John Pelham's older cousins was killed in William Walker's ill-fated Nicaraguan revolution in 1857. During the Civil War one more cousin was torn literally "to pieces" while manning a gun in the horse artillery, while some cousins served with Braxton Bragg and Joseph E. Johnston in Tennessee.[3] The warriors of the Pelham family stood proud of their heritage; they had served their nation and family well.

Soldiering, however, was foreign to John's father, Atkinson Pelham. Born near Maysville, Kentucky, his formative years landed him in medical school. He attended the University of North Carolina at Chapel Hill and afterward graduated from Jefferson College Medical School in Philadelphia in 1826. He practiced surgery there for two years before settling in Person County, North Carolina. Here he met, courted, and married the daughter of Colonel William McGehee, Martha Mumford McGehee, on Sunday, December 22, 1833. Atkinson was thirty-six; Martha, twenty-five. The marriage lasted nearly forty-three years until Martha's death at age sixty-eight on August 16, 1876. Atkinson outlived her by nearly four years, dying on July 7, 1880, at age eighty-two.[4] Two photographs exist of Atkinson Pelham, showing a balding man with a steely glint, broad chest, and firm jaw. The only known photograph of Martha, evidently a pre–Civil War pose, evidences an attractive, aging woman of patrician quality with an equally glinting stare but gentle features.[5]

Martha, reportedly a cousin of the famous legislator and would-be president Henry Clay, gave birth to her first child, a son Charles, on March 12, 1835. A year and a half later, William was born on September 14, 1836. Soon after the birth of their second child, Martha's father, Colonel William McGehee, moved to the virgin land of northeast Alabama in Benton County. Within a short while, the colonel beckoned his daughter and son-in-law to join him. Although Atkinson's medical practice was flourishing, he packed his family and belongings for Alabama in 1837.[6]

At first the family of four lived with Colonel McGehee, his wife, Elizabeth, and their twelve children. Although eighteen people existed under the same roof, the house, called Mahlep, was a good-sized log structure able to accommodate them. The two-story building, situated on a moderate-sized hill, overlooked Cane Creek, standing about five miles north of Anniston and nine miles southwest of the county seat in Jacksonville. A beautiful pine forest covered a good part of the McGehee land. Meanwhile, Atkinson busied himself constructing a house of his own, nearly three miles down Cane Creek, for his family that soon would grow one more in size as Martha was pregnant again. Though nearly finished, Atkinson and Martha's new dwelling remained unlived in when their third son, John, was born on September 7, 1838. Within a short time, Atkinson moved his wife and three sons into his new home.[7]

The new house would serve the Pelham family until late 1847. Atkinson continued his labors as a country doctor, but with the purchase of a large parcel of land, he now balanced his time as a farmer as well. Clearing the pine forest for cotton fields took long hours of backbreaking work, and the daylight hours were spent at this laborious task. However, Atkinson's nights were devoted to his family. Martha gave birth to a fourth son, Peter, on April 25, 1840. Less than twenty months later the family added its first daughter, Eliza Lewis Pelham, nicknamed "Betty,"[8] on December 6, 1841. Within the next six years three more sons were born. Sadly, baby Richard, sickly from birth, lived only three days, but the births of Samuel Clay Pelham on August 6, 1845, and Thomas Atkinson Pelham on April 20, 1847, filled out the family roster—six sons and a single daughter. The six sons all went on to serve the Confederacy.[9]

In 1847 the family moved to the county seat of Jacksonville. Meanwhile, Atkinson purchased about a thousand acres of farmland from his father-in-law near the town of Alexandria. Two years later Atkinson bought four acres of land in Alexandria and built a new home. This sturdy house of seven rooms, surrounded by large oak trees, remained the family home until Atkinson died in 1880. No longer owned by the Pelham family, it stood until 1931 when it was torn down.[10]

Atkinson became a pillar in the small community of Alexandria, now upward of three hundred inhabitants. He joined the local Masonic Lodge and remained one of the few Henry Clay and Whig Party supporters in that area of Alabama. He also avidly opposed secession, which led to countless debates with his neighbors. On Sundays the family worshiped at the local Presbyterian church where the Pelham children studied the *Westminster Catechism,* and each day began and ended with a reading from the Bible. Atkinson, according to a relative, "was one of the noblest men on earth. Their mother was equally worthy. . . . I never knew a happier family than they were."[11] The family owned approximately thirty slaves that Atkinson used to work his growing land acquisitions. On January 27, 1855, he purchased 120 more acres in Benton County. He continued his limited medical practice as well. All of the Pelham children attended the local school, Jacksonville Academy, which opened two years before John's birth. Here the rudiments of education were passed on to the students by various teachers who often found the switch more effective than a daily recitation. Young John loved history and geography and had a grudging respect for mathematics. He also possessed some talent and enthusiasm for drawing. A lack of interest quickly developed, however, for grammar, and spelling remained his nemesis.[12]

Atkinson's busy schedule often kept him away from home until evening; consequently, his wife, Martha, who stood 5'9" tall, became the family disciplinarian for their six sons and tomboy daughter. It was no easy task reining in "those wild Pelham boys," and one neighbor, Jacob Forney, flatly predicted, "Some day they're all gonna hang."

Occasionally, some were aghast at their behavior. Walking a considerable distance to school, the Pelham boys passed the pasture of Isaac Ross Green. Unbeknownst to farmer Green, the Pelham lads took to riding his cows. Green noticed a considerable drop-off in their milk production, but the puzzled farmer knew not why. One day he observed the young riders whooping it up as they rode through his pasture. Admonishing them for their outrageous activity, he sternly suggested they ride his yearling bull. Not to be outdone, the Pelham boys put their minds together to outwit the ferocious bull, but all their subsequent efforts ended in disaster. John, being "the most adventuresome member of that adventurous group," hatched a plan. Mounting an open gateway, John straddled the edges and motioned his brothers to drive the bull through the opening. John daringly dropped on the back of the bull and rode off while being bucked, yelling with delight. He soon had the animal conquered. Two purposes were served: farmer Green's cows went back to their normal milk production, and the Pelham youths had tamed the bull to where even Betty could ride it.[13]

The Pelham brothers' penchant for mischief occasionally became acrimonious. Once while at school brothers John and Charles received a thrashing from their teacher, a red-haired Irish martinet, whose name unfortunately has been lost to history. Also lost is the reason for their punishment. In retaliation, the Pelhams plotted against the stern educator. One evening they nearly dismantled the schoolhouse. In addition they took school benches and desks that were stowed away in a neighbor's barn. This did not end their pranks. They later locked the teacher from the schoolhouse, tossed his books down a well, smeared his clothes with ink, chucked wads of paper during class at his unsuspecting back, and reworked his chair so it collapsed when he sat down. Atkinson was called in to explain this rude behavior, and he meted out the necessary punishment. Soon a committee of concerned parents decided the schoolmaster had to go, and a new one was brought in from the North. This new instructor evidently appealed to the Pelham boys, who, from then on, behaved in an exemplary manner. The Northern teacher was a firm but resourceful man who taught John and the others until 1855.[14]

One prank seemed innocent enough when it entered the minds of the three eldest Pelham boys: Charles, William, and John. After a Fourth of July picnic, they conspired to fool their father, the doctor, by smearing a Negro boy from head to toe with the blood of a slaughtered hog and then push the boy into their father's office that evening. The Negro child, of course, needed no prompting from the Pelham brothers to cry from this abuse, and he screamed hysterically as he was led to the doctor's office. Startled by this bloody image, Dr. Pelham quickly deduced that the blood had come from a hog, not the boy. Atkinson ordered the boy washed clean and proceeded to look for the culprits. It did not do to ever lie to their father, and the three Pelham boys fessed up to their crime. After a stern lecture Atkinson gave the boys a severe spanking. It was the last such whipping the three boys would receive from their father.[15]

No dare was too great for the Pelham brothers, no adventure too perilous. A natural rivalry existed among the youths; each constantly tried to outdo the other. Sister Betty even entered the contests, which sometimes deteriorated into friendly brawls. Neighboring lads often came into these frays as well. Once, John fought a rather bloody battle against a boy much larger than himself. Repeatedly, the older, more experienced opponent knocked John to the ground. Older brother Charles offered to step in, but John's competitive juices would not allow for a substitute. The one-sided melee ended when John finally fell exhausted to the ground.[16]

Exactly when John Pelham first showed interest in the military and entertained the thought of attending West Point cannot be determined. Surely, the stories told after supper in front of the fireplace of his fighting ancestors provided a certain enchantment for the boy. Perhaps, as surmised by some, it was the flashy uniform donned by army cadet and fellow Jacksonville native John Horace Forney, at home on furlough from West Point around 1850. Forney, with his shoulders pulled back at near-attention pose, made a striking appearance to the folks in the rural town. The young Pelham boy, nine years younger than Forney, must have been fascinated by the handsome cadet, strutting before the townspeople. Although unproven, it has been suggested that Pelham possibly sought an audience with Forney to discuss the academy and what it took to become a soldier at such an illustrious place. The Forney and Pelham families were not particularly close. The Forneys attended Sunday services at St. Luke's Episcopal Church and supported the Democratic Party—both contrary to the convictions of Atkinson Pelham and his family. Whether the conversation between John Pelham and John Forney ever took place, it was observed that Pelham became more serious as a student after Forney's furlough.[17] John became "very studious . . . [with a] cheerful, happy disposition," according to his brother Peter. "[He was a] very hard student. [He] worked on father's farm. Went fishing on Saturdays [and] studied the Westminster Catechism on Sunday."[18] Throughout this formative period, John developed a true sense of religion. His belief in God was possibly surpassed only by the love and respect he willingly bestowed upon his parents.

Young Pelham's boyhood friends included Edward T. Clark and Thomas Benton Bush. As close as the three of them were, a good-natured rivalry often existed. Once John and the Bush boy had been scheduled to deliver an oratory for the graduation ceremony at the Mt. Zion Academy, and the two families showed up in force to support their respective speaker. Both boys did well, but Charles Pelham later declared, "The hardest fight I ever saw was between Mrs. Bush's carriage driver and my mother's trying to settle the question as to whether John or Benton made the 'best speech' at a country school examination at Mt. Zion Academy." Charles further stated, "My mother and Mrs. Bush and the negroes had arranged it for two of the Pelham boys to marry the Bush girls and for Benton Bush to marry our only sister."[19] None of these projected marriages ever took place, but some of the Pelham slaves, in fact, married those of the Bush family. Two slave brothers, Willis and Newton, owned by the Pelham family, became playmates for John and his brothers, and both would accompany John when he entered into the service of the Confederacy. One slave mammy, Myrian, took care of the Pelham children for many years, but left the Pelham homestead at the end of the Civil War.[20] John's childhood sweetheart appears to have been a Miss Fannie Gladden. For this he became an easy target for his brothers' unmerciful teasing.

For John Pelham this area of Alabama seemed perfect for his activities. Rivers existed for excellent fishing, a favorite pastime, especially on Saturdays. Swimming holes were a favorite gathering place for the entire Pelham brood. The area teemed with wildlife; he often ventured to hunt with his ever-present dogs. Riding horses, at which John excelled, always topped his list. This talent he imparted to sister Betty's playmates. He was a "friend of all his sister's girl friends," stated Peter Pelham's future wife. "He was a splendid equestrian & gave us girls lessons in horse-back riding."[21] From this physical activity John grew lean and hard, a superb athlete. He stood nearly six feet tall, of reedy build, weighing about 150 pounds, neatly framed, with slender hips, broad shoulders, and sinewy muscles. He carried himself in an erect manner, making him appear even taller.[22] His grace in bearing made him a fine dancer, another lesson he garnered from his mother. As he grew older, his temperament calmed down, yet his own brothers described him as "tense and high-strung," never backing down from a fight. His blondish hair and sparkling blue eyes made him a favorite among the ladies. "A perfect picture of Pelham cannot be had," declared one of his future soldiers, "because the most remarkable feature was his eyes. In social life they were gentle and merry 'laughing eyes,' but in the animation of battle his eyes were restless, and flashed like diamonds."[23] His pleasant demeanor also caused him to be adored by his many cousins, aunts, and uncles, as well as neighbors.

At age sixteen John had proven himself able enough to handle adult responsibilities. Atkinson, now running two farms, decided to send John to supervise the work on a few hundred acres at one of the farms, known as the Crow place. Together Atkinson and John selected six blacks to assist John in this project. One of the blacks brought along his wife to do the cooking. Setting out in May 1855, John took a valise packed with an extra pair of clothes, his Bible, and a few other books he planned on reading. Atkinson's instructions sounded simple: clear out the woods and make a crop. Located six or seven miles from the Pelham homestead, the Crow place assignment was no easy task. Living by himself in a pine log cabin, John spent weeks alone except for the slaves who helped him. Eventually, he made "quite a success" of this activity, as Atkinson realized a "handsome profit."[24] In his spare time John proceeded with another hobby: drawing pencil sketches and painting watercolors.

Exactly when John told his mother and father of his desire to enter West Point is unknown. Assured of John's conviction of becoming a soldier, Atkinson used whatever influence he had to secure the appointment by writing to a few influential friends. Meanwhile, John's schooling continued in preparation for what he hoped would be an appointment to the academy. The Reverend L. H. Parsons, a Presbyterian minister, assisted John in this effort by tutoring him twice a week, and John worked conscientiously to improve his academic skills. By early March 1856, at the age of seventeen, John Pelham received notification of his appointment to the United States Military Academy at West Point from Secretary of War Jefferson Davis. The letter also stated clearly that scholastic success at the academy depended largely on an individual's aptitude in mathematics. It further warned that lack of ability in this area should be considered in order to "escape the mortification of failure for himself and family."[25] Although mathematics was not one of John's strongest suits academically as he would plainly show in his first two years at the academy, he would worry about his deficiencies later. His selection resulted from the recommendation of an influential political leader, Senator Miles Washington Abernathy, a friend of his father's. Conferred by Congressman Sampson Willis Harris of the Seventh Congressional District of Alabama,[26] it would not only change the routine John had fallen into, it would alter his life. Beaming with pride, John sat down and wrote a short note in reply to Jefferson Davis, dated March 18, 1856:

Sir,

I have the honor to acknowledge the receipt of your communication of the 8th March informing me that the President has confirmed upon me a conditional appointment of Cadet in the Service of the United States, and to inform you of my acceptance of same.

Yours Respt.,
Jno. Pelham

Atkinson then took the pen and wrote beneath John's letter:

I hereby assent to the above by my son of his conditional appointment as Cadet, and he has my full permission to sign articles by which he shall bind himself to serve the United States, eight years unless sooner discharged.

Pelham.

Later that evening Atkinson led John to his office for a physical examination. Afterward Atkinson prepared another brief letter to Jefferson Davis:

Alexandria, Ala. Mar. 18, '56
Hon. Jefferson Davis
Secretary of War,
Sir,

I am much gratified at the appointment of my son (John Pelham) as conditional Cadet. He was 17 years old in Sept. last, and fills <u>all</u> the physical regulations of the Circular attached to the appointment. He has my consent to enter into any engagement with [the] U. S.

Very respectfully,
Your Ob. Ser't.
A. Pelham[27]

For the next couple of months the Pelham family prepared for John's departure to the military academy. Even more worrisome to Atkinson and Martha was the fact that Betty, two years younger than John, would also be leaving home to attend Maysville Seminary, a prestigious school for young ladies in Kentucky. Packing for John would not entail much effort as West Point severely limited one's possessions and necessities—a small valise for toiletries and a few personal items plus a suitcase for some extra clothing. His sketch pad, some pens, paper, and envelopes for writing letters home and a leather-covered Bible, a gift from his mother, were neatly stowed. John had promised his mother that he would write home regularly and read his Bible daily. John also took along $60 in cash, a sum that most students brought with them. The money would be placed in the safe of the adjutant general to be used by the cadet in emergencies.

With an underlying excitement, John said good-bye to his parents and the others in the Pelham homestead. Older brother Charles drove him in the family buggy to the railhead at Blue Mountain. Certainly, Charles offered his younger brother some mature advice on a variety of subjects as the two rode toward their destination. Along the way the two brothers stopped at a neighbor's house that belonged to some friends of the family. Seeing a number of girls at the homestead, John, for some unanswered reason, refused to get out of the buggy. When asked why John was reluctant, Charles replied: "Ask him in; what's the use? John would rather face the U.S. Army than a girl."[28]

A quick good-bye to his brother at the railhead and John was off on the train heading to Selma, a roundabout trek but the best way to link up with the railroad heading north. Another switch and he would move on to Montgomery and then to Atlanta. On up through Tennessee and across the state of Virginia to Richmond and another one hundred miles into Washington, D.C.—farther north than John or his immediate family had ever been. Entering the free state of Pennsylvania posed no difficulty, nor did the final trek by rail into New York City. A stay overnight in a New York hotel room was interrupted by dawn, and John boarded a steamboat to go up the Hudson River, through mountains that may have reminded him of home, a beautiful ride of fifty-two miles.

John Pelham would soon cross the threshold into the spartan life of a West Point plebe. He officially entered the academy on Tuesday, July 1, 1856.

2

"We Are a Class beyond the Common Ones"

[Pelham was] the kind of man whom you felt instinctively, "Here is a friend."

—Adelbert Ames, classmate

To a country boy from Alabama, the one-thousand-mile trip northward to New York must have seemed like traveling to the end of the world. Disembarking from the vessel with his scant luggage, Pelham walked up the steep pathway to his new home. Entering the grounds of the famed campus, one was awed by its solemn, spectacular beauty and prestigious history. Established by President Thomas Jefferson with the consent of the U.S. Congress in 1802, West Point stood on forty acres overlooking the Hudson. Granite and limestone buildings sat on the perimeter of the area known simply as "the Plain." Two rows of large elm trees surrounded the tranquil setting. One of the newer constructions, finished in 1850, was the Cadet Barracks, a four-story, L-shaped, medieval-looking edifice on the south side. Each floor contained four rooms, starkly furnished, with a solitary fireplace. Other buildings could be viewed in most directions: a triple-turreted library containing twenty thousand volumes; a lovely chapel, built in 1836, with mandatory attendance; and a three-story hospital, erected in 1839, which included twelve rooms and a dispensary where First classmen were compelled to study hygiene, sanitary engineering, and the standard methods for attending the sick and wounded. West of the Plain stood the quarters of the superintendent, the commandant, professors, and instructors.[1] Because Secretary of War Jefferson Davis had instituted a new five-year plan for cadets in 1854, John Pelham's next half decade would be spent here—but only if he could withstand the fierce regimentation that tended to force so many back into civilian life.

New plebes, collectively called "Animals," signed an oath of allegiance and went through the prescribed physical and mental examinations. Dated July 1, 1856, the form to which Pelham affixed his signature stated his age at "seventeen years, nine months" and vowed to "serve the Army of the United States for eight years." Pelham further solemnly swore to "bear true faith and allegiance to the United States of America" and to "serve them honestly and faithfully against all their enemies or opposers whatsoever, and observe and obey the orders of the President of the United States, and orders of the Officers appointed over me, according to the Rules and Articles of War." The physical exam, administered by an academy surgeon, preceded the mental test, deemed "extremely simple," in the old Academic Hall.[2]

Assigned to Company D, consisting mostly of Southern boys, Pelham soon made acquaintance with a Virginia-born, Texas-reared plebe named Tom Rosser. The two lads hit it off from the beginning. Rosser seemed the complete antithesis of Pelham. Nearly two years older at nineteen and standing about 6'2" tall, Rosser, with his black hair, dark brown eyes, muscular frame, and swarthy complexion, resembled a pirate. Conversely, Pelham, of smooth, pale skin, blond hair, and blue eyes had an almost girlish look about him. Yet, they held much in common; both were fighters of the first order, and each was an expert horseman. They remained roommates and the closest of friends during their tenure at the academy, and both walked out of the institution two weeks before graduation in 1861 on the same day.[3]

After the formalities of admittance, the plebes spent the months of July and August in encampment. This time was allotted to familiarize them with the harsh aspects of military life as well as to deplete the ranks of those who did not belong. Assigned four to a tent in the muggy summer heat, the hottest recorded up to that time in the Hudson Valley, many an unprepared youth opted to drop out and return home rather than scorch during the daily exercises, regimentation, and unceasing hazing under the watchful eyes of the skeptical and demanding upperclassmen in charge. Tent mates Pelham and Rosser, used to the heat of their native soil, withstood the rigors in excellent fashion. A typical day commenced at 5:00 A.M. with the unwelcome sounds of reveille. Drill occurred from 5:30 to 6:30 followed by roll call and a half-hour march to the mess hall for a less than nutritious breakfast. More drill instruction ensued with little time off until another march to the mess hall for dinner at 1:00 P.M. Again the bland menu was of a lower quality than most of the plebes were familiar. Classmate Adelbert Ames later reported that the fish served on Friday "in odor and taste is sometimes disgusting." He added matter-of-factly, "I have become accustomed to the sight of it, but never eat it." A brief respite followed the meal, but the drilling continued until a 7:00 P.M. dress parade. A meager supper, which most of the boys sloshed down with coffee, followed. Tully McCrea, a graduate in the Class of 1862, disdained the watered-down coffee, preferring the bread and water provided, and compared his provisions to those of a "prisoner confined in a dungeon." After supper the plebes were given time to clean up; another roll call followed, and then the cadets prepared for bed. Tattoo sounded at precisely 9:30 P.M. "We sleep like logs," noted McCrea, "when the old cadets will let us." The constant drilling showed vast improvement in the cadets' technique as their early awkwardness evolved into a unified precision and grace. Gradually, "the rigid discipline and cast-iron routine of every-day life, which at first seem so artificial and needlessly emphasized," observed Morris Schaff, "became familiar and really easy of observance." At noon on August 29 the dull, boring, but strenuous camp was struck, and the plebes marched back to the barracks. Inseparable, Pelham and Rosser moved their modest belongings into the south end of the west barracks. Classmate Henry du Pont spoke for all when he penned, "It is a great luxury to sleep on a mattress with sheets."[4]

The rooms at West Point were singularly stark and gloomy. Furniture included an iron bedstead topped with a mattress and two blankets—one to sleep on, one to sleep under—a small table, a lamp, a mirror, a washstand with pitcher and bowl, and an uncomfortable straight-backed chair. In winter, without a proper heating system, water froze in the pitchers. Virtually no comforts of home were allowed. Reveille rudely began each day at 5:00 A.M., and tattoo abruptly sounded at 10:00 P.M., making every day seventeen hours of drudgery. Food, served in somewhat meager portions, was a long way from the home-cooked meals the newcomers were used to. Only the basics, cooked in nearly unpalatable military fashion, were consumed: bread and butter, sometimes rancid; potatoes (invariably boiled); boiled meat or fish; and "hash," clearly made from the previous day's leftover meat dish with an ample portion of fresh potatoes or rice mixed in. Desserts mostly consisted of a boiled pudding along with an extra cup of tepid coffee or tea. An 1860 survey of cadets indicated that they universally complained more about the victuals than anything else. "Bugs will be found in the sugar," wrote Adelbert Ames, "and cockroaches in the soup." Furthermore, no food was allowed in the barracks' rooms. Social status prior to enrollment at the academy meant nothing. One simply had no money to spend. The rules forbade any money from home, and the $30 per month given to each cadet immediately went for the essentials of the commissary: razors, clothing, and such.[5]

The demerit system also remained anathema to the cadets. Once explained, the rules seemed simple enough: anyone tallying two hundred in a year or one hundred in six months was summarily dismissed, or "found," in the vernacular of the cadets. The problem was these demerits, nicknamed "skins," were meted out for an unending variety of offenses, sometimes petty in nature. Being late, improper saluting, buttons undone, shoes unshined, equipment tarnished, speaking out of order, untidy rooms, bedding improperly made, an unshaven face, gambling or playing any game of cards, sitting while on sentry detail—the list looked endless. Consumption of alcohol usually guaranteed the culprit expellable, but he could be spared from this indignity if his entire class "took the pledge" for abstinence. Multiple "skins" also could be exacted virtually at the discretion of the officers doling them out. "I don't like this mode of life at all," wrote one unhappy cadet to his father, "it is too much like slavery to suit me." Pelham's first demerit occurred for "bedding not properly aired at morning inspection." Other "skins" were given to Pelham early on for "laughing in the ranks," "boyish conduct" in class, and "relaxed ways" as a sentry. At one time he neared the danger point with five fewer than necessary for dismissal from the academy.[6]

Fortunately, not all the regimen brought grief or discomfort. Cadets were allowed to indulge in an assortment of athletic events including boxing, fencing, horseback riding, and ice skating or sledding on the frozen Hudson River in the winter. Most Southern boys were hearty outdoorsmen, but their winter skills, of course, lacked any sort of athleticism. Wobbly legs on ice skates resulted in many a cracked head, twisted ankle, or bruised ego. Periodic dances were held at the academy, although women were allowed to attend only on rare occasion. Consequently, the boys usually danced with each other. Invariably, Pelham and Rosser could be seen as partners. Because of the two- to three-inch discrepancy in their heights, Pelham increased his size by neatly folding paper and placing it in his shoes.[7] Numerous societies and clubs also existed where cadets showed off their various skills. For those who lasted two years at the Point, a two-month furlough was granted to visit one's family.

Another diversion, attractive to many, was a trip to Benny Havens. This establishment, located no more than a mile south of the academy in Buttermilk Falls, offered fine cuisine and beverage. It remained off-limits to cadets, but like a magnet, it drew them as a light does insects. The proprietor, Benny himself, was an affable, fun-loving sort who acted as chef, bartender, and raconteur. For years he had practically seen it all at West Point. His excellent food, a welcome change from the bland fare served at the Point, along with his remarkable ability to remember names and relate charming stories made his place a popular gathering spot. Benny's favorite tale seemed to be an incident that occurred in the late 1820s when cadet Jefferson Davis made a mad dash, fell over a cliff, and nearly killed himself while escaping from a raid on the place. Although lacking formal education, Benny offered solid advice and even tutored the cadets in mathematics.[8]

Seventy-two plebes began their service as part of the Class of May 1861, but the attrition rate, as usual, lowered the numbers considerably. Forty-five actually graduated. Many of Pelham's classmates who stuck out the five-year program were destined for honor and notoriety in the Civil War. Most fought on the bloody battlefields; some became generals; too many were wounded and killed; five won the coveted Medal of Honor.

- Adelbert Ames, hailing from Maine and graduating fifth in his class, received six brevet ranks as well as the Medal of Honor. His friendship with Pelham was forged early at the academy, as they shared the same quarters. He later fathered six children, one of whom, Butler, graduated from West Point in 1894. Adelbert served as a senator and governor of Mississippi following the Civil War, and he volunteered to fight in the Spanish-American War. Ames also had the distinction of being the last surviving Civil War general, dying at age ninety-seven on April 13, 1933.
- The brilliant Orville Babcock from Vermont, number three in this class, served on Ulysses S. Grant's staff. He would later personally escort Robert E. Lee to the Wilmer McLean House for the formal surrender. His reputation would be severely attacked as a party to the scandals of the Grant administration. Babcock died heroically on June 2, 1884, drowning while attempting to save others.

- Eugene Beaumont, a Pennsylvanian and number thirty-two in the class, won a Medal of Honor for his heroics at the Harpeth River in Tennessee. Following the Civil War, "Beau," as his classmates called him, taught at West Point and fought Indians in the West under Ranald Mackenzie.
- Another Medal of Honor recipient was New Yorker Samuel Benjamin, number twelve in the class. An outstanding Civil War artillerist, Benjamin received his medal for his actions during the Seven Days Battles. Severely wounded twice during the war, Benjamin ultimately returned to the academy to teach mathematics. Crippled by rheumatism, he died at age forty-seven on May 15, 1886.
- Charles Campbell from Missouri resigned from the U.S. Army after graduation to fight for the Confederacy. During the war he sent John Pelham a personal letter; following the war he fathered four sons, one of whom he named John Pelham Campbell.
- Charles E. Cross finished second in his class and served as a military engineer during the Civil War. At the Battle of Fredericksburg, perhaps John Pelham's greatest day as a soldier, Cross helped put in the pontoon bridges over the Rappahannock River. He was killed six months later on June 5, 1863, while placing bridges over the Rappahannock at Franklin's Crossing. As a testimony to his ability, commanding officer John Sedgwick noted, "[Cross's] life was worth more than a thousand bridges."
- Justin E. Dimick, number twenty-three of forty-five in his class, roomed with Pelham's artillery mate Mathis Winston Henry. He fell mortally wounded at the Battle of Chancellorsville.
- Henry Algernon du Pont, from Delaware, graduated number one in the class and was elected class president. Popular with all of his classmates, he became a close friend of Pelham's while at the academy. He was awarded the Medal of Honor for his valor at the Battle of Cedar Creek in 1864. When Federal general David Hunter torched Virginia Military Institute (VMI) in 1864, du Pont helped save the home of Superintendent Francis Smith, a West Point classmate of du Pont's father. While serving as a U.S. senator in 1913, du Pont sponsored a bill to pay VMI for the destruction during the war. He died at age eighty-nine on December 31, 1926.
- New York–born William Elderkin served with distinction in the Federal army and evidently was a close friend of John Pelham.[9]
- Charles Edward Hazlett, a New Yorker and number fifteen in his class, lost his life at Gettysburg in the fighting at Little Round Top at age twenty-five.
- Pennsylvanian Guy Henry, number twenty-seven, won a Medal of Honor at Cold Harbor in 1864 for leading his regiment in an assault and having two horses shot from beneath him.

- Also hailing from the Keystone State, Mathis Winston Henry, graduating next to last, served under Pelham in Jeb Stuart's horse artillery. Orphaned at an early age, Henry grew up in his sister's home in Kentucky. Illness plagued him at West Point, as did the rigorous rules and classroom work. The recipient of numerous demerits, he was arrested twice for wandering into hospital wards "not his own" and for playing cards with his friends on another visit. Prior to his service in Pelham's horse artillery, Henry had been in Stuart's cavalry. Following his tenure in the horse artillery, he transferred into John Bell Hood's division as the chief of artillery. In all three instances Henry displayed honorable abilities as a soldier. Stricken with paralysis, Henry died on his thirty-ninth birthday, November 28, 1877.[10]
- Llewellyn Griffith Hoxton, a Virginian, graduated number six in the class. "Lou," as he was known to his classmates, resigned from the army in May 1861 to join the Confederate forces. He served in the Western Theater as a chief of artillery and commanded all the cannon against the Federals at the Battle of Franklin. His younger brother, William, became a lieutenant in the horse artillery under Pelham's command.
- Mississippian James Kennard, who resigned a month before Pelham, fell mortally wounded at First Manassas, dying five days later at age twenty-two, the first in his class to die on the field of battle.
- Pennsylvanian Jacob Ford Kent, graduating thirty-first, was captured at First Manassas and held by the Confederates for over a year. Gruff and opinionated, he often ruffled feathers in the high command, displaying a particular abhorrence for George Custer. Kent actively served in the Spanish-American War and retired with the rank of major general. He died at age eighty-three on December 22, 1918.
- Hailing from New Jersey, Hugh Judson Kilpatrick graduated number seventeen in his class and became a general. He was best known for his blustery persona and less than efficient cavalry tactics, earning him the negative nom de guerre "Kil-Cavalry" among his own men. The diminutive Kilpatrick died of Bright's Disease at age forty-five on December 2, 1881, in Santiago de Chile.
- Illinois-born Henry Walter Kingsbury, number four in the class and considered by many of his classmates to be the finest soldier in the group, was wounded four times at Antietam and died the following day at age twenty-six, September 18, 1862.
- Handsome Edmund "Ned" Kirby, a New Yorker ranking number ten, opposed Pelham's guns numerous times. At Chancellorsville his severe thigh wound developed an infection, causing surgeons to amputate. Kirby's condition worsened and he died later at age twenty-three on May 28, 1863.[11]

- Charles Patterson, from Iowa and ranking number sixteen, resigned shortly after graduation to fight for the Confederacy. At age twenty-five, he died from wounds incurred at the Battle of Shiloh two days after the battle on April 9, 1862.
- John Scroggs Poland, who eventually rose to the rank of brigadier general, hailed from the Hoosier State and graduated number thirty-four. A member of D Company at the academy, he became one of Pelham's closest chums. He served in the Army of the Potomac through numerous battles. A photograph of Poland, taken early in the war, was later found in Pelham's personal belongings. Apparently smuggled through the lines, the photograph contains the penciled words "Yours ever faithfully" on the front and "To Jno. Pelham" on the back. Below the brief inscription Pelham wrote: "Jno. S. Poland, Lt. U.S.A." Poland died at age sixty-two on August 8, 1898.
- Virginian George Thornton exited the academy on the same day as Rosser and Pelham, fellow members of D Company. Thornton's photograph was among the possessions that Pelham carried home in 1861. Although Thornton survived the war, his final outcome is unknown.
- Mercurial-tempered and humorless Emory Upton, a native of the Empire State and an abolitionist, finished eighth in the class. Rising to the rank of brigadier general, his heroism at Spotsylvania won him glowing accolades. A shell fragment severed his thigh muscles, exposing the femoral artery at the Battle of Winchester in September 1864, and only the use of a tourniquet saved his life. Upton authored two books on military tactics, but his life and health turned sour, and he committed suicide with a bullet to the brain at age forty-two.[12]

This impressive array of plebes now entered into their most trying period: classroom studies. Classes, normally of about fifteen students each, met throughout the day from 8:00 A.M. to 4:00 P.M. Monday through Friday and again from 8:00 A.M. to noon on Saturdays. With chapel services, inspections, drilling, parades, and studying, little personal time remained. Cadets listened to lectures and sweated through the daily demands for recitations. Not knowing an answer and readily admitting it was, in academy jargon, labeled a "fess"; worse by far was a "found"—to be seriously delinquent. If many a student did not last through the physical trauma at West Point, even more were dropped for lack of classroom ability. Course work included mathematics, English, drawing, French, Spanish, ethics, chemistry, tactics in infantry, cavalry, and artillery, and engineering. Semiannual examinations were administered in January and June. These rigorous demands once prompted President Andrew Jackson to label West Point "the best school in the world."[13]

Heading the institution was the crusty and austere superintendent, Richard Delafield. Delafield's career had been long and illustrious. Graduating first of twenty-three in the Class of 1818, he was assigned to the Army Corps of Engineers. Twice he held the superintendent's post at West Point, totaling eleven years.[14] Efficiency and discipline keyed his administration. With a small budget he streamlined the academy into a model of military proficiency. Not one to delegate authority, he demanded that all decisions be made through his office. Although his office remained open to cadets each day from 7:00 to 8:00 A.M., Sundays excluded, his acerbic personality often rendered this welcome ineffectual. He tyrannically punished the slightest violation of the regulations and meticulously exhorted his faculty to perfection. Consequently, he was no more popular in his first administration than in his second. With his autocratic demeanor, nervous temperament, and narrow eyes peering through steel-rimmed spectacles, he reminded one of a buzzard. His arbitrary and petty rules made him the least popular man at the academy. Henry du Pont remembered him as one "who has poked his long nose into everything you can think of" and later declared, "I have come to the conclusion that he is insane!" For reasons unexplained, John Pelham "hated" Delafield as well.[15]

The teaching staff at West Point contained many names of future prominence. Lieutenant Colonel William J. Hardee, a strict disciplinarian with a stern martial bearing, served as commandant of cadets and taught classes in cavalry, artillery, and infantry tactics. First Lieutenants John Pegram and John Schofield were assistant instructors in cavalry tactics and philosophy, respectively. Perhaps the most feared instructor, Albert E. Church, headed the Mathematics Department. Assisting him was First Lieutenant Oliver Otis Howard. Noted for his sympathetic manner toward his pupils, Howard led the chapel services as well. Dennis Mahan headed the Engineering Department. Although "bereft of all natural feeling," noted one cadet, Mahan's brilliance in his field was widely recognized. The Reverend John W. French was professor of geography, history, and ethics. "He is no more qualified to fill the place than the man in the moon," wrote Tully McCrea. John Pelham nicknamed French "Old Visionary" because "he wanders about so much like a specter." Henry L. Kendrick, an instructor in chemistry, mineralogy, and geology, and a veteran of the Mexican War, remained one of the favorites of cadets. Patrice de Janon taught Spanish and sword instruction. Other instructors included Charles W. Field, Edward Porter Alexander, John F. Reynolds, William B. Hazen, Alexander Webb, Gouverneur Kemble Warren, and John Gibbon. Perhaps more important than the faculty was the unique aura that was everywhere evident within the gray stone walls of the academy. "West Point is a great character builder, perhaps the greatest among our institutions of learning," wrote Morris Schaff. "The habit of truth-telling, the virtue of absolute honesty, the ready and loyal obedience to authority, the display of courage . . . to establish these elements of character, she labors without ceasing."[16]

Without effort, John Pelham quickly became a favorite among the other plebes. His modest personality, genteel manner, and soft-spoken Southern demeanor set him apart. Adelbert Ames later noted, "He was easily the most popular man of the Corps in my time. Everybody liked him. I never heard anyone say a word against him. He was that kind of man, the kind of man whom you felt instinctively, 'Here is a friend.' No; he was quiet, simple, unassuming, unpretentious. There was a reserve about him that we got to know covered an inward strength. . . . There was something about him that drew you to him."[17] To many cadets Pelham was simply called "Jack," but during his first year, Pelham, because of his near-girlish looks, picked up the nickname "Sallie." According to Edward Porter Alexander, "[Pelham] was a very young looking, handsome, & attractive fellow, slender, blue eyes, light hair, smooth, red & white complexion, & with such a modest & refined expression that his classmates & friends never spoke of him but as 'Sallie' and there never was a Sallie whom a man could love more!"[18]

For all his easygoing manner and calm disposition, Pelham quickly proved he was no one to be trifled with. Two weeks after his arrival at the academy, he was turned in and given a demerit for reading his Bible on a Sunday instead of General Winfield Scott's treatise on military tactics. His accuser, a "handsome" senior from New York, detailed Pelham's offense to the authorities. Charges brought against Pelham's dereliction of duty ensued into a mock court-martial. When the official part of the incident ended, the outraged Pelham challenged the New Yorker. The senior replied he "couldn't fight one so young, so small & so far beneath him in class." Soon a fellow senior from Mississippi offered to be Pelham's second, declaring, "That will make him your equal." A group of cadets paraded out to the dueling ground to witness the fight. The New York senior, being bigger and stronger than Pelham, quickly had the young plebe on the ground. Pelham merely protected himself, as best he could, until his antagonist tired out. The strategy worked. When the senior appeared exhausted from throwing excessive blows, Pelham turned on him with a vengeance. For several brutal moments Pelham "whipped" the senior. So disgraced from the beating by a plebe, the senior at once tendered his resignation from the academy and abruptly left.[19]

The first year's curriculum stressed calculus and English. John struggled with mathematics, as did so many other plebes under the watchful and critical eye of aging professor Albert E. Church. More than one plebe found the class entirely too difficult and packed for home. "It was in this department," noted Morris Schaff, "that the ground was strewn . . . with the bones of victims." One unknown plebe scrawled on the flyleaf of a calculus book, "God damn all mathematics to the lowest depths of hell!!"[20] Of the seventy-two plebes who entered in the Class of 1861, only fifty-nine remained at the end of the first year. Academically, Pelham ranked in the bottom half of his class. In mathematics he stood forty-third; in English thirty-first. In general merit he ranked thirty-fifth and totaled seventy demerits, affectionately called "slugs" by the cadets. John described one of his "slugs," which occurred on November 11, 1856, for "sitting down in chair and reading while sentinel."[21]

More important than his studies appeared to be the friendships he fostered and his natural gifts for athletics. Considered by many as the "best athlete at West Point," Pelham excelled in fencing, boxing, and horsemanship. Being lithe, agile, and cat quick, he mastered the art of fencing. His boxing skills were praised by many. "It was beautiful to watch his quickness and his dodging of blows," reported Tom Rosser. "You could see it was always fun for him, even when he got hurt." His equestrian abilities were "marvelous and went down from class to class as a sort of tradition, and long years after he met a soldier's death the cadets would relate to gaping plebes how Pelham rode."[22]

Most important, he made it—the first year, with the culmination of June exams, had ended successfully. With him were fifty-eight classmates. Thirteen had not been so fortunate. Only two had been "found." As Cadet du Pont boasted, "It is very unusual for so few to be found . . . but we are, you know, a class beyond the common ones." Sadly one of those who had not made it was twenty-year-old William H. Woods from Indiana. Troubled by consumption, Woods died in the cadet hospital on May 27, 1857, after a lingering illness. With a few of his classmates serving as pallbearers, he was buried at the West Point Cemetery. All classes and military exercises were suspended on the afternoon of the funeral, and the entire corps wore black armbands in his honor for thirty days. The following year classmates Henry Kingsbury and Henry Hasbrouck selected a monument that was erected over his grave site. The inscription poignantly read, "Let it serve as a symbol to all who 'lie forgotten.'"[23]

3
"Fear God and Know No Other Fear"

I do not think a man can be strictly honorable unless he is brave.

—John Pelham

Thus, the second year of John Pelham's West Point service began. No longer a lowly plebe, he was now considered a cadet. During the summer encampment of 1857, Tom Rosser became embroiled in an altercation that nearly resulted in his expulsion from the academy. Two cadets were involved in a squabble; one of them refused an order and even raised a sword in defiance.[1] Impulsively, the hotheaded Rosser jumped into the fracas and punched one with his meaty fist while drawing his sword, threatening the other with further harm. When quiet had been restored, Rosser endured a court-martial. Found guilty of "conduct prejudicial to good order and military discipline," Rosser was "restricted to ordinary Cadet limits for the period of four months" and alternating weeks "to be kept in solitary confinement in the Cadet's Light Prison." Although uninvolved in the incident, John Pelham undoubtedly offered sympathy to his hot-tempered Texas roommate.

Meanwhile, the new class of plebes entered West Point. Seventy-nine bright-eyed rookies took their places among the cadets. Perhaps the most compelling of the newcomers was seventeen-year-old George Armstrong Custer. His irreverent and rollicking attitude made him an instant favorite. Nicknamed "Fanny," Custer had a penchant for demerits that bordered on insanity. In his own words, "My career as a cadet had but little to recommend it to the study of those who came after me, unless as an example to be carefully avoided." Perhaps Custer's most talked-about high jinks occurred one day in Spanish class. Walking in tardy, Custer promptly asked Professor Patrice de Janon how to say "class is dismissed" in Spanish. Unconsciously, de Janon replied, "Basta para hoy," whereupon the rambunctious Custer led his laughing classmates out of the room.[2] Assigned to Company D, the same as Pelham and Rosser, Custer fit in especially well with the Southern boys. With a respect for Pelham that never waned, Custer admired Rosser even more. Although facing each other from opposite sides during the Civil War, Custer and Rosser remained friends forever.

Added to the curriculum in the second year was French, a class that Pelham struggled with, and horsemanship, in which Pelham and Rosser excelled. Pelham also continued to impress his fellow cadets with his personality and athletic skills.

Boxing remained a favorite diversion. Rosser once admiringly remarked, "[He was] the mildest, gentlest man out of a fight and the fiercest man in a fight I ever knew." But mostly Pelham inspired those around him with his gentle and soldierly bearing. It was said that when he walked across the campus, he ventured "straight as a 'bee line' and never looked back, no matter how much noise the other cadets made in his rear." No doubt his mother's serious training of her children's posture paid off as numerous cadets observed with a keen eye John's erect bearing. Adelbert Ames possibly spoke for the entire corps when he stated, "[Pelham] was a gentleman in the highest sense of the term. A discourteous act was wholly foreign to his nature. . . . His kindly heart, sweet voice and genial smile carried sunshine with him always. What he instinctively claimed for himself he graciously conceded to others."[3]

By the end of the second year, Pelham's class had lost seven more members and numbered fifty-two. Cadet Jefferson Davis Bradford, nephew of the now Senator Jefferson Davis, was "found" by the Medical Board after spending a year on medical probation. In January 1858 a cadet was expelled for violation of Paragraph 113 of the academy's regulations: he was caught drunk at Benny Havens. Five others were "found" for academic deficiencies. Pelham's class ranking remained about average. He stood thirty-fifth in mathematics, thirty-eighth in English, and thirty-third in French. In general merit he ranked thirty-fourth. His "slug" count for demerits totaled ninety-two.[4]

Like all cadets, Pelham was granted leave for home, a place he had not seen in nearly twenty-four months. The ten-week furlough was considered a luxury since the cadets received virtually no other extended time away from the academy during their five-year tenure. Anticipating the venture home, John wrote his father on March 29, 1858. The letter discussed the cost of the trip, whether or not John was to stop in Maysville, Kentucky, to pick up his sixteen-year-old sister, Betty, who attended school there, and the parental request for the furlough to be addressed to the academy: "I think it almost time to write for money. Most of the class have already written. . . . If you and Ma are going to meet me at Maysville—then it will not take much—if not then I will have to take Sister home. . . . I also want permission to go on furlough. They are generally written in this form, 'I request that my son John Pelham be granted a leave of absence the ensuing encampment.'"[5] With the logistics worked out, John prepared for the trip home.

Dressed in the typical furlough uniform, Pelham boarded the train on Monday, June 14, 1858. The blue uniform with a stiff collar had a single row of gold buttons and was topped off by a high military hat, adorned with a brass plate with the letters U.S.C.C. etched on it. Handsomely dressed, Pelham sat proudly for a photograph in a New York City studio. Certainly, he anticipated the family welcome and the hugs from his siblings. After stopping off in Maysville to pick up his sister, John and Betty continued their trip home by train. After a joyous homecoming,

John told stories of his two years at the academy and the friends he had met. He ate heartily, as his mother's home cooking was a major change from the bland portions dished out at the mess hall. He spent a goodly amount of time with neighbors and taught the young girls in the area the proper way to ride a horse. He also planted a seedling from a New York sugar maple he had brought home. Most of his activities during his ten-week sojourn are unrecorded, but one story was told repeatedly by his amused family. At one point some of the Pelham boys, including John, ventured off to Atlanta in a wagon to buy horses. The money for the purchase was hidden in the wagon bed with younger brother Peter sleeping on it and acting as an innocent guardian. In the event they were stopped and questioned by strangers, the boys had been given strict instructions to say that Peter was an "invalid" traveling to see a doctor. John thought it funnier, however, to relate that Peter was an "infidel" en route for his health. Following his ten-week respite and the sad farewells to his family, Pelham returned to West Point at 2:00 P.M. on Saturday, August 28, to enter his third year.[6]

Now back at the academy, John found time to write to family. He penned two letters to his brother Charles in the fall of 1858. The first, dated September 25, offered much brotherly advice on women.

> Remember the best weapon for conquering women is flattery. Don't talk to them about History or Grammar, nor the Philosophy of Socrates, Plato or Zeno, but tell them about the Moon, spoons, the Starry Heavens, and moonlight walks &c. Flatter them, and be certain and let all your words be sentimental. I would like to be back in Ala[bama] again, although I am almost a follower of Machiavelli. . . . Nothing will please me more than to hear all the movements of the Calhoun Girls and the maneuvers of the Boys. . . . My heart may become susceptible to the impressions of "woman's wiles, woman's smiles and woman's blandishments." . . . You may rest assured that I will never be dismissed on studies or demerit—but they may discharge me for some mischief, fighting, etc.[7]

The second letter, dated October 12, rambled on a variety of subjects, particularly the rumor that the five-year course had been officially reduced to four.

> I have been sick with the Chills and Fever for more than a week. Am still unwell. Every feeling of sickness and discontent was overcome for a while by the good news of yesterday. <u>The Course has been reduced.</u> The order was published yester-evening at Parade. . . . Without some misfortune I will graduate in <u>June 1860.</u> . . . The intelligence of the change was received by the Corps with becoming merriment and rejoicing. As soon as we broke ranks every one put forth a shout that set at defiance all control, and might have caused

even a party of savages to cease with shame their hideous yells. The Officers essayed to stop it but in vain. They threatened to place any one they heard make a noise in arrest—but they could not hear any particular one the shout was too general. After supper we formed a procession of about 150. The <u>band</u> went in front. It was composed of one fiddle, one tambourine, one accordion, two pieces of sheet iron, one large tin box (upon which your humble bro' performed) and five or six swords to clang together—most of the others followed with brooms. All this may appear very foolish to you but we were full of enjoyment.

John closed the letter with a personal note: "I am very glad you have quit the use of <u>tobacco</u> but don't commence lecturing me yet. I would not discontinue the use of it for a good deal now."[8]

On February 26, 1859, John wrote two more letters, one to his mother and one to his brother Samuel. To his mother he stated, "Our 2nd class course is generally acknowledged to be the most difficult of any other." He further stated that the West Point band, consisting of forty-three musicians, was "the best band in the United States." He also mentioned being the "unworthy vice-president" of the Dialectic Society, a campus organization that discussed political issues and other contemporary topics. Changing subjects, John related, "We have an excellent gymnasium in which I exercise about an hour every evening, Sundays excepted. . . . I think the exercise is indispensable to health after being confined as much as we are. . . . I am in good health and doing well." He also spent a sizable amount of space discussing the latest ministers who preached on Sundays. Lastly, in his first mention of Richard Delafield, Pelham referred to him as "an arbitrary Superintendent, and a hypocritical and deceitful man." In the letter to Samuel, John quoted a poem and underlined the last line: <u>"Fear God and know no other fear."</u> He further offered some sound advice: "I do not think a man can be strictly honorable unless he is brave. If he fears and cringes to other men, he cannot fill the full definition of a man." He then admonished his brother not to be "contentious and quarrelsome, it shows a want of true courage. Cats are very quarrelsome and spiteful to dogs, but they always run when the dog pursues them."[9]

In a different letter to his niece, dated March 20, 1859, John possibly divulged a little-known characteristic when he penned, "I love you as much as I do myself." In the same letter he further mentioned that his dog, Brite, "has entirely recovered."[10]

Letters frequently arrived home from Pelham. On May 29, 1859, he wrote to his father, who seemed concerned about his son's class standing. Evidently Atkinson believed John was falling in love. John apologized that "I have caused you so much uneasiness—next year I will try & make my standing such as to free you from much care." As to his possible love interests, John mused, "I was greatly surprised and somewhat amused at the little fear you expressed. . . . If you knew me well your fear would be short. . . . So far from being in that condition, I think any and every one is incapable of prostrating me at that shrine. Unlike the arrows of fate they are easily warded off—I wish all your fears for me were as groundless as that one." John also proudly mentioned "no demerits this month."[11] Vowing never to get serious with a girl while at the academy, John joined a group called the Bachelors' Club. This select assemblage of eligible males made it their sworn duty to remain single.

Less than a month later, John wrote his mother, Martha. He mentioned his pending examinations. One test, which he labeled "a very good examination," had already been administered in Spanish class. He continued, "The worst part of it is being caged up in Barracks these beautiful days. . . . I have been pretty busy reading, but without much improvement to myself—the books I have read have been only entertaining for the time I waste in reading them, but I intend to read better and improving works." John then changed subjects and referred to the upcoming graduating class. Some of them were sporting mustaches, "though it is contrary to the regulations." John wrote of one who "went to inspection this morning with a very diminutive one [mustache], and the inspecting officer, not knowing what it was, reported him for having a 'dirty face.' Many others were reported and ordered to shave." His closing paragraph referred to his bachelor status and his vow to his father concerning women: "The Point is swarming with ladies. I sometimes amuse myself by observing them with a small telescope as they are passing about. There is a beautiful walk around the Plain, and some are continually on it. I have not spoken to a lady since my return. Think I will make a good <u>Bachelor.</u> I do not think the 'Bachelor Club' will be very large this encampment." In another letter John told of an elderly Alabama gentleman who arrived with his daughters as visitors to the academy with the intention of seeking out his Alabama "boys." Disdainful of the term "boys," John wrote, "I wonder where he thinks the <u>men</u> are."[12]

Closing out his third year at West Point, John wrote a letter to his brother detailing his class standing and the elite Color Guard. But most revealing was his detestation of Superintendent Richard Delafield, emotions John Pelham seldom showed.

> I did not try to hide the result of my June Examination from you. I came out low—lower than I expected, but I hope not lower than I deserved—and am not ashamed of it—42 in Philosophy—46 in Drawing & Painting—33 in Spanish—and I don't know where in General standing. . . . The "Color Line" was established on the 10th. I took "First Colors"—have got the prettiest & cleanest gun in Camp—it is a <u>beauty.</u> I have heard a whispered rumor that the Comd't will be relieved in Sept. I <u>hope</u> he will be. I <u>hate</u> him—<u>hate</u> him & <u>despise</u> him more than any man living. . . . He always congratulates the

Graduates on the successful termination of their course. I would like to hear him congratulate me—I would give him an insult he could never regret—and one he dare not resent. I have the time, now but not the feeling or substance to write more—[13]

Pelham's "slug" count for his third year numbered ninety-five. Some of these demerits occurred for "floor in alcove not cleanly swept"; "books and papers on tables not neatly arranged"; "floor dirty"; "noise in room"; and "inattention to the rules and regulations." The last offense was meted out for "chewing tobacco in quarters." Although Pelham's class ranking had slipped in his third year, his classmates continued to praise him. "[Pelham] did not apply himself particularly to his studies," recalled classmate Henry du Pont, who remained number one in class rankings, "[but] he was a young man of high tone and decided character, and his proficiency in military exercises and in all that pertained to the details of a soldier's life made him a cadet non-commissioned officer and a cadet officer." Adelbert Ames, always a Pelham supporter, beamed, "It is a pleasure to recall his memory. He was a general favorite at the Academy, and I think I am safe in saying that he was the most popular man in his class."[14]

Highlighting Pelham's career at West Point was his selection to the elite and coveted Color Guard. This prestigious honor went only to cadets who evidenced exemplary standards of preparation. According to Ames, "success depended on military bearing, cleanliness of gun, and condition of dress and accoutrements, including every possible detail." A cluster of willing classmates went about the serious business of assisting Pelham in this process. After brushing his uniform to perfection, one of the eager cadets procured a cleaner waist-belt, another brought a finer bayonet scabbard, while a third wiped his rifle with a handkerchief "to remove any possible neglected particle of dust; time, effort and interest they would hardly have given to themselves." During this operation, Pelham modestly and near embarrassment "was protesting they were too kind, and acknowledging his appreciation of their attention with merry laugh and twinkling eyes."[15] Topping it off came the five-pound, seven-inch high, black leather cap, with an additional eight-inch black plume. When finished with the process, Pelham was resplendent. Ames proudly added, "He made the Color Guard." It was a satisfying moment for the blushing Alabama farm boy.

Pelham's acclimation to the academy now seemed complete, as he later wrote to Judge A. J. Walker of Alabama: "I am very glad that you approve of my going into the Army. I don't think I could be satisfied with any other profession—in fact, I think I am better suited for the army than anything else. Its hardships I do not dread—its temptations, drinking & gambling, I can resist."[16]

That summer of 1859 Pelham stayed at the academy. Many of his friends, however, ventured home for a visit. All too often cadets made the mistake of stopping off in New York City and purchasing the services of a local prostitute before heading home. Gonorrhea could be the result, which frequently led to a harrowing appointment with the post surgeon for painful treatment. Evidently, this never occurred with Pelham, but it is exactly what happened to his wild young friend George Custer.[17]

Throughout the days and months of 1858–59, a tranquility of brotherhood had existed at West Point. Southern and Northern boys alike worked in harmony while the nation continued toward the seemingly inevitable clash of arms. "Not a word was said about politics," noted Morris Schaff, as "the days came and went." However, he wisely noted that pent-up emotions and hostilities existed under this façade, with "haughty disdain on the one hand, crouching hate on the other."[18] By the fall of 1859 these antagonisms were jarred loose by an alarming incident in the South that would have far-reaching consequences.

Not long after Pelham had entered his fourth year at West Point, the cadets, as well as the nation, were stunned by news from Virginia. At midnight on Sunday, October 16, radical abolitionist John Brown and his followers seized the federal arsenal at Harpers Ferry. Innocent hostages were taken by the extremists, including Lewis Washington, the great-grandnephew of George Washington and the father of cadet James Barroll Washington. For nearly two days local townspeople and state militia battled to capture these raiders. Five townspeople, including the mayor of Harpers Ferry, died in the fracas. Among the slain was George W. Turner, a West Point graduate from the Class of 1831 and a personal friend of Henry du Pont's father. Ultimately, ninety-three marines, under the leadership of Colonel Robert E. Lee with the assistance of a young lieutenant, James Ewell Brown Stuart, successfully ended the insurrection.[19] Instantly, the nation focused on the trial of John Brown. Emotions boiled over as the sectional conflict took center stage. Many predicted that a civil war was inevitable. For one of the few times at isolated West Point, sectionalism interrupted the revered brotherhood of cadets. At least one bloody fistfight occurred as two enraged cadets refused to hold back their anger.

Found guilty of murder, treason, and inciting a slave rebellion, John Brown was hanged in Charles Town, Virginia, on December 2, 1859. The day after his execution some Southern cadets strung up an effigy of him in front of the barracks building. It remained there until cut down by policemen. On the same day du Pont wrote to his mother about the existing tensions at the academy: "A great many here seem to think the Union is going to be dissolved." Schaff prophetically labeled Brown's raid "the first dying wail of an age." Calling Brown's raid a "devilish plot," Schaff recalled that "many of the Southern cadets broke out into natural and violent passion, denouncing in unmeasured terms the Abolitionists, and every one in the North who shared their antipathy to slavery." Although his feelings certainly favored the Southern thinking, John Pelham attempted to steer a quiet course of preventive action. Henry du Pont praised Pelham's low-key approach to the sectional differences: "social relations between Northerners and Southerners were not very close as a rule. Pelham, however, while preserving his sectional affiliations, was popular with everybody, his manly deportment and pleasant manners making him universally liked."[20]

Not all of the cadets, however, were able to control their emotions. On one December night tempers flared uncontrollably as the sanctimonious Emory Upton flaunted his Northern viewpoints, ridiculing some of the Southern boys. Taking exception to Upton's "dirty abolitionist" attitude was the stout South Carolinian Wade Hampton Gibbes, who further made a racial slur concerning Upton to another cadet. An apology was demanded, none was given, and Upton challenged Gibbes to a fistfight. In this noteworthy brawl Upton took a bloody thrashing. Even the Northern cadets, who often spurned Upton for his pious thinking, sympathized with the upstart New Yorker. Schaff called the fight "the most thrilling event in my life as a cadet, and . . . the most significant in that of West Point itself." According to him, it foreshadowed the ominous days ahead.[21]

Although Pelham seemed to stay out of the fisticuffs, he acted as second for the aristocratic and scholarly Henry du Pont, who fought two lads from New England who were upset with du Pont's high class ranking. Wrote du Pont, "I turned at once to John Pelham, who was my second in a pugilistic encounter of twenty-one minutes from which I emerged victorious." Even Pelham's fun-loving friend George Custer nearly became embroiled in a sectional skirmish of his own. A large and ill-tempered Southern cadet overheard Morris Schaff, an Ohioan, speak of the virtues of Senator Ben Wade, an abolitionist. When the argument came nearly to blows, Custer jauntily strolled up with classmate Leroy "Deacon" Elbert, an Iowan of goodly proportions. Said Custer, "If he lays a hand on you, Morris, we'll maul the earth with him." That ended the confrontation.[22]

Despite some bitter antagonisms and lingering hard feelings, classmates found time to design their graduation rings. With each class designing its setting and stone, Pelham's Class of May 1861 selected a ruby-red stone. Etched into the stone was the class crest, a drawn saber encircled with a minute chain, and the class motto, "Fidele a outrance" (Faithful to the uttermost). On one side of the gold ring appeared the insignia of the "Engineers," "Cavalry," and "Ordnance"; the other side contained a likeness of the Judge Advocate General's Office along with the emblems of the "Artillery" and "Infantry." Each ring cost a mere $25. Worn on the small finger of the left hand, Pelham's was inscribed, "John Pelham, Graduating Class of 1861." A leather-bound class album was another item greatly sought by the cadets, who collected photographs of their classmates to fill the pages. Although expensive—$50 per album—most eagerly purchased one as a remembrance of their acquaintances at the academy. "They are well worth the money," stated Tully McCrea, "for when we part here on graduation day we don't know but it will be the last time, for never have a class all met again after graduating and leaving West Point."[23]

Later that month John wrote his father a lengthy letter. He related how he had been hospitalized "with pains in my ears and chest, caused from cold." John also told of attending a wedding in the chapel of a Lieutenant Samuel Henry Lockett, a fellow Alabamian from the Class of 1859. Reiterating his pledge to remain a bachelor, John wrote, "rather early to take a companion! I think a young officer ought to play his hand alone for four or five years at least after graduating. He ought to rough it on the frontier for several years and learn whether Fate is propitious and in what direction Fortune showers her favors. That is the road I'll take." He further informed his father that "eight or nine" cadets were "hived" (found drunk) and arrested, and he supposed they would be court-martialed. Not only did Pelham vow not to marry, but he mentioned that he and several others "are on a pledge to abstain from all intoxicating liquors." He closed his letter with a powerful description of his frigid room: "My room is so cold that water freezes in my bucket at all times of the day. . . . The thermometer stands 9 degrees below zero, and the wind is so bitter that it is too cold to skate. Old Bentz, the bugler, accounts for it by supposing the Southerners won't let the south winds come north since the 'Harper's Ferry' affair. He says they won't have many enemies to fight if they hold their warm southern breezes much longer."[24]

On January 25, 1860, John penned as lengthy a letter to his mother. He began by telling her that he was in the hospital again, this time from a horse's kick. The leg he described as lame and severely swollen: "A crutch is indispensable when I move about." The incident happened two days earlier while in the riding hall. "We have heads, rings, lances and bars arranged . . . which we have to cut thrust, parry and jump, each one taking his turn. Sometimes miscuts are made and the horses ears or legs are struck—this makes them foolish and hard to get out of the ranks. While attempting to force a vicious one—I do not mean my horse . . . he let fly both feet, which took me on the leg—My leg is quite sore but the bone is not injured—the kick was not on the bone but on the muscle." This compelled him to dismount and go to the hospital. John stated that he enjoyed the hospital stay since some "nice eatables" were sent by his classmates every day. "I have a tolerably pleasant time. . . . Seven or eight other cadets are in here with whom I can talk." Also "ten or twelve come down to see me every evening and stay till 'call to Quarters.'" In his last paragraph, John admitted breaking his vow to the Bachelors' Club. In humorous fashion he related how he called on a young lady and immediately "about twenty cadets commenced hollering, 'Look here fellows Pelham has turned lady's man—he is going to make calls' 'John is getting spoony, he is going to the hotel.' etc." He then ruefully acknowledged that soon other crowds took up the chants "until there was at least 100 or 150 hollering at me." Seemingly hurt by this unwanted attention, John pouted, "other cadets [were] going to call on ladies at the hotel with me, but no one said anything to them."[25]

The Dialectic Society elected John president on May 12, 1860, during a meeting he failed to attend while he "called on some ladies." He casually mentioned this in brief to his father in a letter written the following day. This organization, which normally refrained from discussing sectional issues, had by now become more political. Topics related to the possible separation of the Union were even brought up. As president, John attempted to downplay the bitter sectional tone, not always with success. In one meeting Morris Schaff witnessed a bit of swordplay between a Southern cadet and a Northern one that could have gotten out of control. Virginian Jack Garnett and pompous New Yorker Judson Kilpatrick squared off in a mock duel as part of a play. As the contest proceeded, the two combatants, both excellent swordsmen, "lunged at each other in great style," which elicited cheering from their respective geographic sections. When two Southern cadets shouted, "Kill him, Jack, kill him!" Northern voices countered with, "Go it, Kil!" Luckily, the competition ended with laughter before any harm occurred. Schaff later wrote, "It was the funniest performance, I think, I ever witnessed."[26]

As the Class of 1860 prepared to graduate from the academy, George Custer decided to set up a farewell party for four of them—Stephen Dodson Ramseur, his roommate Wade Hampton Gibbes, who had only recently beaten up Emory Upton, Wesley Merritt, and Alexander Pennington—at Benny Havens's establishment. Other underclassmen invited were John Pelham, Tom Rosser, who helped Custer with the arrangements, Adelbert Ames, and a few more, possibly including Henry du Pont. With the tavern off-limits, the dozen or so cadets bunched pillows and clothing under their blankets to form a fake human body on their beds, a ruse undoubtedly thought up by Custer. From there they slipped off to Benny Havens, where the amiable host had a row of mugs, filled with "flip," a popular drink made of rum, sugar, and egg, waiting. After a preliminary toast to the four guests of honor the friends sang, drank, laughed, and danced long into the night. Benny even brought out his banjo to pluck in accompaniment to their singing and dancing. Sometime before the party broke up in the wee hours of the morning, Custer stood to toast what he called the finest class ever to go through West Point.[27]

Nearing his examinations and the close of his fourth year at West Point, Pelham penned a letter to his father on June 4. He mentioned an illness that pervaded the family back in Alabama and that he was requesting a furlough to visit his ailing relatives. He further indicated that he would need a forward of "traveling expenses" but vowed to be "economical." The remainder of the letter explained an exhaustive inspection made by the Board of Visitors, causing the "whole Point" to be "in a stir." In literary fashion John stated, "The boats are constantly landing to belch forth their loads. All the carriages and omnibusses are crowded with <u>crinoline.</u> The Point is inundated with the gay throngs. The whole Plain & Flirtation Walk are radiant with the smiles of beauty leaning . . . on [the arm of] the military. In almost every room in Barracks bouquets & flowers are to be seen in profusion. In short everything is gay, animated and pleasing." He also proudly related that during the inspection by the Board of Visitors, the president of the board "complimented [me] very highly on the neatness & cleanliness of my room." He then coyly added, "Some of the Board said there was no necessity for us to marry for we could keep our rooms in good order without a wife, while the ladies said 'we were the very ones to marry for we were the very kind they loved most.' "[28]

After examinations John's scores were in. In a class remaining at fifty, he finished twenty-sixth in ethics, thirty-first in both infantry and artillery tactics, nineteenth in cavalry tactics (his highest standing), thirty-third in chemistry, and fortieth in drawing. He had received 156 demerits and stood thirty-fourth in general merit. Some of his "slugs" were for "smoking in room," while two were given for "childish conduct in Ethical Section" and five more for "making use of highly profane language while on duty at riding hall."[29] Pelham's friend Henry du Pont continued to be number one in the overall class.

But all the academia was now behind him, for the time being, as he boarded a train for home in mid-June 1860. The lingering illnesses at home were nearly over when he arrived. His sister, Betty, took the longest to recover. This vacation from the rigors of the academy afforded John some badly needed relaxation. Once more he could roam his beautiful homeland followed by his ever-present dogs. Fishing the local streams was, as always, his favorite. The precious time spent with his family was also his time to show off his improved boxing and riding skills. He further dazzled them by slicing buttons off brother Charles's coat with his West Point saber without disturbing the cloth.[30] With time passing all too quickly, John said good-bye to his loved ones and headed back to West Point in early August for his senior year. Little did he know that this final year at the hallowed institution would force him to render the most important decision of his life.

4
"Madness and Fanaticism"

I had hoped . . . to graduate here. . . . but Fate seems to have willed it otherwise.

—John Pelham

One month shy of his twenty-second birthday, John Pelham began his last year at West Point. His class was scheduled to graduate in early June 1861. First, however, came the substantial and grueling classroom studies in such courses as engineering, ethics, and ordnance and artillery.

Shortly after his return, John wrote his father on August 13 and reported that he was "Officer of the Day." His duties entailed making the rounds and inspecting every "relief" into the wee hours of the morning. He further stated that it was a "miserable rainy day" that left him "drenched through." Switching subjects, he gladly related that "the Commission appointed to examine into the affairs of the Academy I think will report favorably of us (cadets). They are going to have our Mess fare improved—give us wood fires in winter, etc. But they will not report favorably for the 4 years course for Jeff Davis is on the Commission." He then gave attention to his daily schedule: parade and artillery drill for one and a half hours in the morning, followed by two hours of practical engineering, topped off with riding in the afternoon. He closed the letter with an interesting statement: "I have almost changed my mind about the dragoons—I am <u>now</u> inclined to prefer the Infantry."[1]

What Pelham most likely never mentioned to his father occurred during his last summer camp in mid-August. On the twenty-first of the month John found the time to entertain a number of visiting ladies and apparently did not notice a commanding officer, Colonel William Hardee, approaching. Neglecting to stand at attention and salute, Pelham was sent to his tent to await further punishment. In a letter to his brother, dated September 18, John wrote: "I guess you think it strange that I have not written. If you knew how busy I had been this last encampment you could not have blamed me much. I devoted all my time, talents, and energies to the fair sex." John then explained the encounter with Colonel Hardee, who ordered him to be confined to the Guard Tent "for 7 days!" His demerit log read: "Highly disrespectful conduct—not rising and saluting his superior officer -5." Although John labeled Hardee "a bearded monster," he took the punishment in stride and seemed to relish his detention. "I got five or six baskets (of food) every day," he wrote his brother, "and enough cigars for half a dozen men to smoke." John further mentioned a "belle" from New York who was "ahead of any thing in . . . beauty ease and gracefulness of manner I ever saw. She had numerous admirers of course. But I got full share of her company and attention." John also stated that "by putting me in the Guard Tent, they [the ladies] lionized me. I ran ahead of my competitors in that line. . . . A good many of the ladies came to see and sympathize with me—but I told them I hated sympathy except when in some tangible form." Referring to the entire episode as "a splendid time," John closed by stating, almost proudly, "I am doing pretty well—got a great many demerits in Aug[ust]." This letter undoubtedly explains why young Pelham's class standing did not improve in his last year at West Point.[2]

In the first weeks of October 1860, eastern newspapers headlined the American visit of Albert Edward, the so-called Baron of Renfrew and Prince of Wales, heir to the British throne.[3] Edward's particular interests were in the areas of horsemanship and the military, so quite naturally his entourage planned a trip to West Point. Cadets were abuzz with his impending visit, scheduled for Monday, October 15. Selected as a member of the guard of honor, Pelham helped Prince Edward disembark from the yacht, *Harriet Lane,* named for President James Buchanan's niece. From there the prince was escorted to Cozzen's Hotel, where he would enjoy his own exquisite suite, while his extensive entourage was lodged in twenty-four rooms. Meanwhile, cadets spruced up and awaited his presence. An estimated six thousand people patiently sat, including special guest General Winfield Scott, as well as the entire faculty in full military dress, while the cadet corps stood in precise lines for three hours until he arrived. Loud applause greeted the prince as he entered the Plain late that afternoon, seated on a fine stallion and dressed in a tall silk hat, surrounded by his escort. The cadets, dressed in their finest, held a military review replete with horses and cannons. Tully McCrea noted that the visit came at a splendid time of the year "for the mountains look really beautiful with their many-colored trees." A cannon salute greeted the prince as he rode forward, which he acknowledged with a gentlemanly tip of his hat. The cadet band then welcomed him by playing "God Save the Queen" and the "Flower of Edinburgh." The prince enjoyed it all, broadly smiling and applauding vociferously. He was then led to the superintendent's headquarters for an official greeting. Cadet McCrea stated that "[The prince] saw the prettiest military spectacle he ever will have the chance to see. Every cadet had his pride aroused and did his best."[4]

That evening the cadets invited Edward to a ball, but he politely declined. He was receptive, however, to an invitation to the next day's classrooms. Seemingly bored by the academics, the prince warmed considerably to the demonstration of equestrian skill in the riding hall. He applauded the showmanship of Mississippian James Kennard, who nearly fell from the saddle in one demonstration but athletically regained his seat by swinging his body back onto his mount. The prince particularly complimented young Pelham on his abilities and presented him with a meerschaum pipe as a memento before leaving.[5]

Most of the cadets seemed to enjoy the royal visit and were impressed by the prince's stature and mannerisms. Some, however, were not the least thrilled. "Well, the Prince has come and gone, and we have all been able to live through the mighty event," scowled the always honest McCrea. "The conclusion the cadets have come to is that the Prince is a grand humbug in the shape of well-dressed Dutch boy with monstrous big feet. He looked to me not very intelligent."[6]

A few newspaper editorials also blasted the visit as too showy and expensive, and further criticized the prince for not seeing more of the United States. Pelham responded to this negative analysis in a letter to his sister dated October 18. "I enjoyed the Prince's visit vastly. . . . I intended to send home the 'New York Herald' containing an account of his visit, but the reporter is a fool as well as a villain—and his account is worth nothing. It says 'the Cadets were offended because the Prince did not wear his uniform.' This is a falsehood—no one was offended—we liked his conduct very much." In the same letter, John casually mentioned that he wasn't receiving too "many demerits."[7]

By mid-October the talk at the academy, as well as the nation, centered around the upcoming presidential election. Four candidates had been nominated earlier in the year in what appeared to be the most sectional campaign in the nation's history. Representing the Republican Party was Abraham Lincoln, labeled a "Black Republican" by many in the biased Southern press. His support undoubtedly would come exclusively from the North. The oldest existing party in America, the Democrats, had virtually ruined its chances when it split over the sectional issues. The Northern Democrats nominated their old standby, Stephen Douglas, now a disillusioned and alcoholic has-been. The Southern Democrats, espousing their states' rights theory, nominated the current vice president, Kentuckian John Breckinridge. John Bell, an aging Tennessean, received the nomination from the Constitutional Union Party, a group ascribing to the belief in the Constitution and keeping the Union together "at all costs."

Many predicted a permanent split in the young nation if Lincoln were elected. This realization impacted the cadets at West Point heavily since it would rupture their sacrosanct brotherhood. In a letter home Henry du Pont warned, "I am glad the elections will soon be over. . . . There is a most insane spirit here rampant on the secession question." On October 26 some Southern boys held a meeting to decide what they would do if Lincoln won. Some determined to leave immediately, but the majority held firm: show restraint and wait for further outcomes. A few wondered if legally they could leave since they had sworn allegiance to the Constitution and the laws of the United States. Recognizing that cooler heads must prevail, Pelham took an active role in calming a possible volatile situation. "No one's bearing under such circumstances was more wise, more discreet than John Pelham's," observed Adelbert Ames. "When we separated in the spring of 1861 none took with him more affectionate regard than he."[8]

As the election of 1860 drew nearer, anxiety at the academy swelled. In September a group of cadets held a mock presidential election. Of the 278 total corps, 214 cast their ballots. Breckinridge prevailed with 99 votes, followed by Douglas with 47, Bell 44, and Lincoln with a mere 24 ballots. A number of Northern cadets were peeved with the results, claiming that the election was a fraud. Another election was later held. With 64 of the 210 cadets casting their ballots for Lincoln, the Southern boys were both surprised by and indignant at the result.

Election day came on Monday, November 6, and the results ensured what many had forlornly predicted. By midnight the ominous news of Lincoln's victory reached the academy. Sometime in the wee hours of the cold morning, a few Southern cadets hung an image of Lincoln in effigy. Shortly after daybreak some Northern cadets, including Custer, cut it down. Morris Schaff labeled it "the most exciting and certainly the most fateful [election] which our country has gone through . . . the very air was charged. . . . the day for compromise had gone by."[9]

Although Lincoln was not due to be inaugurated until March 4, some of the Southern cadets refused the pleadings of Pelham and Rosser and opted to leave West Point immediately. The first was South Carolinian Henry S. Farley from the Class of 1862, who left on the night of November 19. His resignation was quickly followed by another South Carolinian, James Hamilton. "The future certainly looks very dark and threatening," wrote the astute Henry du Pont to his family, "and I cannot look forward to graduation with that pleasure I did formerly. And if it is to be our lot to be employed in cutting our countrymen's throats and fighting our dearest friends and class-mates, I am very sorry I ever came here."[10]

No doubt, John Pelham and his faithful roommate, Tom Rosser, spent long hours after "lights out" discussing their personal plight over the secession issue. Both desired to graduate, but the intense pressure of loyalty to their home states seemed to outweigh the oath of allegiance to the corps. While awaiting the woes of the nation to climax, each of them wrote to an influential state leader seeking advice. Rosser chose the ex–Indian fighter and hero of Texas independence, Governor Sam Houston. Houston, an avowed Unionist, responded on November 17. "I cannot for a moment entertain the belief that any cause for secession or disunion exists," wrote the governor, "or that the masses of the people would be ready or willing to precipitate the country into all the horrors of revolution and civil war. If madness and fanaticism should so far prevail as to bring about this disastrous state of affairs, no human being could calculate the injury that would be inflicted upon mankind. Anarchy and confusion . . . then Monarchy. . . . Rapine plunder and devastation would follow in its footsteps. Brother would be in arms against brother." Houston closed with a terse admonition: "My advice is that you give your whole time and attention to your studies in order that you may be prepared to assume that position to which your graduation would entitle you."[11]

Pelham wrote to Alabama Supreme Court Chief Justice A. J. Walker. His reply arrived at West Point on December 11. "I advise you to resign immediately after Alabama secedes," Walker suggested in contradiction to what Houston had advised, "and tender your sword to her." Pelham explained this in a letter to his father written on the same day. Pelham further stated, "[Chief Justice Walker also] said he would write me again as soon as the Convention acts and give me further advice. He expressed a deep interest in my career and offered to assist me whenever he could. . . . I wrote to Governor [Andrew B.] Moore a day or two ago. With your advice and theirs I ought to be able to act judiciously." To his father Pelham sadly noted, "I had hoped, fondly hoped, to graduate here. It would be exceedingly gratifying to me and I know to the family also for me to receive a Diploma from this Institution, but Fate seems to have willed it otherwise. I don't see any honorable course other than tendering my resignation when Ala. leaves the Union, and offering my services to her. In this I did not wish to act precipitately, but in a manner worthy of myself, of my family and of my section of the country." John closed the letter concerned about his own personal finances. "We are in a terrible fix about <u>money.</u> Army officers can't get their pay. . . . The sup't has placed our equipment funds out at interest—the treasury is empty. . . . I don't know what we are to do."[12]

On December 18 John wrote his mother. "You may expect to see me at home by the 1st of Feb. 1861," he said. "I regret the circumstances which make it necessary but I don't see any remedy—Alabama seems to be determined to leave the Union before the middle of Jan[uary] and I think it would be dishonorable in me to withhold my services when they will be needed. It seems pretty hard that I should toil for four years & a half for a diploma and then have to leave without it. I am studying pretty hard and I think I will be higher after the coming Jan. examinations than I have ever been before . . . but my <u>standing</u> will not do me any good." He also mentioned his ailing knee and problem teeth. "My teeth are troubling me a good deal—I have had two drawn—and caught cold in my jaw—all my face is on one side—I have had three filled—the Dentist will be down tomorrow and I am going to have ten filled. I hope the engagements will not be so pressing as to prevent his doing it all tomorrow." John's last paragraph reassured his mother that his religious training had not been forgotten. "I always (nearly always) get over my lessons and read a chapter in my Bible a short time before 11 P.M. . . . I am not allowed to have a light after [this hour]." He admitted staying up past "lights out" to draw by "put[ting] a quilt up over my windows . . . sometimes as late as 1 or 2 o'clock. . . . For the past two years and a half I have read my Bible very regularly—one chapter almost every night—and when I neglected it one night I made it up the next."[13] Although Pelham seemed emphatic about leaving the academy if Alabama seceded, he continued to wait for the inevitable.

On Thursday, December 20, 1860, ominous news arrived. South Carolina became the first state to secede from the Union at 1:15 P.M. that day. The state legislators in Charleston had voted to sever their ties with the rest of the nation by an overwhelming tally of 169 to 0. Certainly other states would follow the Palmetto State's lead. Calling South Carolina's severance from the Union "a step down the stairway of their tragic fate," Morris Schaff noted that the West Pointers, especially the Southern boys, followed the secession with "absorbing and painful interest."[14]

Tensions continued to mount at West Point. Pelham's father, Atkinson, and brother Charles sent word for John to remain calm and wait before making any decision. Not all Southern cadets, however, were as patient. Alabamian Charles P. Ball from George Custer's class stood in the mess hall before the gathered cadets and announced his decision to leave. He called out to the assembled crowd, "Battalion, attention! Good-bye boys! God bless you all!" His fellow classmates cheered him loudly and carried him off on their shoulders down to the Hudson River.[15] In the meantime the Christmas holidays passed and still no word for Pelham from Judge Walker or the Alabama Convention.

Soon after the holiday season had ended, word did arrive, but not from Alabama. On January 9, 1861, Mississippi voted to secede, and a handful more cadets tendered their resignations. The next day Florida became the third state to leave. And then the news arrived. Alabama's state legislators at Montgomery, by a vote of 61 to 39, pulled out of the Union on Friday, January 11. Although anxiety-ridden by the news of his home state's secession, John Pelham remained steadfast, still hoping to graduate. Pelham's determination to remain at West Point was respected, especially by the Northern boys. Numerous cadets marveled at his restraint and general bearing in such troubled times.

By this time Pelham had grown to full manhood. Morris Schaff described him as "gracefully tall, fair, and a beautiful dancer, and it may well be asserted that Nature was in a fine mood when she moulded his clay. Her final touch was to give him a pronounced cowlick on his forehead, which added a mounting swirl to his blond hair. His eyes generally were cast thoughtfully downward, and a little wrinkle on his brow gave just the faintest suggestion of a frown on his otherwise unclouded face." Even in the perilous year of 1861, the cadets found ways to amuse themselves. "The larger number [of cadets]," continued Schaff, "would congregate in the fencing-hall and dance to music by members of the band. How often I sat with [classmate Clifton] Comly—for dancing was not among our accomplishments—and watched the amazing couples, Rosser and Pelham, 'Cam' [Campbell] Emory and [Adelbert] Ames, [Nathaniel] Chambliss and [Llewellyn] Hoxton, [Jacob] Kent and [Eugene] Beaumont, [Peter] Hains and [Alonzo] Cushing, [James] Dearing and [George] Gillespie, [Henry] du Pont and [Francis] Farguhar, and many, many others! Yes, that was the way we were passing the time in that January of 1861, on the verge of the Civil War."[16]

On January 19, Georgia became the fifth Southern state to secede. Georgian Pierce M. B. Young expressed his situation, and that of Pelham and the other remaining Southern boys, to his parents in a letter that day, saying, "You and others down there don't realize the sacrifice resigning means. It is a hard thing to throw up a diploma from the greatest Institution in the world when that diploma is in my very grasp." Chief Justice A. J. Walker penned a letter to Governor Andrew B. Moore that same day. "I take the liberty of recommending to you John Pelham as an applicant for a military appointment," Walker wrote. "His standing in the Academy is high and he promises to make a soldier of the first order. I have letters from him and they show that his whole heart is with his state."[17]

There was some good news for John Pelham on January 23: the much-despised superintendent, Richard Delafield, resigned. His replacement was Pierre Gustave Toutant Beauregard. Schaff labeled the resignation "an incident of historic importance in the life of the Military Academy." Beauregard may have been a welcome addition as superintendent to Pelham and the remaining Southern cadets, but his tenure lasted a mere five days. His outspoken Southern sympathies forced his early dismissal.[18] Three days after Delafield left the academy, Louisiana seceded from the Union. Then, on February 1, Texas withdrew as the seventh Southern state. On the same day Atkinson Pelham sent his son written permission to resign from the academy: "In consequence of the troubles and unhappy condition of our Country, I hereby give my son John Pelham, a Cadet at the U.S. Military Academy, West Point, New York, permission to tender his resignation to the Superintendent or other proper officer of that Institution." When John received this message, he neatly folded the paper and put it away, doing nothing more for the time being.[19]

Delegates from the seceded states, charged with the immense task of forming a "confederacy," met on February 4 in Montgomery, Alabama. They quickly appointed a twelve-man committee, under the chairmanship of Christopher Memminger, to write a constitution. One of the members, brilliant constitutionalist Alexander H. Stephens, remarked that their objective was "not to tear down so much as to build up [a government] with greater security and permanency." Over the next few weeks, the committee formulated a new constitution and government, the Confederate States of America. For the all-important job as president, the committee selected Jefferson Davis on February 18, 1861. Sworn in four days later on Friday, February 22, at the temporary capital in Montgomery, Davis, with his hand on the Bible, took his oath of allegiance. From the portico of the state capitol building, Davis delivered an uninspired inaugural speech to a large, enthusiastic audience.[20] Exactly ten days later Abraham Lincoln took a similar oath in Washington, D.C.

Tensions still ran high at the academy. The tirelessly abrasive mouth of Judson Kilpatrick forced a memorable fistfight with Kentuckian William Dunlap just outside the mess hall. While Southern cadets rooted against the hated Kilpatrick, many Northerners, including George Custer, cheered Dunlap as well. Schaff called it a "lively encounter" but also viewed it suspiciously: "A funnier row I never saw in my life." Later many of the West Pointers witnessed one of the most poignant scenes in their years at the academy. On this unseasonably warm night, February 22, the academy band marched across the Plain playing "Washington's March." As the band passed through the sally port, the musicians struck up the stirring notes of "The Star-Spangled Banner." The haunting melody echoed across the Plain, and the cadets, Northern and Southern alike in D Company, began raising their windows for a better view. As the band marched toward the barracks, the music swelled louder. Eyes misted, as the boys may have realized the finality of the moment. As the notes softened into silence, a tumultuous and shrill cavalry cheer surged from the Northerners. "I believe it was begun at our window by Custer," wrote Schaff, "for it took a man of his courage and heedlessness openly to violate the regulations." When the screaming ended, the band played the vibrant "Dixie." As the final notes faded, the Southern lads, led by Rosser, broke into an equal cacophony, soon to be known as the "Rebel Yell." Thereafter, the Northern and Southern boys took turns shouting for the band to replay their favorite of the two songs. "Ah, it was a great night!" related Schaff. "Rosser at one window, Custer at another."[21]

On February 27 Pelham and Rosser wrote letters to Jefferson Davis offering their services to the Confederate government. Pelham's letter read:

> Being still a member of the Mily Acad'y [Military Academy], I don't think it would be exactly proper for me to offer my services to the new Government, but I am anxious to serve it to the best of my ability. If you think it would be better for me to resign now than to wait and graduate which will be in June, a single word from you will cause me to resign and as soon as my resignation is accepted, I will consider myself under your orders, and repair to Montgomery without delay. I am a member of the 1st Class which graduates in June next—you know the importance of that portion of the Course still to be completed and also whether my services are needed at present. May I expect a recall if needed?[22]

No letter was immediately forthcoming from President Davis, so the two cadets temporarily stayed.

While waiting for any sort of response, Pelham wrote his sister-in-law, the new wife of brother Charles, on March 9. In perhaps his most moving letter, he stated:

> You need not be afraid of piquing my southern feelings by respecting the "Stars and Stripes." Although I am a most ultra Secessionist, I am still proud

of the American Flag. It does not belong to the North any more than to us, and has never had anything to do with our wrongs. I think that both sides ought in justice to the illustrious dead lay it aside as a memento of our past greatness and of our Revolutionary renown. I would fight harder and longer to tear the "Stars and Stripes" from every Northern battlement than for any other cause. They have no right to use it and we should not permit them. It should be stored away with our other household goods, cherished and preserved spotless and unstained "not a single stripe erased or polluted, not a single star obscured."

Changing subjects from this patriotic fervor, he noted: "I am courting all the girls around here—making friends of all of them, in order to render my imprisonment as easy and pleasant as possible. Isn't that diplomatique?" Of his own "Sister Bettie," John wrote, "She is the best girl I ever saw—possesses more virtues and fewer faults than any girl I ever saw—in short she is a perfect model of a sister." Then returning to his earlier, more serious tone, he wrote: "I am still clinging to a faint hope of graduating—but each day's news is [more] portentous . . . than its predecessor. I think my chances are few and small—hope almost gone—still I swing on with one hand and strive to ward off the threatening convictions which force themselves on my mind with the other. But I don't really think I can ever graduate—and so near it too!"[23]

Dr. Atkinson Pelham evidently believed that it was time for him to intercede on his son's behalf. On March 15 he wrote a lengthy letter to Jefferson Davis explaining John's plight: "If you think proper to reply to my son's letter, please inclose [*sic*] to me at this place. The reason given by Mr. Rosser & my son for making this request is that a communication to either of them from Montgomery <u>might</u> be opened before reaching them. . . . If my son's services are not immediately needed I would much rather he should remain where he is till the next Annual Examination but will cheerfully yield to your judgment and suggestions in this matter." Atkinson then proceeded to rattle off the impressive list of his many relatives who had served in the military since the Revolutionary War. "I lately sent my son permission to resign but urged him to remain as long as it was prudent to stay & left it discretionary with him." Atkinson closed the letter by stating: "John Pelham is in his 23rd year has been at West Point nearly 5 years. He is intelligent, athletic, & well proportioned. I think he will make a good soldier." Whether the letter had an impact on Davis is not known, but the following day Confederate Secretary of War Leroy Pope Walker sent a signed commission for John Pelham to be admitted as a first lieutenant of artillery.[24]

Later that month John penned a letter to his cousin Marianna in Philadelphia. This unpublished letter is presented here in its entirety.

West Point N.Y.
March 26th/'61

Dear Cousin

I am just in receipt of your kind letter of the 23rd Inst.

I would like above all things to meet your Mother and Sister [Martha and Ellen Wright] in Phila.—it may be the only opportunity I will ever have of seeing them. I am most anxious to see them, but can not say when I will leave. If I remain to get my diploma I will have to wait till 15th June. But whether I will stay till then is the question. I am not master of my own acts at present. I have been appointed a 1st Lieutenant in the Army of the "Confederate States of America." My appointment has been confirmed by the Congress. The appointment was made without my consent or knowledge. I cannot accept an appointment from them as long as I am a member of this institution, but if I am recalled by the Authorities, I will obey it. I have thus far resisted every overture, on the part of my friends, to resign, disregarded their advice and braved their anger. My father and brothers alone wished me to graduate. I had no idea I was so well supplied with friends. All seemed to vie with each other in attempting to force me to resign. I have worked almost five years for my diploma, and it pains me to give up the undertaking now—besides all this, it chagrins me to be forced to leave an undertaking unfinished. I believe there [are] only two Cadets here at present from the Seceded States—Myself and a classmate from Texas [Tom Rosser]. We will leave together—in June—or before, as the fates will it. We have been living together for three or four years, and I feel like we are inseperable [*sic*]—like his presence is necessary to my happiness. If we leave before June, it will be in about two weeks. You must allow me to introduce him.

I suppose you have heard of Bro' Charles' Marriage, through Aunt Ann [Ann Pelham Miller] or some of our Kentucky kin. I believe Aunt Martha knew Bro' Chas—if so, tell her, he married one of the nicest ladies in Ky. So they all write—I have never seen her.

I had a letter from Henry Pelham [a Kentucky cousin of John's] a few days since, he says all are well in Ky. Sister is almost crazy about her Sister—it is the first she has ever had. I think it would be doing her a kind and brotherly act to present her with another, but none of the girls will have me. It's the most unaccountable thing I ever heard of—don't you think so?

I can let you know definitely in a week or two whether I will have the pleasure of visiting you before you leave Phila.

If anything could compensate me for giving up my dearest object—graduating—it is the pleasure I would have in visiting your family, you, Mother & Sister.

Tell Cousins Belle & Emily [Marianna's daughters Isabel, 15, and Emily, 13]
we may get another ride together—and then I will teach them to ride like
Cavalry officers. Give them my best love. Remember me kindly to Mr. Mott
[Marianna's father].

Affectionately
Jno. Pelham[25]

Evidence exists that Pelham's intentions of resigning were not kept secret from
the Northern cadets. On March 27, Henry du Pont wrote his mother, "Rosser [and]
Pelham . . . are here and still do not intend to resign until they receive official notice
of their having been appointed & will then hand in their resignations so as to enable
them to accept the appointments as soon as they are released from their engagements to the United States." On the last day of March Pelham responded to a letter
he received the day before from Judge A. J. Walker: "Until [your letter] came I was
quite uncertain whether I could graduate. Now, I think I shall." He further stated
that Jefferson Davis had "advised some of his friends here in my class to graduate,
by all means." He then commented: "Mr. Lincoln does not seem to be very anxious for war, and I guess everything will remain quiet till June—in the mean time
I will better qualify myself for a position in life especially for the military profession. . . . The army suits me better than anything else—and I feel a confidence that
I can succeed in it. I am studying very hard at present—not only the textbooks of
the Acad'y, but other useful military works." He closed by saying he would resign
as soon as he graduated and hoped the Confederate Army would allow him in.[26]

On April 8 Henry du Pont's mother wrote her son concerning the dilemma facing Pelham and Rosser: "I cannot comprehend how they can honorably hold two
commissions at once—or how any soldier educated by the government can employ
his talents to overthrow that government to which he has sworn allegiance." Two
days later Henry responded to his mother's logic in a return letter expressing sympathy and respect for the dilemma of Pelham and Rosser: "You do not understand
the position in which Rosser and Pelham are in. They are not in the service of the
Southern Confederacy now, as they have not accepted the appointments; in fact,
they know nothing more about it than you or I do, only having seen it in the paper.
Take Pelham. . . . a man of nicer and more honorable feelings never lived. Some
months ago the Governor of his state wrote to him offering him a high rank in the
state forces if he would resign and come home. He would have nothing to do with
it & did not even answer the letter and had not applied for any position in the Confederate troops. But, like many others, they have appointed him a first lieutenant,
that is, have published in the newspapers his appointment. . . . He does not intend
to serve in the army but will resign as soon as he graduates. . . . He will, though, as
an honorable man, never accept a commission from the Confederate States until
he has resigned the one he holds in that of the United States."[27]

Henry's mother wrote back to her son without a change of heart: "You defend your friend Pelham very ably, but do not convert me from [my] opinion." Henry's father also felt the necessity to write his son concerning the impending resignation of his son's friends: "I consider an officer in the service of the Government owes his allegiance to the United States and not to any State of which he may be a native. . . . He belongs to the flag, and it is his duty to stand by it when the Government is threatened with Treasons, Rebellion, or War."[28] Following these admonishments from his parents, Henry saw fit not to write more on the dilemma of his two Southern friends.

Distressing news arrived on Friday, April 12. That morning at 4:30, Confederate cannons opened fire across Charleston Bay at Fort Sumter. Inside the fort were 127 Federal personnel under the command of Major Robert Anderson, a Kentuckian. P. G. T. Beauregard, now a general and an ex-artillery student of Anderson's at West Point, directed the Confederate gunners. Over four thousand Confederate shells blasted for better than thirty hours, without any fatalities, but Anderson was forced to surrender on Sunday, April 14. Thus, the Civil War began without a formal declaration from either side. "The news of the firing on Sumter reached West Point some time between eight and half-past nine in the morning," remembered Schaff. "That whole livelong day we thought of and talked of nothing else."[29]

Pelham, Rosser, and the remaining Southern cadets knew what this meant. All last-minute arrangements for their departure from the academy were worked out. Meanwhile, a delegation of Northern cadets signed a petition, dated April 14, and sent it off to Lincoln's secretary of war, Simon Cameron, requesting permission for an early graduation. It read in part: "we the undersigned members of the graduating class of the Military Academy, do respectfully request to be allowed to graduate now, and take our places among those who are serving their country and defending its flag."[30] No answer was immediately forthcoming. The following day President Lincoln called for seventy-five thousand volunteers to put down this armed insurrection and drag the seven rebellious states back into the Union.

On April 17 John Pelham formally tendered his resignation to Secretary of War Cameron. At the bottom of the official form appeared John's signature and his handwritten words: "I have accepted no place or appointment from any state or government." Tom Rosser resigned the same day. John also submitted the letter he had saved from his father (dated February 1) giving him written permission to resign. Pelham's resignation was approved and signed by the commandant of cadets, John F. Reynolds, who marked it "Approved and Respectfully forwarded."[31]

Pelham's last recorded action at West Point brought demerits: "absent from breakfast" on April 18. No crowd of cadets gathered to usher Pelham and Rosser off on their shoulders. None cheered their departure as had been done for the cadets exiting earlier. They left at night, April 22, slinking away, fearful of being placed under arrest. Years later Pelham's friend Henry du Pont remembered their departure: "After a very sorrowful parting [Pelham] left the Military Academy for the south early in 1861 and I never saw him again." Adelbert Ames, too, was touched by Pelham's exit, writing nearly forty years later, "I am not disloyal when I tell you we heard with secret pride of his gallant deeds on the field of battle. It was what we had the right to expect of him—he was our classmate for five years—he was one of the best of us—who should win honors and glory if not he?" During a class reunion held in 1909 classmate and friend Adelbert Buffington recalled: "It seems as though it were yesterday that Pelham and I walked together in '61. 'Buff,' he said, turning to me suddenly, 'I am going home. I shall be in two or three fights and then be killed.'"[32]

Forty-five of Pelham's classmates stayed on for the early May 6 graduation. Had Pelham remained, he would have stood twenty-ninth in engineering, sixteenth in ethics, twenty-ninth in ordnance and gunnery, with 139 demerits.[33] Thus after four years and ten months at West Point, and just a mere two weeks shy of graduating, Pelham left the academy with some meager possessions, including a few photographs and approximately thirty autographs of his classmates. The one item he most desired he left without—a diploma.[34]

In the ensuing weeks, four more states seceded and joined the Confederacy. Virginia left on April 17, followed by Arkansas (May 6), Tennessee (May 7), and North Carolina on May 20. Eleven states now constituted the Confederate States of America. Soon the capital was moved from Montgomery, Alabama, to Richmond, Virginia. This new capital became the target of Lincoln's plan to break the enemy resistance.

5
"We Predict for Them a Brilliant Future"

I could see that the neighbors thought that the money spent upon John's
military was as good as thrown away.

—Charles Pelham

The trip home for Pelham and Rosser was fraught with perils and often tested
their mental skills. On occasion, Pelham's talent for amateur theatrics and quick
thinking helped their trek through the North. A steamboat carried them from West
Point to New York City where a friend, Ben Wood, aided them in escaping the
city. Before leaving Pelham and Rosser stopped in a photographer's studio to have
pictures made. Pelham mailed the *carte de visite* back to Jacob Counselman, a friend
at the academy from the Class of 1863. Purchasing railroad fares, they made their
way to Philadelphia, where they visited John's cousin, Marianna, as he promised
in his letter of March 26, and then detoured to Harrisburg to avoid arrest. The
train was searched at least twice by the authorities, who questioned Pelham and
Rosser, suspiciously dressed in their West Point uniforms. Pelham responded they
were on their way to Washington, D.C., to report for duty. His answer sufficed.
At another spot they observed a number of hangman's nooses tied to a crossbeam
with a crudely lettered sign reading, "for Southern traitors."[1]

Averting more patrols, Pelham and Rosser decided to head west through Pennsylvania, Ohio, and Indiana. Once they crossed the Ohio River into the slave state
of Kentucky, they figured they would be safe. But crossing the Ohio might prove
difficult. In the small community of New Albany, Indiana,[2] near the river, they
were again questioned. This time Pelham brazenly announced they were carrying
dispatches from General Winfield Scott to New Port Barracks in Kentucky.[3] The
authoritative manner in which Pelham answered their queries evidently made him
believable.

The Indiana town of Jeffersonville rested across the Ohio River from Louisville,
but the river was constantly patrolled. Getting across posed a problem. Here John,
using his good looks and charm, persuaded a nameless but supposedly beautiful
lady to paddle them to the Kentucky shoreline in her rowboat. Through Kentucky and
Tennessee to Calhoun County in northern Alabama, the trip was less complicated.
After more than ten days of tension, they arrived at the Pelham home on May 2.
The *Jacksonville Republican,* the hometown newspaper, heralded their arrival:

Lieutenants Pelham of this county and Rosser of Texas, arrived here last night, on their way from West Point to Montgomery. They have both received appointments in the Confederate Army, and are hastening on to Montgomery for orders, and a "place in the picture."

We had the pleasure of a long interview with them. . . . They report that the populace all through Pennsylvania are worked up to the last degree of frenzy and madness by their abolition leaders. They talk of nothing but shooting, and gibbeting the "traitors of the South." . . . They were, themselves, narrowly watched, & scrutinized, and questioned as to their destination, but managed by a little finesse to pass unmolested.

All Southern officers who offer to resign now are being arrested before they can get out of the country, if possible.

Lieuts. Pelham and Rosser are a couple of handsome, well educated and promising young officers; and will be quite an acquisition to our army at this time. We predict for them a brilliant future.[4]

For little more than a week Pelham and Rosser stayed with Atkinson and Martha Pelham. John's homecoming was celebrated by roasting a barbecued pig on an outdoor spit. Family members and neighbors joined in the celebration.

During his brief stay at home, John endured a most discomforting episode. The story was revealed many years later by his brother Charles. Because of his military training, John was asked to drill a company of the newly organized Tenth Alabama Infantry by its commander, Captain Woodruff. This unit consisted of some "big boys" noted for their rowdiness who did not take kindly to the smallish and fancy Pelham giving them orders. A crowd of Alexandria's finest, including many Pelhams, watched the proceedings. After much shouting from John, the boys lined up smartly. "I remember John had an awful time," stated Charles, "trying to get them to 'assume the position of a soldier.' " However, some of them began moving out of line and misbehaving, much to the embarrassment of young Pelham, whose face turned bright red. John, along with his chagrined family, seemed relieved when Captain Woodruff proposed to adjourn for dinner. As Charles related, "None of us said much but I could see that the neighbors thought that the money spent upon John's military was as good as thrown away. At least a dozen of them took dinner with us but my mother was not as proud of her boy as she expected to be."

A neighbor, named McAuley, one of the "staunchest friends" of the Pelham family, wasn't content to end the day in this manner. He proposed that John try his hand again late in the afternoon "when the sun would not be so hot." The Pelham family, according to Charles, "delighted" in the idea of John receiving another opportunity to redeem himself and "[show] the ladies what he could do" with the ill-bred company.

Captain Woodruff cynically consented to give John a second try "at a few West Pint maneuvers," but to the "utter amazement" of all, John rigidly declined the invitation. When all recovered from their astonishment, "they insisted, even pleaded with him, but to no avail." Martha Pelham was "mortified," and Atkinson "didn't like the looks of things at all." Atkinson appeared perplexed. As Charles relates, "he had tried to rear his sons so that they would do just what he wanted done without an order. Besides I think there was a vague impression on his mind that John would not drill that Co[mpany] then even if he did 'Order' it, though John had always been an obedient affectionate son & had never disobeyed him. I could see there was a 'heap of trouble on the ole man's mind.' . . . It seemed that the scepter of his authority was slipping from his grasp!!"

Meanwhile, Atkinson, Charles, and John decided to "take a stroll and look at the stock," and John soon regained his spirits. Atkinson also seemed to retrieve his as well, but none of them referred to the drill. At last in conversation, Charles bravely asked John why he had declined to drill the men a second time. John replied he would not have drilled that company "to have saved their lives." Charles further asked why John had so embarrassingly declined, and John responded that the men had "insulted" him, "insulted him outrageously," and he almost "swore at them." Atkinson's eyes "fairly danced as they blazed with anger and indignation." "I felt that trouble was coming for Father," continued Charles, "though a quiet Christian, peaceable man." Atkinson, according to Charles, did not like Captain Woodruff at all, "and [Father] would fight & fight to hurt bad & didn't fear men or numbers any more than John did. . . . And I was awfully worried lest Father and John would involve us in a fight with all of Capt[ain] W[oodruff]'s Company." "Father stopped John," continued Charles, "looked him straight in the eye with a glitter in his eye somewhat similar to the light that comes in a woman's when she admits she has lovers, and demanded to know the extent and particulars of the insult." John, growing increasingly angry at the recollection of the incident, with "pressed rage" told them that the " 'volunteers' hadn't only repeatedly 'stuck their hands in their pockets' but had actually 'chewed tobacco in ranks!' " When their tempers calmed down, the three had a substantial laugh. Over the next few years Charles "teased Father no little about his wanting to charge Captain Woodruff's Company for 'insulting' John."[5]

Pelham and Rosser reported for assignment to Adjutant General Samuel Cooper in Montgomery on May 10. Five days later the two young men were commissioned as first lieutenants in the Confederate service. Rosser's assignment took him to North Carolina for coastal duty; Pelham, designated to the artillery as an ordnance officer, was destined for Lynchburg, Virginia. Though they were separated, their paths would cross again.

Anxious to get to his post, John packed some belongings and said farewell to his family. He hugged and kissed them, his mother last in line. "God bless you John,"

Martha tearfully said. "Bring you back safe to us." With a smile and his blue eyes
sparkling, John replied, "If we win Mama, your boy wants to come back. But if we
lose, pray God to take [me] safe from the battlefield."[6] Two of Atkinson's slaves,
Willis and Newton, went with John as his wartime servants. They remained with
him throughout his military service.

John arrived at Lynchburg at the end of May. Although Pelham was excited
about his new role, ordnance duty quickly settled into a rather mundane assignment. Action seemed to be brewing farther north in Virginia, and John longed to
be a part of it. Luckily, he received word from the War Department of his immediate transfer to General Joseph E. Johnston's Army of the Shenandoah stationed
in Winchester, Virginia. Arriving in Winchester on June 15, John immediately reported to the general.

Johnston had three batteries of artillery under his command: the Rockbridge
Battery, led by Colonel William Pendleton; Groves's Culpeper Battery, under Lieutenant Robert F. Beckham; and the Alburtis Battery, commanded by the aging and
sickly Captain Ephraim G. Alburtis, who suffered from lumbago. Pelham was assigned as a drill instructor to the Alburtis Battery. Gladly relinquishing a good deal
of his authority, Alburtis seemed pleased to have Pelham aboard. Whether Pelham
had learned from his experience in attempting to drill the Alabama company back
home, he quickly established himself as a leader with his new battery. One of the
recruits supposedly stated with respect, "He took us over then and there and we
knew he was boss before we went to sleep that night."[7]

One Confederate onlooker noted Pelham's prowess as a drill instructor:

I recollect one morning . . . hearing a voice with a long and peculiar drawl
drilling a squad of men. The difference in sound and pronunciation of the
various orders were so marked that my curiosity was excited to know who
this drill instructor was. . . . I saw a youth who was apparently not over 18
years of age [Pelham was actually twenty-two] with a fair complexion, blue
eyes, smooth face, light hair, lightly built, about medium height, and remarkably sinewy. His boyish appearance, manly looks, handsome face, and soldier
bearing riveted my attention as he and his long, drawling, peculiar accent of
the west pointer drilled the awkward squad that had been assigned to him.

There was something about this youngster at this time that was pecu-
liarly attractive, but I little dreamed that this military stripling in a few short
years would make the world ring with deeds of daring. . . . Little did I think
when occasionally chatting with this youngster that later on he was to be the
favorite soldier of Lee, Jackson, and Stuart. . . . My acquaintance with this
heroic soldier was very limited, and of short duration, but I became drawn
to him at first sight, and followed his splendid, brilliant, but brief career
with gratification mingled with admiration, and for personal courage and

knightly daring, he was not excelled by any of the hosts of brave and gallant
men who fell on either side in the war between the states.[8]

Pelham knew his work was cut out for him. The Alburtis Battery consisted of
sixty-two men, of little or no experience, in a variety of uniforms, representing numerous states across the South. Worse yet was the dearth of proper equipment—
four outdated smoothbore 6-pounder cannon with a scarcity of gunpowder and
projectiles. Added to this were forty-three horses, four broken-down caissons and
limbers, and one forge wagon. Turning this ragtag battery into a well-drilled and
precise unit would be an amazing accomplishment, especially in the time allotted,
but Pelham worked wonders. He began with seven hours per day of nearly constant
drill for his men. Little time was wasted as rumors spread that the Union army in
Washington, D.C., would be on the move at any moment. Pelham worked diligently alongside his gunners as they fashioned crates and old boxes into caissons.[9]
Items deemed as throwaway for some quickly became essential to Pelham's reorganization. The young first lieutenant's work ethic filtered down to the men in the
battery. Within a month it had become a respectable cog of disciplined men eager
to do battle. Pelham's efforts had not gone unnoticed by his superiors. Joe Johnston
praised the newfound efficiency of the unit and its drillmaster. Two others who
took note were Colonel Thomas J. Jackson, who commanded an infantry brigade
under Johnston, and Lieutenant Colonel Jeb Stuart, who headed Johnston's cavalry. Pelham also gladly received his first remuneration of $100 from the Confed-
erate government for his services from May 15 to July 1.[10]

And now the rumors, prevalent in the Confederate camps for so long, proved to
be true. Federal armies were on the move. Northern newspaper editorials for weeks
had been clamoring for a push to the Confederate capital at Richmond. President
Lincoln, knowing his troops were far from ready but realizing his three-month
volunteer enlistment period was about to expire, reluctantly ordered his generals
"On to Richmond." It amounted to a two-pronged invasion. Forty-two-year-old
Brigadier General Irvin McDowell with an army of thirty thousand headed out of
Washington, D.C. Moving with his inexperienced force was a huge gathering of
civilian spectators anxious to witness what many predicted would be the only battle
of the war. Entire families out for a midsummer "picnic" accompanied McDowell's
army. Newspapermen and politicians joined to report on the upcoming battle. Two
theatrical groups as well as numerous prostitutes tagged along. A second force of
fifteen thousand, headed by General Robert Patterson, an aging veteran of the War
of 1812, pushed toward the critical Shenandoah Valley. The Shenandoah, known as
the "South's Breadbasket" because of its fertile soil, stretched nearly 150 miles, an-
gling southwest to northeast. Bordered on the east by the Blue Ridge Mountains
and the west by the Alleghenies, its value to the Confederacy was immense. Joe

Johnston and his eight-thousand-man army were responsible for the safety of the Shenandoah.

Meanwhile, the Confederate Army of the Potomac,[11] numbering about twenty-four thousand and headed by P. G. T. Beauregard, defended a somewhat obscure railroad junction called Manassas. This junction, approximately twenty-three miles southwest of Washington, D.C., lay directly in the path of McDowell's force. By capturing Manassas Junction, the Federals would cut a crucial railroad link between the Shenandoah Valley and Richmond. Hence, Beauregard positioned his men to guard against the possibility of such a calamity.

When Confederate spies stationed in Washington observed the Federal movements in mid-July, they quickly informed Beauregard. Knowing he needed reinforcements to defend Manassas, Beauregard sent word to the Confederate government, asking for Johnston's men out of the valley. "Send forward any reinforcements," pleaded Beauregard, "at the earliest possible instant and by every possible means."[12] Jefferson Davis ordered Johnston to give Robert Patterson the slip and head to Beauregard's awaiting army. Luckily for Johnston, the maladroit Patterson, totally out of his realm as a commander, posed little problem to the Confederate escape. Jeb Stuart would simply remain behind with a contingent of cavalry to delude Patterson into thinking the entire Army of the Shenandoah was intact. The ruse worked, largely due to Stuart's uncanny skill.

Johnston's major difficulty lay in getting his army from Winchester to Manassas, a distance of sixty miles, over some rugged terrain. At daybreak on Thursday, July 18, Johnston ordered his army to cook three days' rations and prepare to break camp at noon. Excitement mounted as his men seemed to know the importance of their mission. Near midday in the growing heat, the Army of the Shenandoah began moving eastward along the dusty roads. Newly promoted general Thomas Jackson and his First Brigade led the way. At dusk the men waded through the waist-deep Shenandoah River. After passing through the Blue Ridge Mountains at Ashby's Gap, a rugged climb for worn men, the army took a deserved rest. It was near 2:00 A.M. when the soldiers collapsed for the remainder of the night. Twenty miles had been traversed that day. As the men slept, John Pelham scouted the perimeter of the camp, checking on the sentinels before he, too, fell asleep.

The following morning Joe Johnston hit upon a novel idea. To conserve time his infantry would use the nearby railroad for quicker transportation. It entailed a six-mile march to Piedmont Station where the Manassas Gap Railroad ran through. Piedmont to Manassas was another thirty-four miles. Surely the railroad would save them precious time. No time was wasted, as once again Jackson spearheaded the march, which started before dawn. By 7:00 A.M. the first men from the Army of the Shenandoah had reached Piedmont. The small community turned out to feed and cheer the Confederate soldiers. After a brief rest the first men climbed into the boxcars for the ride to Manassas. Since space was at a premium, only infantrymen would ride the train; the artillery with their cannons, horses, and caissons remained on foot. Stuart's cavalry, which successfully fooled Patterson into thinking the entire Confederate army was "bottled up," had completed its trip through Ashby's Gap. The cavalry would accompany the artillery to Manassas. The first wave of infantry from the valley reached Beauregard's army at 4:00 the following morning.[13] The combined artillery and cavalry remained on the dusty roads. With the adroitness of a veteran, Pelham kept his men from straying and in line as well as his cannons from falling behind.

The grueling march in the mid-July sun continued. By 8:00 A.M. the bone-weary men reached a small settlement called Salem. Here the few townspeople provided a nourishing and welcome breakfast. Much attention was bestowed on the soldiers, especially Pelham. The prettiest ladies gathered around the dashing soldier, ensuring his plate remained full while flirting with him. Back on the road, the men brutally pushed themselves onward. They reached Manassas at 1:00 A.M. on Sunday with little more than two hours' rest. It was a forced march for which they could be proud. And now a well-deserved sleep, for later that day they would become battle-hardened veterans.

6
"War Is Not Glorious"

I felt as cool and deliberate under the showers of lead and iron as if I had
been at home by our fire-side.

—John Pelham

With the arrival of Joseph E. Johnston's army, Beauregard's apprehensions seemingly were assuaged. Beauregard now awaited the arrival of the enemy, led by his
former West Point classmate Irvin McDowell. His plan of battle had already un-
knowingly gone astray when Robert Patterson allowed Johnston's army to escape—
a fact McDowell was unaware of. Confidently, McDowell planned an attack on
Beauregard's extreme left to drive the Confederates back toward Richmond. One
of McDowell's subordinates, Colonel William Tecumseh Sherman, claimed this to
be "one of the best-planned battles of the war."[1]

Meanwhile, Beauregard, unsuspecting of McDowell's plans, hoped for a Federal attack that would place his army in a more tolerable defensive stance. The combined armies of Beauregard and Johnston stretched some eight miles in a diagonal
position from the Warrenton Pike on the left to Union Mills Ford on the right.
The lazy stream, Bull Run, meandered along Beauregard's front. Although ford-
able at nearly any spot, Bull Run offered a modest defense with its relatively steep
banks. The feisty Creole, however, changed his mind concerning defensive fighting and boldly decided to attack the Federals. His plan called for an all-out thrust
on McDowell's right flank. McDowell's army, however, succeeded in moving first.
Thus, the Battle of Manassas Junction (or Bull Run) commenced on the Confederate left. It was Sunday, July 21.

That morning before dawn John Pelham received information that Ephraim Alburtis was ill, too sick to lead the battery. Thus, the battery Pelham had trained for
the past few weeks would be his this day. Confident that his men would fight well,
John stood waiting for orders and preparing his outdated 6-pounder cannons. His
orders to move to the action did not arrive until the battle was a few hours old. But
when they came, he was ready.

On Beauregard's extreme left, guarding the Stone Bridge, were one thousand
men under the command of Colonel Nathan "Shanks" Evans. This glint-eyed South
Carolinian, whose nickname came from his noticeably skinny legs, was acclaimed
for his irascible temper and ability to consume whiskey in huge proportions. He
looked older than his thirty-seven years. But Evans was a fighter, and on this morn-

ing, his ability would be sorely tested. At 6:00 A.M. a Federal division appeared along Warrenton Pike and suddenly opened fire with a 30-pounder Parrott gun. Almost immediately, more Union cannon, positioned in the hills a half mile north of the run, targeted Evans's men, and began blasting.[2] Stunned by the sudden pounding, Evans bravely stood his ground. Soon eleven thousand Federals moved on his position, and the Confederate left was in danger of collapsing. Evans's men valiantly staved off the Federal onslaught for nearly an hour until reinforcements could be hurried in to help him.

The self-assured Beauregard was confident no longer. As surprised as Evans had been by the Union offensive, Beauregard now had to shift gears. His plan for an offensive thrust on McDowell's right was quickly shelved. In order to save his army, men were needed desperately and quickly at the Stone Bridge. In near panic, Beauregard ordered as many available units forward. Coming in from different locations, some as far as three miles away, were the brigades of Generals Bernard Bee and Thomas Jackson, along with Colonel Francis Bartow, who personally signaled the Alburtis Battery to move. Beauregard also ordered in the six hundred men, just arrived from Richmond, under Colonel Wade Hampton. Marching like veterans, all these men hurried into the fray. Beauregard and Joe Johnston rode to the area to direct the fighting, but it would be some time before they arrived.

Meanwhile, "Shanks" Evans was being overwhelmed. He courageously held his position on Matthew's Hill with Bee and Bartow's men until thrown back by superior numbers. Collectively they fell back to the most prominent geographic feature of the battlefield, Henry House Hill, nearly a mile away. Awaiting them were the five regiments and nine cannon of Thomas Jackson. Arriving shortly before the retreating men, Jackson critically eyed the terrain. Without orders from his superiors, Jackson quickly placed his brigade in an excellent position along the inner edge of the ridge facing the Henry House about two hundred yards distant. Jackson then directed the Alburtis Battery toward the Robinson House six hundred yards northeast on his extreme right.[3] Young lieutenant John Pelham's blood was up as he was about to see his first action.

Much confusion existed among the Confederates, as they tried to coordinate their defenses along Henry House Hill. The laconic and steady Jackson, however, gave needed stability to the dazed men, as he methodically positioned more artillery pieces along the ridge. Fighting continued to seesaw near the Henry House until after 1:00 P.M. At one point Bernard Bee, a tough South Carolinian and decorated veteran of the Mexican War, rode up to Jackson and said, "General, they are beating us back!" Calmly, Jackson retorted, "Sir, we'll give them the bayonet." Rallying his disorganized men, Bee shouted his immortal words: "There is Jackson standing like a stone wall. Let us determine to die here, and we will conquer!"[4]

For over seven hours the fighting at Bull Run had been dictated by the Federals. They held the initiative and set the tempo of the battle from its onset. The climatic encounter, however, was now at hand near the Henry House. McDowell sent thousands of men forward in an all-out attack, while the Confederates girded for the assault. Amid the smoke of musketry and the acrid odor of gunpowder, the Federals surged ahead. Blasted back, they regrouped for a second advance. This time McDowell, sensing victory, ordered up five batteries of artillery, twenty-four pieces in all, to assist in the onslaught. Pelham and the rest of the Confederate gunners, most of them using obsolete 6-pounders, opened fire. For the next few minutes cannons belched their projectiles in a deadly hail with neither side wavering. Excitedly, Pelham pushed his guns dangerously forward to an exposed position. One of his officers, sensing the peril of the situation, turned and fled, remarking, "If Pelham's fool enough to stay there, I'm not."[5]

McDowell then ordered two of those batteries, eleven guns in all, magnificently led by Captains Charles Griffin and James B. Ricketts, to move in closer. Recklessly advancing to within canister range, these young Federal gunners poured repeated volleys into the Rebel lines. Griffin and Ricketts remained in their dangerous position, continuously firing, even when Jeb Stuart's cavalry drove back Federal infantry coming to their assistance. The Henry House and all things around it took a severe beating from Federal and Confederate shelling.[6] Suddenly Jackson's Thirty-third Virginia Regiment under Colonel Arthur Campbell Cummings rushed forward toward the two Yankee batteries. Captain Griffin readied his gunners to blast canister into the Virginians. However, in the confusion of the battle, Griffin became persuaded these approaching men could be Federals. Meanwhile, at a distance of seventy yards, Cummings's men let fly with a barrage of bullets. Forty men and seventy-five horses fell dead or wounded. Ricketts took four wounds and was captured. Griffin's gunners managed somehow to drag off three of the guns, but the remaining eight cannons became a prize that both sides coveted. For the next few terrible minutes a terrific struggle ensued. Finally, the Confederates seized the cannons, turned them around, and fired repeatedly at the fleeing Federals.

Meanwhile, during a furious counterattack, Jackson ordered his artillery to the rear for safety. As the men and equipment were moving back, a Federal brigade, commanded by Colonel William Sherman, threatened Jackson's undefended right flank. Luckily, John Pelham observed this newfound danger. William T. Poague, a twenty-five-year-old gunner of the Rockbridge Artillery standing nearby, heard Pelham remark, "I'll be dogged if I'm going any further back." Quickly, Pelham moved his battery forward to blunt this counterstroke. Ordering his men to fire blasts of canister, Pelham's gunners let loose. Sherman's brigade, hit by the deadly one-inch iron balls, hastily retreated.[7]

Federal soldiers had finally reached their physical limit. Little fight remained in their exhausted bodies. Then on the far left, a dust cloud swirled; another body of troops was approaching. Could it possibly be Robert Patterson's army from the Shenandoah Valley? If so, Confederate hopes for victory were dashed. For long moments soldiers from both sides paused to watch the advancing dust cloud as it neared their positions. Anxiety festered, especially when flags were observed, but no one could make out any more than color. And then, dramatically, a midsummer breeze kicked up on this excessively hot day. A tumultuous cheer arose from the Confederate lines. As the flags unfurled, there was no longer any doubt; they were red, white, and blue, but not the "Star and Stripes" of the Union. These were the "Stars and Bars" of the Confederacy, signifying Yankee defeat. This fresh brigade belonged to Colonel Jubal A. Early, the foul-mouthed and cynical Virginian who had earlier voted against secession. His manners were somewhat crude, his popularity not the best, but no one doubted his ability as a fighter.

Early's brigade hastened forward and literally drove the disheartened Federals away from Henry House Hill and back across Young's Branch. All Federal hopes collapsed and a full-scale retreat for the Union army ensued. Pulling back along the Warrenton Pike, McDowell's army trudged away from the battleground. Jubilant Confederate artillerists fired some parting cannon blasts. And then, like an apparition, appeared a sixty-seven-year-old, with long white hair flying in the wind. It was Edmund Ruffin, the hero of Fort Sumter, astraddle a cannon barrel, with "a Yankee rifle grasped in one hand and a Confederate musket in the other," tearing after the retreating enemy. Halting, old man Ruffin spied a mass of confusion on the bridge over Cub Run. Frightened Federals had become jammed inextricably with caissons, wagons, ambulances, and a crowd of northern civilians, all anxious to flee toward the safety of Washington, D.C. Ruffin measured the situation and fired a blast from his cannon. The shell landed squarely on the bridge, killing twelve to fifteen soldiers and wreaking havoc on the panic-stricken survivors, who lost all control and rushed mob-like to get away. The old man delighted in his triumph.[8]

What followed was a frantic retreat that turned into a rout as Union soldiers threw down their weapons and rushed pell-mell to the rear. The fanciful picnickers and observers became a part of the senseless release from the battlefield in a rush to get back to Washington, D.C. "There was never anything like it," wrote Ohio congressman Albert G. Riddle, who became a part of the rout, "for causeless, sheer, absolute, absurd cowardice, or rather panic. . . . Off they went, one and all; off down the highway, over across fields, towards the woods, anywhere, everywhere, to escape. . . . no mortal ever saw such a mass of ghastly wretches."[9]

Confederate pursuit was limited and mostly nonexistent. Most of the exhilarated Confederates found the time to congratulate one another and collect the booty left behind by the Federals. Among the many items confiscated were twenty-eight cannons (seventeen of them rifled, including a 30-pounder Parrott gun), thirty-seven caissons, six forges, four battery wagons, sixty-four artillery horses, numerous harnesses, nearly five thousand rounds of artillery ammunition, over five hundred rifles with a half-million rounds of small arms ammunition, and nine battle flags.[10] Pelham had lost only two of the sixty-two men in his battery. At the end of the battle Pelham strolled over his part of the field of battle looking at the wreckage, possibly for something salvageable. Finding an abandoned cannon from Griffin's battery with its nose shoved into the earth, Pelham eyed the gun suspiciously, as if it were a long-lost friend. Slowly rubbing his fingers over the raised initials "U.S." brought a smile to his face, as he immediately recognized the cannon as one he had trained on while a cadet at West Point. In fact, Charles Griffin had been an artillery instructor at the academy beginning in 1860, and the gun Pelham brought in was one of the pieces that Griffin hauled from West Point.

Various stories concerning Pelham, some true, some questionable, swirl around the young gunner about the end of the battle. It is reported that Pelham observed a congealed pool of blood near the captured cannon, not knowing that it came from a severe leg wound of classmate and friend Adelbert Ames, who served in Griffin's battery. Pelham then fell to his knees and became violently ill from the sight. This tale is possible, but more likely improbable. Another exists that Pelham personally brought in a captured horse that he had ridden at West Point, claiming that the horse knew him, and that the stoic Stonewall Jackson made certain that Pelham kept the animal. This story appears to have some credibility. It was reported in the *Jacksonville Republican* that Pelham's horse was shot from beneath him during the battle. This story, although dramatic, appears to be false. Finally, it has been written that Pelham also captured the captain of this battery, his former artillery instructor Charles Griffin. There is no truth to this one, as Griffin narrowly escaped capture while James Ricketts, who never taught at West Point, was captured but not by Pelham.[11]

It had been a frightful day for casualties. Total Confederate losses included 387 killed, 1,582 wounded, and 13 missing. Federal losses were nearly the same: 460 killed and 1,124 wounded. Only in the numbers missing did a huge discrepancy appear—1,312 missing Yankees. Among the Confederate killed were General Bernard Bee and the promising colonel Francis Bartow.[12] For so many who survived this first taste of battle, the visuals of watching men die or suffer horrible wounds were overwhelming. Two days after the battle, Confederate Philip Henry Powers still felt stunned by and sickened while viewing the aftermath of the struggle. Describing the bodies, alive and dead, in a heap, he wrote his wife: "To pass by it was enough to soften and sicken the hardest heart. I will not dwell upon the awful scene. . . . Nothing—Nothing could lessen the horrors of the field by moonlight. . . . May God, in his infinite mercy, avert a second such calamity."[13]

An assessment of the battle reveals some substantive facts. The Confederates had been variously lucky and skillful. Fresh units showed up at critical times, something unplanned by Rebel leaders. The avoidance of Robert Patterson's army in the Shenandoah, albeit brilliant, was fortuitous for the Confederacy mainly because of Patterson's deplorable inactivity. His forces at Manassas would undoubtedly have meant a Federal victory. Numerous Confederate officers, particularly Stonewall Jackson, evidenced an uncanny knack for not waiting for direct orders to act upon their own intuition. Jackson's deliberate actions on Henry House Hill turned a dejected force into one of stability, and much credit for the victory surely goes to him. Above all else, the Rebel soldier proved his worth as a fighting man. Under positive leadership these men were a force to be reckoned with.

On the Federal side there might be consolation in defeat. For an ill-trained army, executing some difficult offensive maneuvers, the men had fought well. Some of their officers can be faulted, however, for the overall failure at Bull Run. Lack of proper coordination, inefficient communication, and inexperience helped doom their efforts. No such criticisms, however, can be placed on the glorious work of Charles Griffin or James Ricketts. With fighters such as these, the Union side need not worry about future battles. A few cynics from the North ripped into the heart of the Union fighting man. "Our men are not good soldiers," complained Sherman. "They brag, but don't perform . . . and what is in store for us in the future I know not." Pelham's classmate Emery Upton bitterly stated, "The effect of this disastrous battle, which gave the enemy all the advantages of the initiative . . . was to paralyze military operations for more than six months."[14]

The Confederate high command praised the labors of its men for this day of battle with much of the accolades bestowed on the artillery. Lieutenant Pelham and the Alburtis Battery received some of the flattery. Beauregard, describing the action at Henry Hill, reported: "A Federal brigade was lurking along under cover of the ridges and a wood in order to turn my line on the right, but was easily repulsed by [Captain A. C.] Latham's battery . . . aided by Alburtis's Battery, opportunely sent to Latham's left by General Jackson, and supported by fragments of troops collected by staff-officers." He added, "[all the batteries displayed] that marvelous capacity of our people as artillerists which has made them, it would appear, at once the terror and admiration of the enemy."[15]

Without mentioning names of individuals or units, Joe Johnston was equally effusive. "The efficiency of our infantry and cavalry might have been expected from a patriotic people accustomed, like ours, to the management of arms and horses," he reported, "but that of the artillery was little less than wonderful. They were opposed to batteries far superior in the number, range, and equipment of their guns, with educated officers and thoroughly instructed soldiers . . . yet they exhibited as much superiority to the enemy in skill as in courage. Their fire was superior both in rapidity and precision." The pious Presbyterian Stonewall Jackson, as was his wont, praised the Almighty first: "The blessing of God . . . gave us the victory." But here the reticent genius also lauded "the battery under Lieutenant Pelham [that] came into action on the same line as the others; and nobly did the artillery maintain its position for hours against the enemy's advancing thousands."[16] A small approval, but from Jackson it was a rare and well-deserved acclaim.

Congratulations for Pelham's heroics rolled in from elsewhere. In response to a letter Pelham sent him describing the battle, the Honorable A. J. Walker from Alabama wrote: "It affords me indescribable pleasure to learn from your letter that you had discharged your duty in such a manner as to elicit praise from your commanding officers. My gratification was greatly enhanced by the reception of a letter from Colonel Martin,[17] informing me that you acted admirably throughout the engagement. I know you have done more and better than your modesty permitted you to describe. If I have ever shown you any friendship I am amply compensated by the knowledge that you have acted so nobly, so bravely, and so skillfully. I have sent your letter to your father. The great victory which has been achieved does not finish the war." The judge added: "You are fighting for great principles. Justice and right are upon your side. Future generations will bless you for the deeds of daring and patriotism you are doing." Wrote future Confederate general Joseph Wheeler, "The handling of the guns at the First Battle of Manassas established [Pelham's] reputation as a fearless officer and a skilled artillerist."[18]

Thus, John Pelham showed his mettle in the opening battle. He was proud of his accomplishments, especially with a group he had trained for such a short duration. He was equally proud of the Alburtis Battery. He let the men know of his satisfaction and promised even greater accomplishments for the future. Pride would have swelled inside Pelham, as well, had he known of his classmates and friends who had fought at Bull Run. From his own class were Emory Upton, who suffered a wound, Edmund Kirby, Henry Hasbrouck, William Elderkin, Francis Davies, John Williams, Charles Gibson, Jacob Kent, wounded three times and captured, Sheldon Sturgeon, who was also captured, Henry Kingsbury, who served as an aide-de-camp to Irvin McDowell, and Mississippian James Kennard, who resigned from the academy a month before Pelham. Poor Kennard took a mortal wound and died five days later, the first of Pelham's classmates to fall. But mostly Pelham's interest would have been for roommate Tom Rosser, who gallantly fought with the elite Washington Artillery of New Orleans, and good friend Adelbert Ames, who took a bullet through his leg near the Henry House and was later awarded the Medal of Honor for his heroics. It would have pleased Pelham to also know that his flamboyant and lovable friend George Armstrong Custer fought with the Second United States Cavalry.[19]

Two days after the battle ended, Pelham proudly penned a letter to his father. Its poignancy, grace, and style mark it as a classic in wartime correspondence. It is produced here in its entirety.

I just write to let you know that we have had one of the most desperate battles ever fought on American soil. It was the <u>most</u> desperate—the enemy fought long and well, but victory is ours, it was a splendid victory too. Jeff Davis made his appearance on the field, just as the last of the Yankees were in full retreat. I was under a heavy fire of musketry and cannon for about seven hours, how I escaped or why I was spared a just God only knows. Rifle balls fell like hail around me. Shells burst and scattered their fragments through my battery—my horse was shot under me, but did not give out until the fight was almost over. I was compelled to take one of my Sergeant's horses and ride through. At one time I dismounted and directed the guns—one of the gunners asked me to dismount and shoot the Federals' flag down. I did so— you ought to have heard the cheers they gave me. I directed all of my guns three or four times apiece. My men were cool and brave and made terrible havoc on the enemy. They fought better than I expected they would. The highest praise is due them. We shot down three U.S. flags and dislodged the enemy from several positions. I was complimented several times on the field of battle by general officers and a great many times after the battle was over by other officers.

You may want to know my feelings—I felt as cool and deliberate under the shower of lead and iron as if I had been at home by our fire-side—I did not feel fear at any moment, I can't see how I escaped. A merciful Providence must have been watching over us and our cause. We slept on our arms last night but were not disturbed—the battle began about 8 o'clock but did not become general until 10 o'clock. We fought desperately about 9 ½ hours, but I was under fire only about 7 ½ hours. The enemy attacked our left flank and then tried to turn it. We had to change our line of battle and fight them on their own ground.

We whipped old [Winfield] Scott on Sunday—the great fighting fortunate day, on ground of their own choosing in open field. They poured down overwhelming numbers on us. I firmly believe they had three to our one— but I don't know positively how many they had—but certainly between 50,000 and 100,000 men.[20] A great many prisoners told us, they expected confidently to whip us here and then go to Richmond. We have got about 1,000 prisoners and the cavalry are bringing them in continually. We took the celebrated Rhode Island battery of rifled cannon, also Sherman's great battery of the same kind of guns[21]—also the West Point battery that I have drilled with so often.

They say we have taken 90 pieces of Artillery—I have not seen all of them but I have seen a great many. They had the best Artillery trains and equipage I ever beheld, but <u>we</u> have them now. I have no idea how many small arms we took, a great many. The victory was splendid and complete. Col. [William] Forney's Regt. (Tenth Alabama) was not engaged—but the 4th Ala. Reg't was cut all to pieces. They fought desperately. The Col. and Lieut. Col. and Major were all shot down but neither of them was mortally wounded.[22] I don't know what the intention of our General is but I hope I will be able to write you from Washington City before many weeks. Johnston's forces were encamped at Winchester, but we all moved down here on getting a dispatch from Beauregard. We got here the evening before the fight—Beauregard repulsed them with considerable loss a few days ago.

I have seen what Romancers call <u>glorious war.</u> I have seen it in all its phases. I have heard the booming of cannon, and the more deadly rattle of musketry at a distance—I have heard it all near by and have been under its destructive showers. I have seen men and horses fall thick and flat around me. I have seen our own men bloody and frightened flying before the enemy. I have seen them bravely charge the enemy's lines and heard the shout of triumph as they carried the position, I have heard the agonizing shrieks of the wounded and dying—I have passed over the battle field and seen the mangled forms of men and horses in frightful abundance. Men without heads, without arms, and others without legs. All this I have witnessed and more, till my heart sickens; and war is <u>not</u> glorious as novelists would have us believe. It is only when we are in the heat and flush of battle that it is fascinating and interesting. It is only then that we enjoy it. When we forget ourselves and revel in the destruction we are dealing around us. I am now ashamed of the feelings I had in those hours of danger. The whistling bullets and shells were music to me, I gloried in it—it delighted and fascinated me—I feared not death in any forms; but when the battle was won and I visited the field a change came over me, I see the horrors of war, but it was necessary.

We are battling for our rights and homes. Ours is a just war, a holy cause. The invader must meet the fate he deserves and we must meet him as becomes us, as becomes men. As President Davis said several months ago, "A small mound of earth marks the place where the invader fell."[23]

For John Pelham his first battle had been a combination of exhilaration and repugnance. No one questioned his bravery and competence; he had demonstrated remarkable ability for one so youthful and inexperienced. The positive remarks of his commanders and peers portended impressive accomplishments to come. But his military career was about to take a dramatic turn.

7
"An Honour to Be One of Them"

The [horse battery] under the energetic management of Pelham . . . will tell a tale in the next battle.

—Jeb Stuart

The days following the opening battle at Manassas were critical for the Union. Severe criticism blistered the Lincoln administration. Formerly chastised by newspaper editorials for not sending his army into action sooner, Lincoln now suffered outright condemnation by the same hostile press for making war before his men were ready. Headlines labeled him an "Imbecile" and demanded an explanation for his rashness. Lincoln wisely recognized that changes were necessary to boost morale and instill confidence in the Northern people for the overall war effort ahead. The three-month volunteer time had expired, so his first priority became a three-year army. Lincoln called for four hundred thousand volunteers, and tens of thousands of recruits poured in from the North, forming the new Army of the Potomac. When ready, this force collectively made up the largest and most powerful army ever seen on the North American continent. To train and command this fighting force, Lincoln selected thirty-four-year-old George Brinton McClellan on July 27, 1861. Arriving in Washington, D.C., McClellan found the reception overwhelming. "I find myself in a new & strange position here," he wrote his wife, Ellen, "Presdt, Cabinet, Genl Scott & all deferring to me—by some strange operation of magic I seem to have become <u>the</u> power of the land."[1]

Small in stature, McClellan made up for any physical deficiency with a towering ego. Handsome and charming, McClellan cut a true military pose. With his penetrating eyes, full mustache, and a wisp of hair on his lower lip, he enchanted his friends who labeled him "Young Napoleon." His ability to ready an army for combat was second to none. His new army, warmly nicknaming him "Little Mac," loved him for his combined sensitivity to their needs and martial bearing. Above all, he promised them victory. His attitude was contagious. Unfortunately for the Union war effort, McClellan was his own worst enemy. A natural dislike for Lincoln and several members of the cabinet made McClellan petty and spiteful. Unwilling to recognize his own frailties, Little Mac accepted no criticism without blaming others. His actions could be reprehensible, his comments caustic. Described by his critics as the "only man ever born who could strut while sitting down," McClellan was pompous in the extreme. His most fatal military flaw, overexaggerating the enemy strength, would save the Confederacy on more than one occasion. This foreboding kept any major battles from being fought for months in the Eastern Theater.

In the meantime on the southern side of the Potomac River where self-confidence prevailed, the Confederate army continued to recruit and reorganize. Individual commanders, under the watchful eyes of Pierre Beauregard and Joseph E. Johnston, attempted to steady this assurance and render it a positive. For Lieutenant John Pelham the next few weeks were spent in training and resupplying his battery. Donations to the Alburtis Battery included two cannon captured from McDowell's fleeing army—a 12-pounder howitzer and a 3-inch rifled gun. These could easily replace some of the old 6-pounders he had used so effectively during the fighting at Bull Run. His battery also received more horses, the number increasing from fifty-three on August 1 to sixty-one by month's end. In mid-August Pelham's battery was given much-needed ammunition: thirty-six rounds of canister, twenty-four rounds of solid shot for the 6-pounders, plus various amounts of shot and shell.

Then in early September Pelham received word that he was being transferred from the Alburtis Battery. His new assignment would find him in charge of Captain George A. Groves's Culpeper Battery. Upon his arrival at Centreville, Pelham saw a unit badly in need of reconditioning. Pelham eventually reported merely twenty-four officers and men present, with sixteen desertions and another six on sick leave. Pelham tersely wrote: "Most of the desertions took place before I was assigned to the Company & I don't know at what time they left." Only determination and diligence would save this unit, so Pelham rolled up his sleeves and started to work. Recruiting and transfers helped fill the sagging ranks. On October 9, Pelham also requested three caissons from the Confederate War Department.[2]

The War Department complied with Pelham's requests, sending the cannons as well as his pay: $228 for services through July 31. Thereafter, his pay, $100 per month as a first lieutenant, generally arrived about ten days after the end of each month. Further promotion in the artillery would, of course, raise his monthly pay: captains earned $130, majors $150, lieutenant colonels $185, and colonels $210. Although the youthful and clean-shaven Pelham probably was not considering promotion at this time, he jokingly commented to another lieutenant in his battery, "If I had a beard, it would be worth a brigadier's commission to me." Good news also arrived concerning Tom Rosser. As of September 17, Rosser ranked as a captain of the Second Company of the Washington Artillery.[3] Although Rosser and Pelham were not rivals, Rosser's promotion certainly spurred Pelham for his own advancement in rank. But welcome news soon arrived for Pelham as well.

Other parts of the Confederate army were also being revamped. As early as the beginning of August, Joe Johnston sought to reorganize the cavalry and recommended Jeb Stuart's promotion to brigadier general. "He is a rare man," wrote Johnston to Jefferson Davis, "wonderfully endowed by nature with the qualities necessary for an officer of light cavalry. Calm, firm, acute, active, and enterprising, I know of no one more competent than he."[4] With the commission confirmed on September 24, Stuart set out to refashion the entire cavalry. Consisting of six regiments, Stuart's cavalry included some of the South's finest horsemen. But according to its masterful leader, something was lacking. Possibly, a familiar Napoleon axiom he had learned at West Point possessed Stuart's thoughts. "It is the artillery," Napoleon stated emphatically, "which generally decides my battles, for as I have it always on hand, I can bring it to bear, whenever it becomes necessary." Stuart, therefore, desired a unit of horse artillery attached to his command. This group, as Stuart perceived it, would consist of two to six cannon with the men and guns as mobile as his own cavalry. Obviously, such a unit required a distinctive leader, one of dynamic personality and rare skills. For such a demanding post, Jeb selected twenty-three-year-old John Pelham.[5]

What prompted Stuart to request the services of one so young and relatively inexperienced as Pelham? First, Stuart possessed an amazing eye for talent. Age and youthful looks mattered not; Stuart desired leadership and extreme capability. Next, the cavalryman's attention had been drawn to Pelham for the "masterly manner" in which he handled himself, his men, and his guns at Manassas. The skills demonstrated by Pelham could not be overstated; his deftness and composure in the midst of crisis made him just the man Stuart sought. On November 11, 1861, Secretary of War Judah P. Benjamin sanctioned the formation of the Stuart Horse Artillery, but the secretary remained painfully slow in authorizing Pelham as the commander. Stuart expressed his anxiety over the delay in a letter to his wife dated November 24: "Pelham wants it and he may get it, and next to Rosser probably no graduate would do better, but whoever is to be should be appointed at once and come directly here. I need a commander very much to organize the battery forthwith. What is he doing in Richmond? If he is to command this Battery he should be here now. If he is not let me know it so I can get someone else. He ought certainly to get either yes or no out of the Department." Five days later Pelham was ordered under Special Order No. 557 to report to Jeb Stuart. But, much to the consternation of Stuart, the Confederate government woefully dragged its feet in officially commissioning Pelham as a captain of the group. In a second letter to his wife, dated December 4, Stuart again verbalized his dissatisfaction. "The Horse Artillery is growing rapidly," wrote the disgruntled commander, "the only chance is 'vox populi' [the voice of the people]. Pelham is in command of it and there are three acting lieutenants."[6] The rank of captain would not materialize until the following May, but the formation of the unit continued.

Pelham quickly fell into his role and exhibited exceptional prowess in organizing this elite group of fighting men. When completed, the horse artillery would consist of 153 men, including four captains, six lieutenants, one assistant surgeon, one chaplain, two orderly sergeants, one color-bearer, four sergeants, six corporals, two buglers, and 126 privates. By December 21, Pelham had 94 horses on hand for his detachment. At the same time he requisitioned proper forage for the animals from the War Department. He later requested "20 skillets and 20 Camp Kettles for 150 men," calling it "necessary for the public service."[7] The government complied. To begin filling the ranks, Pelham took twenty gunners from Groves's Culpeper Battery. Pelham then obtained a furlough to return to Alabama to recruit more men. The visit to his homeland was preceded by a rather grandiose article in the *Jacksonville Republican* announcing his request for additional manpower. It read in part:

Mounted Flying Artillery

CAPT. JOHN PELHAM, of Calhoun county . . . is authorized to raise two hundred volunteers for mounted Artillerists, to serve during the war. The Confederate States will furnish 240 horses, and eight splendid brass cannon, wagons, caissons and equipments complete for men and horses.

The artillery of 8 splendid brass guns—200 men rank and file, and 250 horses, has the novelty of being the only one in our service—in fact the only one in America. All the men or cannoneers are mounted on horses furnished by the government.

This doubtless will be the most desirable, pleasant, and efficient service in our entire Army. The service will be active and energetic; the men will never be detailed to guard forts, fortifications, baggage or prisoners; neither will they be quartered in one place long at a time. The career of this company is destined to be a brilliant one; and whenever or where ever there is likely to be a fight, they are bound to be in the front. . . .

If there be any young men who desire to enlist for the defense of their native sunny South—who desire eminent distinction, glory or renown, here is no doubt the finest opening that has yet been offered.

It may be asked, who is John Pelham. It is with pride and pleasure we say he is the son of Dr. A. [Atkinson] Pelham, and was raised in this county, near Alexandria. He was educated at the military school at West Point—was five years there—has been in the military service ever since—was in the battle of Manassas on the 21st July, had command of a battery that day and did gallant service, having his horse shot under him in the midst of the fierce conflict. He is a young man of fine attainments—high military culture—has been tried on the field of battle, and found equal to the emergency. If he has the honor to command this splendid company, we are satisfied that his men, his native State, and his Country will have cause to be proud of him.

We will close this article with an extract from a private letter from Capt. Pelham to a friend:

"Now is the time to serve your country—enlist the interest of the Ladies— tell them I want to do something to render myself worthy of them, and they must aid me in furnishing men. I have got the finest equipment and the finest guns in the service, and I want good men to man them."[8]

Pelham remained in Alabama visiting his family and friends, continuing to recruit until March 1. As many as forty Alabamians were brought back to Virginia when he returned to the Confederate army on March 10. Some of these were enlisted in the Talladega area with the help of Pelham's boyhood friend, William M. McGregor. Besides McGregor and his brother Jesse, the Alabamians included Jesse A. Adams and William Bolinger. Others came in from Mobile and New Orleans. Part of this contingency consisted of French Creoles. These exuberant warriors entertained the others with their lusty singing of the "Marseillaise" and their high-spirited practice on the new 12-pounder Napoleon cannon. Pelham proudly referred to them as the "Napoleon Detachment," and he especially befriended one Creole named Jean Bacigalupo, merely a boy in his mid-teens, who displayed workmanlike ability as a "sponger."[9]

Still requiring additional manpower, as well as supplies, Pelham ventured to Richmond, Centreville, and Culpeper where he enlisted more men. His new recruits included a twenty-year-old blacksmith, Jonathon Connor, who brought along two or three of his slaves, one of whom boasted that he once shoed "Traveler," Robert E. Lee's famous mount, in a mere five minutes. Samuel Taylor Evans, a Virginian in his early teens, joined up and would later be severely wounded at Fredericksburg. James C. Murdock, who had attended the University of Edinburgh in Scotland before the war, offered his services. One of the most intriguing of the new men was Thomas Kinloch Fauntleroy of Clarke County, Virginia. Better known as "Flintlock," Fauntleroy had previously served in the First and Sixth Virginia cavalries before transferring to the horse artillery. As described by Edward Porter Alexander, "[Fauntleroy] combined in himself the reddest head, the most freckled face, the worst crossed eyes & the most terrible stammering I ever heard, with the most perfect sang-froid & self possession, & absolute freedom of self consciousness, that I ever met."[10] Other incoming recruits transferred from various cavalry regiments. Another unit of relatively untrained men soon arrived from Floyd County. As artillerist George Shreve stated proudly, "Our Battery was very cosmopolitan in its make up. We enrolled men from Maryland, Virginia, South Carolina, Georgia, Alabama, Mississippi, Louisiana, and Tennessee." On March 15, Pelham received a $600 bounty from the Confederate government for his success in gaining more volunteers.[11]

The soldiers of the horse artillery quickly realized that their smooth-faced leader was a combination taskmaster and perfectionist. The men endured long hours of practice, often sunrise to dusk. Constant drill included the art of horsemanship. Unlike some artillery units, all of Pelham's men rode, as he recognized the need to keep up with the hectic pace set by Stuart's cavalry. Pelham stressed speed in movement over a wide variety of terrains. He forced his men to practice stopping and starting, quick and intricate maneuvers to right and left, and jumping homemade obstacles until their muscles ached. Technique was perfected in swiftly detaching caissons from cannon and then rapid firing of the guns. When these procedures were mastered, Pelham labored his men at firing and abruptly moving the guns to a new position. He desired no enemy cannons to draw a bead on the location of his guns, a key to much of his Civil War success. The men toiled at firing from long-range shooting of over a mile to near suicidal distances of less than fifty yards. All of this training would signify boldness and mobility plus an esprit de corps un-known to most artillery units. Above all, Pelham determined to forge the horse ar-tillery as a powerful and integral cog in Stuart's fighting machine. "What fairly dis-tinguished the young Alabamian from the rest," wrote John Esten Cooke at a later date, "was his remarkable genius for artillery."[12]

Beginning with eight field pieces, Pelham assigned eighteen men per cannon. These guns included the 6-pounders, a 12-pounder Napoleon, and some 12-pounder howitzers donated to the unit by Virginia governor John Letcher. At various times his men employed a wide assortment of cannon: Blakelys, Whitworths, and 3-inch ordnance rifles. The Napoleon and Blakely appeared to be Pelham's personal favor-ites. The bronze, smoothbore Napoleon's tube weighed an average of 1,227 pounds and fired a 12.3-pound projectile from its 66-inch barrel. Commonly the preferred cannon of many artillerists, its accuracy and killing power were effective from long or short range. Capable of firing solid shot 1,680 yards, the Napoleon was deadly when loaded with canister and fired less than 300 yards. The howitzer, with its shorter barrel and lighter weight of 778 pounds, lobbed shells and was a potent antipersonnel weapon when loaded with canister or case shot. The Blakely and Whitworth cannons were both British made and rifled. Although accurate, the Blakely displayed more proficiency when loaded with British ammunition. The Whitworth proved deadly from 1,500 to 1,800 yards, and tests indicated when fired over a mile away, the shell deviated no more than twelve feet. The 3-inch ordnance rifle remained one of the war's most popular weapons. Its lighter, 820-pound barrel could propel a projectile 2,000 yards with a mere elevation of five degrees. Theo-retically, the ordnance rifle had a range of 4,000 yards.[13] The horse artillery might haul a meager two cannon into combat, or sometimes over a dozen, but Pelham's men could later proudly boast that in over sixty fights with Federal troops, they never lost a single gun.

Ever the perfectionist, Stuart carefully observed the development and train-ing of the horse artillery and verbally displayed his pleasure. "The [horse battery] under the energetic management of Pelham," he wrote his wife, "is going ahead and will tell a tale in the [next] battle." He then proudly added, "It has taken the name of the 'Stuart Horse Artillery.'" The following day Stuart held the first of many reviews, or public drills, of his cavalry to impress a gallery of various generals. He commented, "I was congratulated on my performance—putting them through as no Cavalry was ever put through before. I had 8 full squadrons present. They drilled admirably." No mention was made of Pelham and the horse artillery participating.[14]

Whether or not Pelham's gunners were on display, others on Stuart's staff, watching the horse artillery in training, equally beamed with enthusiasm for their efforts. The "'Stuart Horse Artillery' consisted of volunteers of many nationalities, and embraced Englishmen, Frenchmen, Germans, Spaniards, and Americans," wrote Heros von Borcke, the verbose Prussian who later served as Stuart's chief of staff. "Many of these men had not brought to the standard under which they served an immaculate reputation, but they distinguished themselves on every field of battle, and established such an enviable character for daring and good conduct that the body was soon regarded as a corps d'elite by the whole army, and it came to be considered an honour to be one of them. I have often seen these men serving their pieces in the hottest of the fight, laughing, singing, and joking each other, utterly regardless of the destruction which cannon-shot and musket-ball were making in their ranks. They were devoted to their young chief, John Pelham."[15]

By mid-March the ranks had filled enough for an election of officers. Pelham's selection as captain, without the official rank, was a mere formality. Stuart's influence, of course, prevailed, particularly in the choice of Pelham's first lieutenant, James W. Breathed. Barely twenty-four years old, Breathed had been practicing medicine on the western frontier when the Civil War broke out. As chance would have it, Stuart and Breathed shared the same train east to tender their services to the Confederacy. Struck with Breathed's "manly and bold bearing," a friendship ensued, and when the horse artillery began, Stuart persuaded Breathed to join. Stuart then induced the men to select Breathed as Pelham's number one officer. None of this seemed to distress Pelham, as he and Breathed became close friends. Pelham soon learned to admire Breathed's courage and fighting ability, as well as his organizational skills.[16] William M. McGregor, a year younger than Pelham and a lawyer from Talladega, Alabama, became the second lieutenant.[17] Fellow Alabamian William C. Elston was elected third lieutenant. The fourth lieutenant was Virginian James S. Touro Shepherd. The sergeants, mostly Virginians, included Walter S. Dabney, Ashton Chichester, Joseph Holmes, Daniel Shanks, G. Wilmer Brown, J. D. Cook, and Charles Edward Ford.[18]

During April, Pelham sent in three additional requests for forage, a testimony to the harshness of the preceding winter. On April 16 Pelham asked the Quartermaster Department for another fifty horses; the request was soon granted.[19] By the end of the month Pelham had 153 men, 130 horses, and eight cannons, including six howitzers, one 12-pounder Napoleon, and one 3-inch Blakely rifle. The ranks of the Stuart Horse Artillery were now completely filled and arrayed for battle. Unfortunately, many of the men suffered illness from drinking polluted water from the nearby streams. Measles and various other ailments added to their woes, particularly the new recruits who had seldom been away from home.[20] Food, although available, was occasionally in short supply according to Private William P. Walters. "We don't get our coffee and sugar," he wrote his wife on April 30. "We had to eat parched corn and beef with out salt for 3 days, but we have provisions now."[21]

Pelham saw to it that his battery received constant drilling in preparation for the inevitable clash with the Federals, now on their way southward. Discipline remained paramount to his battery; skulkers were not tolerated. "He didn't say much. He didn't need to," stated color-bearer Robert Mackall emphatically. "He would look at you and you felt his eyes going through you and all of a sudden you felt pretty mean. I saw the fellows stammer and blush before him; the biggest and the strongest just wilted when he called them into account. And I tell you, I wouldn't have liked to have been those two who stole away to Richmond against orders. They were the sickest looking pair you ever saw when he told them what he thought of them and gave an order, 'Sergeant, have these men walk up and down over there with their arms folded—keep 'em at it for a week.' No, sir! It wasn't good to fool around with orders around John Pelham!"[22]

Pelham's accomplishments as an organizer were not favored by at least one observer in the Richmond War Department: Quartermaster General Abraham C. Myers. A veteran of the Seminole Wars and the Mexican War, Myers complained in writing to Joe Johnston, accusing Pelham of "a needless and oppressive seizure" of private property (a wagon, team, and mules) from a Mr. Lyons. Myers stated that nothing "justified this injury." He further said that Pelham participated in another "unmilitary exercise" when Pelham, "without the color of propriety or necessity, seized two valuable mules and harness from the wagon of a citizen (a Mr. Quarles) of Henrico County." Myers further asserted that "Captain Pelham was supplied fully with the means of transportation and was not compelled by any want of animals to commit this wrong. . . . I regard this as a wanton act of oppression on the part of Captain Pelham, and as such report it to you. . . . The burdens of war are severe enough upon our people, without their being made more onerous by the arbitrary conduct of military officers." Johnston promptly turned the complaint over to Jeb Stuart, who bristled at the criticism and heatedly defended his chief artillerist.

Stuart stated that Pelham's actions were "necessary, legitimate and unavoidable" and objected to Myers's arbitrary accusation "without a knowledge of the facts in the case." Stuart also shot back that Myers himself was guilty of "an extraordinary ignorance" pertaining to the circumstances. Jeb further argued that "the wagons were all returned except one," which was soon given back to Mr. Lyons as well. Continuing with his censure, Stuart stated: "Upon reaching Richmond [Pelham's] command was increased 100 men—without any increase of transportation. My experience certainly forbade the attempt to procure any from the [Quartermaster]

Dept at Richmond. With his usual perseverance Capt P started with what he had but before proceeding far found it absolutely necessary to procure two mules & harness giving the owner assurance of restitution or ample compensation—receipting for the property." Stuart then admonished, "If purchasing of Mr. Quarles at full value his mules be a hardship on the people of Henrico they have much to learn. A people who have literally fattened on the war may well bear some of its burdens. Yet our artillery must stick in the mud while the streets of Richmond are thronged with spanking teams, enjoying immunity, when the very act of wanton oppression complained of was a measure directly tending to the defence & protection of the city. . . . Col. Myers sweeping declaration against Capt Pelham amounts to nothing, for you & I know what a high-toned, zealous, and efficient officer he is."[23] With that the incident was closed.

Hard work paid dividends for Pelham and his men. The gunners in his battery developed a workmanlike technique and precision unknown to other artillery units in the Confederacy. For Pelham it brought promotion. The authorized document, now housed in the Alabama Archives, is dated May 1, 1862, retroactive to March 23. At the top is the official seal of the Commonwealth of Virginia. It reads in part, "To John Pelham. . . . Know you, that from special trust and confidence reposed in your fidelity, courage and good conduct, our GOVERNOR, in pursuance of the authority vested in him by an Ordinance of the Convention of the State of Virginia, doth commission you a 'Captain of Artillery.'" At the bottom of the citation is the large, scrawling signature of Governor John Letcher. The long wait for the overdue promotion was finally over. Boisterous cheering by the men in the ranks greeted the news. Knowing he deserved it, Pelham still blushed with embarrassment when Stuart announced the tidings. With the new ranking, Pelham also received $76.59 in back pay for the captaincy.[24] Especially proud, Jeb Stuart enjoyed taking Pelham with him and introducing him as "Captain Pelham, my Chief of Artillery." Embarrassed by all the attention, Pelham attempted to grow a beard for a more manly look. He may have been a fighting man, but his boyishness and blondish fuzz made the endeavor a brief, and somewhat humorous, experiment.

The makeshift horse artillery spent the winter of 1861 at Camp Qui Vive (French for "Who goes there?"), located in northeastern Virginia between Centreville and Fairfax Court House. An abandoned farmhouse, the Mellon Place, served as Stuart's headquarters. Always easy to spot, Stuart's headquarters building kept a Blakely cannon positioned to its front with an enormous, hissing raccoon tethered to the gun. "Black, wary, with snarling teeth, and eyes full of 'fight,'" the ferocious animal was regarded by Stuart "as the pearl of sentinels, the paragon of 'coons.'"[25] Making it equally simple to find was the constant noise of song and mirth emanating from the structure. Although Pelham remained outside Stuart's official headquarters' staff, the energetic cavalry leader insisted Pelham stay with the group. Here lasting friendships were forged with a diversity of talented officers, all selected by Stuart.

Methodist chaplain Dabney Ball, affectionately known as "The Fighting Parson," served also as Stuart's chief commissary officer. His nickname was well earned at Bull Run, where he rode within ten paces of the New York Zouaves and calmly emptied his pistol "as if he were practicing at a target."[26] Somewhat physically disabled from rheumatism and erysipelas, an inflammatory skin disease, the great pain he suffered never interfered with his performance of duty.

Stuart's two chief scouts, Will Farley and Redmond Burke, were men of great daring and alacrity. South Carolinian Farley, barely twenty-six years old, had studied at the University of Virginia. Suffering from a severe case of measles and fever until he could barely stand, he fought throughout the day at Bull Run, winning the plaudits of his commanders. Prior to the war he had traversed northern Virginia in detail, giving him a technician's knowledge of its terrain and making him indispensable to Stuart. A gentle writer of poetry, Farley often evidenced another side of his personality. He once responded to a question, "I don't know how many of the enemy I've killed. I never counted. A good many." When asked if it might have been "a dozen," Farley calmly replied, "Oh yes, I can remember six officers. I never counted the men." Stuart described Farley's ability by reporting, "His name is in this army synonymous with intrepidity, bravery, good judgment, and intelligence."[27] Redmond Burke served as a scout and aide-de-camp to Stuart. His background is shrouded in mystery as no birthplace or date of birth exists. Well liked for his capacity to entertain the camp with his marvelous stories, no one doubted his stamina or sagacity as a scout.

Also serving as aides-de-camp were Lieutenants Chiswell Dabney and William Henry Hagan. No two men could have been more unalike. At merely seventeen, Dabney was the youngest on Stuart's staff. Unusually handsome, the quiet Dabney was the "Adonis of the staff." Conversely, Henry Hagan, a Marylander by birth, presented a giant frame, with a heavily bearded face "almost to his eyes" topped off by a deep, hoarse voice. A particular favorite of Stuart's, Hagan also served as chief of couriers. When complimented, Hagan's enormous face "puffed up" in gratitude. It was said that Stuart once promoted him to see "if the giant was capable of further swelling."[28]

Included in the assortment of staff officers were chief engineer William Willis Blackford, surgeon Talcott Eliason, and voluntary aide John Esten Cooke. Highly skilled and versatile, Blackford hailed from nearby Fredericksburg. A graduate of the University of Virginia, he represented a family devoted to the Confederacy. Four of his brothers served in the Confederate army, and all survived the war. Noted for his engineering talents, Blackford was a capable warrior who could boast he had had three horses shot from beneath him. Dr. Eliason, whose father ranked number one in the West Point class of 1821, attended Jefferson Medical School in Philadelphia. Originally from North Carolina, Dr. Eliason joined Stuart's staff in January 1862. His ability with a scalpel endeared him to the men of the cavalry only slightly less than when he occasionally led a charge against the enemy. Scion of a fine Virginia family, John Esten Cooke dutifully served his cousin-in-law Jeb Stuart in a number of capacities. A writer by profession, Cooke glorified Stuart during the war and following Stuart's death. Ironically, Jeb seemed to tire of Cooke's presence and didn't particularly care for him. "John Esten is a case," Jeb penned his wife, "and I am afraid I can't like him." Evidently, Cooke reminded Stuart too much of his father-in-law.[29] Although Stuart never let on to Cooke his earlier feelings, the two became much closer as the war progressed.

Joining Stuart's staff in June 1862 was Johann August Heinrich Heros von Borcke. "Von" immediately became a favorite of Jeb, who was one of the first to befriend him. Hailing from Ehrenbreitstein, Prussia, von Borcke sailed to America and landed in Charleston, South Carolina, on May 24, 1862. Standing 6'4" and weighing 240 pounds, von Borcke truly was a giant. He carried a huge sword of Saracen proportions. With his long, pointed Prussian mustache and trimmed beard, he looked the part of an ancient warrior. His good looks, charismatic personality, and sense of humor delighted Stuart's camp. Broken English and all, he fit right in. Von Borcke held a number of positions on the staff, including aide-de-camp, adjutant general, and inspector. A venerable soldier, von Borcke proved to be a capable writer but weakened his status by often claiming the accomplishments of others.[30]

An ex officio member of the staff was anemic-looking John Singleton Mosby. Weighing no more than 120 pounds with a cadaver-like countenance, Mosby appeared anything but a soldier. But his frail looks were deceiving. Inside this man beat the heart of a lion. A lawyer prior to the war, Mosby proved one of the most daring and skillful of the partisan rangers. His exploits were chronicled far and wide in the Confederacy.

Ruling over this assemblage like a medieval king was James Ewell Brown Stuart. Perhaps no Civil War personality is more compelling. "Beauty," a nickname acquired before his graduation from West Point in 1854, was possibly bestowed for reverse effect; his luxurious beard supposedly covered a weak chin.[31] Standing nearly 5'10" and weighing 175 pounds, Jeb's body seemed somewhat out of proportion. His long legs supported a barrel chest. Broad shoulders and sinewy muscle, however, indicated a man of athletic ability. His catlike movements, restlessness, and agility gave him an air of authority. Possibly his most dominating feature were his penetrating blue-gray eyes, sparkling when he laughed, fierce when angered. His full, cinnamon-colored beard reached down to his chest. He combed his hair back, accentuating his large forehead.

Stuart's self-designed uniform was resplendent, the coat often opened to reveal a vest with gold watch and fob. The ornate, gold piping on the sleeves matched his sash with its swaying tassels. White buckskin gauntlets, stretching halfway to his elbows, covered his large, muscular hands and forearms. Highly polished jackboots reached above his knees and were highlighted by a pair of solid gold spurs given to him by some admiring ladies of Baltimore. Occasionally, a rose or a small bouquet of flowers adorned his coat. Often he wore a red, silk-lined cape made expressly for him by his wife, Flora.[32] Stuart's fawn-colored hat, complete with gold cord and decorative acorns, held a curved black ostrich plume, his proudest piece of apparel. A sparkling, polished saber rested in an immaculate metal scabbard; a 9-shot LeMat revolver was holstered in black leather.

Stuart's personality matched his gaudy appearance. Prone to obstreperous laughter, Jeb's playful demeanor was that of a boy. Practical jokes and mild debasement took much of his time. "It was his delight to jest at the expense of each and all," stated John Esten Cooke, "and he was perfectly willing that they should jest at him in return. If he hurt someone's feelings, he would put his arm around the individual, laugh, and say, 'Come, old fellow, get pleased. I never joke with anyone unless I love them.'" The melodic, baritone voice added distinction whether in battle or merely singing. "There was so much music in his voice," said an admiring Fitzhugh Lee, who soon served under Jeb's command, "sounding like the trumpet of the Archangel."[33] And always music resonated at his campsite. Stuart enlisted the talents of banjo-picking Sam Sweeney and "Mulatto Bob," Jeb's personal servant, who sang and displayed accomplishment at playing bones, fiddle, and guitar. Bob possessed a "dandified appearance—the air, indeed, of a lady killer—and an obvious confidence in his own abilities to delight, if not instruct and improve, his audience."[34] Entertainment also included black-faced minstrels, mimes, and ventriloquists. Although welcomed into this delightful atmosphere, Pelham tended to stay in the background. Perhaps his natural shyness halted him from joining in the gaiety; perhaps he felt the need to prove himself first.

For all the merriment around the camp, Stuart shunned liquor—a promise he had made to his mother as a twelve-year-old—tobacco, and foul language. His staunch Methodist beliefs never wavered. Undoubtedly a ladies man, women willingly threw themselves at Stuart. Entirely comfortable around the opposite sex, Jeb relished the attention and was not above a hug or a kiss on the cheek or hand.[35]

In camp Stuart romped with his two Irish setters and kept an outstanding stable of horses. His favorites—Skylark, Lady Margrave, Highfly, and Star of the East—were all thoroughbreds noted for their amazing speed and endurance. The common notion in camp that "Stuart was born in the saddle" seemed true. George M. Neese, one of the gunners of the horse artillery, remembered with reverence the panache and elegance of Stuart at a review: "He is the prettiest and most graceful rider I ever saw. . . . his every motion in the saddle was in such strict accord with the movements of his horse that he and his horse appeared to be but one and the same machine."[36]

Showmanship was not all that made Stuart legendary. His capability as a cavalryman endures as a testament of his legacy. Unerring judgment and nonpareil instinct headed his virtues. Remarkable powers of observation and resourcefulness marked him as a born leader. "In very dangerous and critical situations," Cooke gushed, "I have seen him throw his leg over the pommel of the saddle, drum his knee carelessly, and then give his orders so quietly that it was difficult to believe it was 'touch and go' whether he would extricate his command, or be cut to pieces." Federal general John Sedgwick assessed Stuart as "the best cavalryman ever foaled in North America."[37]

Glowing reports might be tempered by Stuart's one major flaw: the compulsion to take excessive risks. Other blemishes existed, as even the adoring Cooke admitted: "Foibles he had—a hasty temper, an imperious will, a thirst for glory, the love of appearance, and a susceptibility to flattery that all observed." Although in the minority, some despised Stuart. "[He] carries around with him a banjo player and a special correspondent," observed Confederate general Lafayette McLaws, "[and] this claptrap is noticed and lauded as a peculiarity of genius, when, in fact, it is nothing else but the act of a buffoon to get attention." The surly Confederate general William E. "Grumble" Jones constantly criticized Stuart's flamboyance and literally hated him. "By God . . . you know I had little love for Stuart," groused Jones, "and he had just as little for me," but Jones would later declare, "[Stuart's death] is the greatest loss that army has ever sustained except for the death of Jackson."[38]

Into this roistering world of Jeb Stuart's camp appeared John Pelham. Only five and a half years separated the two in age, yet they were miles apart in personality: one boisterous and jocular, the other shy and retiring. However, they struck up an immediate friendship with Stuart playing the role of the older brother. One trait they shared: the love of the sting of battle. Stuart admired Pelham's tenacity and trusted him implicitly in a fight; Pelham prized Stuart's leadership and patrician manner. Pelham once frankly remarked to another officer, "There never was another man like Stuart." Their partnership became one of the war's most distinctive tandems. As the historian John Thomason stated, "There was love and mutual admiration between the two of them, and no abler combination, sabre and light artillery, has ever been arrayed for battle."[39]

For now the frivolity was over; word arrived that McClellan and his massive army were on the move.

8
"Like a Duck on a June Bug"

Pelham's battery was speaking to the enemy in thunder tones of defiance.
—Jeb Stuart

The persistent rumors involving the movement of George McClellan's army proved to be true. Word of this reached General Joseph E. Johnston, encamped at Manassas with thirty-five thousand men, in early March. Knowing his position was less than tenable, Johnston decided to pull his forces back some thirty-five miles southwest behind the Rappahannock River. With snow still powdery on the ground, the withdrawal began on the morning of March 9. Tons of excess supplies, all that could not be hauled away, had to be destroyed, and Stuart's cavalry drew the assignment. The sight of food and clothing going up in flames left many soldiers with a hollow feeling; surely they would need these coveted items in the lean times ahead.

Pelham, of course, had to move the horse artillery, and he was expected to keep up with the quicker cavalry. The trek to Yorktown tested the mettle of his untried battery and the march "was a most intensely disagreeable one." The roads had deteriorated into a morass, streams were swollen, and bridges often had to be rebuilt. Along the way, according to one of the cannoneers, men sickened "from drinking vile stuff that had been designated by the name of water." Just prior to the larger battles about to ensue, Pelham added to his heroics by capturing a Federal soldier at the end of March. This occurred while Stuart's cavalry posted guard over the Orange and Alexandria Railroad near the Warrenton Junction, a few miles west of Manassas. Here a Union brigade showed up doing reconnaissance work, and a brief and minor skirmish took place. Nothing of consequence resulted, but Stuart happily reported on March 31, "Captain John Pelham, of the Stuart Horse Artillery, while riding alone on his way to join me, came suddenly upon a sturdy veteran, armed with an Enfield gun, took him prisoner, and marched him up to me."[1] No more was stated on this episode, but Stuart certainly beamed over his newly appointed captain's accomplishment.

After months of incessant delay and postponement, McClellan began the transit of his behemoth force toward Richmond on Monday, March 17. The Peninsular Campaign, arguably the largest and most complex campaign of the war, had begun. Little Mac outwardly possessed the confidence of a winner. His self-assurance was easily understood; he commanded an army to rival that of Genghis Khan. With more than 100,000 men, McClellan's Army of the Potomac included 44 batteries of artillery, 14,500 horses and mules, an unlimited supply train, and 7 hot air balloons for aerial reconnaissance. Curiously, McClellan did not confront Richmond in conventional style. Instead he chose to sail down the Potomac River into the Chesapeake Bay and disembark on a peninsula heading to the Confederate capital. For this trek he needed an amazing 400 vessels to transport his men and equipment. Less than enamored with the plan, Lincoln sanctioned it because at least McClellan was finally on the move.

The peninsula leading to Richmond runs southeast to northwest, flanked by the York River on the northern shore and the James River on the southern edge. Halfway up the peninsula, the Chickahominy River, less formidable but more difficult for travel, bisects the peninsula and heads toward the Richmond area forming a considerable barrier for an advancing army. At the so-called entrance to the peninsula stood Fort Monroe held by Federal forces. Here McClellan would land his massive army and march up the peninsula toward Richmond, approximately seventy miles away. The York and James rivers easily served as supply sources since his ships could transport materiel as needed. McClellan's most serious problem, however, was not the logistics involved or the enemy that faced him. His dilemma existed in his own mind; to comprehend the thinking of Little Mac, it must be understood that, without exception, he always thought he was greatly outnumbered. "The enemy have from 3 to 4 times my force," he wrote his wife, Ellen. He then added what he thought of Abraham Lincoln: "the Presdt is an idiot."[2]

A small army of 10,000 Confederates, under the command of General "Prince John" Magruder, defended against McClellan's invasion. Magruder's base stood at Yorktown, about fifteen miles up the peninsula. Here Magruder did yeoman's work in convincing McClellan that his force was significantly larger, causing McClellan to creep, nearly snail-paced, in moving forward. Meanwhile, Joe Johnston met with Jefferson Davis to decide where best to place his army. Arguments arose as the proud and stubborn Johnston believed the peninsula to be indefensible. Davis, equally proud and just as stubborn, felt otherwise. To Johnston's consternation, Davis ordered him to the peninsula. Confounding the Confederate difficulties at this time were five Union armies, totaling 63,000 men, spread out in the Shenandoah Valley. Luckily for the Confederacy, Stonewall Jackson, with an army no larger than 16,000, was there as well.

For more than a month, Jackson's small valley army conducted a clinic of military maneuvering and excellence. Urging on his "foot cavalry," Stonewall responded to the critical needs of the Confederacy by moving and attacking at a whirlwind pace. Covering over six hundred miles in thirty-five days, Jackson's remarkable talents shone brightly as he confused, bottled up, and beat all that came against him. These same Federals in the Shenandoah were earmarked for McClellan, who continued to bog down on the peninsula. With these additional forces, Little Mac believed he would have enough men to invest Richmond, even though he still believed his forces outnumbered. Therefore, Jackson's brilliance in the Shenandoah Valley not only held five Federal armies at bay but largely determined the inactivity of McClellan.

While Stonewall Jackson defended the Shenandoah Valley as though he owned it, a disgruntled Joe Johnston arrived at Yorktown. Together with Magruder's small army, Johnston's forces numbered 53,000, including Jeb Stuart's 1,289 cavalrymen and Pelham's battery of 141 men and eight cannons. In one of the war's ironies, Joe Johnston believed Yorktown could not be defended, while McClellan seemed to feel that Yorktown could not be taken by force. In Little Mac's mind the only solution was siege warfare, and to this he made a halfhearted effort. On May 1 McClellan opened up a cursory fire with his field guns. The effect was enough for Johnston to defy orders and retreat toward Richmond.

On the night of Saturday, May 3, Johnston pulled his men from the trenches at Yorktown and began his retrograde movement to the Confederate capital city. Rain had fallen for twenty of the past thirty days, and the roads grew into a mushy quagmire as Johnston's army slogged westward toward the quaint town of Williamsburg, roughly ten miles away. Reaching Williamsburg, Johnston did not tarry long. Pulling back in the heavy rain, he ordered Stuart's cavalry to act as a rearguard. Stuart quickly deployed his troopers for this critical assignment. Posting the Fourth Virginia Cavalry along Yorktown Road near Whittaker's Mill, Jeb rode with the Third Virginia Cavalry to the center of his defenses at Blow's Mill. The Jeff Davis Legion was sent to Stuart's right along Skiff's Creek, and the First Virginia took up position at Eltham's Landing at the York River. The Wise Legion and John Pelham's horse artillery held the line a few miles from Williamsburg.[3] Meanwhile, the army of Johnston continued to withdraw along the single muddy road leading from Williamsburg to the area of Richmond approximately fifty miles distant.

Rain persisted as Stuart formed the rearguard at Williamsburg on May 4. The following day, Monday, May 5, two Federal divisions of infantry pushed their way toward a large redoubt called Fort Magruder and the rearguard of Johnston's army. To counteract this, Johnston sent three divisions to hinder the Federal approach and buy extra time for his retreating army. General James Longstreet, commanding one of the three divisions, took a strong defensive position near the junction of Lee's Mill Road and Yorktown Road in the vicinity of Fort Magruder. Stuart worked in close harmony with Longstreet to ensure the safety of Johnston's escaping army. Here, just a little over a mile outside Williamsburg, the Confederates awaited the enemy's advance. Soon the battle commenced.

From daylight until mid-morning Confederate infantrymen fought to keep Johnston's retreating army safe. Sometime between 10:00 and 11:00 A.M. Stuart sent for the horse artillery. Over seven miles away near Bigler's Wharf when the order arrived, John Pelham urged his battery forward to meet the crisis. For nearly four hours Pelham and his men labored at moving two 12-pounder howitzers and a Blakely through the mud in a backbreaking effort. By the time Pelham appeared at 2:00 P.M., the enemy seemed to be beaten and retreating. Immediately Stuart directed the battery to "press the pursuit to the uttermost" and sent Pelham and his guns to the right and front of Fort Magruder along Telegraph Road. Suddenly, Federal riflemen, hidden in dense woods, opened up. Stuart shouted instructions for Pelham to return the fire, but "before the order could be given," an admiring Stuart later wrote, "Pelham's battery was speaking to the enemy in thunder tones of defiance, its maiden effort on the field, thus filling its function of unexpected arrival with instantaneous execution and sustaining in gallant style the fortunes of the day." Loading mostly spherical case shot, along with some percussion shells, Pelham's men blasted into the trees with lethal effect. Pelham then instructed his gunners to fire one cannon immediately after the other for a continuous effect with himself running from one gun to the next. Other batteries inside Fort Magruder joined in the cannonade. Stuart continued to heap praise on Pelham for "keeping up a destructive fire upon the enemy until our infantry, having reformed, rushed forward, masking the pieces." Confederate soldiers cheered the resourcefulness and daring of Pelham's battery, fighting its first battle as a unit. Inside the redoubt James Dearing of the Lynchburg Battery maintained that the combined firing of the guns "was kept up incessantly by my two guns and one other in the fort, and by Captain Pelham's Horse Artillery outside, until the enemy ceased firing and were out of sight." As one soldier exclaimed, Pelham managed "his guns with the calmness of a veteran."[4]

When it became apparent that other Federal units were not retreating, Stuart gave the order for Pelham to move his guns farther to the left on Yorktown Road and set them in an enfilading position toward Telegraph Road. One officer noted that Pelham and his gunners were "hotly engaged," but the battery soon "raced across gullies and fields to beat a Federal battery to a desirable position." With support from gunners of the infantry, a deadly crossfire was established. Pelham's Blakely soon suffered a malfunctioning elevating screw, but it easily kept pace with the booming of the howitzers. After some bloody fighting, the Rebels broke through the Union lines and captured four guns and an ammunition limber. Six more cannon, there for the taking, were too mired in the mud to extricate and had to be left behind. Although the fighting at Williamsburg was not conducive to cavalry maneuvers, Stuart sent in the Fourth Virginia Cavalry to help finish off the retreating Federals. A swift volley from the enemy, however, sent the horsemen reeling for cover. One of three Virginians to fall was Major William H. Payne. Shot in the face only moments after he remarked that "one could catch [the thickly falling bullets] by the hatful," Payne was carried to the rear for medical attention. Although Payne's bloody wound was thought to be fatal, Dr. Edmund Pendleton saved his life by forcing his fingers into Payne's mouth and squeezing off the severed artery. Both the doctor, still holding tightly to the artery, and Payne were lifted simultaneously into an ambulance heading to Williamsburg. A surviving Payne later remembered: "There was hardly an instant from the time I fell until I was put in the ambulance that the chances of death to both of us were not a thousand to one."[5]

Fighting continued to seesaw as segments of both armies arrived on the field, giving each side an advantage whenever a new unit appeared. General Philip Kearny's division showed up at 3:00 P.M. and saved the day for the Federals. The handsome Kearny, a graduate of Columbia University who had lost his left arm during the Mexican War, ordered a furious counterattack that drove the stunned Confederates back into the woods at Lee's Mill Road.

Presently, the staggered Rebels came alive with the arrival of the brigade under Jubal Early. This same hero from the Battle of Bull Run appeared, as he had at Manassas, in the nick of time. His counterstroke offset the Federal advance, but a rifle bullet struck Early in the shoulder, ending his day of fighting.[6] Further counterattacks ensued from both sides until the rain-soaked day ended with darkness. The bloody stalemate at Williamsburg, including Pelham's repulse of the Federals, cost the Confederates 1,682 casualties. Union losses totaled 2,283. Both sides claimed victory, but the Confederates won a tactical success by holding the enemy back while the bulk of their army escaped. Although McClellan boasted of a great win for the Army of the Potomac, Federal general "Baldy" Smith, who actually participated in the battle, dejectedly labeled it "a beastly exhibition of stupidity and ignorance."[7]

John Pelham modestly described his part in the action on May 5 in his official report:

> Between 10 and 11 A.M. . . . I received orders from brigade headquarters to proceed immediately to Williamsburg. I left five of my pieces [behind] and reported with three (two 12-pounder howitzers and one 12-pounder rifled gun, Blakely) to . . . Stuart . . . about 2 P.M.
>
> I took position to the right and in front of Fort Magruder, and opened fire on the enemy, who occupied the woods on the road to Lebanon Church. Here I detached Lieutenant [William C.] Elston, with two men, to bring off some captured artillery. In a few minutes they returned on foot, their horses having been shot down as soon as they made their appearance at the guns. I held this position under a heavy fire until General [D. H.] Hill's brigade moved up and deployed in front of my battery, when I moved to the left and took position on the Yorktown Road, to enfilade the enemy's lines. Here the

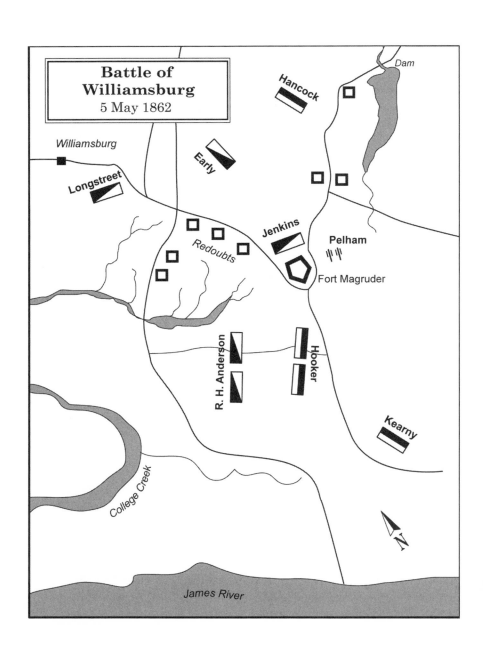

Battle of Williamsburg
5 May 1862

Dam

Hancock

Williamsburg

Early

Longstreet

Redoubts

Jenkins

Pelham

Fort Magruder

R. H. Anderson

Hooker

Kearny

College Creek

N

James River

metal bed of the elevating screw of my Blakely gun gave way; but it was retained on the field and did good service. I remained in this position until 5 P.M., when I withdrew for want of ammunition.

I fired 286 rounds of spherical case and 4 of canister from the 12-pounder howitzers and 40 percussion shell and 30 solid shot from the Blakely gun. Total of 360.

During the entire engagement both officers and men acted with commendable calmness and courage. The example of cool, conspicuous bravery set by Lieutenants Breathed, McGregor, and Elston was emulated by my non-commissioned officers and men.

Casualties as follows: 2 men wounded, Summers and Gibson; 4 horses killed, 3 wounded, and 13 escaped from horse-holders, all of which have since been found except two.[8]

From the saddle, Jeb Stuart wrote his wife on May 9, again praising Pelham:

I consider the most brilliant feat of the 5th to be a dash of the Stuart Horse Artillery to the front, and, coming suddenly under a galling fire of the enemy from the woods from a reinforcement of the enemy, [they] wheeled into action sustaining in the most brilliant manner the fortunes of the day until the infantry could come to its support, and all the time under a continuous infantry fire of 200 yards or less distance. For <u>myself</u> I have only to say that if you had seen your husband you would have been proud of him.

The Floyd County Militia in Pelham's battery behaved in the handsomest style, astounding every one beyond measure.

At one point Jeb added rather ruefully, "I came within an ace of capturing my father-in-law."[9]

The following day Stuart penned his official report on the battle at Williamsburg, further complimenting Pelham and the newly created horse artillery: "[Pelham's battery] was composed mostly of raw militia from Floyd County, Virginia, who had received but a few weeks' drill, yet, under the indefatigable exertions of Captain Pelham, ably seconded by his lieutenants and non-commissioned officers, they that day won the name of veterans. The daring and efficient conduct, under circumstances of great personal danger . . . came under my own observation."[10]

James Longstreet lauded numerous officers and units, and in a few words mentioned Pelham by name: "The artillery was well served . . . [the] Stuart Horse Artillery, under Capt. Pelham." Special praise by Longstreet was given to Stuart: "I am under many obligations to Brig. Gen. J. E. B. Stuart, who, while waiting for an opportunity to use his cavalry, was exceedingly active and zealous in conducting the different columns to their proper destinations and in assisting them to get properly into action."[11]

The next day, May 6, dawned clear and sunny as Johnston's army maintained its struggle back toward Richmond. Stuart's cavalry, including the horse artillery, continued to form the rearguard. Pelham and his gunners spent hours wearily hauling their cannons over the muddy roads. Excessive amounts of fence rails, used to extricate the mired cannons of Johnston's army and then carelessly tossed into the road, further hindered their progress. Periodically Pelham's gunners fired "an occasional shell to remind [the enemy] that we would not be hurried in our march." After a day of backbreaking labor, Pelham's men neared a spot called Burnt Ordinary, a good dozen miles up the peninsula from Williamsburg, where they collapsed for the night at a brick schoolhouse. The following morning Pelham's forces skirmished with two cavalry squadrons, the Third Pennsylvania and the Eighth Illinois, under the command of Colonel William W. Averell. Pelham's report, written the following day, detailed the brief encounter. "About 10 A.M. . . . I received orders from the brigade commander to return to the rear, with a rifled gun and howitzer. The howitzer was left at the Methodist Church, about 1 ½ miles beyond Burnt Ordinary, under Lieutenant Breathed; the rifled gun was placed in position about a mile farther on. The enemy's cavalry made their appearance in the edge of the woods in front of us, and I fired five shots at them. The shot fell, well scattering them, but I could observe no other effect. I then retired in the rear of the main body of our forces."[12]

This brief engagement between Pelham's gunners and an enemy scouting party represented merely one of many such encounters over the next couple of weeks as various Federal units sought to reach the rear of Johnston's retreating army. Stuart's cavalry, ably assisted by the efforts of Pelham's artillery, continued to frustrate these attempts. On May 8 Pelham pushed his artillerists farther northwest up the peninsula to New Kent Court House, a stretch over muddy roads of nearly twenty miles. The weary unit remained in this area for the next six days. On Wednesday, May 14, Pelham received orders to proceed westward to Bottom's Bridge, approximately halfway from New Kent to Richmond. The march to the bridge, located on the Chickahominy River, a distance of about twenty miles, proved uneventful. Upon crossing the bridge, Pelham ordered the structure to be put to the torch. All attempts, however, proved unsuccessful as the heavy wooden beams, saturated by the constant rains, simply would not ignite. Suddenly enemy shells began to spatter the bridge area as two Federal batteries appeared in the distance. Confederate gunner Henry Matthews humorously noted, "we concluded that we did not want to burn the bridge anyway." Moving to a safer position on the north bank of the Chickahominy, Pelham's gunners immediately started digging earthworks, which were "strengthened by railroad iron and ties" from the nearby Richmond and York River Railroad. Their labors were soon completed.[13]

In the last third of the month Pelham continued to stymie some of the lead elements of McClellan's army. On May 20 Pelham, in what was becoming typical behavior, boldly fired a half-dozen shells into the forward section of Erasmus Keyes's Fourth Corps near Bottom's Bridge. Although the skirmish amounted to little, Keyes seemed impressed by the quickness and surprise of the action. "The enemy," reported the Federal general, "threw five or six shells before any of our artillery replied at all." The overall effect of Pelham's brashness was not lost on the morale of his men, whose confidence soared with each engagement. "Our little battery seems to keep McClellan's whole army at bay," wrote Private William P. Walters to his wife on May 20. "If they only knew that we was here with as little force as we have got they would be on us like a duck on a June bug."[14]

On May 24 another clash took place near a crossroads known as Mechanicsville, consisting of nothing more than four houses and a blacksmith shop. The importance of this settlement, however, rested with the fact that its location was merely eight miles northeast of Richmond, making it an invaluable striking point from which to assail the Confederate capital. Although Pelham arrived too late to participate in this bout, he was pleased to later learn that Captain Tom Rosser, commanding the Washington Artillery, added to the heroics of the fighting. Although the details remained scarce, Pelham learned that Rosser and three others were wounded by a Federal shell that fell in their midst. A severe gash had opened up on Rosser's right arm above the elbow, but he valiantly stood directing the fire of two cannon while holding a bloody cloth to the wound. It further pleased Pelham to find out that his Texas friend would receive medical attention and survive.[15]

For the previous two weeks, Joe Johnston's fatigued troops somehow had managed their way over bad roads and rugged terrain. Some mules, bogged irretrievably in the mud, had to be shot; some were said to have completely disappeared in the ooze. Hunger plagued the men as equally as the inclement weather. Illnesses, brought on by the soggy climate and brackish drinking water, struck down scores, especially the newer recruits. Severe diarrhea and measles flattened many men, disabling them from the most mundane of soldierly chores.[16] Luckily, McClellan's army pursued slowly, and no battles of consequence occurred. Finally, after days of superhuman effort, Johnston's men began trickling into the Richmond area. Johnston wisely placed his forces behind the flooded Chickahominy River, less than ten miles from the outskirts of the capital city. Stuart's cavalry and horse artillery made camp, which Jeb named Quien Sabe (Spanish for "Who Knows?"), just outside Richmond. Here the Confederates waited for any advance from the Army of the Potomac.

As McClellan's men approached the Chickahominy, they were appalled by the nature of the river. One described it as "a narrow, sluggish stream flowing through swamp land . . . covered with a rank, dense, tangled growth of trees, reeds, grasses and water plants. Vines climb and mosses festoon the trees; . . . its stagnant water is poisonous; moccasins and malaria abound; flies and mosquitoes swarm."[17] In approaching Johnston's army, McClellan's troops would be forced to cross this swampy morass. Johnston's good fortune continued as McClellan found it necessary to split his army across the Chickahominy. While three full corps sat north of the river, two corps, those of Major Generals Erasmus Keyes and Samuel Heintzelman, remained isolated on the southern side. The Fourth Corps, under the capable leadership of Keyes, positioned itself dangerously close to the outskirts of Richmond, at a small community called Fair Oaks. From this spot, merely five miles west of the capital along the Richmond and York River Railroad line, Keyes's men could set their watches to the church bells chiming within the capital city itself. Keyes's left flank extended about a mile southward to the village of Seven Pines. The indecisive Heintzelman and his powerful Third Corps encamped five miles farther east of Keyes on the Williamsburg Road. The populace of Richmond fairly panicked at the intensity of the situation.

Faced with an enemy of extraordinary numbers breathing directly down on Richmond, Joe Johnston prepared a plan to attack Keyes's Fourth Corps at Fair Oaks. Two divisions would hold the main portion of the Federal army north of the Chickahominy. His remaining three divisions were assigned to attack Keyes simultaneously on the three nearly parallel roads leading to Fair Oaks and Seven Pines.

On Saturday, May 31, Johnston's battle plan broke down immediately. Without written orders for his generals, Johnston's verbal orders became confusing on the march. Swampy grounds and rain-soaked roads further hindered movement. By mid-afternoon Federal reinforcements arrived. The proposed Confederate simultaneous attack had disintegrated into a disjointed slugfest. By nightfall, the Rebels called off the battle.

In the shadows of the early evening random shots were still being fired. Joe Johnston sat on his horse along Nine Mile Road, two hundred yards north of Fair Oaks, keenly observing the situation to his front. Beside him sat a staff officer who automatically ducked low on the saddle each time bullets whizzed by. Johnston laughed and reassured him, "Colonel, there is no use dodging; when you hear them they have passed." At that moment an expression of pain came over the general's face, as he knew he was hit. Johnston fell unconscious to the ground but later described the wounding: "About half-past 7 o'clock I received a musket-shot in the shoulder, and was unhorsed soon after by a heavy fragment of shell which struck my breast. I was borne from the field—first to a house on the roadside, thence to Richmond."[18]

Including killed, wounded, and missing, the Confederates sustained 6,134 casualties; Federal losses were put at 5,031. Countless guns and various pieces of military equipment littered the battlefield. The Confederates captured an assortment of cannon, one of which, a 12-pounder Napoleon, was given to John Pelham for his battery. Wagons continually hauled the dead and wounded into Richmond for the next several hours. One of those severely wounded, of course, was commanding general Joseph E. Johnston. He had lost a considerable amount of blood, and surgeons found several broken ribs.[19] Johnston would survive, surgeons announced, but he remained sidelined for the next six months.

In Richmond Jefferson Davis made possibly his most important decision of the war: Robert E. Lee, who had been a desk general and advisor to the president, would take field command. Lee reached the army, now officially known as the Army of Northern Virginia, at 2:00 P.M. on Sunday, June 1. Few in this army knew what to expect from Lee. Born into a military tradition—his father was the famous "Lighthorse Harry" Lee who fought under George Washington—Robert, now fifty-five years old, graduated number two in the West Point class of 1829. During the Mexican War, Lee was brevetted three times and given the extreme compliment "the very best soldier that I ever saw in the field" by his commanding general, Winfield Scott. As a career officer and former superintendent of West Point, Lee knew the men who served under him as well as those he served against. Most of his pre–Civil War years had been spent as an engineer, and his propensity for digging entrenchments earned him the ignominious nickname "King of Spades." Recognition, however, was given to his dignity and moral strength of character. His appearance was certainly that of a soldier. Comments ranged from "Lee looked a very god of war" to "a born king among men." What his army could not perceive at this time was his audacity as a general. This they learned in the next few days.

In assessing his new opponent George McClellan viewed Lee interestingly. Ironically, in describing Lee to Lincoln Little Mac appeared to be characterizing himself. "[Lee is] too cautious & weak under grave responsibility," commented McClellan, "wanting in moral firmness when pressed by heavy responsibility & is likely to be timid & irresolute in action."[20]

For nearly two weeks, the Army of Northern Virginia, under Lee's orders, dug entrenchments and constructed field fortifications. The men grumbled and complained to one another as they labored. Whether a King of Spades or too weak to handle his responsibilities, Lee was certain of one immutable fact: defending Richmond with sixty-five thousand men against McClellan's superior forces could not be done. To successfully drive McClellan from the capital city, Lee must take the offense and push Little Mac's enormous army to a safe position, far beyond the limits of Richmond. To do this, Lee required a strong defensive base to secure his planned offensive operation—hence the fortifications. He also needed Stonewall Jackson's army from the Shenandoah Valley. Lastly, Lee must have information on any weakness of the Army of the Potomac.

Lee believed McClellan's extreme right flank, near the Pamunkey River some fifteen miles north of Richmond, was vulnerable. From his command post at the home of widow Mary C. Dabbs, Lee outlined a special plan for Stuart to raid and disrupt McClellan's supply and communication line. On June 11 Lee drew up the official orders, carefully worded, and gave Stuart his copy. Riding secretly to the rear of the Federal army, Stuart was to gain "intelligence of [the enemy's] operations [and] communications." Wagon trains were to be destroyed as well. Lee further cautioned Stuart to use "utmost vigilance" in his trek and finally added "not to hazard unnecessarily your command."[21] Of course, utmost secrecy, even from his own cavalry, must be kept, so Stuart alone knew what lay ahead. Knowing that his father-in-law, Philip St. George Cooke, headed McClellan's reserve cavalry put that special light in Stuart's eyes. Jeb champed at the bit for this assignment.

Ordering his men to cook three days' rations and carry sixty rounds of ammunition each, Stuart further indicated they would need some rest. He did not speak of their destination but told them to be ready at a moment's notice. Stuart selected the 1,200 cavalrymen for the venture. Included in the group were Colonel Fitzhugh Lee (Robert E. Lee's nephew) of the First Virginia, Colonel "Rooney" Lee (Robert E. Lee's son) of the Ninth Virginia, Lieutenant Colonel Will T. Martin of the Jefferson Davis Legion, and an assortment of aides: Heros von Borcke, John Mosby, Redmond Burke, Will Farley, John Esten Cooke, and Henry Hagan. Although two cannons, a 12-pounder howitzer and a 6-pound English rifled gun, along with a group of gunners from the horse artillery, were selected, strangely, John Pelham was not involved. Instead, Lieutenant James Breathed took command of the guns with nineteen-year-old Lieutenant William M. McGregor second in command.[22] Stuart also made sure that some of his riders included locals who knew the territory's roads and hidden trails.

At 2:00 A.M. on Thursday, June 12, Stuart awakened his aides abruptly. Immediately, "Boots and Saddles" rang out, and shortly the energized men saddled up. Excitement pervaded the camp as the troopers readied for their unknown destination. Although no one among them, except Stuart, knew their objective, the troopers readily guessed that they were heading to the Shenandoah Valley to join Jackson's forces. As Stuart rode forward to lead the column to its unknown target, someone asked how long he would be gone. Laughingly, the cavalier Stuart replied, "It may be for years and it may be forever."[23] Leaving the Richmond area in the still night air, the 1,200-man column headed north along Brook Turnpike toward the South Anna River. Stuart's much-heralded ride had begun.

∾

After an exhausting ride that carried Stuart and his troopers completely around the Army of the Potomac, Stuart walked into Lee's headquarters just before dawn on June 15. Pleased to see his cavalry chieftain, Lee sat patiently as Stuart filled him in on the details of the 150-mile venture, completed in little more than seventy-two hours. Coming up from the rear, Stuart told him, were 165 prisoners and 260 captured horses and mules. Stuart had lost only one killed, a handful of wounded, and one captured. Most important was the necessary information on the Federal right flank: Fitz John Porter's Fifth Corps lay exposed, or "in the air," as Stuart said.[24]

Robert E. Lee beamed with pride at Stuart's stunning achievement. "The general commanding announces with great satisfaction to the army," wrote Lee, "the brilliant exploit of Brig. Gen. J. E. B. Stuart." Virginia governor John Letcher presented Stuart with a fine ceremonial sword. General Daniel Harvey Hill stated that "no more dashing thing [was] done in the war." The "Ride around McClellan" was an elixir to the demoralized people of Richmond. It further bolstered the sagging confidence and morale of the Confederate army. Newspapers splashed headlines, "A MAGNIFICENT ACHIEVEMENT" and labeled it "Unparalleled and Brilliant." Whether Stuart's ride deserved such high accolades is still debatable, but Confederate historian William Allan may have saluted it best when he tersely stated that the raid "mortified McClellan, and lessened his waning influence with his [own] government."[25]

Stuart's exhausted troopers arrived in Richmond the following morning to a tumultuous crowd of cheering onlookers. Bands played and handkerchiefs waved, as the valiant riders enjoyed their welcome. Stuart lavishly praised his men in his official report and asked for the prompt promotion of many. To John Pelham, elated to have his commanding officer return, Stuart reported both guns intact. Pelham could take much pride in the words of Colonel William T. Martin's report: "I would take occasion to mention the energy displayed by Lieutenant Breathed in overcoming the difficulties encountered in moving his piece of artillery, and the promptness shown in preparing for action on several occasions when there was reason to believe that the enemy were about to attack."[26]

A few days passed, and at 3:00 P.M. on June 23, two riders appeared at Lee's headquarters. Both men showed signs of dustiness and an apparent weariness from a lengthy ride. As they dismounted at the Dabbs House, only one entered—Stonewall Jackson. Leaving his men in the Shenandoah Valley, Jackson had been summoned to meet with Lee. The commanding general described the exposed right flank of McClellan's army and proposed that Jackson's army march to link up with the Army of Northern Virginia.[27] The King of Spades was preparing to strike McClellan's jugular.

The upcoming campaign was destined to further bolster John Pelham's career as a premier artillerist.

9
"We Are Going to Whip the Yankees Like the Mischief"

No field grade is too high for [Pelham's] merit and capacity.

—Jeb Stuart

From his headquarters at the Dabbs house, at noon on Monday, June 23, Robert E. Lee summoned Generals James Longstreet, A. P. Hill, D. H. Hill, and Stonewall Jackson for a discussion of strategy. Longstreet was the senior officer of the foursome. Noted for his poker playing and occasional social drink, "Old Pete's" personality had changed considerably when three of his children died early in 1862 from a scarlet fever epidemic that ravaged Richmond.[1] A. P. Hill, sensitive and proud, originated from a respected Virginia family. Aggressive to a fault, "Little Powell" became a battlefield fixture for the Army of Northern Virginia throughout the war. His red beard and famous crimson battle shirt matched his fiery personality. D. H. Hill, noted for his bluntness and cynicism, was more renowned for being Stonewall Jackson's brother-in-law. A South Carolinian by birth, Hill graduated in the middle of the 1842 West Point class with Longstreet. His cutting remarks offended many, but none denied his ability to fight. Enigmatic Stonewall Jackson rounded out the four. Although his shabby appearance belied the notion, the fanatically religious and soft-spoken Jackson possessed something the others did not: pure military genius.

Once this distinguished group assembled, Lee proceeded to explain his plans for an attack on McClellan. While two-thirds of the Army of the Potomac sat on the south side of the Chickahominy River, Fitz John Porter's Fifth Corps of thirty thousand men lay exposed on the north bank. Lee's four generals would lead their divisions in a coordinated attack, via separate and converging roads, on the Union Fifth Corps near the town of Mechanicsville. Coordination and timing were essential to the plan's success. Jackson's men were to initiate the movement on the morning of June 26. When the meeting ended, the generals proceeded back to their various commands. For Jackson, this entailed a ride of approximately forty miles back to his forces along the Virginia Central Railroad near Beaver Dam Station.

The following day Lee issued Order No. 75, detailing the battle scheme, to his commanders. Jackson's Army of the Shenandoah remained the key to the entire plan. Lee sent Jeb Stuart's cavalry to meet with Jackson's forces at Ashland, some fifteen miles north of Richmond. Here Stuart would screen Jackson's movement from the left and guide the valley forces toward Porter's exposed right flank. Stuart's column included the First, Fourth, and Ninth Virginia cavalry regiments plus Cobb's Legion and the Jefferson Davis Legion. Captain John Pelham directed the horse artillery, which he expertly managed to keep up with the cavalry over the still-muddied roads. Riding toward Ashland, none of the cavalrymen, except Stuart, knew of their destination or purpose, but anticipation ran high among the ranks. Less than a week earlier, Chiswell Dabney excitedly penned his mother, "We are going to whip the Yankees like the mischief in a few days."[2]

On June 25, George McClellan surprised Lee by initiating an attack of his own at a spot called Oak Grove, thus beginning the Seven Days Battles. The fighting continued for most of the day with casualties negligible on both sides. Although Lee was concerned about McClellan's show of energy, it did not deter him from staying with his plan for an attack on Mechanicsville the following day.

After a night's rest, the forces of Jackson and Stuart readied for the move on Mechanicsville. Difficult and confusing roads made the going slow, as did the scorching heat. Surprisingly, Jackson seemed in no extreme hurry. As the men trudged along, reports came in of Federals destroying a bridge over Totopotomoy Creek ahead. This bridge was essential to Jackson's movement, and Stuart quickly summoned John Pelham. Taking two howitzers, Pelham hurried to the site. Eyeing Federals in the woods across the creek, Pelham ordered a quick load or two of canister fired in their direction. The enemy fled rapidly, while W. W. Blackford and a few men extinguished the flames and saved the bridge. After this episode Pelham and his gunners rode to the front in the event of further trouble.[3]

Hours dragged by as Jackson languidly moved forward. By 3:00 P.M. with Jackson's army long overdue, A. P. Hill impetuously decided to go ahead with his attack on the Federal Fifth Corps. Five brigades of Hill's division proceeded to frontally assault Porter's strong position, strategically located behind the marshy lowlands of Beaver Dam Creek. With Federal artillery in full control, A. P. Hill's men suffered heavily. Anticipating Jackson's arrival, the Confederates fought on until nightfall. Apparently unaware of the other's situation, Hill fought while Jackson dawdled. At Hundley's Corner, merely three miles from the fighting, Jackson inexplicably ordered his men to bivouac. That night, as Jackson's men slumbered, Hill's men attempted to save the wounded and fetch the dead around Beaver Dam Creek. Confederate losses numbered 1,475 while the Federals placed their casualties at 361.[4]

Lee's complex plan to bring nearly 56,000 men against Fitz John Porter had failed miserably. Responsibility for this debacle partly rested with the commanding general himself—his orders, based on precise execution, were at times confused and faulty. His major subordinate generals also must share part of the blame. Incredibly, McClellan decided to pull Porter's forces from their strong position at Beaver Dam Creek to a spot five miles southeast at Gaines' Mill. Equally as incredible, Robert E. Lee planned to attack Porter again the next day.

The Federal commander, competent Fitz John Porter, formed his lines into a semicircle over two miles in length. His right stretched nearly to the community of Old Cold Harbor; his left extended toward the Chickahominy River. With 27,000 men positioned mostly on a plateau behind a meandering marsh known as Boatswain's Swamp, Porter held a rock-solid line of defense. Adding to his advantage were twenty batteries of artillery, finely placed, along with abatis and rifle pits. An open plain, about a quarter of a mile in width, stretching across Porter's front offered excellent range for his riflemen and artillerists. Three brigades of reserve infantry stood behind Porter's lines, not far from the McGehee homestead.[5] Ready to assist his main forces, these reserves also guarded the four nearby bridges, spanning the Chickahominy, which linked the rest of McClellan's army south of the river.

In the meantime, Robert E. Lee devised an assault all too similar to that of the preceding day at Mechanicsville. Lee's four divisional commanders, with close to 50,000 men, would advance on Porter's corps and drive it southeast from its location. Once again, the planned attack called for coordination from Lee's generals. Friday, June 27, dawned hazy and warm, as Porter's veterans girded for a morning Confederate advance. Hours passed and nothing of consequence occurred. Not until 2:30 P.M. was the Battle of Gaines' Mill begun in earnest, as A. P. Hill, displaying his impetuous nature, pushed his large division forward instead of waiting for Jackson's men as Hill's orders stated. For two desperate hours, Little Powell's men rushed ahead, time and again, against Porter's formidable defenses. Federal artillery and riflemen blasted them back repeatedly with staggering losses. Both valor and lives were sacrificed with each assault. Frustrated and angry, A. P. Hill decided to back off and wait for Stonewall to arrive. Hill's men halted for the better part of the afternoon without any sign of Jackson.[6] For two consecutive days, the question "Where is Jackson?" hounded the Confederates and was left momentarily unanswered.

Jackson's approach, delayed considerably by taking an incorrect road, which forced him to backtrack over the same route, cost him valuable time. Indeed, Confederate cavalryman George W. Beale noted: "Our march for some time seemed rather away from the Federal army on the Chickahominy than towards it."[7] Tangled woods and poorly drawn maps added to Jackson's woes. Hours behind schedule, his forces would not reach their destination until 4:30 P.M. Along the way, Stuart's cavalry drew the assignment of protecting Jackson's flank. Stuart detached the Jefferson Davis Legion and the Fourth Virginia, both commanded by Lieutenant Colonel Will T. Martin, to scout the area around Old Church. Pelham's horse artillery rode alongside them. As they moved forward on Old Church Road, Federal cavalrymen were spotted ahead. Martin ordered Pelham and his gunners to disperse this nuisance. Quickly, Pelham pushed his gunners forward, and just as quickly, they opened up with canister. The Union horsemen, caught unaware, scattered. Martin later reported this incident in his official report: "A piece of the Horse

Artillery was advanced, under Captain Pelham, and fired in the direction of the church. Subsequently it was ascertained that this firing put to flight a force of 1000 or 1500 of the enemy's cavalry in this vicinity."[8] The slow march continued.

Finally, at half past four, Stonewall Jackson's nine brigades made their way to the Gaines' Mill area and were placed on Lee's left near the men of D. H. Hill. Suddenly, two batteries of Federal artillery, a total of twelve guns, began a rapid fire on Jackson's men, whose own artillery units had not yet reached the front. Jeb Stuart, showing good sense and his usual bravado, ordered John Pelham and two of his cannons forward. Reacting expeditiously, Pelham brought up his cannons, a rifled Blakely and a 12-pounder Napoleon—the same captured piece given to him after the Battle of Seven Pines. All twelve Federal guns, the batteries of Stephen Weed and John C. Tidball, instantly turned their attention toward Pelham's two cannons.[9] The first salvo from the Federal gunners completely damaged the carriage and trail of the Blakely, and Pelham ordered it to the rear. Now, with the single Napoleon, the Creoles of the Napoleon Detachment moved dangerously close to the enemy and opened fire. Astonishingly, for nearly an hour, close to the Old Cold Harbor tavern, Pelham's lone cannon dueled two enemy batteries to a standstill. Stuart's staff officer, John Esten Cooke, noted that "Pelham [was] still fighting like a trump." In his choppy journal notations, Cooke remembered: "Artillery duel in full roar. Shells hot and furious. Enemy's battery at last quieter." From afar, Stonewall Jackson inquired of Stuart the identity of the officer directing that accurate fire versus such overwhelming numbers. Stuart proudly identified him as Captain Pelham, "fighting like a tiger!"[10] Jackson, momentarily spellbound by the scene before him, soon ordered up three batteries of his own to assist Pelham. With the additional Confederate firepower, the Federal gunners withdrew from the field.[11]

William P. Walters, a member of Pelham's horse artillery, described the action a few days later in a letter to his family.

> its only providence that saved us for we went on the left of general Jackson's army and commensed on the yankeys withe our rifle gun and napolian gun but our too guns was a pure show against 8 or 9 yankys canons which was throwin balls and shells at us fast enuff, but worse than all our rifle piece broke its elevating screw and left us there withe one gun I ramed the balls down as fast as I cood we all worked hard captin pelham helped us himself and general Stuart holered give it too them boys you soon will have help and it come in good time for we was nearly broke down when 6 guns fell in our rite and 4 guns on our left they was fresh batterys and commensed a quick fire on the yankeys which done them as mutch harm as it done me good the captin told us to quit firing and rest rest dose good eaven when it is taken under a shower of balls for we soon commensed agane like fresh set of boys and soon heard the last Gun of our enemy groaning threw the are.[12]

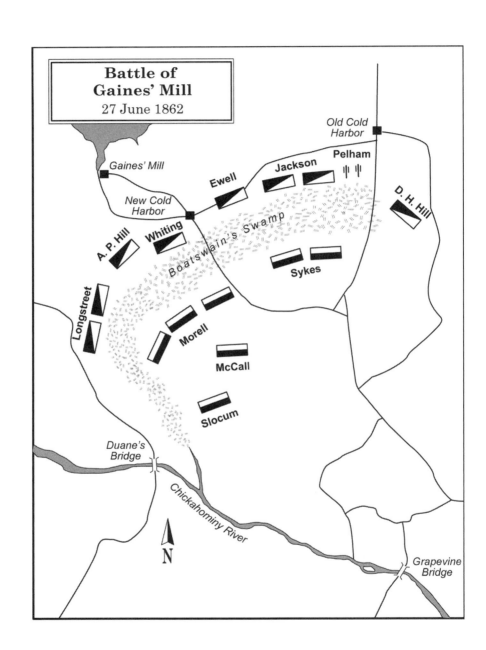

Battle of Gaines' Mill

27 June 1862

Old Cold Harbor

Gaines' Mill

Pelham

Jackson

Ewell

New Cold Harbor

D. H. Hill

A. P. Hill

Whiting

Boatswain's Swamp

Sykes

Longstreet

Morell

McCall

Slocum

Duane's Bridge

Chickahominy River

N

Grapevine Bridge

Afterward, Stuart beckoned Pelham to join him for an introduction to Stonewall Jackson. Pelham appeared, streaked with the souvenirs of battle: grime, dust, and black grease smeared on his face and hands. "This is Captain Pelham, General," said Stuart. "He has fought with one gun that whole battalion on the hill, at point-blank range, for nearly an hour." Jackson said nothing but extended his hand in a gesture of respect and congratulations. Saying nothing in return, the awestruck artillerist bowed low and blushed "like a girl." Pelham then rode back to his gunners. He had fought the battle "with blood hound pertinacity," recalled one veteran.[13]

Stuart effusively detailed the episode in his official report written seventeen days later:

> The only artillery under my command being Pelham's Stuart Horse Artillery, the 12-pounder Blakely and Napoleon were ordered forward to meet this bold effort to damage our left flank. The Blakely was disabled at the first fire, the enemy opening simultaneously eight pieces. . . . Then ensued one of the most gallant and heroic feats of the war. The Napoleon gun, solitary and alone, received the fire of those batteries, concealed in the pines on a ridge commanding its ground, yet not a man quailed, and the noble captain directing the fire himself with a coolness and intrepidity only equaled by his previous brilliant career. The enemy's fire sensibly slackened under the determined fire of this Napoleon, which clung to its ground with unflinching tenacity. I had the opportunity of calling General Jackson's attention to the heroic conduct of the officers and men of this piece, and later he, by his personal efforts, re-enforced it with several batteries of rifle pieces, which, firing, advanced en echelon about dark and drove the enemy from his last foothold on the right.[14]

Jackson, who did not file his report of the incident until eight months later, remembered the heroics of Pelham "[who] bravely dashed forward and opened on the Federal batteries posted on the left of our infantry. Reenforced by the guns of Brockenborough, Carrington, and Courtney, of my command, our artillery now numbered about thirty pieces. Their fire was well directed and effective, and contributed to the successful issue of the engagement."[15]

Pelham's valiant duel certainly did not win the Battle of Gaines' Mill, but it may have shaken the lethargy from Jackson. "This affair must hang in suspense no longer," shouted the inspired Jackson, "sweep the field with the bayonet!" Some 18,000 of Jackson's Confederates surged ahead, but the fighting appeared to be a stalemate as Porter's men bravely stood their ground. Near darkness, with all the Confederate divisions advancing, a breakthrough occurred at 7:00 P.M. directly in the center of the Federal stronghold. Led by Brigadier General John Bell Hood, his "wild Texans" at first halted due to the persistent firing of a Union battery of artillery. Jackson sent word, "Tell General Hood I will have that battery silenced at once." Turning to a staff officer, Jackson ordered, "Bring up several batteries to assist Pelham and tell them to drive that battery away or destroy it!" Momentarily, the Confederate gunners, led by Pelham, halted the firing of the Federal guns. Hood's Texans now cracked through the Union middle, their screams, according to one of Longstreet's veterans, "sounded like forty thousand wild cats." Forcing their way across innumerable natural obstacles, the Texans plunged forward and struggled in hand-to-hand combat with the enemy. A sizable gap occurred in the Union lines, and Confederate reinforcements showed up to widen it even more. With victory at hand, after a most difficult and intense day, the Rebels swept to triumph. The headstrong and fearless Hood proved he was a man to be reckoned with. Standing 6'2," the blond-haired, sad-faced Hood relished combat. Although not a strategist of note or an intellect, Kentuckian John Bell Hood consistently proved that men are inspired by dynamic leadership. He would be heard from again.[16]

As the Confederates broke through Porter's lines at twilight, the Federals pulled back and retreated across the Chickahominy River to the railroad junction of Savage Station, destroying the invaluable bridges along the way. Losses for both sides at Gaines' Mill staggered the war's statisticians: Federal casualties numbered 894 killed, 3,114 wounded, and 2,829 captured, while the Confederates reported 1,483 killed, 6,402 wounded, and 108 missing. More than 25 percent of the Rebel losses occurred in A. P. Hill's division. Said James Longstreet, "There was more individual gallantry displayed upon this field than any I have ever seen." The Federals also left behind 10,000 rifles and at least 22 cannons. Truly, Lee had won his first real victory in the war as well as the admiration of his men. "The great Lee seemed to be ubiquitous," wrote an admiring Confederate.[17] Only the tardiness of Stonewall Jackson kept the Confederates from scoring a decisive victory.

Surveying the battlefield, Confederates witnessed scenes of unspeakable dimension. Stonewall Jackson called it "the most terrific fire of musketry I ever heard." Later viewing the terrible carnage where Hood's Texans broke through the Federal lines, Jackson tersely remarked, "The men who carried this position were soldiers indeed." John Esten Cooke recalled "Dead Yankees as thick as leaves. Hundreds of red legged Zouaves lying on their backs—toes up. No pity for them." For some the immense strain and horrific consequences of the battle proved too much to bear and left nerves jangled as evidenced when a staff officer found John Bell Hood "sitting on a cracker-box, crying."[18]

That June night, as the moon shone brightly, John Pelham slowly walked over the field, eyeing the profusion of battlefield remnants. Something caught his attention. He bent down and slowly lifted an Episcopal Book of Common Prayer. Carefully, he placed the book in his pocket as a keepsake.[19]

For McClellan the Battle at Gaines' Mill, which he hoped would be "decisive of the war," marked the end of his offensive against Richmond. Little Mac decided to pull his enormous supply base from the York River to Harrison's Landing, twenty-six miles southeast from Richmond on the James River. To accomplish this, McClellan's army, replete with supply trains, had to cross the peninsula. Robert E. Lee, who now held the trump cards and the initiative, was certain to follow.

At dawn on June 28, Lee ordered Jeb Stuart and his cavalry to proceed to White House Landing where the York River Railroad crossed the Pamunkey River. The White House area served as an immense supply depot for McClellan; however, it was better known as the historic home of Robert E. Lee's son, Rooney. Here at this picturesque six-room plantation over a century before, George Washington had courted his bride to be, widow Martha Dandridge Custis. Now the area contained tons of McClellan's supplies, which he planned to move to Harrison's Landing. Stuart's assignment was to cut McClellan's communications and destroy the supplies. Meanwhile, Lee would continue to pressure McClellan's army with the Army of Northern Virginia. For the next two days portions of Lee's army harassed McClellan in mostly rearguard actions near Savage Station.

Stuart's cavalry, with Pelham and his gunners, made their way east some fifteen miles toward White House Landing. Along their advance, they cut telegraph wires and damaged the tracks of the York River Railroad running from White House Landing to Richmond. These two actions would hinder McClellan if he still planned to attack the Confederate capital. At a spot known as Tunstall's Station, less than five miles from the White House, Stuart's forces approached Black Creek bridge, recently destroyed by the Federals. Closer observation revealed a detachment of enemy cavalry and what appeared to be a battery of artillery on the opposite bank. Stuart quickly ordered Pelham to "disperse the enemy." Unlimbering two howitzers and placing them in a concealed position, Pelham's gunners sent a concentrated salvo across the creek. The Yankees hastily fled. Pelham's keen eye then noticed a bit of movement in some underbrush. A few rounds of canister flushed out more hidden Federals; the artillery, however, proved to be fake cannon set up as a ruse. For the next few hours, Blackford's men labored to repair the bridge.

That night Stuart's men camped along Black Creek, but the red glow of the sky east of them indicated McClellan's men had torched the White House area. "All night long the conflagration continued," observed Blackford, "and the country for miles around was as light as day, while vast clouds of smoke rose hundreds of feet in air, and explosions of shells and other ammunition were of frequent occurrence, sounding sometimes like a battle." The following morning Stuart's troopers found two rifled cannon, which the scurrying Federals from John C. Tidball's battery had left behind in their hasty retreat. Stuart presented the guns to Pelham and his battery for their marksmanship the day before.[20] Stuart's cavalry now proceeded to White House Landing as clouds of black smoke billowed to their front.

Supposedly five thousand Federals guarded the White House supplies. Therefore, as Stuart approached the enormous repository, he decided to fool the Yankees, who vastly outnumbered him. Parading his men within sight of the White House, Stuart hoped the Federals would see a greater force than actually existed. Stuart also summoned Pelham to fire artillery shells from long range while constantly changing positions to reinforce the deceit of having superior firepower. The ploy apparently succeeded as the enemy put up no resistance and escaped via ships on the Pamunkey River.

As Stuart neared within a quarter mile of the abandoned Federal supply base, he observed an enemy gunboat, the USS *Marblehead,* closing in on the shore. The powerful *Marblehead,* armed with 11-inch naval guns, carried three companies of the Seventeenth New York Infantry as well. Stuart once again summoned Pelham, who moved to a concealed position with a howitzer. Also ordered forward were seventy-five sharpshooters, at forty-yard intervals, carrying rifled carbines. As the Confederates deployed for a fight, a company of Union soldiers manned two boats and rowed toward the banks of the Pamunkey. After wading ashore, the Federals began shooting into the Rebels. Suddenly, in a simultaneous action, Jeb's sharpshooters and Pelham's cannon opened fire. The landing party of New Yorkers quickly headed back to their rowboats and furiously paddled away. Pelham, meanwhile, zeroed in on the *Marblehead* and directed spherical case shot fired directly over the decks. The Federal captain aboard the vessel possessed the greater firepower, but he remained confused due to Pelham's hidden position. To add to the Federal's bewilderment, Pelham rapidly changed the location of his lone gun. Although only one Yankee aboard the vessel was hit, the captain of the *Marblehead* directed his ship back down the river. While Stuart's cavalrymen moved into the White House area, Pelham, watching the exit of the *Marblehead,* decided to give chase. Limbering up the howitzer, Pelham and his crew of gunners headed along the shoreline, parallel to the enemy vessel. Only stopping to fire occasional blasts at the departing ship, Pelham hounded the *Marblehead* until a severe bend in the river hindered his movement. Pelham then returned to Stuart, who laughingly offered his congratulations. "Well done, Captain," said Stuart. "You certainly handled the Union Navy as roughly as you do the Army of the Potomac."[21]

An amused Stuart offered his rendition of the episode in his official report:

Armed with rifle carbines [my troopers] advanced boldly on the monster, so terrible to our fancy, and a body of sharpshooters were sent ashore from the boat to meet them. Quite a determined engagement of skirmishes ensued, but our gallant men never faltered in their determination to expose this Yankee bugaboo called gunboat. To save time, however, I ordered up the howitzer, a few shells from which, fired with great accuracy and bursting directly over her decks, caused an instantaneous withdrawal of sharpshooters and precipitate flight under full headway of steam down the river. The howitzer gave chase at a gallop, the more to cause the apprehension of being cut off below than of really effecting anything. The gunboat never returned.[22]

The smoldering ruins of the White House caught Stuart's attention first as his cavalry slowly rode toward the supply depot. Only the stone chimneys remained intact, and Jeb became livid at the ugly sight. His wrath manifested itself when he wrote of "the deceitfulness of the enemy's pretended reverence for everything associated with the name of Washington, for the dwelling-house was burned to the ground, and not a vestige left except what told of desolation and vandalism." Rooney Lee's thoughts, as he saw the ruins of his home, are unknown.[23]

Despite the fact that literally tons of supplies had been destroyed by the fleeing Federals, sumptuous amounts remained for Stuart's hungry cavalrymen. Delicacies of every description lay as far as the eye could see: tropical fruits, vegetables, meats, lobster, fish, oysters, barrels of sugar, tons of ice, eggs, French rolls, Havana cigars, candy, bottles of beer, and assorted liquors. John Esten Cooke marveled at the massive amounts of leftovers as well as their fine quality, referring to them as the "debris of sutlerdom. . . . The greatest luxury of all was iced lemonade. The day was terribly hot, and the men, like their horses, were panting with the combined heat of the weather and the great conflagration." Indeed, Stuart sat on the banks of the Pamunkey gulping a large container of iced lemonade, a satisfied look on his bearded face. Nearby John Pelham and James Breathed relaxed under a shade tree and enjoyed a feast of pickled oysters and fresh fruit. As Blackford sagely noted, "it was no wonder that McClellan's men had rather run away than get killed."[24]

Following the enjoyment of Federal food and the swapping of old equipment for new, the men commenced destroying what could not be salvaged. At the dock nine barges, filled with supplies of unknown value, were put to the torch. However, several locomotives, which obviously could not be taken, presented a problem. After a bit of discussion Stuart decided to turn the matter over to John Pelham. With a unit of gunners and Breathed to assist in the project, Pelham blasted shells into the middle of the boilers at a distance of fifty yards, easily scrapping the locomotives. With darkness coming and a full day of glorious activities ended, Stuart decided to spend the night at White House Landing. Tomorrow the refreshed cavalrymen would resume their destruction of the remaining supplies.

On Monday, June 30, Stuart's horsemen spent a leisurely morning finishing their handiwork. Then Stuart's cavalry left White House Landing and headed south some ten miles to cross the Chickahominy River at Forge Bridge. Nearing the river, Stuart sent the Jeff Davis Legion and the Fourth Virginia Cavalry, both under the command of Lieutenant Colonel Will T. Martin, to reconnoiter the bridge for possible Federals. John Pelham went along with two howitzers. Observing a concentrated force of Union infantry, cavalry, and two cannon posted across the river in the thickly wooded hills, Pelham once more was called upon to clear the path ahead. The young artillerist selected an advantageous position approximately four hundred yards from the bridge. Sighting each gun, Pelham gave the order to fire. Instantly, a wicked fire drove the Federals back into the hills. George W. Beale, looking on with interest, described his view of the action: "Suddenly, as we were watching from our sheltered position, Pelham dashed forward, with two guns, down the incline and across the plain, and taking position near the river, opened on the guns on the hilltop. He had already received their fire. The duel became rapid and exciting. It was quickly apparent that Pelham's guns were aimed with fatal effects. At each discharge of them a man, or a horse, was seen to fall or flee. In a few minutes after the firing began, the Federal guns were in full retreat. As they dashed along the road in the distance, we saw the branches of the cedars falling about them, cut down by Pelham's parting shots." Staff officer James Hardeman Stuart noted in his diary, "Capt. Pelham's battery . . . was in engagement with the Yankees posted on the other side; our practice was very good."[25]

Later, as the Confederate horsemen trotted across the bridge, Federal artillerists again opened fire. This signaled Pelham into action a second time. Placing his guns directly on the bridge, Pelham renewed the accurate and deadly hail of shells. Federal artillerists halted and sent a few rounds toward the bridge before pulling back to safety. The shells from the Union cannons fell dangerously close to Pelham and his men, who continued without injury. Stuart later reported of the skirmish: "Captain Pelham engaged the enemy across the Chickahominy [with two 12-pounder howitzers] and after a spirited duel against one rifle piece and one howitzer the enemy was driven from his position with the loss of 2 men and 2 horses killed, we escaping unhurt." The following day, while crossing over Forge Bridge, Beale eyed the results of Pelham's marksmanship: "[I] saw a dead horse, and under the cedars farther on two freshly made graves—silent witnesses of Pelham's death-dealing shots seen by us the day previous."[26]

Perhaps the most reliable account of the fighting at Forge Bridge was offered by Will T. Martin:

Monday, June 30, my command, with Pelham's artillery, now moved toward the Forge Bridge, encountering a few of the enemy's skirmishers. It was discovered, as the bridge was approached, that the enemy already held the position with infantry, cavalry, and artillery. Captain Pelham was advanced with two of his pieces to a point within 400 yards of the bridge, and opened with his pieces (howitzers). He was replied to by two rifled pieces, but soon silenced them, and they withdrew to the hills beyond the river.

A reconnoitering force was crossed over the river to examine the position assumed by the enemy, and was charged upon by cavalry in the afternoon. In order to clear the road of this cavalry Captain Pelham was ordered with two

12-pounder howitzers to take position on the bridge and shell the road. Just as he unlimbered the enemy opened upon him with two rifled pieces, one at only 400 yards distance. As the gun had to be trained upon the road occupied by the pieces of Captain Pelham its fire was very accurate and rapid, yet in fifteen minutes the enemy was driven away with a loss of 2 men and 2 horses killed and several wounded.

Martin subsequently added to his lengthy report: "Among the officers . . . I would mention favorably . . . Captain Pelham."[27]

Seemingly in no hurry to reach the Army of Northern Virginia, Stuart ordered his cavalrymen to spend the night at Forge Bridge. That same day Robert E. Lee's soldiers fought McClellan's Army of the Potomac in a bloody battle known as Frayser's farm, near the small town of Glendale. Lee planned a coordinated attack with six divisions of 71,000 men with the intention of cutting McClellan's army in half. However, unforeseen circumstances spoiled his chances of complete victory. During the night, McClellan's army retreated less than five miles south to the strong position of Malvern Hill. The day cost Lee 3,673 in killed, wounded, and missing. The losses of the Army of the Potomac numbered 3,797 with roughly half of those missing in action.

At 3:30 on the morning of Tuesday, July 1, Jeb Stuart was awakened by a courier from Robert E. Lee with orders to rejoin Stonewall Jackson. Stuart's horsemen readied themselves and began their lengthy ride. The day dawned exceptionally warm, and by afternoon the temperature soared. Blistering summer heat took a toll on the riders and their mounts. Ordering frequent rests, Stuart allowed his sweat-drenched cavalrymen and their tired horses to move slowly ahead. Periodically, Captain Pelham needed time to unhitch the weary horses and harness fresher ones to the task of pulling the heavy guns.[28]

What had transpired in the absence of Stuart was the sanguinary Battle of Malvern Hill. McClellan's forces positioned themselves on the formidable plateau, 150 feet above the surrounding swamps and ravines. From atop this slope, the Federals dominated every view of the valley below. Here McClellan's chief of artillery, Colonel Henry Jackson Hunt, strategically placed 100 cannons to the front with another 150 protecting the flanks. Lee, sensing no other option, determined to assault the Union lines after weakening their position with his own artillery barrage. At 1:00 P.M. Lee's batteries of artillery opened up; Federal guns answered quickly. For the next two hours, an artillery duel ensued with the Federal gunners having the better of it. By 4:00 in the afternoon, Lee's battle lines had formed, but fragmented attacks against a near impregnable position ended in a Confederate disaster. Horribly raking the Confederate lines with canister, Hunt's gunners increased the carnage until long after darkness that evening. As predicted, Rebel batteries "were no match" for Federal iron, and the Confederates severely struggled with "disjointed and badly managed charges." Statistically, the Battle of Malvern Hill tallied into a nightmare. Confederate losses totaled 5,650 with 869 killed, 4,241 wounded, and 540 missing. The Army of the Potomac suffered 3,007 casualties including 314 killed, 1,875 wounded, and 818 missing. "It was not war," D. H. Hill submitted tersely, "it was murder."[29] That same evening McClellan began pulling the Army of the Potomac seven miles southeastward to Harrison's Landing on the James River.

On the night of Wednesday, July 2, Jeb Stuart summoned John Pelham for a special and dangerous assignment. Taking one howitzer and a squadron of First Virginia cavalrymen under Captain Charles R. Irving, Pelham would proceed in the darkness to the area of Westover near Harrison's Landing. His mission was twofold: to locate the position of McClellan's army and to shell the enemy if it attempted to escape down the James River during the night. Ordering James Breathed to remain with the rest of the horse artillery, Pelham selected a handful of gunners to accompany him. Lieutenant William McGregor served as second in command; the others came mostly from the Napoleon Detachment. Off into the sultry darkness they rode as a heavy rain began pelting them.

Hours later, in the early morning of July 3, a courier swiftly rode to Stuart's camp with an astonishing note from Pelham. "Genl: Our pickets are now below Mr. Allen Bradley's farm—," wrote an excited Pelham. "I fired on the enemy's pickets and drove them in. Capt. Irving sent a scouting party out. They report the coast in front of us clear. I questioned Mr. Bradley about the position of the enemy." At this point Pelham inserted a crude, hand-drawn map at the bottom of the page showing Evelynton Hill overlooking where Herring Creek runs into the James River. "He says in Westover and Berkeley they have all their wagons and cattle—It is a beautiful plain, commanded by Eventon Hills [Evelynton Heights]—one mile and 36 yards—he says that guns placed on the hill commands [*sic*] everything as far as the [James] river—The hill is two miles from our present position. He reports the roads leading to this Depot blocked up with wagons & stragglers—He also says they have a considerable force there—All they have. Mr. Turner knows this Bradley and says he is a reliable man."[30] Incredible, indeed! Pelham had found McClellan's entire army, tightly bunched along a three-mile front. Even more astounding, McClellan was trapped on low ground with the James River to his back and unguarded Evelynton Heights looking down on his demoralized army. Stuart quickly notified Jackson of this fortuitous situation; Jackson, in turn, hurried off a note to Lee. Stuart, with his cavalry riding behind him, immediately set out to join Pelham.[31]

When Stuart arrived, Pelham directed him to Evelynton Heights. There, a handful of Federal cavalrymen were captured and, under intense questioning, informed

Stuart that McClellan's entire army lay encamped at the foot of the Heights. Down below the men of the Army of the Potomac had spent a horribly uncomfortable night. Incessant rains had soaked them through. Furthermore, in attempting to pitch their shelters in the mire, tent poles slipped in the morass and could not be driven. Many of the men slept in the mud, demoralizing them even more. Most amazing of all, McClellan had posted no guards. Here was a golden opportunity, one that had not existed so blatantly in the previous Seven Days Battles, to annihilate McClellan's Army of the Potomac. Stuart excitedly set up a skirmish line of sharpshooters on the plateau and ordered Pelham to be ready with his howitzer.

By 8:00 that morning, Stuart and Pelham watched as the Federals, blithely unaware of their predicament, prepared breakfast. Stuart faced a difficult decision. He had been told that the infantry divisions of James Longstreet and Stonewall Jackson were headed to the Evelynton Heights area to attack McClellan's army, but the question remained: when would they arrive? If Stuart continued to wait, McClellan would certainly become aware of the unguarded Heights and proceed to brush Stuart's small force aside and fortify the strategically critical position. Time passed, and Stuart made his decision; he ordered Pelham "to let them have it!" and commence firing on the Federal encampment with his single howitzer.

Pelham hurried into action and placed the howitzer along Herring Creek beyond the spires of Westover church. Just before 9:00 A.M. his first shells fired toward the Federal boats anchored on the James River. Pelham then shortened his range to carry in the direction of the Union troops. "Judging from the great commotion and excitement below," Stuart jubilantly reported, "it must have had considerable effect." Other than causing a startled confusion in the Federal camp, Pelham's shelling did no major damage. The artillery shells, fired from a single cannon, however, alerted McClellan to the importance of the Heights.[32]

Union gunboats, along with a battery of artillery, commenced firing shells in Pelham's direction, forcing him to change locations. Moving a half mile back, Pelham continued his one-gun barrage. Pelham then moved his cannon more often to avoid being a stationary target and to give the effect of having more firepower. "I had no apprehension, however," reported Stuart, "as I felt sure Longstreet was near by."[33] The entire affair appeared ludicrous, a 12-pounder howitzer versus the Army of the Potomac. Soon McClellan sent Federal skirmishers to drive the pesky Confederates from their advantageous position. In retaliation Stuart ordered his sharpshooters forward, and the Federals dispersed.

With the Federal gunboats blasting their 11-inch naval shells, Stuart summoned a battery to fire Congreve rockets into the Union camp. Spreading "liquid damnation," as the soldiers called it, these rocket explosions set Federal tents ablaze and scalded some horses and mules. "Great consternation was occasioned among the camps of the enemy," wrote Blackford, "as these unearthly serpents went zigzagging about among them." Occasionally, however, the unstable and often unpredictable rockets hit and ricocheted, flying in any direction. When a few of them buzzed back toward the Confederates, Stuart called off the Congreves.[34]

For five miraculous hours, until 2:00 P.M., Pelham withstood all attempts of the Federals to dislodge his howitzer. Finally, a battery of Union gunners crossed the troublesome Herring Creek and made its way dangerously close to Pelham's position. Still, the young captain somehow continued to hold his own. At this time, Stuart, who had been anxiously awaiting the arrival of infantry support, received word that Longstreet had taken an incorrect road and was still six miles back at Nance's Shop. Stuart ordered a retreat, none too soon, as Pelham reported only two projectiles left in his arsenal. "Although Pelham reported but two rounds of ammunition left," reported Stuart later, "I held out, knowing how important it was to hold the ground till Longstreet arrived. . . . Pelham fired his last round, and the sharpshooters, strongly posted in the skirt of the woods bordering the plateau, exhausted every cartridge, but had at last to retire; not, however, without teaching many a foeman the bitter lesson of death." Quickly, the Confederates pulled back to safety. The amazing episode ended with McClellan's men atop Evelynton Heights.[35]

Longstreet arrived later that night; Lee and Jackson followed the next morning on July 4. With McClellan's men safely entrenched on the Heights, Lee called off any further attack. Many severely criticized Stuart for his headstrong and theatrical decision to shell McClellan's army. It assuredly revealed a position of undeniable worth to both armies and, more important, alerted McClellan to the potential danger his army faced from Evelynton Heights. A cavalry brigade with a single cannon could not, under any circumstances, defeat or even deter as powerful a force as the Army of the Potomac. Theoretically, however, had the Army of Northern Virginia been present, McClellan would have been doomed. Stuart, believing Longstreet's division to be well on its way, should have waited to unleash the cannon blasts. His excuse, possibly a feeble one, was that McClellan would soon know of his disadvantage anyway, so why not open fire with the hope that Longstreet's arrival would occur at any moment? In retrospect, Stuart should have waited for the approach of the infantry to reveal his position of strength, but his impulses and bravado betrayed his patience.[36]

Satisfied that McClellan no longer proved a threat to the Confederate capital, Robert E. Lee moved the Army of Northern Virginia closer to Richmond. Meanwhile, McClellan's Army of the Potomac continued to sit along the James River safely out of range of the Confederate capital city. President Lincoln offered to send 50,000 reinforcements, but McClellan snidely remarked that he needed more. By the early days of August, McClellan pulled his army back toward Washington, D.C. Thus, the Peninsular Campaign ended.

The Seven Days Battles, starting on June 25 at Oak Grove and ending at Malvern Hill on July 1, had cost both sides dearly in manpower. Federal casualties numbered 15,855 with 1,734 killed, 8,066 wounded, and 6,055 missing. In the Army of Northern Virginia Robert E. Lee lost 22 percent of his starting forces, or 20,204. These included 3,494 killed, 15,758 wounded, and 952 missing.[37] Federal losses also comprised 52 cannon, 35,000 rifles, and enormous quantities of supplies captured or destroyed. Lee's immediate plan to save Richmond had been accomplished by beating McClellan to the punch and shoving his huge army safely away from the capital. However, his design to destroy the Army of the Potomac failed.

An appraisal of the two sides reveals much in contrast. George McClellan, a master of preparing an army, displayed little ability when it came to taking advantage of a smaller enemy. His belief that the Confederates outnumbered him continued to be his Achilles' heel. In Robert E. Lee, the Confederacy possessed a magnificent leader whose battlefield technique possibly bordered on genius. His daring, guile, and capacity for taking the initiative set him apart from McClellan and other future Federal generals. Perhaps Lee needed to temper his audacity for attack; he certainly needed to coordinate his commanders more skillfully.

Other Confederate generals deserve a look. James Longstreet, A. P. Hill, and John Hood strongly evidenced dynamic leadership and rare fighting ability. The most enigmatic general during the entire Peninsular Campaign, however, was Stonewall Jackson. Displaying an uncanny brilliance while in the Shenandoah Valley, Stonewall reacted rather unJackson-like throughout the Seven Days Battles. His sluggishness during that week stayed a topic of conversation for days. Some attributed Jackson's success in the valley to those he faced with lesser talent. A combination of factors caused Jackson not to be himself. Lacking proper maps and information on the terrain of the peninsula hurt Jackson tremendously. Moreover, his physical stamina had simply been depleted from the grueling days in the valley. Halfway through the Seven Days, Robert L. Dabney, Jackson's chief of staff, mentioned Stonewall falling asleep "with his supper between his teeth."[38] With proper rest Jackson would emerge as his old self.

One of the younger officers receiving commendation was Pelham. "Captain John Pelham, of the Horse-Artillery," reported Jeb Stuart, "displayed such signal ability as an artillerist, such heroic example and devotion in danger, and indomitable energy under difficulties in the movement of his battery, that, reluctant as I am at the chance of losing such a valuable limb from the brigade, I feel bound to ask for his promotion, with the remark that in either cavalry or artillery no field grade is too high for his merit and capacity. The officers and men of that battery emulated the example of their captain, and did justice to the reputation already won."[39] Pelham was proving the axiom of Napoleon: "Artillery and cavalry must be the complements, the one to the other." Pelham's pride further emanated for his

West Point roommate, Tom Rosser, now a permanent fixture in Stuart's cavalry.[40] Rosser reportedly fired a few random shots at McClellan's observation balloons during the Peninsular Campaign, and rumors persisted that he actually shot one of them down. In his report of the campaign Stuart praised Rosser, saying he "inspired his men with such determined resistance—arranging them so as to resist to best advantage—that the enemy failed."[41]

For the Army of Northern Virginia, a well-deserved rest was in store before the next campaign. Robert E. Lee decided to revamp the army in the interval, which meant changes for the cavalry and John Pelham. Across the Potomac River, President Lincoln also contemplated change.

"I Have Had My Revenge Out of Pope"

[Pelham] was as brave as Julius Caesar.

—W. W. Blackford

Following the Seven Days Battles, Robert E. Lee divided the Army of Northern Virginia into two infantry "Commands"—one under James Longstreet, the other led by Stonewall Jackson. Changes also occurred in Stuart's cavalry, which now became an expanded division of two brigades. Leading Stuart's brigades were Brigadier Generals Fitzhugh Lee and Wade Hampton, who presented an antithesis in personality and style. The Virginian Fitz Lee, merely twenty-six years of age, had graduated from West Point near the bottom of the class in 1856. His flamboyance and playful demeanor endeared him to Jeb Stuart. Hampton, a forty-four-year-old South Carolinian, had no prior military training. Better known for his vast plantation holdings, the oft-wounded Hampton proved a leader of remarkable skill. His age and solemn bearing, however, placed him second on Stuart's favored list to Fitz Lee.

That summer Stuart added two new faces to his growing list of staff officers: Norman Richard FitzHugh and Richard Channing Price. FitzHugh, an adjutant and later quartermaster, was widely respected for his diligent work ethic and outgoing personality. He often entertained the other staff officers around the campfire with descriptive tales of his life with the Indians out West. Stuart, who forged a close friendship with FitzHugh, became the godfather to FitzHugh's son on July 27, 1862. Nineteen-year-old Channing Price joined Stuart's staff on August 8. Serving as aide-de-camp and later as assistant adjutant general, Price astounded nearly everyone with his phenomenal ability to memorize rapid dictation and later write out several separate orders verbatim. Historian Douglas Southall Freeman claimed that Price "as A.A.G. in the field . . . had no superior in the Army."[1]

Promotions also came to many that summer, the most notable to Jeb Stuart himself. Rising to the rank of major general at the age of twenty-nine, Stuart proudly announced the advancement, which became official on July 25, to his jubilant division. No advancement in rank, however, arrived for Captain John Pelham. Promotion for artillerists came slowly in the Army of Northern Virginia. But by mid-August, young Pelham would see his promotion and added responsibility to the horse artillery.

Stuart established his campsite on July 12 at the home of a Mr. Timberlake, near Atlee's Station, along the line of the Virginia Central Railroad. This beautiful residence, located ten miles north of Richmond, was situated in a picturesque forest of giant oaks and hickory trees, surrounded by lush green fields. Timberlake, whose two sons rode in Stuart's cavalry, amiably hosted the general and his staff. Two days later, Jeb's wife arrived with their two children, four-year-old Flora, named after her mother, and two-year-old Jimmie, who "were the pets of the whole camp."[2]

On July 17 Stuart held a review of his cavalry for the locals, mostly females, who sat in carriages out of the sun watching with excitement. Thousands of well-trained horsemen, including Pelham and his horse artillery, paraded for the ladies, who applauded their every move. When the ceremonies ended, Stuart, accompanied by Pelham, proudly walked from carriage to carriage introducing young Pelham as "my eligible artillerist." Quickly, the blushing Pelham smiled and acknowledged the compliments of the ladies. The general "loved [Pelham] dearly," wrote Blackford, "so innocent looking, so 'child-like and bland' in the expression of his sparking blue eyes, but as grand a flirt as ever lived. . . . He was tall, slender, beautifully proportioned and very graceful, a superb rider, and as brave as Julius Caesar." Stuart cordially invited all the ladies, who enthusiastically agreed, to visit his campsite.[3]

Pelham's early summer included a mixture of relaxation and business. While continuing to train the horse artillery and keep them in top fighting condition, he ordered and received forage for 180 horses from the Confederate Quartermaster's Department. This amounted to twelve pounds per horse or 2,160 pounds total. On July 19 he received a varied amount of cooking utensils for his men. With his ranks up to capacity at 150, Pelham's cannon count numbered six: two 12-pounder Napoleons, three 12-pounder howitzers, and a single Blakely. He also received some needed caissons, projectiles, and other assorted goods that had been captured from McClellan's army during the Peninsular Campaign. During this period, Pelham made use of his spare time courting some ladies from the surrounding area. He also attended dances and parties, as well as visited homes and churches. He even appeared to overcome his social shyness somewhat by occasionally joining in the singing of choruses led by Stuart's minstrels.[4]

On Monday, July 21, Stuart moved his camp to Hanover Court House and established his headquarters, that evening, in a small red brick building. Located atop a hill, the campsite afforded the staff officers a magnificent panorama of the beautiful rolling Virginia fields stretching for miles before them. Less than two to three miles away resided Dr. Lucien Bonaparte Price and his family at their exquisite plantation home, Dundee.[5] Since Stuart was related to the Price family, he, Pelham, and other staff officers spent much time here relaxing in the shadows of the giant oak trees. Price's two beautiful teenage daughters, Elizabeth and Nannie, gladly hosted the officers.[6] Nannie enjoyed teasing John Pelham about his bashfulness, and the two became close friends. Pelham later gave her a photograph of himself in civilian clothes. Von Borcke seriously courted Elizabeth, and the two were eventually engaged to marry. The marriage plans ended, however, when the jealous Von one day observed Elizabeth on the front porch of Dundee talking to another officer sitting beside her. The giant-sized von Borcke insisted on plopping his body between them, and evidently an argument ensued. This ended their relationship.[7]

Romance was in the air for other members of Stuart's cavalry. On a brutally hot summer's day, Tom Rosser rode into Hanover Court House and called out to a young boy, Will Winston, "Little Fellow, if you'll bring me a drink of water, I'll come back and marry your sister." The lad of eight or nine years of age hurried to fetch the water for the handsome officer. Sometime later, Rosser happened to be in the area again, and young Will Winston remembered the face of Rosser although the officer did not recall the boy. Quickly, Will brought his nineteen-year-old sister, Betty, to meet Rosser with the words, "Sis Betty, here's that man come to marry you." A love affair developed and the couple planned on marrying May 28, 1863. John Pelham was to be the best man.[8]

As always during the days of encampment, Stuart enjoyed the camaraderie of teasing his favorite officers and staff personnel. One such incident, vividly described by Val C. Giles, a soldier in John Hood's infantry, occurred at Hanover Court House.

> I was detailed to guard some army supplies in the warehouse there. General Fitzhugh Lee was sauntering up and down in the platform near my post waiting for the Richmond train. General Stuart, Major [*sic*] Pelham, and half a dozen cavalry officers rode up to the depot and dismounted from their horses. They stopped near me and I heard their conversation. General Stuart said, addressing young Pelham, "My boy, when I grab him, you swing on too, for he is as strong as a young bull."
>
> They all went up to General Fitz and engaged in conversation. A few minutes later I heard the whistle blow and the passenger train pulled in from Fredericksburg. The officers surrounded General Fitz, wished him a good time in Richmond, and bade him good-by. A few mail bags were thrown from the train, the bell rang, and the cars began to move. General Lee waved his hands to his friends and started to board the slowly moving train, when Stuart and Pelham grabbed him. Several other officers closed in on him.
>
> He tried hard to release himself, but it was no use, they had him foul. The old train went flying down the road toward Richmond, and the soldiers raised a big laugh at the expense of General Fitz. He didn't appear to be amused as much as the others, but they soon got him in a good humor when the kidnaping business was explained. General Jeb said to Fitz after they had

released him, "See here, young man, I'm going to break up this jularky business. You have been gallivanting around about long enough. 'Possum and 'taters for dinner at Headquarters today. Bring the prisoner along, boys."

The affair was a premeditated plan, and they had brought a saddle horse along for General Fitz to ride to camp. Mounting their horses they all went galloping off, General Stuart singing "Sweet Evelina, dear Evelina, my love for you shall never, never die." They were splendid soldiers, all in the heyday of life.[9]

Periodically during these hot midsummer days, John Pelham and his gunners were called upon to halt lurking Federal forces along the Rappahannock River. It was a natural sight to see Pelham leading his men, armed with a cannon or two, out of camp, sometimes in the wee hours of the morning. Others in the Army of Northern Virginia became accustomed to the sight. Young artillerist Charles Browne Fleet of the Fredericksburg Artillery remembered such an occasion. "We had heard Pelham's guns and as he dashed by us with two guns," recalled Fleet. "I greeted him with 'Going for them, are you Captain?' 'Yes,' he replied with a bright smile, 'been after 'em all the morning and am going down the river to pepper 'em again' and dashed by us. He looked like a bright beardless boy, his face all lighted up with the gaudium certaininis [the joy of contest]."[10]

Seldom did a day pass without numerous guests arriving to visit Stuart's camp. The merriment surrounding the camp was nearly legendary, but the reviews and singing around the campfires came to an abrupt halt as a new Federal threat appeared on the horizon. While George McClellan's Army of the Potomac continued to stagnate at Harrison's Landing, President Abraham Lincoln proceeded to create a new army. Named the Army of Virginia, this force consolidated the scattered commands of Nathaniel Banks, Irvin McDowell, and John Fremont. Selected to lead this newly created army of forty-five thousand men was the controversial Major General John Pope. Fresh from his two victories on the upper Mississippi River (New Madrid and Island No. 10), Pope yearned to transfer eastward to be an integral part of the fighting in Virginia. Lincoln, tired of McClellan's feeble excuses and enamored by Pope's heroic feats in the West, granted Pope his request.

Pope almost immediately alienated his army by issuing a lengthy proclamation full of insults and bellicose rhetoric. In part, it read: "Let us understand each other. I have come to you from the West, where we have always seen the backs of our enemies; from an army whose business it has been to seek the adversary, and to beat him when he was found; whose policy has been attack and not defense." He further brashly announced to the press that "His headquarters would be in the saddle." Not only the common fighting man shunned Pope's antagonistic words, but other generals found him reprehensible as well. "I don't care for John Pope one pinch of owl dung!" roared Samuel Sturgis. McClellan smugly predicted of Pope, "the paltry young man who wanted to teach me the art of war will in less than a week either be in full retreat or badly whipped."[11]

Even Confederates found Pope's arrogance a bit too much. Wrote Stuart's tireless scout John Mosby, "Pope opened his campaign in northern Virginia with a bombastic manifesto that, by an invidious comparison, gave offence to his own side and amusement to ours." An artillerist simply referred to Pope as "the prince of braggarts." W. W. Blackford most likely spoke for the entire Army of Northern Virginia when he wrote, "we looked forward with keen delight to see this inflated gas bag punctured by the keen rapier of our great commander."[12]

Despite the criticism, Pope moved his army across the Rappahannock River deep into Virginia, along the Orange and Alexandria Railroad line in the direction of the town of Culpeper. Only twenty-five miles south of Culpeper nestled the town of Gordonsville on the Virginia Central Railway. If Pope captured this railroad line, he would dangerously cut off Richmond from the vital Shenandoah Valley. As he made his way into Virginia's midsection, Pope ordered his army to "subsist upon the country." In doing so, Pope plundered farms, arrested innocent and defenseless civilians, and destroyed private property. Richmond newspapers identified him as "an enemy of humanity." Even Robert E. Lee, who normally referred to the enemy as merely "those people," turned his wrath on Pope, labeling him a "miscreant" and ordering him "to be suppressed."[13]

At the end of July Lee summoned Jeb Stuart to discuss Pope's movement. Lee wanted to know Pope's intentions and whether there was any truth to the report that Federal detachments were moving to the east near Fredericksburg. On August 4, Stuart set out with four cavalry regiments and Pelham's horse artillery. That day they pushed ahead about twenty miles to Bowling Green and camped for the night. The following day, possibly the summer's hottest, Stuart's forces neared the town of Port Royal, located on the Rappahannock River, about 11:00 A.M. After a hearty meal, the entire force pushed ahead, reaching Round Oak Church, twelve miles from Fredericksburg, near sunset. Here they spread their blankets and camped for the night with still no signs of a strong enemy force.

Before dawn on August 6 some of Stuart's scouts reported a large column of Federals leaving Fredericksburg laden with a string of supply wagons. This Union force of more than eight thousand, located on Telegraph Road, intended to strike the vital Confederate supply depot at Hanover Junction at the intersection of the Virginia Central and Richmond & Fredericksburg railroad lines. Although outnumbered nearly five to one, Stuart determined to stop them. Heading a few miles west, Stuart's cavalrymen hastened toward the Massaponax Church area to intercept the Yankees. When Stuart reached his destination, he observed that the main body of Federal troops had separated from the supply wagons. Approaching unseen, Stuart divided his forces. Two regiments of cavalry, joined by John Pelham and two cannon, were sent to pursue the main body. Another regiment was ordered to capture the wagon train, while a third regiment, along with the remainder of Pelham's guns, stayed in reserve.

The Federal supply wagons, seemingly Stuart's main objective, came under fire first. With the teamsters caught unaware, a confused jumble of wagons and horses filled the road. The Confederate troopers made short work of capturing the supply train and routing any opposition from the escort troops. Eighty-five prisoners fell into Confederate hands as well as eleven wagons, filled with provisions, and one hundred Enfield muskets. Two of Stuart's cavalrymen fell with mortal wounds.[14]

Meanwhile, Pelham moved ahead, strategically placing a lone cannon on each side of Telegraph Road at the rear of the Federal column. Then, with complete surprise a bugle sounded the attack. Pelham's gunners opened up with canister from both sides of the road as Fitz Lee's yelling troopers charged in, according to Stuart, "like a thunderbolt." These Federals, also caught off guard, fled in wild disorder. Stuart decided to break off the fight when the main Federal force pulled around to do battle. Stuart positioned his cavalrymen, armed with carbines, to halt any Federal advance. As the Federals moved forward, the Confederates opened fire with their carbines before falling back. To protect the rear of Stuart's retreating men, Pelham placed his cannons on a slight elevation and opened fire. Although the Blakely's troublesome elevating screw malfunctioned again, the howitzer continued to blast almost nonstop. Enough time was given for the remainder of Stuart's men to escape. Federal soldiers fired exploding rifle bullets "which made a crack like a pistol when they struck a tree," according to Blackford, "and must have been very uncomfortable things to be hit with." When the Confederates were safely out of range, Stuart trotted back toward the enemy and, removing his plumed hat, gracefully bowed before returning to his men.[15]

It had been an eventful day for Stuart's cavalry. One private in the Ninth Virginia referred to the day's activities as "a grand little fight." Stuart perhaps overstated the results of the day as he later reported "that this wholesome check to the enemy prevented any further raids upon the railroad, and kept him in a state of trepidation for fear of attack in the rear for the remainder of the summer."[16]

Stuart led his forces back to Bowling Green, where they camped for the night. The next day, August 7, the troopers rode back to Hanover Court House. Here Stuart presented the booty captured: prisoners, eleven wagons and teams, and fifteen cavalry horses. A note arrived from Robert E. Lee congratulating the cavalry general for his excellent service on the raid. For the next ten days the cavalry received a well-deserved rest.

The results of Stuart's raid had been most successful. Not only had he captured prisoners, horses, and wagons, he had blunted a major attempt by the Federals to destroy a Confederate depot of supplies and saved the crucial Virginia Central Railway. Furthermore, he had demoralized the Federals while losing only two men. Pope was outraged by the lack of success. No more Federal raids were conducted on the Virginia Central Railroad line. John Pope now brought his Army of Virginia southward with his advance guard reaching as far as the town of Culpeper in early August.

While the two armies readied to square off against one another, John Pelham received some magnificent news: his promotion to the rank of major had come through in mid-August. A Federal prisoner, who witnessed the announcement of the promotion, detailed the following account:

> I was captured and taken to the field headquarters of General Stuart. . . . While talking to me, an orderly rode up with a dispatch, which was evidently welcome, as a pleased smile illumined the general's features. "Call Pelham," he ordered. A youth entered. Pelham, Pelham, thought I; I've heard of Stuart's artilleryman, but what boy is this? "Pelham, my boy," said Stuart, "accept my sincere congratulations. General Lee wishes me to say that, in his opinion, the masterly handling of your guns today contributed in no small measure to our success; also that you are to receive a major's commission." Well! I was astounded. There stood the young boy, embarrassed, blushing. I give you my word, gentlemen, I thought the whole thing a cruel joke, with our young friend the butt. But the news quickly got out, and the way those soldiers of all arms crowded around and cheered the young officer soon convinced me that the incident was genuine. The occurrence impressed me profoundly. In spite of the enthusiasm of the Confederates, I could hardly believe it was justified, and I kept asking myself, "Can this boy fight?" My question was soon answered—answered by the boy himself. He delivered it at the cannon's mouth, and it was convincing.[17]

Although the commission would not be official until six weeks later, a celebration was held that night at Stuart's headquarters. With Sam Sweeney magically picking the banjo, accompanied by James Dearing on the guitar and Jim Hawkins rattling the bones, the camp filled the air with music, song, and mirth. Stuart sang in his beautiful baritone voice. Near the general sat twenty-three-year-old John Pelham. Those around the young artillerist noticed a definite change in his normal blushing and shy demeanor. That evening Pelham sang along as loudly as the others.

With the promotion came more responsibility for Pelham as a new battery under Captain Roger Preston Chew was added to the Stuart Horse Artillery. Nineteen-year-old Chew had attended Virginia Military Institute and was a student of Professor Stonewall Jackson. In the early stages of the Civil War he had the distinction of forming the first horse artillery unit in the Confederacy under cavalry general Turner Ashby. With exceptional prowess this young artillerist won fame and laurels as a man of supreme talent and courage. "There was not an officer in the army of his rank," wrote Tom Rosser after the war, "who stood higher in the estimation of our higher officers, in point of courage, military ability and enterprise than he. . . . I regard him as one of the very best artillery officers I ever knew, and indeed, one of the very best officers of his rank in the Confederate army." His battery served with Pelham until mid-September 1862 when he returned to the Shenandoah Valley.[18] Eventually, on September 2, an additional battery transferred to Pelham's command—Captain James Franklin Hart's Battery from South Carolina. Pelham would handle his new responsibilities with his usual excellence.

Mid-August also brought ominous news. George McClellan, still commanding the Army of the Potomac at Harrison's Landing, began his long-awaited move to join with Pope's Army of Virginia. Together, by sheer weight of numbers, these two armies might easily crush Robert E. Lee's forces. Luckily for Lee, McClellan, who first received his marching orders from Washington, D.C., on August 4, procrastinated for ten days before moving. His delay allowed Lee to make one of his boldest decisions of the war: he would divide his smaller forces and attack the "miscreant," John Pope, before McClellan arrived.

To create his daring plan of action, Lee summoned Jackson, Longstreet, and Stuart to his headquarters at Orange Court House, seven miles north of Gordonsville. That morning Lee detailed his plans for an attack on Pope. Pope's army lay in a sideways "V," with the vertex to the east, between two rivers: the Rappahannock at his rear, the Rapidan to his front. Pope's supply line was the Orange and Alexandria Railroad running directly through his camp at the open end of the "V." By positioning his Army of Virginia in this precarious situation, Pope was exposed to disaster. Thus, Lee designed his battle plan based on Pope's vulnerability. Lee assigned Stuart's cavalry the task of crossing the Rapidan River below Pope's left flank and proceeding to the enemy's rear where he would capture the bridge at Rappahannock Station as well as seizing the railroad supply line. This would seal off Pope's main path of retreat while Longstreet hit Pope's left from the rear and Jackson attacked the left from the front in pincer fashion.[19] The plan, if executed correctly, would cut Pope off from McClellan's reinforcements and Washington, D.C., rendering him defenseless.

Later that day, August 17, Stuart and his staff enjoyed dinner at Jackson's headquarters. Near dusk, Stuart, Mosby, and von Borcke ascended Clark's Mountain to the Confederate signal station. The precipice offered an unimpeded view for miles. In the distance, they witnessed the Federal army. Years later Mosby penned, "A worse position for an army could not have been selected for Pope by an enemy. . . . General Lee never again had such an opportunity to destroy an army."[20] None of them knew, of course, that within hours a singular and seemingly meaningless incident would force Lee to alter his plans severely.

Stuart sent verbal orders ahead to Fitz Lee to bring the cavalry from Beaver Dam to Raccoon Ford on the Rapidan River, a distance of thirty-two miles, where

Jeb would commence his march on Pope's left. Figuring Fitz Lee could cover that stretch in one day, Stuart decided to ride on toward Verdiersville, a mere handful of houses located on the Orange Plank Road and only ten miles from Raccoon Ford. Here Fitz Lee would pass directly on his way to rendezvous with Stuart. Riding with Stuart were a half dozen trusted men, including von Borcke, adjutant Norman FitzHugh, John Mosby, and eighteen-year-old aide-de-camp Chiswell Dabney. Shortly after midnight on August 18, the riders approached the tiny crossroads hamlet of Verdiersville. With no sign of Fitz Lee, Stuart sent Norman Fitz-Hugh on ahead to try and locate the errant cavalryman. Meanwhile, Stuart and the others bedded down on the porch and in the yard of the Rhodes house. With no indication of Federals in the area, guards seemed unnecessary. The saddled horses stood nearby as the Confederates unbuckled their belts and removed their weapons. Quickly, the men fell asleep in the warm and inky August night.

At just past 4:00 A.M. horses' hooves in the distance awakened them. Certainly, it was the overdue Fitz Lee being led to them by FitzHugh. Stuart sent Mosby and another to guide the approaching horsemen. Suddenly pistol shots rang out. Instead of Fitz Lee and his cavalry, these were members of the First Michigan, under the command of Colonel Thornton F. Brodhead, along with others of the Fifth New York.

Stuart instinctively leaped on his thoroughbred, Skylark, and vaulted a fence, leaving his plumed hat, haversack, sash, and cape with the red silk lining behind. All of the others narrowly escaped as well. Once assured of his safety, Stuart slipped back to the scene at Verdiersville and observed the joyous Federals from a distance. The lucky ones carried off his personal possessions. The plumed hat was taken by Adjutant Second Lieutenant Fordyce Rogers of the First Michigan Cavalry.[21]

Later that morning Stuart gathered the other fugitives together. Riding along, they marveled at their narrow escape. Undoubtedly, Stuart wondered at the whereabouts of Fitz Lee and Norman FitzHugh. Within a matter of hours, Stuart found the answers to these two riddles. Fitz Lee, apparently confused by Stuart's verbal orders, simply did not comprehend the urgency of his punctuality and arrived late. FitzHugh, in searching for the cavalry in the darkness, was captured by the same Federals who surprised Stuart at Verdiersville. Bad enough to lose one's plumed hat and accoutrements, but Stuart's personal adjutant had been gobbled up as well. Stuart's worst loss that August morning, however, was the contents of FitzHugh's haversack, now in the hands of the Federals. It contained the signed orders from Robert E. Lee to Stuart disclosing Lee's planned attack on Pope's left flank for the next day. With this critical document in John Pope's hands, no attack would be made, as Pope would either change the position of his army or sit and wait for Lee's surprise.

Stuart must be held responsible in three instances for neglect or error in judgment concerning the incident at Verdiersville. First, his orders to Fitz Lee were obviously unclear. Lee, a highly talented officer who cherished Stuart, fell short of his obligation as a result of the lack of clarity in Jeb's verbal directions. Next, Stuart's complacency in posting no guards at the Rhodes house is inexcusable. Only luck spared the Confederacy from the capture of a major general, a loss Robert E. Lee could ill afford. Did Stuart need reminding that a commanding officer is always accountable for an enemy surprise? Finally, Stuart's decision to place critical orders in the hands of FitzHugh and send him off alone into the darkness remains reprehensibly irresponsible. Any one of the other officers available should have been selected to search for the cavalry. This last error virtually ended Robert E. Lee's hope for a complete victory over Pope and jeopardized the Confederacy's chances for success.

Stuart's ride back to Lee's camp brought animated jeers of derision from the infantry. Shouts of "Where's your hat?" greeted him all along the line. Good-naturedly, Jeb smiled outwardly, but inside, the cavalryman seethed. Later, in writing to his wife, Stuart stated: "I intend to make the Yankees pay dearly for that hat." Alerted to the danger of enemy attack, John Pope removed his army northward behind the safety of the Rappahannock River on August 19.[22] Robert E. Lee and James Longstreet disgustedly watched the retreat from the heights of Clark's Mountain. With George McClellan's Army of the Potomac moving slowly toward Pope, Lee determined to alter his plans and set after Pope once more.

On Wednesday, August 20, Stuart exacted a modicum of revenge for his lost hat. In retreating across the Rappahannock, Pope left a large body of cavalry on the south side of the river near Brandy Station, guarding the Orange and Alexandria Railroad. Stuart, with orders to drive the Federals from the area, ordered two brigades to cross the Rapidan River at daybreak. Fitz Lee's brigade, along with John Pelham and his gunners, began crossing Raccoon Ford on the Rapidan at about 4:00 A.M., heading in the direction of Kelly's Ford. The depth of the river made it difficult for the cannons and caissons to cross, but Pelham managed the task well. Separating his forces, Stuart led a brigade in the direction of Stevensburg.

Fitz Lee quickly ran into some Federals, and Pelham hurried his guns up in support. Fitz Lee's troopers, firing from the saddle, with help from Pelham's gunners, forced the Federals back toward Kelly's Ford, where the bluecoats offered stiffer resistance. Stuart later reported that "by vigorous attack" Lee "secured several prisoners and a cavalry color." Pelham's gunners continued to fire on the enemy, bringing a smile to their commander's face. As one of his cannoneers stated, "You could see it was the kind of fighting he liked most, that it was meat and drink to him."[23] The overmatched Federals withdrew across the Rappahannock, where well-placed artillery and infantry ended the Confederate pursuit. Although a successful day for Jeb Stuart and his cavalry, it still did not make up for Verdiersville and the lost hat.

On the evening of August 21, Stuart met with Robert E. Lee, suggesting a most daring plan. Offering to take 1,500 cavalrymen, Stuart proposed to ride to the rear of Pope's army and sever the Union supply line along the Orange and Alexandria Railroad by burning the bridge over Cedar Run. The plan had strategic value, but it entailed much danger. Lee decided to mull over the idea and give his response to Stuart in the morning.

Near dawn on the following day Stuart moved his men through the rain five miles northwest to Freeman's Ford on the Hazel River, a tributary of the Rappahannock. Here Stuart's horsemen met stubborn resistance from enemy infantry under Brigadier General Robert H. Milroy with Captain Aaron C. Johnson's Twelfth Ohio Battery of artillery posted on the north bank. Pelham brought up four guns and, with much difficulty, dueled the Federal artillerists. Stuart later briefly reported on the stiff opposition of the Federals: "The ford was commanded by the enemy's artillery and infantry, and four pieces of the Stuart Horse Artillery, under . . . Pelham, tried in vain to silence the enemy's guns. Having advantage in position, he handled the enemy severely, though suffering casualties in his own battery." Pelham's constant blasting convinced Milroy that his forces faced far more iron than merely four cannons, but the Federal general rightly praised Johnson's Twelfth Ohio Battery: "Too much praise cannot be awarded the captain [Johnson] for the promptness and skill exhibited in bringing his battery into position. In less than five minutes after receipt of the order he had his pieces in action amid a perfect shower of shot, shell, and canister from three of the rebel batteries, and in ten minutes after had silenced their heaviest battery. He continued engaging the enemy for about two hours, compelling them to constantly change the position of their guns."[24]

Milroy claimed the rebel gunners did not cease firing until approximately 3:00 P.M. and admitted he lost "2 killed and 12 or 13 wounded by canister and shell."[25] Pelham lost at least one man wounded, Private Edward McCaffrey, who took pieces of shell in his chest and arm.

But the fighting had not ended for the day. Roger Preston Chew's battery appeared and unlimbered its weapons against the reluctant Federals, who brought up three fresh batteries. For two solid hours shells blasted back and forth between the two lines with Chew's men constantly at their guns. Fitz Lee and John Pelham rode up to observe Chew's gunners and noticed a few of his men tiring from the endless shelling. Dismounting from their horses, Lee and Pelham began assisting in serving the guns, with Lee, as one gunner remembered, "ramming the shell home with the promptness and dexterity of a born cannoneer" and Pelham, "the gallant and courteous Alabamian, kindly taking my place." Stonewall Jackson had also sent some guns to help with the pesky Federal artillerists. When the duel finally ended, the Confederates reported one killed—Private John Stewart, who had been hit by a piece of shell—and two others wounded. Two horses had also been killed. Federal captain Michael Wiedrich described the accuracy of Pelham and Chew's gunners: "The fire of the enemy was very hot where the two sections of my battery were posted. Here we had 5 killed and wounded. . . . we also had 2 horses killed and 10 others rendered unfit for service, which had to be shot." Wiedrich added that a limber chest caught on fire and exploded.[26]

At 8:00 A.M. that same day Lee sent his approval of Jeb Stuart's bold plan. Ordering Stuart to "rest your men . . . refresh your horses, [and] prepare rations," Lee then stated Stuart's objectives: gather information "of fords, roads, and position of enemy," destroy the Orange and Alexandria Railroad bridge, and cut the enemy's communication and telegraph line. Within two hours Stuart had his cavalry ready to move. Accompanying him were portions of Fitz Lee's and Robertson's brigades, plus two guns from Roger Chew's horse artillery.[27] As the troopers rode out of camp, Stuart passed by John Mosby. With a smile Stuart said, "I am going after my hat."[28]

~

Riding all day and into a heavy night rain, Stuart's horsemen finally approached Catlett's Station near 8:00 P.M. Under a pitch black darkness Stuart carefully engineered his plans for the surprise attack. The unsuspecting Federals literally gave in without a fight. Stuart's troopers began rounding up prisoners, torching wagons, and cutting telegraph wires. Unfortunately, the railroad bridge, a main target of the venture, could not be destroyed due to its particular structure. At 3:00 A.M. Stuart ordered his men to exit Catlett's Station. Confederate losses numbered four killed, one wounded, and seven missing. Stuart would return to Lee's army by the same route.

The plunder hauled off during Stuart's raid on Catlett's Station was bountiful: more than 300 prisoners, including many officers, and over 400 horses and mules. The most pleasurable prize for Stuart must have been the items taken from John Pope's personal baggage: his hat and dress uniform coat, plus $500,000 in greenbacks and $20,000 in gold from the Federal army's money chest. Pope himself had just missed being captured, according to one of the prisoners; he had left his tent sometime earlier on personal business. Tom Rosser reportedly captured Pope's horse and orderly. Fitz Lee even walked off with Pope's supper from his table.

Upon returning to the main army, Stuart, Rosser, Fitz Lee, and the others were greeted by overwhelming cheers. Fitz Lee slipped behind an oak tree and donned the hat and long coat of Pope. "In a moment or two," wrote a startled Confederate officer, "[he] emerged dressed in the long blue cloak of a Federal general that reached nearly down to his feet, and wearing a Federal general's hat with its big plume. This masquerade was accompanied by a burst of jolly laughter from him that might have been heard for a hundred yards."[29]

Stuart later penned a note to Pope: "General, you have my hat and plume. I have your best coat. I have the honor to propose a cartel for a fair exchange of the prisoners." Pope never acknowledged Stuart's memo. The famous coat was paraded throughout the entire camp and later sent to Governor John Letcher in Richmond.

He had it displayed in a bookstore window on Main Street with a card reading "Headquarters in the Saddle" and "The Rear Taking Care of Itself."[30] It was later placed in the state library.[31]

Pleased with his accomplishment, Stuart wrote: "What a demoralizing effect the success of this expedition had upon the army of the enemy, shaking their confidence in a general who had scorned the enterprise and ridiculed the courage of his adversaries." To Flora, Jeb wrote: "I have had my revenge out of Pope. I captured part of his staff, all of his baggage and baggage train, horse and equipments. . . . Captured his Quartermaster, safes—also his Field Quartermaster and 290 prisoners, of whom eleven were officers. Killed many. Loss slight."[32]

Although disappointed that the bridge over Cedar Run still stood, Robert E. Lee complimented his bold cavalry leader in a report to Richmond: "I take occasion to express to the Department my sense of the boldness, judgment and prudence he displayed." To President Jefferson Davis, however, Lee downplayed Stuart's raid, saying "[he] accomplished some minor advantages, destroyed some wagons, and captured some prisoners."[33] What may have pleased Lee most were the contents in the pocket of Pope's dress coat. There, in a leather wrapping, were Pope's personal dispatches. From these Lee learned Pope's intentions and numbers. He further discovered from these pages that three of McClellan's corps—Samuel Heintzelman's Third, Fitz John Porter's Fifth, and Jesse Reno's Ninth—had already joined Pope's Army of Virginia. With these additions Pope numbered 80,000. Undeterred by his numerical disparity, Lee with 55,000 must attack before the remainder of McClellan's Army of the Potomac arrived.

II

"Who Could Not Conquer with Such Troops as These"

My God, Pelham, if you're fool enough to stay out here, I'm not.

—Major L. M. Shumaker

Robert E. Lee ventured to Stonewall Jackson's headquarters on Sunday, August 24, with a new and audacious plan of attack. Separating his smaller army into two groups in the face of the enemy, thus violating a cardinal rule of textbook strategy, Lee suggested that Jackson march his twenty-five thousand men across the Rappahannock River, far beyond Pope's right flank, and move through Thoroughfare Gap to strike Pope's rear. Jackson's target, as Lee explained, was the capture of the Orange and Alexandria Railroad, Pope's vital supply line, linking his forces with Washington, D.C. With his lifeline of communications and supply ruptured, Pope would have to stay and fight or retreat. Secrecy of Jackson's movement and the precision of his "foot cavalry" constituted the two key elements in the plan. Meanwhile, James Longstreet and Lee, remaining behind with the other half of the Army of Northern Virginia, would pin down Pope's army and move to Jackson's support, depending upon his success and Pope's reaction to it. Jackson nodded his head in agreement; the plan called for Stonewall's excellence in moving an army and allowed him a chance of redemption for his sluggish activity during the Seven Days Battles. The dangers of such a plan were obvious. Jackson's march would be lengthy, and the weather promised to be hot. Any error in the undertaking could lead to an attack by Pope on either Jackson's isolated army or Longstreet's army protecting Richmond, thus ensuring disaster. The element of surprise, however, rested with the Rebel army.

The role of Jeb Stuart's cavalry was to make certain that Jackson had an unimpeded start on his march and then to catch him and act as a screen for his movement behind Pope. In this endeavor John Pelham and his horse artillery would be a significant factor. For more than a day, Pelham and his gunners, with help from some of Stuart's troopers, held off Federals from capturing Waterloo Bridge spanning the Rappahannock. Pope evidently desired the destruction of this bridge to hinder any endeavor by Lee to gain an advantage on the Federal right flank. With little or no sleep, Pelham and his gunners peppered away at the Federals for hours, foiling their attempts to capture the bridge. Jackson's getaway, in the meantime, succeeded. Late on Monday night Pelham and his men lay down for a well-deserved and much-needed rest. At 1:00 A.M. Pelham's slumber ended abruptly as Stuart gathered his men for a forced march to catch the forces of Stonewall Jackson. Within an hour, Stuart had his men moving. By this time, Jackson and his "foot cavalry" had marched nearly halfway to Pope's rear.[1]

Jackson's column had begun its march from Jeffersonton with General Richard S. Ewell's division taking the lead at 3:00 A.M. on August 25. Stripped of all but the barest essentials, Jackson's army moved without any excess baggage as only ambulances and ammunition wagons were allowed. Bypassing Waterloo Bridge, Jackson headed northwest and splashed his men through the Rappahannock at Hinson's Mill. As usual, only Jackson knew their destination. The August sun burned down on the men, who kept up an amazing pace of three miles per hour, as Jackson steered the column northeast toward Orleans. "Our rations of unsalted beef, eked out with green corn and unripe apples," wrote Allen C. Redwood of the Fifty-fifth Virginia, "formed a diet unsuited to soldiers on the march, and there was much straggling." J. F. J. Caldwell remembered the march as a solemn testimony to the men's endurance. "We were in wretched plight," wrote Caldwell. "Many men were barefoot, many more without a decent garment to their backs, more still ill with diarrhea and dysentery, and all half-famished." As the men trudged onward, Jackson continued to urge them with his constant admonition of "Close up! Close up, men!" From Orleans Jackson turned his column farther northeast toward the town of Salem, eleven miles distant, located on the Manassas Gap Railroad. As his weary soldiers marched into Salem, Jackson, sitting on his horse, observing, was heard to proudly announce, "Who could not conquer with such troops as these?"[2] Here the men camped for the night after an arduous twenty-six-mile march.

Meanwhile, Jeb Stuart with three thousand sabers and the horse artillery rode through the darkness and neared the rear of Jackson's column as it headed out of Salem at dawn on August 26. Stuart immediately fanned out his troopers to the right of Stonewall's men as a screen for the second leg of the march. Marching southeastward, Jackson pushed his men forward toward Thoroughfare Gap in the Bull Run Mountains. No Federals guarded the pass as the Confederates marched through. John Pelham, astride a powerful sorrel, made certain his gunners kept up the strenuous pace at the rear of Jackson's army. Miles behind this entire force, Lee and Longstreet began to move in the same direction as Jackson on the afternoon of August 26.

With Thoroughfare Gap behind them, Jackson's army marched on, reaching Gainesville where the Warrenton and Centreville Turnpike intersected the Manassas Gap Railroad. At this juncture Stuart's cavalry joined Jackson, who turned his infantrymen farther southeast toward Bristoe Station, merely five miles ahead. Along the way, friendly farmers informed Jackson that the Federals posted only a token guard at the Bristoe Station railroad bridge where the Orange and Alexandria Railroad fortified Pope's army with reinforcements and supplies. Good news indeed.

Near dusk of August 26, Jackson's forces captured Bristoe Station on the Orange and Alexandria Railroad after a brief skirmish with a small detachment of Federals. Soon afterward, a Federal train roared through the station before the Confederates prepared to stop it. Pope would certainly be alerted to the disturbance in his rear. Jackson ordered the railroad tracks torn up. Next Jackson sent Brigadier General Isaac Trimble's infantry brigade and Stuart's cavalry ahead to capture Manassas Junction, located less than five miles to the northeast where the Orange and Alexandria Railroad intersected with the Manassas Gap Railroad. Jackson would follow them the next day.

Pope, now aware that the enemy lurked in his rear, made ready for action by ordering his troops toward Manassas Junction. He had also been alerted that more Confederates were on the move a few miles away. These troops, under Robert E. Lee and James Longstreet, did not appear to concern Pope as he blithely set out to crush Jackson's men. Unaware of the potential trap being set for him, Pope brazenly stated of his army, "We shall bag the whole crowd, if they are prompt and expeditious."[3]

The forces of Stuart and Isaac Trimble arrived at Manassas Junction at dawn on August 27 and captured Pope's precious supply depot. Before them, they saw at least a hundred railroad cars and sutlers' wagons plus warehouses bulging with a cornucopia of supplies.[4] Later that morning Jackson's army arrived to share in the plunder.

Jackson's march to the rear of Pope's army served as a military classic for preeminence in precision and timing. In the full heat of summer his foot soldiers had traversed fifty-four miles in two days, taken three hundred prisoners, captured eight cannon, demolished two trains, and severed the enemy's communications and supply lines. Moxley Sorrel, of Longstreet's staff, stated: "Jackson's marches, in swiftness, daring, and originality of execution, were almost extraordinary." Perhaps W. W. Blackford put it best when he wrote of the consequences to the enemy: "the dread of their lives had his fangs in their vitals ready to tear them to pieces."[5]

As the men began helping themselves to the plethora of goods, a Union brigade under General George William Taylor appeared. Believing he faced a mere raiding party, Taylor ordered his men forward. Instantly, the Confederates sent a fusillade of lead into the Federals. Positioned for an enfilading fire, the Rockbridge Artillery also opened up at about 300 yards distant. Then Joseph Carpenter's battery began shelling from the front. This hail of canister and shell riddled the Federals unmercifully. Driven back by the overwhelming numbers, the Federals quickly retreated at about 11:00 A.M. across the bridge, with General Taylor mortally wounded in his left leg. Of the 1,200 bluecoats that entered the fracas, 201 were captured and another 138 lay dead.[6] Afterward the Confederates torched the railroad bridge and the cars that brought the Federals.

Arriving sometime after the action had ended, Pelham and his gunners spent a good part of the day salvaging munitions and equipment. Prized among his possessions were two unused 3-inch rifled guns. Pelham quickly ordered his men to unhitch two old howitzers and take them into the woods while summoning others to attach the new guns to the horses. Stuart later reported, "Pelham, arriving late, was indefatigable in his efforts to get away the captured guns, which duty was intrusted specially to him."[7]

The plundering of the Manassas Junction storehouses now began in earnest. For the foot-weary and empty-bellied soldiers of Jackson's army, it was a day like no other in their lives. "Then came a storming charge of hungry men, rushing in tumultuous mobs over each other's heads, under each other's feet," recalled Lieutenant Edward McCrady Jr., "anywhere, everywhere, to satisfy a craving hunger, stronger than a yearning for fame." John Worsham of the Twenty-first Virginia Infantry wrote, "Were you, when a boy, on some special occasion allowed to eat as much of everything you wanted? Were you ever a soldier, who had eaten nothing but roasting ears [of corn] for two days? . . . Only those who participated can ever appreciate it. . . . Now here are vast storehouses filled with everything to eat, and sutler's stores filled with all the delicacies, potted ham, lobster, tongue, candy, cakes, nuts, oranges, lemons, pickles, catsup, mustard, etc. . . . It was hard to decide what to take."[8]

"Fine whiskey and segars circulated freely," wrote James F. J. Caldwell, "elegant lawn and linen handkerchiefs were applied to noses hitherto blown with the thumb and forefinger, and sumptuous underclothing was fitted over limbs sunburnt, sore and vermin-splotched." Father James Sheeran, chaplain of the Fourteenth Louisiana, remembered, "Just imagine about 6000 men hungry and almost naked, let loose on some million dollars worth of [supplies]. . . . Here you would see a crowd enter a car with their old Confederate greys and in a few moments come out dressed in Yankee uniforms." Writing to his mother ten days afterward, artillerist Ham Chamberlayne, still in disbelief, noted, "To see a starving man eating lobster salad & drinking rhine wine, barefooted & in tatters was curious; the whole thing is indescribable."[9]

For all the merriment and gorged stomachs, Jeb Stuart had not forgotten John Pelham and his gunners, who, as of yet, had not participated in the carnival atmosphere at Manassas Junction. Stuart summoned von Borcke and sent him with a sutler's wagon, described by the Prussian as "one of those large gaudily-painted vans drawn always by four excellent horses." Von Borcke first exchanged the four bay horses for sturdier artillery horses and then proceeded with the wagon, laden with luxuries, to Pelham's impatient men on the outskirts of Manassas. Von later gleefully reported that the artillerists "collected round the wagon in large numbers, and received the contents with loud demonstrations of delight." The contents of the wagon contained "shirts, hats, pocket-handkerchiefs, oranges, lemons, wines, cigars, and all sorts of knick-knacks." Pelham immediately had the horses unhitched from the wagon and harnessed them to one of the new 3-inch rifles confiscated earlier. Later some of the infantrymen professed a certain jealousy that cavalrymen and artillerists could carry more booty than the man of the trenches. Pelham acknowledged this unfair advantage, then laughingly said, "You know the saying—If you want to have fun, jine the cavalry!"[10]

That night Jackson ordered all the remaining supplies at Manassas Junction burned. As the flames consumed the balance of the Federal stores, leaving a reddish cast in the sky, Jackson marched his men five miles northward to the hamlet of Groveton where the Warrenton Turnpike intersected with Sudley Springs Road. Here, some ten miles from Thoroughfare Gap, Jackson found a solid position to deploy his army in a fighting stance. And now the wait began: for Pope's army to arrive and, hopefully, for Lee and Longstreet.

As Jackson's forces settled into camp, John Pelham placed his battery in a defensive mode, about six miles from the infantry along the turnpike near Centreville. Early the next morning, Stuart ordered Pelham to take his battery to Jackson for support in the event of Pope's arrival. Moving quickly, Pelham limbered his battery and headed southwest toward Jackson's army. Pelham later wrote of his movement:

> I left Centreville . . . in rear of General Jackson's corps. I marched without interruption until I had crossed Bull Run at Lewis' Ford, when a small party of the enemy's cavalry appeared in my rear. I detached Lieutenant [James] Breathed, with one piece, as a rear guard, and moved on with the rest of my battery. A few well-directed shots from Breathed's gun drove the enemy off. I moved up the Warrenton pike, and when near the Jim Robinson house I overtook the rear of General A. P. Hill's division, which had just left the turnpike and was moving along a by-road to the right. I moved to the right of this division and passed it. I moved on and parked my battery in a field where General Jackson had ordered all his artillery to await orders.[11]

Told to be ready at a moment's notice, the gunners rested for the time being at Sudley Church. Jackson, meanwhile, arranged his men for battle. Slightly more than one mile west of the old Judith Henry House, Jackson's forces sat just north of the Warrenton Turnpike on a rise covered with thick woodland. The heavily treed area offered an ideal spot to conceal his men for an ambush. The trees, however, would hinder the use of his artillery. His right flank extended to the Brawner farm and his left beyond Dogan's Branch.

John Pope had spent most of the day groping around, unsuccessfully searching for the elusive Jackson. Perhaps angry at his lack of good fortune, Pope now disregarded Lee and determined to employ his entire force against Jackson. Reaching Manassas Junction on the morning of August 28, Federals found the remains of Jackson's devastation, but nothing more except a few Confederate stragglers. Intense questioning of these Rebels brought erroneous information that Jackson was at Centreville. Later in the day, however, Federals found Centreville clean of Confederates as well. Where, Pope wondered, had Jackson disappeared to? It was as though the ground had opened up and thousands of men had vanished. During the afternoon, Pope's separated forces searched for the ghostlike Jackson without fruition. The longer the search, the more Pope itched for a fight.

Jackson's men now rested during the hot part of the day. Relaxing in the shade, the soldiers enjoyed cold buttermilk brought to them by the farmers nearby. "The men were packed like herring in a barrel," wrote Blackford. "There was scarce room enough to ride between the long rows of stacked arms, with the men stretched out on the ground between them, laughing and playing cards in all the careless merriment of troops confident in themselves, their cause, and their leader." Blackford, however, observed Stonewall Jackson's apparent anxiety while waiting for word from Longstreet or the arrival of Pope's army. "When [Jackson] was uneasy he was as cross as a bear, and neither his Generals nor his staff liked to come near him if they could help it. The expression of his face was one of suppressed energy that reminded you of an explosive missile, an unlucky spark applied to which would blow you sky high." Later Jackson's tension was greatly alleviated when a courier arrived about 3:00 P.M. with a message from Robert E. Lee: Longstreet, a mere twelve miles away at Thoroughfare Gap, would arrive in the morning. Jackson broke into a smile and said, "Where is the man who brought this dispatch? I must shake hands with him."[12]

At nearly 6:00 P.M. 10,000 Federals marched eastward along Warrenton Pike directly in the front of Jackson's hidden 24,000-man army. Watching their movement with a critical eye, Stonewall Jackson, his fighting blood up, could not resist the ready target. Turning to his staff officers, Jackson sternly ordered: "Bring out your men, gentlemen!" Immediately, Confederate guns opened up on the left flank of the unsuspecting Federals. Frantically the Federals formed a defensive line and managed to regain their composure. With no more than seventy-five yards separating the two armies, the battle intensified all along a one-mile line. Volleys of musketry sent men and officers reeling on both sides.

Confederates, under divisional commanders Richard Ewell and William B. Taliaferro, stormed down the slope only to be halted by the stubborn resistance of John Gibbon's "Black Hat Brigade." Neither line wavered as the air filled with minié balls. Luckily for some Federals on the low ground, many Confederates overshot

their targets. After a few horrible minutes of colossal struggle, both sides sent in reinforcements, which only heightened the fury. Officers fell in amazing numbers.
John Neff, the twenty-eight-year-old commander of the Thirty-third Virginia in
the Stonewall Brigade and one of Jackson's finest colonels, was riddled by bullets
and died instantly. From the same brigade, Lieutenant Colonel Lawson Botts of
the Second Virginia fell from his horse with a horrible mortal wound as a bullet
tore through the left side of his face and ripped out part of his skull before exiting behind his ear.[13] Two Confederate generals also went down with ugly wounds.
William Taliaferro was hit in the neck, foot, and arm with the last injury being the
most serious. Perhaps Jackson's greatest loss of field commanders occurred when
feisty Richard Ewell took a bullet in the left kneecap. The minié ball shattered the
kneecap, as Ewell knelt on the ground, and continued up the femur bone of the leg
until it exited the upper thigh. A tourniquet stanched the hemorrhaging, but the
severity of the wound necessitated amputation.[14]

During this fighting, John Pelham and much of the Confederate artillery had
remained to the rear out of action. Now, as shadows lengthened across the battlefield, Jackson called for his gunners. Eagerly responding to the summons, Pelham pushed his men into action. Swinging behind the Confederate lines in the
darkness, the horse artillery, consisting of three 3-inch rifles, covered one and a
half miles in twenty minutes, much of the distance through the Groveton woods.
Along the way on the uncertain and sinuous roads, one of the cannons turned on
the wrong path, and when Pelham arrived, he had only two guns. Jackson sent
Major Lindsay M. Shumaker of his artillery to guide Pelham and his guns into position on the extreme right of the Confederate lines near Taliaferro's division. In the
darkness Federals of the Nineteenth Indiana, a regiment of Gibbon's "Black Hats,"
fired a volley from little more than fifty yards away, thus revealing their position
to Pelham. Quickly ordering his gunners to load double canister, Pelham momentarily waited; when ready, he rose in his stirrups and shouted, "Fire!"[15]

The deadly effect of the blasts stunned the Federals who courageously mounted
a counterattack with two companies firing directly into Pelham's gunners. Shumaker, fearing for his life, turned to the leader of the horse artillery, shouting, "My
God, Pelham, if you're fool enough to stay out here, I'm not." Shumaker darted
for cover as Pelham was forced to move his men to a more tenable location. From
this new position Pelham continued firing at extremely close range for more than
an hour. For a few of those minutes, Federals nearly surrounded Pelham's gunners.
"We fully expected to take them," said a Federal later taken prisoner. "It's almost
unbelievable to me that we didn't." For a while Pelham was forced to fight with
merely one gun. Soon Jackson ordered three regiments of Taliaferro's riflemen forward to support Pelham's effort. Surging into the yard of the Brawner house, Confederate infantrymen fired on the stubborn Hoosiers. Major Shumaker, regaining
his courage, shouted for Pelham to withdraw his cannons. Since one of his guns

was immobile due to a damaged pole, Pelham refused the order and maintained his firing with a solitary cannon. The Federals eventually pulled back out of range and the fighting ended for the day at about 9:00 p.m.[16] Pelham rounded up his gunners and cannons and ordered his men to rest for the evening.

For more than two-and-a-half hours the two sides had fought a bloody contest with neither gaining more than a few feet of territory. The fighting at Groveton had proven little except the mettle of soldiers, both Union and Confederate. The Stonewall Brigade lost 340 of 800 men engaged—more than 40 percent. Of the nearly 2,000 Federals in Gibbon's "Black Hat Brigade," 750 were counted as casualties. "The best blood of Wisconsin and Indiana was poured out like water," lamented Rufus Dawes, "and it was spilled for naught." In both armies it is estimated that one of every three men who fought that day was killed or wounded.[17]

Late that night Stonewall Jackson summoned John Pelham to offer his personal congratulations for the outstanding artillery work demonstrated by the young officer. Months later Jackson remembered Pelham's heroics in his written report of the battle. Dated April 27, 1863, the memo read: "Owing to the difficulty of getting artillery through the woods I did not have much of that arm as I desired at the opening of the engagement; but this want was met by Major Pelham, with the Stuart Horse-Artillery, who dashed forward on my right and opened upon the enemy at a moment when his services were much needed." Jeb Stuart also added his compliments: "Capt. John Pelham's battery . . . acted a conspicuous part on the extreme right of the battle-field, dashing forward to his position under heavy fire."[18]

Stuart later influenced Pelham to write his own report of the fighting at Groveton. Pelham penned his account on January 10, 1863, but his self-effacing manner caused Stuart to urge the young artillerist to write another, fuller version. Complying with Stuart's wishes, Pelham wrote a second report dated March 7, 1863. The following constitutes both narratives:

> Just before night-fall General Jackson ordered twenty pieces to be sent rapidly to the front. I took three pieces at a gallop through a thick woods. . . . I crossed the old railroad about 1 mile from Groveton and took position between it and the turnpike. . . . One of my guns was unable to keep up and was lost from the battery, it being dark and the road narrow and winding. I reported to General Jackson, and he told me his chief of artillery, Major Shumaker, would show me a position. By this time it had become dark, and, Major Shumaker not being aware of the exact position of the enemy, we crossed the old railroad about a mile to the right of Groveton, and moved but a short distance beyond, when the enemy apprised us of his presence by firing a volley into the head of the column, distance about 40 paces. I immediately put my guns in position and engaged them at about 50 or 60 yards. We con-

tinued the fight for an hour or more, when, our re-enforcements coming up, we drove the enemy back. . . . Major Shumaker ordered me to fall back. Owing to the pole of one of my guns being broken I could not obey the order, and continued firing until the enemy were driven back. During the latter part of the fight I had but one gun, the other having been taken off by the order of some mounted officer (it was dark and no one could tell who), while my attention was wholly directed to the right piece.

Lieut. M[athis] W[inston] Henry . . . displayed the greatest courage and daring during the engagement. Every non-commissioned officer and private acted so gallantly I cannot particularize. After the fight was over I collected the other pieces of my battery and reported to General Stuart the next morning.[19]

Receiving the news of the combat at Groveton, John Pope came to the conclusion that he had Jackson trapped. With this erroneous thought in mind, Pope summoned his separated troops to converge on Groveton for what he thought would be the decisive battle the following day. As Pope announced to his staff officers, "the game is in our hands." Scattered Union forces began moving toward Jackson's army. Aware that Longstreet's army of thirty thousand men and twenty-two batteries of artillery were but a few miles off, Pope's tunnel vision refused to recognize this force as a threat. The defeat of Jackson consumed the Federal commander entirely.

During the night Jackson deployed for the expected Federal attack on the morrow. Pulling his men back to the unfinished railroad cut, Jackson spread his army along nearly two miles of the embankment. On his left, extending almost to Sudley Church, stood the powerful division of A. P. Hill with Fitz Lee's cavalry guarding Hill's flank. Ewell's division, now under the command of Alexander R. Lawton, held the center, while Taliaferro's division, led by William E. Starke, maintained the right. Strong as the formation appeared, it offered three apparent weaknesses: the thickly treed area negated much of Jackson's artillery, the cover of foliage afforded the enemy some concealment in attacking the Confederate center or left, and the extreme right flank remained exposed until the arrival of James Longstreet's forces. Only the third could Jackson remedy; he sent the brigades of Jubal Early and Henry Forno west of Brawner's farm. Jackson now waited with little more than 20,000 men for Pope's combined strength of 62,000. The key to Jackson's survival continued to be Longstreet's army, still a few miles off to the west.

Later that night Jackson and Hunter McGuire, his chief surgeon, rode from Groveton toward Bull Run Mountains. After a fashion Jackson dismounted and put his ear to the ground in hopes of hearing the trampling feet of Longstreet's army. He listened for several moments, then disappointedly stood up. "I shall never forget the sad look of the man that night as he gazed toward Thoroughfare Gap," wrote McGuire, "wishing for Longstreet to come." Back at Groveton Confederate soldiers felt the same despair and anxiety. "Before us was Pope, with at least the bulk of the Federal army," wrote J. F. J. Caldwell. "Behind us was no base, no subsistence, no reinforcement. . . . God, Jackson and our own hearts were our dependence."[20]

12

"The Lord of Hosts Was Plainly Fighting on Our Side"

If you have another Pelham, please give him to me.

—Stonewall Jackson

Just after dawn on Friday, August 29, Federal skirmishers began moving on Jackson's left flank in a feeling-out process with possible thoughts of outflanking him. With skirmishing beginning up and down the Confederate line of entrenchment, Jackson knew a large Federal attack would soon commence. At 8:00 A.M. the anxious Jackson ordered Stuart and part of his cavalry to locate Longstreet and guide him there.

Soon musket barrels flashed smoke and fire as the Federal First Corps of nine thousand men initiated a full assault. Pope's plan called for a series of attacks along Jackson's front to pin him down while Fitz John Porter's Fifth Corps headed to Gainesville nearly five miles to Jackson's right. If successful, Porter's control of the Gainesville area, at least in Pope's mind, would seal Jackson's doom by cutting off reinforcements and blocking his escape route. The railroad embankment suddenly came alive as fierce and bitter fighting appeared to mirror the scenario of the preceding day. For the better part of the morning and on into the afternoon, Pope sent wave after wave of Federal soldiers in piecemeal attacks, and still Jackson's men desperately held on.

One of these assaults occurred at 10:00 A.M. when two brigades of Philip Kearny's division swung wide of Jackson's left, beyond A. P. Hill's division, along Sudley Springs Road. Moving along rather blindly, these Yankees suddenly posed a critical problem as Jackson's ambulances and trains loomed ahead, virtually unguarded. Jeb Stuart, starting on his way to find Longstreet, observed this threat when "my party was fired on from the woods bordering the road, which was in rear of Jackson's lines and which the enemy had penetrated." Realizing the grave danger, Stuart ordered six companies of the First Virginia Cavalry, under Major William Patrick, "to interpose in defense of the baggage, and use all the means at hand for its protection." Jeb further ordered the baggage trains at once to start for Aldie.[1]

Suddenly, John Pelham appeared with his battery to the front of the Federals and opened a deadly hail of canister. The Napoleon Detachment of Creoles lurched to the forefront and blasted at a furious pace. Stuart later proudly reported:

"Captain Pelham, always at the right place at the right time, unlimbered his battery and soon dispersed that portion in the woods." Meanwhile, Major Patrick's troopers dismounted, firing carbines. "Our sharpshooters were quickly dismounted and placed behind a fence," remembered von Borcke, "where they received the enemy with a very well-directed fire; while Pelham, who had come up at full gallop with his guns, threw from a favourable position such a deadly shower of grape and canister upon the advancing lines of the foe, as brought them suddenly to a halt."[2] Heroically, Pelham and Patrick, ably assisted by some infantry Jackson had detached as well as the arrival of Captain Louis E. D'Aquin's Louisiana Battery, combined to rout the enemy and help ensure the safety of Jackson's wagons.

Federals now scrabbled for safety between Pelham's gunners and those of D'Aquin. "We had to pass through a perfect hail of grape and canister," wrote John Reuhle of the Second Michigan, "which ripped the sod under our very feet." Unfortunately for the valiant Confederates, Major Patrick, at age thirty-nine, fell mortally wounded. Stonewall Jackson mentioned Patrick in his report as an "intrepid officer, who fell in the attack while setting an example of gallantry to his men well worthy of imitation." Wrote Jeb Stuart of Patrick's death: "He lived long enough to witness the triumph of our arms, and expired thus in the arms of victory. The sacrifice was noble, but the loss to us irreparable."[3]

Before Stuart departed to find Longstreet, he sent Pelham to report to Jackson. Upon Pelham's arrival, Jackson asked the young artillerist to ride with him. Calmly, Jackson pointed out the landmarks of the field, including strengths, weaknesses, uneven terrain, and enemy positions. Then Jackson gave Pelham arbitrary orders to place his cannon that day where he deemed best and "to act as the occasion might require."[4] This from a general who so often trusted no one's judgment but his own! Although Pelham must have been proud of his actions that morning, he modestly did not mention them in his report of the battle. Instead, he selflessly wrote: "Early on the morning of the 29th the enemy showed himself on our left and seemed to be moving toward Sudley Hill. General Stuart placed my battery in position and opened fire upon them. After remaining here for nearly an hour he ordered two other batteries to this position and sent me to the right of our line."[5] That and nothing more—not a word on the saving of Jackson's trains. For the time being, Pelham parked his battery behind A. P. Hill's division and waited.

Pelham, however, received much praise for his efforts that morning in saving the wagons and ambulances from his superior officers. Stonewall bestowed his gratitude by stating: "During the day a force of the enemy penetrated the wood in my rear, endangering the safety of my ambulances and train. Upon being advised of this by General Stuart I sent a body of infantry to drive them from the wood; but in the mean time the vigilant Pelham had unlimbered his battery and dispersed that portion of them which had reached the wood." Robert E. Lee briefly praised "the Stuart Horse Artillery, under Major Pelham [who] effectually protected General Jackson's trains against a body of the enemy who penetrated to the rear."[6] But the work of the horse artillery and its leader had not ended for the day.

Soon divisions of Samuel P. Heintzelman's Third Corps made a direct frontal attack against A. P. Hill's division on the Confederate left. For a few awful moments the sector became a bloodbath as the brave Federals attempted to dent the strongly entrenched Rebel line. As the bluecoats began falling back, Hill organized a counterattack. To support his efforts, Hill sent for Pelham's guns to assist his own three batteries. Pelham, stationed in Hill's rear, pushed his men and six guns forward to the heart of the action. Selecting an excellent position to unlimber his guns, Pelham began firing from a ridge overlooking Groveton. For two hours his cannons blazed away at the Federal artillery until five of his guns exhausted their ammunition. Ordering James Breathed to take the five empty guns to the rear, Pelham stood his ground and directed the fire of the solitary cannon. Without reinforcements to help him and the trail of his lone cannon being splintered by Federal gunfire, Pelham finally gave the order to withdraw. Invaluable service in the repulse of the Federals also came from Fitz Lee's cavalry positioned on the far right near Sudley Church. Crossing Sudley Ford, the horsemen swooped in on the Federal right, inflicting many casualties. Pelham could be proud of his ex-roommate, Tom Rosser, whose Fifth Virginia Cavalry captured, according to von Borcke, some five hundred prisoners.[7]

Although the battle continued until after dark, Pelham's fighting for the day had ended. His first report, written on January 10, 1863, summed up this part of the contest at Groveton in merely two rather bland sentences: "General A. P. Hill sent for some artillery to be thrown rapidly forward, as the enemy were giving way. I placed my battery in position near the railroad and opened on some batteries and a column of infantry posted on the hills around Groveton." Stuart, as mentioned earlier, urged Pelham to submit a second, more detailed account. Pelham's second report, dated March 7, 1863, reveals a far more comprehensive narrative of the support given to A. P. Hill:

A courier reported that the enemy were falling back, and that General A. P. Hill wanted the artillery to press forward. I moved toward Groveton, and saw two batteries coming into position to play on the enemy's artillery near the town. I passed these batteries about 200 yards, and took position on the point of a ridge and opened upon their artillery. The position was held for nearly two hours, when the ammunition from all my guns except one was expended. The three batteries that were supporting me retired about the same time, and I was left alone, with one gun, exposed to the fire of a long line of batteries with a direct and flank fire. I dispatched Sergeant [William] Hoxton to General A. P. Hill to inform him of my condition and ask him to send re-enforcements. After we had continued this unequal contest for fifteen or twenty minutes Sergeant Hoxton returned and reported that he could not find General Hill. I then determined to retire, not, however, until the trail of my only gun had been struck and shivered. The accuracy with which my guns were fired and the rapidity with which they were served during both days was very gratifying, and the execution they wrought was very great.

It gives me great pleasure to speak in terms of the highest praise of Lieuts. James Breathed and William [M.] McGregor. The example they set was worthily emulated by the non-commissioned officers and men. Sergt. W[ilson] H. P. Turner behaved with conspicuous gallantry until he was killed; also Sergt. R. T. [Robert P. P.] Burwell during the entire engagement, and Sergt. W. [Walter] S. Dabney acted admirably when left alone with his gun to fight at least twenty. He fired his gun with the same precision and accuracy as before. All the corporals and privates acted so well that it would seem invidious to particularize.

I moved my battery to the rear to procure ammunition, but could only get a very limited supply.

I held my battery in readiness on the field for action during the 30th, but it being the only battery of horse artillery, would be very much needed in case of a retreat or pursuit. General Jackson ordered me to reserve my ammunition for any emergency.[8]

While the Federals persisted in attacking Jackson's front, Longstreet and Lee moved their section of the Army of Northern Virginia at a strong pace but without a sense of urgency. The circumstances changed, however, when Jeb Stuart rode up to Longstreet's column between Haymarket and Gainesville, and proceeded to explain Jackson's situation. Realizing Jackson's peril for the first time, Lee stated, "We must hurry on and help him." Jackson's exigency also seemed clear to Longstreet, who "knew Jackson was hard pressed," according to Longstreet's adjutant, Moxley Sorrel, "and praying for a sight of him."[9] The pace increased as the heat of the late summer morning set in.

Meanwhile, John Pope continued to assail Jackson's army along the railroad embankment. "Our condition appeared critical," moaned John Casler of the Stonewall Brigade, "for we had lost severely and were being hemmed in on all three sides by nearly the whole army of the enemy; our retreat cut off, and no assistance possible until Lee and Longstreet could arrive. . . . We knew assistance was at hand if we could hold out a little longer."[10]

The vanguard of Longstreet's army made its way to Jackson's right before noon. "Old Pete's" forces began forming a line running north nearly to the Brawner farm adjacent to Jackson's extreme right and south to the Manassas-Gainesville Road. Together the two armies patterned a huge inverted "L." Pope, unaware of Longstreet's arrival and the trap about to be sprung on him, continued to storm Jackson's front. "Our own force was large, comparatively fresh, and eager to crush John Pope," wrote Moxley Sorrel, "but for some reason the attack was not made, although I think General Lee preferred it to waiting." Sorrel's analysis was entirely correct. Lee desired an immediate attack, but Longstreet objected, wanting to survey the terrain and position of the enemy first. Longstreet admitted, "General Lee was quite disappointed by my report against immediate attack along the turnpike." But the iron-willed subordinate held firm.[11]

Jackson's army continued its attempt to withstand the tremendous pressure of the Federal attacks, and as the day neared 5:00 P.M., the fighting intensified. Longstreet later admitted this part of the fighting "was fiercely contested till near night" but excused his inertia by saying "no account of it came from headquarters to my command, nor did General Jackson think to send word of it." Three times that afternoon, however, Robert E. Lee urged Longstreet to attack, but each time Old Pete declined. Finally, Longstreet persuaded Lee that the lateness of the day prevented any sound reason to attack. He promised Lee instead that "we [would] have all things in readiness for a good day's work" on the morrow. To this Lee hesitatingly assented.[12]

The harrowing day of battle continued for Jackson until 9:00 that evening. Six major Federal assaults had been repulsed at great loss to both sides as the fighting raged all along Jackson's front. Darkness ended the fighting on the twenty-ninth with the lines virtually unchanged from what they had been that morning. Believing he had pushed Jackson's men into retreat and that he had won a "great victory," Pope cheerfully wired Washington, D.C., "Today we drove them from the field." He now stood ready to follow up his "victory" with a final assault the following day. Still unaware of Longstreet's arrival, Pope was, in fact, about to flounder helplessly into Lee's trap.

Saturday, August 30, dawned dry and hot. That morning John Pelham and his reliable lieutenant James Breathed had breakfast together and discussed what role the horse artillery might have that day. Jackson's infantry maintained its position with the artillery excellently placed on high ground. The guns in the center held a commanding location with a two-thousand-yard clearance toward any advance made by the Federals. Hours passed as the Confederates waited for the Federal assault to begin. That morning Robert E. Lee called a meeting attended by Longstreet, Jackson, and Stuart. He outlined what measures would be taken in the event the Federals did not attack. Following the meeting, Jackson asked Stuart's permission to again enlist the services of Pelham and the horse artillery. Stuart granted the request, but only smiled when Jackson said, "If you have another Pelham, please give him to me."[13]

During the day, the Confederates rested as hour after hour passed with little activity save some random skirmishing. By 3:00 P.M., however, Pope's army began moving forward as he resumed the offensive. Soon massed Federal troops stormed Jackson's right flank with three lines. Thousands of Confederate riflemen responded by raising up in the railroad cut and sending a barrage of minié balls into the attackers. Jackson's artillery opened up as well. This fire caused the Federals to fall back momentarily before regrouping. Heroism was commonplace as soldiers from both sides kept up a murderous volley. Caught up in the fervor of the battle, Major Andrew Jackson Barney of the Thirtieth New York Infantry rode his horse up the embankment while shouting for his men to follow him. Enthralled by his valor, Confederate riflemen briefly held their fire. Shouts of "Don't kill him! Don't kill him!" came from the Rebels. Then instantly a shower of bullets came in Major Barney's direction, and he toppled from his horse with a bullet through his head.[14]

Many of Jackson's soldiers began running critically low on ammunition. Some ran down the embankment to procure cartridges from the dead. Others had collected rounded stones "as big as one's two fists" to hurl at the oncoming enemy. "Such a flying of rocks never was seen," wrote a startled eyewitness. "One such stone was as good as a cannonball," recounted Blackford, "so far as the men it hit on the head was concerned." Fitz John Porter verified the intensity and excellent aim of some of the rock throwers: "Many of the enemy . . . had not time to reload, and received us with stones, severely wounding many and killing some of our men."[15]

As the minutes wore on, Jackson needed Longstreet's help; he sent a staff officer to find Old Pete. The characteristically methodical James Longstreet continued to watch the battle waged by Jackson's hard-pressed veterans, who had fought Pope's army for nearly thirty-six hours. By 4:00 P.M., however, Old Pete observed what he had been waiting for, as the Federals began losing their initiative and started to make their way to the rear. Robert E. Lee, astride his horse on the Warrenton Turnpike, watched the same scene and decided it was time to close the jaws of his magnificent trap. Nearly simultaneously, Lee and Longstreet ordered the advance of twenty-five thousand Confederates to strike the exposed left flank of the retreating Federals. The long-awaited counterstroke by Longstreet's command was about to begin.

The fleeing Federals began to cluster on Henry House Hill, a natural area for defense, while the veterans under the commands of Longstreet and Jackson pushed forward. Stuart's cavalry, defending Longstreet's right flank in the advance, performed meritorious service. Colonel Tom Rosser displayed his excellence when given command of four artillery batteries. Moving the guns forward in advance of Longstreet's pursuit, Rosser effectively fired an enfilading barrage into the retreating Federals. Pelham's horse artillery joined in by riding forward and blasting rounds of canister in a "destructive flank-fire on the dense ranks of the Yankees," according to von Borcke. Stuart later reported the results of the counterattack:

"The Lord of Hosts was plainly fighting on our side, and the solid walls of Federal infantry melted away before the straggling, but nevertheless determined, onsets of our infantry columns."[16]

Nightfall ended the Battle of Second Manassas. Pope's defeated and demoralized army retreated back to Centreville under cover of darkness. Rainfall hindered any further pursuit by the Confederates. Federal losses numbered 14,462. They also abandoned thirty cannons and 20,000 rifles. Confederate casualties totaled 9,112.

The images of the battle's horror were revealed by Chaplain James Sheeran of the Fourteenth Louisiana Infantry as he viewed the scars of war at the railroad cut: "Oh! May I never again witness such scenes as I saw this day. . . . The Yankees in front of RR . . . were lying in heaps. . . . Some with their brains oozing out; some with the face shot off; others with their bowels protruding; others with shattered limbs. . . . They were almost as black as negroes, bloated and some so decomposed as to be past recognition." Confederate Val Giles described his own feelings after the battle: "I was just about half dead and felt . . . as weak as branch water." At 10:00 P.M. Robert E. Lee dispatched word of his victory to Richmond. William Allan underscored the brilliance demonstrated by Lee in the victory on that day: "In no other of his great battles do the skill and good judgment of [Lee] show to better advantage than in that of the 30th of August."[17]

Meanwhile, John Pelham, exhausted from his duties of the preceding forty-eight hours, gladly succumbed to a night of blissful and needed sleep. A fellow member of the horse artillery marveled at Pelham's stamina by observing, "His endurance here was truly something to wonder at." Without mentioning Pelham by name, infantryman Val Giles paid a handsome compliment to the Confederate artillery: "During the war I used to think that the artillerymen were the bravest men on earth. They could pull through deeper mud, ford deeper streams, shoot faster, swear louder, and stand more hard pounding than any other class of men in the service."[18]

Dawn of Sunday, August 31, found John Pope's forces on elevated ground, facing west, at Centreville. Jeb Stuart, who had spent considerable time scouting that morning, reported Pope's whereabouts to Robert E. Lee. Later that morning Pope would send word to Washington, D.C., that if Lee attacked again, the Confederates might destroy his army, but Lee's intentions were not to directly attack. Instead he would send Stonewall Jackson's men in a circuitous march to the north to try to cut off Pope's retreat. With rain beginning to fall, Lee sent Jackson and Stuart to "tail" the enemy. By early afternoon Jackson's exhausted men began crossing Bull Run at Sudley Springs Ford. Pushing on ahead, Stuart was assisted by Pelham and the horse artillery. Because the roads were wet, Pelham and his gunners struggled to keep up the pace and fell behind.

Pope remained at Centreville until the afternoon of Monday, September 1, when he retreated to Fairfax Court House. Jackson's army, with Stuart's cavalry nearby, continued pushing southeast down the Little River Turnpike to the site of a mansion known as Chantilly. Again Pelham's gunners struggled mightily to keep up on the glue-like roads.

With storm clouds rolling in on the horizon from the western sky, skirmishing began in the late afternoon. Controversy shrouds the opening segment of the battle and Pelham's possible place in the fighting. Pelham biographer Philip Mercer cites John Esten Cooke in describing Stuart ordering Pelham to bring forward a Blakely to fire on a wooded area in the distance, stating: "Major John Pelham commanded this gun in person, and General Stuart superintended the firing." A few well-placed shots into the trees drove out some hidden Federals, but suddenly enemy sharp-shooters came from the right of the woods and fired a concentrated volley of minié balls at Pelham's gunners. "The enemy's lines were about one hundred yards dis-tant, and as the gun was without canister, it was, after a few shots, withdrawn." The Battle of Ox Hill, commonly called Chantilly, had begun.[19]

By sunset the fighting became intense as soldiers from both sides battled with a fury common to the previous three days. Soon the blackened clouds opened up with a ferocious downpour mixed with lightning, thunder, and high winds. With rain falling in horizontal sheets directly into the faces of the Confederates, the battle continued for two hours. The soaking rain drenched weapons and gunpowder, ren-dering many of them useless. Some men wielded rifles as clubs or resorted to the bayonet. Darkness, accompanied by the horrible thunderstorm, ended the fighting at Chantilly. One thousand Union casualties littered the field; Confederate losses numbered about half as many. That night Pope continued his withdrawal beyond Fairfax Court House to Alexandria and the safety of Washington, D.C. Without sleep, John Pelham and his gunners, along with some of Stuart's cavalry, tailed the retreating Federals through the blackness.

On the morning of September 2, Stuart's forces were joined by the brigade of Wade Hampton and James F. Hart's battery of six guns, who had been previously assigned to picket duty near Richmond. Although Pope's main body of troops had safely reached Alexandria, much of his cavalry and artillery remained in the Fairfax Court House area as a rearguard. Hampton's fresh sabers, accompanied by Hart's gunners, attacked the Federal rearguard at Flint Hill, two miles north of Fairfax. Pelham joined the fracas with two guns of his own. Speedily deploying his guns, Pelham began firing solid shot as Hampton unleashed his sharpshooters at the same time. Together their volley drove the Federals into a hasty retreat. As Stuart approached, he observed a number of farmhouses set ablaze by the scurrying bluecoats. Angered by the sight, Stuart turned to von Borcke and ordered, "bring up some of Pelham's guns at full gallop, that we may give a parting salute to these rascally incendiaries." Soon Pelham's gunners were shelling the rear of the Federal column with such accuracy that "leaving their dead and wounded, they galloped off in the greatest confusion."[20] With Hampton's brigade pouring in from the left joining Fitz Lee's Virginians, Jeb Stuart led the cavalry in hot pursuit. Meanwhile,

Pelham's gunners continued shelling over the heads of the Confederate riders into the retreating Federals. As Stuart's troopers rode into Fairfax Court House from one side, the escaping enemy departed the town from the opposite end.

Stuart later reported on the skirmish at Flint Hill: "Getting several pieces of the Stuart Horse Artillery in position, Brigadier-General Hampton opened on the enemy at that point, and our sharpshooters advancing about the same time, after a brief engagement the enemy hastily retired. They were immediately pursued, and Captain Pelham, having chosen a new position, again opened upon them with telling effect, scattering them in every direction."[21] Darkness and a concentrated fire from enemy infantry and artillery hidden in the woods halted further Confederate pursuit. The day had cost Stuart the loss of only one trooper.

Unbeknownst to the Confederate high command and perhaps to John Pope himself, President Lincoln and his general in chief, Henry Wager Halleck, held a meeting with George McClellan at 7:30 A.M. that same September 2. Lincoln spoke briefly on Pope's badly beaten army and its retreat and further informed Little Mac of the extreme peril facing the capital city. Then, according to McClellan, Lincoln "asked me if I would, under the circumstances, as a favor to him, resume command and do the best that could be done. Without one moment's hesitation . . . I at once said that I would accept the command and would stake my life that I would save the city."[22]

Later that afternoon, McClellan donned his finest dress uniform and rode out to confront the demoralized forces of Pope as they filed into Washington, D.C. Without exchanging words, Pope and McClellan saluted each other; Pope then rode off and the two Federal generals never saw one another again. Word spread rapidly of Little Mac's return, and the rejoicing resembled jubilation as line after line of exhausted soldiers obstreperously shouted their approval. "The effect of this man's presence upon the Army of the Potomac—in sunshine or rain, in darkness or in daylight, in victory or defeat—was electrical," wrote one admirer. "A Deliverer had come," penned another. "Men threw their caps high into the air, and danced and frolicked like school-boys."[23]

On the following day, Stuart sent Fitz Lee's brigade, accompanied by Pelham's battery, in the direction of the fleeing Federals. By the afternoon of September 3, they had ventured to within seven miles of Washington, D.C., as Pelham positioned his guns on Barrett's Hill overlooking the community of Falls Church. With no more Federals within firing range, Pelham pulled his guns back to the village of Dranesville the next day.

Later the next day Jeb Stuart sat down and penned a message to his wife, briefly describing his adventures of the previous few days: "Long before this reaches you I will be in Maryland. I have not been able to keep the list of the battles, much less give you any account of them. My present position on the banks of the Potomac will tell you volumes." Stuart then added a humorous postscript: "I send $200 in draft and $50 in notes. Can you pay my tailor bill?" He also jotted a quickly scrawled note in pencil: "The Horse Artillery has won imperishable laurels!"[24]

John Pope's star in the east had risen and descended at an amazingly rapid speed. Perhaps no other Civil War general found himself propelled so quickly to top command only to fall with such ignoble disgrace in so short a time. His bluster, grandiose statements, and insults to his troops targeted him as a marked man from the onset. With little camaraderie among his subordinate officers, his destiny was prophesied before the Second Manassas campaign commenced. To his own detriment too many of his generals displayed incompetence or a loyalty to George McClellan. In ridiculing the common soldiers, who fought valiantly throughout the campaign, Pope lost the thread of esprit de corps that, conversely, held the Army of Northern Virginia together so tightly. Furthermore, once in battle, Pope never understood his opponent. To him it was incomprehensible that the enemy would dare divide smaller numbers and have the audacity to attack. In disrespecting or disregarding the daring of a more skillful foe, Pope simply doomed himself.

Not unlike many losers, Pope refused to acknowledge his shortcomings and quickly blamed others. Yet, the negative tone of his subordinates, which seemed universally against Pope, revealed the true culprit in the Federal debacle at Second Manassas. "The campaign was destined to end in humiliation," snarled one of Pope's officers. Michigan general Alpheus S. Williams went further: "It can be said of [Pope] that he had not a friend in his command from the smallest drummer boy to the highest general officer. All <u>hated</u> him." "Great God how humiliating," wrote a Federal surgeon in a letter to his wife. "Pope is sunk lower than Hell—where he belongs."[25] Most admitted simply that Pope had been "outgeneraled."

Pope later offered his excuse for defeat, which resembled all too familiarly McClellan's feeble reports of his own disasters, in his written account: "At no time could I have hoped to fight a successful battle with the superior forces of the enemy which confronted me, and which were able at any time to outflank and bear my small army to the dust." As Pope passed from the scene, his last official orders, dated September 6, directed him to "proceed immediately" to the state of Minnesota in the Department of the Northwest where the bloody Santee Sioux Indian massacre was nearing its end.[26]

The Confederate side of the ledger for the Second Battle of Bull Run clearly evidenced positive claims. Robert E. Lee, in his first full campaign as commander of the Army of Northern Virginia, displayed boldness and clarity of thought unknown to most Federal leaders at this stage of the war. His magnificent leadership, willingness to take chances, and rare ability to force the enemy into mistakes had once again compelled a larger opponent into a disastrous defeat. Moreover, Lee's selection of Stonewall Jackson, James Longstreet, and Jeb Stuart as his chief subordinates had paid great dividends. Jackson rebounded from his sluggish moves on the peninsula and demonstrated brilliant precision and independent leadership. Long-street, although criticized by some for his sluggishness in moving to Jackson's sup-port, showed superiority in managing a large body of troops and a resourceful determination as a fighter once he resolved to go into action. As always, Stuart con-firmed his reputation as the tireless horseman who continued to outfight Federal troopers. Nor were the exceptional skills demonstrated by this quartet wasted on the thinking of the subordinates. "[Lee] & his round table of Generals are worthy of the immortality of Napoleon & his Marshalls," wrote Ham Chamberlayne to his mother. Young, talented General Dorsey Pender of A. P. Hill's "Light Division" seconded those thoughts: "Gen. Lee has shown great Generalship and the greatest boldness. There never was such a campaign, not even by Napoleon."[27]

Others, too, exhibited outstanding qualities, including John Bell Hood, A. P. Hill, Maxcy Gregg, Jubal Early, Stephen Dill Lee, and Richard Ewell—although Ewell's presence would be missing for months until he repaired from his leg ampu-tation. Lesser-ranked officers also received commendations from the top. One of those cited numerously was John Pelham. Perhaps, however, a compliment from the common soldier has more meaning. "It was something to be proud of, I can tell you," recounted one of Pelham's gunners. "You heard about Pelham everywhere you went. But it didn't surprise us a bit. We knew him and we trusted him. We would have followed him anywhere, I think. As a matter of fact, I guess we did."[28]

Following the battle, the Confederate army buried its dead and tended to the wounded. The jubilation of victory became tempered by the exhaustion of the pre-vious days' rigors. Most of Lee's army welcomed a much-needed rest. Lee, however, decided against relaxation and boldly determined to keep the initiative by carry-ing the war into the North. Justifying his decision, Lee said, "We cannot afford to be idle."

13
"The Lord Bless Your Dirty Ragged Souls"

If all goes well I hope that the war will be over soon.

—John Pelham

Encamped approximately thirty miles northwest of Washington, D.C., near the town of Leesburg, the Army of Northern Virginia awaited Robert E. Lee's call to action. During the brief interim between battles, fresh troops had been added to Lee's command. From Richmond came Daniel Harvey Hill with two divisions of infantry. Also Wade Hampton's brigade of horsemen became a permanent fixture for Jeb Stuart's cavalry. The batteries of Roger Preston Chew and James F. Hart now augmented Pelham's horse artillery. Beverly Robertson's transfer placed his cavalry brigade in the capable hands of Colonel Tom T. Munford, an 1852 graduate of Virginia Military Institute. Extraordinary fighting men all, but certain questions persisted. Did Lee have sufficient numbers to invade enemy soil against an opposing army known to be vastly larger than his own? Was the physical condition of Lee's men up to the enormous challenge before them, especially considering the extent of abuse they suffered in the preceding campaign? Certainly Lee's confidence held as he stated of his army, shortly after entering Maryland, "the material of which it is composed is the best in the world, and, if properly disciplined and instructed, would be able successfully to resist any force that could be brought against it."[1]

Pelham spent his hours preparing and conditioning his men, horses, and equipment for the campaign ahead. From his campsite at Goose Creek, near Leesburg, Pelham found time to pen a letter to his parents. "We whipped General Pope last week at Manassas," he wrote. "Now General Lee is leading us into Northern territory. Tomorrow we'll cross the Potomac and enter Maryland, where they tell us a lot of men are anxious to join our cause. I understand that General Jackson wants to invade Pennsylvania in order to strike the coal mines and railroads so as to cripple the enemy's industry and transportation. If all goes well I hope that the war will be over soon and then we can all be together again—at least that is my prayer."[2]

While awaiting orders, the soldiers found few victuals to sate their appetites, but as one of Jackson's men noted, "We heard with delight of the 'plenty' to be had in Maryland." Word arrived on September 4, and the Army of Northern Virginia, with Jackson's command in the lead, exited Leesburg. In a farewell gesture one elderly woman stood "with upraised hands, and with tears in her eyes exclaimed: 'The Lord bless your dirty ragged souls!'"[3] Marching five miles north to White's Ferry, the army began wading through the Potomac River into Maryland.

For many Confederates the invasion of Northern soil seemed to violate their religious principles. The Almighty had certainly favored the defense of their homeland with a string of powerful victories; however, the crossing of the Potomac might bode less favorably in the eyes of their Maker. Therefore, far too many of Lee's soldiers refused to tempt fate and simply stayed on the Southern side of the Potomac, alongside those too weak to keep up, leaving Lee's army a skeletal force of thirty-seven thousand. Yet, those who chose to set foot into Maryland appeared to delight in their own self-assurance. Stuart's three brigades of cavalry stayed at Dranesville until the following day and then rode to White's Ford, where they began splashing into the cool waters of the Potomac.

The cavalry took most of two hours in crossing, while Pelham and his horse artillery waited patiently for their turn. Near midnight the guns were hauled into position, and the arduous work commenced. The river at White's Ford was four hundred yards wide and approximately two-and-a-half feet deep, causing Pelham's men great difficulty in pulling their heavy cannon across. Fortunately, an island, nearly a half-mile wide, sat in the middle. This offered much help, as the gunners labored to haul the cannon onto the island before shoving into the waters again. Finally, with the task completed, the weary artillerists stretched out under a grove of trees and bivouacked for the rest of the night. They would catch up with the cavalry after daylight. The cavalry and horse artillery rendezvoused near Poolesville the following day, as the main army, stretching more than twenty miles in length, marched toward Frederick, Maryland. Badly in need of horses since the exhaustive campaign at Second Manassas, Pelham added twenty-eight fresh ones on September 6.

The following morning Stuart divided his cavalry into three segments, each taking a battery of Pelham's horse artillery, and spread them out on a twenty-mile line to seal off any roads between the main army and McClellan's Federals. Pelham and his battery went with Fitz Lee's brigade to New Market, some twenty miles to the north, to guard the main road between Frederick and Baltimore. Stuart, meanwhile, rode to the quaint town of Urbana, seven miles east of Frederick, to establish his headquarters.

As the bulk of the Army of Northern Virginia marched into Frederick, curiosity aroused the townspeople to turn out in large numbers and witness the transit of this mythical, seemingly invincible force. Although their battle record was nearly flawless, Lee's ragamuffin veterans presented a startlingly unkempt sight to the Marylanders. "They were the dirtiest, lousiest, filthiest, piratical-looking cutthroat men I ever saw," noted one young man of Frederick. "A ragged, lean, and hungry set of wolves. Yet there was a dash about them that the Northern men lacked. They rode like circus riders." Over one-third of them remained shoeless, and often, uniforms were threadbare. Many wore blue Union uniforms confiscated during the preceding campaign. Not surprisingly, the lack of proper diet, together with the exhausting previous weeks of struggle, debilitated the Rebels and gave them a skeletal appearance. A Confederate private poignantly wrote: "there was not a man whose form had not caved in, and who had not a bad attack of diarrhea. Our under-clothes were foul and hanging in strips, our socks were worn out, and half the men were bare-footed, many were lame."[4]

Despite their appearance, an air of confidence prevailed in their mannerisms and attitudes. They, too, seemed to know they were the best army on the continent. Strict orders had been issued against any form of theft or vandalism, and the Rebels, for the most part, adhered to these dictates. "I saw thousands of troops pass the very orchards, whose red and golden burdens overhung the road," noted J. F. J. Caldwell proudly, "without touching a fruit." Still many of the native Marylanders viewed the Confederate army as a frightening invader. "They fear us with a mortal terror," noted one Rebel. "Many of them seem to think us Goths and Vandals and Huns, they tremble sometimes when spoken to, and are astonished to see us without the torch and tomahawk."[5]

Naturally, attention was drawn toward the patrician leaders of this army: Lee, the gentlemanly yet audacious commander; Longstreet, the solid warrior of unsurpassed steadiness; Jackson, whose skills by now were legendary; and Stuart, whose flamboyance and rare ability set him apart from all other horsemen. Oddly, three of these leaders had suffered recent injuries, rendering them less than the titans depicted in newspapers. On August 31, Lee's hands were painfully hurt from a fall. Longstreet had rubbed an ugly sore on his heel, causing a severe limp. Jackson, presented a new horse on September 6, proceeded to spur the animal, which inadvertently fell backward, sending the rider sprawling to the ground in a heap. For the next few days his pain was conspicuous by his board-like gait and occasional wincing. Only Stuart remained healthy on the trek into Maryland.

Pelham soon joined Stuart at Urbana, where the general had established his headquarters. On Sunday, September 7, the artillerist celebrated his twenty-fourth birthday. As a surprise present, gunner Moses A. Febrey brought in a huge pig, which a few culinary artists began roasting. Although Confederates had been forbidden to steal from Maryland civilians, Febrey explained his felonious adventure by saying the pig had "attacked him," and thus he killed it in "self-defense." This brought hearty laughter from Pelham and those lucky enough to join in the repast of barbecued pork later that day. Although the hardships of the war had tested Pelham's manhood and pushed his endurance to the limit, he retained his boyish good looks and youthfulness. One old Maryland farmer attested to the innocence of Pelham's appearance by observing the beardless face, girlish smile, and slender figure, and

then skeptically remarking to Jeb Stuart, "Can these boys fight?"[6] Pelham's aptitude for battle, as well as the fighting spirit of the entire Army of Northern Virginia, would be severely tested beyond their wildest imagination in little more than
a week.

For a few brief days Stuart and his staff officers enjoyed the cordiality of a Mr.
Cockey, a local Confederate sympathizer, who generously offered the lovely, shady
grounds surrounding his home as a campsite. Cockey's attractive daughters, Martha
and Virginia, anxious to meet Stuart and the other handsome officers, made certain the strangers felt welcome. By chance the girls' cousin, a red-haired beauty
named Ann, was visiting from her native state of New York. Ann belied her Northern heritage by admitting her allegiance to the Southern persuasion, which further
endeared her to both Stuart and von Borcke. Stuart took particular pleasure in
teasing Ann for "deserting" her cause and nicknamed her the "New York Rebel."
Von Borcke seemed smitten by her charms and followed her around as though tied
by a leash. During the evenings, Pelham commonly walked arm in arm with the
beautiful dark-haired Virginia, while his dashing lieutenant, James Breathed, accompanied Martha. Stuart, von Borcke, and the "New York Rebel" often joined in
these moonlight walks.[7]

The hours passed by quickly, and the thoughts of war naturally subsided in the
splendor of these exquisite settings. One such stroll brought them to the Female
Academy at Urbana, located on the edge of the village and deserted since the war's
beginning. Von Borcke described it as a "large building, crowning the summit of
a gentle hill . . . from which a broad avenue of trees sloped downwards to the principal street. . . . Each story of the house had its ample verandah running round it,
and from the highest of these we had a magnificent view of the village and the surrounding country." The extraordinary grandeur of the murky structure suddenly
snapped Stuart from his pensive mood. Turning to von Borcke, his excitement could
not be concealed. "Major," he nearly shouted, "what a capital place for us to give a
ball in honour of our arrival in Maryland!" All readily agreed with the date set for
the following night. With little time for preparation, Stuart and the Prussian divided up the duties. "I undertook to make all necessary arrangements for the illumination and decoration of the hall, the issuing of the cards of invitation," wrote
von Borcke, "leaving to Stuart the matter of the music, which he gladly consented
to provide."[8]

The following day, September 8, as von Borcke hastily organized a decorating
committee for the dance hall, Robert E. Lee, at his headquarters in Frederick, issued an official statement to the people of Maryland. Carefully worded, it expressed Lee's political objectives for entering Maryland and assured the citizens of
the state that his intentions were noble. Explicitly Lee listed the violations of rights
"usurped" upon these people "with scorn and contempt" by the Federal government. Of his own mission he wrote, "our Army has come among you, and is pre-

pared to assist you with the power of its arms in regaining the rights of which you have been despoiled. . . . No constraint upon your free will is intended, no intimidation will be allowed."[9]

While the grim business of war continued from the top commander's headquarters, Stuart's staff officers prepared for the "Sabers and Roses Ball" at Urbana. All day von Borcke, assisted by Pelham, Breathed, and various officers, worked diligently at sweeping and airing out the dusty academy building. Von borrowed regimental battle flags to decorate the dingy walls and saw to it that roses "festooned" the place to detract from the musty odor. Candles, held in ornate brass containers, illuminated the room. Over the entrance doors Pelham added a decorative touch by attaching two large colored lanterns. Invitations had been sent out by von Borcke to all the available ladies of the neighborhood, no matter what their allegiance in the war. As promised, Stuart provided the musicians, as the Eighteenth Mississippi Infantry band showed up. Scheduled to begin at 7:00 P.M., it could not go unnoticed that a full moon arose that warm September night.[10]

Pelham and Breathed, attired in their finest dress uniforms, called at Mr. Cockey's home to fetch Martha and Virginia. Von Borcke made his obligatory stop there as well to escort the "New York Rebel." A large array of guests arrived at the academy for the promised gaiety of the evening. Although expecting no difficulty, "The officers came prepared for any emergency, fully armed and equipped," according to Blackford, "picketing their horses in the yard and hanging their sabres against the walls of the dance hall." Stuart officially began the merriment by welcoming everyone and declaring he had the honor of leading the Grand March into the hall while the musicians struck up a rousing chorus of "Dixie." "Amid the loud applause of the numerous invited and uninvited guests," wrote the proud von Borcke, "we now made our grand entree into the large hall, which was brilliantly lighted with tallow candles."[11]

Sometime near 11:00 P.M., the dancing abruptly halted as the rumbling of cannon and faint clatter of rifle shots echoed in the distance. Almost as suddenly, a courier entered the hall to inform Stuart that Federal cavalry had surprised Wade Hampton's pickets on the outpost. Females and guests fairly panicked, as the Confederate cavalrymen quickly buckled on their sabers and made for their horses outside. Stuart calmly announced that the dance would proceed as soon as these bluecoats were attended to. Within five minutes spurs kicked horseflesh, and the Rebels departed eastward.

Five companies of the First New York Cavalry had indeed run into the First North Carolina, under the command of Colonel Laurence Simmons Baker, along the Washington pike near Hyattstown, merely three miles from Urbana. Although Baker's forces had temporarily halted the bluecoats, Stuart, according to von Borcke, ordered Pelham and his gunners forward to fire canister in the direction of the Federals. "Pelham, with his guns in favourable position," stated the Prussian, "was soon pouring a rapid fire upon their columns." Then Stuart sent in his cavalry to finish the job. The task appeared easy, yet both sides accrued casualties. With the situation quelled, Jeb led his would-be dancers back to Urbana.[12]

By 1:00 A.M. the horsemen arrived at the academy to find most of the ladies anxiously waiting. Stuart's riders scurried through the sleepy town, summoning those who had departed. The musicians picked up their instruments, and the sounds of gaiety once again swelled into the night air. At 4:00 A.M. the trampling of heavy feet at the doorway attracted the attention of Blackford's dancing partner who "clasped her hands and uttered a piercing scream," as stretcher bearers hauled wounded men inside from the earlier skirmish. Quickly, the academy became a hospital as the ladies "like a flock of angels in their white dresses . . . bent over the wounded men, dressing their wounds . . . with their pretty fingers all stained with blood."[13]

~

On Tuesday, September 9, Robert E. Lee summoned Stonewall Jackson to his headquarters, where he outlined the boldest of plans. Lee proposed separating his army on enemy soil with Jackson capturing Harpers Ferry. In Lee's mind the plan made sense: the twelve thousand Federals garrisoned at Harpers Ferry offered a serious threat to the Army of Northern Virginia's rear. Besides, valuable supplies awaited there, necessities that reluctant Marylanders had been thus far hesitant to part with. Jackson nodded his approval. James Longstreet suddenly appeared at Lee's tent and listened to the details. Knowing McClellan's larger Army of the Potomac lurked somewhere to their front, Old Pete voiced his opposition. Lee listened patiently to Longstreet's rejection but overruled. The blueprint remained the same.

Lee dictated Special Orders No. 191 to his adjutants, who in turn made eight handwritten copies to distribute to his highest-ranking generals. The daring strategy authorized Lee's army to be split five ways. The plan called for three separate columns, all under Jackson's overall leadership, to converge on Harpers Ferry from different directions. One would capture Bolivar Heights to the west, another would seize the 1,462-foot Maryland Heights to the east, and a third would scale 1,190-foot Loudoun Heights to the south of the town across the Shenandoah River. This entire endeavor involved twenty-six of Lee's forty brigades. Having little communication on the march, these three forces would coordinate their movements on the Federals at Harpers Ferry, force the surrender of the town by September 12, and return to Lee's army in seventy-two hours—a near impossible task by Lee's timetable. Meanwhile, Lee further gambled by dividing his remaining army into two parts. Longstreet's command was ordered to Boonsboro with the reserves and supply trains. (He would later be directed another thirteen miles northwest to Hagerstown.) Finally, Daniel Harvey Hill's division, sent to South Mountain, formed the rearguard, protecting the scattered armies from the Federals. Jeb Stuart's cavalry would be split among the various armies to assist them in their assignments.[14] John

Pelham with one of his three batteries, along with Tom Rosser, heading the Fifth Virginia Cavalry, was sent to aid Hill at South Mountain. The following day constituted the target date for putting the plans into action. Continuing to realize the enormous danger of the plans, Longstreet, through gritted teeth, stated to Lee, "General, I wish we could stand still and let the damned Yankees come to us!"[15]

Reading over their individual copies of Special Orders No. 191, each general obviously recognized the overwhelming importance of secrecy. "I was so impressed with the disastrous consequence which might result from its loss," wrote John Walker, "that I pinned it securely in an inside pocket . . . Longstreet, as an absolutely sure precaution . . . memorized the order and then 'chewed it up.'"[16] Sitting by a campfire, Jackson memorized his copy and destroyed it in the flames. What the others did with their copies remains unknown. What is known, and what could possibly alter the course of history, is that Stonewall Jackson, mistakenly believing that D. H. Hill would not receive a copy, handwrote a duplicate and had it sent to Hill's headquarters.

Lee's confidence would have only been bolstered had he known that McClellan, whose 87,000-man army outnumbered his own by 50,000, still deluded himself in believing the Confederates had the superior numbers. This ill-conceived conclusion was fostered by McClellan's own imagination as well as the reports of his scouts. Alfred Pleasonton, chief of McClellan's cavalry, reported on September 9, "Jackson crossed with 80,000 men and Longstreet with about 30,000."[17] Jackson's forces began moving out of Frederick by daylight of September 10. Other Confederate columns were soon on the move.

In the meantime Pelham had stayed busy. On September 9 his artillerists fired a few shells at the pesky New Yorkers just east of Hyattstown, but nothing more of consequence occurred. The following day the upstart Empire Staters left the region, satisfied that they had caused Stuart's forces enough grief for the time being. This allowed Pelham, a few of his gunners, and the Fifth Virginia Cavalry under Colonel Tom Rosser to wander along the National Pike unimpeded. In the area of Poplar Springs these Confederates, evidently with Pelham's approval, began raiding the barns of local farmers with the intent of taking the finest horses for their use—the justification being that the campaign ahead would be most strenuous and the horse artillery needed these animals.[18]

On September 11 a chilly, steady rain fell on the marching troops, dampening their bodies but not their spirits. That same day Stuart received orders to pull his remaining cavalry out of Urbana and act as a rearguard for the Confederate forces heading toward Boonsboro and Hagerstown. Shortly after 2:00 P.M. Yankee cavalrymen entered the village where, only three days earlier, Rebel officers had enjoyed the music and dancing. Saturday, September 13, began as a typical fall day. Although hours behind schedule, the three individual columns investing Harpers

Ferry neared their destination. Together the three armies could blast the Federals into submission, but more precious hours would be required to complete their mission. Meanwhile, Longstreet's forces remained at Hagerstown while D. H. Hill continued to guard the passes at South Mountain.

Stuart's responsibilities, of course, loomed equally large as his troopers screened the invading Confederate forces, scouted the roads for elements of the Federal army, and acted as the rearguard for Lee's men. Fitz Lee's cavalry, assisted by Pelham and part of his gunners, headed toward the area of Hamburg by crossing the Monocacy River north of Frederick. Orders soon arrived from Stuart directing Lee and Pelham to move farther north of Frederick, scout the Federals in the area, and possibly move to outflank the enemy where found. Running into a strong detachment of bluecoats, Lee determined that the flanking maneuver could not be accomplished and decided to move back through Hamburg. Along the way as darkness fell, Pelham inexplicably separated from the others and became lost. Upon Fitz Lee's arrival at his destination, Pelham, to the amazement and concern of the others, was nowhere to be found. His capture by the Federals became the inevitable conclusion. "We were greatly distressed at learning that the leader of our horse-artillery, Major Pelham, who had marched with Fitz Lee, had been cut off, and was a prisoner in the enemy's hands," wrote von Borcke. Much relief was indicated when, the following morning, Pelham arrived at the campsite without explanation. "He turned up," related the joyful Prussian, "having cut his way through the Yankee lines, and saved himself by his never-failing coolness and intrepidity."[19]

Near dusk that same evening of September 13, a civilian stranger on horseback approached Stuart's pickets near Turner's Gap claiming he had a message of utmost importance for the general. Shown to Stuart's tent, the man told an unbelievable story. Before noon in Frederick, he said, McClellan had been in an informal discussion with a few businessmen of the town, when suddenly he was interrupted by another officer who handed him a piece of paper. McClellan, according to the stranger, raised his arms, as if victorious, and shouted that he knew Lee's intentions in Maryland. Inconceivably, Little Mac held a copy of Special Orders No. 191! Exactly how the paper, soon known as the Lost Order (or Lost Dispatch), came into Federal hands was unknown by the man, but this seemed to interest Stuart little. Stuart's immediate concern centered on the extreme peril of Lee's divided forces. Lee must be notified at once. Two hours passed before a rider reached Lee at Hagerstown with the ominous news.[20]

With his army spread out, separated by as much as twenty-five miles in mountainous terrain with sprawling rivers, Lee refused to panic. He ordered Longstreet to move his divisions at dawn to Boonsboro in support of D. H. Hill, whose defense of the South Mountain passes against McClellan's advancing forces became crucial. Longstreet balked, maintaining his men would be worn out by the thirteen-mile march and in no condition to fight. The commanding general overruled. Next

Lee sent orders to Stuart: "The gap [Turner's] must be held at all hazards until the operations at Harper's Ferry are finished."[21]

The story of the Lost Order began when McClellan's Army of the Potomac marched into Frederick on the morning of September 13. Townspeople, who had welcomed Lee's army only a few days before, now greeted the Federals. At this point McClellan remained in doubt concerning Lee's intentions. Soldiers pitched tents on the outskirts of town in the same area where Confederate debris still littered the countryside from their own evacuated campsites. As McClellan's soldiers rested, two of them noticed a curiosity: three cigars in the grass, seemingly wrapped with paper. The cigars proved a prize for the soldiers, but the paper revealed an astonishing title: "Headquarters, Army of Northern Virginia. . . . Special Orders No. 191." The treasured paper soon made its way through the chain of command to George McClellan.

Little Mac's reaction and relative inactivity concerning the Lost Order have been well documented. McClellan dispatched a message, brimming with confidence, to President Lincoln: "I have the whole rebel force in front of me, but am confident, and no time shall be lost. . . . I think Lee has made a gross mistake, and that he will be severely punished for it. The army is in motion as rapidly as possible. . . . I have all the plans of the rebels, and will catch them in their own trap." Certainly, McClellan held the trump cards: a numerical superiority of fifty thousand men, fighting on his own soil, and now, the full knowledge and position of his enemy's widely separated army. Perhaps no general in history had the advantages of McClellan. "Had Lee whispered into the Federal General's ear his inmost plans," wrote Moxley Sorrel, "the latter could have asked for nothing more than the information brought him on that fatal paper."[22]

For all the information revealed by the Lost Order, two items of particular consequence went unmentioned by the paper: Longstreet's forces being located at Hagerstown and, more important, the manpower of Lee's individual divisions. Consequently, McClellan continued to believe that Lee had superior numbers. Later that evening, McClellan evidenced this fabricated notion in a wire to Washington, D.C.: "It may, therefore, in my judgment, be regarded as certain that this rebel army, which I have good reasons for believing amounts to 120,000 or more." Furthermore, Little Mac appears to have fallen under the mystique of Lee's invincibility that fatally harmed so many other leaders of the Union army before and after McClellan. In McClellan's words, "[Lee] was a general not to be trifled with or carelessly afforded an opportunity of striking a fatal blow."[23] Whatever evoked caution in Little Mac, he mysteriously refused to budge his army during September 13 after promising bold movement. Thus, Lee's army was given a reprieve, albeit it a momentary one.

A final question remains concerning the missing copy of Special Orders No. 191: Who lost it? Evidence appears inconclusive as to the actual culprit, although for years D. H. Hill received the blame since the Lost Order was specifically addressed to him. W. W. Blackford clearly states in his book, "Gen. D. H. Hill, in leaving his camp, dropped this order and it fell into the hands of McClellan." Hill vehemently denied ever seeing the copy from Lee's headquarters, but he readily admitted receiving the duplicate handwritten copy from Stonewall Jackson. This copy he retained until his death as "evidence" of his truthfulness.[24] In all likelihood the facts will never be known.

D. H. Hill's immediate dilemma was not so much defending himself regarding the Lost Order but the near impossible task of defending South Mountain against McClellan's inevitable attack. South Mountain, a spur of the Blue Ridge, stands northeast to southwest across Maryland and reaches an elevation of 1,300 feet. Three roads, bisecting this formidable height, run roughly parallel to one another: National Road at Turner's Gap to the north, Old Sharpsburg Road at Fox's Gap in the middle, and Burkittsville Road at Crampton's Gap to the south. On the morning of September 14, Hill's small army, teamed with Stuart's cavalry and Pelham's horse artillery, were all that stood between McClellan's advancing army from the east and Lee's still scattered forces on the western side of the mountain. The obstinate and sometimes cantankerous Hill realized his precarious assignment was "to prevent the escape of the Yankees from Harpers Ferry . . . and also to guard the pass in the Blue Ridge near Boonsborough."[25] Longstreet's divisions left Hagerstown to the northwest at dawn that morning, en route to Hill's rescue. But, until they arrived, nearly nine hours later, the onus fell on Hill and his thinly drawn lines.

Exactly which passes to guard and how strongly to fortify them with sparse forces troubled Hill, as each crossing held its own importance. Turner's Gap, the main thoroughfare, stretched directly toward Boonsboro and the direction from which Longstreet would be coming. Here Hill placed his strongest force, a mere three thousand men. Six miles south lay Crampton's Gap, where a Federal capture would split the Confederates at Harpers Ferry from Longstreet's advancing army. Hill assigned Colonel William A. Parham's regiment to its defense, along with Tom Munford's cavalry and Roger Chew's battery of horse artillery. Fox's Gap, a mile south of Turner's, necessitated attention since its capture would allow Federals to break through the center and outflank the defenders at Turner's Gap. To this post Hill designated the five regiments of Brigadier General Samuel Garland's brigade. Tom Rosser's Fifth Virginia Cavalry and John Pelham's battery joined Garland. Collectively stretched to the limit, the inadequate force of Rebels awaited the onslaught. The possible fate of the Confederacy hinged on their ability to defend South Mountain.

At 9:00 in the morning the battle for the mountain commenced. At Crampton's Gap Federal general William B. Franklin began moving his Sixth Corps of twelve thousand men toward the Confederates, who were outnumbered ten to one. For several hours the valiant underdogs, with the support of reinforcements, held their position against the sporadic attacks. However, sheer numbers determined the outcome at this sector. Soon the Confederates broke, falling back to the western side of the slope. Luckily, Franklin overestimated the enemy strength and eventually halted his assault.

Meanwhile, Federal forces, commanded by Ambrose Burnside, hit Hill's small army of defenders at Turner's Gap. As this portion of the battle developed, Burnside detoured part of the Ninth Corps, led by Brigadier General Jesse Reno, toward Fox's Gap. Awaiting them, Samuel Garland spread out his five regiments of mostly inexperienced North Carolinians on both sides of the Old Sharpsburg Road. Pelham, always with an eye for favorable terrain, positioned his cannons at the edge of some woods that overlooked the Federals. Close by, Tom Rosser dismounted his men and stationed them solidly behind a stone fence. While his gunners anxiously watched the deployment of the Federals, Pelham calmly reminded the men to shoot low. Suddenly, the Yankees surged forward, and Pelham ordered his artillerists to open fire. For several stunning seconds the cannon shots disoriented the Federal attackers. Regrouping, the Federals came on again. This time Garland's Tarheels sent a volley into the advancing bluecoats, who fought back with renewed vigor. The thirty-one-year-old Garland, once referred to by D. H. Hill as "the most fearless man I ever knew," received an ugly head wound from an enemy sharpshooter and fell to the ground in writhing agony. A few inaudible orders issued from his trembling lips before he died. Without their leader many of the raw Carolinians fled for safety down the opposite side of the mountain. Others bravely fought on until their ammunition ran out before surrendering. On the verge of extinction, the remaining Confederates courageously held their ground and suffered to regain some order.

Luckily, Pelham's accurate gunners, assisted by a lone battery of the Jeff Davis Artillery from a position about five hundred yards south and to the front of Pelham, continued to find the range on the Federals. Their persistent blasts hindered the advance and fooled the Union leaders into thinking they faced several batteries. Rosser's Virginians, meanwhile, stood up from behind the stone fence and unleashed numerous volleys the deluded Yankees believed came from reinforcements. Pelham then pulled his guns farther back to a safer position and blasted shell and canister, adding to the enemy confusion. The ruse worked as Federal commanders stalled the attack for the next two hours. As the sun began to set, Federal reinforcements arrived and attempted a last push to capture the Old Sharpsburg Road. Rosser's troopers continued to fire a steady barrage as Pelham's guns, according to one Confederate general, were "speedily placed in position a short distance in our rear on the Braddock [Old Sharpsburg] road. A few well-directed shot and shell drove the enemy up the hill, leaving the road in our possession." The fighting ended on that successful note. Rosser's Fifth Virginia cavalrymen and Pelham with two guns covered the withdrawal from Fox's Gap before pulling back toward Boonsboro.[26]

Lead elements of Longstreet's column began arriving from Hagerstown at 3:30 P.M. It was none too soon as the beleaguered Confederates atop South Mountain were nearly spent from over six hours of battle. Upon their arrival, Hill directed them to Fox's Gap, where Pelham's battery had helped stave off a Union victory all afternoon. Among the vanguard, John Hood's Texas Brigade surged forward and demonstrated once more why it was considered by many to be Lee's most feared fighting unit. The battle continued with neither side giving in to the fury of the other. On into the darkness, Confederate reinforcements, aided by their regrouped artillery, mounted counterattacks that held the Federals from their objective.

That night Lee, Longstreet, and D. H. Hill all deemed it best to abandon South Mountain before daylight. Lee's plan for the invasion of Pennsylvania had to be discarded, and by midnight Confederate forces began withdrawing toward the town of Sharpsburg, ten miles southwest of Boonsboro. During the retreat, Stuart's cavalry and Pelham's battery served as rearguard to hinder any thoughts of McClellan's army pursuing. With their duties completed, Stuart's cavalry rendezvoused at Boonsboro. The battle for South Mountain had ended with significant losses for both sides. The Federals numbered 325 killed, 1,403 wounded, and 85 missing, totaling 1,813; Confederate casualties included 325 killed, 1,560 wounded, and 800 missing for an aggregate 2,685. The following morning Federals witnessed the awful scenes of the previous day's fight. Clusters of bodies lay in various areas of the mountain showing the agony of their deaths by the grim looks on their stilled faces. The burial of the dead was left to the Union forces.

McClellan openly displayed extreme delight with the results of the battle, calling it a "glorious victory" and referring to the Confederates as "demoralized." True, he had taken South Mountain, but D. H. Hill's stubborn defense had given Lee an additional twenty-four hours, invaluable time to gather his forces and for Stonewall Jackson to complete his task at Harpers Ferry. If, in fact, McClellan won at South Mountain, the Confederates were saved by their own defeat. Little Mac assuredly wasted the colossal advantage of Special Orders No. 191.

Abraham Lincoln, too, appeared elated with McClellan's announcement of success. "God bless you, and all with you," wired Lincoln. "Destroy the rebel army," then the President added ominously, "if possible." In the meantime, Robert E. Lee realized his predicament and ordered his scattered forces to return to Virginia. Only this decision could hope to save his army. However, a welcome message arrived, dated "Near 8 A.M., September 15, 1862," which caused Lee to change his mind. "Through God's blessing," read the note from Stonewall Jackson, "Harpers Ferry and its garrison are to be surrendered. . . . The . . . forces can move off this evening [as] soon as they get their rations. To what point shall they move?"[27] Bolstered by this uplifting news, Lee rescinded his order to retreat and sent word to Jackson to head to Sharpsburg as soon as his business at Harpers Ferry concluded. Survival depended on Jackson's final capture of Harpers Ferry and his return to the Army of Northern Virginia.

That same morning, McClellan, with the way now open, put his forces into action, sending them through the gaps at South Mountain. Pelham, who had rejoined Fitz Lee's cavalry during the night, watched from concealment along the National Turnpike as the Federals poured through Turner's Gap toward Boonsboro. To gain additional time for the Confederates to concentrate at Sharpsburg, Pelham's battery, along with Fitz Lee's sharpshooters, attempted to hold back the Federals. Severely outnumbered, Fitz's cavalrymen were forced to retreat, but Pelham's gunners unleashed a barrage that temporarily stunned the bluecoats. Returning the fire, the Federals regrouped and came on a second time. This forced Pelham to seek new ground a few hundred yards back. Here he helped support the Third Virginia Cavalry under the command of Lieutenant Colonel John T. Thornton. Federal forces eventually pushed the Rebels back into Boonsboro, where other dismounted Confederate troopers of the Ninth Virginia stood idly waiting orders, unaware of the advancing Federals. Soon the rearguard, "retreating at full speed," rode headlong into the stunned members of the Ninth, so that "the street became packed with a mass of horses and horsemen, so jammed together as to make motion impossible for most of them." A narrow, covered bridge that funneled traffic at the south end of the town made conditions even worse. As chaos prevailed for awhile at the bridge, much of the turmoil was alleviated when Pelham placed his guns in a defensive stance to deter any Federals from advancing. Luckily for him, and the somewhat embarrassed troopers of Fitz Lee, the Federals slowed their pursuit.[28]

While Confederate cavalrymen hurried to escape, Pelham and Fitz Lee made another stand to hinder the surging Federals along the road leading southwest to Keedysville. Firing a last few rounds, Pelham ordered his men to limber the guns and proceed toward Sharpsburg. Although overwhelmed and forced to retreat, the Confederates had performed a critically important service: two parts of Robert E. Lee's army had crossed Antietam Creek and safely reached Sharpsburg. The remaining three continued their mission at Harpers Ferry.

⁓

Surrounded by elevations, Harpers Ferry remained an indefensible location, a "death trap," and the garrison at Harpers Ferry awaited the inevitable. Stonewall Jackson, who had been stationed there early in the war, freely acknowledged that he would "rather take it forty times than to undertake to defend it once."[29]

When Jackson penned his note to Lee on the morning of September 15, his three Confederate columns had surrounded Harpers Ferry. Jackson's troops had captured Bolivar Heights and now positioned guns pointed directly at the town. John

Walker's division had scaled Loudoun Heights only to find no Federals had been stationed there. With five rifled guns, Walker faced Harpers Ferry from across the Shenandoah River. Lafayette McLaws's men confronted 1,600 Union soldiers defending Maryland Heights, as well as the unenviable task of scaling the formidable mountain. Driving the Federals off Maryland Heights proved easier than the enormous difficulty of dragging cannons up the elevation, but McLaws's soldiers did just that. With all three summits well fortified, Jackson now ordered an artillery barrage, and shortly the Federals raised a white flag signifying defeat. Jackson demanded an "unconditional surrender" and then generously paroled all the Federals, allowing the officers to retain their sidearms and personal baggage.

Besides the more than 11,000 prisoners taken at Harpers Ferry, other spoils added greatly to the Confederate victory: 13,000 small arms, 73 cannon, over 1,200 mules, and 200 wagons loaded with assorted supplies—and at a loss of only 39 killed and 247 wounded. Once again, much like Manassas Junction, Jackson's men feasted. "We fared sumptuously," noted one. "In addition to meat, crackers, sugar, coffee, shoes, blankets, underclothing, &c., many of us captured horses roaming at large, on whom to transport our plunder."[30] While the men enjoyed their capture, Jackson sent a message to Robert E. Lee verifying the triumph. Awaiting Lee's response, Jackson handled the formalities of the surrender, thanked God, and found time to write his wife. The news from Harpers Ferry could not have been more meaningful to Lee's downcast and troubled veterans.

By 1:00 A.M. on September 16 Jackson put his column on the road out of Harpers Ferry heading north toward Sharpsburg, seventeen miles distant. A. P. Hill's division remained behind, attending to the parole of the Federal prisoners and caring for the captured supplies. The divisions of John Walker and Lafayette McLaws, still positioned on their respective elevations, soon pulled out and began marching toward Lee's army as well. All three columns, therefore, would reach Sharpsburg at different times. Meanwhile, Lee sat with fourteen Confederate brigades facing six corps of the Army of the Potomac. One immutable fact persisted: if McClellan attacked before the divisions at Harpers Ferry arrived, the Army of Northern Virginia was doomed. Fortunately for the Confederates, Little Mac foolishly kept inactive for hours.[31]

After an all-night march, Jackson's bone-weary men reached Sharpsburg by noon of September 16. Quietly, they slid into the cool grass for a much-needed rest. Their arrival heartened the spirits of Lee's men and brought the Confederate strength up to twenty-two brigades. Walker's men came in during the afternoon, but McLaws's ten brigades were still on the way. When Walker approached Robert E. Lee, he fully expected the commanding general to be "anxious and careworn," but to his surprise, he found Lee "calm, dignified, and even cheerful."[32]

That day Jeb Stuart and John Pelham had wisely selected a prominence, known as Nicodemus Heights,[33] to place Pelham's guns. It was to be a most fortuitous decision, as these heights would control much of the following day's fighting. This rise lay one and a half miles north of Sharpsburg on Lee's extreme left and fronted Hagerstown Road. Only four cannon remained with Pelham since James Hart's and Roger Chew's batteries were with Hampton's and Munford's brigades. By now Joseph Hooker's First Corps had crossed the Antietam at Upper Bridge and, armed with ten batteries, moved forward to the Joseph Poffenberger farm.

Near dusk the Pennsylvania Reserves pushed even farther ahead to the farmhouse near the North Woods. Suddenly the Keystone Staters came under attack from Nicodemus Heights as Pelham's gunners opened up with a cannon barrage. Abner Doubleday ordered more of his brigade forward and later reported, "As we came on, we were assailed by one of the enemy's advanced batteries, the first discharge wounding several of [Marsena] Patrick's men and dismounting three orderlies." Patrick assessed the situation similarly: "Although taking no part in the action, several of my men were wounded by the enemy's fire before and while taking position in the wood." Federal artillerists now answered with hot metal of their own. Confederate G. W. Beale of the Ninth Virginia Cavalry remembered "shells from two directions were passing over our heads, their burning fuses gleaming like meteors." William Allan described the brief fight as "spirited" with darkness ending the duel. "The affair," according to Allan, "was hardly more than a skirmish between the advance of the two armies."[34] Inexplicably, Hooker, a veteran soldier, either did not fathom the advantage of controlling Nicodemus Heights or simply chose to ignore its considerable importance. His report that "[Jackson] planted field batteries on high ground on our right and rear, to enfilade our lines when exposed during the advance" clearly acknowledges his understanding that Confederate guns held the position. Undoubtedly, the brief cannon duel of that evening should have convinced him of its dominance, yet he made no attempt to clear or seize it.[35]

After readying the guns for further service, Pelham enjoyed a dinner with Heros von Borcke. By 9:00 P.M. it started raining and Pelham sought the shelter of a haystack near a post-and-rail fence on the reverse slope of Nicodemus Heights for needed sleep. Meanwhile, the ever-vigilant Jeb Stuart checked on troop deployment and readiness before returning periodically to his headquarters at the Grove house to rest. Stonewall Jackson stayed in close communication with Stuart during the night and slept occasionally on a sofa at Stuart's headquarters. Thus taking turns sleeping, it appears that either Jackson or Stuart was on the field at any given time during the evening.[36]

During one of Stuart's restless prowls around the Nicodemus farmstead, he must have observed the danger of Hooker's army lurking closely in the darkness. Attempting to locate Pelham for a warning, Stuart prodded his horse through the blackness over ground covered with sleeping Confederates. Artillerist Robert McGill Mackall remembered being startled "by the tramp of a horse near my head."

Incensed by this rude intrusion, Mackall challenged the rider for an explanation. Certainly once Stuart identified himself Mackall's anger ceased, and Pelham's resting place was pointed out. Mackall listened as Stuart's melodic voice awakened Pelham. "My dear fellow," chided Stuart, "don't you know that the corn field at the foot of the hill is full of Yankees? and that you ought to have your guns in position now, for if you wait until daylight the hill will be swarming with blue coats." The admonishment from his superior brought Pelham to his feet, and he instantly roused his gunners for action. Before dawn the battery guns, under Pelham's supervision, were hauled to "the <u>highest</u> point" of Nicodemus Heights. A satisfied Stuart later wrote: "I . . . crowned a commanding hill with artillery, ready for the attack in the morning."[37]

That night, as the two armies rested in the darkness, a decided anxiety ran through the ranks, for possibly unlike other battles, the soldiers appeared to realize what the morrow held. As evidenced by their many letters, a certain dread existed, a comprehension that the next day would yield the most unholy of conflicts. "There was a drizzling rain," wrote Rufus Dawes of the Sixth Wisconsin, "and with the certain prospect of deadly conflict on the morrow, the night was dismal. Nothing can be more solemn than a period of silent waiting for the summons to battle, known to be impending." Federal brigadier general Alpheus Williams, in a letter to his family, later described this night as "so dark, so obscure, so mysterious, so uncertain . . . but with a certain impression that the morrow was to be great with the future fate of our country. So much responsibility, so much intense, future anxiety!"[38] For many the pent-up emotions surfaced quickly when, before dawn, a sleepy New York recruit tripped over a reposed dog, sending the soldier headfirst into some stacked rifles. The nerve-racking clatter stirred nearly everyone within earshot, and precious minutes passed before officers could calm the disturbance.

14
"Put on the War Paint!"

With a Pelham on each flank, I believe I could whip the world.

—Stonewall Jackson

As they awakened on the morning of Wednesday, September 17, the 1,300 civilians who lived in and around the sleepy town of Sharpsburg, Maryland, must have realized that their attractive countryside would soon harvest a grisly battle. Two opposing armies, only a few thousand yards apart, sat poised to clash in the surrounding woodlands and fields. Robert E. Lee had meticulously placed his lines in a defensive stance to repel any attacks from the insuperable numbers of McClellan. Lee's left extended north of Sharpsburg along Hagerstown Pike, where Jackson's depleted forces hunkered on the property of two area farmers, Alfred Poffenberger and David R. Miller. Although no entrenchments had been dug and the ground appeared relatively flat, the perception remained deceiving from afar. Numerous low spots and swales dented the soil while limestone outcroppings, mostly imperceptible to the Federals in the distance, protruded above the landscape. Lee's middle, anchored by the veterans of the fighting at South Mountain and under the command of D. H. Hill, stood 1,500 yards northeast of Sharpsburg along an irregular and unnamed sunken road. This road, actually little more than a rutted dirt path, served the William Roulette family to the north of it and the Henry Piper family to the south as a means of transporting harvested crops to a gristmill. Beginning roughly at Hagerstown Pike, the sunken road traversed eastward and then veered sharply southward to Boonsboro Pike. Parts of it had fallen away to more than a man's height, offering a pocket of strength to Hill's undermanned brigades. Lee's right rested south of the town. There the brigades of David R. Jones defended a bluff overlooking picturesque Antietam Creek, meandering north and south below them. Rohrbach Bridge, named for Henry Rohrbach, who lived nearby, spanned the stream and provided passage over the shallow water. From his headquarters, just west of Sharpsburg, Lee could supervise the day's activities from a centralized location.

Lee's selected position would serve his army well with one major exception: the Potomac River lay to his rear, blocking a possible escape route, leaving the only accessible course to Virginia more than an hour's march to the south at Boteler's Ford. McClellan had established his headquarters at the Philip Pry house, located east of

Antietam Creek. The high ground afforded him the capability of watching the up-coming battle from a distance of more than a mile away. McClellan admitted, how-ever, in a letter to his wife that Lee "possessed an immense advantage in knowing every part of the ground, while I knew only what I could see from a distance."[1]

Before dawn, Robert E. Lee dispatched a rider to A. P. Hill at Harpers Ferry with orders to dispense with his activities there and immediately move his division to Sharpsburg. Hill left at 7:30, but he faced seventeen rugged miles of marching, a good eight hours, even for the accomplished "Light Division" under his command. By 3:00 A.M. most of the Confederate forces at Sharpsburg stood in readiness for the awaited Federal attack. Pelham, still stationed on Nicodemus Heights, arranged his gunners for action, unaware that the ridge he held would be so fiercely vital to the existence of Lee's left flank that morning. Deploying his guns at a perpendicu-lar angle from whence the Federal attack would commence, Pelham would have clear shots into the advancing enemy and could dominate the battlefield immedi-ately to his front. Stonewall Jackson, recognizing the extreme value of Pelham's po-sition, decided to send three additional Virginia units—the Staunton, Alleghany, and Danville batteries—raising Pelham's firepower to approximately fifteen guns. More amazingly, the powerful Federal long-range rifled artillery atop Porterstown Ridge could reach all other Confederate artillery positions on the field that day with the exception of those planted on Nicodemus Heights, some 4,300 yards distant.[2]

Time crept by slowly, inexorably. Finally, the sun arose at 5:43, with the tem-perature standing at sixty-five degrees. By mid-afternoon, with an additional ten degrees,[3] it should have yielded a gorgeous, late summer Maryland day. Within minutes, however, shortly after daybreak, the sound of guns promised to spoil the splendor of the setting, creating scenes of unfathomable horror.

Joseph Hooker's First Corps of the Army of the Potomac contained three di-visions of 8,600 fighting men, ably led by Brigadier Generals Abner Doubleday, James B. Ricketts, and George Meade. This corps drew the assignment of attack-ing Jackson's 7,700 men on Lee's left, yet as daylight neared, many of these blue-coats continued to sleep or were now merely awakening. Alarming them from their doldrums, Pelham ordered his gunners, at a distance of approximately 800 yards, to open up with a startling barrage at 5:30 A.M. One of the first blasts severed the throats of two horses in a New Hampshire battery. A Federal officer described the cannonade as "exceedingly brisk," while another reported that "round shot, shell, and canister" hit his men. All along Hooker's front scores of frantic Federals scur-ried to find places to hide. Others "recovered from their astonishment" and began manning their guns for reprisal. All the while Pelham's gunners proceeded to un-leash "a stream of shells" into Hooker's soldiers. Pelham's advantage rested with the element of surprise and the fact that his clustered guns sat in an area of Nicodemus Heights of unusual irregular terrain, making it difficult to pinpoint by the Federal gunners. Conversely, Pelham's gunners were almost assured of hitting their intended targets.[4]

Although Union artillery encountered difficulty in sighting in on Pelham's gunners, some of their shells overshot their mark and reached Fitz Lee's cavalrymen along the western base of Nicodemus Heights. One of their early blasts smashed viciously into a woodpile near some officers with terrible effect. Fragments of shell and splintered cordwood flew in all directions. Lieutenant Colonel John T. Thornton of the Third Virginia Cavalry fell with a horrible wound. One chunk of hot, spinning iron ripped into his saddle. A piece of cordwood, or possibly a hunk of shell, violently smashed his arm from the shoulder down to his hand, leaving a severely bleeding appendage. "I was near [Thornton] at the moment," wrote G. W. Beale, "and witnessed the shrugging of his shoulders and quivers of the muscles of his face, as he felt the shock of the piece of shell." The amputation of Thornton's arm could not save his life, and he died later that evening.[5]

To the Federal front lay the thirty-acre cornfield of David R. Miller with the stalks fully ripened and over five feet tall. It was time for Hooker to launch his infantry attack. He set his sights on the high ground beyond where the small, whitewashed Dunker Church[6] stood among a cluster of trees. The bluecoats' progress along Hagerstown Pike placed them at right angles to Pelham's guns. Suddenly Pelham shouted for his gunners to open fire, blasts that stunned the Federals within their range. Then Jackson's men, crouching near the cornfield, opened with musketry, causing the bluecoats to reel. Hooker wisely directed thirty-six cannon to rake the cornfield. Simultaneously, twenty-four 20-pounder Federal Parrott guns found the same target. This combined hail of shell ripped into the cornfield, sending parts of Confederate bodies hurling through the air. Throughout the barrage, Pelham's battery continued a deadly firing of its own. Soon Brigadier General Henry Jackson Hunt, commanding portions of the Federal artillery, turned his guns in Pelham's direction from the heights above Antietam Creek.[7] Shells hit Nicodemus Heights, killing some of Pelham's horses and causing him to alter his range on Hunt's batteries nearly a thousand yards distant. As a testament to Pelham's distinguished marksmanship and superb leadership, neither Stonewall Jackson nor Jeb Stuart interfered in any manner. For Jackson, in particular, to relinquish any role in guiding the artillery and allowing a mere twenty-four-year-old to manage the guns on Nicodemus Heights was the ultimate compliment. His trust would not be misplaced.

During this artillery duel, shells passed frighteningly close to the attractive home of the Nicodemus family. Suddenly, a group of women and children "like a flock of birds," according to Blackford, came running from the house terrorized by the cannonade and "tumbling at every step over the clods of ploughed field. Every time one would fall, the rest thought it was the result of a cannon shot and ran the faster." Blackford found the episode worthy of laughter, but shouting and waving could not make the occupants return to the house. Pelham, anxious for their safety, yelled for his men to cease firing. From his side of the lines, Hunt chivalrously did the same. With the impromptu cease-fire in effect, Pelham mounted his horse and, with a few staff officers, galloped to the rescue.[8] Once the women and children were safely out of range, the bombardment continued.

Fighting seesawed as soldiers from both sides fell in heaps. Regimental and brigade losses reached as high as 50 percent as officers and men were whittled away. Jackson, impressed by Pelham's stout defense, dispatched the excellent Rockbridge Battery, led by William T. Poague, to reinforce the young artillerist. Now, with nineteen ready field pieces, Pelham's battalion opened a telling fire of double canister on Hooker's attackers. Near Dunker Church, Colonel Stephen Dill Lee possessed an unimpeded view of the Federal approach. Opening up with his four batteries, Lee joined in with Pelham's gunners to catch the Federals in a murderous two-sided box of devastation. Federal cannon from the north and east maintained a ferocious fire of their own, causing Lee to label it "artillery Hell."[9]

Into this maelstrom marched John Gibbon's "Black Hats" of the Iron Brigade, who instantly met with a terrible fire from the Confederate cannons. "No sooner was the column in motion than the enemy opened fire on us with their artillery, and so accurate was his aim," a Federal lieutenant later wrote, "that the second shell exploded in the ranks, disabling thirteen men." The percussion shell exploded against a threshing machine on the Alfred Poffenberger farm. Hunks of spinning shell fragments and jagged shards of metal from the demolished thresher whirled mightily through the air and landed amid them, killing two and wounding eleven, including one who had both arms severed. Another Federal captain had a foot torn off by the same explosion. Other advancing Federals suffered the same harrowing consequences as Pelham targeted his prey along the edge of the North Woods. Members of the Ninth Pennsylvania Reserves marched from the apparent shelter of the trees into the open only to be forced back in the North Woods "owing to the enemy's battery on the right having obtained our range." A member of the Twelfth Massachusetts Infantry echoed these words, stating "that dreadful battery on our right" maintained a steady barrage that was "ploughing through our ranks."[10]

Those who sought shelter in the North Woods discovered to their dismay that the trees offered little protection. The constant shelling from Pelham's gunners, added to those of Stephen Dill Lee, found their mark among the crouching Federals. Limbs, sliced from the trees by solid shot, fell among the men, adding to their nightmares. For some the shelling proved too much, and they ran in fright.

Bullets and canister balls continued tearing through the corn, striking men down in sheaves. Yet the Federals bravely, unconsciously moved ahead toward the David R. Miller farmhouse. "There was . . . great hysterical excitement, eagerness to go forward," wrote Rufus Dawes, "and a reckless disregard of life, of every thing but victory." Suddenly the tide began to turn, as many of Jackson's overwhelmed men headed back to the safety of the trees to their rear. For a few harrowing moments it seemed that only Pelham's battalion of guns offered any resistance. Then part of Doubleday's men swung to their right in an attempt to dislodge Pelham's cannons. Only a few made it through the blasts to Nicodemus Heights before being forced back. One of those, a mounted Federal officer, bravely rode directly toward Pelham's Napoleon Detachment. Abruptly, the officer toppled from his horse, felled by a mighty blow to the head from a wooden sponge wielded by Pelham's teenage friend Jean Bacigalupo.[11]

As the Federals continued to make headway into the cornfield, Pelham's position became dangerously close to the enemy's concentrated rifle fire. Jeb Stuart appeared to anticipate this new peril and sent word to Jackson for reinforcements. Stonewall found General Jubal Early and his brigade at the rear of the West Woods. "General Jackson in person ordered me to move my brigade to the left," reported Early, "to support some pieces of artillery which Major-General Stuart had in position to the left of our line." Early moved his forces immediately and readily received Stuart's suggestion that he form his line at the rear of Nicodemus Heights. Here Early's men remained about an hour until needed. For now Pelham continued to throw shells into the Federals without immediate help. Meanwhile, back at the Pry house, McClellan received heartening news that his attack on Lee's left was successful. "All goes well," he remarked. "Hooker is driving them."[12]

McClellan's boast was not unsubstantiated; in fact, Hooker's attack had nearly seized the entire Miller cornfield. Desperately in need of support, Jackson, at 7:00 A.M., summoned John Hood's division of dynamic warriors. When the order came, Hood's hungry men were beginning to prepare hoecakes on the ends of their ramrods in the West Woods behind Dunker Church. With their empty bellies still unsated, Hood's angry Texans answered the call to arms, a "disgusted bunch" and as "mad as hornets." Two brigades, numbering nearly 2,400, marched northward with a vengeance directly toward the cornfield. Some of the Texans "carried the half-cooked dough on their ramrods and ate it as they went forward." With Hood in the lead, his men stepped over the bodies of those who had fallen in the preceding hour of battle. "Never before," Hood later wrote, "was I so continuously troubled with fear that my horse would further injure some wounded fellow soldier, lying helpless on the ground." Then, with a fury, Hood's screaming brigades rushed forward to halt the oncoming Iron Brigade. This bloody counterstroke broke the Federal advance and sent the bluecoats back through the same ground they had captured only minutes before. The next Federal artillery blast, however, proved deadly. Switching to double canister, the Federal shot scored a direct hit in the midst of Hood's men; parts of humans and assorted accoutrements flew in all directions. Although they suffered staggering losses, the Texans cleared the cornfield.[13]

Hooker's attack of the First Corps was spent, but he sent word for the Twelfth Corps to come forward and renew the struggle. Meanwhile, most of Hood's shattered division, which had saved the day, retreated for safety. Losses in the first hour and a half had been staggering. Hooker's corps tallied nearly 2,600 casualties with the Iron Brigade's killed and wounded numbering 343, or 43 percent of those sent into action. At least 50 percent of the Confederates engaged had fallen. Hood's division suffered horribly for its heroics with a 60 percent casualty rate. At least 1,000 of his men went down in the carnage. When later asked by a fellow officer, "Where is your Division?" Hood emotionally responded, "Dead on the field."[14]

During this phase of the fighting, Pelham's position on Nicodemus Heights became less tenable as Federal batteries from the area of Joseph Poffenberger's farm began finding their mark. Furthermore, Pelham found that as Jackson's lines wavered, his own marksmanship was less pronounced. In the smoky cornfield his gunners simply could not distinguish their own men from the enemy, thus Jackson's soldiers might sustain hits from friendly fire. Watching the situation closely, Jeb Stuart judiciously decided to move Pelham's batteries. After holding Nicodemus Heights for nearly an hour and a half against the Union forces, Pelham gave the order to pull out.

As the Union Twelfth Corps, commanded by Major General Joseph K. F. Mansfield, strode toward the Miller cornfield, John Pelham deftly moved his cannons to Hauser's Ridge, approximately one thousand yards south of Nicodemus Heights. Here Pelham's guns held a sweeping command of all Federal approaches from the Nicodemus house on his left to Dunker Church on the right. Only ten feet lower than Nicodemus Heights, Hauser's Ridge also offered some of the same irregular terrain that made the previous position so worthy for artillery placement. Furthermore, the ingenious move placed Pelham's artillery in a position where it remained relatively free from the constant barrage of Hunt's strong guns. "No one movement on either side," admired the historian Jennings Cropper Wise, "bore a greater influence upon the final issue of the battle than did the advancement of Pelham's group during the interim between Hooker's and Mansfield's attacks." Perhaps giving too much credit to Pelham and not enough to Stuart, Wise continued: "This was a move on the chess board, though perhaps by a pawn, which baffled the most powerful pieces of the enemy. It was one of those master strokes by a subordinate of highly-developed initiative, which has so often been found to play a major part in the tactical success of the superior." Labeling Hauser's Ridge "the key to the whole of Jackson's position," William Allan declared: "Its retention was vital to the Confederates."[15]

Carefully surveying the oncoming Federals, Pelham waited for the critical moment to shout the orders to fire. "This position we held the balance of the day," remembered Private John W. Bryan of Captain Asher W. Garber's battery. Bryan continued with particular praise for Pelham: "I wish to say that soon after taking this last position we were joined by that gallant and brave artillery officer, Major

Pelham of Stuart's Horse Artillery, who remained with us throughout the day working at one of our guns as a gunner, and by his conduct and bravery greatly assisted us in repulsing every charge made against our battery, and that they were very frequent."[16]

Nearly half of the 7,200 men in the Twelfth Corps had never been exposed to gunfire. Joseph Mansfield at age fifty-nine had only been in command of his corps for two days, but the white-haired, white-bearded general represented a father figure to his mostly inexperienced soldiers. Now at 7:30 A.M. Mansfield, astride his horse, trotted out into a situation for which he had little knowledge or preparation. Jackson's men and Pelham's gunners suddenly opened fire on the unsuspecting Federals "with still more terrible effect than before." Federal general Marsena Patrick witnessed the results: "The whole force now in the wood moved forward, when its advance was suddenly checked by a terrific fire on the left and front. As before, the lines of our troops were broken and thrown into confusion." It was a maddening, continuous blast that tore huge gaps in the Federal ranks. Mansfield, attempting to restore order, rode directly into the confusing melee. Within moments his horse was hit and a second bullet tore into Mansfield's chest. Taken to the rear, Mansfield died the following day only a few hours after receiving field command.[17]

Although beaten back, the Twelfth Corps, together with remnants of the First Corps, rallied and pushed forward again. This time they moved ahead all the way to Dunker Church, driving Stephen Dill Lee's batteries from their position. Confederate losses continued to mount. Desperately in need of reinforcements, the call went out to D. H. Hill's division at the sunken road for more men. Hill responded by sending three brigades. At best these men provided a temporary stopgap, but more help was imminently required. Luckily for the Rebels, Pelham's gunners furnished a continuous blanket of shell and canister to assist in preventing a complete Federal breakthrough. Again, Wise praised Pelham's accomplishment: "While the Federals had gained all the ground north of the church and east of the pike, Jackson's left, by means of Pelham's guns, had held fast. No troops, however brave, could cross the space which Pelham's group so perfectly commanded."[18]

Another hour and a half of struggle in and around the cornfield left the two sides panting with exhaustion, as commanders feebly attempted to renew the fighting spirit of their men. The Miller cornfield, according to William Allan, had become "a scene of dreadful carnage." The corps of Hooker and Mansfield "had been literally fought to pieces." On the back of his white horse Hooker took a serious wound to the foot from an enemy sharpshooter. Soon an eerie lull settled over the battlefield, as only random shots and the pitiful groans of the wounded could be heard. Both armies gravely needed additional help from fresh men—the Federals to continue their drive to crack Lee's left, the Confederates to keep their lines from caving in. Sensing a victory, McClellan ordered in the Second Corps. Lee coun-

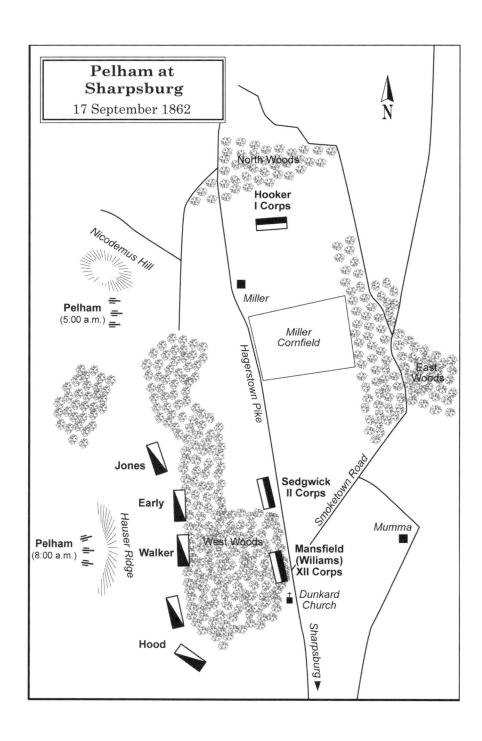

Pelham at
Sharpsburg

17 September 1862

tered this move by summoning troops just arrived from Maryland Heights, as well as the division of John Walker, positioned far to the right. The strange silence persisted as these unused troops marched onto the field. It was just after 9:00 A.M.

Sixty-five-year-old Major General Edwin Vose Sumner, nicknamed "Bull," commanded the Second Corps of the Army of the Potomac. Although his courage could not be faulted, his judgment remained suspect. Sumner's corps, one of the largest in the army at 15,200 men, consisted mostly of veteran soldiers under the divisional commands of John Sedgwick, William French, and Israel Richardson. Without proper reconnaissance, Bull Sumner confidently rode at the front of Sedgwick's 5,400 men coming from the East Woods into the fields carpeted with the bodies of those who had fallen in the three awful hours of preceding battle. Now climbing fences and wheeling southward along Hagerstown Pike, the lead elements of Sedgwick's division exposed themselves to Pelham's cannons posted on Hauser's Ridge. Shot and shell blasted into the faces of these Federals, cutting a sizable swath in their lines. "The projectile that went over the heads of the first line," wrote a Federal officer, "was likely to find its billet in the second or third."[19] Continuing to push forward, the courageous Federals simply made better targets for Pelham's gunners.

With at least two dozen guns posted on Hauser's Ridge, Pelham had concentrated a nearly impregnable wall blasting iron directly into Sedgwick's men. When Stuart sent two additional cannon, Pelham helped drag them to the apex of the ridge. Volunteers from the Thirteenth Virginia Infantry assisted him in the arduous task. Captain Samuel D. Buck of this regiment recounted: "We charged, skirmished and then went to work assisting the horses to pull the artillery in position. . . . Major Pelham was trying to get two Napoleon guns on a hill commanding their position but the horses could not pull them over the plowed fields and up the hill so every fellow regardless of the shot and shell, took hold and almost carried both pieces into position and therein [sic] front of a corps of the enemy the Gallant Pelham fought those pieces, aiming and firing each piece as fast as the men could load, while our men supported him and poured the lead into their flanks."[20]

The wicked blasts of these massed guns were nearly too much for Sedgwick's men to bear, as they could almost taste the iron from the double charges of canister. Clustered together as they marched, the Federals made inviting targets that Pelham's batteries could not miss. "Instantly my whole brigade became hotly engaged," remembered Brigadier General Willis A. Gorman of the Fifteenth Massachusetts Infantry, "giving and receiving the most deadly fire it has ever been my lot to witness. Although the firing was not so rapid, it was most deadly, and at very close range. We also had to stand the most terrific fire of grape and canister, which told fearfully on the three right regiments of the brigade."[21]

Suddenly, the forward elements of the reinforcements that Robert E. Lee had designated for support burst forward. Sedgwick's division, quickly boxed in on three sides, stood directly in the vortex of a living hell. During the confusion, many of the Union men spun around to fire and shot directly into other Federals standing behind them. Others, caught in the ungodly crossfire of the Confederates, died before they had a chance to lift their weapons into firing position. In a matter of ten to fifteen minutes, the Federals lost nearly half, or over 2,300, of their men. Sedgwick suffered three wounds and was carried to safety.[22] Henry Jackson Hunt's Federal artillerists opened a deadly barrage on the Confederates in an attempt to save Sedgwick's remaining men, and many of the shells landed among Pelham's gunners on Hauser's Ridge. Some of Pelham's guns were damaged and many horses hit. This left part of his batteries immobile until after the battle when fresh mounts became available.

Meanwhile Sedgwick's brigades could no longer hold in the West Woods, and orders were given to retreat to safety. With only one path of escape to the north, Sedgwick's men hurried in that direction toward the Miller cornfield. Some of the Confederate infantrymen ran after them in an attempt to continue the slaughter. Pelham ordered his gunners to limber up the cannons and follow, stopping only occasionally to fire blasts into the backs of the fleeing Federals. Stuart, too, saw the opportunity to exploit the hard-pressed bluecoats and gathered what serviceable guns he could find and began to pursue. Occasionally, he halted the guns to fire a few hasty rounds into the running Federals. Stuart pressed the enemy "for half a mile" until he found himself once again occupying Nicodemus Heights. Only the marksmanship of four Federal batteries held the Confederate pursuit in check. Other than sporadic shots, firing on this end of the line died out shortly after 10:00 A.M.

The importance of Stuart's retaking Nicodemus Heights cannot be understated. Once again the weakened Confederate left renewed its strength against a possible Federal flank attack. When Stuart informed Jackson of his accomplishment, Stonewall issued immediate orders to "hold this advanced position." Contemplating a counterattack, Jackson pledged to send all the infantry he could muster "to follow up the success." The fighting now intensified farther to the south.[23]

Miraculously, Lee's left had withstood three devastating attacks from two full Union corps and portions of a third. More than twelve thousand men lay dead, dying, or wounded in the fields and woods to the right and left of Hagerstown Pike. The Miller cornfield had changed hands six times during the awesome struggle. The battle-scarred countryside covered an area, roughly rectangular in shape, bordered by the North, East, and West woods with Dunker Church to the south. Within this perimeter occurred some of the war's most horrible fighting, as parts of bodies, literally torn from human torsos, meshed with piles of groaning and stilled men, attesting to the bitter struggle. Survivors of this ghastly ordeal gasped for breath and certainly realized that only fortune had spared their lives. One member of the

Iron Brigade later sadly wrote: "Whoever stood in front of the corn field at Antietam needs no praise."[24]

The arduous labors of Pelham and his artillerists, during those four hours, displayed what one modern military expert has labeled "pure genius." With an amazing propensity for selecting terrain to his absolute advantage, Pelham invariably placed his guns where they could inflict the severest damage without suffering as much in return. His quickness and daring established a true dominance over superior numbers and weaponry. Above all, Pelham's superb and uncanny timing kept the enemy off guard.[25] His accomplishments understandably earned high recognition from his superiors. "The gallant Pelham displayed all those noble qualities which have made him immortal," wrote Jeb Stuart the following day. "He had under his command batteries from every portion of General Jackson's command. The batteries of [William] Poague . . . and [James M.] Carrington . . . did splendid service, as also did the Stuart Horse Artillery, all under Pelham. The hill, held on the extreme left so long and so gallantly by artillery alone, was essential to the maintenance of our position."[26] Stonewall Jackson echoed Stuart's sentiments: "The bold use of artillery secured for us an important position which, had the enemy possessed, might have commanded our left." Jackson later gave Pelham the supreme encomium: "He is a very remarkable young man. He commanded to-day nearly all the artillery of the left wing of the army, and I have never seen more skilful handling of guns. It is really extraordinary to find such nerve and genius in a mere boy. With a Pelham on each flank, I believe I could whip the world." Stuart added to this informal conversation, "Pelham has covered himself all over with glory!"[27] Although the fighting now shifted to other parts of the battlefield, Pelham was not finished for the day.

~

In the middle of Lee's army Daniel Harvey Hill awaited a new onslaught six hundred yards south of Dunker Church in the sunken road, soon fittingly labeled "Bloody Lane." With only two unused brigades left to him Hill positioned these men in the natural entrenchments of the sunken road, where they held strong positions behind rail fences. Hill's total strength amounted to 2,500. Robert E. Lee stood next to Hill, both men observing a new wave of blue approaching in the distance.

Brigadier General William French headed a division of Sumner's Second Corps. French apparently was to follow Sedgwick's division into battle but somehow veered farther left and now advanced on the sunken road with ten regiments totaling 5,700 men. As they passed through the pastureland and apple orchards of the Roulette farmstead, they presented a spectacular aura. Reaching a slight rise overlooking the sunken road, they aligned for battle. Colonel John Brown Gordon described the next few moments: "Now the front rank was within a few rods of where I stood . . .

and with all my lung power I shouted 'Fire!' My rifles flamed and roared in the Federals' faces like a blinding blaze of lightning. . . . The effect was appalling. The entire front line, with few exceptions, went down in the consuming blast."[28] French sent in one brigade after the other, only to see men shot down with alarming effect. By 10:30 that morning French's attack had ended at a cost of 1,750 dead and wounded Federals.

From the left of French's beaten men came the last division of the Second Corps, 4,000 veterans under the able leadership of Major General Israel B. Richardson. Known as "Fighting Dick," Richardson had won the sobriquet honestly. His division, considered to be one of the finest in the Army of the Potomac, was filled with men of the same ilk as their commander. Countering this new adversary, Robert E. Lee sent in the last of his reserves, 3,400 men led by Major General Richard H. Anderson, who quickly filed his soldiers in support behind D. H. Hill.

The Irish Brigade, led by colorful Thomas Meagher, spearheaded the drive of Richardson's division. They came forward quickly, paused, and then rushed in. Viciously driven back, two of the regiments lost 60 percent of their fighting force within minutes. Now the Fifth New Hampshire, under Colonel Edward E. Cross, prepared to move forward. The red-bearded, bald-headed Cross was an imposing warrior of the first order. Already bleeding from a shrapnel wound to the head, he shouted to his men, "Put on the war paint!" Facing toward him, the Granite Staters witnessed a demoniacal apparition. There stood their leader with his customary red silk handkerchief tied around his head, a mixture of blood, sweat, and gunpowder smeared over his face. Inspired by his example, the men blackened their faces with gunpowder, as Cross bellowed: "Give 'em the war whoop!" Suddenly, the New Hampshire boys charged in, thundering an Indian war cry that gave credence to their state motto: "Live Free or Die."[29] A slugfest ensued that all too closely resembled the sanguinary fight at the Miller cornfield earlier that morning.

"Fighting Dick" Richardson, furious that Federal artillery appeared nonexistent in this area, gathered up a battery of 6-pounders and led them forward. Moments later he lay prostrate, grievously wounded in the side by a shell fragment from a spherical case shot. Borne to McClellan's headquarters, Richardson died on November 3, 1862, in Philip Pry's bedroom after infection set in.[30] With Richardson down, the fight seemed to go out of the Federals. Lee's wrecked lines stood nearly where the fighting had begun, but stood shattered. With 7,000 men D. H. Hill had resisted furious onslaughts from not less than 10,000 Federals. By 1:00 P.M., after three and a half hours of frenetic combat, 3,000 Federals had fallen. Hill's losses totaled nearly 2,600. The sunken road, now called "Bloody Lane," yielded a shocking visage.

Surveying the bloody ground, Longstreet later admitted: "It was easy to see that if the Federals broke through our line there, the Confederate army would be cut in two and probably destroyed, for we were already badly whipped and were only holding our ground by sheer force of desperation."[31] One more organized lunge by the Federals would almost certainly have demolished Lee's center, thus wrecking the Army of Northern Virginia and its frantic hope for survival. But not only had McClellan withheld Porter's powerful Fifth Corps, he kept the Sixth Corps of William B. Franklin and the cavalry of Pleasonton in reserve as well. Illogical as it seems, the only logical reason for this monumental blunder was Little Mac's dogmatic belief that he remained outnumbered.

∽

Meanwhile, on Lee's extreme right the Federal Ninth Corps, consisting of four divisions totaling 12,500 men, stood poised for battle for the better part of the morning to the east of Antietam Creek. Thirty-eight-year-old Major General Ambrose Burnside commanded this sector and was better known for his intriguing appearance than his ability. Burnside's problem that morning did not appear overly troublesome. Since his corps vastly outnumbered the Confederates at this end of the line, he could overwhelm them and drive Lee's right flank into the Potomac. But complications existed for Burnside. First, a rather steep hillside, rising 150 feet, began directly on the other side of the stream where Confederates had judiciously dug a series of rifle pits at the top. Next, Burnside's own vacillation and sluggishness plagued him from the beginning, as evidenced by his total lack of reconnaissance before the battle and indecision once the fighting started. Burnside's most formidable difficulty, however, remained the stream itself and exactly where and how to cross it. No steep banks existed on his side of the Antietam, and the creek was neither particularly wide nor deep and contained no perceptible current. Burnside's attention focused on the Rohrbach Bridge, a stone structure 125 feet in length and little more than twelve feet in width, which picturesquely arched over the stream. When called upon, Burnside, for some unwarranted reason, would make his attack across this span, renamed Burnside Bridge after the battle.

At ten minutes after nine that morning, a messenger arrived from McClellan's headquarters with orders for Burnside to attack. Yet almost a full hour passed before any movement began. Only the 3,000-man division of Brigadier General David R. Jones remained to guard the entire south end of Lee's line. Approximately 450 Georgians of Jones's division were pushed far forward and looked directly down on the bridge. The Georgians readied their rifles as the Federals in the distance deployed for attack. No other Confederates remained available for support with the exception of A. P. Hill's division, still more than five hours away on the road from Harpers Ferry.

Burnside's divisions now approached their target—Rohrbach Bridge. Amazingly, for the next few hours, no one ordered any of the Federal troops to wade through the stream, making the narrow bridge an ugly bottleneck for the Federal crossing and an easy target for the elevated Georgians. Why Burnside did not order his army across the stream en masse has never been explained and remains a controversy today.[32] The detestable assignment of spearheading Burnside's assault on the bridge fell to the Eleventh Connecticut, led by Colonel Henry Walter Kingsbury. A former classmate and friend of John Pelham, the twenty-six-year-old Kingsbury was considered an outstanding soldier despite his relative inexperience. Under a hail of bullets the boys from the Constitution State attempted to reach the bridge, and although some of them did, one-third of the regiment fell dead or wounded. Riddled by four bullets, Kingsbury was taken to Henry Rohrbach's farmhouse, where the promising officer died the following day.[33]

Now other units of the Ninth Corps took their turns in storming the bridge. Some of the Federals lined up parallel to the stream and ran along the water's edge toward the bridge, more than two hundred yards ahead of them. These efforts failed as the Georgia sharpshooters laid down an unmerciful fire. Finally, at 1:00 P.M. with the Georgians running low on ammunition and beginning to retreat, Federals began successfully crossing the blood-slicked Rohrbach Bridge. All Confederate hopes appeared in doubt, but Burnside ordered a halt until some of his men could be resupplied with ammunition. Thus the counterstroke would not begin for another two hours. Meanwhile, A. P. Hill's division continued its push from Harpers Ferry.

～

With a constant eye for offensive operations, Robert E. Lee about noon requested that Stonewall Jackson prepare a movement around McClellan's extreme right. This counterstroke would possibly relieve the inordinate pressure on D. H. Hill at Bloody Lane, as well as regain the initiative for the Confederates. Jackson, excited at the prospect, selected Stuart to lead the foray and began to gather what troops were available.

Amassing a force of five thousand men was no simple task, but together Stuart and Jackson succeeded. They collected seven regiments of cavalry, mostly from Fitz Lee's brigade, the Forty-eighth North Carolina Infantry, and twenty-one cannons, a portion of them under the direct command of John Pelham. Pelham gathered eight serviceable guns, all rifled pieces: three from William H. Turner's Virginia Battery, two from Brockenborough's Baltimore Artillery, two from the Lee Battery, and one from Poague's Rockbridge Artillery.[34] How long it took to collect the entire force has not been determined, but the men, once assembled, awaited Jackson's signal for the attack. It would not come until nearly sundown.

～

At 3:00 P.M. Burnside had his columns, nearly 9,000 men, ready for the assault. Awaiting the attack, David R. Jones could muster less than 2,800 soldiers along with twenty-eight guns. Unbeknownst to Burnside or any others of the Federal high command, A. P. Hill had ridden to Lee a half hour earlier with the welcome news that his division was now crossing Boteler's Ford, approximately one hour's march away. Lee instructed Hill to bring his men forward immediately and support Jones. Until Hill's "Light Division" arrived, however, the onus fell on Jones's beleaguered and heavily outnumbered soldiers.

As the first Federals made their way up the slope, Rebel artillery greeted them with severe blasts. The Confederate riflemen then took over and launched a hail of bullets into the advancing bluecoats. After minutes of regrouping and repeated charges, the Federals won the elevation, as many Confederates fled back through the streets of Sharpsburg. By 4:00 P.M. with much daylight remaining, the Ninth Corps appeared victorious.

Suddenly, from the Federal left along Harpers Ferry Road emerged A. P. Hill and two thousand men of his "Light Division." The thirty-six-year-old Virginian Ambrose Powell Hill fought like a demon in battle. When called upon to move an army into action, no one did it better. Yet Hill's personality presented a paradox. Charming and affable, he was admired and adored by his subordinates. However, his petty bickering and squabbles with his commanding officers were already legend in the Army of Northern Virginia. His mysterious health problems also baffled his contemporaries as well as modern scholars. Too often Hill's maladies forced him out of battles, with the consensus labeling the illness "psychosomatic." In truth, his enigmatic behavior resulted from recurring painful effects of venereal disease contracted while at West Point.[35] Robert E. Lee greatly valued Hill's ability. "Next to these two officers [Longstreet and Jackson]," Lee once remarked, "I consider A. P. Hill the best commander with me. He fights his troops well and takes good care of them."[36]

A. P. Hill had been called upon that day for the most critical venture of his military career. Marching over rugged terrain in the heat of the day, he must arrive in time to save Lee's army. That is precisely what he did. In eight hours he pushed his men, often at the point of his sword, over a seventeen-mile stretch. Dressed in his flaming red flannel "battle shirt," he epitomized the perfect warrior as he prodded his men forward. Many fell out of line, exhausted from the severity of the trek, but a savior had come for the Army of Northern Virginia. Wasting no time forming battle lines or aligning his men, Hill sent them in with a thunder. "[He] struck with the right hand of Mars," wrote Kyd Douglas. Hill's three brigades stunned and halted Burnside's corps.[37] For the next thirty minutes the fighting intensified to a slugfest, nearly equaling the two rounds earlier in the day.

By 4:30 the Ninth Corps began falling back over the same ground it had only recently captured. With Confederate cannon finding their mark, Federal gunners pulled back as did the infantrymen, moving in reverse toward the heights overlooking the bridge. Lee's right flank had miraculously been saved, but more important, the pathway to his escape at Boteler's Ford remained open. Hill had only 63 of his division killed and another 283 wounded, but combined with those killed and wounded in David Jones's command, the losses totaled over 1,000 men. Conversely, the Ninth Corps took 2,350 casualties. Once again McClellan refused to commit any of his reserves.

With the exhaustive fighting completed, Robert E. Lee now summoned the force of cavalry and artillery he had ordered Stonewall Jackson to muster at noon near Nicodemus Heights. Amazingly, after nearly twelve hours of what can only be described as a ferocious bloodbath, Lee was ready to take the initiative. Stuart received orders to engage the Federal right, and accordingly, he sent Pelham and his gunners forward across Nicodemus Heights. Fitz Lee's cavalry brigade accompanied them. Heading north toward the Joseph Poffenberger farm, this Confederate force found the formidable Federal division of Brigadier General George Meade in a sturdy position. With only a narrow passageway between Meade's forces and the Potomac River, Stuart decided to send Pelham and his gunners to test the enemy strength. Moving far to his left to avoid detection, Pelham found a stretch of trees to deploy his guns less than five hundred yards from the Federals. To his front rested thirty rifled Union cannons strategically placed on high ground. Moving farther ahead against this massed Federal artillery seemed more than foolhardy to many of the Confederate gunners. "We artillery captains didn't know the object of the movement, and were disposed to criticize Pelham for turning us loose within 500 yards upon an immense battery . . . in plain view and easily counted," reported a disconsolate Poague. Seriously disputing the wisdom of such an attack, he added, "We protested against attacking such an overwhelming force." Pelham brushed aside the complaints with a laugh: "Oh, we must stir them up a little and then slip away." Poague added gloomily, "And so we did stir them up, and with a vengeance they soon stirred us out."[38]

To the amazement of his men and over the protests of Poague and the others, Pelham ambitiously ordered his gunners to commence firing. Before the first piece could be discharged, however, the Federal guns sent a salvo of "twenty-nine projectiles of various kinds and sizes . . . flying towards that unfortunate battery." For less than a quarter of an hour the lopsided duel continued as Pelham persisted in staying his ground. Poague admitted, "Fortunately we were concealed in a body of small trees and they could only mark our places by the smoke rising above them." Still the Federal gunners found their mark. A member of the Lee Battery stated that "almost every second a bomb would burst over our heads and among us." Another referred to the blasting as a "slaughter-house," while Poague's losses included "1 officer and 5 privates wounded, 14 horses killed and wounded, and 3 limber-chests and 1 wheel badly damaged." Pelham had seen enough, and in Poague's words, "[He] skilfully [sic] led us to one side out of range of the murderous fire." Poague added, "There were too many for us and soon shut us up." Captain J. Albert Monroe of the First Rhode Island Light Artillery proudly stated the Federal artillerists had silenced the enemy "in about ten minutes." The uneven contest ended as Pelham ordered his men to limber up and move back to Stuart. Faced with too large and strong an opponent, Stuart prudently called off the excursion.[39]

Discouraged by Pelham's seemingly unnecessary audacity, William Poague penned his less than complimentary report five days later: "Along with six or eight other guns, under the direction of Major Pelham, an attempt was made to dislodge the enemy's batteries, but failed completely, being silenced in fifteen or twenty minutes by a most terrific fire from a number of the enemy's batteries." However, in his memoirs Poague greatly tempered his feelings and endorsed Pelham's actions that afternoon:

> Major Pelham with three other guns, who, by direction of superior officers beginning with General Lee himself, was trying to see if McClellan's right could be turned. . . . We protested against attacking such an overwhelming force. We battery commanders thought Pelham had gotten permission to look up a fight and were down on him for what we regarded as a most indiscreet proceeding. In my report you may read between the lines my feelings. But we did him injustice. We know now that General Stuart in compliance with instructions from General Lee through Jackson, took this method of determining whether McClellan's flank could be turned. I suppose Pelham knew what he was sent there for.[40]

Perhaps the most disappointed Confederate in calling off the counterattack was Stonewall Jackson himself, who remarked: "It is a great pity,—we should have driven McClellan into the Potomac."[41]

Pelham's ill-fated advance against the Federal right ended the fighting at Antietam—the bloodiest single day of the Civil War. Sharpsburg and all the surrounding area became a living nightmare for those who survived the horrors of September 17. Houses, barns, churches—any available building that could be used as a makeshift hospital—became gruesome reminders of the day's tragedy as the struggle now ensued to save lives instead of destroying them. Bodies were hauled to Dunker Church where half of the single-room structure was used to sever limbs while the other half served as an embalming area. Throughout the night stretcher bearers carried dazed and screaming men toward the dimly lighted buildings. In ten catastrophic hours Federal losses totaled 2,108 killed, 9,549 wounded, and 753 missing. Confederate casualties numbered 1,512 killed, 7,816 wounded, and 1,844 missing. One of every three Confederates and one of every four Federals who saw action that day became grim statistics on the casualty rolls. Officers fared no better than the common fighting men. Each camp lost three generals killed or mortally wounded, and twelve more fell from wounds, six per side. Fifteen Confederate colonels were killed or mortally wounded while thirty-six others incurred wounds; thirty-four Federal colonels took battle wounds with nine killed or mortally wounded. When adding all the losses from both sides, the final figure of 23,582 ranks Antietam as the most appalling day of battle throughout American history.

That night Lee held a conference at his headquarters to determine the army's next move. Among the generals attending were Jackson, Longstreet, D. H. Hill, Hood, Early, David Jones, and A. P. Hill. After listening to the solemn accounts of these commanders, Lee may have astounded them all by boldly announcing that the Army of Northern Virginia would remain in its present position and see if McClellan would offer battle on the morrow.

For John Pelham the day had been filled with moments of exhilaration and triumph, near mishap, and exhaustive efforts against superior gunnery. Starting with his brilliant showing at Nicodemus Heights and Hauser's Ridge, Pelham had strongly assisted in repelling the advances of three Federal corps in the Miller corn-field and Dunker Church areas. Then in the late afternoon he had been called upon to force an artillery duel near the Poffenberger farm against weaponry greater in number and killing power. Before he slept that night, he made certain that his re-maining cannons and gunners were prepared for what might take place the follow-ing day. He could sleep taking solace that his horse artillery had performed invalu-able service. Pelham had countless admirers but possibly none more so than John Esten Cooke, who wrote:

> At Sharpsburg he had command of nearly all the artillery on our left, and di-rected it with the hand of a master. . . . With every fight in which I witnessed his superb and headlong courage, his coolness, dash, and stubborn persis-tence, my admiration for him had increased. . . . I admired now, more than ever, the splendid genius for artillery which this mere boy possessed. There is a genius for every thing—Pelham's was to fight artillery. He was born for that, and found his proper sphere in command of Stuart's guns. With what unyielding obstinacy he fought! With a nerve and courage how gay and splendid! No part of the ground escaped his eagle eye—no ruse could de-ceive him. He fought with the ardor of a boy and the stubborn obstinacy of gray hairs. Rushing his guns into position upon every hill, there he staid until the enemy were almost at the muzzles and were closing in upon his flanks. Then, hastily limbering up and retiring, under a storm of bullets, he took position on the next elevation, and poured his canister into the advancing columns as before.[42]

Indeed, Pelham's heroics and the extraordinary leadership of Jeb Stuart that day had helped save the vulnerable Army of Northern Virginia. Stuart, who virtually acted as Stonewall Jackson's chief of artillery, summoned all his skills in massing ar-tillery, concentrating fire, and moving the pieces precisely at the proper time. Jack-son's trust in Stuart had not been unwarranted. Stuart's reliance on the expertise of

Pelham proved equally wise. Together these two had again confirmed a partnership of rare ability, unmatched in the war to this time. Pelham unfortunately wrote no post-battle report. Neither did he seek accolades for his invaluable services that day. Instead he later penned a note honoring a mere private, Thomas Clifford Dudley, for his valor in the previous weeks of fighting: "In two days of fighting at Groveton Heights and at Sharpsburg, South Mountain and various heavy skirmishes [Dudley] was conspicuously gallant. He is attentive . . . eminently qualified to command and discipline a company."[43]

When the new day dawned, battle-weary men, Union and Confederate, braced for another day of fighting, but all remained quiet. Both sides received reinforcements during the night, raising McClellan's level to sixty thousand and Lee's to over thirty thousand—yet neither offered battle. After 8:00 A.M. McClellan analyzed his preceding day's performance in a letter to his wife: "I feel some little pride in having, with a beaten and demoralized army, defeated Lee so utterly and saved the North so completely. I feel that I have done all that can be asked in twice saving the country." He added proudly, "Those in whose judgment I rely tell me that I fought the battle splendidly and that it is a masterpiece of art."[44] The morning passed into a warm afternoon with still no indication of either side desiring battle. Finally a white flag from the Federal lines signaled a request for a joint burial of the dead. For the next few hours blue and gray labored side by side in an effort to put as many corpses into shallow graves as they could before sundown.

That moonless night in a drizzling rain, Lee's army began its retreat toward the Potomac River. Although the noises clearly indicated Lee's intention, at no time did McClellan move to intervene. Approximately a mile below Shepherdstown, the weary Confederates reached Boteler's Ford, a crossing three hundred yards wide and knee-deep. Here the wagon trains, artillery, and infantry, in that order, crossed into Virginia. The cavalry, acting as a rearguard, followed behind with Fitz Lee's horsemen and John Pelham with his battery bringing up the extreme rear. Von Borcke described the ride to the Potomac as "one of the most disagreeable of my life." The incessant rain had turned the dirt road into a quagmire, causing Von and his horse to fall "not less than five times." Hours passed as the Army of Northern Virginia slowly splashed through the cool water, and still no signs of McClellan's army in pursuit. Lee, meanwhile, sat astride Traveler in the middle of the shallow Potomac, watching for hours as his army trudged across the ford. When at last the men had completed their crossing into Virginia, Lee bowed his head and sighed, "Thank God!"[45]

15

"An Exile from His Own Land of Alabama"

Don't you think all this romance will spoil your love of fighting?

—Stuart to Pelham

Dawn, September 19, exposed a hideous sight around the town of Sharpsburg. As far as the eye could see, scores of silent, bloated forms littered the landscape. The joint burial from the preceding day had interred many bodies in temporary grave sites, but the hours of exhausting labor failed to complete the task. "When we marched along the turnpike on the morning of September 19 the scene was indescribably horrible," wrote Rufus Dawes. "Great numbers of dead, swollen and black under the hot sun, lay upon the field. . . . Friend and foe were indiscriminately mingled."[1]

Meanwhile, the Confederate army lay temporarily safe on the Virginia side of the Potomac. After weeks of exhaustive marching and near constant fighting with provisions at a minimum, the proud Army of Northern Virginia possessed a haggard appearance. J. F. J. Caldwell described the men as "sunburnt, gaunt, ragged, scarcely at all shod, specters and caricatures of their former selves. . . . they had fed on half-cooked dough, often raw bacon as well as raw beef, had devoured green corn and green apples, they had contracted diarrhea and dysentery of the most malignant type, and lastly, they were covered with vermin. They now stood, an emaciated, limping, ragged, filthy mass, whom no stranger to their valiant exploits could have believed capable of anything the least worthy."[2]

Near dawn on September 19, Robert E. Lee decided to send Stuart and the cavalry fifteen miles farther upriver toward Williamsport. The cavalry's purpose was twofold: to check McClellan, if he opted to follow Lee's army, and to demonstrate against the Federals, giving the impression Confederate forces might be reentering Maryland near Hagerstown. Stuart's forces, accompanied by Pelham and a portion of the horse artillery, set off in the chilly morning fog. By midday Stuart led his troopers across the Potomac to Williamsport. Before proceeding in the direction of Hagerstown, they skirmished with Federal cavalry. A heavy bombardment by Pelham temporarily drove off the enemy. One teenage girl of Williamsport, so impressed with Pelham and his gunners, insisted on joining up with his battery. Pelham's arguments could not deter her. Only when he allowed her to fire one of the cannons did she agree to go home. The gunners cheered her heartily and nicknamed her "The Girl Cannoneer of Williamsport."[3] Driving the Federals into Hagerstown, the Confederates pursued to the outskirts of the town, but Yankee infantry stationed there forced them to withdraw. Stuart's forces remained in Maryland throughout the day observing Federal movements.

On the next afternoon Pelham, who had spent the day reconnoitering the Federals, rode up to von Borcke and explained he had found a peach orchard five hundred yards ahead where the two of them could watch Federal cavalry as well as partake of the ripened fruit. The two friends "were soon seated amid the branches of a large peach-tree, eating and looking out to our great satisfaction." Their happy sojourn rewarded them with not only luscious peaches but a view of Federal cavalry amassing in the distance. Presently, large swirls of dust clouds on the horizon alerted them that McClellan's army must be pushing forward. Grabbing a few extra peaches and filling their pockets, Pelham and von Borcke exited the tree and rode back to inform Stuart.[4] Having finished his work in Maryland, Stuart ordered his men across the Potomac that night.

Pelham's gunners hurriedly splashed through the river and set up facing the Maryland side to assist in detaining any approaching Federals. As Stuart's troopers reentered Virginia, Pelham's battery unleashed a series of blasts at the Federals in the distance. Union artillery answered with a salvo of its own, and soon houses and buildings in Williamsport blazed from the constant shelling. Von Borcke described it as a "one of those magnificent spectacles which are seen only in war." When all the Confederate cavalry had safely crossed at 11:00 P.M., Pelham limbered up his cannons and followed the troopers to safety. The Federals stopped at the northern riverbank, too tired to pursue, while in the darkness, Stuart pushed his horsemen another six miles in the direction of Martinsburg before calling a halt for bivouac. Safely out of Federal sight, Stuart would later pen his observations of the recent days: "There was not a single day, from the time my command crossed the Potomac until it recrossed, that it was not engaged with the enemy. . . . Their services were indispensable to every success attained, and the officers and men of the cavalry division recur with pride to the Maryland campaign of 1862."[5]

On the following day, Sunday, September 21, Stuart directed his sabers into Martinsburg around noon and established a campsite about a mile outside the town. Here he could continue to observe any Federal movement and give his men a well-deserved rest. That evening Pelham received a dinner invitation from the family of Ephraim G. Alburtis, a resident of Martinsburg and the former commander of Pelham's artillery battery during the Battle of First Manassas. Alburtis had relinquished command of the unit because of illness and had recently led the Wise Battery of Martinsburg, until poor health forced his permanent retirement from the military. Alburtis had followed the exploits of Pelham, but he desired to renew acquaintance and hear the details. Shortly after dark, Pelham and his guest, Heros von Borcke, called on the Alburtis family. After enjoying a quality meal, the three men relaxed around the dinner table and discussed the war, the rest of the Alburtis family listening intently. Von Borcke relished being the star performer and entertained the family with his stories told in broken English. The Prussian's anecdotes and hair-raising tales pertained to his own escapades, quite naturally, but his most vivid accounts were of the dashing deeds of his blond-haired friend. Pelham, for his part, spoke little what with Von dominating the conversation, but he blushed as his feats were recounted with flair and possible embellishment by the master raconteur. The two visitors stayed late before shaking hands, hugging, and shedding a few tears with their hosts. For many years Alburtis loved to recall that special evening: "Why . . . that boy he hadn't changed a bit! He was just exactly the same as when he came to my battery! And, good Lord, how he did blush when Major von Borcke told us all about him. I never saw anybody get quite so red as that boy. And yet he laughed about it too."[6]

One day later Stuart moved his campsite to the tiny village of Hainesville, where he spread out his cavalry to cover all Federal operations on a thirty-mile front from Williamsport to Harpers Ferry. At Hainesville the weary, dust-covered staff officers delighted in finding their wagons filled with fresh clothing and eatables nearby. The grounds of a small tavern furnished a suitable campground, and tents were soon pitched. That evening Pelham and von Borcke, now spruced up and tidy, mounted mules and visited the bivouac of the First North Carolina. Sipping punch with Colonel Laurence S. Baker and Major James B. Gordon, the foursome, according to von Borcke, "had a very pleasant symposium, laughing and talking over the adventures of our recent campaign."[7] Once more Pelham and Von arrived rather late back at their own encampment.

The next few days remained an idle time of comparative leisure to what the preceding weeks had been. Pelham's orders directed him to the town of Millwood, where he set up camp at Carter Hall, the lovely residence of Major George H. Burwell. Here Pelham learned of his long-awaited and much-deserved promotion to major—dated September 22 to rank from August 9—as well as authorization that formally attached him to Stuart's staff. During the next few weeks, a massive reorganization occurred in the Army of Northern Virginia that greatly affected not only the higher echelons of command but Pelham's horse artillery as well. One day after the Battle of Antietam, the Confederate Congress approved a new rank of lieutenant general in order to streamline the command structure within its armies in both the Eastern and Western theaters of war. Robert E. Lee selected James Longstreet and Stonewall Jackson, whose elevation in rank gave them leadership of the First Corps and Second Corps, respectively. John Bell Hood and George Pickett received promotions to the rank of major general. Hood's advancement was a given; Pickett's, however, raised a few eyebrows. Wounded in the shoulder at Gaines' Mill in late June, thirty-seven-year-old Pickett had missed the bloody campaigns at Second Manassas and Antietam. High-spirited and an effective leader,

Pickett was known to be Longstreet's "pet" general. Some believed that Jubal Early or Isaac Trimble might have warranted the promotion in his stead. Fifteen new brigadier generals completed the honor roll, including Rooney Lee, who would soon command a brigade in Stuart's cavalry. Being the son of the man in charge of the Army of Northern Virginia obviously did not hurt Rooney's chances for promotion, but he had more than proven his worth. By the end of September the army had reconditioned itself into sixty-two thousand effective fighting men; within ten days it was up to seventy thousand.

Reorganization also occurred in the artillery, and for John Pelham this meant increased responsibility. Pelham's new command included five batteries, twenty-two guns, and six hundred men. His old battery was divided into two separate units: the First Stuart Horse Artillery under James Breathed, and the Second Stuart Horse Artillery commanded by Mathis Winston Henry. Both Breathed and Henry received their commissions as captain on the same day that Pelham obtained his promotion. Breathed received most of the Marylanders and Virginians from Pelham's former battery, while Henry's battery contained the Napoleon Detachment, a few Virginians, and new recruits. The other battery commanders included Roger Preston Chew, James Franklin Hart, and Marcellus Newton Moorman, whose Lynchburg Battery transferred into the horse artillery.[8] Chew's battery consisted of six guns while the others had four each. Weaponry embodied mostly Blakelys, Napoleons, and a few of Pelham's old howitzers. Carter Hall remained the campsite of the horse artillery, and Pelham trained the men daily. One day he smiled when he overheard the teenage veteran Jean Bacigalupo admonish a new recruit: "The Capitaine, he never raise hob with us, but when he look at you—you do wat he say."[9]

Exactly how Breathed and Henry were selected to take over the coveted command of Pelham's former battery, and whose input weighed the most in their promotion, however, is uncertain. Brigadier General William N. Pendleton, the fifty-two-year-old chief of artillery for the entire Army of Northern Virginia, obviously had a strong voice in their selection.[10] Jeb Stuart, too, would have been heavily consulted, and his endorsement was paramount to their approval. Whether John Pelham's opinion was solicited is not known, but it seems that Stuart would have deemed his judgment as essential to their selection. One fact is certain: James Breathed and Mathis Henry were warriors of the first order.

Breathed, age twenty-four, was a Virginian by birth but had spent most of his early years in Hagerstown, Maryland. John Pelham seemed to recognize Breathed's talents immediately, and a friendship was struck between the two. "They [Pelham and Breathed] were both fearless and courageous to a very high degree," remembered artillerist H. H. Matthews in 1908. "Pelham was dashing and, at the same time, cautious. Breathed was reckless and not at all cautious—would take his battery in places that would make your hair stand on end, depending on the bull dog fighting qualities of his men to bring him out safely." A wartime photograph shows a handsome face of soldierly quality with piercing eyes, receding hairline, mustache, and a chin beard.[11]

Mathis Winston Henry, now twenty-three, was born in Bowling Green, Kentucky, the youngest of twelve children. His father died before Mathis was born, and his mother passed away when he was seven, forcing him to be raised by an older sister. He entered West Point at the same time as Pelham, but unlike his fellow artillerist, Henry stayed the course, graduating next to last on May 6, 1861. He resigned from the U.S. Army on August 19, 1861, and joined Jeb Stuart's cavalry before transferring to the horse artillery on February 15, 1862. Henry's reddish hair, light complexion, and boyishly thin, frail face gave the appearance of someone soft and fragile. The facts belie this superficial observation. West Point classmate Charles Loeser wrote: "Gentle as a woman with those he loved, he was as cool as the nether millstone when deadly peril threatened."[12]

On Sunday, September 28, Stuart moved his headquarters to the Bower, the luxurious residence of Adam Stephen Dandridge. The three-story, fourteen-room brick house, located in Jefferson County near Leetown and built in 1805, stood atop a hill overlooking Opequon Creek. A large front porch, set off by half a dozen columns etched with fluting, faced west, exposing a magnificent view of the sunset and powerfully gnarled oak trees. A second-story porch on the back of the house offered an enchanting vista of the Blue Ridge Mountains. White pine trees bordered a rose garden to the rear of the house; giant sycamore trees lined picturesque and quiet Opequon Creek.[13] In the front yard Stuart and his staff officers pitched their tents, sheltering approximately one hundred men. Stuart's tent, centered in the camp with a Confederate banner fluttering above it, stood under a massive tree known as Stuart's Oak.[14] Some two hundred tethered horses lazed nearby. The men dined at a long table in the open air, and food was plentiful for the officers and their steeds. Their month's stay at the Bower remained the most cherished time for many in the long and bloody four-year struggle. Highlighting the sojourn were the beautiful weather, clear nights, star-filled skies, and gentle breezes. "The month passed at the Bower," wrote Blackford, "was the most remarkable combination of romance and real life that it had ever been my fortune to encounter."[15]

Dandridge, who owned over a hundred slaves, kept the residence and grounds nearly spotless. He and his wife made certain that the cavalrymen felt welcome. After breakfast Mr. Dandridge often sat with Stuart sipping coffee and enjoying each other's company. Dandridge, a distant relative of Martha Dandridge Washington, and his "charming . . . and attractive" wife impressed the officers as "fine specimens of Virginia country gentry . . . hospitable, cultivated, and kind-hearted." The Dandridge family consisted of ten children, five sons and five daughters. The two older boys had already enlisted in the Confederate army and another was attending Virginia Military Institute, leaving the two youngest at home. Of the five daughters, the youngest, three-year-old Mattie, often enjoyed sitting in front of Jeb as he made his rounds riding through the camp. However, Sallie and Serena, along with a cousin Lily, attracted the most attention among the amorous cavalrymen. Blackford pronounced them "all grown and all attractive—some very handsome"; von Borcke seconded the description by adding, "some of whom were exceedingly handsome." These grown-up ladies greatly enjoyed the chivalry of the handsome young officers. In the dramatic words of Blackford, "To the eyes of the lovely girls who peeped through the curtains of their chambers in the light of the early morn, we were heroes of romance fresh from the fields of glory—patriots ready and pining to die in the cause of their country."[16]

Quite naturally, handsome and shy John Pelham, ever the ladies man, drew much notice from the damsels at the Bower. He had met Sallie, Serena, and Lily, as well as Belle Boyd, a year and a half earlier when they visited the Army of the Shenandoah in training at Winchester. Pelham, a mere lieutenant in the Alburtis Battery at the time, easily made friends with the girls. Evidently, Belle Boyd found Pelham irresistible and later presented him with a Bible inscribed:

To John S. Pelham
From
Belle
With the sincere hope he
will read carefully and attentively
for his own if not for her sake.
Nov. 1st, 1861
Martinsburg,
Va.

Later in the same Bible Belle penned a poem, dedicated to Pelham, which read in part:

I know thou art loved by another now,
I know thou wilt ne'er be mine,
But take from me still my heart's pure vow,
I ask thee not now for thine.[17]

Who then was Pelham's real love hinted at in Belle Boyd's inscription? Some believe that Pelham courted many of the ladies at the Bower and elsewhere. "Pelham was badly struck as he always was," wrote Blackford. "Three girls went in mourning for him, poor fellow, when he fell." But Blackford quickly explained that love came easily for those under the mysterious spell of the Bower: "it was impossible to help being wounded by such darts under such circumstances." The lady Pelham fell in love with was Sarah "Sallie" Pendleton Dandridge. Much about Sallie appealed to John. He admired her radiant, dark brown eyes, wavy auburn hair, beautiful complexion, and attractive figure. Although reserved in nature, she possessed a vivacious personality, enhanced by a captivating femininity, not unlike other Southern belles of her age and class distinction.[18] Many men sought her, but John won her heart. Seldom apart while at the Bower, they held hands and strolled together in the rose garden, rowed in the moonlight on the Opequon, and often went for rides in an old yellow army wagon confiscated from the Federals in an earlier fight. Stuart liked to tease the smitten Pelham by sometimes shouting, "Don't you think all this romance will spoil your love of fighting?"[19] John Esten Cooke witnessed Pelham's romance at the Bower and, being a romantic himself, reflected:

> It was in an honest old country-house, whither the tide of war bore him [Pelham] for a time, that the noble nature of the young soldier shone forth in all its charms. There, in the old hall on the banks of the Opequon, surrounded by warm hearts who reminded him perhaps of his own beloved ones in far Alabama; there, in the tranquil days of autumn, in that beautiful country, he seemed to pass some of his happiest hours. All were charmed with his kind temper and his sunny disposition; with his refinement, his courtesy, his high breeding, and simplicity. Modest to a fault almost—blushing like a girl at times, and wholly unassuming in his entire deportment—he became a favourite with all around him, and secured that regard of good men and women which is the proof of high traits and fine instincts in its possessor. In the beautiful autumn forests, by the stream with its great sycamores, and under the tall oaks of the lawn, he thus wandered for a time—an exile from his own land of Alabama, but loved, admired, and cherished by warm hearts in this. When he left the haunts of "The Bower," I think he regretted it.[20]

The Sallie Dandridge–John Pelham relationship appeared to be more than merely a brief wartime romance. Numerous sources indicate that the two became engaged with plans of marriage in the not too distant future. Presumably, John wrote his family concerning the engagement, which led to correspondence between Atkinson Pelham and Stephen Dandridge. Moreover, John supposedly wrote letters to Sallie in the ensuing months of his life; unfortunately, if true, these letters have disappeared.[21]

Even with the romantic setting, Pelham attempted to keep his mind on business, ostensibly making certain his gunners were constantly prepared if needed. Although he trusted his subordinates' abilities, Pelham made at least one routine visit to Breathed's campsite. Even in this instance, it was noted by H. H. Matthews, Pelham brought along Sallie and her female relatives: "I remember Pelham bringing the ladies over to our camp, showing the guns and the men under his command. He seemed to be so proud of them. From gun to gun he would go, petting each piece as affectionately as if they were animals. He would tell them the history of each gun—how at a certain place a particular gun had wrought such terrible execution among the Yankees, and so on to the end."[22]

Pelham was also known to have visited the nearby plantation of Glenvin, the home of Nathaniel and Dorothy Burwell. Two of Burwell's sons, Robert Powell Page and George Harrison, served in Mathis Winston Henry's battery. After a stint in the Second Virginia Volunteer Infantry, Robert transferred to the horse artillery. Pelham believed in the abilities of Robert and prompted his promotion to the rank of lieutenant. On October 5 Pelham sent the following letter to Robert Burwell:

I have issued an order to Captain Henry to assign you to duty as Lieutenant. I have recommended you for promotion, and expect your commission will be shortly forwarded to these headquarters. I am satisfied you will do credit to my selection and prove worthy of the trust reposed in you. The recommendation was made, not only because I know you would make a competent and efficient officer, but also as a reward for distinguished gallantry on many a field. I congratulate you on the high character you have won and sustained so nobly. Your reputation for gallantry is deserved, and no one will be more ready to do justice to it and to yourself than,

Your Friend,
John Pelham[23]

While staying at the Bower, romance afflicted others as well. On one of his sojourns to Glenvin, Mathis Winston Henry was introduced to Susan Randolph Burwell, the seventeen-year-old sister of Robert and George. Whether love struck young Mathis and Susan immediately is unknown, but they would marry thirteen years later on October 25, 1875.[24]

For all the staff officers the month spent at the Bower resembled a stay in paradise. Hunting, fishing, boating, riding, picnicking, and relaxing constituted much of the days' leisure time. Abounding with game, the plantation provided "partridges, pheasants, wild turkey, hares, and grey squirrels" for the amusement of the marksmen. Von Borcke proclaimed the breast meat of the pheasant "the best game I had ever eaten," and he enjoyed hunting excursions, occasionally accompanied by the musician Sam Sweeney. Often Von and Pelham toured the countryside in the same yellow army wagon that Pelham escorted Sallie in at a slower pace. "We hitched our horses and drove all over the country," wrote an excited von Borcke, "though the rapid motion of the vehicle with its hard springs over the rough rocky roads nearly shook our souls out of our bodies."[25]

Nighttime, however, remained the most memorable and pleasant of times at the Bower, as all assembled in the lower floor great hall for singing and dancing until a late hour. Sweeney picked the banjo "with amazing cleverness" and astonished everyone with the variety of "sentimental, bibulous, martial, nautical, [and] comic songs out of number" in his repertoire. Assisting Sweeney were two couriers, labeled by von Borcke as "musicians of inferior merit," who labored on the fiddle. Stuart's servant, "Mulatto Bob," livened each session by joining in with his extraordinarily dexterous playing of the bones. "[Bob] became so excited that both head and feet were in constant employment," marveled von Borcke, "and his body twisted about so rapidly and curiously that one could not help fearing that he would dislocate his limbs and fly to pieces in the midst of the breakdown." Stuart himself seemed to enjoy these boisterous evenings more than anyone else and became irritated if any of the staff officers, fatigued from the full day of activities, left early. Jeb would find the officer's tent and "rouse him from his slumbers to take part in the revelry." All the evenings' festivities ended with a noisy rendition of "If you want to have a good time, join in the cavalry," with Stuart's melodic baritone voice heard well above the others.[26]

Not all the days at the Bower were idyllic for the staff officers, as two of Pelham's friends proved the old adage that familiarity breeds contempt. An incident occurred when von Borcke and W. W. Blackford became tent mates, an agreement to which Blackford reluctantly agreed. Von related that Blackford "had a wonderful talent for making himself comfortable." Evidently the Prussian intended this as a compliment, although the meaning could possibly be misconstrued. Blackford, on the other hand, gave von Borcke a backhanded endorsement, saying the Prussian "had many attractive qualities, particularly on the surface. . . . General Stuart was very fond of him at first but got a little tired of him towards the last. . . . He owed everything to General Stuart and it was a debt he was inclined sometimes to forget latterly." Whatever the reason for the disagreement, the two men quarreled and refused to speak to one another for days. Both, however, carefully guarded the petty dispute from Stuart, who frowned upon such matters especially among his staff officers. Eventually the problem surfaced before Stuart, who called them into his tent individually for a lecture. Afterward Jeb met with them at the same time and ironed out the difficulty. Von Borcke and Blackford shook hands in front of their chief, the incident finished.[27]

On Wednesday, October 1, President Lincoln visited McClellan's camp—relatively inactive since the Battle of Antietam. Ostensibly, the president intended to review the Army of the Potomac. But, inwardly angered by the idleness, Lincoln hoped to get McClellan to move on Lee's army. The visit lasted four days, but none of Lincoln's cajoling worked. Although McClellan refused to move his massive infantry, he did order his cavalry to cross the Potomac River on the day Lincoln arrived. Perhaps Little Mac used this display of force to assuage the president's ire. Whatever the reason, Brigadier General Alfred Pleasonton led his cavalry and a battery of artillery, seven hundred strong, across the Potomac at Shepherdstown and forced his way into Martinsburg, less than ten miles from the Bower.

A breathless courier arrived at the Bower to alert Stuart of the predicament, and within minutes the troopers saddled up and rode to the rescue. Pelham brought along Breathed's battery for the occasion. Upon arriving Stuart was informed that the brigades of Rooney Lee, temporarily in charge of Fitz Lee's unit since Fitz had suffered a disabling kick from a mule only a short while earlier, and Wade Hampton were in retreat from the surprise attack. Entirely vexed by the situation, Stuart shouted, "Gentlemen, this thing will not do; I will give you twenty minutes, within which time the town must be again in our possession." With that order, Rooney Lee charged his brigade from the front down Winchester Turnpike, and Hampton supported the attack with a simultaneous charge on the Hainesville Road toward the enemy's right flank. Stuart led an attack directly at the Federals down the turnpike leading into Martinsburg. Pelham, meanwhile, unlimbered his four cannons on a hill overlooking the Federals and opened a "spirited fire" directly over the heads of the dashing Rebels into the van of the bluecoats. All of this proved too much for Pleasonton's cavalry, which turned and fled north of the town. Following close behind were Rooney Lee's men and Pelham's gunners, who limbered up and gave chase. Effectively placing his guns on a hill a mile north of the town, Pelham opened a deadly "rapid and very effective fire upon the dense columns of the enemy," according to eyewitness von Borcke. A six-gun battery of Federal artillery, however, appeared to cover the retreat of their fleeing cavalry. The Federals completed their escape through the darkness, as Stuart showed up to lead his horsemen personally in driving the enemy across the Potomac. An unknown number of Federals lay dead, with thirty prisoners taken. Stuart had hoped to capture Pleasonton, a man he intensely disliked, but the Federal general escaped.[28]

Late that night the Confederates pulled up to the Bower. Surprisingly, the entire Dandridge family awaited their arrival with a full table of food spread for the returning heroes. Most of them enjoyed the cold Virginia ham, which they dived into "with a greater amount of destruction," according to von Borcke, "than we had done during the day into the ranks of the enemy." The hungry cavalrymen enjoyed the food as much as the Dandridges delighted in listening to the tales of driving off the Yankees that day. One of Stuart's men conspicuously absent from the table, however, was John Pelham, who passed up the food to walk hand in hand with Sallie in the rose garden.[29]

Spending the next few days in delightful repose, Stuart, Pelham, and the other staff officers relaxed in the comforts surrounding the palatial Bower. Each evening Stuart assembled "guests, officers, couriers, and negroes" at a roaring log fire in the center of the camp. Here the officers listened to the ringing banjo renditions from Sam Sweeney, followed by the harmonious voices of the staff officers who joined in with a variety of songs. "Join in the cavalry," as always, ended the oratorio, "which was much more noisy than melodious." Then the inspired troopers marched up to the Bower for an evening of entertainment and dancing. Blackford readily called Stuart "the life of the party" but indicated that he was ably assisted by von Borcke,

Pelham, and other staff officers. This reference certainly signified that Pelham's noted bashfulness was slowly disappearing. Von Borcke, for all his enormous bulk, proved an exceptional dancer "with a step as light as a feather." On more than one occasion the Prussian also demonstrated a rare talent for staging bizarre and hilarious theatricals. Most often Colonel Luke Tiernan Brien, Stuart's assistant adjutant general and chief of staff, joined von Borcke as stars in these productions. The thirty-four-year-old Brien with his flowing mustache and wispy sideburns, much in the Burnside style, was a natural performer and paired perfectly with the ostentatious Prussian.[30]

One evening von Borcke and Brien teamed up for a performance titled "The Operation." The great hall of the Bower was filled to capacity as the Dandridge family, Stuart and his entourage, guests, and even many of the plantation's blacks packed into the room or sat on the staircase to witness the presentation. Pelham and Sallie held hands sitting on a sofa watching intently. A large sheet draped across a doorway served as the staging area. Only a few candles, lighted behind the sheet, offered any illumination and served to silhouette the principal characters that performed behind it. The drama began with the enormous von Borcke lying on a sofa groaning in extreme pain. The ample belly of the gigantic Prussian was made to appear outrageously puffed up by the use of numerous pillows stuffed under his nightshirt. Colonel Brien appeared, dressed ludicrously as a "doctor." The patient, continuing to groan with "twitches of agony," proceeded to list for the doctor a full menu "comprising beef, venison, oysters, cabbage, etc." that he recently consumed at a dinner party. The doctor fell into his professional gibberish and explained to the patient that his condition necessitated an operation. With that the doctor seemingly forced his entire arm down the patient's throat "with great effort of muscular power expended in jerks and tugs" and began extracting a variety of articles, which he held up individually for the audience's inspection. Out came a whole cabbage, five ears of corn, an entire leg of lamb, deer's horns, beef's horns, two dozen oysters, a whole watermelon, and finally a pair of cavalry boots. With each extraction the audience roared its laughing approval, and the patient's belly continued to reduce in size, aided by a hidden assistant who periodically removed a pillow. The patient, apparently healed, jumped from the couch, embraced the doctor, and began swigging from a mysterious bottle of medicine. The doctor joined in the drinking, and the twosome closed the performance with "an uproarious dance." Blackford recalled the "effect on the audience was convulsive." The blacks especially enjoyed the play "and their intense appreciation of the scene, and their rich, broad peals of laughter added no little to its attractions."[31]

The overwhelming reaction to the comedic thespians caused them to plot a different show for a grand ball held at the Bower on Tuesday, October 7. This time invitations were sent out to the surrounding countryside, and entire families came for the gala festivities. Sometime during the ball, von Borcke and his sidekick,

Brien, entered dressed in incredibly preposterous costumes that, amazingly, concealed their identities. Von Borcke referred to the pantomime as "The Pennsylvania Farmer and His Wife," while Blackford labeled it "Paddy and His Sweetheart." Brien appeared "disguised as an Irishman dressed in holiday clothes." Von Borcke's metamorphosis into a gigantic female of hideous proportions was a sight to behold. Wearing an old white dress, formerly belonging to Mrs. Dandridge, von Borcke sashayed about in an absurd fashion. "Half-a-bushel of artificial flowers" adorned his long braided hair. "Skillfully arranged pillows" boosted his bosom. Jewelry, ribbons, a bonnet, and much rouge and powder completed his ensemble, except for a large fan with which "she flirted coquettishly." Unbelievably no one recognized the behemoth. Stuart exploded with laughter as he carefully examined the pair. Suddenly the music changed to a waltz, and as the tempo quickened, so did the farcical duo as they twirled around the floor. Only when the dress flew up to reveal von Borcke's big cavalry boots underneath did the audience identify the Prussian. Then to applause and "convulsive roars of laughter from the delighted audience," the couple waltzed out an open door. With the demand for encores, the twosome repeated their performance until von Borcke pretended to faint. Later when von Borcke appeared in his cavalry uniform, Stuart joyously threw his arms around the Prussian's neck in approval.[32] At dawn the ball ended and all the exhausted participants headed for a welcome sleep.

The following day Robert E. Lee sent Jeb Stuart an order of the highest confidentiality. For some time Lee had contemplated a cavalry raid into the North to determine McClellan's exact position and possible intentions. Lee further desired that the cavalry journey north of Chambersburg, Pennsylvania, to destroy the bridge over a branch of Conococheague Creek. The Cumberland Valley Railroad line passed over this span, and by burning it, the Confederates could disrupt the direct shipment of supplies to the Federal railhead at Hagerstown. Lee further directed Stuart to select 1,200 to 1,500 men, ride into Pennsylvania, inflict any damage at his discretion, capture any governmental officials to exchange "for our own citizens that have been carried off by the enemy," and supply his men with confiscated horses as needed.[33] Knowing Stuart's occasional penchant for recklessness, Lee cautioned: "Having accomplished your errand, you will rejoin this army as soon as practicable."[34] Lee's orders were specific enough, yet he gave his cavalry chieftain a bit of latitude and enough leash for his own decision making, even to the point of allowing Stuart to decide his route back to the army. It was a task that Stuart relished and coveted.

That afternoon Stuart summoned his acting adjutant, Lieutenant R. Channing Price, to draw up the orders. Couriers immediately sped to Jeb's three brigade commanders with orders to make "ready for an important movement" and to select six hundred men in each unit for an unknown destination. Stuart wisely kept the details to himself. Only the strongest horses and best men would be chosen. Stuart's three brigade commanders—Rooney Lee, still replacing his injured cousin Fitz, Wade Hampton, and William E. "Grumble" Jones, now in command of the Robertson-Munford brigade—would each lead a six-hundred-man unit. Only Jones posed a potential problem as his hatred for Stuart was universally known. John Pelham was also selected and told to bring four cannons with enough horses and men to service them. Pelham picked out two guns each from Hart's and Breathed's batteries along with sixty of his best men. Stuart's orders further directed that the entire force rendezvous at Darkesville the next day at noon. For the next few hours the process of deciding on men and horses took place. Even Stonewall Jackson strongly desired to go along as a common cavalryman. Those not chosen, quite naturally, remained disappointed, as they smelled a hint of the adventure that lay before the others. Surprisingly, Heros von Borcke, who seemed to share in all Stuart's enterprises, stayed behind.

That evening Stuart and his staff officers hosted a farewell party at the Bower. "We had a pleasant time," wrote Channing Price, "music and dancing, until 11 o'clock." Then the festivities ended and the officers filed back to their tents. Pelham and Sallie Dandridge walked along the banks of the Opequon, as Stuart, by candlelight, sat in his tent finalizing some paperwork. At 1:00 A.M. the couple heard the sounds of music supplied by Sweeney's banjo and the bones of "Mulatto Bob." Above the minstrelsy floated the unmistakably melodic voice of Jeb Stuart, who stood on the porch of the Bower, serenading the Dandridges one last time. Jeb sang four of his favorites: "Sweet Evelina," "Oh Lord, Gals, One Friday," "Lorena," and "Dixie," while a number of ladies applauded from their bedroom windows.[35]

On October 9, a force of 1,800 troopers assembled in Darkesville, a small village located five miles northwest of the Bower. When all had gathered, Stuart read the following command:

> Soldiers: You are about to engage in an enterprise which, to insure success, imperatively demands at your hands coolness, decision, and bravery; implicit obedience to orders without question or cavil; and the strictest order and sobriety on the march and in bivouac. The destination and extent of this expedition had better be kept to myself than known to you. Suffice it to say, that with the hearty cooperation of officers and men I have not a doubt of its success—a success which will reflect credit in the highest degree upon your arms. The orders which are here published for your government are absolutely necessary, and must be rigidly enforced.[36]

Further orders to the individual commanders included the following: one-third of each unit would seize horses while the remainder of each command stood ready for action at all times; receipts were to be given to all civilians for any article taken; other than horses, no private property was to be touched; "individual plundering for private use" was "forbidden, and every instance must be punished in the se-verest manner"; public functionaries (such as magistrates, postmasters, or sheriffs) were to be taken as hostages to trade for captured Virginians and would be "kindly treated"; and no private property in the state of Maryland would be touched. Stu-art concluded: "The attack, when made, must be vigorous and overwhelming, giv-ing the enemy no time to collect, reconnoiter, or consider anything except his best means of flight." Succinct and clear, the orders indicated a raid beyond Maryland into Pennsylvania. But the exact destination and route were known only to Stuart. The profound secrecy only served to intensify the mystique of their mission, but knowing Stuart one thought prevailed: with Jeb anything was possible. As one ar-tillerist who had ventured with the Rebel cavalryman before remarked: "When Stuart started out we never knew where he would land us."[37]

From Darkesville Stuart led the column west of Martinsburg, due north. Pelham put Hart's two cannon with the van of the column; the other two pieces from Breathed's battery brought up the rear. Pelham rode alongside Stuart. Another ten miles of slow and deliberate pace brought them after dark to the hamlet of Hedges-ville, approximately five miles from their crossing point on the Potomac. The night approach was necessitated by a Federal signal station on the Maryland side of the river, and Stuart hoped to remain unnoticed by the enemy as long as he could. The column bivouacked that night without campfires. Stuart and his staff officers, in-cluding Pelham, slept in a haystack in an open field.

At 4:00 A.M. on October 10 amid a misty fog, the men stirred from their sleep. Again, no campfires were allowed and no breakfast eaten. Prior to the approach of McCoy's Ford by the main force, Hampton sent a party of thirty-one men to wade through the river above the ford and overwhelm a Federal patrol stationed there. The Confederates succeeded in driving off the bluecoats, wounding one and con-fiscating several horses. By dawn Stuart's van splashed into the ford and headed into Maryland. At 7:00 A.M. the last of Pelham's guns, bringing up the rear, traversed the ford, and all had crossed merely ten miles from the Pennsylvania state line.

Unknown to Stuart at the time, his crossing had been observed by a pro-North-ern civilian who relayed the information to some nearby Federals about 5:30 that morning. Telegraphed reports exaggerated the strength of Stuart's force, stating that 2,500 Confederates and eight guns were moving northward toward Mercers-burg, Pennsylvania. Quickly, Union telegraph operators dispatched what limited information they had to various Federal command posts in the surrounding area as well as to Washington, D.C. Indeed, within hours nearly the entire Army of the Potomac had been alerted.[38] Ahead of Stuart's cavalry lay enemy country, filled with Federal cavalry and infantry, signal stations, and a giant network of tele-graph communications. But in traversing the Potomac River, Stuart had crossed his Rubicon.

Fig. 1. John Pelham. (Cook Collection, Valentine History Center, Richmond, Virginia.)

Fig. 2. John Pelham in furlough uniform. (Library of Congress, Washington, D.C.)

Fig. 3. John Pelham, 1861. (John Pelham Association
Archives, Jacksonville, Alabama, Public Library.)

Fig. 4. Tom Rosser. (Library of Congress, Washington, D.C.)

Fig. 5. Sallie Dandridge. (John Pelham Association Archives, Jacksonville, Alabama, Public Library.)

Fig. 6. The Bower. (Photograph taken by the author.)

Fig. 7. Unfinished cross-stitched bookmark with the words "To My Dear Mama." Found among Pelham's possessions, after his death, with possible bloodstains. (Alabama Department of Archives and History, Montgomery.)

Fig. 8. Pelham grave site. (Photograph taken by the author.)

16
"Stuart Has Euchered Us Again"

So long as [I heard Pelham's cannon] in action, I knew the way was still open.

—W. W. Blackford

On into Maryland rode Stuart's raiders. Ahead lay another ten miles before reaching the Pennsylvania border. The troopers galloped on to the old National Road, which connected Hagerstown to Hancock. Near this location an important Federal signal station atop Fairview Heights was seized by Wade Hampton and twenty of his men. From a few captured bluecoats Jeb learned that six regiments of enemy infantry with two batteries of artillery, under General Jacob Cox, had passed by this same road only an hour before. With the cover of fog still hovering on the ground and the near miss by this larger Federal force, Jeb realized his good fortune and wisely decided to ignore Cox's army.

Stuart's column, now stretching four miles in length, proceeded quickly on a remote road toward Pennsylvania. Good luck held as the morning fog shrouded the troopers from any enemy observation posts. Hampton's brigade, accompanied by Pelham and two guns of Hart's battery, took the lead. Next came the brigade of Rooney Lee followed by "Grumble" Jones with two guns under James Breathed. Anxiously, the troopers anticipated the approach of the Pennsylvania line. "The men were wild with enthusiasm," noted Blackford, "and eagerly watched for the line across which the fun would begin."[1] Crossing into Pennsylvania at 10:00 A.M., Stuart halted the men and read an order of his expectations for his troopers' behavior "in enemy country." Mercersburg lay less than ten miles ahead, and the march hastily resumed.

Once inside Pennsylvania, the raiders began taking horses from the farmers. This task fell to the six hundred men of Rooney Lee's brigade, who fanned out from the middle of the main column in individual parties numbering six each and approached the farmhouses. Again the weather played into the hands of the Confederates as an occasional rain shower reduced the telltale sign of the column's dust to a minimum. Furthermore, the wet fields kept the farmers inside their barns threshing wheat, unaware of the sudden advance of the troopers. Scores of horses, tethered together in threesomes, were brought back, led by an individual rider. Most of the horses, however, were of the Belgian or Norman breed, too large and cumbersome for cavalry, more suitable for pulling cannon. Henry McClellan observed, "as far as scouts could extend the country was denuded of its horses."[2]

Often the Rebels amused themselves by pretending to be Federals from Geroge McClellan's army impressing horses for the Federal government. This sham usually elicited storms of rage from the farmers who cursed "the Government, the army and the war in general." Although forbidden to seize private property, many took the liberty of pilfering food from the pantries and kitchens of the various homesteads. Blackford stated that the local custom of baking bread once or twice a week "was a godsend to us." He further claimed that men returned from some homes with "a vista of roasted turkeys, hams and . . . beef strapped to the saddles, [with] brown rolls peeping out from haversacks and crocks of cream and rolls of butter."[3]

Shortly before noon on October 10, the vanguard of the column reached the outskirts of Mercersburg. Pelham placed two guns in the town square while frightened townspeople scampered indoors. Many of the inhabitants, however, remained blithely unaware of the identity of the intruders. The first of Stuart's troopers to enter the town rushed to a merchant's establishment, where they purchased shoes and boots. They were met with initial congeniality, and it wasn't until they paid in Confederate script that the surprised store owner realized their true loyalty. One Rebel remembered "the astonishment depicted on the faces of the natives to see live rebels in their midst."[4] Refusing to tarry in Mercersburg for long, Stuart gave the order to leave, and the column departed by 2:00 P.M.

Five miles outside Mercersburg the column halted briefly to feed the horses directly from the corn in the Pennsylvania fields. Heavy rain began to fall as Stuart steered the troopers toward Chambersburg, less than twenty miles to the northeast. The roads turned muddy now, and the going became rougher, but the raiders pushed on. Whenever a horse appeared to tire, one of the stolen mounts replaced it. Pelham frequently ordered a temporary stop to unhitch the fatigued horses, pulling his guns and caissons, and reharness fresh ones. Throughout the remainder of the afternoon and beyond sundown, the men labored to reach Chambersburg—with still no sign of Union opposition.

Rain continued to fall, making the riders uncomfortable. "Rain, rain, nothing but rain," complained H. H. Matthews. Fortunately, a number of the gunners had confiscated straw hats from the farmers around Mercersburg, and these gave added protection from the elements. Stuart, of course, took note of the new headwear and was not the least shy in making his opinion known. "The appearance of the battery was grotesque, indeed," noted Matthews, "so that Gen. Stuart on riding through the battery asked Pelham where he got all the farmers from." The artillerist remembered: "The name farmer stuck to us for quite a while."[5]

By 8:00 P.M. the vanguard of Stuart's column saw the lights of Chambersburg through the "pitchy dark" in the distance. Forty miles had been left behind them since the troopers departed their rendezvous point in Virginia. And now as they peered ahead at the town of seven thousand residents, one question remained: was Chambersburg occupied by Federals? In case of trouble Pelham strategically positioned two guns on a knoll overlooking the town. Stuart ordered Wade Hampton, commanding the lead horsemen, to send in a party of men under a flag of truce to demand surrender. Chambersburg had evidently been alerted to the Confederate approach, and three selected representatives of the community met the Rebel squadron at the town's edge. One of the three civilians was A. K. McClure, a colonel in the local militia as well as a newspaper editor and Republican politician; of course, he kept his military affiliation to himself. The terms were blunt: unconditional surrender and any resistance would result in a cannon shelling within three minutes. The nervous locals quickly acquiesced.[6]

Hampton's brigade entered Chambersburg first, and soon all of Stuart's troopers had gathered in the public square. The local magistrates had apparently disappeared, and Stuart grandiosely appointed Hampton the military governor of the town. The only Federal soldiers in Chambersburg were 275 sick and wounded found in the hospital, and these Stuart directly paroled. Military orders, which included the cutting of the telegraph wires, were followed to the letter. Colonel Matthew Calbraith Butler of Hampton's brigade entered the town bank to obtain the available funds, but the cashier insisted that the money had been removed that morning. Inspection of the cash drawers and vault proved the cashier's statement honest. Stuart ordered "Grumble" Jones and a select group of his brigade to ride north of the town and destroy the railroad bridge over Conococheague Creek. The provost guard made certain that private property remained untouched. With his good fortune still intact, Stuart decided to allow his troopers a night's rest in Chambersburg. Pelham ordered Breathed to park his two-gun battery in the public square with the battery flag tied to the spoke of a wheel, signifying ownership, albeit temporary, of the town.

Prior to cutting the telegraph lines, however, and unknown to Stuart, an urgent message had been tapped out on the telegraph to Governor Andrew Curtin in Harrisburg informing him of the town's capture. Curtin promptly wired Secretary of War Edwin Stanton in Washington, D.C.: "The people have surrendered Chambersburg." By 9:10 that evening Stanton informed McClellan of the situation with the ominous warning: "Not a man should be permitted to return to Virginia. Use any troops in Maryland or Pennsylvania against them." McClellan wired back: "Every disposition has been made to cut off the retreat of the enemy's cavalry."[7] With Stuart's 1,800-man cavalry completely isolated on enemy soil and directly at the rear of the Army of the Potomac, it finally appeared that McClellan would react.

Meanwhile, Stuart's men attempted to rest in the constant drizzle and chill of the October night. Most of the raiders simply camped in the streets, attempting unsuccessfully to ward off the rain. Some made their way to McClure's home. Although the Pennsylvanian feared for his property, he was "bewildered" by their "uniform courtesy." McClure soon found himself sipping coffee and enjoying their "conservation on politics, the war, the different battles, the merits of generals of both armies, etc." Soon others came "until nearly a hundred had been supplied with something to eat or drink." At 4:00 A.M. the bugle sounded "Boots and Saddles," and the Rebels arose to depart.[8]

Three times that night an anxious Jeb Stuart awakened Benjamin Stephen White, his guide through Maryland, and inquired as to whether the constant rain would make the fords leading back into Virginia impassable. White, born in Montgomery County, Maryland, and familiar with the roads and fords, each time assured Stuart they would make it safely back. Furthermore, "Grumble" Jones returned sometime during the night with bad news. The railroad bridge over Conococheague Creek was made of iron, and all efforts to destroy it with fire and axes had failed. Discouraging news indeed, for the destruction of the bridge had been the primary target of the raid. However, Stuart had a much larger concern weighing on his mind: what route to take in returning to Virginia. Surely the Federals would swarm to block his path, and most likely they would expect him to return the way he had come. Conversely, riding around McClellan added three times the distance and would bring his troopers dangerously close to the Army of the Potomac. But the longer trip might surprise the enemy and would certainly bring greater glory. Without consulting anyone else, Stuart "after mature consideration" boldly made his decision: he would take the circuitous route.[9]

While his cavalrymen as well as the townspeople assembled in the Chambersburg square, Stuart rode among them. Although private property remained untouched, Stuart gave his men permission to pilfer the supplies at the Federal army depot near the railroad station. This repository housed mountains of clothing including overcoats, underwear, socks, hats, and pants, along with five thousand new rifles and a copious number of pistols and sabers. For the next few frenzied moments the Confederates hurriedly exchanged what worn-out equipment and uniforms they possessed for brand-new Yankee gear. To the surprise of nearly everyone assembled, Stuart ordered the column eastward toward Gettysburg. John Pelham, possibly instructed of the ruse, shouted to Breathed's gunners, "You're to have first whack in Gettysburg to make up for being late in Chambersburg!"[10] Stuart, of course, intended to ride eastward but had no design of going as far as Gettysburg.

Calbraith Butler's South Carolinians, designated to form the rearguard, were assigned to destroy the unused supplies and ammunition at the depot. Remaining in Chambersburg until his task was completed, Butler carefully moved the civilians away from the storehouse and then torched the building. Butler's troopers rode out of Chambersburg at 9:00 A.M. also heading east and caught up with Stuart's main body of cavalry little more than ten miles away at Cashtown.[11] With the column once again intact, Stuart called for a brief halt to feed the horses. The respite lasted less than thirty minutes, during which Jeb leaned against a tree and slept. When awakened, Stuart ordered a change of direction. Instead of continuing on to Gettysburg, the raiders veered southward toward the Maryland line more than ten miles ahead. Most of the Rebels now realized they were about to encircle McClellan's Army of the Potomac—a repeat performance of their glorious feat accomplished five months earlier.

The weather continued to be a blessing as the skies cleared and the rain halted. The constant wetness of the foregoing hours again kept the dust clouds down as they moved along. Three scouts, searching the horizon, rode 150 yards in front of the advance guard squadron, which preceded the main body of the column. Two hundred yards farther back from the advance guard trotted Pelham with Breathed and his two cannon. Immediately behind Pelham's gunners rode the 600 men of Rooney Lee's brigade. Next came the 600 of Jones's brigade, whose duties included leading the stolen horses and taking more animals until they reached the Maryland line. The 600 men under Wade Hampton brought up the rear with the remaining two guns of Pelham's battery under James Hart's command following immediately behind. At another 200-yard interval rode the rearguard with three more scouts behind at a distance of 150 yards. The entire column stretched five miles in length. Stuart generally stayed at the front of Lee's 600 while issuing standing orders that only sabers would be employed in case of Federal attack since the noise of firearms would only call attention to the force.

In the meantime the Federal high command prepared to trap Stuart's raiders. The telegraph wires dispatched urgent messages to various units along the Potomac with orders to be vigilant in watching for the Rebels. Couriers hastened in different directions with the same alarm. Infantry divisions began moving, and the cavalry forces of Alfred Pleasonton and George Stoneman prowled the countryside. From Hancock to Harpers Ferry thousands of Federals took up positions to halt the return of the Confederate troopers. Satisfied with his preparation, McClellan informed Washington, D.C., that he had troops covering all the roads and fords to cut off the Rebel escape. Confidently he stated, "I hope we may be able to teach them a lesson they will not soon forget."[12] With the web spun, the Federals confidently waited to ensnare its prey.

In the early evening of October 11, Stuart's caravan crossed the state line into Maryland. Approximately 1,200 horses had been taken in Pennsylvania, but orders prohibited any from being stolen once they crossed into Maryland. The town of Emmitsburg lay a short ride ahead, and Benjamin Stephen White took over the duties as guide. Since leaving Chambersburg that morning, the Rebels had traveled thirty-one miles without a single sign of Federals. Blackford described the lack of Federal intervention as "incredible," but McClellan seemed content to stay south of Stuart's raiders and wait for their arrival.

The Confederates rode into Emmitsburg shortly after sundown to the complete surprise of the townspeople. "If we had fallen from the clouds the people could not have been more astonished," wrote Blackford. But the bewilderment quickly passed, and "we were hailed by the inhabitants with the most enthusiastic demonstrations of joy," noted Stuart. Baskets of food were provided by the ladies, and Henry Matthews remembered giving the females "our straw hats as souvenirs" in return.[13] One young lady, visiting friends in Emmitsburg, however, mistook the Rebels for Federals and instantly spurred her horse beyond the town. No amount of shouting could dissuade her thinking, and Pelham, fearful she intended to alert the Federals, rode out after her. The chase lasted a good mile before he overtook her and explained the identity of the raiders. The blond lady clarified the reason for her panic, and the two slowly rode back to Emmitsburg, laughing at her confusion.[14]

After a mere thirty minutes Stuart's column pulled out of Emmitsburg in the darkness and headed south in the direction of Frederick. The guide, Benjamin White, rode at the front with Pelham and two of his cannons close by. Captain F. W. Southall commanded the advance guard. The remainder of the column filed in behind. Forty-five miles of difficult travel now separated the raiders from the fords leading back into Virginia. Knowing the Federals would be swarming the countryside, Stuart determined to push his men throughout the night without sleep. At one point Jeb rode forward near Southall and Pelham, advising them, "Keep this pace. Slow the gait for nothing, and ride over anything that gets in the way."[15]

Approximately six miles south of Emmitsburg at a village known as Rocky Ridge, the Confederates in the lead spied a lone Federal rider. Quickly, Southall and Pelham apprehended the bluecoat and took him to Stuart. The frightened young man proved to be a Federal courier with critically important data in his dispatch pouch. The papers revealed that a strong Federal force, commanded by Colonel Richard H. Rush, existed in Frederick—directly in the path of Stuart's column. This command included Rush's Lancers, two infantry regiments, the First Maine Cavalry, a battalion of Maryland horsemen, and a New York battery of artillery. Furthermore, Stuart learned that Pleasonton and eight hundred cavalrymen were now heading toward Mechanicstown, a site only four miles west of Stuart's present location. Studying a map with his guides, Jeb determined that he must swing his column farther east to avoid these Federals. Crossing the Monocacy River, the Rebels headed for the hamlet of Woodsboro, another five miles ahead. Sometime near 9:00 P.M. a small force of Pleasonton's cavalry appeared in the distance, and in the confusion of the darkness, they almost ran into the lead Rebels. Pelham shouted, "Halt or we fire!" but the Federals turned and fled before any shooting took place.

Once through Woodsboro, the column swung southeastward toward Liberty where Stuart halted the column for a bite of food and to change horses. Pelham's battery horses, more exhausted than the others from pulling their heavy loads, had to be exchanged and reharnessed three or four times during the night. South of Liberty on a dangerously steep downgrade, Pelham's two guns lost control and rolled forward, crashing down the trail. For a few frantic moments it appeared that the pieces would be lost, but the superb efforts of his gunners, with their energy nearly spent, saved the cannons. On into the night the caravan proceeded.

Federal activity continued to be confused and hectic as rumors ran rampant through the various camps. Maddeningly, for many it was like chasing a ghost. That night Richard Rush and Alfred Pleasonton received news of Stuart's whereabouts, but neither had the luxury of fresh horses, so their efforts to apprehend the enemy failed.

Confederate troopers had been in the saddle almost constantly for twenty hours since being summoned to the square in Chambersburg at 4:00 A.M. Aching with sleepiness and numbed bodies, many of the men began dozing off. The light the moon cast through the trees availed no landmarks in the near black surroundings, causing Blackford, in his eyelid-drooping stupor, to envision castles and houses that vanished and then reappeared. Noted Blackford, "to be sleepy and not to be allowed to sleep is exquisite torture." For relief from their weariness, he and a few others often dismounted and walked alongside their horses. Pelham battled his drowsiness by periodically waving his hand above his head to enhance his blood circulation.[16]

On through the night they rode, past New London and then New Market with still no Federals in sight. Continuing their course on little-used roads, they reached Monrovia. Here the Baltimore & Ohio Railroad line stretched perpendicularly across their path, heading southwest to Harpers Ferry. Stuart ordered logs placed on the tracks as an obstruction and the telegraph wires cut. Only a few hours of darkness remained, and the Potomac River was still a good twenty miles ahead. Even with the most dangerous leg of the journey facing him, Stuart found time for frivolity. Remembering a promise he had made to the ladies of the Cockey family in Urbana back in September, Jeb rode up to Blackford with an extraordinary proposition. Laughingly, Jeb inquired, "Blackford, how would you like to see the 'New York rebel' tonight?" Up ahead lay a side road that cut southwest six miles to Urbana. They could easily separate from the main column, pay the visit that Stuart had promised, and return to the caravan in a few hours. Informing Pelham and a handful of others of his intentions, Stuart rode off accompanied by Blackford, a few staff officers, and ten men from the First North Carolina. The rest of the column continued southward toward Hyattstown. Blackford later downplayed the seriousness of this escapade.[17]

Reaching the Cockey house beyond midnight, Stuart and the others dismounted and entered the yard. Not a soul stirred in the darkened house. One of the officers broke the silence with a loud knock on the door. A moment passed without response, and then a frightened female voice from an upstairs window asked meekly, "Who is there?" One of the men answered, "General Stuart and staff." The lady barely poked her head out the window for a better look and softly screamed with delight. For a few seconds excited voices were heard inside, but no one opened the door. Soon another skeptically asked, "Who did you say it was?" Stuart stepped forward and with a ringing laugh bellowed, "General Stuart and staff. Come down and open the door." Suddenly much shrieking occurred upstairs and then a commotion of putting on dresses and shoes before a mad dash to open the door. Hugs and kisses abounded as the ladies delighted in seeing their heroes in the moonlight. Stuart allowed only thirty minutes at the Cockey house before ordering the men back to their saddles. Smiles and tears mingled as the officers and ladies said their good-byes. Stuart and Blackford waved their farewells in the distance.[18]

In the meantime the main body of troopers continued on their course. Numerous times during the night Pelham and his gunners had to change the worn-out horses attached to the cannons and caissons in order to keep up the grueling pace. "As fast as one team was broken down," remembered Henry McClellan, "the horses were turned out and others were substituted . . . and the march was made without delay or interruption." H. H. Matthews concurred: "Everything now depended upon the rapidity of our march as Pleasonton was advised of our movements. . . . When we reached the Potomac we did not have a single horse that we started with, except a few that were ridden by the cannoneers."[19]

Traveling southeastward from Urbana, Stuart and the others successfully linked up with the main column at Hyattstown before daylight on October 12. Thirty-three miles had been traversed since leaving Emmitsburg, but another twelve miles lay beyond to the Potomac. These last miles would surely be the most hazardous as the Federals gathered to block the escape of the Rebels. Soon the light of day would expose the column more readily to the enemy. The openness of the country ahead and the exhaustion of the men added to the difficulties. The line of the caravan remained essentially the same as it had been. Ahead to the west loomed Sugar Loaf Mountain, where a Federal signal station could pass on information of the approaching Rebels. Stuart sent the order down the column: they must move faster.

For the next few miles the countryside changed radically. From relative flatness they now faced rolling hills, steep ravines, and thick woodlands. Skilled horsemen could negotiate the difficulties with some ease, but Pelham's cannons presented a problem. A branch of Bennett's Creek offered such an obstacle with its steep banks, murky water, and muddy bottom. Refusing to recoil from the possible morass, Pelham spurred his horse forward and splashed into the blackened water. With a relieved smile he shouted back to his gunners, "The Lord's been good to us! It'll hold well. It's all right. Come ahead!"[20] The guns passed safely across. Pushing on, the head of the column reached Barnesville. Information confirmed what Stuart already suspected: George Stoneman with four thousand to five thousand men held Poolesville, a town south of Barnesville and directly in Stuart's path, guarding the lower fords of the Potomac.

With four possible fording points available, Stuart faced a dilemma. Edwards' Ferry, a logical crossing south of Poolesville, now seemed ill-advised due to Stoneman's forces. Six miles farther north sat Conrad's Ferry, but this, too, would be carefully watched by Stoneman. Another five miles up the Potomac was little-used White's Ford, but getting to White's remained a tricky course over difficult roads with Stoneman's men on one side and Pleasonton's on the other. Two miles farther the Monocacy emptied into the Potomac near Hauling's Ford. Here Pleasonton had arrived with four hundred troopers and two guns commanded by Lieutenant Alexander C. M. Pennington Jr. With 1,600 men from the Third and Fourth Maine infantries guarding this crossing, Pleasonton set out with his cavalry and guns to find the elusive Stuart. Meanwhile, McClellan, whose entire Army of the Potomac had been encircled once again, sat back and waited for the prey to be snared. "I did not think it possible for Stuart to recross," wrote McClellan, "and I believed that the capture or destruction of his entire force was perfectly certain."[21]

Jeb halted the column to confer with his guide, Benjamin White, who had once run a store in Poolesville. The guide calmly suggested White's Ford, a crossing that Stuart possibly was unaware of. White further described an uncharted pathway a few miles ahead that ran southwestward through a wood, thus concealing them from the Federal signal station atop Sugar Loaf Mountain. Stuart posed numerous questions to White, but the risk seemed worth the gamble. Once more the column started up and headed south to Beallsville. To the casual observer the route seemed suicidal as the troopers rode directly toward the Federals beyond at Poolesville. Stuart's intentions were meant as a ruse to make the Federals believe his destination was Edwards' Ferry. The key to his ploy remained the obscure road that lay in the woodland ahead.

Halfway between Barnesville and Beallsville, Captain White veered from the main road sharply to his right and entered the wooded area with the others following closely behind. Although somewhat overgrown, the road between the trees appeared passable. At various places rickety wooden fences blocked their path, but the troopers quickly tore them down. On they rode, mysteriously out of sight, for more than a mile. By 9:00 A.M. the first of Stuart's raiders emerged from the wooded trail and eyed an open field to their front. Another eight hundred yards farther lay the main road, connecting Beallsville to the southeast and the mouth of the Monocacy to the northwest. The shortcut had led Stuart's column directly between Stoneman's men at Poolesville and Pleasonton's forces at Hauling's Ford. Turning right toward the Monocacy, Captain White guided the men forward.

Suddenly, ahead of them the Confederates observed Federal troopers, part of Pleasonton's men, blocking their path. The Federals hesitated, apparently confused by the blue overcoats, the same ones pilfered from Chambersburg, now worn by the approaching Rebels. Friendly gestures from the Confederates further puzzled the Yankees as did the slow, deliberate gait of the advancing horsemen. Then, with a shout, Stuart and the head of his column drew their sabers and charged madly at the baffled Federals, who fired one volley and fled rapidly.

Not satisfied with merely scaring off the Federals, Stuart led his advance guard in pursuit for nearly a mile. Stuart halted the chase on the south side of the Little Monocacy River. Here Rooney Lee's sharpshooters dismounted and deployed, facing Pleasonton's main force across the river. Opening fire with their rifles, the Rebels held their ground until John Pelham appeared with one of Breathed's guns. While his gunners unlimbered the cannon, Pelham's keen eye observed a long ridge, a commanding position where artillery could rain shells on the Federals with pinpoint accuracy. Some well-directed fire drove the fleeing Federals across the Monocacy to join Pleasonton's larger army. Federal gunner Pennington brought two of his pieces forward and proceeded to trade shots with Pelham. Stuart later proudly reported: "Quick as thought Lee's sharpshooters sprang to the ground, and, engaging the infantry skirmishers, held them in check till the artillery in advance came up, which, under the gallant Pelham, drove back the enemy's force upon his batteries beyond the Monocacy, between which and our solitary gun quite a spirited fire continued for some time. This answered, in connection with the high crest occupied by our piece, to screen entirely my real movement quickly to the left, making a bold and rapid strike for White's Ford, to force my way across before the enemy at Poolesville and Monocacy could be aware of my design."[22]

The impetuous chase, initiated by Stuart only minutes before, fortuitously worked to his benefit, as the deluded Federals became convinced that the Confederate objective was Hauling's Ford. In fact, Stuart's target remained White's Ford, nearly two miles behind him with an old farm road leading directly to the crossing. The ridge not only provided Pelham's gunners with a location to defend any approach made by the Federals, it shielded the path of escape for Stuart's column. Leaving enough of the sharpshooters to assist Pelham, Stuart directed the remainder of Rooney Lee's men to head to White's Ford. Orders were immediately sent back to the commands of "Grumble" Jones and Hampton to hurry forward to the crossing at a gallop. Stuart dispatched Blackford forward to make certain the water-deprived horses did not stop in the ford to quench their powerful thirst, thus bottlenecking the remainder of the column behind. Meanwhile, Stuart remained with Pelham, knowing the artillerist's station was paramount to the escape of the caravan.

With Pelham's gunners attempting to hold Pleasonton back, Rooney Lee's command took the hidden farm road behind and streaked for White's Ford. One of Pelham's guns under Breathed's command accompanied them in case Federals dominated the crossing. Pelham's task became highly troublesome as Pleasonton rushed his men forward, along with Pennington's battery, a total force of more than one thousand. Pelham immediately responded by launching a series of deadly blasts into the approaching bluecoats. The accuracy of the solitary cannon halted the enemy and forced the Federal artillerists to change their position three times. More important, the heavy firing from Pelham's gun convinced Pleasonton that the Rebels intended to cross at the mouth of the Monocacy. Pleasonton, therefore, appeared content to remain and wait for reinforcements to halt the attempted Confederate breakthrough. Thus, two hours of precious time elapsed as Pelham held the Federals at bay.[23]

All the while, Rooney Lee pushed his exhausted men and horses toward White's Ford. The success of his escape clearly depended on whether or not Federals held the crossing in force. Benjamin White rode alongside Lee, apprising him of the prospects ahead. The Chesapeake and Ohio Canal on the Maryland side of the Potomac would afford decent cover to the ford, the guide assured him. White cautioned, however, that a rock quarry, an ideal spot for an ambush, overlooked the crossing. If the Potomac hadn't swelled from the recent rains and if Federals weren't hiding at the quarry, the crossing at White's Ford could be effected with ease.

Reaching the ford, Lee observed Federals at the rim of the rock quarry. The force consisted of two hundred men of the Ninety-ninth Pennsylvania Cavalry under Lieutenant Colonel Edwin R. Biles, who later stated that he "took up a position to completely cover the ford with our rifles." Although no enemy artillery was discernible on the rise, Lee grasped his predicament. "A serious resistance from such a force, in such a position, at such a time," wrote Blackford, "must have caused considerable delay, and possibly enough to have enabled the large forces near by to assemble and destroy us."[24] New to command and not wanting to make a decision for himself, Lee sent a courier back to Stuart requesting his presence. Jeb, however, returned the messenger with explicit orders: the crossing must be made at once.

During the interim, Biles, uncertain of the strength of the force below him, ordered up some skirmishers. After a few momentary shots, the Federals came back, reporting a considerably large army of Confederates with two cannons. (By this time a second cannon had arrived from the rearguard to support Lee.) According to Biles thirty minutes elapsed as the Confederates waited approximately eight hundred yards away. Twenty-five-year-old Rooney Lee carefully studied the terrain to determine his course of action. Suddenly, a bold plan struck him: why not deceive the Federals from their strong position? Deeming it worth the risk, Lee scrawled a note informing Biles that Stuart's entire cavalry was on the scene and that he wished "to avoid unnecessary bloodshed." Biles was given fifteen minutes to decide. A Rebel courier rode toward the quarry with a white handkerchief tied to his upraised saber. Amazingly, after fifteen minutes the Federals relinquished their strong position and "with flags flying, drums beating, [and] in perfect order," retreated eastward. The audacity of the bluff would have made Stuart proud.[25]

With the way to White's Ford unimpeded, Lee ordered his men to move at

9:30 A.M., and the weary horsemen clattered into the dry bed of the Chesapeake and Ohio Canal. Ahead of them went one of the cannon to be placed on the opposite shore to hold off any pursuing Federals. The other gun would remain on the Maryland side of the river to defend any approaches. Reaching White's Ford, which stretched four hundred yards across the Potomac, the Rebels retained their good fortune—the recent rains had not swollen the river. Although Blackford admonished each company commander not to allow the animals to stop and drink, the savagely thirsty horses "sometimes . . . would stop in spite of everything and plunge their heads up to their eyes into the water to take deep draughts of what they so much needed."[26]

With Lee's men and horses safely across, the command of "Grumble" Jones made its way to the ford. Plunging in, they, too, made it over. Hampton's men brought up the rear. In the meantime, John Pelham, who had managed to hold off the Federals, adroitly moved his cannon from one position to another and backpedaled his way to the ford. Here, he placed his gun in an excellent stance to abort any final rush by the Federals. As Hampton's troopers crossed the ford, Pleasonton's forces appeared at the right from Hauling's Ford. Concurrently, Stoneman's men from the Edwards' Ferry area began massing for an attack from the left. Stuart ordered Pelham to stop both armies, a near impossible task. Limbering his cannon to a spot along the river where he could defend both approaches, Pelham set up for the awaited Federal advance. Soon he was firing up one bank of the river and then turning his gun nearly around, blasting down the opposite shore, while often changing his location. Repeatedly, Pelham sent projectiles in two directions to halt the Federals from joining forces. Stuart later fondly reported that "Pelham continued to occupy the attention of the enemy . . . withdrawing from position to position." Blackford marveled as "Pelham pounded away . . . first one side and then the other, with great spirit, on the heads of their columns in full view of us."[27]

As Hampton's men traversed the ford, Stuart rode up to Blackford. With a horrified look clouding his usual smiling countenance, Jeb spoke in deliberate tones "in a voice choked with emotion . . . his eyes filling" tearfully. "Blackford, we are going to lose our rear guard." Stuart explained that Calbraith Butler's men had not come up yet and were in danger of capture to the rear. Blackford volunteered to try to find them. Stuart shook Blackford's hand, saying, "All right; if we don't meet again, good-bye, old fellow." The engineer spurred his horse, Magic, a gritty and powerful mare that had carried him on the entire raid, and headed up the bank to the rear. Stuart called out after him, "Tell Butler if he can't get through, to strike back into Pennsylvania and try to get back through West Virginia. Tell him to come in at a gallop." Once out of Stuart's sight, Blackford remembered that he "passed Pelham who with one gun, kept back for the purpose, was rapidly firing alternately up and down the river at masses of the enemy plainly in view not over a quarter of a mile away." Blackford further recalled that he and Pelham "waved our hats at each other as I passed."[28] Pelham's unenviable duty remained to hold back the Federals until Blackford returned.

Riding at a gallop, Blackford retraced the trail taken only hours before by the Confederate raiders. Along the way he ran into the couriers that Stuart had dispatched earlier in the day in search of Butler. Each reported that Butler could not be found. Blackford continued, covering nearly four miles without a trace of the rearguard. In despair and virtually giving up all hope of finding Butler, Blackford rounded a bend and happily eyed the missing men. Without delay the two officers led the regiment toward the ford in breakneck fashion. Butler's one cannon, a piece from Hart's battery, had much difficulty in keeping up the grueling pace, and Blackford strongly suggested cutting the horses loose and abandoning the gun. Butler, however, insisted that the cannon not be left behind, and the gunners somehow managed with liberal use of the whip to keep the gun from lagging.

Approaching the ford at about noon, Blackford listened for the boom of Pelham's cannon, for "so long as that [sound] continued in action, I knew the way was still open." Hearing the repeated blasts, Blackford confidently headed toward the ford, but the more cautious Butler ordered his men to draw sabers. Dashing forward, they spotted Pelham in the distance, personally directing fire on the enemy—at the same spot where Blackford had waved to him on his way to find Butler. Better yet, the young artillerist had cleared a corridor from which the entire regiment could pass safely to the ford. As Pelham's single cannon staunchly held the enemy back, Blackford and Butler led the splash into White's Ford. With Butler's men now in the water, Stuart sent Channing Price with a note for Pelham to disengage the enemy: "Major Pelham, get your gun across the river—that's an order. Stuart." Quickly, Pelham ordered his gunners to the opposite shore. When Pelham and his men reached approximately halfway across the Potomac, Federal rifles opened up on them with a "galling fire . . . the bullets splashing the water around us like a shower of rain." The blasts ended abruptly, however, as his other guns on the Virginia shoreline answered the Federals with a deadly bombardment of their own. As the last of Pelham's guns reached safety, Stuart and Wade Hampton jumped into the shallow water and helped muscle the cannon up the steep embankment.[29]

While the last of Stuart's column finished crossing White's Ford, many of Pleasonton's Federals swarmed down to the banks of the Potomac. Union horses, however, had become "so thoroughly exhausted," admitted Pleasonton, "as to be unable to move the guns up the steep hills on the road the enemy took." Some of the Federals attempted to push the cannons up the inclined terrain by hand. Pleasonton concluded: "This rendered our movement so slow that the enemy had time to cross the river." Just in case Pelham ordered his gunners to send a few farewell shots across the river as a warning to the Federals against pursuit. But Pleasonton appeared to have no inclination to follow. The gloom on the Federal side of

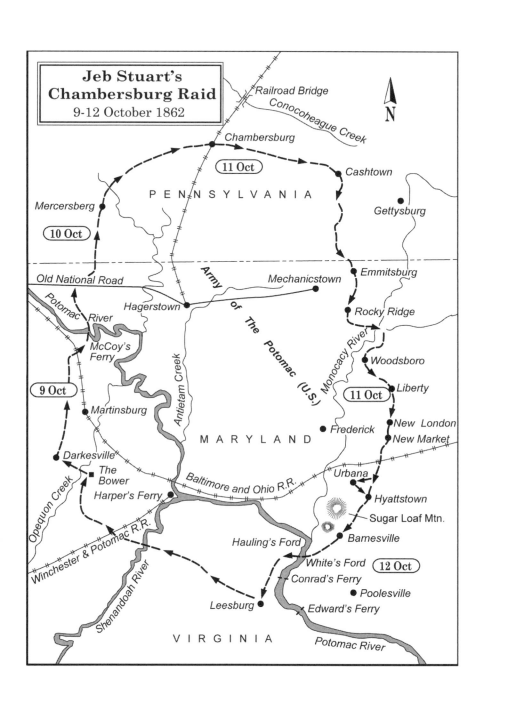

the river contrasted sharply with the exhilaration displayed on the opposite shore. Tired but rejuvenated, Stuart smiled broadly as he rode among his warriors. "Exulting cheers . . . greeted Stuart as he rode along their lines," penned a proud Henry McClellan. "Stuart's joy at the successful termination of his expedition was unbounded."[30]

Within half a mile from the crossing Stuart allowed the bone-weary horsemen a rest. Many simply fell from their horses to the ground in a stupor. Stuart then led the bulk of the column southwest toward Leesburg, a ride of less than five miles. Townspeople hailed the dusty horsemen as they trotted slowly into town. Here they camped for the night "as weary a set as ever dismounted," recalled Blackford, but even a torrential downpour of rain could not dampen their spirits.[31]

The ride around McClellan covered 126 miles in three days, almost all of it within enemy country. Incredibly, the last ninety miles from Chambersburg, which included a forced night march, came with only one halt of half an hour within twenty-seven hours. At its climax Stuart had forged an escape through Federal forces, which greatly outnumbered his own, while leading exhausted men. "His march from Chambersburg," wrote the boyishly enthusiastic Henry McClellan, "is one of the most remarkable on record." The booty gathered was even more astonishing: 1,200 Pennsylvania horses, thirty civilians of prominent social rank destined to Richmond and later traded for captured Confederate citizens, the parole of 280 Federal soldiers from Chambersburg hospitals, and supplies and railroad property destruction with an estimated value of $250,000. Losses were negligible: none killed, one wounded, two captured, and sixty lame horses left behind. Stuart's personal loss included two of his prized mounts, Lady Margrave and Skylark. This occurred when Stuart's servant, "Mulatto Bob," who had an affinity for applejack, consumed too much of the beverage and passed out along the roadside. Later awakened, but still in a stupor, "Mulatto Bob," along with the two horses, fell into Union hands.[32]

What reasons existed for the overwhelming success of the raid? The Confederate high command shoved aside all petty bickering and former disagreements, such as the feud between Stuart and "Grumble" Jones, to work as a team. Outnumbered and in enemy territory, the raiders harmoniously strove to attain an objective as a single unit, a goal the Federals sometimes ignored. The weather chanced to play into the hands of the Rebels. Rain restricted the dust the Yankees could normally have spied to track the trail of the raiders. Fog, conversely, hindered the view of the Federals from the various signal stations along the way. The stolen horses in Pennsylvania offered the Rebels a much-needed change of horseflesh during a nearly unbroken march. The Federals, on the other hand, had no such reserves, causing breakdowns when speed was essential. Stuart's decision to ride through the night literally stole a march on the enemy since stopping for the darkness would have doomed the expedition. The elements of surprise and swiftness cannot be disregarded: Stuart realized, as usual, that keeping the enemy on its heels, guessing at his intentions, gave him the advantage. Daring must also be considered. The entire raid, when laid out on a map, appeared suicidal. Yet the audacity of the entire notion of a raid around McClellan's army enhanced the chances for exploiting the Federals' uncertainty. Furthermore, the exceptional work of the guides, in particular Benjamin Stephen White, through Pennsylvania and Maryland provided Stuart with a secret weapon. The effectiveness of John Pelham and his gunners also gave Stuart a decided edge. Essential to the final crossing at White's Ford, Pelham's diligence and steadfastness decided the fate of Butler's rearguard. If this segment of Stuart's cavalry had fallen into Federal hands, as it nearly did, the raid would have been deemed a failure. The adroitness of Pelham and his able artillerists saved the day and allowed Stuart to later bask in the glory. Luck, always a considerable factor in such enterprises, can never be discounted, and Stuart was blessed with it. However, Stuart forced some of his good fortune with his "shrewdness and sagacity and boldness," according to Blackford. "Take him all in all—capacity, daring, skill, swiftness, *élan*—," wrote Kyd Douglas, "America never produced Stuart's equal as a cavalry commander. . . . There was but one Jeb Stuart."[33]

And what blame can be placed on the Federals for letting their prey escape? Certainly the Federals from McClellan down reacted slowly, and often clumsily, to the invasion by the Rebels. Much blame has been placed on Little Mac's subordinates, especially Alfred Pleasonton. However, the historian Stephen Z. Starr, a noted expert on the Federal cavalry, exonerates Pleasonton from all wrongdoing. Starr maintains that Yankee scouts determined that Stuart's destination was the Monocacy River, and Pleasonton gave chase to the best of his ability. Later, when Pleasonton reached White's Ford with his available four hundred men after a grueling seventy-eight-mile march, Stuart had already crossed safely "without . . . molestation."[34]

After a good night's rest the column made its way back across the Blue Ridge Mountains. Stuart and his staff officers rode on ahead to the Bower where "great demonstrations of joy" greeted them. The remainder of the caravan arrived hours later. The Dandridge family once more rolled out the welcome mat for the heroes. Various foreboding rumors, including one that Stuart had been killed and his command captured, had reached the Bower in the preceding days. Quite naturally, great concern swept through the family members, especially Sallie, who fairly wept when John Pelham rode up. The unexpected presence of staff officer Major Norman Fitzhugh, captured at Verdiersville back in mid-August, made the return to the Bower even more joyous. Once the warriors were fed and rested, they shared their stories and exploits from the previous days. The non-participants in the raid reveled in the tales told by the others. Lieutenant James H. Williams of Chew's battery listened and wished he had been involved: "Stuart has made the entire compass of the enemy's lines, a dash more brilliant than any yet. . . . Major Pelham, Chief of his Artillery, has just told me of it, many amusing incidents. . . . What plunder."[35]

Stuart's written report concluded with praise for his subordinates and the accomplishments of the raid as a whole: "The conduct of the command, and their behavior towards the inhabitants, are worthy of the highest praise, a few individual cases only were exceptions in this particular. . . . The results of this expedition, in a moral and political point of view, can hardly be estimated, and the consternation among property holders in Pennsylvania beggars description."

Presuming that divine providence had intervened on his behalf, Stuart closed the report with thanks to the Almighty. The succinctness of the report, minus Stuart's usual verbiage and self-praise, indicated a growth in maturity on his part as a military communicator. Only when he referred to his trek from Chambersburg as "a march without parallel in history" did he revert to his old form.[36]

Some criticized the entire raid as a waste of horseflesh and energy. Many in the infantry wondered aloud if the excursion's value equaled the risks taken. Certainly the fact that the railroad bridge above Chambersburg remained intact initiated some of these complaints and rendered them legitimate. Since the core of the raid depended on the destruction of the bridge, critics labeled the entire affair "pointless." Even one of Stuart's own troopers referred to the expedition as nothing more than "horse stealing" and "abuse of old folks." Others felt Stuart used it as an opportunity to enhance his reputation and earn promotion. William Dorsey Pender, a classmate of Stuart's at West Point, penned his wife: "Beaut is after a Lieut. Generalcy." Wade Hampton saw the incursion a bit differently but still criticized Stuart: "I suppose Stuart will as usual give all the credit to the Va. Brigades. He praises them on all occasions, but does not often give us credit."[37]

For the most part, however, praise rolled in. Richmond newspapers nearly deified Stuart for his exploit, claiming the raid "cheered" the Confederacy and calling it "a morale victory of some magnitude." The extraordinary boost in morale cannot be denied. Robert E. Lee's opinion, of course, carried the heaviest weight, and the commanding general's reports to the War Department greatly sanctioned the accomplishments of the raid, declaring the expedition "eminently successful."[38]

Perhaps overlooked in the results of the raid is the remarkably negative effect it had on the Federal high command. From its outset to well beyond its conclusion, Union officials bickered and feuded like schoolchildren. McClellan constantly complained that "this exhausting service completely broke down nearly all of our cavalry horses and rendered a remount absolutely indispensable before we could advance on the enemy." To Lincoln he lamented, "Horses are absolutely broken down from fatigue . . . sore-tongued, lameness and sore backs." The president shot back an unsympathetic response: "I have just read your dispatch about sore-tongued and fatigued horses. Will you pardon me for asking what the horses of your army have done since the battle of Antietam that fatigues anything?"[39] The incongruous relationship that existed between Lincoln and McClellan for the many preceding months was all but shattered. Lincoln received word of Stuart's escape into Virginia while relaxing with friends aboard a boat on the Potomac River. When questioned about McClellan, the president picked up a stick and drew a circle on the deck, explaining, "When I was a boy, we used to play a game—three times around, and out. Stuart has been around McClellan twice. If he goes around him once more, gentlemen, McClellan will be out."[40]

Complaints rolled in from other Northern sources. Gideon Welles, Lincoln's loyal secretary of the navy, concluded: "It is humiliating, disgraceful. . . . It is not a pleasant fact to know that we are clothing, mounting and subsisting not only our troops but the Rebels also." Robert Gould Shaw, the future colonel of the famed Fifty-fourth Massachusetts Infantry, in a letter home wrote: "The raid of Lee's cavalry into Pennsylvania makes us feel pretty cheap; they must have had an exciting time of it." One colonel stated: "I fear our cavalry is an awful botch." Perhaps the simplest assessment of the raid dripped from the pen of a *New York Times* correspondent: "That shrewd gambler, Stuart, has euchered us again."[41]

Stuart wrote his "Darling Wife" shortly after the raid: "It is a march without a parallel. . . . Whether it will be appreciated as highly as Chickahominy and Catlett by our people I can't tell of course. But if my wifie is proud of me I am satisfied."[42]

So delighted with his accomplishment, Stuart decided on a "grand celebration ball" to be held on the evening of Wednesday, October 15. Invitations went out to the folks of the countryside, and wagons, drawn by the stolen Pennsylvania horses, were detailed to gather up the people. Music once more filled the air at the Bower as Stuart's musicians played long into the night. Von Borcke and his accomplice, Tiernan Brien, added to the entertainment with another "popular extravaganza." Pelham in full dress uniform escorted Sallie on his arm, and later the two engaged in a late-night stroll along the banks of the Opequon. Jeb's wife, Flora, arrived that evening for the festivities and danced repeatedly with her husband. As the hours passed that blissful evening, Stuart's party makers also reveled in the attention given them. Their adventurous tales of the time spent on Northern soil thrilled the ladies and guests. The daring escape at the eleventh hour at White's Ford climaxed the evening's narrative. When at last the merriment died down and the guests were escorted home, the troopers wearily strode to their tents, gratified by the results of the preceding days. Dawn would bring them a rude awakening.

17
"Like Some God of Battle"

I always thought [the Federals] must have known when Pelham was opposed to them.

—John Esten Cooke

Before dawn on October 16 the troopers at the Bower awakened to the staccato sounds of "Boots and Saddles." Only moments before a courier had arrived to inform Jeb Stuart of a large movement of Federal soldiers south of the Potomac River. These columns, led by the talented Brigadier Generals Andrew A. Humphreys and Winfield Scott Hancock, contained divisions of infantry, regiments of cavalry, and ten cannon. Moving southward separately via Shepherdstown and Harpers Ferry, the bluecoats drove in Stuart's pickets and posed a serious threat. Stuart quickly reported this peril to Robert E. Lee, while requesting infantry reinforcements. Within minutes, Stuart had his men saddled and ready for action.

Exiting the Bower, Jeb led his staff officers, along with Pelham and Breathed's battery, to the turnpike running between Shepherdstown and Winchester. Near the hamlet of Kearneysville, Stuart found Fitz Lee's brigade doing battle with the advance guard of Humphreys's command. The powerful numbers of the Federals drove the Confederate cavalrymen back to a new position. Observing dust on the horizon, indicating more Federals, Stuart reluctantly ordered a withdrawal. Pelham, accordingly, moved his guns forward to stave off the Federal advance and allow the Rebel cavalrymen a successful retreat. Von Borcke noted the retrograde action was "happily well protected . . . by the excellent service of our horse-artillery under the untiring Pelham."[1] Although later reinforced by a brigade of infantry, Stuart found it expedient to continue pulling back. Near dusk, Humphreys surprisingly called off the Federal advance and bivouacked for the evening. By sundown Stuart doubled his outpost arrangement and covered it with two of Pelham's guns strategically placed on the crest of a hill. With the scare momentarily over, Jeb led his staff officers through the darkness back to the Bower a few miles away.

Arriving in a fierce downpour of rain, Stuart and his staff gladly accepted the invitation of Stephen Dandridge to come in and warm themselves before a fire. Providing hot coffee and food to the weary horsemen, Mr. Dandridge introduced two distinguished visitors, Francis Lawley of the *London Times* and Frank Vizetelly of the *Illustrated London News,* to Stuart and the others. Guests at Robert E. Lee's headquarters, the two correspondents had arrived at the Bower earlier in the day with the promise of interviewing Jeb Stuart. The cavalry chieftain, never one to dodge publicity, spoke to them for a few hours that evening before retiring. He pledged more time for their interview on the morrow.

Early the following morning, however, the Federals renewed their advance, again pressing Stuart's outposts. Angered by this second interruption and believing his stay at the Bower ended, Stuart ordered all tents struck and wagons loaded before moving off to the front. Bidding hasty farewells to their hosts, the saddened cavalrymen rode away from their paradise along Opequon Creek. Stuart apologized to the two Englishmen, who abruptly left for Lee's headquarters with the promise of a return visit. Later, nearing the field of action, Stuart, with Pelham's assistance, arranged the horse artillery in a semicircle to quell any Federal notion of further advancement. By 9:00 A.M. A. P. Hill's division of infantry arrived to strengthen the Rebel position. Skirmishing resulted before the Federals withdrew and began pulling back across the Potomac. The Federal purpose in the two days of brief combat remains a matter of debate. Von Borcke maintained it resulted from the "ill-feeling" and resentment fostered in the North by Stuart's recent venture into Pennsylvania. Whatever the reason, Stuart and his staff officers delighted in returning to the Bower, where they once more pitched their tents and made camp. For the next ten days the war faded into the background as the sounds of music again filled the air. Laughter and gaiety, dancing and romance constituted the bill of fare. Young John Pelham returned to the arms of Sallie Dandridge as they nightly strolled the banks of the Opequon. During the gorgeous fall days of that Indian summer, "the couple," as they were fondly labeled by a staff member, spent all their available time together.

True to his word, Frank Vizetelly ventured back to the Bower, where he remained for a number of days. Vizetelly soon ingratiated himself with the others by his varied abilities as an artist, chef, and notable raconteur. All agreed his nightly narratives, filled with allegorical descriptions and bawdy humor, set him apart as an accomplished storyteller. "Vizetelly was the most interesting narrator I have ever listened to," complimented Blackford. "There was not a disreputable or reputable place of prominence in the civilized world that he did not know all about, and his accounts . . . were as interesting as a novel. We had a shrewd suspicion that he drew a little on his imagination for his facts, but what difference did that make to us. . . . Vizetelly was fascinating." Moxley Sorrel simply described the Englishman as one who "could drink like a fish, and did so."[2]

The idle times at the Bower also allowed Stuart to catch up on his correspondence. To the adjutant and inspector general, Samuel S. Cooper, Stuart wrote a strong appeal for Pelham's promotion on October 24:

> Owing to the conspicuous gallantry, ability and efficiency of Major John Pelham in action, I have the honor to request that he be appointed <u>Lieutenant Co-</u>

lonel to date from the 17th September, when at the Battle of Sharpsburg, in charge of the batteries on the left wing he exhibited a dare-devil spirit that broke the enemy and forced back his left in utter confusion half a mile. As a fit reward for distinguished service then and since, I ask for his promotion as my Chief of Artillery, and also with the view of enabling him in action to take charge of and control batteries that may be brought together at critical periods and important points, such as occur in every battle.

On the same day Stuart recommended that Colonels Thomas T. Munford and Tom Rosser be promoted to the rank of brigadier general. Of Rosser, Stuart wrote: "No officer that I have met within the Confederacy combines in a more eminent degree the characteristics of the Cavalry Commander. . . . He is an officer of superior ability, possesses in an extraordinary degree the talent to command and the skill to lead with coolness and decision of character . . . he has displayed the highest qualities of a veteran commander. In judgment he is older than his years, and there are few gray heads of riper military intelligence."

Stuart further vented his anger over the promotion of "Grumble" Jones to the rank of brigadier general in a letter to Robert E. Lee: "I do not regard Brigadier Jones as deserving. . . . I must beg the Commanding General to avert such a calamity from my division."[3]

～

On Sunday, October 26, McClellan's Army of the Potomac began crossing the Potomac River below Harpers Ferry near the small community of Berlin. Eight days would pass before his entire army rested on Confederate soil, but the advance Federals deployed east of the Blue Ridge Mountains in a threatening position to Robert E. Lee. Uncertain of McClellan's intentions, Lee countered this move by dividing his forces: Jackson's corps would position itself near Winchester in the Shenandoah Valley, while Longstreet placed his corps approximately fifty miles south at Culpeper. Stuart's cavalry was ordered to the gap between the two armies with instructions to keep an eye on the enemy and prevent any attempted Federal drive through the passes of the Blue Ridge Mountains. For the next two weeks the role of the cavalry remained decidedly taxing; not only were they to defend a large area, they must face five thousand Union troopers under Pleasonton, George Bayard, and William Averell. Furthermore, Fitz Lee's brigade numbered only a thousand sabers due to an affliction, "greased heel and sore tongue," which agonized the horses.[4] Luckily, this malady had little or no effect on Pelham's artillery horses.

A hazy dawn with drizzling rain greeted Stuart's troopers on Wednesday, October 29. For Stuart, Pelham, and the staff officers the weather matched the prevailing mood among the men as they finished their packing and said their farewells to the folks at the Bower. Perhaps many of them realized they would not return to the delightful haunts of this place of rare beauty. Pelham, who had spent every possible hour with Sallie while there, attempted to allay her tears by saying, "Don't worry, Sallie, we'll drive General McClellan out of Virginia and return to the Bower before Christmas." To this she replied, "That would be the nicest Christmas present we could have."[5] The rain ceased and a blustery, cold wind blew into the men's faces as they departed from the Bower, many of them "musing on the joyous hours that had passed away," penned von Borcke. "We all rode down to the house to take a last, sad farewell of our kind host and his charming family," remembered Blackford, "whose tears fell fast as they bade us good-by."[6]

Taking Fitz Lee's depleted brigade, Stuart headed southward then crossed through the Blue Ridge onto the eastern side at Snicker's Gap. Here bodies of men and horses lay, dead and wounded, as a grim reminder that his pickets had fought off Federal cavalry in his absence. Meanwhile, Pelham veered farther south to pick up six guns at Millwood before traversing the mountains at Ashby's Gap. Along the way farmers provided food to Pelham's gunners and politely offered lodging to their leader. Pelham gladly allowed his men the victuals, but he graciously declined the overture for shelter until he reached the area of Upperville, where his men would spend the night. Pelham placed his guns on Seaton's Hill, the most imposing eminence in the area. Five hundred yards from the hill stood Welbourne, the estate of John Peyton Dulany, the father of Lieutenant Colonel Richard Henry Dulany, commander of the Seventh Virginia Cavalry. When Mr. Dulany offered Pelham and his aide, Lieutenant George Walker, an invitation to spend the night in his house, Pelham accepted.

Soon after wakening Pelham appeared in a hurry to leave, but Mr. Dulany insisted the two officers have breakfast. While waiting for the food to be prepared, Pelham paced the floor impatiently, constantly peering out the window at his guns on Seaton's Hill, apparently aware of the danger of Federals. After breakfast, Pelham thanked his host and rushed on to the hill to collect his gunners. In leaving Seaton's Hill, Pelham observed to Lieutenant Walker what a fine place this elevation made for artillery placement, as it offered a full view of the surrounding plains. Pushing on, Pelham and his gunners rendezvoused with Stuart's cavalry near the small town of Bloomfield, where they bivouacked on the night of October 30.

Starting on the next morning with a skirmish at Mountsville, Stuart and his cavalry fought the Federals almost nonstop in what would be called the Ten Days Battles. Thirty-two separate engagements took place between the opposing cavalries on the eastern side of the Blue Ridge Mountains. The battle area covered hundreds of square miles between the Blue Ridge and Bull Run Mountain ranges: from Snicker's Gap to forty miles south at the Hazel River, from Markham to twenty-five miles east at Aldie. The terrain altered sharply between steep hills, open plains, and thick woodlands, an excellent testing ground for cavalry maneuvers. Although never conclusive, the battles demonstrated a marked improvement in the fighting ability of the Federal cavalrymen. Perhaps their leadership and tactics progressed as well. Although often forced to fall back from sheer numerical disadvantage, Stuart continued to display his mettle as a leader by never allowing the enemy to break through his lines. In nearly all the engagements, however, the superiority of Pelham's horse artillery proved the difference as his talents overmatched the Federal gunners. Little wonder that Stuart praised him so highly when the fighting ended.

The Ten Days Battles began on the morning of Friday, October 31. Near dawn Stuart learned of a small Union force posted along the Snicker's Gap Turnpike near Mountsville, no more than six miles away. Heading southeastward, Stuart guided his sabers on a little-used road, hoping to surprise the Federals. Three companies of the First Rhode Island Cavalry lay ahead, resting, totally unaware of the approaching enemy. Stuart sent the Ninth and Third Virginia forward for the attack. The Rhode Islanders nearly panicked as the Virginians rode hard at them, screaming the Rebel Yell, "dispersing the whole without difficulty," according to Stuart. "We were upon them before they could prepare to resist us," reported a member of the Ninth Virginia. He added: "Many of them surrendered without attempting to run." Some of the Federals did attempt resistance, however, causing a "brief and fierce conflict."[7]

In the short encounter fifty-one Federals fell into the hands of the Confederates, while most of the others were killed or wounded. The surviving Yankees fled toward the town of Aldie, five miles southeast of Mountsville, where the strong brigade of Brigadier General George D. Bayard was posted. Members of the Third Virginia kept up the pursuit, hotly following the fleeing Federals down the pike. As the Third Virginians neared Aldie, they recoiled from the blasts of Bayard's superior forces drawn up to meet them. Stuart now turned the advance over to the Fourth Virginia Cavalry, which made it to the edge of the village before being forced back by Bayard's artillery posted on the hills west of the town. Since Pelham's artillery had not yet arrived, the Federal gunners found their mark with precise accuracy as several Confederate troopers and their horses went down in the consuming blasts. Watching from a nearby hill, Stuart seethed at the ugly situation. Mounted next to him, John Esten Cooke observed, "I never saw him more impatient." Stuart turned to Cooke and ordered, "Tell Wickham to form on the hill, and bring up Pelham at a gallop!"[8]

Cooke delivered the message to Williams C. Wickham and then went in search of Pelham. "I found him advancing, alone, at a walk, riding a huge artillery horse," penned Cooke, "his knees drawn up by the short stirrups." Pelham courteously smiled and inquired innocently, "The pieces are coming up a gallop, anything going on?" Cooke frantically explained the situation ahead and the absolute need for Pelham's guns. "All right," reassured Pelham, "they'll be there." Within minutes Pelham led his gunners to the fight near Aldie, where "Pelham was again in his element." Wheeling his guns to the top of a hill, Pelham sighted in on Bayard's artillery and began firing solid shot with a "destructive fire." The third blast disabled a Federal gun and forced Bayard's men to change their position. Other Yankee gunners soon felt the accuracy as well. "I always thought they must have known when Pelham was opposed to them," penned an admiring Cooke. "In the Southern army there was no greater artillerist than this boy." With the Federals forced to withdraw into the woods, von Borcke added his accolades: "Our flying artillery, under the intrepid and energetic John Pelham . . . had, as usual, done admirable service, disabling several of the enemy's guns, and contributing greatly, by the terror it carried into their advancing columns, to the final result."[9]

With his position solidified by Pelham's battery, Stuart brought up his horsemen in support. Suddenly, a courier appeared announcing that a large enemy force was approaching from the rear. With Bayard's five thousand men at his front and more approaching from behind, Jeb's small brigade faced the danger of being surrounded. Quickly ordering his troopers to fall back, Stuart left Pelham and his gunners to cover the retreat. Within minutes the Confederate cavalrymen safely escaped the clutches of the Federals and made their way five miles southwestward to Middleburg. Meanwhile, Bayard inexplicably pulled his forces back to Chantilly. The courier's warning had not been a hoax: Pleasonton's cavalry, supported by Pennington's horse artillery, were making their way toward Stuart from Leesburg.

Reaching Middleburg near dusk, the Confederate horsemen found the entire community aroused with an excitement that Cooke viewed as "indescribable." Men, women, and children of all ages flooded from their homes with a "joyous insanity" to greet the gray-clad warriors. Cheering wildly with tears in their eyes, the townspeople became ecstatic when Stuart finally appeared. Pulling his horse to a halt, Stuart smiled and bowed before his admirers, who began kissing his gloves and the hem of his uniform coat. Cooke later mused, "When Stuart lay down in his bivouac that night . . . I think he must have fallen asleep with a smile on his lips."[10]

The infantry troops Stuart had requested from Robert E. Lee had now pushed through Ashby's Gap and encamped near Upperville. These men consisted of Daniel Harvey Hill's battle-tested veterans. On the morning of Saturday, November 1, Stuart ordered his troopers to cover Hill's front, but new Federal movements caused him to alter his plans. Pleasonton's cavalry had begun moving westward from the slopes of Bull Run Mountain in the direction of Philomont,[11] with Snicker's Gap as the apparent objective. Stuart immediately pushed his small brigade of cavalry in that direction to intercept the Federals. Pelham and his gunners went along for assistance.

Heading through the hamlet of Union, Stuart and Pelham reached Pleasonton's forces along the Snicker's Gap Turnpike near Philomont. For the bulk of the day the fighting amounted to little more than a sparring match between the lead elements of both cavalries as they sought an opening. Late in the day, however, part of Pleasonton's horsemen pushed the advance guard of Stuart's troopers back through a wooded area. It was the breach the Federals desired. Shoving the Rebels back, the bluecoats proceeded after them only to run directly into the muzzles of Pelham's cannons. Double canister stunned the Federals and forced them back. Pleasonton later reported, "the enemy bringing up his artillery, no further advance was made."[12] With darkness setting in, both sides pulled back to bivouac. Stuart's forces once again encamped in Middleburg where the men watered and fed their horses, knowing that the next day would bring more serious fighting.

On the morning of November 2 Stuart learned that Pleasonton was moving again. This time, however, Pleasonton's cavalry had been reinforced by a brigade of Abner Doubleday's infantry under the command of Lieutenant Colonel J. William Hofmann supplemented by the First New Hampshire Battery of artillery. Jeb's information indicated that this sizable Federal force had appeared on the road toward the town of Union with its obvious goal being Ashby's Gap through the Blue Ridge Mountains. Woefully short of manpower, Stuart summoned his troopers—the Federals must be stopped.

Racing toward the town, the Confederates arrived in time to espy Pleasonton's cavalry with Hofmann's infantrymen following. Stuart ordered his men to the heights above the town where they dismounted and crouched behind a number of stone fences—a fortuitous position for the outnumbered Rebels. Pelham supported them by placing his guns at one end of the line. Meanwhile, Pleasonton arranged his men for an attack. Charging the half-hidden Confederates, the Federal horsemen came on strong only to be driven back by the opposing riflemen. Regrouping, the Federals advanced a second time to within fifty yards of the Confederate position. Here Pelham's artillery "became very quickly and effectively engaged," remembered G. W. Beale. Pelham's gunners opened up with a hail of double canister that assisted the riflemen, mistakenly reported as "infantry" by Pleasonton, in repulsing the bluecoats. "On no other field did the gallant Pelham appear to us who supported his guns on the field, to a greater advantage," noted Beale. "The rapidity and accuracy of his fire elicited rounds of hearty cheering from those of us who could see its effects."[13] Pleasonton decided to counter the strong Confederate location by employing his artillery in coordination with a succession of hit-and-run tactics from his cavalrymen before bringing in the infantry for the breakthrough. Although successful in killing a few of the Rebels, as well as some of Pelham's artillery horses, the Federal attack continued to flounder. Stuart later reported his version of the action:

> About eight o'clock the enemy began to deploy in our front both infantry and cavalry, with six or eight pieces of artillery. Our dispositions were made to receive him by putting artillery advantageously, and the cavalry dismounted behind the stone fences, which were here very numerous, and, consequently, afforded the enemy as good shelter as ourselves. Having to watch all the ave-

nues leading to my rear, my effective force for fighting was very much diminished, but the Stuart Horse Artillery, under the incomparable Pelham, supported by the cavalry sharpshooters, made a gallant and obstinate resistance, maintaining their ground for the greater part of the day, both suffering heavily.[14]

During the struggle, a detachment of Federal sharpshooters made their way to a wooded area in the valley below Pelham's battery. Periodically they came out of their concealment and fired a volley with deadly effect, killing several of Pelham's artillery horses. After discharging their weapons, the snipers retreated to the woods to reload. Pelham seethed at the loss of his horses and his own inability to draw a clear bead on the Yankees. Federal artillery under the capable Pennington, meanwhile, rained iron on Pelham's position, and two of his gunners, Corporal Christian Costigan and Private John Isaac Phillips from Breathed's battery, were hit by the vicious shelling. Costigan's wounds were immediately fatal; Phillips died the next day.[15] For one of the few times thus far in the war Pelham was forced to move his cannons to another position not of his own choosing.

Pelham's anger boiled when moments later a well-aimed Federal artillery shell detonated one of his caissons, horribly wounding two other privates, John Culbreth and John M. Bollman. Corporal Henry "Hal" Hopkins fell with less severe injuries. Another shell wounded three more men including Private Henry H. Matthews, who was struck near the hip bone.[16] The screams of these agonizingly wounded men, with their blood-soaked uniforms, prompted Pelham to instant action. Commandeering his nearest howitzer, Pelham summoned a crew of his gunners to follow him. With horses drawing the cannon, the men made their way toward the woods hiding the Yankee sharpshooters. Upon reaching a thick undergrowth, which the horses could no longer manage, Pelham had the animals unhitched. From there the gunners muscled the howitzer to a slight rise, beyond the help of Stuart's riflemen, where they waited for the reappearance of the troublesome sharpshooters. Moments later the Yankees appeared for another foray. From their hidden position, Pelham's gunners waited, the howitzer loaded with double canister. As the Federals cleared the wood and came into view, Pelham gave the order, "Fire!" Instantly, canister sprayed from the howitzer's muzzle into the faces of the unsuspecting Federals. Bluecoats toppled grotesquely as the one-inch iron balls found their mark. The surviving Yankees wildly panicked and fled for safety. Seizing the opportunity, Pelham shouted, "Come on men, let's charge them!" With Pelham in the lead, his gunners hurried after the Federals into the trees. Moments later, Pelham and his artillerists returned from the woods with their booty—captured men and horses, arms and equipment, and a Federal standard—all without the loss of a single Confederate life.[17]

Stuart's later report summed up Pelham's heroics and praised the artillerist for "sustaining in this extraordinary feat no loss whatever." Von Borcke also witnessed his young friend's incredible exploit:

> We had the opportunity here of witnessing one of those daring feats which Pelham was so constantly performing. He had been greatly annoyed during the day by a squadron of Federal cavalry which operated with great dash against his batteries. . . . they had already killed or disabled many of his horses, when our gallant major, losing all patience, suddenly advanced with one of his light howitzers at full gallop toward the wood. . . . the Yankee squadron . . . without the slightest suspicion that a cannon loaded with a double charge of canister was directed upon them from a point only a few hundred yards off. All at once, the thunder of the howitzer was heard, and its iron hail swept through the ranks of the Yankees, killing eight of their number, among whom was the colour-bearer, wounding several others, and putting the rest to flight in hopeless stampede. Pelham and his cannoneers now emerged from the wood in a run . . . amid loud shouts of applause. Before the Yankees could recover from their astonishment, the howitzer was removed, the horses were hitched to it again, and it had arrived safely at the battery.[18]

For the next few hours the fighting continued with Stuart's outnumbered troopers holding their ground. By late afternoon, however, Pleasonton wisely employed the available infantry to assist his cavalry in striking the Confederate flanks. When the pressure became too great, Stuart decided to abandon his position and ordered a withdrawal through the town of Union. As usual, Pelham drew the assignment of protecting the retreating men. Constantly firing and repositioning his cannons from one ridge to another, Pelham held the Federals back and prevented a breakthrough. Von Borcke again applauded the efforts of the Alabamian: "The retreat through Union was admirably covered by Pelham with his artillery, and was executed with great steadiness and order under a perfect hail of shot and shell." This constant barrage of Federal projectiles set ablaze various stables, buildings, and haystacks in the village of Union and "added to the terror and confusion of the scene, which now became truly frightful." Once clear of the town, Stuart halted his troopers on a rise. Here they caught their breath and girded for another attack by the enemy. Within minutes the Federals arrived and again forced a withdrawal by the Confederates.[19]

In the late afternoon Stuart pulled his forces in the direction of Upperville near Welbourne. Remembering well his stay there only three days earlier, Pelham positioned his six cannon on nearby Seaton's Hill, the same dominating eminence he had placed his guns on October 29. The Federals soon arrived, rolled twelve guns forward, and commenced a ferocious artillery duel with Pelham's gunners. For several furious minutes shells splintered trees and plowed holes into the ground as horses bolted from the awful noises. Unsuspecting farm animals, calmly grazing in the surrounding fields, suddenly became part of the melee, running frantically in all directions. One projectile exploded in the midst of a herd of sheep; amazingly, none appeared to be injured.

The Yankees made numerous attempts to push forward only to be driven back repeatedly by the accurate firing of Pelham's cannoneers. Stuart's later report described the fighting succinctly: "The enemy were held at bay until dark at Seaton's Hill,[20] which they assailed with great determination, but were each time signally repulsed by the well-directed fire of the Horse Artillery." Stuart then added a terse sentence to describe a phenomenal occurrence: "Major Pelham, directing one of the shots himself at the color bearer of an infantry regiment, struck him down at a distance of eight hundred yards."[21] That and nothing else—no other explanation, description, or plaudits emanated from the cavalry commander's usually loquacious pen. The circumstances behind this noteworthy accomplishment deserve further detail. During Pelham's confrontation with the Federal artillerists, a detail of the Seventh Indiana Volunteers appeared in the open, moving on his flank. Rolling up his shirtsleeves, Pelham personally took over one of his guns. Sighting in on the Hoosiers, Pelham was heard to say: "Here goes one for Costigan and Phillips!" and then, "Here goes one for that flag!" Pelham pulled the lanyard and awaited the result. Seconds later the projectile found its mark with perfect accuracy, wreaking havoc among the Indiana infantrymen. From a half a mile away, Pelham's one blast killed the color-sergeant and his color-corporal while wounding nearly a score of others. The surviving Hoosiers turned and fled back into the woods for safety.[22] In his report Lieutenant Colonel J. William Hofmann, commander of the Federal infantry, attested to the exactness of Pelham's shot: "As we advanced on the enemy they again opened up on us with shell, one of which struck the line of the Seventh Indiana, killing the color-sergeant and 1 color-corporal and wounding a number of others. We then took possession of a wood beyond the church, on the left of the road. . . . The enemy in the mean time continued throwing shell, causing a number of casualties."

With dusk falling, Stuart once more decided to pull back his forces. Pelham, of course, covered the retreat with his usual acumen, compelling the pursuing Federal infantry to withdraw. Hofmann again confirmed the accuracy of Pelham's gunners: "As we were crossing an open field, a shell struck the line of the Fifty-sixth Regiment Pennsylvania Volunteers, killing 2 men of Company G and mortally wounded 2 others."[23] Darkness ended the fighting for the day. Stuart bivouacked a mile east of Upperville along Pantherskin Creek with Pelham's weary artillerists the last to enter camp. As Pelham walked in, his face streaked with grime, sweat, and grease, Stuart greeted him with an exuberant bear hug. "Pelham, my boy," roared Jeb, "it was bully—bully!" Acknowledging the praise with his typical blush and nonchalance, Pelham softly admitted, "Well, it was a pretty good day."[24] It had, in fact, been a miraculous day, perhaps the most superlative the young Alabamian had sustained to date in the war.

Sometime that day distressing news came to Stuart—not from the battlefront but from far away Lynchburg: his four-year-old daughter, Flora, "La Petite" as he called her, was deathly ill. Word of the tragic circumstances arrived in a letter from Jeb's brother-in-law, who prevailed on the cavalry chieftain to leave his post and go to the family at once. Although deeply touched by the dolorous information, the professional soldier within Stuart forced him to stay with his cavalry. He explained this in a letter to his wife:

> If my darling's case is hopeless there are ten chances to one that I will get to Lynchburg too late. If she is convalescent why should my presence be necessary? She was sick nine days before I knew it.
>
> Let us trust in the Good God, who has blessed us so much, to spare our child to us, but if it should please him to take her from us let us bear it with Christian fortitude and resignation. . . . At all events, remember that Flora was not of this world, she belonged to another, and will be better off by far in her heavenly habitation.[25]

Meanwhile, Pleasonton's forces, now strengthened by the addition of William Woods Averell's cavalry and the horse artillery of John C. Tidball, possessed a distinct numerical superiority over Stuart's command. Pleasonton meant to press his advantage, and by 9:00 A.M., Monday, November 3, the Federals, according to Stuart, were advancing "by all the roads and fords." For the next few hours, combined Federal infantry and cavalry pushed forward in what von Borcke described as "a mighty avalanche." Stuart yielded ground, but he stubbornly refused to retreat to safety. Pelham's crew of artillerists was again called upon to resist any Federal breakthrough. Although the fighting intensified, Stuart adamantly rejected the notion of withdrawing. "Stuart's face was stormy," remembered John Esten Cooke, "his eyes like 'a devouring fire.' . . . The veins in his forehead grew black, and the man looked 'dangerous.'" Only when the Federals began outflanking Stuart's position and word arrived that McClellan's entire army was moving southward did Jeb call for a retreat. "In consequence of the long delay of our commander in issuing the orders," criticized von Borcke, "[the withdrawal] was managed, I am sorry to say, with a great deal of haste and confusion, and came very near being a rout."[26]

While Stuart pulled his forces out of Upperville and headed toward Ashby's Gap, Pelham moved his guns from one location to another in order to slow the advance of the Federals. By late afternoon, Pelham had placed his cannon west of Upperville on Fairview Hill. Here, all six of his pieces in Breathed's battery opened a concentrated fire at the Federals, allowing Stuart's forces to escape successfully. Von Borcke praised Pelham's magnificent effort:

Too much credit cannot be given to Pelham for the great forethought and coolness with which he had taken his artillery along a little by-path around the village to a point about a mile distant, where, placing his guns in a favorable position, he skillfully covered our retreat, and, by the accuracy and rapidity of his firing, saved us from greater disaster. My brave friend was himself hard at work in his shirt-sleeves, taking a hand with the cannoneers in loading and aiming the pieces. Meanwhile the united efforts of General Stuart and the members of his staff had availed to put a stop to the stampede; our regiments were re-formed and our lines re-established. But the scene was still frightful.[27]

Angered by Pelham's dominance, Pleasonton sent a detachment of sharpshooters from the Third Indiana Cavalry to halt the Confederate cannons. Galloping to a thick stone fence some two hundred yards from Pelham's guns, the Hoosiers dismounted and aligned themselves behind the barrier. Raising their carbines above the fence, the Yankees began a deadly fire into Pelham's gunners and horses. The steady blasts of double canister from Pelham's guns had little effect, as the iron balls merely caromed off the stone barricade. Von Borcke rode up with two squadrons of cavalry and attempted to charge the Federals behind the wall, but to no avail. When the riders made it to within eighty yards of the fence, they dispersed from the rapid, deadly fire and returned to the site of Pelham's guns. Switching to solid shot, Pelham opened again on the stone fence with satisfying results. "Every ball demolished large sections of the fence," wrote Von, "scattering the fragments of the stones all around, killing and wounding many of the sharpshooters behind it, and driving off the rest, whom we pursued, cutting down and taking prisoners nearly all of them."[28] Pelham, von Borcke, and the others soon exited Fairview Hill and followed Stuart's forces toward Ashby's Gap.

By 6:00 P.M. they came upon Stuart's campsite at the base of the Blue Ridge Mountains. Far to their rear Pleasonton's forces followed and seemed intent on continuing the day's running fight. However, Stuart had received some help of his own in the form of a battery from the command of D. H. Hill's division stationed near Ashby's Gap. This Alabama battery, ably led by Captain Robert A. Hardaway, included a British-imported 12-pounder Whitworth rifle noted for its long-range killing power. Wheeling the breech-loading Whitworth forward, Hardaway's gunners let fly with a blast sending the projectile at the Federals over three miles away. A direct hit among the Yankee artillerists forced them back, and the fighting ended for the day. Confederates marveled at the gun's amazing accuracy. "At a single shot," wrote Stuart, "it drove away an enemy battery near Upperville, three or four miles away." Stuart also did not overlook the excellence of his own gunners: "Breathed's battery, of the Stuart Horse Artillery, added to its many laurels on these hard-fought fields." Indeed, Pelham's cannoneers had virtually exhausted their ammunition that day. Luckily, Edward Porter Alexander's ordnance train passed nearby, and Alexander supplied the horse artillery with 300 rounds of 3-inch projectiles and 500 friction primers. Pelham quickly dispersed these necessary articles among Breathed's gunners.[29] The weary men now settled in around their campfires for a night's rest.

Shortly after midnight Stuart summoned Tom Rosser and Pelham. Stuart explained that within minutes he would be leaving to confer with Stonewall Jackson near Millwood, a ride of nearly twelve miles. Jeb confirmed temporary command of Fitz Lee's Brigade on Colonel Rosser and instructed the Texan that after sunrise he was to take the cavalry to Piedmont Station on the Manassas Gap Railroad and pick up two regiments that Stuart sent as a rearguard to protect his supply trains. From Piedmont Rosser would head east to Markham and link up with Hampton's Brigade. Pelham's artillery would follow Rosser and keep the enemy off his tail. Stuart then shook hands with the two young officers and dismissed them. As they made their way back to their bivouac, Pelham and Rosser glanced at each other and smiled. So long ago, as they shared the same room at West Point, they had dreamed of the chance to fight side by side. So many hours into the night they had discussed this moment. Now the time had come. They would get their chance on the morrow.

It was not to be an easy day for Rosser and Pelham. Early that November 4 morning, Rosser, as directed, led his cavalrymen to Piedmont Station. Finding the two regiments already gone, Rosser ordered his sabers on to Markham, where he hoped to rendezvous with the brigade of Wade Hampton. Before the juncture was established, however, Federal cavalry under the command of William Woods Averell sliced in on Rosser's rear, compelling the Rebels to withdraw. Pelham, with the guns of Mathis W. Henry's battery and assisted by a detachment of James Gordon's First North Carolinians, drew the difficult assignment of holding off the Federals. For the better part of the day Pelham's gunners fired and fell back, successfully protecting Rosser's rear. Late in the day as Federal attacks became stronger, Pelham realized that despite his accomplishment, he would be forced to make a stand. Guiding his gunners to a nearby hill, Pelham ordered the cannons unlimbered. Mounted on a spirited black horse, the blond Alabamian eyed the terrain in the distance where New York cavalrymen wound their way toward the hill. After a few moments of silence, he shouted, "Stand to it men! Load with double canister! Hold your fire until I give the word!" As one Federal observer later remarked, "[Pelham had] put on his fighting clothes."[30]

While Pelham's gunners waited further orders, Gordon led his valiant Tarheels down the slope, hoping to break the New Yorkers with his audacity. The Federals grouped behind a stone fence and fired a deadly volley into the oncoming North Carolinians. Veering somewhat off course, Gordon's troopers stumbled into a hidden ditch, which unhorsed many of the riders. Another volley forced the Rebels to remount quickly and beat a path back to Pelham's guns. Incensed by the hasty retreat, Gordon, his face "flushed with rage," rode up to Pelham who greeted him with a serene smile. "Don't annoy yourself, Colonel," reassured Pelham, "they won't ride over me."

There Pelham sat his horse, calmly, almost contemptuous of the advancing Federals. "He did not move a muscle," remembered John Esten Cooke, "but his teeth were clenched beneath the thin lips, and the blue eyes blazed." On came the Empire Staters. When they reached within one hundred yards of his six cannons, Pelham stood in his stirrups and with all his lung power screamed "Fire!" Instantly, the field pieces belched forth sheets of flame, and hundreds of canister balls tore into the attackers, driving them rearward. "Pelham's reply was overwhelming," wrote an admiring Federal soldier. "The attack was instantly repulsed, and the New York boys were swept down the hill like chaff, leaving their dead and wounded in swaths." The badly shaken bluecoats regrouped and dismounted, sheltering themselves behind trees and boulders. In the meantime, Pelham calmly ordered the guns reloaded.

Suddenly, an entirely new threat came from Pelham's rear. Another Federal detachment had made a circuitous path behind Pelham's guns and swarmed toward the artillerists out of the woods. Simultaneously, the New Yorkers to his front renewed their charge. Caught in the middle of the bluecoats, Pelham sprung into action with the order, "Action rear!" Two of Captain Henry's guns instantly swung toward the rear in an attempt to halt the onrushing Yankees, while the other four continued to pound the front. With the determination of men possessed, the Federals hurled themselves forward, many reaching the very muzzles of Pelham's guns. Drawing his saber, Pelham rode among the enemy, furiously wielding the blade against those who dared to capture his guns. For nearly thirty minutes the struggle continued with Pelham's men surrounded. "None but the very best troops could have sustained the shock," wrote a Federal participant. "Indeed . . . Pelham should have surrendered. His situation seemed hopeless, desperate; and no imputation of lack of courage could have lain against him had he delivered up his command then and there. . . . [But] Pelham . . . moved calmly among his trained bulldogs, exhorting them to stand by the guns. . . . Standing, as if rooted to the soil, he struck . . . first with one hand and then with the other. . . . Cheered on by the words and example of their boyish commander, the grizzled veterans, officers and men alike, handled that superb artillery so efficiently that the cannon's mouths seemed to breathe a living fire in our very faces."[31]

Then from the mouths of the Napoleon Detachment arose a sound, nearly inaudible at first, above the cacophony of screaming men and horses and the thunder of the guns. At first indistinguishable, the melodious sound soon became recognizable—the "Marseillaise" being sung while the men loaded, fired, swabbed, and reloaded the cannons. "There was something in the voices of these men inexpressibly defiant and determined," penned John Esten Cooke. "The martial chorus rang out splendid and triumphant; it seemed to say, 'Come! we will die here, where we stand!' Above them, on his horse, towered the form of Pelham, and his voice made the men grow wild. Never have I seen such a fight."[32]

Both columns of Federals now aligned themselves for a final push toward the cannons. As they rushed forward, another familiar sound pierced the air. From the right came the galloping horsemen of Tom Rosser, sabers drawn, screaming the terrifying Rebel Yell. The valiant Federals, who had so nearly captured the prized cannons, fell back in disorder and ran for safety. "In an instant we were brushed from the hillside—almost annihilated," wrote a surviving bluecoat. "With a sort of fascination my gaze followed Pelham wherever he moved; and at the moment when he saw relief was at hand, I, though badly wounded, distinctly saw the young officer lift his cap in salute to the staggering, bleeding ranks in recognition of their splendid valor, and heard their triumphant cheers in reply." With darkness rapidly falling, Rosser and Pelham decided they had had enough fighting for one day. Rosser gave the order and the weary men headed south toward Barbee's Cross Roads. However, instead of stopping there, Rosser, perhaps leery of further Federal attacks, moved seven miles farther on to the village of Orleans.[33]

Oddly enough, Stuart had witnessed part of the engagement and retreat, watching from an elevation in the Blue Ridge Mountains. Without knowing the heroic struggle that Rosser and Pelham had endured that day, Stuart immediately assumed they had been routed. Getting back to Rosser would take hours through the darkness and the meandering pathways of the Blue Ridge, but Stuart's party started out immediately. Along the way they stumbled across a local of "wild and haggard appearance" who might serve as a guide. "You lead us to Barbee's Cross Roads, over there," said Stuart curtly with a gun pointed at the local, "and I'll give you a reward. Betray us, and I'll shoot you down quick as thought." Near midnight, the struggling party reached Barbee's, where Stuart promptly handed the delighted guide a fifty-dollar bill. Finding only a small detail of Rosser's men standing picket at the Cross Roads and learning that the main body was another seven miles beyond, Stuart grew livid. Summoning von Borcke, Stuart's orders were explicit: find Rosser and bring the entire command to the Cross Roads at once "that we may be ready to receive the enemy at this place at daylight." Riding through the night, the exhausted Prussian located Rosser, who, though "exceedingly annoyed" by the orders, made his way to Stuart before dawn.[34]

Before daybreak on November 5, Hampton's brigade arrived at Barbee's Cross Roads bringing Stuart's numbers to roughly three thousand. Hampton's men also wheeled in two brass cannons, which their wealthy commander had imported from Europe at his own expense. Exceptional at long-range firing, these guns remained too heavy for Pelham's horse artillery, according to von Borcke's assessment. Stuart now deployed his men for the expected Federal attack: Hampton's brigade on the left, Fitz Lee's brigade, still under Rosser, on the right. Pelham positioned Captain

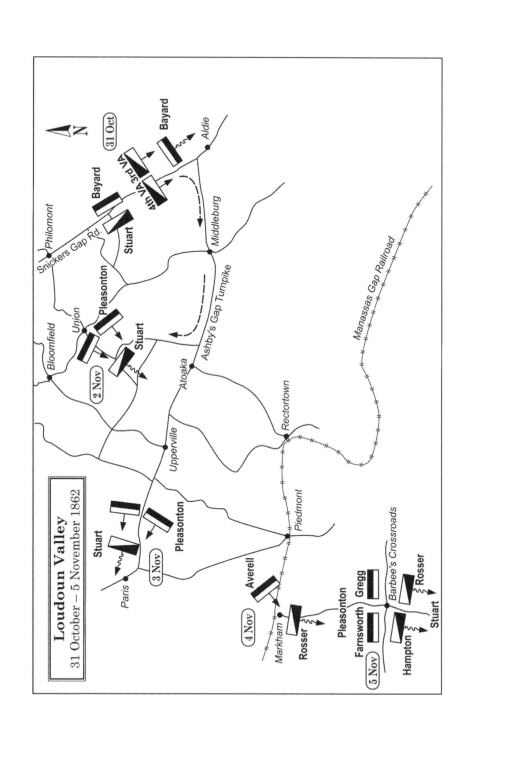

Loudoun Valley
31 October – 5 November 1862

N

31 Oct

Bayard

Bayard

4th VA

3rd VA

Stuart

Aldie

Philomont

Snickers Gap Rd.

Middleburg

Ashby's Gap Turnpike

Pleasonton

Bloomfield

Union

Stuart

2 Nov

Atoaka

Upperville

Rectortown

Manassas Gap Railroad

Stuart

Pleasonton

3 Nov

Paris

Piedmont

Averell

4 Nov

Markham

Rosser

Barbee's Crossroads

Rosser

Pleasonton

Gregg

Farnsworth

5 Nov

Hampton

Stuart

Mathis Henry's two pieces on a hill north of the Cross Roads. "The crest of the hill immediately north of the town," according to Stuart, "was occupied by our artillery and sharpshooters, with a view to rake the enemy's column as it moved up the road."[35]

By 9:00 A.M. Pleasonton's forces arrived, and the fighting commenced with a spirited artillery duel in which Pelham's boys more than held their own. Again his adversary was the worthy Alexander Pennington, whose gunners continued to show signs of marked improvement. Pleasonton, meanwhile, aligned his forces for the assault. Bugles blared and the Federals moved forward. Stuart noted that "the enemy at length approached under cover of ravines and woods," but maintained that his cavalry strongly held "the cross-roads, where our artillery had complete control of the approaches." Jeb's assessment of the situation may have been a bit exaggerated since Federal cavalry forced Pelham to move his guns by threatening his flank. But after repositioning, Pelham fired some deadly canister rounds into the Eighth Illinois Cavalry.[36]

Heavy skirmishing occurred all along the Confederate defensive line as Stuart's sharpshooters, ably assisted by the accurate firing of Pelham's gunners, withstood the onslaught. By mid-afternoon, however, Stuart received a report that other Federal forces had reached Warrenton to his rear. This information, later proven untrue, forced Stuart to order a retreat toward Orleans. As his men pulled away, James Gordon's North Carolinians on Stuart's left had to fight their way out. Slowed by the jumbled terrain, some of Gordon's troopers fell from their mounts, causing momentary confusion, and concealed Federal riflemen opened fire. "A number of men and horses were shot down," reported Gordon, who had no alternative but to order a withdrawal. "To my surprise," continued Gordon, "I saw a large body of cavalry charging upon us from the right, which had been concealed from view by a hill. . . . I lost in this affair four men killed, seventeen wounded and captured." Gordon may have understated his losses. Pleasonton reported that the Federal charge "routed the enemy and sent them flying in all directions. Thirty-seven of the rebel dead were left on this field, and more than that number of arms, horses and prisoners were captured."[37]

Pelham, once more, drew rearguard duty, and his blazing guns withstood any attempt at pursuit by the Federals. Pelham's stubborn resistance allowed Stuart's column the luxury of an hour's rest at Orleans to feed and water their horses. In the remaining hours of daylight Stuart led his cavalry southward to Waterloo Bridge, where they camped for the night.

In the early morning with darkness still shrouding Stuart's bivouac, an urgent telegram arrived. The sleepy von Borcke opened it and read "the most painful intelligence": little Flora had died on November 3 and was buried the next day. Shaking with grief, von Borcke awakened Jeb, and without a word, handed him the message. Stuart read the tragic news silently, "threw his arms around my neck," stated the Prussian, "and wept bitter tears upon my breast." Later that day Stuart summoned his courage to write his bereft wife:

> I was somewhat expecting it and yet it grieves me more, the more I think of it. . . . my heart is ready to burst. I want to see you so much and to know what her last words were. . . . She is up in Heaven where she will still pray for her Pa and look down upon him in the day of battle. Oh, if I could see her again. No child can ever have such a hold on my affection as she had. She was not of earth however. . . .
>
> I have been in battle every day since I heard of Flora's sickness and that was November 2nd. She died November 3rd and I heard of it November 6th. . . . God has shielded me thus far from bodily harm, but I feel perfect resignation to go at his bidding, and join my little Flora.[38]

Ten days later Stuart shared his anguish in a letter to his friend Lily Parran Lee, stating, "May you never feel such a blow." Stuart added that his wife was still "not herself." Stuart's pain stayed with him for the remainder of his life. "His devotion towards his young wife and children attracted the attention of every one," wrote John Esten Cooke. "Many months afterward, when speaking of [his daughter], the tears gushed to his eyes, and he murmured in a broken voice: 'I will never get over it—never!' "[39]

Little activity occurred on Stuart's front for most of the morning of Thursday, November 6. By midday Stuart had led the remainder of the brigade across the river in a reconnaissance. Before long a large Federal force appeared and in a lively action drove Stuart's heavily outnumbered troopers in a "disgraceful stampede" back across Waterloo Bridge. Luckily Pelham's alert gunners and a body of concealed sharpshooters waited at the bridge to hold back the Federals, which allowed a clean, but embarrassing, escape. Fighting carried on around the bridge until nightfall, when Stuart decided to retreat farther southward toward the village of Jeffersonton. Stuart had already prepared for such a hurried departure by readying Waterloo Bridge with flammable material. In the darkness the wooden span was set ablaze to hinder the Federals from following.

That night winter came to upper Virginia. Snow fell and gusty winds blew, chilling the men to the bone. Stuart and his staff found a dilapidated, abandoned wooden house in which to spend the night. With no panes in the windows and cracks in the walls, the snow swirled into the shanty. A crackling fire aided in staving off the bitter winds, but the men slept little under the unfavorable circumstances. Pelham, most likely, slept outdoors with his gunners, who carefully guarded the area. By dawn the snow mixed with rain soaking the men through. Furthermore, men and horses had gone twenty-four hours with virtually no food. Stuart again decided to pull back across the slippery, miry roads with the Federals following.

The artillery horses had much difficulty pulling the guns over the icy paths, and at one point the Confederates had to bury two of the pieces. The subject of these guns became a serious point of contention between the Federal and Confederate commands with Pleasonton boasting that he captured them and the Rebel high command denying his claim. "[Pleasonton's] report is entirely without foundation," scoffed John Esten Cooke. "[Pelham] never lost a gun there or anywhere else."[40]

For the next three days the ragged and mud-splattered Rebels somehow negotiated the morass, stopping to scuffle with the enemy at Amissville, Gaines' Cross Roads, and Newby's Cross Roads in what W. W. Blackford referred to as an "endless series of skirmishes."[41] Each time Stuart's weary men retreated with Pelham's cannoneers acting as a rearguard to hinder Federal pursuit. The continuous movement, nearly constant fighting, and lack of supplies against a larger and better-fed enemy cavalry wore heavily on the men and horses. The ugly weather added to their woes.

Monday, November 10, brought the last of the Ten Days Battles at a place known as Corbin's Cross Roads, near Amissville, a little more than ten miles north of Culpeper. Stuart, possibly tired of retreating and reinforced by two regiments of infantry, determined to take the offensive against Pleasonton's forces. His plan called for simultaneous attacks by the brigades of Hampton and Fitz Lee (still under the command of Rosser) with a battery of Pelham's horse artillery. By 10:00 A.M., Stuart's lead horsemen under Rosser clashed with the pickets of the Federals, and the bluecoats immediately backpedaled from the surprise. Unfortunately, Hampton did not receive Stuart's orders so his troopers did not take part in the fighting, leaving Rosser to initiate the battle himself. Still his sabers pushed the Federal pickets back more than two miles. Pelham's guns helped break the Yankees. Watching the Federal horsemen of the Fifth New York Cavalry, von Borcke could not help but admire the enemy's "excellent behaviour . . . [when they] received with the greatest coolness the heavy fire of our battery, maintaining perfect order while shell after shell exploded in their ranks, and saddle after saddle was emptied—quietly filling the gaps in their lines, and finally only giving way when we charged them with several squadrons." Falling back to the main column, the retreating Federals alerted Pleasonton to the danger.[42]

Pleasonton ordered up his artillery, and soon several Union batteries opened up on Pelham's guns. Taking a beating from the Federal bombardment, Pelham doubled his effort. Unfortunately, one of Pelham's lieutenants, William M. McGregor, suffered a debilitating injury. An enemy shell exploded thirty feet from McGregor, and a piece of the bursting projectile broke both bones in his right leg so "that it dangled loosely from his side." McGregor bravely insisted on remaining with the guns, but Stuart ordered him off the field to the help of a surgeon.[43] Private Jesse A. Adams also took a wound during this intense shelling.

When a large force of Federal infantry appeared on Stuart's flank, Jeb called off his offensive and began pulling back toward the Hazel River. At one point Pelham, defending Stuart's escape, leaped from his horse and assisted in manning the guns. Angered by the push of the Federals, Stuart summoned twenty-five or thirty sharpshooters to aid Pelham and "punish effectively the impudence of the Yankees." Sending the riflemen to a stand of trees, Stuart ordered them not to fire until the enemy approached within two hundred yards. Meanwhile, Stuart, still astride his horse, remained hazardously close to the action. Von Borcke, nearby, sensed the danger and warned his chief to seek a safer location, but Stuart "was in a very bad humour." Jeb turned on the Prussian and responded tersely "that if this place seemed too hot for myself, I was at liberty to leave it." Von Borcke sought the shelter of a tree close by as the firing intensified around them. Three bullets smashed into the tree, causing Von to cast a glance at Stuart. "I saw him pass his hand quickly across his face," remembered von Borcke, "and even at this serious moment I could not help laughing heartily when I discovered that one of the . . . bullets . . . had cut off half of his beloved mustache as neatly as it could have been done by the hand of an experienced barber."[44]

With the Federals eventually backing off, Stuart and the others withdrew to the Hazel River. The appearance of the Confederate horsemen attested to the hardships they had encountered over the previous two weeks. Some of the officers had cut holes in blankets and pulled them over their heads serape style. Von Borcke estimated that nearly five hundred men were sick or disabled. Horses, too, had broken down, and many had to be led along by hand. Pelham and his artillerists soon joined the cavalrymen gathered at the ford. Confederate sharpshooter J. W. Bush described the crossing and the further heroics of Pelham:

> The stream was ordinarily so low that anyone could leap across it, but the rain had swollen it to the extent that many horses had to swim, delaying the crossing. . . . Upon the crest of the hill Major Pelham had placed a battery of four guns. . . . The wind was blowing from the northwest directly into our faces, and there was an occasional rift of snow. Pelham was mounted on a black horse, long and rakish, with keen round legs, beautiful neck and fiery eyes—every now and then he would put out one foot pawing the earth, then the other. Pelham was dressed in high top boots, a close-fitting gray overcoat with bright brass buttons, and buckskin gauntlets; a small sword hung by his side. His cheeks were as rosy as a maiden's, with every appearance of a boy about sixteen years old. As we lay on the ground we looked up at him with the greatest admiration, because we knew he was every inch a soldier.

Federal gunners suddenly appeared and began a cannonade on Stuart's slow-moving, weary warriors. Pelham responded with a fierce barrage of his own. Bush continued: "Imagine this boy soldier fighting four pieces of artillery against eight. . . .

In his anxiety he cried out: 'Tell General Stuart to cross his men, or I will not have a man left to work a gun!' He leaped from his horse, aimed a gun and fought with his men. Sometimes, when the Federal batteries would fire, I would throw my face to the ground, expecting, when I looked up, to see Major Pelham shot into fragments."[45]

As dusk set in the Federals backed off, and the crossing of Hazel River was completed. Stuart then pulled his forces southward toward Culpeper where Longstreet had positioned his corps. That night Stuart sent von Borcke to Robert E. Lee's headquarters to report on the day's action, a matter that Jeb would normally have taken care of himself. However, the embarrassing loss of his mustache may have precluded the cavalry chieftain from doing his duty. That night at supper, Von related the "recent adventures" of Stuart's cavalry and especially enjoyed reciting the story of Jeb's mishap that day. Robert E. Lee and his staff officers found the tale of the half-gone mustache, "a personal ornament upon which they knew [Stuart] much prided himself," exceedingly amusing.[46]

Stuart situated his bivouac, humorously calling it "Camp No Rest," near Culpeper. For the most part, however, his troopers did rest for the next week. Mrs. Stuart arrived with their youngest child, three-year-old Jimmie, who resembled his father in both appearance and action as evidenced by his fascination with the horses in the camp. Other visitors came as well, including the British correspondents Frank Vizetelly and Francis Lawley. Robert E. Lee stopped by for a brief visit to offer his solemn condolences to Flora Stuart. Even Tiernan Brien, von Borcke's fellow amateur thespian, reappeared to renew acquaintances.

With the Ten Days Battles ended, Pleasonton submitted his report, claiming victory. Stuart's report, written over a year later, ended with justifiable plaudits for his cavalry; however, he all but credited Pelham with the entire success of the campaign:

> In all these operations I deem it my duty to bear testimony to the gallantry and patient endurance of the cavalry, fighting every day most unequal conflicts, and successfully opposing for an extraordinary period the onward march of McClellan.
>
> The Stuart Horse Artillery comes in for a full share of this praise, and its gallant commander (Maj. John Pelham) exhibited a skill and courage which I have never seen surpassed. On this occasion I was more than ever struck with that extraordinary coolness and mastery of the situation which more eminently characterized this youthful officer than any other artillerist who has attracted my attention. His coup d'oeil [quick survey or glance] was accurate and comprehensive, his choice of ground made with the eye of military genius, and his dispositions always such in retiring as to render it impossible for the enemy to press us without being severely punished for his temerity.

His guns only retired from one position to assume another, and open upon the enemy with a fire so destructive that it threw their ranks into confusion and arrested their further progress.[47]

Others echoed Stuart's praise for his young artillerist. John Esten Cooke maintained that Stuart trusted Pelham implicitly, "and those who witnessed, during that arduous movement, the masterly handling of his guns, can tell how this confidence was justified. It was the eye of the great soldier, the hand of the born artillerist, which was evident in his work during those days of struggle. . . . Thus fighting every inch of the way from Aldie, round by Paris, and Markham's, he reached the Rappahannock, and posted his artillery at the fords, where he stood and bade the enemy defiance." Henry B. McClellan added: "Two spirits more congenial than Stuart and Pelham never met on the field of battle. Stuart's fondness for the use of artillery was almost excessive; Pelham's skill in its management amounted to genius. Stuart and Pelham imparted to the horse artillery an independence of action and celerity of movement which characterized it to the end of the war, and which was nowhere equalled or imitated." McClellan later stated, "[Pelham] won the hearts of all with whom he came in contact. Certainly no similar organization in the Army of Northern Virginia contained more officers who were distinguished by excessive daring than did the cavalry division; yet, much as Stuart valued and admired them all, no one could to him supply the place of his 'incomparable Pelham.'" Later in the month of November Stonewall Jackson, with Pelham at his side, rode through a part of the camp of the Army of Northern Virginia. "There was no need to tell the Second Maryland Infantry it was Pelham," wrote John G. White. "Somehow I had come to find out that the infantry worshiped Pelham like some god of battle." Another stated that Pelham fought "with a pertinacity and unfaltering nerve which made the calm face of Jackson glow."[48]

But the talk of the camp, from the highest-ranking officers down to the common fighting man, stemmed around the ouster of George McClellan as the head of the Army of the Potomac.

18
"We Have a Magnificent Position . . ."

[Pelham] looks like a man who would make his mark upon the world.

—Helen Bernard

McClellan's days as head of the Army of the Potomac had long been numbered. His inactivity and constant bickering with President Lincoln caused an irreparable rift with the administration. Thus, Lincoln decided McClellan must go. At nearly 11:30 P.M. on Friday, November 7, McClellan was presented with the orders for his removal. Later that night McClellan finished a letter to his wife: "They have made a great mistake," he penned sadly. "Alas for my poor country!" For the next few hours a line of officers appeared at McClellan's headquarters offering their condolences. Some threatened to resign en masse in protest of his removal. A handful of these subordinates even boldly suggested that Little Mac march on Washington, D.C., and oust President Lincoln to establish himself as military dictator of the country. Rumor had it that the instigator was none other than George Armstrong Custer, a devoted member of McClellan's staff.[1] This information most likely never reached either John Pelham or Tom Rosser, but both kept warm memories of their West Point friend and his well-remembered high jinks.

Three days later the admiring soldiers of the Army of the Potomac lined up to bid a tearful farewell to McClellan. For Little Mac, it was the supreme and final compliment. McClellan's departure prompted a variety of responses in the Army of Northern Virginia. Robert E. Lee regretted the decision, saying to Longstreet, "We always understood each other so well. I fear they may continue to make these changes till they find some one whom I don't understand."[2]

McClellan's replacement to command the Army of the Potomac was thirty-eight-year-old Ambrose Burnside. Twice before he had been offered command of this army but had abruptly turned the assignment down, each time asserting a lack of confidence in his own abilities. Replacing the popular McClellan, who remained one of Burnside's closest friends, weighed heavily on his mind as well. What Burnside needed, possibly above all else, was the confidence of his subordinates; this, too, seemed lacking. Burnside, however, moved quickly to restore some faith from his men. He began by altering the corps command structure into three "Grand Divisions," each headed by a major general: the Left Grand Division under William Buel Franklin, the Right Grand Division led by Edwin Vose Sumner, and the Center

Grand Division commanded by Joseph Hooker. Burnside's choices for leadership can certainly be questioned, but the fact remains that the Army of the Potomac, with 125,000 men and 320 cannon, continued to be one of the most formidable armies in the world.

Changes occurred as well in the Army of Northern Virginia for Stuart's cavalry. On Monday, November 10, word officially arrived, via Special Orders No. 238, of the Cavalry Division's reorganization, which included a new fourth brigade. Brigadier Generals Wade Hampton, Fitz Lee (finally returned from his injury), W. H. F. Rooney Lee, and William "Grumble" Jones commanded each of the units. Pelham's horse artillery now consisted of five batteries, individually led by Captains James Breathed, Roger Preston Chew, James Franklin Hart, Mathis Winston Henry, and Marcellus N. Moorman, whose Lynchburg Battery was officially added nine days later. The creation of the new brigade of cavalry greatly pleased Stuart, but the retention of Jones did not. Pelham's lack of promotion also plagued Stuart, who repeated his efforts for the artillerist's upgrading in rank the following day: "I have the honor to renew my application for the promotion of Major John Pelham to the rank of lieutenant-colonel of artillery in my division. He will now have five batteries; and always on the battle field, batteries of other divisions and the reserve are thrown under his command, which make the position he holds one of great responsibility, and it should have corresponding rank. I will add that Pelham's coolness, courage, ability and judgment, evinced on so many battle fields, vindicate his claims to promotion. So far as service goes he has long since won a colonelcy at the hands of his country."[3]

The well-deserved promotion was, however, not forthcoming. Pelham apparently displayed no outward emotion with the oversight, but Rosser felt somewhat betrayed as a result of his own lack of promotion, and his feelings toward Stuart cooled considerably.[4]

Stuart's entire command now totaled 603 officers, 8,551 enlisted men, and 30 staff. Pelham's duties included gathering more equipment and horses for his artillery batteries. "Greased heel" continued to plague the entire cavalry and now made its way to the artillery horses, but the cavalry was on the move in little more than a week. Meanwhile, Pelham, in order to streamline his organization, divided his batteries among Stuart's brigades: Hart's battery of South Carolinians accompanied Hampton's men; Breathed's battery teamed with Fitz Lee's brigade; Moorman's battery rode with Rooney Lee; and Chew's battery followed Jones's brigade. Pelham kept Henry's battery with the Napoleon Detachment as his headquarters section.[5] This segmentation of the horse artillery offered greater flexibility to the cavalry and evidenced the confidence Pelham had in each of his commanders to act independently. Although the leaders of each battery retained a certain amount of autonomy, all of them still fell under Pelham's jurisdiction.

In mid-November Burnside put his army on the move. He planned to swing his massive force toward Fredericksburg, about fifty miles north of Richmond, cross the Rappahannock River, and march on the Confederate capital before Lee could react. It was a bold plan with winter coming on. But Burnside reckoned that speed and surprise would outmaneuver Lee, whose army remained separated with Stonewall Jackson across the Blue Ridge Mountains at Winchester miles apart from Longstreet at Culpeper. Never one to allow initiative to the enemy, Lee directed Longstreet's corps to Fredericksburg to position itself between the Federals and Richmond. Lee further summoned Jackson's corps, which would take days to arrive.

Burnside's army won the race for Fredericksburg arriving at the heights of Falmouth on the northern side of the Rappahannock on November 19. A token force of merely five hundred men from Longstreet's corps had taken position on the opposite side of the river at Marye's Heights with the remainder of the corps slowly filtering in. Advised to cross the Rappahannock immediately and seize the heights, tentatively held by the Confederates, Burnside refused. To do so would split his forces across the formidable Rappahannock without a viable access for retreat. Instead Burnside desired to await the appearance of his pontoon bridges, which would simplify the fording of the wide river and allow a retrograde movement if necessary. Burnside's decision to halt any advancement for the pontoons became the fatal error of the campaign. Days passed before their arrival, giving the Confederates ample time to fortify the bluffs south of the Rappahannock.[6] Thus the last days of November became a waiting game: Burnside biding his time until his pontoons arrived, the Army of Northern Virginia anticipating Jackson's corps, which left Winchester on November 22.

Jackson's legendary marches had become part of Southern lore by this time, but his 120-mile trek to Fredericksburg remains one of his lesser-known classics. The difficulties of this masterpiece included horrendous weather as rain, sleet, and snow hindered the ill-clad veterans. Many of his men lacked shoes or proper winter apparel as they slogged through the muddy byways toward their destination. Cowhide strips, tightly wrapped around bare feet, offered little protection. But Jackson pushed the men onward with faith in his God, a perfect sense of military duty, and the news from his wife, Anna, of a baby daughter, Julia, born on November 28. In eight days Jackson reached the Fredericksburg area with barely any straggling. One Second Corps veteran proclaimed the journey "one of the longest and hardest marches on record."[7] Jackson posted his weary soldiers to the right of Longstreet's men overlooking the Rappahannock River.

Pelham and his headquarters battery had been sent to the area of Port Royal, eighteen miles southeast of Fredericksburg. Here the Rappahannock widened to nearly one thousand feet, offering Burnside use of his gunboats and a possible crossing point around Lee's army. Pelham's sphere of defense ranged from Port Royal northwestward six miles to Skinker's Neck, where the Rappahannock narrowed and twisted back in the direction of Fredericksburg. On numerous occasions Stuart personally accompanied Pelham in scouting the various locations along this route where artillery would best be utilized against enemy gunboats. For several days Pelham's gunners remained on the alert, periodically firing a blast at vessels that ventured too far up the river. As Pelham put it, "We'd just better let 'em know we're here."[8]

Often during their travels up and down the Rappahannock between Skinker's Neck and Port Royal, Stuart and Pelham dropped in to visit the Bernard family, cousins of W. W. Blackford's wife. The Bernard plantation home, Gay Mont, in Blackford's words, "was a lovely old place, all embowered in trees. . . . The house was a large, rambling structure, built at different times, and furnished with the elegance which the refined taste and ample means of the family supplied." The visits, although frequent, generally were of short duration as Stuart and Pelham enjoyed a cup of tea, while conversing with the ladies and warming themselves by the fireplace, before leaving.[9]

On Sunday, November 30, the ladies at Gay Mont became excited upon hearing that Stuart and part of his staff would soon arrive. Assuming the general and his officers would have supper and spend the night, the ladies worked diligently making preparations. Soon Stuart arrived with Pelham, Major Andrew Reid Venable, Lieutenant Walter Q. Hullihen, and Will Farley. "With considerable difficulty," wrote Helen Bernard in her diary, "we contrived to give them tea and prepare beds, when lo! Like a comet, Gen. Stuart was gone, nor would he allow any of his train to remain saying that it was unsoldierly to sleep in a house." Helen avowed her disappointment by adding, "We feel worn out with the hustle & excitement of the day."[10]

Two days later, however, Stuart again appeared with members of his staff. Rooney Lee soon dropped in as well, and Helen described him as "the very model of a young soldier in appearance & manners. Tall, robust, athletic, yet polished, courteous & with a gentleness of manner almost like a woman's." Although Helen was impressed with Stuart, her comparison of the two men left Stuart lacking: "Genl. Stuart does not impress me so favorably, a bold and dashing soldier, he doubtless is, but without the striking marks of high breeding which distinguishes Gen. Lee." Her diary entry for Stuart's artillery chieftain remains compelling: "Major Pelham also pleased us extremely, a mere youth apparently, beardless & slender almost to a fault, but quick & energetic in his movements & with an eagle eye that shows his spirit. He reminds me of Gov. [Henry] Wise in his fiery expressive countenance & looks like a man who would make his mark upon the world."[11]

Rooney Lee and Stuart freely discussed the seemingly dangerous situation of the Federals nearby. According to Helen, Lee "advised us to leave, but Genl. Stuart said he thought we need not be in a hurry, as if it became necessary to put troops around the house & there was danger of the house being knocked to pieces, we might still escape or take refuge in the cellar." Helen's apprehension intensified when she overheard Lee say to Pelham, "I shall depend upon you for that artillery," and to another, "We shall want sharpshooters along the river tonight." Furthering her anxiety was a report that Stonewall Jackson had shown up at a nearby signal station asking to see Stuart. In Helen's words, "We are inclined to think that when 'Old Stonewall' appears upon the field, the time for action has come." The following day, December 3, soldiers of D. H. Hill's division came to the Port Royal area. Helen reported that Lee, Pelham, and other staff officers spent the night at Gay Mont. Her fears of an impending battle were obvious when she penned, "Officers & men are constantly coming in to report to the Genl. We have a guard around the house. . . . The tramp of armed men on all sides produces a strange feeling of excitement that banishes sleep."[12]

Helen Bernard's angst proved insightful. On December 4, four Federal gunboats—the USS *Anacostia, Currituck, Coeur de Lion,* and *Jacob Bell*—steamed into the Port Royal area. With a combined crew of five hundred sailors and twenty-one guns, the vessels blasted shells into the town. "Scarcely was dinner over when we were startled by the sound of cannon near at hand," wrote Helen. "And then broadside after broadside was poured into poor inoffensive little Port Royal. . . . Nearly every house in the place was struck. . . . No one was seriously hurt. This brings the war to our very door, yet we cannot believe that it is necessary to leave home. It is astonishing to find how calmly one looks danger in the face upon its near approach."[13]

Pelham and D. H. Hill, however, had ably prepared for such an occurrence. At about 3:00 P.M. Captain Robert A. Hardaway with his Alabama battery began firing upon the gunboats with his imported British Whitworth from a distance of three miles. With water splashing on the decks from the shells of the Whitworth, the Federal vessels fired back, but their projectiles fell woefully short of their mark. When attempting to steam in to closer range, the gunboats faced Confederate riflemen, strategically placed along the hills overlooking the river. "These piratical cruisers," mused D. H. Hill, "which have bombarded so many unoffending private residences, and have carried desolation to so many peaceful homes, shrank from the wager of battle and kept close under the shelter of town, so that the flank batteries could not fire upon them without endangering it. Hardaway still kept up his pelting in front until dark, when they fled down the river."[14]

Steaming downriver the four gunboats headed to apparent safety, "but now a worse fate awaited them," reported D. H. Hill, as they were caught by the deadly fire of Pelham's two, 3-inch rifled Blakelys borrowed from Moorman's battery under the supervision of Lieutenant Charles R. Phelps. From atop a hill Pelham personally superintended the guns, dangerously located three hundred yards from the gunboats. Opening a salvo upon the enemy vessels, Pelham's first two shots blasted directly through the side of a ship, smashing the deck and sending Yankee sailors scurrying for cover. The angry Federals "replied with grape," wrote Rooney Lee, "and one of [Pelham's] gunners had his leg carried off."[15] For the next few minutes Pelham and his gunners held the upper hand in the duel until the gunboats pulled farther away and out of range. Von Borcke complimented his young friend: "Pelham with his horse-artillery had met with his usual good fortune, inflicting much damage upon the enemy, and driving off the gunboats, which, from the narrowness of the stream and the height of the cliffs where our guns were posted, had scarcely been able to respond at all to the destructive fire which was pouring down upon them at so near a range."[16]

That night through a driving snowstorm, Rooney Lee and Pelham returned to Gay Mont to warm themselves before a fire and relate the day's events to the Bernard family. Both officers and their commands, however, remained vigilant in the Port Royal area in case of further trouble with Yankee gunboats.

Accolades again poured in for Pelham's defiant stand against the Federal vessels. D. H. Hill commended "the gallant [John] Pelham [who] placed [his guns] near the water's edge, [and] gave them a parting salute."[17] Submitting a note to Robert E. Lee, Stuart spoke of "the gallantry displayed by Major Pelham and the officers and men under his command," and lauded "the brigade of Brig. Gen. W. H. F. Lee [which] is doing gallant service on the Lower Rappahannock." In a note to Stuart, Robert E. Lee stated: "Major Pelham and his men deserve great credit for the manner in which they co-operated in the attack of General Hill's battery upon the gunboats. I beg you to express to all the officers and men my gratification and appreciation of their services." The commanding general, however, expressed some regret regarding the incident to the War Department: "I desired to drive them [the gunboats] out of the river without drawing their fire upon the town. . . . I fear the boats did not suffer as much as I intended they should."[18]

The freshly fallen snow added new diversions from the preparations for battle back at "Camp No-Camp." Dawn, December 5, brought sporadic playfulness as many soldiers, especially those from the deep South who had probably never witnessed such a thick, white blanket, tossed the well-packed spheroids at other human targets. Soon the random throwing took on the aspect of a full-scale battle as hundreds of Lafayette McLaws's men advanced toward the division of John Bell Hood. Officers from both divisions appeared and quickly began shouting commands while the soldiers fought back and forth over the field between them. Neither side gave quarter as the combatants shrieked with excitement. Thousands of the projectiles hurtled back and forth until "the air was darkened with the snowballs." Hood's Texans, to no one's surprise, fought with a possessed spirit they had demonstrated on countless battlefields and soon had McLaws's men on the run. Reinforcements soon arrived to help "save" McLaws's beleaguered Georgians. As the joyous melee ended for the day, casualties included infinite bruises and scratches, with lumps aplenty. Surgeons also attended to one of Hood's men, down with a broken leg, as well as one of McLaws's veterans who forfeited an eye.[19]

The grim reality of war all too soon replaced the frolicsome mood in the camp. Although Ambrose Burnside continued to feign an advance in the area of Port Royal, he had already decided to attack across the Rappahannock River in the vicinity of Fredericksburg. From atop Stafford Heights, Burnside's chief of artillery, Brigadier General Henry Jackson Hunt, concentrated 147 of his total 312 guns. The remaining guns would be employed as part of the strike force once the river had been traversed. But Burnside continued to postpone the crossing until his pontoons arrived and could be emplaced.

In the meantime Lee's army took up strong positions on the western side of the Rappahannock. The quaint, historic town of Fredericksburg, with nearly five thousand residents, lay on their side of the river. Behind the town on several hills Lee had placed his seventy-five thousand men in a line stretching nearly seven miles in length. On the left atop Marye's Heights sat the First Corps of James Longstreet, who saw little need for digging entrenchments due to the entirely favorable position and the hardness of the ground. Adjacent to Longstreet stood Jackson's corps, which reached to Hamilton's Crossing on the far right. With the Confederate infantry forces packed strongly and ample batteries of artillery in place, the Army of Northern Virginia held its most formidable defensive line thus far in the war. "We have a magnificent position," boasted Brigadier General Thomas R. R. Cobb, recently promoted and new to Longstreet's command.[20]

Burnside also received some negative feedback from various officers familiar with the terrain regarding his proposed attack across the Rappahannock. One predicted, "If you make the attack as contemplated, it will be the greatest slaughter of the war." Another simply stated: "The carrying out of our plan will be murder, not warfare." Neither warning deterred Burnside, who displayed outward confidence now that his pontoon equipment had finally arrived. Confederate self-assurance had not waned either. Predicted John Bell Hood, "I think we will whip [Burnside] badly. Our army is in good trim for an old-fashioned fight." Moxley Sorrel, however, may have put it best when he said, "Burnside could and would fight, even if he did not know how."[21]

With the amassing of Federal troops clearly evident from the Confederate side of the Rappahannock, Robert E. Lee prepared a circular urging all Fredericksburg citizens to evacuate the town. Most families remained in their homes as the first exodus of men, women, and children trickled to safety. Still, the view of forlornly moving people touched the hearts of many Rebel veterans. "The evacuation of the place by the distressed women and helpless men was a painful sight," remembered Longstreet. By December 8 most of the townspeople began to flee in droves with only a handful steadfastly remaining behind. Robert E. Lee commended the people on their raw courage: "History presents no instance of a people exhibiting a purer and more unselfish patriotism, or a higher spirit of fortitude and courage, than was evinced by the citizens of Fredericksburg."[22]

While the Army of Northern Virginia sat perched on the hills west of Fredericksburg, Robert E. Lee designated the Mississippi brigade of Brigadier General William Barksdale to occupy the nearly empty town and watch for the possibility of a Federal crossing. The assignment of Barksdale's 1,600 riflemen was not to halt the enemy crossing but "to delay [and] annoy him as much as possible."[23] Stuart, meanwhile, had deployed his brigades at various sectors of the main army to maximize their effectiveness. While John Pelham's batteries continued to be detached to the various cavalry brigades, Pelham himself stayed at Port Royal to oversee his gunners in case more enemy gunboats appeared.

On Saturday, December 6, Stuart, von Borcke, and a few other staff officers rode to Port Royal. They arrived at Gay Mont rather late in the evening, but the Bernard family welcomed their guests. "[I]n the snug library, before a glorious wood-fire, we warmed our half-frozen limbs," remembered von Borcke, "and remained in delightful conversation with the ladies till a late hour of the night." The following evening the Bernards hosted a fine meal for the officers with Pelham joining them. Part of the conversation between Pelham and Stuart undoubtedly pertained to the lack of Federal gunboats in the area and the build-up of Federal forces near Fredericksburg. For this reason Stuart ordered Pelham to return with them to the main army the next day.[24]

Returning to Camp No-Camp, Stuart's new bivouac, the following evening, Stuart, Pelham, von Borcke, and the others delighted in finding that Francis Lawley and Frank Vizetelly, anxious to report on the impending battle, had returned. The correspondents introduced a guest, Captain Lewis Guy Phillips of the British Grenadier Guards, who had obtained a temporary leave from his post in Canada. After formal introduction of the youthful officer, the party sat in Stuart's tent leisurely chatting and sipping hot coffee. Phillips made an immediately positive impression on his hosts. "The young English Captain was a fine fellow," pronounced Blackford, "whom we all liked." Von Borcke concurred, referring to Phillips as "a portly grenadier, whose engaging manners had endeared him to us all."[25] The gregarious officer especially took a liking to Pelham and appeared to know of his many exploits on the various fields of battle. Pelham and Phillips talked long into the night with the Englishman asking probing questions regarding Pelham's military techniques. Pelham politely answered the queries though he blushed in his typical manner when he remained the center of attention.

On a cold and windy December 10, Private Thomas Frazer Chancellor, a courier for Stuart, arrived at Camp No-Camp with exciting news. A country ball would be held that evening at the crossroads known as Chancellorsville, barely ten miles away, and the general and his staff were cordially invited to attend the festivities.

Stuart declined the invitation, but he allowed a handful to show up provided they return to camp the following morning. The select group included Pelham, von Borcke, Blackford, Major Lewis Terrell, Lieutenant Chiswell Dabney, and Captain Phillips. Banjoist Sam Sweeney, "Mulatto Bob," and two fiddlers were conscripted to provide the musical entertainment. Following supper at 6:00 P.M., the party hitched four "spirited" mules to the much-used yellow ambulance and fashioned improvised seats by laying planks across the wagon bed. Then nine of the ten men clambered aboard with "Mulatto Bob" riding a horse behind in case their guest, Captain Phillips, found the wagon too uncomfortable. Von and Major Terrell sat in the front as drivers.

Jouncing along in the starlit, blustery night, the elated men sang songs and huddled together to keep warm. Adding to their joy were the many soldiers who "ran out and cheered us as we passed," recalled von Borcke. As the overcrowded wagon disappeared from view of the camp, the drivers increased the speed, hoping to arrive at the dance on schedule. Soon von Borcke turned over the reins to Terrell, who fancied himself a par excellence reinsman, so the Prussian could join the others in the back for the songful gaiety. Terrell urged the mules even faster along the "frozen, rough country roads . . . and away we jolted at a furious rate," wrote Blackford.

Suddenly a loud crash resonated into the night, and the ambulance abruptly overturned, scattering its surprised occupants in all directions. A large, snow-covered stump, "several feet in circumference and as many feet in height," unseen by Terrell, had brought the wagon to a rude halt. Assessing the damage, the shaken party found no one seriously injured. Pronouncing the mules unhurt, the men pushed the yellow wagon back onto its wheels and adjusted the harnesses. All laughingly agreed to their good fortune in the near disaster but concluded that the oft-used wagon was done for as a future conveyance. Terrell again took up the reins and recklessly pushed the mules as fast as before.

As the wagon creaked and groaned through the night, Blackford, occupying the rear, opened the tailgate and draped his legs over the back. This he mistakenly surmised would allow for a faster getaway in case of another disaster. Four miles from their destination the rear axle snapped in two, causing the back of the wagon to come crashing down harshly, expelling the occupants a second time. Again the distraught passengers surveyed the damage. To their dismay they found Blackford, out cold, bleeding heavily from a wound where the discarded wheel had cracked his forehead. The men frantically pooled their handkerchiefs to stanch the bleeding, "no longer in a frame of mind to laugh over our misfortunes," rued von Borcke. "When I came to myself," remembered Blackford, "all the party were collected around looking very mournful, for the profuse bleeding and my being unconscious led them to think I was seriously if not fatally wounded." Still four miles from the dance, the group of men held a "council of war" to determine whether their ill-fated efforts justified continuing. All agreed that a return to camp would prove just as hazardous, but they left the final decision to their guest, Captain Phillips. The grenadier opted to go on, and for good measure the entire party, including the injured Blackford, voted unanimously to persevere on to Chancellorsville.

Readjustments, of course, had to be made. Discarding the main body of the ambulance, the men placed the still woozy Blackford on the shattered wagon bed immediately behind the front wheels. Captain Phillips, along with Dabney and von Borcke, sat uncomfortably on the axletree. Pelham, Terrell, Sweeney, and "Mulatto Bob" mounted the mules; the two musicians rode double on the horse. Collectively, the shaken men continued toward their destination, albeit at a considerably slower pace. "After an hour of torture, during which the headlong speed of our team over the rough plank-road had given to the sufferers on the axletree the sensation of riding on a razor," lamented von Borcke, "we reached the scene of the evening's festivities."

Private Thomas Chancellor greeted the beleaguered travelers and proceeded to introduce them all around. Feeling stronger from his travails of the journey, Blackford noted, "Great was the pleasure among the rustic beauties assembled at our arrival for they had given us up." Within moments Sweeney and his fellow musicians had tuned their instruments and soon their melodious notes filled the air. Pelham, Von, Blackford, and the others grabbed willing partners, and the long-awaited dance commenced. The treacherous winter trip was quickly forgotten by the "many pretty faces and sparkling eyes worth looking into," remembered von Borcke, "and it was quite delightful to see our foreign friend [Captain Phillips] winding through the mazes of many bounding quadrilles and Virginia reels with an evident enjoyment." Near midnight the entire party feasted on a sumptuous meal before returning to the dance floor until nearly 3:00 A.M. Remembering their promise to Stuart, the officers and musicians bade farewell to their amiable hosts, who commandeered a new wagon to replace the storied yellow ambulance. Only Blackford, still feeling the effects of the mishap on the road, remained behind to sleep in a "delightful feather-bed" with the assurance he would return to camp on the morrow. Pelham and the others arrived at Camp No-Camp shortly before daybreak and immediately fell asleep.[26]

⁓

By 2:00 A.M. on Thursday, December 11, William Barksdale reported that the enemy could be heard moving pontoon bridges into position. Then through the fog and darkness of the morning, Barksdale's riflemen opened up on their nearly invisible targets, killing one engineer and wounding two other officers and several enlisted men. When daylight came, the Confederate sharpshooters were afforded a clearer view of the Federals and forced them back with withering fire. With three bridges nearly completed and his men on the run, Burnside ordered Henry Jackson Hunt to blast the town. Sixty-five Union guns began firing on the buildings in Fredericksburg, but Barksdale's riflemen stalwartly held their ground. Five consecutive times the bluecoats appeared to finish the pontoon bridges, but each time Barksdale's veterans drove them back. Losing all patience with the pesky Rebel snipers, Burnside angrily gave the order for a full-scale barrage of the town at 12:30 P.M. For the next two hours 183 Union guns bombarded the small garrison of Confederates stationed in Fredericksburg.

Churches, warehouses, stores, and private homes suffered irreparable damage. Many civilians who had refused to evacuate their dwellings clamored like rats into their cellars and huddled together to ward off the awful shelling. Hunt, witnessing the massive destruction through his field glasses, said, "There was no such necessity" for this "barbarous" action and called off the cannonade. But Burnside angrily countermanded the order, and the intense blasting continued. W. W. Blackford, who had returned from Chancellorsville, witnessed the devastation to his hometown and recalled: "It was a fearful but a grand sight. . . . the very ground we stood upon shook like an earthquake." Rebel Benjamin Stiles noted with hatred: "I do believe . . . I could murder the devils in cold blood." In a rare display of anger Robert E. Lee stated: "Those people delight to destroy the weak and those who can make no defense. It just suits them!"[27]

Throughout the two-hour Federal barrage, Lee refused to allow his artillery to fire back, thus saving ammunition and wisely not revealing the positions of his guns. Pelham and numerous other battery commanders impatiently watched as the unimpeded Union guns continued to hurl their projectiles into the town. Finally, Burnside mercifully called off the bombardment and sent another team to finish the bridge construction. Then from the rubble and half-standing buildings came the unmistakable and deadly rifle fire of Barksdale's Mississippians, who miraculously had withstood the punishing cannonade. Burnside's rage ballooned as he shouted, "The army is held by the throat by a few sharpshooters!" Meanwhile, Robert E. Lee sent a courier to inquire of Barksdale and his men. The stout leader returned a message a few moments later: "Tell General Lee that if he wants a bridge of dead Yankees, I can furnish him with one."[28] In exasperation Hunt suggested to Burnside that the unused pontoons could serve as landing craft to haul hundreds of infantrymen, under artillery support, across the river to dislodge Barksdale's riflemen. By nightfall, the last of Barksdale's men had withdrawn from their shelters and retreated up Marye's Heights, while teams of Federals had completed six pontoon bridges above and below the town. Burnside now appeared content to wait another day before ordering his army to cross the river. That night candles burned late in Stuart's tent as he, Pelham, von Borcke, Blackford, Captain Phillips, and a handful of other staff officers sat up until daylight speculating on Burnside's intentions.

On December 12 under the cover of a heavy fog, the Army of the Potomac finally came across the Rappahannock on the swaying pontoons. Once inside the town, many Federals resorted to acts of vandalism in the fine Fredericksburg homes. Within moments of their arrival priceless mirrors, the finest china, vases, furniture, and heirlooms were dispatched into tens of thousands of minute particles by Federal rifle butts. Fully stocked wine cellars emptied quickly, which heightened the ransacking. One New Yorker stated: "Fredericksburg, once a proud and wealthy city is now nothing but a sacked and ruined town."[29]

Hours went by as Burnside's Grand Divisions made their way across the Rappahannock, and still Robert E. Lee seemed satisfied to offer no resistance. The massing of the Army of the Potomac in the Fredericksburg area convinced Lee to summon the divisions of Jubal Early and D. H. Hill from Skinker's Neck and Port Royal. Other than that, Lee sat patiently waiting. The day passed with the Confederates observing the impressive build-up of the Federal forces in preparation for an obvious attack. That night, long after most had fallen asleep, John Pelham and Captain Phillips sat up discussing a variety of subjects including the tactics of the British artillery and the possibility of England offering full support and recognition to the Confederacy. Eventually their conversation drifted to the anticipated battle, certain to be fought on the morrow. Later the two friends bade each other good night and settled into their own quarters for some much-needed rest.

As Pelham lay there, his mind may have wandered to his mother and father down in Alabama. Would he ever see them or his brothers and sister again? He most likely thought of his gentle Sallie back at the Bower. It had been slightly more than six weeks since he had last seen and held her. War certainly had a harsh way of keeping lovers apart, but another great victory might possibly cause Lincoln to ask for a cessation of arms. Then John could take Sallie back to his native state to meet his family and finalize plans for the wedding. Perhaps he contemplated a family of his own. And maybe, as his mind raced, he thought of his military accomplishments over the past year and a half. Yes, it had seemed an eternity since, as a naïve twenty-two-year-old lieutenant commanding the Alburtis Battery in his first combat at Manassas, he had won praise from Stonewall Jackson himself. . . . And months later at the Battle of Williamsburg when he first led his horse artillery into action. . . . And then during the Seven Days Battles when he won the mutual praise of Jackson and Stuart for his heroics at Gaines' Mill. . . . And how his gunners had fought and driven off the USS *Marblehead,* and later held off the Federal artillerists with merely one gun for five full hours at Evelynton Heights. . . . Late August at Groveton when Stonewall had given him the supreme compliment of discretionary orders for his gun placement. . . . And then on to Sharpsburg where his gunners may have saved Lee's army from defeat while blazing away from Nicodemus Heights. . . . The Chambersburg raid in early October where with one gun he allowed Stuart's troopers to cross White's Ford and return safely. . . . The Ten Days Battles where his brilliance possibly outshone all his other endeavors. A handful of major battles, scores of bloody engagements—and all without a serious injury, much less any wound whatsoever. Why had he been so fortunate when thousands of others on both sides had not? And what would tomorrow bring with the massive Federal army preparing for an assault? These thoughts and countless others may have darted through John Pelham's brain as he dozed off that night.

Pelham was awake and at his post before dawn. Captain Phillips appeared and removed a narrow red and blue striped necktie, which he handed to Pelham. Briefly explaining that the colors represented those of his own British regiment, Phillips requested that Pelham take the necktie into battle with him. "Wear it," said the Englishman. "It's to be your good luck talisman today, a souvenir for me after the battle." Blushing deeply, Pelham lowered his head and accepted the ribbon, which he carefully tied around his cap before galloping off to his battery.[30]

Burnside's forces had begun moving through the fog before daybreak. On this day—Saturday, December 13—the war gods smiled on John Pelham more than ever before. For within a time span of less than two hours, the twenty-four-year-old artillerist would perform an act so brilliant, so daring, and so unconventional that it remained the talk of the Army of Northern Virginia for the rest of the winter.

"You Men Stand Killing Better than Any I Know!"

General Lee has spoken of him as "the Gallant Pelham," and that settles it.
—Henry Kyd Douglas

Although sunrise occurred at 7:17 A.M. on Saturday, December 13, little could be seen by either army as a dewy mist rolled in, shrouding the countryside. Eyes squinted painfully to see little more than fifty yards ahead. Nearly two hours would pass before the fog burned off enough to offer a clear view from the hills surrounding Fredericksburg. In the predawn the temperature stood at a chilly thirty-four degrees, but by midday the thermometer would rise nearly thirty degrees to a balmy sixty degrees Fahrenheit—all in all a lovely day of unseasonably mild weather, even by Virginia standards. By sundown, however, the aesthetic beauty of the Fredericksburg landscape would appear manifestly ugly by the thousands of pockmarks from artillery shells and the eighteen thousand dead and mangled youth that strewed the shadowy grounds.

The Confederate high command had gathered at Lee's headquarters on an elevation, anxiously awaiting the advance of an enemy they could not yet see. Presently Stonewall Jackson rode up looking "resplendent with gold lace and marks of rank." He further sported a new black felt hat and an untarnished sword. Always thinking in terms of offense, Jackson again made his pitch to attack the Federals before the fog cleared. This would negate the effectiveness of the enemy artillery as well as push the bluecoats toward the trap of the Rappahannock River. Stuart saw things the same way as Jackson, and together the two generals attempted to sway Lee to their thinking. The commanding general, however, agreed with Longstreet; they would hold their ground and wait for the Federals to come to them. A few moments passed and the fog began to lift, revealing enemy forces in huge numbers.

Never had the Army of Northern Virginia been in a better stance to wage a battle. Seventy-five thousand soldiers, stretched along a seven-mile front, stood ready for a fight. Longstreet had massed his corps from Taylor's Hill on his extreme left running southeastward to Deep Run on his far right. Most of Old Pete's men were stationed on Marye's Heights, a formidable position without weakness. A sunken road and a four-foot-tall stone fence, both manned by Longstreet's stalwarts, at the foot of the Heights added to the strength of First Corps' location. Jackson's thirty-five thousand men covered only two miles of front to the right of Longstreet's command from Deep Run southeastward to Hamilton's Crossing. Jackson's position, though not as decidedly elevated as Longstreet's, contained definite advantages. With considerably less terrain to cover, Stonewall could double and even triple stack his units for additional strength. Furthermore, much of the area held by the Second Corps was wooded, giving the men added protection. Conversely, the Federals facing him would have to approach in relatively open ground.

Only two weaknesses existed in Jackson's deployment. The extreme right at Hamilton's Crossing might be exposed to a flanking movement by the Yankees, although this appeared unlikely with the Federals' present configuration. Stuart's cavalry and Pelham's horse artillery stood guard in this sector in case the Yankees had such a notion. Far more consequential was an unmanned triangular-shaped boggy area five to six hundred yards in A. P. Hill's sector. This spot, generally known as the Gap, existed between the right of James Lane's brigade and the left of James Jay Archer's brigade. Because of the swampy, marshy, dense entanglement of the area, Hill saw no reason to fortify the Gap, although Lane and Archer had issued warnings of its susceptibility to attack. Hill decided that Maxcy Gregg's brigade, stationed in reserve behind this sector, along with well-directed artillery fire could protect this weakness. Unlikely as it seems, Jackson himself may not have been aware of the Gap until he rode back along his lines that morning. Observing the seriousness of the omission of troops there, he stated simply, "The enemy will attack here," and further predicted it as "the scene of the severest fighting."[1]

That morning Robert E. Lee had carefully scrutinized virtually his entire line with the placement of the artillery possibly drawing his closest attention. Determining the Hamilton's Crossing region to be potentially the weakest area, Lee advised Stuart to have the horse artillery prepared in this sector. Although the warning made great sense, John Pelham had already addressed the problem. Before dawn Pelham requested additional guns from Colonel Stapleton Crutchfield, Jackson's chief of artillery. Dipping into the artillery reserve, Crutchfield sent two batteries, bringing Pelham's cannon total up to eighteen. There Pelham waited, poised and ready for action, like a cougar eager to pounce on its victim. Von Borcke remembered seeing "Pelham's eighteen pieces of horse-artillery in favourable position, the young leader longing for the combat, and anxious to open the ball with some of his light guns."[2]

Crutchfield also strengthened the area by massing fourteen more guns on Prospect Hill, adjacent to Pelham's position, under the command of the talented Lieutenant Colonel Reuben Lindsay Walker. Furthermore, the awesome Whitworth rifle, still manned by deadeye Captain Robert A. Hardaway, was placed approximately a mile and a half southeast of Pelham's post just across Massaponax Creek on a wooded height. With other batteries strategically sprinkled to the left of Walker's spot on Prospect Hill, the Confederate cannons along Jackson's line of deployment appeared to have all the possible Federal approaches defended. Even the seldom satisfied Jackson appeared confident with the placement of the guns.

Longstreet's guns along Marye's Heights may have been even better placed than Jackson's. Lieutenant Colonel Edward Porter Alexander reported that "A chicken could not live on that field when we open up on it." Longstreet obviously delighted in the report. Confederate Armistead L. Long noted that the Battle of Fredericksburg was the first time in the war that "the Confederate artillery was systematically massed for battle."[3]

On the Federal side of the lines, Burnside strangely delayed the orders to his commanders for advancement though all three of his Grand Division leaders favored an attack at dawn. With patches of fog still lingering, the Federal high command first decided to launch an artillery barrage against the Confederate lines to weaken the Rebel position before the infantry assault. Soon the horrific sounds of the Federal guns shattered the relative silence of the morning. At no time, however, did Confederate field guns fire back as the gunners strictly obeyed Lee's orders not to wage an artillery duel.

With much of the fog beginning to dissipate, William Franklin's massive force began its movement in front of Stonewall Jackson's position, prompting the general to observe: "I am glad the Yankees are coming." Calmly, Jackson penciled a note for Stuart, summoning Pelham's artillery to commence firing on the Federals. Only a few minutes earlier, Stuart had sent Robert E. Lee a message: "Jackson has not advanced, but I have, and I am going to crowd them with artillery."[4]

Chosen to spearhead the Federal assault was the seasoned Pennsylvania veterans of George Meade's division. Collectively, they marched across the nearly level plain that had become soft and sticky from the recent thawing. With John Gibbon's division protecting their right flank and Abner Doubleday's division held in reserve on their left, Meade's 4,500 men pressed forward confidently. After crossing the Richmond Stage Road, also known as Bowling Green Road, they paused for a moment to realign their forces into the tightly packed, almost phalanx formation. Suddenly, solid shot enfiladed their extreme left from an unseen enemy. The outright shock of this stunning assault brought Meade's entire division to an abrupt halt, like a sucker punch disorients an unsuspecting combatant, rendering him groggy and reeling. Stuart had been true to his word and was "crowding them with artillery" from John Pelham's battery as he had promised.

Shortly before this rude attack, Pelham had begged Stuart's permission to move one field piece forward from Hamilton's Crossing along Massaponax Road[5] a half mile northeast to the intersection at the Richmond Stage Road. Here Meade's unwary Federals would pass at right angles to Pelham's gun. Stuart quickly assessed the situation and saw immediately the peril of advancing too far in front of the main army, especially with merely a handful of men and a solitary cannon. Stuart's instincts said no; it was too reckless. But Stuart had learned to trust the intuition and skills of his young artillerist. Pelham was no grandstander, and his genius for gunnery had been proven countless times. "Go," said Stuart with an admonition to be careful and to return in plenty of time. Pelham had already selected his piece, a 12-pounder Napoleon, the same weapon captured from the Federals at Seven Pines and used so effectively by the Alabamian at Gaines's Mill. Captain Mathis Winston Henry with part of his gun crew, along with the Napoleon Detachment, accompanied Pelham who, according to von Borcke, "went off . . . at a gallop, amidst the loud cheering of the cannoneers."[6]

Wasting no time, Pelham set his men in motion. Boldly moving forward, the gunners followed their leader beyond the relative safety of their own lines. Irregular ditches and cedar hedges, along with patches of fog, concealed their movement from the approaching enemy. Pelham motioned for a halt at the southwest corner of the road intersection, "where an old gate stood on a small knoll." Here Pelham signaled for his field piece to unlimber. Maneuvering his gun to a more manageable position, Pelham sought lower ground than the oncoming Federals to further conceal his location. Gunner George W. Shreve recalled, "We came to a cross hedge row, of cedar, behind which we noiselessly formed 'In Battery.'" The long lines of bluecoated Federals now swung into a perpendicular angle from Pelham's gunners at a distance of four hundred yards. Peering through the hedge and over the uneven ground, Shreve and the others observed "a grand spectacle of marshaled soldiery in readiness for the fray, spread out in vast proportions on the level plain in our immediate front."[7] The voices of the Yankee officers could be distinguished above the steady trample of thousands of feet. A hazy sun broke through the clouds. It was 10:00 A.M.

Pelham opened up with solid shot, which plowed directly into and stunned Meade's Pennsylvanians. For split seconds many of the bluecoats stood in momentary bewilderment, but soon the natural instincts of these veterans sent them sprawling facedown to the ground. "A cannon boomed out on our left, at close range," recalled a private of the Pennsylvania Reserves, "seemingly on the Bowling Green road, a shot whizzed high in the air passing over our heads from left to right along the line. Naturally supposing, from its position, 'twas one of our own batteries. We thought our gunners had had too much 'commissary' this morning and so remarked." Another of the reserves who hit the ground a bit faster simply stated: "[I was] pressing down hard . . . and flattening out that I might not interfere with any of the flying iron." From the site of the Confederate cannon George W. Shreve had a different perspective. "Fearing annihilation at their hands in such close range of their infantry, we commenced firing. . . . Instead of rushing for us and overwhelming us with their numbers, they were evidently afraid of us, judging no doubt that we had a strong force concealed. . . . We were far in advance of any supports, either cavalry or infantry. Our fire must have been very effective and gave them a whole-some fear of us."[8]

Whether the Federal artillerists from across the river fired a shot before Pelham's gun crew blasted a second projectile of its own is debatable, but Shreve remembered it that way. While observing Private Hammond sponge out the barrel from the first Confederate shot, Shreve claimed "a shell from the enemy's gun cut him down, and he had time only to say, 'Tell mother I die bravely.'"[9] Quickly Pelham's gunners readied the Napoleon and began firing as rapidly as they could. One of the earliest shots from the 12-pounder instantly killed John A. Camp of the Eleventh Pennsylvania Reserves. An irate but compassionate George Meade witnessed this and ordered Camp's body to be immediately buried. Federal soldiers, still under fire, hastily dug a shallow grave in the muddy soil with their bayonets and placed Camp's remains in the hole.

In his typically sour mood when things did not go his way, George Meade ordered the closest battery to silence whatever Confederate interference lay out there. Without hesitation Battery A of the First Pennsylvania Light Artillery, commanded by Lieutenant John G. Simpson, rolled forward. Almost immediately, a solid shot from Pelham's piece scored a direct hit on one of Simpson's cannon. Like so many other Federals that morning, Simpson mistook Pelham's rapid and deadly fire for that of a battery: "a battery, which was enfilading our troops as they were advancing to the front, and shortly after entering the action had the axle of my third piece broken by a shot from the enemy, at the same time destroying the sponge bucket, sponge staff and rammer, and lunette strap." A second blast by Pelham's gunners smashed a Federal limber chest, making an ungodly sound and throwing pieces of jagged metal and fireballs through the air. Captain James A. Hall of the Second Maine Battery wrote: "A battery of the enemy . . . was playing upon us, and did us considerable harm for a short time." Even the experienced eye of George Meade mistakenly allowed Confederate resistance to be from a larger amount of guns: "the enemy opened a brisk fire from a battery posted on the Bowling Green road, the shot from which took the command from the left and rear."[10]

Meade impatiently called for more artillery to end this extreme nuisance on his flank that had temporarily stymied his entire infantry, and as many as six Federal batteries would soon move into position. Meanwhile, one of Burnside's staff officers, Brigadier General James A. Hardie, assigned to report the progress of the advance, exaggerated Pelham's resistance even more, claiming "two batteries" were halting the advance.[11] With that ominous information Burnside ordered the heavy artillery from across the Rappahannock River on Stafford Heights into action.

Moving up to assist Simpson's Federal gunners were two more batteries from Meade's division, those of Captains James H. Cooper and Dunbar R. Ransom. Soon two of Doubleday's batteries rolled into action as well, joining the cannon duel against Pelham's single gun. Collectively these five Union batteries—possibly numbering thirty-six cannons in all—along with the 20-pounder Parrott guns from Stafford Heights offered a murderous crossfire from which Pelham and his gun crew should not have escaped.[12] Benefiting Pelham greatly, however, was his selected position. The thick cedar boughs and hedge continued to shield him from the crosshairs of the enemy gunners. Also the mist remained on parts of the battlefield, which aided his concealment. Furthermore, the lower ground selected by Pelham caused many Federal gunners, unable to depress their cannon barrels enough for a score, to overshoot their proposed target.

Approximately twenty minutes had passed since Pelham had first unleashed a projectile on Meade's forces; to some it seemed an eternity. Amazingly, the small band of Confederate artillerists had withstood the Union storm of iron. Astride his horse, Pelham, "dashing and at the same time cautious," according to one of his gunners, calmly ignored the dangers around him and gave deliberate orders to his men to continue the barrage on Meade's prone infantrymen. Soon Pelham shouted and gestured for his gunners to lie down between shots for added safety, while he remained in the saddle "wholly careless of the 'fire of hell' hurled against him." As his men hugged the ground under the wrath of the Federal guns, "a shot struck squarely the head of one of our men," wrote Sergeant Shreve, "and decapitated him as he lay prone on the ground. The rain of shot and shell upon us was terrific, both from their field batteries at close range and also from their big guns on the north bank of the river, but being concealed by the hedge, the enemy's gunners, shot high and so we escaped."[13] After a brief respite Pelham had his gunners up and firing.

Awed Confederate onlookers watched the spectacle as Pelham's gunners had literally halted the advance of the Federal infantry. Oddly, Edward Porter Alexander referred to the stirring episode as "one very petty little incident" but praised "Sallie" Pelham, who "with only 2 guns . . . galloped forward . . . & opened fire on them & soon began to produce a good deal of confusion & delay." South Carolinian J. F. J. Caldwell noted Pelham "enfilading his [the enemy's] lines with great slaughter." Staff officer Channing Price, who witnessed the standoff at Hamilton's Crossing, penned his version to his mother four days later: "The enemy were in dense masses advancing straight towards our line of battle, and Pelham was exactly on their left flank with his gun, with no support whatever. He opened on them with solid shot, and though most of them went amongst the infantry, one blew up a caisson for the Yankees." Price marveled: "Not a gun on our long line, from Fredericksburg to Hamilton's Crossing, had yet fired, only Pelham with his Napoleon." The normally impassive James Longstreet lauded Pelham, "a brave and gallant officer, almost a boy in years," for giving the Federals "lively work."[14]

From his vantage point on Lee's Hill, Robert E. Lee observed the spectacle through his field glasses. Greatly impressed with Pelham's fearlessness and marksmanship, the commanding general, according to Channing Price, "expressed his warm admiration for Major Pelham's distinguished gallantry, but said that the young major general (alluding to Stuart) had opened on them too soon." In fact, Lee was correct. As much as Pelham's gunfire had thrown the entire left flank of the Federal attack into confusion, he should have waited a few more minutes for the bluecoats to have passed his gun barrel before opening up his cannonade. Thus, he could have created an even deadlier crossfire with the massed batteries of Reuben Lindsay Walker atop Prospect Hill.[15] Pelham's instincts, however, had dictated the bombardment start when it did, and now the temporarily paralyzed Federals had been forced to react.

Watching from a distance, Jeb Stuart decided to send some dismounted sharpshooters from the Ninth Virginia Cavalry in Pelham's direction to keep the Federal infantry from closing in on Pelham's position. "It was quickly perceived that we had gone into a lion's mouth," noted Beale, "because of the close proximity of heavy masses of Federal infantry and four batteries, which began to return Pelham's fire. Very serious fears were felt that our gun could not be extricated from its dangerous position, and that the Federal cannoneers, by getting our range, would cut deadly swaths through our ranks." Beale credited two reasons why this did not happen: "the intrepid hardihood of Pelham," who ordered the "rapid fire" of his single gun, and the tinges of fog that shrouded parts of the field. For a while Stuart's sharpshooters did yeoman's work, but the combination of Doubleday's advancing infantry and artillery fire forced most of the Confederates to fall back to safety, once again leaving Pelham and his cannoneers to fend for themselves.[16]

Still observing Pelham's predicament, Stuart summoned John Esten Cooke, who was ordered to bring up a Blakely with another gun crew. Cooke directed the gunners to haul the weapon forward where "[it] was posted nearer the crossing and opened fire." One shot only could be blasted from the Blakely when, from a distance of two hundred yards, Battery A of the Maryland Light Artillery, commanded by Captain John W. Wolcott, scored a direct hit, disabling the piece and killing two of the men.[17] Other Confederates managed to pull the badly damaged Blakely to safety, leaving Pelham, once again, to face the inordinate number of Federal guns with his lone Napoleon.

Quickly maneuvering his single cannon along the undulating ground in the Hamilton's Crossing area, Pelham reverted to his old tactics of repeated firing and moving. This swift blasting and nimble movement to a new location before the enemy could react had become Pelham's hallmark as he proceeded to make the Fredericksburg battlefield his personal arena. The rapidity of his blasts, each from a different position, continued to delude his opponents into thinking they faced an entire battery. One eyewitness called it "the grandest sight he had ever seen." Miraculously, above the terrible din of the contest could be heard the voices of the Frenchmen from the Napoleon Detachment singing the "Marseillaise" as they served the cannon. "It was intensely exciting to watch the effect of [Pelham's] firing," remembered Beale, "as from time to time the shells struck the enemy's lines, and bursting, created no little confusion." Truly, Pelham's unerring marksmanship was a sight to behold. One of Pelham's shots targeted the 121st Pennsylvania Infantry and seven Keystone Staters were injured by the blast. Another literally severed a man in half. An officer from the Eleventh Pennsylvania Reserves fell mortally wounded. Incessant canister balls tearing into the Federal lines even hammered rifles from the hands of unsuspecting soldiers. Having seen the disabled Blakely, Stuart, however, knew his "pet artillerist" was in deep trouble. Summoning Churchill Cooke of the Fourth Virginia Cavalry, Jeb sent him off to find Pelham with the words, "I want to know how he's getting on." Zigzagging along the Massaponax Road, Cooke eventually found the Alabama artillerist still sitting his horse, directing the fire of his gunners. When told of Stuart's concern, Pelham answered coolly, "Tell General Stuart I'm getting on fine and I've only lost one man so far."[18]

Minutes passed and Pelham's gunners proceeded with the uneven struggle. Uncannily, Pelham held his ground, while constantly moving the Napoleon, as Federal projectiles menacingly tore through the cedars. One enemy shell found its mark. The explosion killed one of Pelham's gunners immediately while wounding several others, some of them severely. Among those hit was Jean Bacigalupo, who had survived countless struggles. Pelham dismounted and rushed to him only to find the young Creole bleeding profusely where a piece of shell fragment had torn an ugly wound in his chest. Realizing the wound to be mortal, Pelham attempted to comfort the boy, whose body jerked in agonizing spasms. Pelham summoned two of his men to carry the boy back to a surgeon. Soon von Borcke rode up with orders from Stuart instructing Pelham to pull back "if he thought the proper moment had arrived." Shaking his head, Pelham flashed an angry response: "Tell the General I can hold my ground."[19] Pelham remained on foot for awhile and, along with Mathis Henry, hurried to help his depleted gunners load and fire the single Napoleon the Federals continued to mistake for a battery.

Later a third messenger arrived from Stuart again urging Pelham to retire from the field with the words: "Get back from destruction, you infernal, gallant fool, John Pelham!" Once more Pelham demurred, insisting he could maintain his position. Stonewall Jackson, intently watching the heroics of the young major, dispatched his own messenger, Captain James Power Smith, ordering Pelham to withdraw. "I remember my ride across the field under fire," recalled Smith, "to bear orders to Pelham to retire his guns and how cool and quiet he was as he sat on his horse in the open field in the center of the converging fire of a hundred guns."[20] But only when his limber chests had been emptied of their ammunition did Pelham give the order to pull back. Robert E. Lee could not hold back his enthusiasm: "It is glorious to see such courage in one so young!"[21]

Pelham's display of courage had not, of course, been without damage to his own gunners. The killed included Private Hammond and David R. Barton. Mortally wounded Jean Bacigalupo died later that evening. Eight others sustained wounds, three of them seriously. In a letter to his wife, written on December 17, Private William P. Walters described the eight injured men.

> There were 3 Floyd [county] boys wounded, Joseph [Henry] Phlegar, Samuel [Taylor] Evans and Henderson Boothe. The other 5 were all slightly wounded but 1 man lost his arm. Phlegar lost his right arm. Evans was struck on the breast. The doctor doesn't think he will ever get well. Boothe was struck on the shoulder but [it] did not break the skin. . . . it looked to me like there were cannon balls enough shot at us to kill the whole army. The shells flew as thick as hail [and] burst all around me, but thank God they never touched me yet. They struck so close to me that several times they threw my face full of dirt. We had 14 horses killed, 2 of them were killed [with]in 3 or 4 feet of me. There isn't any fun in this sort of work, so I won't say any more about it, and I expect this is more than you want to hear.[22]

What exactly had Pelham's bold move accomplished that morning from a military standpoint? It stalemated a full Federal corps, of some sixteen thousand men, for an hour or more—no small matter when considering that it was achieved with basically one cannon.[23] In negating the Federal movement, Pelham also gave Union commanders, primarily William B. Franklin and George Meade, cause for concern, albeit too much anxiety, about the Confederate strength on the left. Consequently, Doubleday's division of nearly five thousand men was diverted from its original purpose of supporting Meade's advance to that of a defensive stance for the remainder of the day. Certainly Meade stood a far greater chance for success in cracking Jackson's defensive line later that morning with Doubleday's support than without it.[24]

The effect it had on the morale of the Army of Northern Virginia and on Pelham's growing reputation was possibly even greater. Twice in Robert E. Lee's report following the battle he used the term "unflinching" to describe Pelham's exploit. More significant, Lee bestowed the lasting sobriquet of "the gallant Pelham" on the young Alabamian, and as many have noted, Pelham's name was the only one lower than the rank of general to appear in the commanding general's battle reports. The nickname "Gallant," according to E. P. Alexander, "is still dear to all survivors of the Army of Northern Virginia." Later in the day Lee supposedly stated emphatically to Jackson: "You should have a Pelham on each flank." Stonewall Jackson tersely reported the "brisk and animated contest" that Pelham "kept up for about an hour," and personally thanked Pelham three times for what he had done that morning. Pelham himself left no official account of the episode but did modestly maintain that he would not have kept his solitary gun in such a hazardous spot had it not been for Captain Mathis Winston Henry's encouragement and insistence.

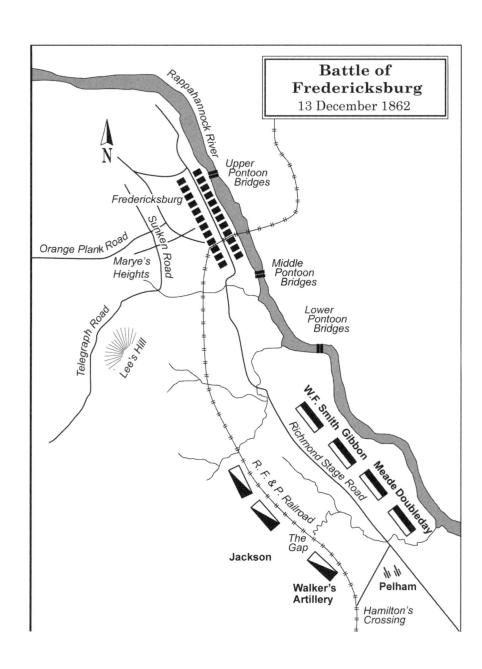

Battle of Fredericksburg
13 December 1862

Confederate John Cheves Haskell, who reportedly interviewed Pelham on numerous occasions, stated that Pelham "freely gave credit to Henry."[25] (See appendix 1.)

Fellow officers and friends also doled out praise for Pelham's fanciful escapade. "This was the climax of his fame," gushed John Esten Cooke, "the event with which his name will be inseparably connected. On that great day [Pelham] covered himself with glory—but no one who knew him felt any surprise at it." Henry Kyd Douglas added his own praise. "No one made so much of a fight and so much of a name in so short a time as . . . John Pelham . . . with his two guns resisting Franklin's attack. Handsome, charming, daring boy! General Lee has spoken of him as 'the Gallant Pelham,' and that settles it."[26]

Perhaps the most telling accolades came from Federal officers. Morris Schaff, a West Point compatriot, marveled at the compliment given Pelham in the nickname "Gallant," stating "and that from Lee was worth more than any rank in any army, more valuable than any title of nobility or badge of any order." Schaff further claimed the nickname to be "almost a household word throughout the South." Following the battle, another unnamed former West Point acquaintance sent a note of congratulations under a flag of truce: "I rejoice, dear Pelham, in your success."[27]

It had been a virtuoso performance, filled with drama and high tension, perhaps unparalleled in the brief annals of Confederate history. Pelham certainly had demonstrated his brilliant talents and panache in other conflicts in this war, but never had he taken on the enemy at such unbalanced odds. Never had he almost single-handedly frustrated and impeded an entire wing of the Federal army. Never had he displayed his abilities so blatantly in front of the admiring Army of Northern Virginia. But, what John Pelham had accomplished that morning was not for the amusement of his Confederate onlookers. What he had done in the gray dawn of December 13 was the stuff of which legends are made. Quite possibly he should have been promoted on the spot to the rank of lieutenant colonel. But the battle was only just beginning.

Without Pelham's interference, Federal gunners were now free to move their pieces forward—some to the exact spot Pelham had only recently vacated. Soon commenced a violent barrage, as "some twenty-five or thirty" Union guns, according to Stapleton Crutchfield, turned their attention toward Prospect Hill. Without returning the fire Confederate artillerists did not reveal their exact positions, leaving the Federal gunners to depend on guesswork. For nearly an hour the earth shook in the Prospect Hill area as myriad Federal projectiles tore into the landscape. Fortunately for the pinned-down Confederates, much of the enemy iron flew beyond the mark, keeping the casualty counts relatively low.

Once more Meade's soldiers rose up from the muddy ground into action. The Federals tramped forward, and yet the Confederate guns remained eerily silent. Suddenly the Union guns ceased firing, adding a bizarre stillness to the scene. "I felt

sorry for those poor Yankee soldiers," penned a Rebel, "as they marched into the
very jaws of death." Up ahead on Prospect Hill sat fourteen well-concealed cannon
under the direction of Reuben Lindsay Walker. The day before Walker and some
of his gunners had paced off distances and noted them with various landmarks at
certain yardages. Walker deemed eight hundred yards the ideal range, so he waited
for Meade's infantry to pass the sited landmark.[28]

Within a few moments, the unsuspecting Yankees were hit by a deadly salvo
from their front as Walker's guns opened up. Almost simultaneously, a murderous
blast smashed into the Federals on their left as John Pelham renewed his efforts
from the Hamilton's Crossing area. This time, however, Pelham had more than one
gun at his disposal. Stonewall Jackson had seen to it that Pelham had fifteen cannon for his immediate use in creating a crossfire with those of Walker's batteries.
"Very soon Pelham's guns were reinforced by two of Lindsay Walker's batteries,"
wrote G. W. Beale, "and the Federal guns opened on them with increasing vigor.
The duel was fast and furious." Other batteries wheeled up to support Walker and
Pelham until the Confederate right had some fifty pieces hurling iron into the Federal ranks. Stapleton Crutchfield commended Pelham, whose "pieces . . . were admirably managed and bravely fought, and perfectly accomplished their objective,"
which was once again to disrupt Meade's advancement.[29]

And disrupt it they did. The combined efforts of the Confederate gunners soon
had many of Meade's veterans recoiling back to the Richmond Stage Road; others
simply fell prone in the mud a second time. Here the Federal infantry caught its col-
lective breath as infuriated and exasperated Union commanders ordered batteries
of artillery forward to meet this new challenge. From across the Rappahannock the
large Federal guns opened up once more with renewed fury. For more than an hour
four hundred guns from the two armies staged a titan clash of artillery fire, both
deafening and deadly, perhaps the largest the war had yet witnessed. And directly
in the midst of the firing John Pelham stood with his assortment of guns. Although
Pelham had requested no additional help, he soon received support with the arrival of two batteries sent by Stapleton Crutchfield—Captain Louis E. D'Aquin's
Louisiana Guards and Lieutenant Asher W. Garber's Staunton Artillery. Crutchfield would later see to it that parts of four other batteries were sent to Pelham, giving the Alabamian the largest contingency of guns under his command thus far in
the war.[30]

All along Stonewall Jackson's right flank the Confederate artillery more than
held its own against the more powerful Federal ordnance. Pelham's gunners persisted in an all-out duel against Lieutenant John G. Simpson's battery of Pennsylvanians. During the intense melee, both D'Aquin and Garber lost a cannon from
the heavy gunfire. Soon D'Aquin, the valiant Louisianan, toppled forward, killed
by a Federal shell. Another projectile struck Garber's horse, mortally wounding

the animal, which darted about for the next moments, crazed with pain. In a frenzied attempt to pull in his maddened steed, Garber instead lost his seat and landed on his head, knocking himself momentarily senseless. More field pieces were dispensed to Pelham with the arrival of two 10-pounder Parrott guns from Captain William T. Poague's famed Rockbridge Artillery. These guns, brought forward by dashing Lieutenant Archibald Graham, remained with Pelham until after nightfall. Also arriving at virtually the same time was the rifled section of the Third Company of the Richmond Howitzers under the leadership of Lieutenant James S. Utz. The advent of these additional guns seemed to animate Pelham, who scurried among the guns "like a boy playing ball."[31]

Within a few moments the last of Pelham's reinforcements arrived: two 10-pounder Parrott guns and a brass rifle from the Second Company of the Richmond Howitzers under Captain David Watson and a 3-inch rifle from Captain Willis J. Dance's Powhatan Battery. Collectively, Pelham's cannons furiously blasted into the Federals, as did Lindsay Walker's from Prospect Hill. Simpson's battery of Pennsylvanians took an ugly hammering as eleven men and sixteen horses fell from the awful barrage. Every field piece in Simpson's battery had been scored by a projectile, and all his caissons suffered damage. Now the Federals, apparently willing to ignore Walker's batteries, turned their fury against Pelham's guns. From as close as 1,100 yards the enemy guns lashed out with swarms of iron determined to end Pelham's resistance. Undeterred, Pelham resolved to hold his position for the second time that morning. Channing Price later wrote that "Pelham was standing [where] the shells were crashing in every direction." Pelham appeared almost invincible, but Lieutenant James Utz, a popular leader of the Richmond Howitzers, was not. Hit by a fragment of shell, Utz died almost instantly.[32]

Moments later Tom Rosser, who had been an observer to the struggle, wheeled his horse and rode slowly to the area where the Parrott guns of the Rockbridge Artillery kept up a steady fire. There he saw his old friend, Steven Dandridge, among the gunners and sought to discuss the hazards of the present situation. After a quick renewal of their acquaintance, Dandridge nervously asked Rosser when he thought Pelham might remove these men from this danger zone. Before riding off, Rosser playfully informed Dandridge that Pelham intended to keep the men in this spot at least until Dandridge was killed. It was a line that would have made Jeb Stuart proud.

Rosser now retraced his steps and ran into John Pelham. Together they watched the artillery duel intensify. For the next few minutes sweaty gunners from both sides rammed home charges and fired into the midst of their opponents. Men fell, horses screamed and reared up in fright, and limber chests exploded from direct hits. One Confederate projectile completely disengaged a Federal cannon barrel from its carriage. Dandridge observed that Pelham was "as gallant a fellow as I ever saw" and was pleased that he reassured the members of the Rockbridge Artillery that when the group experienced a casualty, he would pull the unit back. In fact, the company was "terribly cut up," according to Dandridge, who later stated, "[we] lost 6 killed, and ten or twelve badly wounded." He further reported that a "look of sorrow" was found on the faces of the survivors that evening.[33]

Pelham remained proud of the gunners under his command that morning. Lieutenant Archibald Graham's cannoneers especially impressed Pelham. William Poague remembered: "[Graham's] section fully maintained the reputation of the battery, winning from 'Glorious Pelham' very high compliments—being much impressed with the cool and nonchalant bearing of both Graham and his men." But Poague added solemnly, "The casualty list of both men and horses was heavy." Pelham later complimented the Rockbridge boys by stating, "You men stand killing better than any I know."[34]

Now some of the Federal batteries turned their attention toward the three guns of David Watson's Richmond Howitzers. When a Federal shell targeted an ammunition chest, Rosser and Pelham rode to safety, barely ahead of the exposed gunners. Willis Lee, a member of the battery, remembered, almost cynically, the next few moments of the fight in which his comrades suffered badly:

Our gun was borrowed by Major Pelham of Stuart's Horse Artillery, and taken across a sunken road into an open field beyond the extreme left of the enemy's line. Here occurred a fight that is in history. It was claimed after the war that the gun was of Pelham's battery; quite a controversy arose between Pelham's and Howitzer Battalions. It seems we were sent there to be sacrificed as a military necessity, were to feel the enemy and if there were no heavy guns across the river, Jackson was to "Charge and double Burnside up." If heavy guns were there, we were expected to be wiped out. As soon as we got on the field, we mounted the gun and caisson and rushed at full gallop up to rifle shot of enemy's line, unlimbered and fired shot, shell and canister point blank down his flank, so close was our fire that the line began to waver and crumble. In a few minutes though, a battery of 32 pounders across the river opened on us. Then a light battery of six guns dashed to the infantry line and opened with shrapnel. We were literally smothered with shot and shell: of 12 horses we lost 11; out of 14 men 9 were killed and wounded, 2 killed on the field and 2 others, I think, died of wounds. We were ordered off by Major Pelham. Sergeant Green and I . . . got on our knees to limber up the gun, hoping to get it off with three horses, then standing. As we worked, a shell passed through the limber chest, exploding it, killing or wounding every horse. We then made tracks in quick time for the sunken road, leaving the gun.

General [*sic*] Rosser and Major Pelham, who had watched the fight about a hundred yards to our left, had gotten to shelter ahead of us. The enemy's sharpshooters advanced to the gun, but a few dismounted cavalry of Rosser's, in the sunken road, drove them back. After this [later in the afternoon] we got our detachments together, and brought the gun off by hand, placing it in the sunken road. We again went into action and fired till late at night.[35]

By 1:00 P.M. Meade's infantry, once again ready for another assault on Jackson's flank, began moving forward in three long, massive lines of blue on a one-thousand-yard front. All along Jackson's line artillery pieces exploded as the gray-clad gunners sought to repel the advance. This time, however, the Federals poured past the Rebel artillerists "in defiance of our guns," according to Lindsay Walker, "which were served rapidly and with great havoc upon their dense ranks."[36] In truth the Confederate artillery had lost much of its sting from the furious engagement. Four artillery battalion commanders lay dead; two others had suffered debilitating wounds. Furthermore, a dozen cannon had been put out of action, as well as three limbers and a caisson exploded.[37] Although Pelham's gunners still held their ground, they too had lost much of their effectiveness. Thus the Confederate infantry was about to be severely tested.

Without pausing for breath, the Federals pushed on to the Richmond, Fredericksburg, and Potomac Railroad tracks. It had not been an easy ascent to the railroad. Scores of Meade's best veterans had fallen; one of his three brigade commanders, Brigade General Conrad Feger Jackson, a devout Quaker, took a bullet in the brain, killing him instantly. But the Federals seemed to sense that this was their moment and plunged onward into the Gap, directly between the brigades of James Jay Archer and James Lane.

Five hundred yards beyond rested the South Carolinian regiments of forty-eight-year-old Brigadier General Maxcy Gregg. Noted for his intellect as well as his ability as a warrior, Gregg mistakenly believed that his front was strongly protected and that his brigade, selected as "reserves" for the day, could relax with their rifles neatly stacked. Suddenly, the rushing Federals were among Gregg's men. In the confusion Gregg was hit by a bullet, which severed his spine. Knocked from his saddle, Gregg lay on the ground, conscious, but mortally wounded.[38] Within a few moments his overwhelmed brigade ingloriously fled the field.

Unaware of the dire situation to their rear, Lane and Archer sent couriers back to Gregg in hope of receiving assistance. Instead, their men had to fight desperately for their own survival. With no help available from Gregg's scattered forces, the inside flanks of both Lane's and Archer's lines began to crumble. Unit after unit fell back, surrendered, or panicked, placing the onus on the next regiment of men. Confederate officers vainly sought to restore order in their disjointed lines. The collapse of Lane's entire brigade was inevitable. In fact, with the Federals swarming over Prospect Hill, Stonewall Jackson's once powerful position presently stood in great jeopardy.

And now, as had so often occurred in battles of this war, the side that hurried in reinforcements at the most critical stage of the fighting was destined to win. Good fortune had run its course for Meade and Gibbon, as both commanders sought support that did not arrive. The Confederates, however, still held a trump card in the form of Brigadier General Jubal A. Early's division. And now he unleashed his division directly against the stubborn Yankees who had penetrated the breach. Roaring forward, Early's men attacked with a demonic fury. Heartened by their efforts, Lane and Archer sought with some success to rally portions of their broken commands. Collectively, the Confederates refilled the breach and drove the Federals in flight to the rear.

While the bluecoats hurried to the rear, Confederate gunners again moved their pieces forward and peppered the fleeing enemy with various projectiles. Pelham's cannons stayed close on the heels of the Federals, spraying them with canister balls. Channing Price later wrote: "Pelham continued to advance his guns as the enemy retreated pouring in a terrible enfilading fire all the time." Federal artillerists, however, began finding their target and inflicted numerous casualties of their own, causing the Rebels to back off.[39]

Pushed back beyond the railroad tracks, the Federals finally made a stand that halted Early's pursuing veterans along the embankment. It was now 2:30 in the afternoon. The fighting died down on this flank and shifted to Longstreet's front. Round one of this two-round fight had ceased, although more action would be seen along Jackson's lines before the end of the day. But what a day thus far! Casualty counts had been heavy for both sides. William B. Franklin later tallied his losses in killed, wounded, and missing at 3,787. Roughly half of those came from George Meade's division. A. P. Hill's division had taken the bulk of Jackson's losses— 231 killed, 1,474 wounded, 417 missing—totaling 2,122 men. Of this sum, 1,315 came from the combined brigades of James Lane, James Jay Archer, and Maxcy Gregg. Jubal Early's division took slightly more than one thousand casualties. As the combat ended on this flank, sparks from the weapons ignited the tall sage grass, and some of the flames enveloped wounded soldiers, unable to reach safety. "Agonizing screams" could be heard over the battlefield. "It was a horrible sight to see them burning to death," penned a weary eyewitness. "I never want to see such a sight again." Meade's men had fought valiantly, but the battle lines now existed on this flank as they did nearly five hours earlier. "The expedition [was] a failure," summed up a Federal lieutenant. "The undertaking seemed like madness."[40]

Up to this point the day had belonged to the Confederate artillery with numerous heroics displayed by several talented commanders. Reuben Lindsay Walker and his battery leaders on Prospect Hill had been spectacular. Twenty-one-year-old Captain William Ransom Johnson Pegram, better known as "Willie," deserved rave reviews. Badly nearsighted, the bespectacled Petersburg, Virginia, native looked anything but a warrior. However, in battle he transformed into a veritable tiger, literally fearless. During this struggle when enemy fire drove his men running from their guns, Pegram calmly wrapped himself in the battery's battle flag and walked along his cannons to rally his deserted men. "[He] seemed to love battle more than any man I ever saw," declared A. P. Hill. Labeled a "soldier's soldier" by Lindsay Walker, another paid Pegram the ultimate compliment of pronouncing him "a second Pelham."[41] Captain David G. McIntosh, five years older than Pegram, continued to add laurels to his growing reputation as he battled demon-like against the Yankees.[42] Others, such as twenty-one-year-old Captain Joseph W. Latimer, amazed those who witnessed his composure as he "sat on his horse during the hottest part of the fight . . . and looked as unconcerned as if he had been at a holiday frolic."[43] And certainly the rare marksmanship of Robert Hardaway deserved attention. But when the day had ended, awestruck veterans still spoke with admiration of the exploits of John Pelham and what he had accomplished that morning.

⁓

Three miles farther north from Jackson's position, Longstreet's men had been relatively inactive that morning, as they waited impatiently for some of the action. The eerie silence along Marye's Heights lingered until about 11:00 A.M. when Burnside decided to press forward Major General Edwin V. Sumner's Right Grand Division, thus opening a second front—a decision of unfathomable ignorance that left both sides dumbfounded.

Brigadier General William H. French's division of Darius N. Couch's Second Corps was selected to spearhead the Federal advance. The bluecoats crept through the yards and gardens of the departed residents of Fredericksburg. Many reached a swale, which afforded some protection. Farther ahead, however, the Federals offered themselves as a deadly target to the Confederate artillery, which included two 30-pounder Parrott guns, atop Marye's Heights. In effect, the Confederates had three tiers of infantry and artillery situated to fire over each other's heads directly into the oncoming Yankees. Bravely, French's men scurried upward toward the sunken road and the four-foot stone fence that concealed Confederate riflemen. Getting to within sixty yards of the stone fence, French's men melted back from the violent sheet of flame sent forth by the Rebels.

With French's division spent, orders came to send in the remainder of Couch's corps—the divisions of Brigadier Generals Winfield Scott Hancock and Oliver Otis Howard. One long, continuous roar of musketry sounded from behind the stone fence as tier after tier of Rebels discharged their weapons. Some of Hancock's brave souls came within forty yards of the barrier, but the incessant rifle fire perpetuated the slaughter and drove the survivors running for safety. Couch's three divisions had suffered 4,102 casualties.[44] Ambrose Burnside was far from finished.

Now two more divisions, those of Brigadier Generals Samuel D. Sturgis and George W. Getty, readied for another attack on Longstreet's soldiers at Marye's Heights. Confederate artillery opened up again as the 30-pounder Parrott guns blasted away with superb effect. Federals who escaped the barrage of shells were met by the same sheet of deadly rifle fire at the stone wall. Again it was too much for the bluecoats, who backed off, leaving their dead comrades all along the advance route up Marye's Heights.

The last Federal attacks on Longstreet's position came from two divisions—those of Brigadier Generals Charles Griffin and Andrew A. Humphreys—of Joseph Hooker's Center Grand Division. Fighting beyond sundown, the Federal troops displayed undeniable courage in attacking the stone wall. Humphreys's men struggled to within eighty yards of the barrier before being forced back in confusion. His division had taken 1,016 losses in killed, wounded, and missing; Griffin's casualties had been nearly equal at 923. Longstreet summed up the slaughter: "A series of braver, more desperate charges than those hurled against the troops in the sunken road was never known, and the piles and cross-piles of dead marked a field such as I never saw before or since."[45]

Both Federal attacks on Jackson's and Longstreet's flanks had ended in disaster. But the Battle of Fredericksburg was not quite over. Jeb Stuart had kept in contact with Stonewall Jackson concerning their proposed counterattack. As twilight approached, Stuart's scouts reported the enemy demoralized and backed up defensively against the Rappahannock River. This was enough for the cavalry chieftain, who met with Jackson on Prospect Hill to iron out the details. Knowing the advance was "very hazardous" due to the "judiciously posted" enemy artillery, Jackson still believed it would yield "good results, if successfully executed." A single cannon blast would signal the attack with Pelham's horse artillery and Stuart's sharpshooters moving forward in conjunction with two brigades of cavalry on the enemy flank. With fixed bayonets, Jackson's infantry would smash the middle. Jackson determined to hold off the advance "until late in the afternoon, so that if compelled to retire, it would be under cover of the night."[46]

Meanwhile, the twilight settled in on Stuart's forces, as they anxiously awaited the cannon signal. Time passed, tension mounted, but still no report of a cannon. Impatiently, Stuart gave the order to advance without the prearranged signal, and his men moved forward. "Off we went into the gathering darkness," reported von Borcke, "our sharpshooters driving their opponents easily before them, and Pelham, with his guns, pushing ahead at a trot, firing a few shots whenever the position seemed favourable, and then again pressing forward." For twenty minutes Pelham's gunners and Stuart's sharpshooters led the way through the late afternoon, yet Jackson's infantrymen mysteriously remained stationary. By now the Federals opened up with rifle fire and artillery, making the situation a "critical one," according to von Borcke.[47]

Federal Private John W. Haley of the Seventeenth Maine Regiment, in his first battle of the war, described his view of the action:

We moved to the front and formed ahead of a battery somewhat to the left. . . . If the Rebels had known what was there, they'd have looked before they leapt. We hadn't long to wait, as the Rebels commenced to cannonade our lines about half past four, preparatory to a charge. Our battery replied, and shells went whizzing over us so near that we hugged old Mother Earth most affectionately.

There was a single gun nearly opposite belonging to Stuart's horse artillery and under the command of Major John Pelham. This conceited party must have thought he could silence our battery. His was a large gun and threw a much heavier missile. Our gunners ceased firing for a minute, and never was sixty seconds better employed. They sighted and fired. That shell created a profound sensation in Rebel circles. It burst under Mr. Pelham's gun and not only dismantled the same, but mixed things up dreadfully. Two men and a boy were killed by that one shell. It wasn't necessary to duplicate the dose. The indefatigable Pelham—the incomparable Pelham—and the rest of his crew made haste to depart. No more cannonading that day, nor did the Rebels make the contemplated charge in which they had, no doubt, expected to capture our forces or drive us into the Rappahannock.[48]

During the melee Stuart rashly exposed himself to the bluecoats and barely escaped death as one bullet penetrated his haversack while another cut away the fur collar on his cloak. Suddenly a courier from Jackson galloped up to tell Stuart to call off the attack and fall back to his original position. Stuart stubbornly continued fighting for a few minutes before adhering to Jackson's orders. Only then did Pelham and his gunners, along with the sharpshooters, retreat to safety. Farther along in the darkness, however, D. H. Hill, unaware of the orders to halt, maintained his advance and took moderate losses from the Federal artillery before breaking off the attack.[49]

Jackson's later report explained why he so abruptly canceled the advance: "The first gun had hardly moved forward from the wood 100 yards when the enemy's artillery reopened, and so completely swept our front as to satisfy me that the proposed movement should be abandoned." Other reasons existed for the cessation of the attack. Darkness hindered the swift movement of the troops, and the trees made it difficult to move the artillery smoothly. Confusion among the attackers and poor communication from the leaders, as evidenced by the piecemeal attacks of Stuart and D. H. Hill, rendered the plans hastily prepared and ill-advised. Ammunition shortages may have also been a problem. With the Federal artillery in place to counter such an offensive, Jackson correctly called off the attack. Jubal

Early possibly spoke for the majority when he stated, "There was not a man in the force who did not breathe freer when he heard the orders countermanding the movement."[50]

Amazingly, Stonewall Jackson had not given up the thought of counterattacking the Federals in the darkness. "Word was passed around among us," stated G. W. Beale, "as to how the assault would be conducted and with what weapons. Every man's coat sleeve . . . was to be removed from one arm, which would enable us in the darkness to distinguish friends from foes." Only from the fertile mind of the offensive-thinking Jackson could this notion have been hatched. Exactly how this plan changed is unknown, but according to Dr. Hunter McGuire, the chief surgeon of the Second Corps, Jackson approached him later that night and inquired "how many yards of bandaging I had." The puzzled look on McGuire's face caused Jackson to abruptly explain. "I want a yard of bandaging to put on the arm of every soldier in this night's attack so that the men may know each other from the enemy." Few men dared to challenge Jackson, but McGuire indicated that he did not have enough of the bandaging for this purpose and calmly suggested that the general "would have to take a piece of the shirt tail of each soldier to supply the cloth, but, unfortunately half of them had no shirts!" McGuire did not give Jackson's reaction, but the surgeon stated: "The expedient was never tried. General Lee decided that the attack would be too hazardous."[51] Thus the Battle of Fredericksburg ended.

Total losses from the two sides clearly indicate an overwhelming Confederate victory. The Federal casualty sheet listed 1,284 killed, 9,600 wounded, and 1,769 captured or missing, for an aggregate of 12,653 or 70 percent of the day's losses. The Confederate casualties were broken down as 608 killed, 4,116 wounded, and 653 captured or missing, totaling 5,377. Confederate losses in the artillery approximated 50 killed and 250 wounded. John Pelham's horse artillery had merely three killed and twenty-two wounded, an unusually low total for their highly engaged activities of the day.[52] Moonlight revealed vivid and ghastly images for the living on both sides. "Many died of wounds and exposure, and as fast as men died they stiffened in the wintry air," stated Darius Couch, "and on the front line were rolled forward for protection to the living. Frozen men were placed for dumb sentries."[53]

Ambrose Burnside readily admitted defeat a few days later in his report to Washington, D.C. "Our forces had been repulsed at all points," he acknowledged, "and it was necessary to look upon the day's work as a failure." Burnside, however, proclaimed the attack would resume the next morning, with him personally leading the Ninth Corps into the Confederate center. He then appealed to other generals for support but received, instead, negative and despondent responses. To the amazement of the others, he stuck to his plan. The following morning, December 14, a disheartened Burnside, after again consulting with his leading generals, rescinded the order to attack.[54]

For John Pelham that night brought mixed emotions. Congratulations for his extraordinary day's work were bestowed upon him from those who ventured past his post. Meanwhile, he saw to it that his caissons were filled with ammunition from the artillery wagons. But he had lost a few of his gunners that day, and now he was summoned to the side of Jean, whose wound had been declared fatal by the attending surgeons. There in the darkness Pelham held the fifteen-year-old, encouraging him to "bear it like the brave soldier you are." Some of the Napoleon Detachment had gathered around, tearfully witnessing the agonizing scene as Pelham attempted to console the boy. Jean soon slipped into unconsciousness and died. After composing himself, Pelham remarked, "Poor boy. . . . there was nobody braver."[55]

Later that night Pelham received a directive from Stonewall Jackson ordering the artillery major to the general's headquarters. There Jackson explained the anticipated Federal attack and expressed his concern that the extreme right near Hamilton's Crossing must be fortified. Jackson desired strong earthworks built and entrusted Pelham with the critical task. Pelham could choose the exact site of the earthen fort, but it must be completed by dawn. Jackson then dismissed Pelham, who immediately set out to gather his workers. Throughout the night John Pelham and his selected crew constructed the earthworks. Pelham mostly supervised, but as usual, he often pitched in with the men as a fellow worker. By daylight the earthen fort had been completed to Pelham's satisfaction, and he reported this to Stuart. Nodding to the young artillerist, Jeb smiled and ordered Pelham to get some sleep. Later Stuart and Stonewall Jackson inspected Pelham's handiwork. Proudly, Stuart sat in the saddle, saying nothing, waiting for Jackson's response. Carefully analyzing the creation, Jackson remarked, "Good! Good!" Then turning to Jeb, Jackson stated emphatically, "Have you another Pelham, General? If so, I wish you would give him to me."[56] Together the two generals rode off, content that the extreme right could withstand another Federal attack.

Pelham returned to camp, weary from the long, eventful day and sleepless night. There to greet him was Captain Lewis Guy Phillips of the British Grenadier Guards, who had witnessed the battle from Lee's Hill. Perhaps in all the excitement of the day, Pelham had forgotten the red and blue striped necktie the Englishman had given him to wear. Pelham pulled off his hat and carefully removed the now soiled souvenir. "With a modest smile," recalled von Borcke proudly, "Pelham returned to the Captain the bit of regimental ribbon he had worn as a talisman during the fight, its gay colours just a little blackened by powder-smoke, for it had flaunted from the cap of the young hero in the very atmosphere of Death."[57]

Pelham's flashy heroics had proven he belonged on center stage, but for now, the young lion fell into a deep slumber.

20

"A System of Irritation"

No one of an equal age in either army has won an equal reputation
[as Pelham].

—*London Times*

Sunday, December 14, 1862, was like no other Sabbath in Fredericksburg's 135-year history. No church bells chimed anywhere in the city. Nowhere was there any evidence of townspeople gathering up their gaily dressed families for the stroll or ride to worship services. In fact, little or no sign of residents appeared anywhere in the town. Instead, Fredericksburg resembled an armed camp as two huge monsters, one blue and one gray, peered at each other uneasily. Between them lay a bloody, dismal battlefield where the previous day the two enemies had slugged one another in indeterminable fury. Piles of battered and broken bodies offered grim evidence of the horrible struggle. Occasional movement was observed in this wasteland, and weak, pathetic voices pleaded for help or water. Close observation revealed many dead Federal soldiers had been stripped of their uniforms and footwear during the night. Scrounging Rebels pragmatically reckoned that at least another two to three months of wintry weather remained on the calendar, and the garments would be better served by the living.

All along their elevated lines Confederates continued to wait for a renewal of the enemy assault, which, unknown to them, had been called off by the Federal high command. As they stood at their posts, the Rebels marveled at the gruesome reminders of yesterday's contest in full view below. Although the Federals showed no indication of renewing the offensive that day, a number of bluecoats, sheltered in various clustered haystacks, opened up with rifle fire on the Confederate right. Soon John Pelham brought up some of his guns to silence this nuisance. Within moments shells exploded in the haystacks, setting them ablaze and dislodging the forty or fifty Yankees who had caused the disturbance. "Finding the place too hot to hold," observed von Borcke, "[they] scampered off in a body, accompanied by a loud cheer from our men, and a well-aimed volley, which brought down several of the fugitives."[1] The remainder of the day brought no more of these demonstrations.

That night the men of both sides witnessed what William Poague described as "a magnificent display of the aurora borealis" across the heavens. Beginning at

6:15 P.M. and lasting for over an hour, the Northern Lights saturated the sky with brilliant, flashing hues the likes of which most soldiers had never beheld.[2] It was a strange sight, considering the carnage witnessed the previous day, and may have revitalized the spiritual faith in some who had lost confidence in their belief in a merciful God.

The following day arrived without a trace of Federal intention of attack. Pelham and the other Confederate gunners kept their pieces ready for action in case Burnside showed any change of heart. But the hours passed in relative calm. Somewhat dispirited by this inactivity, Robert E. Lee grasped the notion that the great struggle waged two days earlier had been an empty victory since the Army of the Potomac lay wounded but still intact. Even the offensive-minded Stonewall Jackson appeared to have lost his zeal to unsheathe his saber in a counterstroke. Thus the two opposing armies stayed at bay, satisfied to lick their wounds.

W. W. Blackford, who had grown up in Fredericksburg, toured the town with his brothers, Eugene and Charles, both veterans of the Army of Northern Virginia. Quite naturally, they directed much of their attention to their old homestead, which had been temporarily converted into a hospital. The scene appalled the three brothers. "The room in which we were born," penned W. W., "was half inch deep in clotted blood still wet, and the walls were spattered with it, and all around were scattered legs and arms. The place smelt like a butcher's shambles."[3]

By early afternoon Ambrose Burnside sent two officers under a white flag toward the Confederate lines requesting a truce in order to collect the Federal wounded and bury the dead. Soon Federal ambulances arrived to take away their wounded men, who had lain in the open for some forty-eight hours without medical attention. Hundreds of the wounded were intermingled with the dead, making them difficult to extricate and adding to the horrors of the scene. In some areas piles of dead men reached seven or eight deep.

Confederates pitched in to give their assistance. Together the enemies worked as one with a sense of urgency. Darkness would soon be falling, limiting the time for the joint burial, and the frozen earth snapped many a shovel that attempted to penetrate the rock-hard ground. The men toiled past sundown before ending their efforts, leaving hundreds of bodies still unburied. That night fierce winds blew in from the south and a heavy rainstorm saturated the area. Jeb Stuart fretted during the storm as his instincts told him something was amiss. "These Yankees have always some underhand trick when they send a flag of truce," Jeb sputtered, "and I fear they will be off before daylight."[4]

Stuart's intuition, as usual, proved correct, for that same evening the entire Army of the Potomac—including all its guns, wagons, horses, ambulances, and equipment—had stolen safely across the Rappahannock River on their pontoon bridges. The violent storm with its howling winds had literally muffled the sounds of the escaping bluecoats, whose daring and skillful evacuation had been nothing short of brilliant. Once the crossing was completed, Federal engineers dismantled the bridges.

Early that morning, Tuesday, December 16, John Pelham and Heros von Borcke decided to examine the area to their front only recently evacuated by the Federals. To their surprise they discovered a number of live land mines littering the landscape. These small "torpedoes" had obviously been left behind to hinder any pursuit by the Confederates. Fortunately the overnight rains had saturated the powder inside, rendering the explosives useless. Heading back toward their own lines, Pelham and von Borcke wandered upon an entire Yankee regimental band that had been captured by some Mississippians. These Federal musicians had apparently fallen asleep during the escape and had not been missed by their fleeing comrades. Now they became official prisoners of war. "They seemed but little troubled at their fate," recalled von Borcke, "and cheerfully struck up the tunes of Dixie, to the great delight of our men, who meanwhile set about preparing for them whatever comforts our rough hospitality could afford."[5]

Sometime later that morning, according to Helen Bernard's diary, Rooney Lee, Jeb Stuart, and Pelham paid a visit to Gay Mont. "We were delighted to see them," noted Helen, "especially the first [Lee] & to hear accounts of the battle. It must have been a greater victory for us than we at first supposed as the enemy have all recrossed the river & are now nowhere to be seen."[6]

By this time many of the civilians of Fredericksburg began returning to the city and what was left of their homes. Although some of the houses remained fully intact, far too often fine old residences had been badly damaged or completely destroyed.[7] In many cases the basic structures still stood, but much of the personal belongings within had been scattered, stolen, or vandalized. Numerous scenes of pathos occurred as townspeople wandered the streets tearfully collecting their lifelong possessions. Touched by the poignancy, scores of Confederate soldiers pitched in to assist the residents in putting their belongings back into the battered buildings.[8]

With the Army of the Potomac safely across the Rappahannock and the battle officially over, both sides could assess the outcome with candor. Federal morale had reached its nadir. Absolutely no hint of victory could be gleaned from the fiasco, and only a fool would try to find any solace in the aftermath. There was no pretending; they had suffered a terrible defeat and everyone seemed to realize it. One Union officer sarcastically noted that the only positive gained by the battle was learning to cross a river "in the presence of an enemy." Another simply labeled it "unnecessary slaughter."[9]

Confederate reporting of the battle, conversely and somewhat surprisingly, brought mixed reviews. For some this battle signified the acme of achievement that would guarantee independence. Most simply took pleasure in the tone of the battle and its outcome. Ham Chamberlayne optimistically informed his family "the war . . .

is about ended." D. H. Hill reported: "In no battle of the war has the signal inter-
position of God in our favor been more wonderfully displayed." Others viewed
the battle as a lackluster effort on the part of the Federals, thus leading to an in-
auspicious outcome. Val C. Giles offered his no-nonsense evaluation: "No general that ever lived could have whipped Lee at Fredericksburg. . . . [It] was a complete failure as far as results were concerned. Not one foot of disputed territory was
gained or lost by either army, though nearly 20,000 American soldiers were killed
or wounded there. The only result was a flood of women's tears from the St. Law-
rence to the Rio Grande."[10]

Discussion of the battle continued to center around the performance of John
Pelham, whose achievements had drawn rave reviews and caused even grizzled veterans to shake their heads in wonderment. From Robert E. Lee's fabled comment,
which gave Pelham his immortal nickname, to the common soldiers' talk around
the campfire, all seemed enamored by the young artillerist's heroics. As one of the
gunners boasted, "Pelham is the bravest human being I ever saw in my life." Compliments of that nature were whispered throughout the camp, and predictions were
heard that Pelham could be a colonel or even a brigadier general before long. Stuart
continued to push for his friend's promotion. In a letter dated December 18, Jeb
wrote to Custis Lee: "Pelham won a colonelcy on the field last Saturday. He always
has command of a large number of reserve batteries on the flank and should have
rank to correspond. Do lay his case with the strongest recommendations before the
President. If merit is a criterion or standard Pelham should be rewarded." Even the
foreign press reported his exploits, as the *London Times* stated: "No one of an equal
age in either army has won an equal reputation."[11]

Certainly Pelham enjoyed hearing his name bandied about in veneration by the
officers and men. Praise for his performance came in large doses, but, amazingly,
Pelham showed no outward signs of self-importance. Indeed, he seemed to be more
than willing to pass along the accolades to others. On the morning following the
battle, when many continued to speak of his brilliant actions from the preceding
day, Pelham passed along the information to Captain David G. McIntosh of the
Pee Dee Artillery that Stuart was "highly pleased" with the men for their excellent help. This compliment prompted McIntosh to state in a letter to his mother, "I
am disposed to <u>brag</u> a little."[12] Inwardly Pelham must have swelled with pride and
satisfaction, but on the outside, he remained as selfless as always. Only the occasional flush of color in his cheeks, when others praised him, betrayed his near stoic
demeanor. John Esten Cooke, who would soon be Pelham's tent mate, observed
the lad closely and did not hesitate to applaud his humility: "The character of this
young soldier was so eminently noble—his soul so brave, so true, so free from any
taint of what was mean or sordid or little. . . . His modesty, his gentleness—his
bearing almost childlike in its simplicity. . . . He never spoke of himself; you might
live with him for a month, and never know that he had been in a single action. He

never seemed to think that he deserved any applause for his splendid courage, and was silent upon all subjects connected with his own actions."[13]

Cooke barely modified his comments in one of his other writings:

> I never knew a human being of more stubborn nerve, or shrinking modesty. . . . His color never faded in the hottest hours of the most desperate fighting; but a word would often confuse him, and make him blush like a girl. . . . it was impossible to know him and not love him. . . . The smooth, boyish face was the veritable mirror of high breeding, delicacy, and honor. . . . Quick to resent an insult, or to meet defiance with defiance, he was never irritable, and had the sweetness and good-humor of a child. . . . His modesty did not change after Fredericksburg. . . . He was still the modest, simple, laughing boy—with his charming gayety, his caressing voice, and his sunny smile. . . . He never spoke of his own achievements.[14]

Over the next few days the Army of Northern Virginia began settling into its winter quarters. Longstreet's corps remained in the area around Marye's Heights while Jackson's men moved farther down the Rappahannock in the direction of Port Royal. Jackson himself accepted the invitation of the Corbin family to make his headquarters in the vicinity of their palatial home, Moss Neck. The Corbin property covered 1,600 acres, and Moss Neck sat majestically on an elevation overlooking the woodland, the beautiful fields, and the rolling hills. At first Jackson, ever the spartan, refused to reside in the home, opting instead for his own tent. Later as the weather turned colder, he agreed to make his headquarters in a modest office building some fifty yards from the plantation home.[15]

Pelham and John Esten Cooke became tent mates, and they spent much of their time working hard to winterize their structure. After reinforcing the walls, the two laid a wooden floor and built a makeshift fireplace at the entrance with an ample supply of firewood nearby. Their "cozy" quarters were completed just in time as the balmy temperatures of mid-December now turned bitterly cold with alternating snowstorms and freezing rain. The harsh weather especially took its toll on the horses and mules in the camp. The "poor beasts" suffered, according to von Borcke, "from want of food, exposure, and vermin, [and] was pitiable indeed." The crude lean-tos, built to give protection to the animals, failed to keep out the severe elements, and the horses and mules "stood for the most part knee-deep in water or slush." Soon a malady, first noticed about the hooves but later spreading up the entire limbs, disabled approximately one-fourth of the cavalry and artillery horses.[16]

Life at Camp No-Camp now settled back into a normal routine. Soldiers continued to work diligently on their winter quarters, for as breathtakingly beautiful as the snowfalls were, the harshest part of the season had not yet arrived. With Pelham's lodging completed, the Alabamian oversaw the labors of his gunners to ensure their huts were fit for the winter. Stuart maintained his position as master host, and nightly the harmonious sounds of Sweeney's banjo, accompanied by fiddle music, filled the air. Visitors, as though magnetized, flocked to Stuart's large tent for the warmth of the fire and the camaraderie. British correspondents Frank Vizetelly and Francis Lawley were ever-present in the camp, as were other members of the British military and Parliament. The few days of inactivity gave John Pelham a chance to catch up on his sleep. It also afforded him the opportunity to write some letters home to his family and to Sallie Dandridge, whom he had not seen since October.[17]

Stuart and his staff now planned for a gala Christmas celebration, the second such holiday thus far in the war. With the overwhelming success at the recent Battle of Fredericksburg and the gorgeous wintry weather cooperating at its fullest, Jeb hoped to make this a holiday to be remembered. As usual the details appeared to be haphazardly planned, yet his staff officers, by now used to such goings-on, carried it off to perfection. Cavalry wagons, accumulated for the task of foraging, were sent to all neighborhoods in the surrounding area to round up Christmas goodies. Pelham and John Esten Cooke commandeered one such wagon with amazing results, bringing back a sizable bounty. Other foragers had equal success, as farmers, overcome by the holiday spirit, donated heavily to the upcoming feast. By Christmas Eve, they had amassed turkeys, chickens, hams, thirty dozen eggs, sweet potatoes, breads, and butter, as well as a considerable supply of apple brandy and whiskey. Flora Stuart arrived and stayed half a mile from headquarters at a local plantation. She greatly helped with the preparations as did von Borcke, whose culinary skills were evidenced by the girth of his waistline.

Christmas Eve arrived with an extremely bitter chill in the air. That night the staff officers, a few wives, and various guests—all dressed in their finest—joined together in the warmth of Stuart's tent. Good wishes were extended to each other's health followed by a joyous round of caroling. The carefully prepared feast was long remembered by the privileged participants. Baked turkeys, hams, and chickens filled the tables, and lines of hungry men and women eagerly awaited the repast. Von Borcke served as master of ceremonies and topped off the evening by reading Charles Dickens's *A Christmas Carol*—a lively and spirited rendition tinged with humorous Germanic pronunciations.[18]

Before noon on December 26 Stuart surprised his guests by announcing what he alone had known for some time: he and selected staff officers would leave within an hour to join other mounted men for another raid across the Rappahannock. This one would head toward Federal supply lines in what Jeb hoped would be a "system of irritation." Just enough time remained before their departure to gather the necessary rations and say their good-byes. Then they would be off to join up with 1,800 men—equally divided among the brigades of Rooney Lee, Wade Hampton, and Fitz Lee. Soon Stuart, along with his chosen staff officers, including John Pelham, departed the warmth of Camp No-Camp and headed upriver toward their rendezvous.[19]

Stuart and his staff officers made their way in a northwestward direction along the south bank of the Rappahannock. Gathering up the six-hundred-man outfits from the three brigades took the remainder of the day and part of the next. Pelham had personally selected four of his best guns and enough cannoneers to service the pieces. A winter raid was always difficult for horses and men, but the artillery labored the hardest, maneuvering thousands of pounds of metal over snow- and ice-covered roads. Pelham was certain, nevertheless, that "his boys" were up to the task. Swinging north, the column crossed the Rapidan River at Ely's Ford and the Rappahannock at Kelly's Ford and made its way to the community of Morrisville, where Stuart halted the men for the night. With the sun disappearing, the weather turned bitterly cold that evening.

On Saturday, December 27, exactly two weeks to the day from Pelham's amazing exploits during the Battle of Fredericksburg, Stuart's horsemen were on the move toward the town of Dumfries before daybreak. Dumfries sat on the Telegraph Road along Quantico Creek nearly ten miles south of Occoquan and roughly halfway between Fredericksburg and Washington, D.C. Stuart readily recognized the strategic importance of both Telegraph Road and the town of Dumfries as he pointed out in his later report, "my object being to take possession of the Telegraph road, [and] to capture all the [supply] trains that might be passing."[20] Boldly devising a plan while on the move, he decided to split his forces into three parts to achieve his objective. He sent Hampton far to the left toward Occoquan to seize the northern end of Telegraph Road and cut off any Federal reinforcements that might be gathering in that direction. Fitz Lee received orders to head eastward and strike the road near Chopowamsic Creek. He would then move his column the remaining few miles northward toward Dumfries, where he would link up with the troopers under Rooney Lee. For his part young Lee, under Stuart's supervision, would slam directly into the community of Dumfries, hoping to catch any Federals unaware. It was a brash plan, possibly too grandiose a scheme to pull off, especially considering the coordinated movement necessary in enemy territory in the middle of the winter. But Stuart reckoned that the element of surprise mixed with the skill of his raiders would be enough to guarantee success. Perhaps he further hoped that the holiday festivities had fattened the enemy and generated sluggishness among the bluecoats.

Rooney Lee pushed his six hundred men toward Dumfries without a sign of the enemy until he reached Wheat's Mill located where Telegraph Road and Quantico Creek intersect. Here a small convoy of Federal wagons was observed crossing the creek. The thickly wooded country kept the Rebels from knowing how well the wagons were guarded, so Pelham brought up a gun from Henry's battery to cover a squadron of the Ninth Virginia Cavalry, which boldly dashed forward. A few well-directed shells from Pelham's piece distracted the dozen Federal pickets, who quickly surrendered to the charging cavalry. Inspired by their accomplishment, the Confederates drove on toward Dumfries. Pelham's cannon continued its rapid firing, but the cavalry met a stiffened resistance from two regiments of Federal infantry posted at the edge of the town. Forced to pull back, the Rebels were lucky to escape without serious injury. Now the bluecoats sent in their own cavalry to pursue the fleeing Confederates, but a volley from some Rebel sharpshooters, along with a few timely blasts from Pelham's cannon, discouraged any further pursuit. Stuart then ordered another piece of the horse artillery under Captain Henry to open up with canister, which drove the enemy from its position. Federal cannon now swung forward and engaged in a sparring match with Pelham's horse artillery with little damage done to either side. The Federal garrison soon evacuated Dumfries but, according to Stuart's report, "took position on a commanding ridge overlooking the town—artillery and infantry—in a thicket of pines."[21] The Federals had successfully blunted the Confederate attack, much to Jeb Stuart's disappointment.

Fitz Lee's six hundred men now appeared on Stuart's right. As ordered, Fitz Lee had earlier struck along the Telegraph Road in the vicinity of Chopowamsic Creek. In a brief skirmish there he had driven back a patrol of Federals, captured twenty-two of them, and confiscated nine sutlers' wagons loaded with a wide variety of supplies. Fitz then directed his men farther north for the proposed juncture with Rooney Lee. With these welcome reinforcements, Stuart decided on another attempt at taking Dumfries. Dividing the forces of Fitz Lee, Stuart sent two regiments, the Fifth Virginia under the leadership of Colonel Tom Rosser and the First Virginia led by Colonel James H. Drake, north of the town to distract the Federals. Two rifled pieces of James Breathed's command would in the meantime open on the enemy to pin down their artillery. The coup de grace would be administered by portions of the Second and Third Virginia cavalries sent to drive off the Federals and capture the town in a pincer movement from the south.[22] Skirmishing continued until nightfall, but once again Stuart's fanciful plan failed to dislodge the strongly fortified Federals. Furthermore, Captain John Washington Bullock of the Fifth Virginia suffered a mortal wound.[23]

Stuart dejectedly called off any further attempt at seizing Dumfries "as the capture of the place," he surmised, "would not have compensated for the loss of life which must have attended the movement." Determined to pull his forces away to the northwest along Brentsville Wood Road, Stuart knew the difficulty would be in alerting his split-up forces as to his wishes. Ordering Fitz Lee's remaining men to act as "dismounted skirmishers" and hold back the Federals near Dumfries, Stuart sent two of Pelham's rifled pieces from Captain James Breathed's battery to support Fitz's sharpshooters. The remainder of Stuart's troopers began to withdraw. An "effective fire" kept the enemy at bay until after dark when the rest of the Rebels pulled back in accordance with Stuart's plan. Once safely removed from Dumfries,

Stuart learned, with "considerable anxiety" according to Channing Price, that two of his regiments had not been heard from—the Third Virginia, which held the captured prisoners and wagons, and the Second Virginia, which evidently had not received Stuart's orders to retire. It was eleven o'clock that night before Stuart learned that the Third Virginia had safely escaped but had taken a different pathway out of Dumfries that led them to the community of Cole's Store. The cavalry chieftain continued to fret over the whereabouts of the Second Virginia until 1:00 A.M. when Chiswell Dabney led them into camp.[24]

It had not been Stuart's proudest day. Unable to crack the Federal stronghold at Dumfries, plus the confusion and concern over the retreat from the town, left Stuart perplexed. He further bemoaned the mortal wounding of the popular and promising Captain Bullock. The amount of captured supplies and men could not offset what Stuart felt was a disappointing day. Channing Price listed the captured items as "20 wagons, 100 prisoners, [and] about 150 horses & mules." Federal reports gave their manpower loss as three killed, twelve wounded, and sixty-eight captured. Stuart's report mentioned only the losses in Rooney Lee's brigade as "1 private wounded, 1 non-commissioned officer and 12 privates missing, and 3 horses killed."[25] Eventually on that cold and dismal morning, Hampton's command appeared in the darkness. Hampton, too, had sustained limited success that day. He had driven the Federals from the area of Occoquan while taking nineteen prisoners and eight wagons. Although suffering only one man wounded in the fracas, Hampton's command had allowed the bulk of the Federals to escape southward toward Dumfries.

That night the entire three brigades reunited at Cole's Store. Here Stuart assessed the captured booty as well as the condition of his own men and horseflesh. He decided that the prisoners and wagons would immediately be sent back to Fredericksburg under guard. He further directed that two of John Pelham's field pieces from Breathed's section, which had exhausted their ammunition that day, would also make the trek back to headquarters. By 3:00 A.M. Stuart and his staff officers fed their horses and found some provisions for themselves. An hour later the weary and cold men fell asleep by a large fire. By 6:30 on the morning of December 28, Stuart had the men awakened. Jeb had made his decision, according to Channing Price, "on account of the worn out condition of men and horses," to return his entire command to headquarters.[26]

Then just as suddenly Stuart determined to remain on the Federal side of the Rappahannock and continue the raid. Channing Price attributed the change of heart to "some information given by a man just [arrived] from Fairfax."[27] Whatever news the stranger brought radically altered Stuart's thinking. Conceivably this man informed Stuart that the area around Fairfax, so dangerously close to Washington, D.C., and so sparsely guarded, was ripe for a continuation of the raid. Intelligence of this sort could not be disregarded. Throughout the war, Stuart had sought the slightest opening against the enemy and, once discovered, used it to the fullest advantage even while defying all military logic. Some piece of unknown information had rejuvenated Stuart that morning, and he had his troopers on the go, heading toward the Occoquan River, before dawn.

Stuart soon learned that two Pennsylvania regiments, amounting to about 300 sabers, were pursuing him. Confidently, Jeb ordered Fitz Lee's troopers in the direction of the snooping bluecoats with the columns of Hampton and Rooney Lee close behind. Stuart further detached about 150 South Carolinians under the command of Colonel Calbraith Butler to cut off any Federal reinforcements. Somewhat protected by a patch of dense woods, the Pennsylvanians soon appeared in the distance. With his fighting blood stirred, Stuart sent Fitz Lee's horsemen into action. The First Virginia led the charge head-on, while Rosser's Fifth Virginia swarmed from the left flank. The Federal troopers panicked, fired one hasty volley of pistol fire missing their target completely, and fled. "The Yankees ran like sheep," reported one of the Fifth Virginians, claiming the bluecoats left "dead men, wounded men, & dead horses . . . strewn on the road." Stuart later reported that Fitz's boys "executed the order gallantly," while embellishing that the Confederates advanced "in the face of heavy volleys." Eight to ten Pennsylvanians were killed, according to Stuart, with another hundred or more falling into Confederate hands, while the others fled toward the Occoquan River. Stuart's troopers joined in the chase and pushed the Federals a half-dozen miles to Selectman's Ford, where the bluecoats crossed the Occoquan and headed back toward their camp. One Federal telegrapher indicated that the overwhelmed Pennsylvanians were "going full speed to the rear."[28]

Tom Rosser's Fifth Virginia reached Selectman's Ford along the Occoquan before the other Confederates and immediately splashed into the chilly waters in pursuit. Fitz Lee later commended Rosser's accomplishments that day as "one of the most admirable performances of cavalry I have ever witnessed." Even though Stuart described the ford as "narrow, rocky, and very difficult," and certainly unsuitable to cannons and caissons, John Pelham was not to be outdone by his West Point roommate. Reaching the ford, Pelham ordered his two guns, artillery horses, and full equipment into the hazardous breach. To everyone's amazement, Pelham succeeded in the crossing. Soon the other regiments of horsemen followed. Inspired by Pelham's bit of derring-do, the Confederate troopers pounded rapidly toward the Federal camp. The Yankees remaining at the campsite fired a weak smattering of gunfire and fled for their lives, leaving behind a goodly amount of supplies. Stuart proudly sized up the abandoned camp as "a great many spoils of every description—horses, mules, and wagons, with blankets and other stores." The Rebels helped themselves to the booty and burned what they could not carry with them.[29]

Jeb Stuart's state of mind had certainly changed over the course of the previous twelve hours. Somewhat dejected that morning, he had determined to head

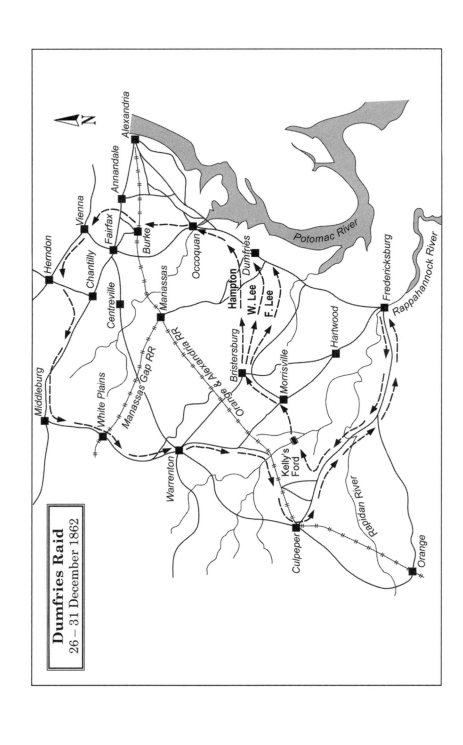

Dumfries Raid
26 – 31 December 1862

back across the Rappahannock with little to show for his efforts. Now, with twilight approaching, Stuart was again his laughing, cocksure self. His next move, if successful, would ensure the legacy of this raid. Three times earlier in this year he had adventurously raided behind Union lines, capturing hundreds of men, horses, mules, and wagons laden with tons of supplies at a minimal loss of his own. In each instance Stuart daringly escaped the enemy with his entire column. In two of those excursions he brazenly looped around the Federals, tacking on numerous miles to his escape route almost in the face of a panting foe. Following all of these raids he received rave reviews for making his opponent appear shamelessly inept. Stuart was about to complete his grand slam.

Rather than heading back southward, the cavalry chieftain decided to go deeper behind Federal lines in the direction of Washington, D.C., itself. With his entire command intact, Stuart proceeded to lead the troopers toward Burke's Station, situated on the Orange and Alexandria Railroad, little more than a dozen miles from the Federal capital. Approaching the station after dark, Stuart sent two or three men "who walked up into the room of the telegraph operator," according to Channing Price, "and with drawn pistols demanded him to surrender the office." The flabbergasted Federal telegrapher surrendered immediately without first sending any warning of the intrusion. Stuart's own skilled telegrapher, a man simply known to history as Sheppard, then sat down to intercept and decipher Federal messages, allowing Stuart the luxury of "detect[ing] what preparations had been made for my reception." Sheppard traveled with Stuart's command on such occasions for this purpose. He also was known for transmitting bogus messages to the Yankees, giving phony accounts of Stuart's whereabouts, thus rendering great confusion among the Federal search parties. Now Sheppard sat for over two hours and listened to the messages being sent between General Samuel P. Heintzelman and the Fairfax Station commander concerning Stuart's raid. "It was very ludicrous," noted Price, "as they were in great alarm & orders were telegraphed to destroy everything in case of our attacking them: meanwhile the track was being torn up and the men helping themselves to oats & some little things found about the depot." While enjoying the ruse, Stuart sent a detachment of a dozen men under Fitz Lee to within eight miles of Alexandria to burn the railroad bridge over Accotink Creek. Fitz completed this dangerous assignment and later linked up with the main command.[30]

Prior to departing the telegraph station, Stuart, in a typically playful mood, bade Sheppard to dispatch a note to the irascible Federal quartermaster general, Montgomery C. Meigs, in Washington, D.C. With impish delight Stuart complained to the enemy War Department concerning the inferiority of the mules he had been stealing and, in mocking jest, threatening not to take any more. In Stuart's own words, "I sent some messages to . . . General Meigs . . . in reference to the bad quality of the mules lately furnished, which interfered seriously with our moving the captured wagons."[31] Once transmitted, this message revealed Stuart's exact location to the Federals, making it imperative that he move his forces immediately. Before departing Burke's Station, Stuart ordered the telegraph line severed and then led his troopers to the northwest in the direction of Fairfax Court House.

Heading up the Little River Turnpike toward Fairfax, Stuart appeared confident that in the darkness he could surprise and capture the town. Once within a mile of Fairfax, however, it was Stuart who received the surprise as Federal infantry under the command of Brigadier General Edwin H. Stoughton had set up an ambush. Stoughton, who cursed the fact that he had no available cavalry, had positioned his infantry in strong breastworks. When the advance unit of the Rebels came within range, Stoughton's riflemen opened fire, resulting in two Confederates wounded and two horses killed. Stuart's men pulled back without returning any gunfire. Convinced of the Federal strength, Stuart decided to leave. First, however, he ordered huge campfires built to fool the Yankees into thinking he had bivouacked for the night. The ruse worked perfectly as "the enemy shelled [the fires] vigorously for some time," wrote Price. The Confederates, meanwhile, proceeded to slip away through the darkness. Stuart also determined to avoid any traps set by the Federals along the way by directing his troopers in another circuitous route farther north and west via Vienna to a spot known as Frying Pan. The men rode on through the night and arrived in the area of Frying Pan near dawn. Here Stuart halted his column for some rest and to nourish the men and horses.[32]

Within a few hours the men remounted and continued to venture farther westward past Aldie to Middleburg. Here Stuart detached Tom Rosser, in whom the cavalry chieftain seemed to be placing more trust, along with fifteen troopers to scout the enemy positions in the area of Leetown. Rosser proceeded through Snicker's Gap, captured some enemy pickets, gathered up the necessary information on the bluecoats, and returned via Ashby's Gap to Stuart's main column in flawless fashion. In the meantime Stuart headed the others due south toward Warrenton. Although a Federal force had been reported there, the town was clear of the enemy, and Stuart's forces confidently rode in and stayed for some time. Later as the Confederate column exited the town, Price and John Pelham stayed behind at the home of a Mrs. Lucas until all the Rebels had departed. Then the two friends followed until they caught up with Stuart's forces. Once again luck was in the cards for Stuart as his horsemen narrowly escaped an encounter with the four thousand troopers of Alfred Pleasonton. Approaching Warrenton from the north, Pleasonton's bluecoats thundered into the town only to find Stuart's men had already disappeared to the south. "As we rode in on one side," noted a Federal, "Stuart's Cavalry rode out on the other side." Disappointed by the results, Pleasonton called off any further pursuit.[33]

The cavalry had traveled thirty-five miles that day, according to Price, and finally pulled into Culpeper Court House, southwest of Warrenton. At Culpeper

Pelham decided to visit Lieutenant William M. McGregor of the horse artillery, who had been seriously wounded in November and left to recuperate at the home of a Dr. Herndon. Channing Price went along. Pelham and Price found McGregor in fine spirits but still a long way from full recovery.[34]

The following morning Stuart's horsemen pulled out of Culpeper and trotted through Stevensburg to Ely's Ford where they camped for the night—a bit tired but excited to be nearly finished with the exhausting expedition. With a little more than fifteen miles to Fredericksburg, Stuart, perhaps anxious to spread the news of his exploits, left his main body of troopers and completed the last leg of the journey, arriving at Camp No-Camp at a late hour on New Year's Eve. Delighted by his most recent escapade behind Federal lines, Stuart, "in buoyant spirits," proceeded with an animated and detailed account of the entire raid.

The next day, Thursday, January 1, the raiders began the final phase of their journey to Fredericksburg. Pelham, still traveling with his comrade Channing Price, did not arrive at headquarters until 7:00 that evening. Price wrote his lengthy epistle to his sister, Ellen, on the following day. "We are all back safe," he gushed, "from the longest, most dangerous and most brilliant expedition that the cavalry has yet given to an admiring public." He later exclaimed, "Gen. Stuart is very much delighted with the success of the trip."[35] And well Stuart should have been. His losses included merely one killed, thirteen wounded, and fourteen missing. Jeb specifically mentioned how deeply he mourned the death of the promising Captain John W. Bullock. Conversely, Stuart acknowledged, "The loss inflicted on the enemy was considerable, but cannot be stated with accuracy." In fact Stuart had bagged an impressive assortment of goods, including nearly 250 prisoners, a like number of horses and mules, 20 wagons laden with saddles, bridles, pistols, and sabers, "as well as 100 or so fine arms & other things too numerous to mention," according to a jubilant Channing Price.[36]

Stuart's report noted that he remained disappointed in two areas. First, "the captures on the Telegraph road were less than had been anticipated." Second, the cavalry chieftain almost apologized for not capturing Dumfries, now guarded "by a full brigade of infantry." Otherwise, he pointed out the various positives of the raid: destroying Burnside's communication with Washington, D.C., capturing enemy property, forcing the enemy to dispense "large bodies . . . as a constabulary force . . . from the Aquia to Vienna," and fooling the enemy in the belief that another invasion of Maryland was likely. The latter result, boasted Stuart, crippled the enemy cavalry as they rode over harsh byways "in the fruitless effort to thwart me in my real intentions." Stuart naturally praised his officers and men, who "returned in astonishingly good condition from this long march," for their "patient endurance, heroic dash, and unflinching courage." Jeb closed his report with special recognition for John Pelham, "[who] with his horse artillery, performed gallant and exceedingly difficult service during this expedition. Ever up with the cavalry, he crossed the Occoquan at Selectman's Ford, which has always been considered impracticable for vehicles."[37]

In his protracted letter to his sister Channing Price further mentioned that Tom Rosser selected some twenty men and crossed the mountains for a visit to the Bower. Price offered no indication of the reason for the venture other than to state, "I hope [Rosser] will succeed in his trip and return safely." It had been weeks since the cavalry camped at the estate of the Dandridge family. Of all the personnel in Stuart's cavalry, Pelham, of course, had the closest tie to the Bower with his purported engagement to Sallie. No further words nor explanation of Rosser's visit, however, came from Price's ebullient pen—nothing to indicate that Pelham sent any messages or even had the notion of doing so. This blatant omission merely adds to the mystique of the relationship between John Pelham and Sallie Dandridge, if in fact a connection now remained at all.

In closing his letter Price penned that "Everything is quiet about here now and the enemy have had all their marching and countermarching for naught."[38] In this regard Price appeared correct. The enemy, to virtually all observers, appeared to have had enough marching and combat for the year, willing to sit complacently until the springtime for another move. Thus, in the Eastern Theater the Army of Northern Virginia had stymied the Federals one final time in the year 1862. And what a magnificent year it had been for the Confederate army.

It was a year in which Stonewall Jackson had shown that quick marching was more popular than a home-cooked meal. Other than his nearly inexplicable stagnation on the Peninsula, Jackson's brilliance in all other campaigns had rendered him an icon across the South. Jeb Stuart, still not even thirty years of age, had also become a household name. His daring raids, courtly manners, and savoir faire had made him the beau ideal of the Confederacy. What other horseman could make a ride around McClellan's monstrous army seem like a Sunday stroll? And what a year for John Pelham. Two promotions—from lieutenant to captain and captain to major—had come his way with certainly more of them due. Rave reviews in abundance for Pelham had come from Stuart and Jackson in virtually all the campaigns, battles, and raids, plus generous praise and an immortal nickname, the "Gallant Pelham," from the commanding general himself. It had truly been a glorious year. There seemed to be no reason to doubt that the oncoming year—1863—would be any different.

"One Could Never Forget Him"

[Pelham] didn't look as though he could ever order anybody to be killed.
—Bessie Shackelford

With the Federals still within striking distance across the Rappahannock River, the Confederate high command continued its diligence with precautionary measures throughout January. Longstreet's corps stayed solidly positioned along Marye's Heights while Jackson had established his headquarters eleven miles farther down the Rappahannock. Stuart meticulously spread his cavalry forces between the infantry corps and beyond in order to forestall any movement of the enemy. Even with all the necessary safeguards in place, the general feeling in the Army of Northern Virginia was that the Federals had spent their last movement for the winter. Some Rebels even ventured optimism that the war appeared nearly over. "Our independence," Brigadier General Frank Paxton, commander of the Stonewall Brigade, boasted to his wife, "was secured in the last campaign."[1]

How exhilarating it must have been for John Pelham to realize that his display of superiority, exhibited at Fredericksburg, had contributed a certifiable measure to this confidence. His exploits, one after another since the war's inception, had added to his mystique as a soldier, culminating with his brilliant performance at Hamilton's Crossing. Yet, there was no secret or magic formula to his success. Pelham simply excelled in three categories: leadership, courage, and ability. As a leader he exuded a quiet confidence and an unparalleled charisma, which gave him the total devotion of his men. He took responsibility at critical times and demonstrated initiative and creativity often without orders. Exhibiting cool judgment, he was able to anticipate changes and improvise when necessary. Pelham's courage was by now legendary—who else would do battle against a division of infantry and numerous batteries with merely one gun? His indomitable drive and will to win put him constantly in the midst of the action. Fearless, and with a true passion for combat, he possessed enough common sense, however, to keep from being unnecessarily reckless. Pelham's finest talent remained his capability as an artillerist. Totally observant of the enemy, he was instinctive to nearly every move they made. This uncanny intuition enabled him to outmaneuver the bluecoats with speed and daring. Perhaps his trump card as a cannoneer was his unerring eye for terrain, resulting in the superb placement of his guns. This is the benchmark of any artillerist, and

Pelham was plainly the best. As John Esten Cooke noted, "He was rightly regarded by Jackson and others as possessed of a very extraordinary genius for artillery; and when any movement of unusual importance was designed, Pelham was assigned to the artillery to be employed."[2]

Others acknowledged his formidable prowess as an innovator. "I have always thought that Pelham is justly entitled to first place [among Confederate artillerists]," observed Rebel John Cheves Haskell. "He was the first who ever demonstrated that artillery could and should be fought on the musketry line of battle. . . . Pelham . . . was, as a fighter, not only the pioneer, and if not the most desperate fighter of artillery, certainly the equal of any." Haskell noted, however, that Pelham was not without flaws. "[Pelham] was not a good organizer and disciplinarian, and seldom had his command in good condition. If he had been confined by his supply of horses to those drawn through the quartermaster's department, he would have been scarcely ever able to transport half his guns. But moving constantly with the cavalry and always at the front, his command picked up fresh horses and equipment, which never passed through the hands of the department. Even with his extra supply, he was often unable to move all his guns when he wanted, but his rule was to go ahead when fighting was to be done and to wait for no stragglers."[3]

Pelham used the off time during the month of January to attend to some unfinished business, including the completion of the shelter he and John Esten Cooke shared. He also spent part of his leisure time catching up on his much-neglected reading and correspondence. Despite the occasional angry, wintry weather, he often traveled about on both business and pleasure. On Tuesday, January 6, for example, Channing Price began a letter to his mother, "Major Pelham is going to Richmond for a few days." No further explanation of the journey or any other details were provided by the normally fussy Price, who casually changed thoughts in mid-sentence.[4] The trip to the Confederate capital city most likely entailed artillery concerns as Pelham possibly sought provisions for the men of his battery. Most of Pelham's travels, however, were of the frivolous variety as he visited friends, including the Bernards at Gay Mont and the Price sisters, cousins of Jeb Stuart, at Dundee. Frequently Stuart and Pelham ventured down the Rappahannock to call on Stonewall Jackson at his headquarters, Moss Neck.

Besides the somewhat difficult weather with which the soldiers had to contend, food remained scarce. At one point the cavalry eased the pangs of hunger by obtaining a wagonload of oysters. But the repetition of consuming the same larder, especially without any seasonings to alter the bland taste, forced von Borcke to confess "that the very sight of an oyster turned us sick." Horses, as usual, suffered far more than the humans as the supply of fodder dwindled daily. Many of the animals resorted to gnawing bark from the nearest tree as a form of nourishment. This lack of proper diet caused such maladies as swollen bellies and "greased heel." William

Poague reported that several details of men were given the unsavory task of washing "with tobacco decoctions, horses of the battery infested with vermin."[5]

Late in January the Confederate army gained the knowledge that Ambrose Burnside planned another crossing of the Rappahannock River. Soon to be ingloriously labeled the "Mud March," this attempt ended in futility and the subsequent removal of the Federal commander. Burnside had long desired to atone for the recent disaster at Fredericksburg, and with a break in the weather, the ground lost its mushiness and became dry and firm. All of his corps commanders strongly opposed such a move, but on Monday, January 19, Burnside sent orders to his commanders to prepare for the march on the morrow. Perhaps never in military annals was a plan so ill-fated from its onset.

The following day the Army of the Potomac assembled in full gear with three days' rations. The Federal army proceeded out of camp under a clear sky, but by midday the skies darkened ominously, and a slight rain began to fall. Soon the heavens opened up with a terrific, unceasing downpour that did not let up for the next two days. On the morning of the twenty-first, soldiers awoke to the incessant staccato of rain striking their tents, and what one of them described as "an ocean of mud" lay everywhere. Howling winds added to their woes. Dry wood of any kind was impossible to obtain, so the ill-humored men answered reveille without coffee in their bellies. Burnside faced an awkward dilemma: to call off the offensive would further damage his army's morale, but to continue would put his uncertain fate in the hands of the weather gods. To the dismay of nearly all, he bade the march go on.[6]

Finding the roads virtually impassable, the sodden soldiers inched and slogged their way forward through the quagmire of knee-deep mud. Cold, clammy uniform cloth stuck to the skin; boots caked with mud weighed an extra five pounds each. Some men's footwear was literally pulled from their feet by the sticky muck. Encumbered by heavy cannon and the massive pontoon boats, the men muscled on as best as they could. Big guns often sank beyond their axles until only muzzles appeared. Hundreds of men pulled futilely on ropes in an attempt to extricate the equipment. Mules were brought forward to help, but the reluctant animals sank, braying wildly, into the muck up to their bellies and even farther. Some men mercifully shot the mules; others simply cut the harnesses and watched as the animals disappeared into the morass. The nightmare continued with all the fury of a biblical plague. By nightfall the undaunted Burnside let it be known that the march would go on the next day. When the weather worsened Burnside finally called off the offensive on January 23. Thus the easiest Confederate victory to date in the war ended, as Federal morale possibly sank to its all-time nadir.

On Sunday, January 25, President Lincoln decided that Burnside's leadership had run its course. The new choice as head of the Army of the Potomac became forty-eight-year-old Joseph Hooker. "Fighting Joe," as he was known to the press, was less than a humble man. His reputation as a purveyor of gossip and a master of intrigue ranked closely behind his fervent use of profanity and love of alcohol. His greatest vice, perhaps, remained his overt association with prostitutes who frequently visited his headquarters, rendering it a place "no gentleman cared to go and no lady could go." "Fighting Joe" seemed perfectly content to allow the wintry weather to run its course and wait for the spring thaw to mount an offensive. Meanwhile, he proceeded to undo the clumsy Grand Divisions of Burnside and reinstate the more conventional corps system. The Army of the Potomac would soon be streamlined into what Hooker deemed "the finest army on the planet."

Throughout January and February, Stuart pushed hard for the reorganization of his cavalry and for the promotion of John Pelham. In a letter dated January 13 to Samuel Cooper, the adjutant general in Richmond, Stuart requested "the urgent recommendation of Major John Pelham to be promoted for gallant conduct to the rank of Colonel of Artillery." He also desired that Will Farley be upped in rank to major of sharpshooters. "Pelham and Farley," wrote Stuart, "have shown and will continue to show the wisdom of such a recognition by the Government of their valuable services in the field." On the same day in a separate letter to Cooper, Stuart called for the promotion of Tom Rosser to brigadier general. Stuart's praise for Rosser would have made Pelham proud: "in battle, a bold and dashing leader; on the march and in bivouac a rigid disciplinarian, but at the same time exacting the confidence of his entire command. He has won a promotion. He would make a splendid General of Cavalry and I am anxious to have him added to my Brigadiers."[7]

Although the Confederate brass in Richmond did not seem overly interested in Stuart's suggestions, he persisted in his requests for Pelham's advancement in rank. On February 10 Jeb sent another dispatch to Samuel Cooper; this one all but demanded Pelham's promotion with certain words underscored:

I have already made several urgent recommendations for the promotion of Major John Pelham, my Chief of Artillery, which have not yet been favorably considered by the War Department. The battle of Fredericksburg, forming a fresh chapter in his career of exploits without a parallel, I feel it to be a duty, as well as a pleasure, to earnestly repeat what I have said in his behalf, and to add that, if meritorious conduct in battle ever earned promotion, Major John Pelham of Alabama, should be appointed Colonel of Artillery.

Pelham's well known ability as an Artillery Officer has won for him the confidence of Generals in Command who unhesitatingly entrust to him the artillery thus brought together from various batteries.

It has been alleged that he is too young. Though remarkably youthful in appearance there are Generals as young with less claim for that distinction, and no veteran in age has ever shown more coolness and better judgment in the sphere of his duty.

In a postscript, Stuart added, "I will thank you to lay this letter before the President."[8]

Others openly wondered why Pelham's promotion had not been acted upon. Even Robert E. Lee stated emphatically, "No one deserves promotion more than Major Pelham." Some sought not only Pelham's promotion but, through political intrigue and crafty maneuver, a transfer to his own command as well. It was no secret that various commanders, including none other than James Longstreet, coveted Pelham's services. Thus, when Stonewall Jackson suggested the promotion and transfer of E. P. Alexander from Longstreet's artillery to Jackson's infantry, a noticeable opening would appear in Longstreet's echelon of officers. To fill the void Old Pete requested Pelham's transfer. Then to soothe Stuart's ruffled feathers, Longstreet cunningly suggested that Pelham's vacancy in the horse artillery be filled by Major Lewis Frank Terrell, an officer Jeb regarded highly. To further complicate matters, Robert E. Lee's chief of artillery, Brigadier General William N. Pendleton, endorsed the entire plan in a letter to his commander. "In reflecting over the list of best officers," Pendleton wrote, "my mind rests mainly on Pelham to command that battalion, he receiving the rank of Lieutenant-Colonel." Pendleton then prudently asked, "Can he be spared from the Horse Artillery?" Nothing came of the suggested plans, however, as Alexander indicated that he preferred to remain in the artillery with Longstreet's corps.[9]

Despite all the scheming, Robert E. Lee continued to seek Pelham's promotion. In a letter sent directly to President Jefferson Davis on March 2, Lee stated: "No class of officers in the army has learned faster or served better than the artillery." The commanding general then suggested various promotions including "Major Pelham, whom I recommend for promotion to lieutenant-colonel to serve with the flying artillery attached to the cavalry, consisting of five batteries." Jefferson Davis reportedly concurred with the promotion and supposedly stated as he reviewed the documents on the subject, "I do not need to see any papers about Major Pelham." Only the mere formality of the president's signature and the approval of the Confederate Senate stood in the way of the new rank.[10]

Pelham certainly knew of the fuss concerning his proposed promotion, and more than once he was asked his opinion on the matter. Never in discussing the situation did he pout, complain, accuse, or lose his composure. Mostly he merely blushed and mumbled something about his youthful appearance as a possible drawback. He further commented that a promotion might mean a transfer from Jeb Stuart and the horse artillery, a possibility that he frowned upon. "There was never anybody like Stuart," he often said, and indicated a strong desire to remain where he was with or without a promotion.[11] Pelham's modesty and selflessness continued to impress his immediate coterie of friends that included Heros von Borcke, John Esten Cooke, and Channing Price. During the wintry months, Pelham had also become fast friends with W. W. Blackford, whose sincerity and intelligence appealed to the young artillerist. "Pelham and I had become more intimate than we had ever been before," penned Blackford. "Our tents were next [to] each other and we had built our stables together. Pelham had some fine horses and, like myself, liked to see them well cared for. I had five and he had three." The two comrades had much in common and often lay awake at night discussing a variety of subjects. Perhaps Pelham soothed Blackford's sorrow from the recent loss of his three-year-old son. They also took turns reading aloud from the Bible and had recently begun Napier's *Peninsula Campaign* in the same fashion.[12]

While tending to his horses and shelter in the sluggish days of February, Pelham was able to catch up on some of his overdue correspondence. One of his letters that still remains, dated February 13, was written to his old West Point crony Llewellyn "Lou" Hoxton, now serving in the Western Theater. Llewellyn's younger brother, William, had served under Pelham's command and had recently been promoted to lieutenant. Evidently, Pelham's intention with the letter was to congratulate Lou on the performance of his sibling as well as to mention that a Whitworth rifle, recently brought from England through the blockade, was being presented to the younger Hoxton brother. In part, the letter stated:

> Your brother Willie is a noble boy. He has fought with me on many a hard field and has always distinguished himself very highly. He bears a reputation for gallantry unequaled in his company, and such a reputation is not a trifling thing in such a company as my old one where all were so brave. He won his commission honestly and fairly. It is not due to any man's friendship or influence, but to his own indomitable courage and soldierly conduct. . . .
>
> Your brother nobly won his commission and wears it with becoming dignity and ease. I have just received a splendid 6 lb. Whitworth gun (English) and have given him the command of it. . . . He is very much pleased with it and I think will make quite a reputation for the gun. . . .
>
> Everything is quiet along our lines at present, and necessarily so. The roads are in such condition that it is absolutely impossible for an army to move. But I hope "Fighting Joe" Hooker will come over and give us a chance as soon as the weather will permit. This army is invincible—whenever you hear of it fighting you may add one more name to our list of victories—for such will certainly be the result.[13]

On the same day, February 13, Pelham wrote a note to First Lieutenant Philip Preston Johnston:

If you have time I wish you would prepare some papers and sign my name to them so that [Andrew] Connor can draw what extra pay is due him as <u>blacksmith.</u> He will hand you this. If you have been able to get the cloth yet, I wish you would have my overcoat cut at the best tailor's. You can find [and] get all the materials and send it down to me to be made. There are a good many ladies down here who have been run out of Fredericksburg and who are willing to sew. You need not have my other clothes cut. Gen. Stuart will be in R. [Richmond] tomorrow. Your friend Jno. Pelham[14]

Eight days after Pelham penned these letters, word arrived of the promotion of Captain Mathis Winston Henry to the rank of major. With the promotion Major Henry, who had so ably assisted Pelham with his heroics at the Battle of Fredericksburg, was transferred to the command of Major General John Bell Hood. Mathis Henry had been a stellar performer for Pelham and would create a definite void in the horse artillery, but his superior abilities necessitated the move. The highly talented William M. McGregor was soon promoted to captain and designated to replace Henry; unfortunately, McGregor's wound from the previous November kept him from returning quickly. Until his arrival, Pelham would have to make do with a temporary replacement.

In mid-February Stuart became increasingly concerned with the weakened condition of the horses in Wade Hampton's brigade. The exhaustive duty of covering some forty miles of picket space along the Rappahannock had caused Hampton's horseflesh to become much debilitated. Stuart sent von Borcke to report on the worsening situation. "It was a mournful sight to see more than half the horses of this splendid command totally unfit for duty," wrote von Borcke, "dead and dying animals lying about the camps in all directions." Wisely Jeb Stuart decided to relieve Hampton's brigade by sending the troopers of Fitz Lee whose winter activity had been less strenuous. Stuart further determined to inspect the two brigades personally. To facilitate his plan, Stuart called together von Borcke, John Pelham, and Lieutenant Thomas Randolph Price Jr., the older brother of Channing Price who, as an assistant engineer, had been added to Stuart's staff merely a week earlier. The general explained that he wanted these three men to ride to Culpeper, thirty-five miles to the northwest, where Fitz Lee's brigade was headquartered. Stuart and the remainder of his staff would later depart by railroad and join them the following day. Pelham, von Borcke, and Tom Price left immediately after breakfast on Tuesday, February 17, in the midst of a heavy and foreboding snowfall.[15]

Heading westward the threesome crossed the Rapidan River at Ely's Ford while the snow, according to von Borcke, "increased in violence every hour." Soon the snow, deeply packed to nearly a foot in depth, had obliterated all sight of the road on which they trudged. By dusk they were still a good ten miles from Culpeper without hope of reaching their destination any time soon. Cold, hungry, and physically worn, they sought shelter from the apparent danger of the blizzard. "No food for man or horse in this barren wilderness," complained Tom Price poetically, "where the ferocity of man has conspired with an unkindly nature to render the entire country a scene of desolation." Miraculously ahead they observed in the faint shadows a house with smoke curling from the chimney into the darkening sky and light emanating from the windows. A sign at the front door proudly proclaimed "Madden—Free Negro." This would hopefully be their haven for the evening. Knocking at the door brought a response from within as a wary Mr. Madden opened the door a few inches to inspect the intruders cautiously. Noticing an invitingly roaring blaze in the fireplace, Pelham identified himself and the others as "Confederate officers" seeking refuge from the snowstorm. Offering to pay the man for his hospitality, Pelham politely awaited an answer. Shouting that he would have "nothing to do with no stragglers," Madden slammed the door in their faces. Stunned by this undesirable reaction, the three nearly frozen men stumbled off the porch to determine their next move.

For some minutes they stood angry, silent, and shivering. Finally Pelham in an uncharacteristic display of emotion vowed, "This won't do at all." According to von Borcke, Pelham went on to explain that in this predicament they had no other option than to spend this wintry night inside Madden's house. Calling it "certain destruction" to remain outside, Pelham hit upon a ruse to fool Madden into letting them enter his home. Without revealing his plan in any depth, Pelham briefly stated that he would "play a trick off on [Madden], which I think quite pardonable under the circumstances." Von Borcke and Tom Price seemed quite willing to go along with any deception as long as it got them indoors. Pelham then stepped to the door and repeatedly knocked until the unwilling black man appeared again with the same discouraging frown as earlier. But before the inhospitable man could refuse their entry a second time, Pelham spoke up quickly: "Mr. Madden, you don't know what a good friend of yours I am, or what you are doing when you are about to treat us in this way." Without as much as a pause, Pelham rattled on, revealing the ingenuity of his impromptu subterfuge. Pointing at von Borcke, Pelham barked matter-of-factly, "That gentleman there is the great General Lee himself." Then motioning toward Price, the artillerist continued, "The other one is the French ambassador just arrived from Washington." The exact reaction of von Borcke and Price is not recorded, but they obviously revealed no sign of the trickery before them. Pelham then introduced himself as "a staff officer of the General's, who is quite mad at being kept waiting outside so long after riding all this way on purpose to see you." Then with a trace of bravado only matched by his performance on a battlefield, Pelham said threateningly, "In fact, if you let him stay any longer here in the cold, I'm afraid he'll shell your house as soon as his artillery comes up."

Von Borcke, who later complimented Pelham for his "perfectly serious countenance" as a thespian, gladly witnessed the complete transformation in Madden's behavior. For now the astonished black man apologized and cordially invited the three men inside "with all manner of excuses for his mistake." First their horses were led into an empty stable, sheltered against the awful weather, and fed abundant amounts of corn. Then the three strangers entered Madden's home where they dried their soggy clothing in front of a crackling fire. Madden disappeared into the kitchen where, according to a ravenous von Borcke, "savoury odours" emanated, indicating "a repast suited to the distinguished rank of his guests." Pelham delightedly continued the ruse throughout the fine dinner and afterward. Following a wonderful night's sleep, the three officers paid Madden a "liberal indemnity" and confessed the truth to the old man. Madden, however, refused to believe their honesty and persisted "to inflate himself with a sense of his own importance at having been honoured with a visit from such distinguished guests." Saying farewell, the three officers mounted their horses and waved good-bye to Madden, whose confused demeanor made each of them smile inwardly.[16]

After a pleasant ride over the remaining few miles they arrived at Wade Hampton's headquarters near the town of Culpeper shortly before noon on February 18. Here they met up with Stuart and enjoyed a good laugh in retelling the amusing episode at the Madden residence. After inspecting Hampton's cavalry they rode on into town to locate Fitz Lee's horsemen. That evening some of Fitz Lee's more accomplished performers put on a combination minstrel and variety show in the spacious Virginia Hotel located on Main Street. Seated in the audience alongside Jeb Stuart were Heros von Borcke, John Pelham, and other staff officers. Some of the local townspeople attended as well. Headlining the entertainment were musicians Sam Sweeney with his joyous banjo and the multitalented "Mulatto Bob" in a virtuoso performance that von Borcke raved "would have rivalled any in London." One of the evening's highlights occurred when some worthy amateurs reenacted the events at the Madden household the day before. When the actor portraying Pelham introduced von Borcke as "General Lee," the entire audience laughed uproariously. Sitting among the bemused spectators, Pelham blushed but laughed heartily. The following morning Stuart informed von Borcke and Pelham that they were free to remain in Culpeper for a few days while he attended to some business in Richmond. The two friends immediately established their temporary residency in the Virginia Hotel where the friendly landlady, whose son served as a private in Fitz Lee's brigade, gave them all the special amenities of home.[17]

Directly across from the Virginia Hotel on an unpaved street stood the lovely home of the Shackelford family. The patriarch of the household was Judge Henry Shackelford, the wise and scholarly adjudicator of the Virginia Circuit Court. Like so many Virginians, the Shackelfords had been Unionists until the vote for secession had removed their state from the ranks in mid-April 1861. Since that time they had remained staunch defenders of the Rebel cause. Wisely, however, the family stayed on good terms with both Federal and Confederate soldiers, who often ventured through Culpeper during the war. It has been suggested that the Federals gladly ignored the Shackelfords' Confederate leanings since Judge Shackelford's brother, Muscoe, a graduate of West Point killed in the Mexican War, was known to various Union generals.[18] More likely, however, it was the hospitality shown by the family and the particular beauty of the judge's daughters that rendered the bluecoats harmless.

The Shackelford family included five daughters: Lucy, Georgia, Kate, Bessie, and Shirley. Unlike most females of the mid-nineteenth century, these ladies had been raised as freethinkers, encouraged to disagree or voice their opinions on a variety of subjects, including religion and politics. A thorough knowledge of music and the arts enhanced their noticeable charm. Less than demure and minus the Victorian mores of their time, the Shackelford women brought an educated and cultured refinement to the small town of Culpeper. Taught to be independent from men, the Shackelford daughters, nevertheless, possessed extraordinary femininity and wiles to quickly attract members of the opposite sex. Although any one of the five could be considered a catch, Bessie, undeniably, was the most desirable. Dark blue eyes, long, raven tresses, and a milky-smooth complexion highlighted her striking beauty. Bessie further parlayed her lovely singing voice and sensitivity into an irresistible mix. With impeccable manners, an enchanting smile, and a witty intelligence, she literally captivated men with her vivacity.[19]

It is difficult to determine precisely when John Pelham first met Bessie Shackelford or to determine the nature of their relationship. Some reported that they attended the minstrel show put on by Fitz Lee's men that first night in Culpeper with Pelham "squiring" Bessie on his arm. Others indicate that Pelham observed Bessie in the crowd that evening, could not take his eyes off her, and begged Stuart for an introduction. Another version has Pelham meeting the Shackelford family shortly after the Christmas raid when Stuart and his staff traversed through Culpeper. Stuart had been introduced to the Shackelfords by Wade Hampton sometime in early January, and it is possible that Pelham was there. Yet none of Pelham's closest friends—von Borcke, Blackford, Cooke, or Channing Price—mentions anything of such a meeting or any iota of a romance.[20] And, indeed, did a romance exist? One source flat out refers to Bessie as John Pelham's "sweetheart," while another labels her as Pelham's "girl friend." If either of these references has credence, did it mean that his supposed engagement and love affair with Sallie Dandridge had completely soured? Pelham by some accounts had mentioned that the Shackelfords were much like his own family back in Alabama and that Bessie reminded him of his sister, Betty—hardly the kind of fuel for an amorous relationship. An attraction certainly existed; whether it went beyond platonic remains unlikely.

No matter the extent of the relationship, Pelham received permission from Bessie to call on her again. The closeness of the Shackelford house to the Virginia Hotel made the jaunt appear simple. However, the rough wintry weather had turned Main Street into a virtual morass of thick mud, literally halting vehicular traffic from moving beyond a snail's pace. Humans could make the journey across but not without clogging, or even ruining, their boots with the muck. A gentleman would never think of tracking this mess into a fine home such as the Shackelfords'. Pelham, therefore, with the able assistance of von Borcke, began working on a solution to the problem the morning after the minstrel show. In the true spirit of chivalry the two friends hauled blocks of stone to fill in the mud. Atop the rocks they carefully placed numerous planks until they had fashioned a makeshift bridge that extended all the way across the street. The Shackelford girls watched from their windows and occasionally called out words of encouragement. Before noon the task was completed; now Pelham and Von could cross over the quagmire without soiling their boots or pant legs, thus keeping the house free of the mud.[21]

Always welcome at the Shackelford residence, Pelham and von Borcke made constant trips across their homemade bridge during the next two weeks. For Pelham it was his happiest time since the treasured days at the Bower. Indulging in a host of enjoyable pastimes, they filled their leisure hours singing, dancing, acting out charades, listening to von Borcke's outrageous stories, or carrying on meaningful conversations. Bessie, an accomplished pianist, often played a variety of songs—lively and melancholy—while her four sisters, along with Pelham and von Borcke, circled around the piano to listen or sing. Occasionally Pelham and Bessie managed to be alone to discuss private matters. Bessie had a natural way of getting the modest young man to open up and talk about his family and friends, and what he hoped to do when this terrible war ended. A closeness, possibly more than friendship, bloomed. Years later, Bessie, now a widow, remembered Pelham fondly:

One could never forget him. A boy, and yet a man, that was Pelham. You couldn't help being drawn to him. He was really fascinating. He had great blue eyes and lovely golden-brown hair and a beautiful face, beautiful manners too. He spoke gently and he moved quietly. He was quick, though—oh, so quick!—just as quick as I was. He would answer a question before you had it half spoken and if there was a joke to be played on some one—well, you had to jump faster than you ever jumped before to get ahead of Major Pelham. We used to dance a great deal too. You didn't get an idea of how strong he was until you danced with him. <u>That</u> was grand. Sometimes I used to sit and just look at him and wonder if it could be true that he was the man they were all talking about, the man who could aim those guns so that they would kill and kill and kill. He didn't look as though he could ever order anybody to be killed. There wasn't a single line of hardness in his face. It was all tenderness and softness, as fresh and delicate as a boy's who liked people and who found the world good. I used to say to myself, "A man like that—this boy?" That is really what he was, you know—a boy, a splendid boy.[22]

Bessie's friends took to Pelham's charms as well, indicated by the following notation: "One of the meetings I prized most was that with Major Pelham . . . a young hero whose name . . . was already on every tongue around us. He was on horseback before . . . [Bessie's] door . . . waiting till I came out to mount for a ride somewhere. A slim boy with a dark, sparkling face is what the splendid Pelham seemed to me in that brief encounter, followed by a little war of wits."[23]

∼

With cavalry units from both sides no longer hesitant to move, Stuart ordered Pelham and von Borcke by telegram to return to Camp No-Camp in late February. Sadly, they said their good-byes to the Shackelford family and made their way back toward Fredericksburg. Upon their return to camp, Pelham spent a few days making the rounds among his batteries, ensuring that the men and equipment continued to be in near perfect working condition. Von Borcke, however, found the next few weeks a boring time that "dragged slowly by, so dull and eventless that existence was scarcely tolerable." The soldiers, according to Von, "looked forward to the commencement of spring and the reopening of the campaign with intense longing."[24]

Satisfied that his batteries passed his rigid inspection, Pelham decided that Sunday, March 8, a rainy and drizzly day, was the ideal time to visit some of his Alabama friends encamped nearby. Taking the better part of the day, Pelham leisurely sat and discussed a variety of topics from the war effort to the more melancholy memories of his youth back in Alabama. By day's end he headed back to his own camp with a novel souvenir, a 12-pound Yankee cannonball accompanied by a note, sent to him by a Miss Moore from his native state. The following day Pelham scribbled out a message, apparently a first draft, to acknowledge and thank the lady for the unusual present:

Near Fredericksburg, Va., March 9th, '63

I visited Col. O'Neal and Sam yesterday. The latter handed me your note and the cannon ball. If he had known with what pleasure I would receive it, I think he would have sent them to me sooner. Permit me to express my sincerest thanks, both for your kind note and for the confidence you show in entrusting the projectile to my care. I promise faithfully it shall be returned to its former owners with all the bitterness and force you could desire and with all the accuracy my limited experience will permit. Nor shall it be carelessly thrown away. I will reserve it till we get to "close quarters"—and then one prayer for Alabama and yourself. You must grant me permission to make an official report to you of the success or non-success of the shot. I hope and believe it cannot fail. I am proud of the honor you do me in allowing me to fire it for you. You were very kind to volunteer the information and spare my modesty the severe shock of having to ask a difficult question. Accept my deep gratitude—and remember me kindly to her. I would like to ask after one or two other ladies I met at W[est] P[oint] if my extreme bashfulness would permit.[25]

Within a matter of days Pelham received a present from a different admirer. This time a letter and a package, containing some homemade candy, arrived at Stuart's headquarters from the town of Orange Court House. The letter, written by Miss Nannie Price, Stuart's attractive cousin and devoted pen pal, offered candy to the general as well as to Pelham. Nannie, who resided at Dundee in Hanover County, had been visiting a friend, and they cooked up the candy as a gift for the two officers. Nannie penned: "Dear General, we had a little candy stew last night, and knowing your fondness for 'sweets' of all kinds, I send you some of it this morning. Miss Brill sends some of it for the 'Gallant Pelham,' which you must be sure to give him." Nannie then added provocatively, "If you could see the burns on our fingers I am sure it would seem much sweeter—."[26]

After sampling the scrumptious contents of the package, Pelham felt obliged to thank the ladies in person. Wisely, however, Pelham did not immediately ask Stuart for permission to leave camp. Knowing Stuart's penchant for refusing furloughs or, even worse, granting them and later callously rescinding them, Pelham retired to his tent to conspire with W. W. Blackford. "General Stuart loved [Pelham] like a younger brother," admitted Blackford, "and could not bear for him to be away from him." The plan therefore had to be one that Stuart would approve and, more important, not quash at a later time. Together they finagled a logical plan. The initial phase of the scheme involved obtaining Stuart's approval for leave, not an easy task in itself. Pelham would approach Stuart that evening, requesting permission to depart the following morning. Stuart might be more apt to agree, so they reasoned, if Pelham would not be leaving for another day. Furthermore, Pelham claimed his ostensible motive was to inspect Moorman's battery, stationed conveniently at Orange Court House. This bit of duplicity certainly did not fool Stuart, as he knew well of Pelham's true intentions, but Moorman's gunners probably could use an inspection—permission granted. Shrewdly, Pelham asked for Stuart's written consent, which the general readily approved by summoning A. A. G. Norman FitzHugh to finalize the order. Thus, Pelham's "little pleasure trip," as Blackford deemed it, had passed its first test.[27]

The second part of the plan—physically getting out of camp, beyond the clutches of Stuart—might prove trickier. But Pelham had provided for such a contingency. With FitzHugh's written order safely tucked inside his uniform coat, Pelham vacated the camp in the darkness, before breakfast, when all remained asleep. Without tarrying for food or any sort of nourishment, Pelham slipped out of sight and headed for his destination. Pelham had planned on having breakfast along the road at an artillery campsite, but upon his arrival, near daybreak, he intuitively decided to move on toward Orange. A mere cup of coffee would do. Ahead the road turned muddy and thick, and Pelham's progress slowed considerably.

Meanwhile, back at Camp No-Camp Stuart and his staff officers gathered for breakfast. The general almost absentmindedly inquired, "Where's Pelham?" When informed that his prized artillerist had left camp before dawn with his written consent, Stuart chafed. Immediately and without humor Stuart ordered FitzHugh to summon a fast courier to bring Pelham back. But Pelham's instincts earlier that morning had served him well; his decision to twice forego breakfast had given him a sizable lead on any rider in case Stuart changed his mind. As Blackford astutely noted, "Pelham knew the General well and feared he would do exactly this thing." By nightfall of Sunday, March 15, Pelham reached the outskirts of Orange Court House where Moorman's men lay encamped. As Pelham rode forward, he heard fierce hoofbeats clattering behind him. He turned in the saddle to observe Stuart's messenger approaching quickly. The courier handed Pelham the written order to return, but Pelham knew he had won the race. A smile broke over his face as he read the order. Looking directly at the courier, Pelham stated: "Sergeant, I'm certain that General Stuart would not want me to wear out my horse by riding back over those roads tonight. I'll return first thing tomorrow." Pelham then spurred his horse on toward Orange. After cleaning up, he dined that evening with Nannie Price and Miss Brill and later escorted the ladies on his arm through the town.[28]

It must have pleased Pelham to have bested his cavalry chieftain this one time. Seldom did anyone, friend or foe, successfully take advantage of Stuart. Certainly Pelham enjoyed the moment, knowing full well he would take his share of grief from his boss once he returned to camp on the morrow. Somewhere back at Stuart's headquarters W. W. Blackford, too, must have found amusement in outsmarting Jeb. Blackford probably smiled and shook his head realizing he had helped his friend Pelham in the ruse. Blackford later penned that on "the day [Pelham] left us to go to Orange C. H. . . . I marked the place we stopped [reading in Napier's *Peninsula War*]." He then sadly remarked: "and I have never had the heart to read more in it since."[29]

22

"Such Is the Fortune of War"

[Pelham] was gone, and his young blood . . . had bathed Virginia's soil.

—Henry B. McClellan

Sometime in the early afternoon of Monday, March 16, a locomotive, carrying a few of Fitz Lee's cavalrymen, arrived in Orange Court House. These men brought information that a large body of Federal cavalry had pushed its way toward the vicinity of Kelly's Ford, thus threatening the Confederate lines of communication. Consequently, Fitz Lee had dispatched these Rebels by rail from Culpeper to obtain ammunition from the local depot with orders to return to Culpeper posthaste. John Pelham had readied himself that day to return to Camp No-Camp, as Stuart's orders indicated, but the exciting news of approaching Federals caused Pelham to rethink his plans. After further questioning the officers on the train, Pelham decided to ignore Stuart's directive and instead join Fitz Lee's men for the trip back to Culpeper. Pelham rationalized that Stuart would want him nearer the action, and besides, his fighting blood was up. After helping load the ammunition and saying good-bye to his lady friends, Pelham climbed aboard the train for the eighteen-mile trip to Culpeper.[1]

Arriving at Culpeper during the late afternoon, Pelham was somewhat surprised to find Jeb Stuart already there. Always happy to see his young artillerist, Stuart quickly passed over any of Pelham's apologies for violating orders by reassuring him he had made the proper military decision. More than likely the cavalry chieftain teased Pelham regarding his presence in Culpeper as merely an excuse to visit Bessie Shackelford. Stuart, meanwhile, gave his own explanation for being in the town: he was to appear as a witness at a court-martial that had ended that same day.[2] Now that the two had reunited, they undoubtedly discussed the situation of the Federal troops. Pelham, who knew little more than what he had learned that afternoon from Fitz Lee's men, listened intently as Stuart described the circumstances. Certainly Fitz Lee had kept Stuart apprised of what had transpired that day along the Rappahannock River, but Stuart himself had only sketchy details of the Federal incursion. In fact, Union general William Woods Averell, commanding three thousand sabers and six pieces of artillery, had specific orders to cross the Rappahannock and "to attack and rout or destroy" the forces under Fitz Lee. Averell selected Kelly's Ford for the crossing "because the opposite country was better known to me than that beyond any other ford, and it afforded the shortest route to the enemy's camp."[3]

Fitz Lee first heard of Averell's movement in a telegram from Robert E. Lee's headquarters late that same morning. Alerting his pickets to this potential danger, Fitz Lee determined to halt the bluecoats with the small, available force at hand. Normally carrying 1,900 troopers on his rolls, Fitz could now only saddle 800. The hard winter had disabled many of his brigade's horses, and a sizable number of men had been furloughed to bring back fresh mounts. He could, however, count on the excellent battery of horse artillery commanded by James Breathed. In the meantime Fitz had to wait for his scouts to report the exact whereabouts of the Federals; only then could he determine Averell's intentions and concentrate his own undersized force. Finally, by 6:00 P.M. Fitz Lee's scouts reported eyeing Averell's cavalry in the vicinity of Morrisville, "a little place," in Lee's words, "6 miles from Kelly's Ford." Fitz Lee ordered forty sharpshooters to reinforce the twenty pickets already stationed at the ford. All the while Averell ponderously moved toward his crossing spot, wasting both time and precious daylight, before ultimately deciding to rest his men for the remainder of the evening.[4]

Back at Culpeper Stuart appeared satisfied with the deployment of Fitz Lee's men and decided that he and Pelham would enjoy themselves that evening. Accepting an invitation from Bessie, Stuart and Pelham made their way to the Shackelford house. With the two officers and her sisters gathered around the piano, Bessie proceeded to entertain them with a variety of classical pieces. Then she requested that her audience join in singing some patriotic favorites. Stuart's well-known and melodic baritone voice sounded above the others as they harmonized to "The Bonnie Blue Flag," "Dixie," "Lorena," and the "Yellow Rose of Texas." Following refreshments, Stuart and Pelham graciously thanked their hostesses and walked to the door. Pelham took Bessie's hand and again thanked her for the wonderful evening. As he said good night, he promised to stop on the morrow to wish her a happy St. Patrick's Day.[5]

Crossing the street and entering the lobby of the Virginia Hotel, Stuart and Pelham found they had an unexpected visitor awaiting them in the person of Captain Harry Gilmor of the Twelfth Virginia Cavalry. Captured in September 1862 when the Army of Northern Virginia crossed into Maryland, Gilmor had been imprisoned until recently. He now sought to meet Stuart and join his staff in some capacity. "I was introduced to them," Gilmor wrote later, "and a jolly time we had of it. Here I first met poor Pelham, the 'boy major,' the renowned young hero of Stuart's horse artillery." Stuart listened to Gilmor's request and promised to give an answer the following day. The three of them then repaired to a room upstairs where they joined with several other officers to enjoy the evening's closing hours. "Little did we anticipate what then awaited us," penned Gilmor. "What a jovial party were assembled that evening in Colonel [Richard Welby] Carter's room. Let them pass before 'my mind's eye': Colonel [Thomas] Rosser, severely wounded next day; Lieutenant Colonel Welby Carter; Colonel Sol[omon] Williams, who married Miss Pegram, and was killed ten days after; Major John Pelham and Major [John William] Puller, both killed next day; Captain A. Rogers, First Virginia Cavalry; Colonel [James Henry] Drake, killed at Shepherdstown the following summer; Colonel [Henry Clay] Pate, killed at Yellow Tavern the day Stuart himself was killed; and myself."[6]

The gathering broke up within a few hours, as the weary men sought a few hours sleep, fully aware that the next day promised much activity. Stuart and Pelham said good night, agreed to meet for breakfast, and retired to their individual rooms. Strangely, another who claimed that he was in the presence of Pelham that night was Confederate officer Pierce Manning Butler Young from the West Point Class of June 1861. Young stated that he and Pelham celebrated at the Shackelford house that evening and Pelham later "shared my couch the night before his death." Yet Gilmor, who took extreme precaution in detailing the names in the room, does not mention Young.[7]

Even before daylight on March 17 Averell's force of three thousand troopers, including six pieces of artillery commanded by Lieutenant George Browne Jr., moved along the muddy roads toward Kelly's Ford. Reaching the ford while the last vestiges of darkness faded, Averell's horsemen ran into resistance from Fitz Lee's handful of skirmishers and sharpshooters positioned on the opposite bank. Averell reported further obstacles as "the crossing was found obstructed by fallen trees, forming an abatis upon both banks, which defended by 80 sharpshooters, covered by rifle-pits and houses on the opposite bank, rendered the crossing difficult." Further complicating matters, the spring thaw and heavy rains had swollen the river to four feet with a swift current. After repeated failures Averell forced a crossing and overwhelmed Fitz Lee's token force of men, capturing twenty-five of them.[8]

The remainder of the Federals now crossed the ford, taking two full hours to complete the task. In particular Lieutenant Browne's six guns found the crossing treacherously difficult and time-consuming. At last with the precarious crossing completed, Averell gave his nearly exhausted men and horses a two-hour respite before setting out anew. Leaving nine hundred of his troopers behind at the ford to protect his rear and help ensure his escape, Averell's command crept slowly along Culpeper Road toward Brandy Station. Averell fully avowed his slowness was intentional and part of his plan for a defensive posture against Fitz Lee.

After John Pelham arose that morning he happened to think that Captain Marcellus N. Moorman's battery, stationed at Orange Court House, would soon be expecting his return. To allay any concern over his delay, Pelham picked up a scrap piece of light blue, ruled paper and with a pencil hastily wrote out his last order:

Culpeper C. H.
March 17th, '63.

Capt.

Be on the alert. Large force of cavalry between Morrisville and Bealton Station. If everything is quiet here I will be at Rapidan Station tomorrow.

Mo. Respty.
Jno. Pelham,
Maj. Art.

Capt. Moorman
Moorman's Battery.[9]

Pelham then joined Stuart downstairs in the dining room of the hotel for breakfast. Sometime during their meal, the two received information that Averell's bluecoats had traversed Kelly's Ford. Without panic they established their plans while finishing their food. Since both had come to Culpeper via the railroad, neither had his horse available, thus borrowed mounts would be necessary. Pelham immediately thought of Sam Sweeney's "rawboned black mare." She would be suitable for the occasion. Stuart, of course, would have no difficulty in finding a horse for himself. Then they would ride out to Fitz Lee's headquarters to assist in repelling these upstart Yankees. Word spread quickly through the town. Harry Gilmor, fast asleep from the previous night's revelry, was awakened abruptly by the shouts of Major John Puller, who burst into Gilmor's room. Before the words were scarcely out of Puller's mouth, Gilmor leaped from bed and made his way to the stable to look after his horse. "Coming back," wrote Gilmor later, "I met Stuart all ready, with Pelham by his side, looking as fresh, and joyous, and rosy as a boy ten years old." Gilmor saluted Stuart and excitedly offered his services as a temporary staff officer. Stuart gladly accepted the proposal, and he and Pelham, already mounted, rode east out of Culpeper to join the fracas. Passing by the Shackelford house, Pelham's eyes met Bessie's as she stood on the balcony waving a white, lace handkerchief. Scurrying along behind them, Gilmor doffed his hat to "the pretty little Miss Bessie" and hastened to catch up. "Alas! What grief possessed her," he later remembered, "before the close of that eventful day."[10]

Gilmor managed to catch up with Stuart and Pelham as they reached the edge of the town. While they trotted along, Gilmor seemed impressed that Stuart and Pelham scanned the surrounding countryside "with rapid glances" in order to select artillery positions in case the enemy should push that far. The roads soon turned into a tricky quagmire that slowed them, but the three riders pressed on. Finally they came upon the Fifth Virginia Cavalry, whose Major John Puller eyed them with a smile. "Harry, leave me your haversack if you get killed!" Puller called out to Gilmor good-naturedly. "Ay, ay, major," Gilmor responded.[11] They continued on toward Fitz Lee's headquarters.

The ever-diligent Fitz Lee, already alerted early that morning of the Federal crossing, moved quickly to stop the bluecoats. Lee feared the enemy troopers might be heading straight toward the Orange and Alexandria Railroad, a little more than four miles north of Kelly's Ford. The potential capture of this railroad line, as well as Brandy Station, would, of course, severely damage Confederate communications and transportation in central Virginia. Consequently, Lee gathered his body of troopers and rode in the direction of Kelly's Ford. To his surprise Fitz Lee found the Yankees had advanced less than a mile west from the ford and now awaited his arrival as Averell had desired. Averell had deployed his men in a line facing northwestward toward Brandy Station. His right extended to Wheatley's Ford, roughly a mile north of Kelly's Ford, on the Rappahannock River. His left, protected somewhat by the thickly treed Jamison's Woods, lengthened beyond the Brooks farmhouse. His middle was strongly anchored by sharpshooters armed with carbines positioned behind a low stone fence that stretched nearly the distance between his two flanks. Lieutenant George Browne's six guns had clear shots at the few approaches toward the stone barrier. To the rear Averell had stationed his mounted reserves to protect the open fields and woodlands where the Confederates might approach.[12] Less than a mile behind the Federals lay Kelly's Ford, an avenue of escape if retreat were deemed necessary. The arrangement had been completed in the most professional manner. Now only two questions remained: Would Fitz Lee order his undersized command to attack as Averell had gambled? If so, would Averell's troopers, so accustomed to whippings from the Rebel cavalry, stand firm?

Stuart, Pelham, and Gilmor rode up and found Fitz Lee looking on toward the enemy forces. Underestimating the enemy's strength but with his fighting spirit rankled, Fitz Lee turned to Stuart. "General," he began succinctly, "I think there are only a few platoons in the woods yonder. Hadn't we better take the bulge on them at once?" Stuart, who had surveyed the Yankee position through his field glasses, concurred. "By all means," he stated. Orders thus went out to the Third Virginia Cavalry to ready for the attack. Meanwhile, James Breathed's battery of horse artillery, still trudging through the muddy and bottomless roads, had yet to come up, so Pelham rode to the rear to hurry them forward. Along the way the careful eye of Pelham noted the best positions for Breathed's four Blakelys once they arrived.[13]

While Pelham was gone, the Battle of Kelly's Ford commenced with early negative results for the Rebels. Fitz Lee had confidently sent in a squadron of sharpshooters on foot under the command of Captain James Bailey preceding the Third Virginia Cavalry. Armed with carbines, these men headed through the thickets and open fields. When the Virginians reached within two hundred yards of the stone fence, they were met by a ferocious volley of lead from the Federals behind their barrier. Simultaneously, four Union field pieces, equally hidden, opened up with shell and canister. Stunned by these blasts, the Confederate sharpshooters fairly panicked and began moving toward the rear. The angered urgings of their officers did not stem the tide. Suddenly, Jeb Stuart was among them, waving his plumed hat, imploring them to stay or "they would leave him by himself." Nearby Harry Gilmor watched in awe as Stuart single-handedly calmed the men and reversed their movement. "Never did I see one bear himself more nobly," wrote an astonished Gilmor. "I stopped to gaze upon him, though I expected every moment to hear the dull thug of a bullet, and see him fall. 'Confound it, men,' said he, 'come back;' and they came." Stuart ordered the remaining sharpshooters behind a raised sod fence a few yards closer but out of view of the Federal riflemen. As the Rebels scampered for safety, however, a shell, fired by one of Browne's New Yorkers, exploded at the top of the sod fence. Jagged metal killed three and wounded seven.[14]

Now the remainder of the Third Virginia, mounted in columns of fours, some with sabers unsheathed, others with pistols drawn, rode into the middle of the melee in "gallant style." Without artillery support this new wave of Virginians, commanded by Colonel Thomas H. Owen, bravely galloped through the clearing of Wheatley's field toward the stone fence, but as they approached, the Federals let loose with deadly results. Gilmor labeled it "a fatal mistake" as the blasts "emptied many a saddle." The determination of the Third, however, could not be denied, and many kept up the attack, riding directly to the stone fence, looking for a gate or some sort of opening to break through. Horses reared up at the fence as many Rebels fired their pistols directly into the faces of their opponents. Others hacked and slashed with their sabers, but an opening could not be found, nor could one be forced. "We found it impossible," wrote Captain William Carter, "to get through the stone fence." Finally, these fearless horsemen were forced to seek shelter and turned toward their left in the direction of Wheatley's icehouse along the Rappahannock.[15]

Two Federal regiments headed in the same direction and took position around the house and in the garden of the C. T. Wheatley home, opening fire on the Confederates. Heading off these bluecoats, the Second Virginia Cavalry entered the fracas with sabers drawn. Minutes passed as the antagonists fought blade to blade on horseback. Then from a pine grove on the extreme flank, help arrived from the First Virginia. This sudden attack from a surprise source startled and drove the pesky Federals back. Now Fitz Lee, still believing the enemy force to be a small one, determined to apply the coup de grace by knifing a regiment to the far left and around to the rear of the enemy, thus cutting off their escape and avoiding that "infernal stone fence." For this assignment he called upon Colonel Tom Rosser and his Fifth Virginia. Under instructions Gilmor rode to find Rosser and to direct him in this mission. With the Rappahannock on their far left and the stone fence some forty yards away to the right, they edged their way through a steep hollow. Without warning

Federal sharpshooters opened fire, enfilading the Fifth Virginia from the fence as well as a few vacant buildings nearby. Only then, according to Gilmor, did the astonished Confederates realize the size of the enemy force. Rosser, sensing the peril, worked feverishly to keep his men in order and from panicking. Shouting directions and offering encouragement, Rosser suddenly spied Major John Puller, who seemed to sit impassively on his horse. "Major Puller," Rosser angrily demanded, "why, in the name of God, don't you assist me in rallying the men?" Nearby, Gilmor swung around to see his friend Puller, the same man who awakened him that very morning and later playfully asked for his haversack, attempt to pull himself upward. "I saw death plainly stamped on his features," remembered Gilmor. In answer to Rosser's admonishment, Puller announced, "Colonel, I'm killed." Rosser's ire quickly turned to sympathy: "My God, old fellow, I hope not; bear up, bear up!" Puller, attempting to straighten himself on his mount, toppled headfirst to the ground. Several valiant troopers extricated Puller's nearly breathless body to an ambulance, hoping surgical help could spare his life, but it was too late. A bullet had smashed into his right breast, passed near his heart, and exited under the left shoulder blade.[16] Rosser managed to pull his troopers from danger, but the effort to outflank the bluecoats was temporarily denied. Despite sustaining a serious wound, Rosser fought on until the battle ended late in the afternoon. This achievement earned Pelham's old West Point roommate the accolades of both Stuart and Fitz Lee.[17]

Now the fighting seesawed back and forth in the open areas as each mounted force attacked and counterattacked without gaining any significant advantage. Most of the conflict was conducted directly from the saddle with saber charges in hand-to-hand conflict.[18] Although neither cavalry appeared to be winning the struggle, several factors gave the Yankees the upper hand. Numerically, the Federals held a three-to-one edge, plus the six-gun battery of the Union horse artillery continued pounding the Rebels, who, as of yet, had no field guns available. Furthermore, the defensive stance taken by the bluecoats particularly stymied their opponents. With a river on one flank and thick woods on the other, any enemy attack was naturally funneled toward the middle where the stone wall, the Federal trump card, literally frustrated the Rebel attackers. Finally, as each phase of the battle passed without Confederate success, the Federal horsemen gained confidence in their own ability to stand up to the legendary gray riders.

Sometime during the action, Pelham rejoined the main body of Fitz Lee's cavalry. Breathed and his four-gun battery soon arrived as well after setting a frantic pace to the battlefield. "I do not think we ever traveled at a more rapid gait than on that occasion," penned H. H. Matthews. "The distance from our camp to where we met the brigade at the Wheatley House is about 3½ miles. We made the distance in about 30 minutes, not more." Pelham directed them to a location near the

Brannin House he had earlier selected as an advantageous site for artillery pieces. Thus far Lieutenant Browne's Federal gunners, without opposition, had unleashed much iron against the Rebels, inflicting significant injuries to men and horses. It was time for Breathed's Blakelys to even the score. Pelham helped sight the guns but allowed Breathed, whom he had trained and trusted, to open the barrage. For the next few minutes the loud concussion of ten cannons dueling in a hot contest filled the air. Pleased with the fact that the Federal guns appeared to be lessening in intensity and volume, Pelham urged Breathed: "Captain, do not let your fire cease; drive them from their position." Breathed acknowledged the order without a word and bade the gunners to keep up the fire without pause. Satisfied with the results, Pelham spurred his horse off to the area where the Virginia horsemen were readying for another attempt at the stone fence.[19] Perhaps the tide of the struggle was about to turn.

Pelham nudged his black mare up alongside the mount of Harry Gilmor, and the two riders sat and watched from the extreme right of the Third Virginia.[20] Gilmor later estimated that approximately thirty minutes had passed since the mortal wounding of John Puller. From their vantage point Gilmor and Pelham witnessed the Virginia horsemen forming into battle array. Meanwhile Federal gunners continued to shell the area, causing some apprehension among the men of the Third. Just then Fitz Lee, who already had had two horses shot from under him on this day, cantered up with a gleam of confidence in his dark eyes. "Keep cool, boys," he admonished. "These little things," referring to the exploding shells, "make a deal of fuss, but don't hurt any one." Bolstered by his words, "the whole regiment gave him three cheers."[21] Fitz Lee then rode forward to oversee the attack.

The events that followed in the next few minutes remain clouded and even muddled since various eyewitnesses, there on the battlefield, all reliable sources, dispute, or possibly distort, the details. Resolving their different stories and reports is virtually impossible because of the varied specifics given and possibly the confusion of the moment. But one undeniable fact stays constant: John Pelham was mortally wounded.[22]

Numerous accounts indicate that Pelham watched intently as the Confederate troopers deployed for the attack. Then as the last of the riders passed by him, Pelham, with the instincts and spontaneity of a true warrior, unsheathed his saber and spurred his horse diagonally across a field toward the head of the column. Repeatedly shouting "Forward" and riding at full gallop, reins in one hand, sword in the other, Pelham wheeled toward some farm buildings on the Wheatley property. Observing that the gray riders had fortuitously found an opening in the stone fence and were rapidly pouring through, Pelham rode up to the gate and reined in his horse. Waving and shouting encouragement to the Rebel horsemen, Pelham urged the men to take full advantage of the breach in the fence. Lifting himself higher in

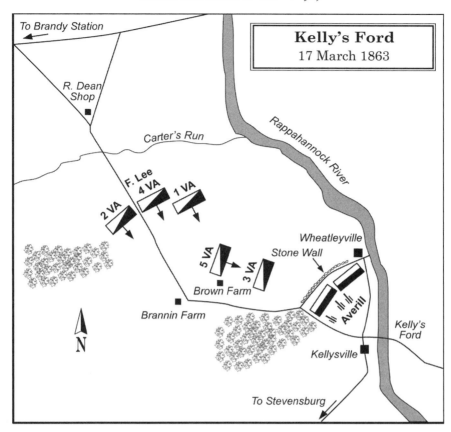

his stirrups and waving his sword aloft for emphasis, Pelham pleaded for the men to hurry.[23] Then a Federal Hotchkiss shell exploded violently overhead, bursting into jagged and twisting hunks or slivers of hot iron. The loud concussion drowned out his words, and instantly he toppled to the ground, landing in a supine position, eyes slightly open, a trace of a smile remaining upon his lips. He appeared dazed rather than severely injured or fatally wounded.[24]

Henry McClellan, then serving as adjutant of the Third Virginia Cavalry, verified this account, stating later that he had witnessed Pelham's wounding. "I saw Major John Pelham rushing to its head [the Third Virginia] with the shout of battle on his lips," wrote McClellan. "After the rear of the regiment had passed through a small enclosure near Wheatley's house, I saw a single cavalryman struggling to place the body of a comrade across the bow of his saddle. I approached to assist, and recognized Pelham. He had been struck in the head by a piece of shell, and life was extinct. By this narrow chance was his body preserved from falling into the hands of the enemy." In summing up the battle McClellan added: "Pelham could not remain inactive on the battlefield. Having no guns to occupy his attention, he rode forward to aid in leading the charge of the 3d regiment, and met his fate."[25]

Some time afterward McClellan, in what appears to be part of his private correspondence, added more detail:

At the moment a regiment of Federal cavalry swept down upon us. Pelham's sabre flashed from its sheath in an instant. At that moment his appearance was superb. His cheeks were burning; his bright blue eyes darted lightning; and from his lips, wreathed with a smile of joy, rang, "Forward!" as he cheered on the men. He looked the perfect picture of a hero, as he was. For an instant he was standing in his stirrups, his sabre flashing in his grasp; for a moment his clarion voice rang like a bugle that sounds the charge, and then I saw him hurled from his saddle under the trampling hoofs of the horses. With a single bound of my horse I reached him. He lay with his smiling face turned upward; his eyes closed. A shell had burst above him, a fragment of which had struck him on the head. He was gone, and his young blood, sacred to the men of his battery and the entire command, had bathed Virginia's soil.[26]

Other contemporaries offer descriptions of Pelham's wounding that are based on hearsay, lack any specifics, or give questionable information. The normally reliable W. W. Blackford, who was not present at Kelly's Ford, for example, wrote:

Pelham rode down to the skirmish line to reconnoitre and select a position for the guns when they reached the field. A light skirmish fire was going on and an officer had his horse hit. He was a friend of Pelham's and he pulled up to talk to him and advise about the treatment of the horse. The officer asked Pelham a question, but receiving no answer looked up and saw his saddle empty. Pelham was stretched on the ground with what his friend supposed to be a bullet through his head. It was, however, only a tip from the ball which did not enter the skull. Thinking Pelham dead, his friend threw the body across a saddle in front of a man and with his head hanging on one side and feet on the other he was taken several miles to the rear before meeting an ambulance; a treatment sufficient to have almost killed a well man, and yet Pelham did not die for twelve hours.

From whom Blackford heard this account he did not say, but he amended the passage by footnoting: "This account of his death I heard at the time, but it since appears that he was killed in a cavalry charge."[27]

Even Pelham's own relatives surprisingly disagreed over the aspects of John's wounding. Mrs. Peter Pelham, John's sister-in-law, claimed in a letter dated November 25, 1898, that John was killed while leading the Fifth Virginia Cavalry on March 16, 1863, but both the unit and the date are incorrect. She further stated that Major J. M. Ryals was by his side when he fell, and that John "died in a few minutes" following the wounding. On the contrary Charles Pelham, John's brother, stated in a letter dated November 21, 1898, that "a fragment of shell crushed his skull. He did not die for several hours, but was never conscious after he received the wound."[28]

Harry Gilmor, who claimed that he sat next to Pelham when the wounding occurred, offered a considerably different version of the entire incident. According to Gilmor, Federal artillery shells continued exploding all around them until he, at least, considered the concussions of the projectiles to be routine. Suddenly, however, he "was deafened by the explosion of one very near." Even so, Gilmor alleged he did not turn around to inspect any damage until he heard Captain James Bailey shout, "My God, they've killed poor Pelham!" Gilmor avowed he had heard no report of a projectile hitting human flesh—the "thug" as he called it—"which you never fail to hear when a man is struck as near as Pelham was to me." Automatically spinning in his saddle at Bailey's dreadful warning, Gilmor observed a riderless horse slowly moving away. Quickly his eyes focused downward where he saw Pelham "lying on his back upon the ground, his eyes wide open, and looking very natural, but fatally hurt."[29]

With Federal cavalrymen lurking dangerously about, Gilmor, Bailey, and Lieutenant Charles Minnigerode, one of Fitz Lee's staff officers, lifted Pelham's body onto Gilmor's horse and carried it to a safer area. Upon inspecting the body, Gilmor found a small wound "bleeding profusely" at the back of the head. Although believing the situation hopeless, Gilmor had Pelham's seemingly lifeless body placed upon the borrowed black mare, summoned two dismounted men nearby, and ordered them to quickly find an ambulance and a surgeon.[30] Gilmor then spurred his own horse and frantically galloped off to find Jeb Stuart.

Within moments Gilmor reined in alongside Stuart, who had been observing the battle. Acknowledging Gilmor, Stuart instinctively noticed the blood on his hands and uniform. Mistakenly assuming that Gilmor had been hurt, Stuart inquired about his injury. "I told him it was not my own blood," stated Gilmor, "but the blood of poor Pelham, killed a few moments before, whose body I had brought off the field." Stuart stiffened at the dreadful news. Gilmor stared into the general's eyes: "I shall never forget his look of distress and horror." In a flash Federal troopers almost surrounded them, but the two literally bolted to safety into a thick stand of trees. There Stuart pulled up and instantly demanded a retelling of all the particulars concerning Pelham. The general fought back tears as Gilmor imparted the sorrowful information of his friend's death. When Gilmor finished, Jeb "bowed his head upon his horse's neck and wept." In his despair he managed to utter, "Our loss is irreparable!"[31] Then regaining his composure, Stuart ordered Gilmor to ride to

Culpeper and dispatch a telegram to Robert E. Lee at Fredericksburg concerning the situation of the battle and the tragedy that had befallen Pelham.

Meanwhile, with Pelham's body being borne from the field, the struggle at Kelly's Ford continued. Regiments from both sides were forced to realign their positions as the fighting wavered back and forth near the Wheatley house. At one stage the Federal horsemen thundered forward only to be met by Fitz Lee's undersized units. A sudden clash of arms and Lee's men, finding themselves outnumbered and overwhelmed, hastily retreated to form a stronger line near the home of James Newby. Averell boasted in his post-battle report that the Rebels were "torn to pieces and driven from the field in magnificent style."[32]

Approximately three-quarters of a mile from his first position Fitz Lee posted his men in a stronger defensive formation across the road leading to Brandy Station. Behind a small, meandering stream known as Carter's Run, the Rebels faced an open field of well over five hundred yards to a thickly wooded area across the way where Averell's cavalrymen would soon be located. More important, Breathed's four-gun battery of horse artillery had set up on the crest of a hill behind the Confederate cavalry. The well-trained gunners rapidly drew a bead on the woodland before them. Within minutes Averell's force appeared at the edge of the woods facing the Rebels. "We never lost a foot of ground," reported Averell, "but kept steadily advancing until we arrived at a stubble-field, which the enemy set on fire to the windward, to burn us out. My men rushed forward, and beat it out with their overcoats." In the meantime four Federal cannon moved into place on the left of the road. Averell then shook out some skirmishers, armed with carbines, and seemed satisfied to let them and the artillery blast away at the Rebels beyond. Breathed's cannoneers now opened up in response with devastating results, killing at least two Yankees, including Lieutenant Henry L. Nicolai of the First Rhode Island Cavalry whose head was knocked from his body, which "turned a somersault." Averell mistakenly claimed the Confederates employed three guns, "two 10-pounder Parrotts and a 6-pounder," whose effect he described as "exceedingly annoying." The Federal commander gave no indication of pushing his advantage, insisting that no artillery horses could be seen through field glasses and that "it was evident that [Rebel guns] were covered by earthworks." He concluded with "our artillery could not hurt them. Our ammunition was of miserable quality and nearly exhausted."[33] Thus Averell remained in his desired defensive posture.

Suddenly, with an impetuosity seemingly bred into Confederate cavalry officers, Fitz Lee ordered an all-out assault from his five regiments. Evidently contemptuous of his opponent's stance, Lee dangerously left nothing behind in reserve other than Breathed's guns.[34] Riding across the field, Rebel horsemen were immediately fired upon by the enemy's carbines as well as double canister and spherical case shot blasted by the artillery. The First, Third, and Fifth Virginia Cavalry regiments, charging from the Confederate left in what one participant labeled as "splendid" and "the prettiest [charge] I ever witnessed," pushed on ahead and drove the Yankees to their front back into the safety of the woods. Content with their success, the Rebel troopers on this flank pulled back and reformed. The Second and Fourth Virginians on the right met greater resistance, especially from the men of the First Rhode Island who simply refused to be shoved back. Once again combatants clashed saber to saber while others brandished pistols at such close range that jackets smoldered from exploding gunpowder. Only the ardor and pronounced stubbornness of the Rhode Islanders saved the Federal guns from being captured. Even a makeshift hospital site had to be abandoned by the Federals as the Rebels moved dangerously close. Finally the Virginians, their forward progress impeded, withdrew to the opposite side of the field. The exhausted but valiant Rhode Islanders lacked the strength to follow and remained at the wood line, satisfied with their heroic struggle.[35]

The next move belonged to General Averell, who continued to hold a number of favorable cards in his hand. He still had numerical superiority, including ample reserves and unused men. Furthermore, Fitz Lee's cavalry had spent itself in charging against its opponent, thus leaving Breathed's pieces at the mercy of the enemy. At least Henry McClellan saw it that way. Averell's decision was greatly swayed by a supposed report "that [Confederate] infantry had been seen at a distance to my right, moving toward my rear, and the cars could be heard running on the road in rear of the enemy, probably bringing re-enforcements." Thus Averell concluded: "It was 5:30 P.M., and it was necessary to advance my cavalry upon their intrenched positions, to make a direct and desperate attack, or to withdraw across the river. Either operation would be attended with imminent hazard. My horses were exhausted. We had been successful thus far. I deemed it proper to withdraw." Averell sent orders to pull back across the Rappahannock. Although most of Fitz Lee's men watched as the Federals retreated, Breathed's gunners continued to pelt the Federals until they were out of range. One newspaper account, with some metaphorical exaggeration, compared the Federal retreat to "whipped curs [returning] to their kennels."[36]

Casualties in the opposing cavalries that day offer testimony to the closeness of the contest. Averell stated in his post-battle report that he suffered an aggregate loss of eighty men (killed, wounded, captured, and missing). Fitz Lee, conversely, broke down his losses as "11 killed, 88 wounded, and 34 taken prisoners," totaling 133. He further noted the severity in loss of horses as 170: "71 killed, 87 wounded, 12 captured." Of course, both generals tended to exaggerate the casualties of their opponent. Averell estimated the Confederate losses as "over 200." Lee labeled the enemy casualties as "heavy," further noting the capture of 29 prisoners, including a captain and two lieutenants.[37]

Quite naturally, the commanders from both cavalries viewed the outcome of the battle differently. Confederate leaders saw an enemy, better equipped and nearly three times the number of their own, advance little more than a mile, fight a one-day battle, and ignominiously retreat at nightfall without any substantial gain. Nothing there to boast about. Referring to the Federals as an "insolent foe," Jeb Stuart called it a "signal victory" and gave high marks to Fitz Lee and his brigade of horsemen. In his view the enemy tucked tail and fled "broken and demoralized . . . having abandoned in defeat an expedition undertaken with boasting and vainglorious demonstration." Stuart closed with the stirring commentary: "Commanders will take care to record while fresh in their memories the instances of personal heroism for future use, and the brigade will have the [battle] of Kellysville inscribed on its banner as its greatest achievement."[38]

Four days following the battle Fitz Lee issued General Orders No. 10, an emotive harangue that tore into the Federals while lauding his own troopers. Although he neglected to use the word "victory" anywhere in the order, he offered "his high gratification and proud appreciation" for his men's "heroic achievements." He accused the "(would-be) horsemen" of Averell's cavalry of invading Southern soil for "infamous purposes"—"to burn, rob, and devastate . . . the property of our peaceful citizens," thus committing their "customary depredations." The Federal aims failed, however, since in his evangelical view they confronted "the holiest cause that ever nerved the arm of a freeman or fired the breast of a patriot." He commended his brigade, which "taught" the Yankees a lesson and thanked his own horsemen who "taught" "certain sneerers in our army that placing a Southern soldier on horseback does not convert him into a coward." He also applauded "Captain Breathed and his brave artillerists" who "behaved, as they always do, with great gallantry."[39]

General Averell perceived the struggle at Kelly's Ford as more of a morale booster than a military triumph. "The principle [sic] result," noted Averell in his post-battle commentary, "has been that our cavalry has been brought to feel their superiority in battle, they have learned the value of discipline and the use of their arms." He closed boastfully, "I believe it is the universal desire of the officers and men of my division to meet the enemy again as soon as possible." Averell's declaration contained some truth, but he could take little solace from the berating later given him by his own commanding general, Joseph Hooker. Claiming "the enemy was inferior . . . in all respects," Hooker believed that Averell "could easily have routed [the Confederates] . . . and inflicted a severe blow upon him." As to Averell's conviction that Confederate infantry would soon appear, Hooker labeled it "imaginary apprehensions" and rated Averell's conduct as "very unsatisfactory."[40] Perhaps Hooker and Averell could have found common ground and a reason to gloat had either of them known that John Pelham was severely injured and barely alive as the battle ended.

⁓

Toward late afternoon near Brandy Station Harry Gilmor observed the two men he had placed in charge of Pelham's body—the same two he had instructed to find a surgeon and an ambulance. Pelham's body had been somewhat carelessly slung, facedown, over the withers of the black mare, arms dangling on one side, legs on the other. Clotted blood and splotches of dried mud masked his normally handsome features. Congealed blood also stained and matted his fine, blond hair and covered his hands. The two soldiers walked rather nonchalantly on either side of Pelham's horse, their pace indicating no emergency. Infuriated by what he saw, Gilmor put spurs to his horse, rode furiously up to the two men, and demanded an explanation for their seeming indifference to his earlier orders. "Imagine my indignation and vented wrath," he later wrote, "when I learned that, instead of looking for an ambulance, they had moved on toward Culpeper, a distance of eight miles, four of which they had already accomplished." Gilmor ordered Pelham's body lifted from the back of the horse and laid gently in the grass of a fence corner. Then bending over the stricken warrior, Gilmor made an astonishing observation that nearly took his own breath away—John Pelham was still alive. Immediately Gilmor summoned an ambulance.[41]

One of those assisting in obtaining an ambulance and helping place Pelham inside was Private Joseph Minghini, serving temporarily as a courier for Jeb Stuart. Once Stuart had heard of the wounding, he directed Minghini to find Pelham and aid in removing his body from the field. Minghini arrived and found Pelham breathing shallowly but miraculously clinging to life. It was quickly decided that Pelham should be taken to Culpeper to Judge Henry Shackelford's house for medical assistance. Pelham was carefully placed inside the ambulance, and the slow trek over painfully bottomless roads commenced. Word of the tragedy was sent ahead so that Bessie and her family could prepare for the arrival. An emergency stop was made along the way at the home of Dr. William A. Herndon, who would travel with the others to the Shackelford home. Undoubtedly, Minghini also sent notice to Stuart that Pelham remained alive.[42]

Back at the Shackelford house Bessie, her sisters, and parents made ready for Pelham. The parlor on the lower floor had been prepared—wash basins, clean cloths, hot water, flannel, bandages, and a bottle of brandy all placed at the bedside. Three surgeons, all sent by Stuart, were on their way. The war had brought untold sorrow and grief to families throughout the nation, but the Shackelfords had thus far escaped the personal sadness and tragedy. Now, teary eyes and choked-back emotion greeted the ambulance at the door of their home. Gentle hands removed Pelham from the vehicle and carried him slowly to the awaiting room. Looking down at the stricken officer, still covered with the gore of his wound, it was hard to imagine that only yesterday he had graced the household with his charm and vibrancy.

Bessie immediately took charge and instructed her sisters, who labored over the still unconscious Pelham. They undressed his body and tenderly washed the mud and blood from his face and hands. Carefully they wrapped his feet and hands in flannel. Some brandy was poured down his throat. The trio of surgeons soon arrived and examined the wound and the extent of the damage. Harry Gilmor stood silently in the room and watched the doctors perform their tasks. "The piece of shell that struck him," Gilmor later wrote, "was not larger than the end of my little finger. It entered just at the curl of the hair on the back of the head, raked through the skull without even piercing the brain, coming out two inches below the point where it entered. The skull was badly shattered between the entrance and exit of the shell." The minute particle of Hotchkiss shell, spinning furiously, had hit the area of the hairline, shattering the bone, and then continued twisting before exiting at the base of the neck. Somehow it had avoided contact with the brain but possibly did fatal injury to the nerves and spinal column. The surgeons gently extracted pieces of Pelham's skull from the wound. "I selected one [of the pieces of skull]," stated Gilmor, "as a memento of one of the most gallant and highly-esteemed officers of the Southern army." The doctors concurred that Pelham's chances of survival were "hopeless," what everyone in the room knew but prayed was not so.[43]

The doctors packed their medical gear and departed. By candlelight, Bessie and Gilmor stood vigil over Pelham, who continued to breathe with some effort. Members of the Shackelford family as well as other friends periodically stepped into the room. Midnight came and went, and still Pelham survived. Nearly an hour later, on Wednesday, March 18, Pelham opened his eyes, looked toward Gilmor with "an unconscious look," and "drew [in] a long breath." He exhaled slowly, closed his eyes, and died peacefully. After the others had left the room Bessie and Gilmor removed Pelham's bloodstained garments and replaced them with a fresh uniform. When they finished their somber task, they sat silent in the nearly dark room.[44]

At about 2:00 A.M. the door opened slowly. Both Bessie and Gilmor peered up to observe Jeb Stuart entering the room. "With measured step, his black plumed hat in hand," wrote H. H. Matthews, "he approached the body, looked long and silently upon the smiling face, his eyes full of tears; then stooping down he pressed his bearded lips to the marble brow. As he did so the breast of the great Stuart was shaken, a sob issued from his lips, and a tear fell on the pale cheek of Pelham. Severing from his forehead a lock of the light hair, he turned away, and as he did so there was heard in low, deep tones, which seemed to force their way through tears, the single word, 'Farewell.'" Stuart withdrew, never again to see the remains of his close friend. That night Gilmor volunteered to stay in the parlor next to Pelham. Gilmor admitted that the long, arduous day had left him "exhausted with fatigue" and that he slept soundly on the floor "beside the mortal remains of a companion who had ridden to the field that morning in unusually fine spirits." But Gilmor added almost blithely, "such is the fortune of war."[45]

23
"I Want Jimmie to Be Just Like Him"

Had he been spared, another great battle would have made him a General,
I think.

—Channing Price

The tragic news of John Pelham's death reached Camp No-Camp approximately
an hour before daybreak when a courier sent by Jeb Stuart galloped in with the
painful information.[1] With little fanfare and "much agitation of manner," according to Heros von Borcke, the rider sadly stated that Pelham was dead. Some
of the details were given to the startled onlookers. For many the announcement
struck like a lightning bolt, as they blankly stared into space. A few of Pelham's
gunners openly wept without shame. Others, however, hesitated to believe that the
handsome young man, who in so many perilous situations had never once been
touched by enemy fire, could now be gone. Most were left to their own thoughts
of how only a few hours earlier Pelham had vibrantly strolled through the camp,
smiling and laughing. "His death created the most profound grief throughout the
army and country," noted one Confederate officer. Artillerist George W. Shreve
agreed: "[Pelham's] death cast a great gloom over us, and we seemed to realize that
no one could fill his place, so brilliantly as he had done."[2] Undoubtedly, many conjured up past events of which Pelham had been such a part. Von Borcke expressed
his own notions of the mood in camp:

> This sad intelligence spread through the whole camp in a few minutes, and
> the impression of melancholy sorrow it produced on all is beyond descrip-
> tion, so liked and admired had Pelham been, and so proud were we of his
> gallantry. One after the other, comrades entered my tent to hear the confir-
> mation of the dreadful news, which everybody tried as long as possible not
> to credit. Couriers and negroes assembled outside, all seemingly paralysed
> by the sudden and cruel calamity; and when morning came, instead of the
> usual bustling activity and noisy gaiety, a deep and mournful silence reigned
> throughout the encampment. I was much touched by the behaviour of Pelham's
> negro servants, Willis and Newton, who, with tokens of the greatest distress,
> begged to be allowed at once to go and take charge of their master's body—a
> permission which I was, however, constrained to refuse.[3]

That same day Channing Price penned a hurried note to his mother: "I have just time to write a few lines to give you some sad news. . . . the Yankees crossed at Kelly's ford and were met by Gens. Stuart & Fitz Lee with part of the latter's brigade: they were repulsed with heavy loss at dark, but poor Pelham was killed." Three days later Price wrote a longer letter to his mother in which he restated his gloom. In part, it read: "It is very dull & quiet at Hd. Qrs., only Capt. [Benjamin Stephen] White, Chiswell [Dabney], Thomas [Price], Capt. [John Esten] Cooke, Frank Robertson & myself being here, and over us all, in spite of the hard-heartedness which war produces, a feeling of gloom is hanging, caused by the loss of one to whom all were so much attached."[4]

John Esten Cooke, in his war journal, wrote: "I have not had the heart to continue this journal from day to day. Poor Pelham is dead—killed in that terrific fight in Culpepper [sic]. It cast a shadow over me which I could not dispel, and is a mournful thought still. He was a brave noble fellow, and I had learned to love him. So we pass." In his sorrow W. W. Blackford confined himself to his tent—the same tent he had so often shared with Pelham. Sadly, Blackford speculated what might have saved his friend from the tragedy on March 17. "If Pelham had stayed for breakfast at headquarters or at the horse artillery camp as he intended; if the locomotive had not come for the ammunition; if Pelham had not gotten a horse; and if his friend had not sent him to the rear as he did, Pelham would not have lost his life when he did. What a pity it was that none of these things had happened differently."[5] So shaken was Blackford that he did not mention Pelham again in his writings.

Perhaps the one soldier in the entire Army of Northern Virginia who would miss Pelham the most was Jeb Stuart. More than a friend and a protégé, Pelham had been Stuart's most consistent warrior in scores of actions, large and small. From its inception the horse artillery had skillfully and prudently allowed Stuart's cavalry to maneuver, thrust, and even escape from countless perilous situations. As the most unique branch of the cavalry, the horse artillery could always be counted on to perform above and beyond expectations. It brought accolades, distinction, and positive headlines to Stuart, who at times irresistibly relished hogging the spotlight. Yet the cavalry chieftain willingly praised his subordinates with unabashed pride. Stuart certainly recognized Pelham's accomplishments and boasted to anyone within shouting distance of the limitless talents possessed by his young gunner. Now that significant cog in Stuart's success was gone, snuffed out from a freakish wound to the back of the head by a tiny shell fragment. Stuart, however devastated, was allowed little time for sorrow. As a professional soldier he had steeled himself somewhat against such tragedies, including the loss of his four-year-old daughter only four months earlier. Presently he needed to muster his own courage and maintain his role as leader of the cavalry.

Before dawn a weary Stuart penned a brief but heartfelt note to the Honorable J. L. M. Curry, congressman of Alabama: "The noble, the chivalric, the gallant

Pelham is no more. He was killed in action yesterday. His remains will be sent to you today. How much he was beloved, appreciated and admired, let the tears of agony we have shed, and the gloom of mourning throughout my command, bear witness. His loss to the country is irreparable."[6]

Stuart had already made provisions for Pelham's body to be displayed in Richmond before being returned to his native soil in Alabama. Placed in a plain wooden box, Pelham's remains were carried aboard a railroad car in Culpeper. From there the train would proceed to Gordonsville and southeast to Hanover Junction before heading south to Richmond, a journey of roughly one hundred miles. That same morning Stuart wired Heros von Borcke to depart Camp No-Camp and head south by train from Fredericksburg to Hanover Junction to meet up with the railroad carrying Pelham. Von Borcke would escort Pelham's body into the capital city and make the necessary preparations for its journey farther south. Taking his responsibilities with the utmost seriousness, von Borcke immediately left camp and arrived at Hanover Junction in time to overtake the train carrying Pelham. The Prussian found several corpses all enclosed in crude wooden boxes in the baggage car, but only Pelham's was guarded by a solitary soldier who stood at attention nearby. Von Borcke described the nameless soldier as "one of our artillerymen, who, with tears in his eyes, gave me the particulars of his gallant commander's death."[7]

Von Borcke telegraphed ahead to the authorities at Richmond, requesting a hearse be readied to transport Pelham's body to the capitol. Then the train slowly began its last leg of the journey, a twenty-five-mile stretch to Richmond. Arriving at the station on the northwest corner of Eighth and Broad streets late at night, von Borcke was much chagrined to find no hearse awaiting nor any official to assist him. Consequently, he gathered some help at the station and hauled the wooden crate onto "a common one-horse wagon." Von Borcke set out immediately to find Governor John Letcher, "who kindly afforded all the assistance in his power, and placed a room at my disposal in the Capitol, where the Confederate Congress held its sessions." Once removed from the wagon, the crude casket was borne into the building and placed in the center of the room. The deep-blue Virginia state flag was draped over the box, and a guard of honor stood at attention nearby. There the remains of John Pelham stayed for the night.

The following day, March 19, von Borcke obtained "a handsome iron coffin." As he helped transfer Pelham's corpse, von Borcke was much "overcome with grief as I touched the lifeless hand that had so often pressed mine in the grasp of friendship." The big Prussian trembled as he sadly noted "[Pelham's] manly features [which] even in death expressed that fortitude and pride which distinguished him." Von then ordered a small glass window to be placed in the coffin over Pelham's face so that his numerous admirers "might take a last look at the young hero."

Pelham's body was moved into the center of the Capitol building and lay beneath the gigantic statue of George Washington for the next thirty-six hours. Mourners came "in troops," according to von Borcke, "the majority being ladies, who brought garlands and magnificent bouquets to lay upon the coffin." John Esten Cooke reported that "some tender hand deposited an evergreen wreath, intertwined with white flowers, upon the case that contained all that was mortal of the fallen hero."[8] For hours soldiers and civilians, young and old, rich and poor, black and white, filed slowly past the plain casket to pay their last respects. One saddened onlooker, known merely as Evelyn, touchingly described the scene:

> I have just returned from the Capitol, and with saddened spirit sit down and write of the dear dead boy now lying there—Alabama's noblest tribute of the whole war. His coffin stands in the hall, upon a pedestal arranged for the purpose. A sentinel passes backwards and forwards beside it. Upon the top are the flags he fought so bravely to sustain; and upon them a mourning wreath of evergreens. Beside it—just over the manly heart, now stilled forever—lies a single snow-white flower. The other prospect is mournful enough, and with moistened eyes a little party of Alabamians gaze upon it. The flag is removed, and there—dear God! I can hardly write it for the blinding tears—there lies the body of my darling friend—noble, noble Pelham! Stiff and stark in death, the loved face white and cold, the same sad smile lingering upon his beautiful lips.[9]

One correspondent estimated that Pelham's body was "visited by most of the ladies in Richmond." At least three young ladies appeared in totally black mourning clothes. One of these, an attractive woman in her mid-twenties, calmly entered the room and knelt beside the casket. Tears fell from her eyes as she prayed silently, her lips barely moving. Only a few in the room would recognize her as Sallie Dandridge, who had bravely made her way through Federal lines to be with her fiancé.[10]

Later that same day, Stuart penned a letter to Flora, "My Darling One," in which he announced the results of the Battle of Kelly's Ford and the loss of Pelham.

> God has preserved me through another conflict and crowned us with victory. Averell's Division on a raid was whipped back with terrible loss by Fitz Lee's Brigade on the 17th. The noble Pelham and Major Puller of the 5th Virginia Cavalry were killed; Colonel T. L. Rosser, 5th Virginia Cavalry severely wounded, though remaining in command of his regiment to the close of the fight, and about 100 killed, wounded and missing.
>
>   Major Pelham's body was sent to Richmond to be sent to his friends. You must know how his death distressed me.

Pelham's untimely death evidently reminded Stuart of his own vulnerability in wartime for he added a maudlin comment, underlining certain words for emphasis:

"I shall religiously observe your wishes respecting ours in case I should survive you, which is so extremely improbable, but I wish an assurance on your part in the other event of your surviving me, that <u>you will make the land for which I gave my life your home, and keep my offspring on southern soil</u> . . . don't stay an instant where you are not contented; there is the whole Confederacy before you and I desire you to seek contentment."[11]

In another letter, possibly composed that day, Stuart wrote of his sadness concerning Pelham's death to his cousin Nannie Price back at Dundee: "To behold that calm sweet face that so quickened at the battle cry in its last moments of consciousness now cold in the sleep of death, wrings tears from the most obdurate."[12]

Still on that Thursday, Commanding General Robert E. Lee sent a somber memo to Confederate president Jefferson Davis: "I mourn the loss of Major Pelham. I had hoped that a long career of usefulness and honor was still before him. He has been stricken down in the midst of both, and before he could receive the promotion he had richly won. I hope there will be no impropriety in presenting his name to the Senate, that his comrades may see that his services have been appreciated, and may be incited to emulate them."[13] Meanwhile Heros von Borcke dutifully fulfilled his obligation in preparing the return of John Pelham's body to his native Alabama for burial. The Prussian tactfully sought the advice of various Alabama members of the Confederate Congress, all friends of Atkinson Pelham, concerning the details. Collectively they decided that "a young soldier, a connection of the family, who had just been released from one of the Richmond hospitals" would officially accompany the remains to their homeland. At 5:00 P.M. the following day, March 20, the coffin was removed from the Capitol and carefully hauled to the Richmond & Danville Railroad Station on Hull Street. At least one remembered the passing of Pelham's coffin: "Far down the street . . . we heard the tramp, tramp, of many feet and the unearthly, mournful sound of the dead march. We knew what it was. They were bearing to his resting place the 'gallant Pelham.' . . . We watched the sad procession file past the door and the music floated to our ears like the wail of a human voice. We wept in sympathy—for one so brave, so young, so fair." A sizable crowd gathered, and with the Richmond battalion of infantry in the lead as an honor guard, the procession slowly moved toward the railroad platform. Without fanfare the body was placed inside one of the cars, and the train began its journey.[14]

Nine different trains traversing four states carried Pelham's body home.[15] The Richmond & Danville Railroad took Pelham southwestward to Burkeville, Virginia, a distance of roughly fifty miles, where it arrived early that evening. Changing cars at Burkeville, the Southside Railroad headed slightly northwest across the High Bridge over the Appomattox River and on through Farmville and Appomattox Station westward to Lynchburg, nearly sixty miles away. It arrived there around midnight. At Lynchburg the Virginia & Tennessee Railroad carried the sad cargo southwestward across the Blue Ridge Mountains to the border town of Bristol,

Tennessee, adding almost another two hundred miles. The train pulled into the station at Bristol on Sunday, March 22. The East Tennessee & Virginia Railroad cut through the eastern part of the state, approximately one hundred miles, to Knoxville. Once again changing cars, the East Tennessee & Georgia Railroad moved southwestward, another hundred miles, to Chattanooga. The darkness of the town was accentuated by the midnight entrance and the surrounding mountains casting deep shadows. Passing into Georgia, the Western & Atlantic Railroad traveled a hundred miles through Dalton and Cartersville on its way to Atlanta. Another eighty miles aboard the Atlanta & West Point Railroad carried the remains to the border community station at West Point.

The varying railroad gauges allowed no transfer at West Point so the body most likely was placed aboard a ferry to cross the Chattahoochee River, the boundary between Georgia and Alabama. Once across the river it was transported by wagon to the Montgomery & West Point Railroad, where it headed to the state capital at Montgomery, a distance of about eighty miles. A large crowd, including Governor Andrew B. Moore, silently awaited the arrival of the train at the station. Removed from the train, the casket was taken to the capitol building under a special military guard and carried to the second floor of the Alabama Supreme Court chamber. A fresh state flag was then draped over the casket and substantial quantities of flowers were carefully placed in the solemn chamber. When all was ready, lines of people patiently entered one door of the room, slowly walked past and viewed the remains of John Pelham, and exited through the opposite doorway. Finally, the doors were shut and a silent sentinel stood guard over the body for the remainder of March 26.

Later the casket was carried down to the Alabama River for the journey to Selma, a distance of fifty-five miles. When the steamboat reached Selma about daybreak, a procession of nine men, led by John Pelham's uncle, Judge Thomas Walker, as well as the city's mayor and a Presbyterian minister, made their way aboard the vessel. The six selected pallbearers who came next then lifted the casket and carried it to the station of the Alabama & Tennessee Rivers Railroad. There a solid hour or more elapsed as the expected train was late, but the additional time gave the crowd that had gathered a chance to view Pelham's face through the glass plate. "He seemed to be asleep," wrote the poet James Ryder Randall, who looked on. "The face was statuesque and unharmed. There was a lovely smile around his lips, and the half-opened eyes." The last leg of the railroad journey, a slow and painful one of more than 130 miles, headed back to the northeast through Talladega to the remote station at Blue Mountain. This stretch of the trip seemed even longer as large crowds delayed the train in every town along the way. "Alabama paid as solemn a tribute of respect to her gallant son," penned von Borcke, "as he deserved to have shown him. As soon as the frontier of the State was reached, a guard of honour escorted the coffin, and at every station on the road ladies were waiting to adorn it with flowers."[16] Pelham's body was removed from the train at 10:00 P.M. on Saturday, March 28. Strong but gentle hands lifted the casket from the railroad car and delicately placed it in an awaiting hearse. As soon as the somber task was accomplished, four snow-white horses began to pull the hearse toward the Pelham homestead, seven miles distant, over dirt roads, where his many relatives and friends awaited his arrival.

～

On the same day Pelham's funeral train pulled out of the Richmond railroad station, Jeb Stuart dictated to his adjutant, Channing Price, General Orders No. 9, a statement officially announcing Pelham's death to the entire cavalry division. It praised the deceased officer's accomplishments and noble character, and proclaimed that the horse artillery and all staff officers would wear a black armband for the next thirty days:

> The major-general commanding approaches with reluctance the painful duty of announcing to the division its irreparable loss in the death of Maj. John Pelham, commanding the Horse Artillery. He fell mortally wounded in the battle of Kellysville, March 17, with the battle cry on his lips and the light of victory beaming from his eye.
>
> To you, his comrades, it is needless to dwell upon what you have so often witnessed, his prowess in action, already proverbial. You well know how, though young in years, a mere stripling in appearance, remarkable for his genuine modesty of deportment, he yet disclosed on the battlefield the conduct of a veteran, and displayed in his handsome person the most imperturbable coolness in danger.
>
> His eye glanced over every battlefield of this army from the first Manassas to the moment of his death, and he was, with a single exception, a brilliant actor in all.
>
> The memory of "the gallant Pelham," his many manly virtues, his noble nature and purity of character, are enshrined as a sacred legacy in the hearts of all who knew him. His record has been bright and spotless, his career brilliant and successful. He fell—the noblest of sacrifices—on the altar of his country, to whose glorious service he had dedicated his life from the beginning of the war.
>
> In token of respect for his cherished memory, the Horse Artillery and division staff will wear the military badge of mourning for thirty days—and the senior officer of staff, Major Von Borcke, will place his remains in the possession of his bereaved family—to whom is tendered in behalf of the division the assurance of heartfelt sympathy in this deep tribulation. In mourning his departure from his accustomed post of honor on the field, let us strive to imitate his virtues, and trust that what is loss to us may be more than gain to him.[17]

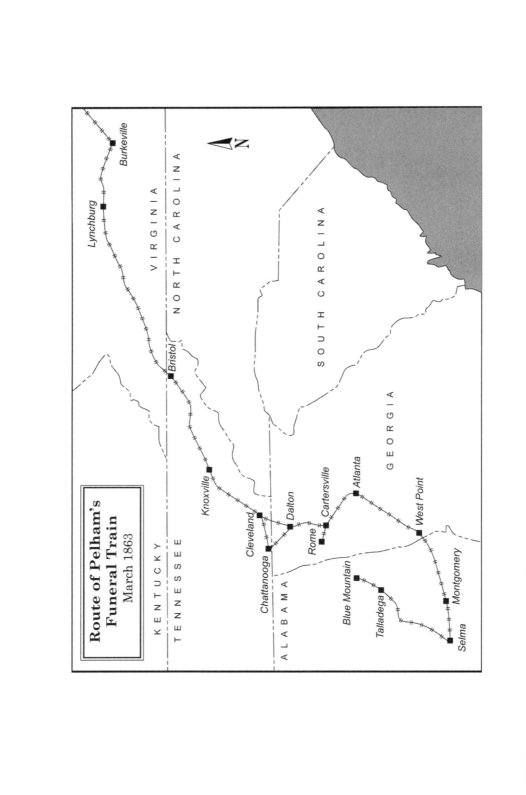

Route of Pelham's
Funeral Train
March 1863

Robert E. Lee endorsed General Orders No. 9 with the brief comment, "Respectfully forwarded for the information of the Department. I feel deeply the loss of the noble dead, and heartily concur in the commendation of the living." Seven days beyond the fighting at Kelly's Ford, the commanding general wrote his brother, Charles Carter Lee, concerning the battle and the loss of Pelham: "Genl Hooker . . . threw his Cavy over Kellys ford. . . . Fitz Lee & his Brigade behaved admirably, & though greatly outnumbered Stuck to the enemy with a tenacity that Could not be shaken off. . . . Fitz did not have with him more than 800. But I grieve over our noble dead! I do not know how I Can replace the gallant Pelham. So young So true So brave. Though stricken down in the dawn of manhood, his is the glory of duty done!"[18]

The next day Stuart rode to Richmond. "Still deeply affected by the loss of his young friend," according to von Borcke, "[Stuart] greatly grieved that he had not been able to attend the funeral ceremonies." Days would pass before Stuart, so sobered by the loss, could muster the strength to write his condolences to Pelham's parents. The cavalry chieftain did, however, send word to John Mosby that briefly told of his sorrow. "I send you an order about our fight at Kellysville," noted Stuart. "It was a hard fight, and a glorious one for us, but the loss of the 'gallant Pelham' has thrown a shadow of gloom over us not soon to pass away." He added succinctly, "Beckham will succeed him."[19]

A full moon helped guide the horses pulling the hearse that carried John Pelham's body over the country roads to the doorstep of the homestead. Mrs. Peter Pelham, John's sister-in-law, who had witnessed his last departure from the house months earlier, poignantly described the scene:

I was in that same home the night his body was brought in in its casket. He had been dead two weeks and the news of his death had gone all over his native County. And they came, old men (the young ones were all at the front) and women, young ladies and children from all over that Country to meet and honor the remains of one so loved and admired. It was a beautiful moonlight night the last of March, and as the casket, covered with white flowers (which had been put on it as the body lay in state in Richmond and then in Montgomery Ala) and borne by white haired old men, followed by girls with uncovered heads, to us who stood in the porch at his home waiting for their coming, it seemed a Company "all in white." And I heard a voice near me say, "made white in the blood of the lamb" and I knew it to be the voice of his Mother.

The Father and Sister were crushed and in sorrow kept their rooms, but that Spartan Mother met her beloved dead on the threshold as she would have done had he been living and led the way into the parlor and directed

where he must be laid where the light would fall on his face when Sunday
came. . . . All day Sunday his dear body lay in the old home and hundreds
came and looked on the quiet face so like life, asleep.[20]

A committee of friends and townspeople met on the morning of Monday, March
30, in the Jacksonville courthouse to arrange the funeral proceedings. Colonel John
R. Clark presided, and John D. Hoke, acting as secretary, recorded the motions entertained and decisions made. Eight pallbearers were selected: William H. Flem-
ming, J. B. Forney, J. H. Wright, W. F. Bush, B. C. Wyly, T. N. Auglin, G. B.
Douthit, and Dr. J. C. Francis. Colonel J. H. Caldwell would serve as honorary
marshal. Chancellor Foster was chosen to deliver the eulogy. The committee further resolved the order of the exercises at the church with the eulogy coming first,
followed by the intercessional, religious exercises, and procession of mourners. Secretary Hoke meticulously listed the order of the funeral procession: "1. Remains of
the deceased with pallbearers, 2. Family and relatives, 3. The Clergy, 4. Officers and
soldiers of the army, 5. Teachers and pupils of the Female Academy, 6. Teachers and
pupils of the Male Academy, 7. Ladies, 8. Committee of Arrangements, 9. Grand
Jury and the Officers of the Court, 10. Citizens, 11. Carriages." The committee also
concurred that the secretary would send a copy of the proceedings of this meeting
for publication in the *Jacksonville Republican*.[21]

On Tuesday, March 31, the body was placed aboard an open wagon and transported to Jacksonville, nine miles from Pelham's birthplace, for the funeral. The
bright spring day brought out hundreds of mourners. So many people attended
that the services had to be moved from the smaller Presbyterian church to the larger
Baptist church to accommodate the sizable crowd. Pelham's sister-in-law later stated
that "the attendance was at that time the largest body of people ever seen together
in Jacksonville, Alabama." Many of Pelham's family and friends openly sobbed in
their bereavement during Reverend Smith's religious services. Afterward the body
was taken to the family plot at the town cemetery and slowly lowered into the
ground. Schoolchildren filled his grave with lilac blossoms before the caretakers
shoveled dirt upon the casket.[22]

Meanwhile, back in the campsites of Virginia, the name of John Pelham had
not been forgotten. John Esten Cooke remembered Stuart's moroseness when the
two of them sat in Cooke's tent and discussed their departed friend: "The Gen.
came back yesterday and had a talk with him today—he wanted to show me his
general order upon poor Pelham's death. It is very excellent: terse and eloquent: in
a style which the Gen. is the best hand at, of any one I ever knew. His face flushed
as he read it—poor Pelham!" Three days later Cooke demonstrated his own sorrow
as he continued writing in his journal in a broken fashion: "Dined with the Gen.
Chat about many things—read me his verse on 'Dundee,' and yesterday on poor

Pelham. He gave me my poor friend's saddle. Yesterday I wrote an obituary, which with the Gen.'s verses, and general order will appear in the 'Sentinel.' He sent it. I wrote an outline about P.[Pelham] for the News, but threw it out, to rewrite. . . . Today (Sunday) after reading my bible [*sic*]—old testament—came to the resolution to kill one Yankee at least with my own hand if possible, before I am killed or the war over. . . . I am writing away as though in the 'little room festooned with roses!' Just read 'Pelham'—good."[23]

Late in March a heartfelt letter arrived at the Pelham residence addressed to Martha from Mrs. William Herndon, the wife of the doctor who attended Pelham before he died:

> Although we are strangers to each other I feel an ardent desire to write to you & tell you that we knew & loved your noble son, the late Major John Pelham. We have known him for twelve months, he was often at our house *&* was beloved by every member of the household—he was brought to this place after he was wounded, was carried to Mr. Henry Shackelfords. Dr. Herndon was sent for to see him & every thing was done for him that could be but death soon claimed him & the demand was irrevocable—he was to see us the Sabbath before he was killed & was so full of hope & life—. His manly image is deeply engraved in our memories & we can never forget him. With best wishes for you & your family, I am yours Mrs. Herndon.[24]

Understandably, Stuart appeared somewhat reluctant to write his feelings to Atkinson and Martha Pelham, knowing fully that the parents of John Pelham suffered more intensely from the death of their son than did he. Nevertheless, he sat down on March 29 to pen his grief to the mournful couple in an earnest letter addressed to Atkinson:

> Hd Qrs Cav Division A. of N. Va.
> March 29, 1863
>
> My dear Sir—
> With the deepest grief, I approach a subject which has doubtless brought to your household sorrowful wailing. I refer to the death of your son—my comrade—<u>friend all</u> but brother,—John Pelham who was to me as a younger brother—whose place on my staff—at my fireside—in my Division—but most of all at the head of the corps to which his genius has imparted so much efficiency and fame—the Horse Artillery—is vacant,—and the vacancy sends pangs to my heart that knew him, and in the space elapsed, a nation's wail is heard from out yon capitol, mourning her lost hero—so noble—so chivalrous—so pure—<u>so beloved.</u>

I know that man's sympathy is emptiness, to one who has lost as you have, the promise and hope of a noble son—but when I tell you, <u>I loved him as a brother,</u> you will permit me to share with you a grief so sacred, so consoling.

He has won a name immortal on earth, and in heaven he will reap the rewards of a pure and guileless heart. I attended church with him the sabbath preceding his death, and marked his close attention to the Word: often have I seen him reading the Sacred volume, and I doubt not in its Sacred truths the young soldier founded a hope of a bright immortality above.

If you would know his military exploits, (and I know he was too modest ever to have informed you) read my official reports since the commencement of the war, <u>these are his biography,</u> and had he lived he would have risen to the highest honors in the nation.

Major Pelham lost his life in the battle of Kellysville on the 17th inst in the <u>strict</u> and <u>legitimate</u> discharge of his duty—with no display of <u>rashness</u> and <u>excessive zeal</u> as some have insinuated—but displaying the same coolness and selfpossession for which he had always been distinguished.

I enclose his ring for his mother, it was taken from his finger at the time of his death, and as he has often made allusion to this ring, I am anxious to commit it to her charge.

A tribute to his memory, sent by my staff, who loved him dearly, to the Richmond papers will I trust accompany this letter—together with some verse, and General Division orders announcing his death. His remains were sent to you in charge of his cousin and I hope have reached you.

His trunk with its contents just as he left it, his sabre, two servants, and two horses, awaiting your orders as to their disposition.

In conclusion let me beg of you a favor to send over any photograph or daguerreotype you may have of our dear departed comrade and friend, in order that I may have it copied, to keep as a precious token, to recall in future years his noble face.

I shall be glad to hear from you, and will cheerfully render you any service in my power.

Most Respectfully
and truly yours
J. E. B. Stuart
Major Gen'l
Commanding[25]

Others continued to salute Pelham in their writings. Channing Price, much affected by Pelham's death, penned a sorrowful letter to his mother on March 30. Interestingly, Price's glowing tribute does not mention Pelham by name:

Major [Norman] FitzHugh will see to getting crape for the members of the division staff, which in accordance with our own wishes & Genl Orders announcing the death, we are to wear for 30 days in memory of the noble Chief of Artillery. I declare, nothing has happened in the progress of the war which I have felt more keenly than his death: although, like myself, not very demonstrative, he was sincerely attached to me I think, & I loved him almost like a brother. His was a noble character: such generosity & unselfishness I never saw in any man before & his dauntless personal courage is proverbial through our young Confederacy. Had he been spared, another great battle would have made him a General I think. But it was otherwise ordained & we must bow humbly & submissively to the decree which robs us of a cherished & loved companion & the service of one of its bravest & most devoted defenders. His successor is a very fine young man & capable officer.[26]

From his home in Alexandria, Alabama, Atkinson Pelham wrote a note to Stuart on April 4 offering a keepsake to the general:

Will Gen. J. E. B. Stuart please accept a trifling present from a berieved [sic] and afflicted family? A friend intended the enclosed Buttons as a present to our much lamented son John Pelham. I intended to have sent to him about this time. They are of no intrinsic value; I know of no one to whom he felt more indebted for kindness & friendship than yourself.

Accept the gratitude of myself & family for your kind & disinterested attentions to our lamented boy. May you be long & safely shielded & protected in this horrible war is the fervent & sincere wish of your friend & humble Servt.[27]

Stuart gladly received the mementos, and in an undated letter to his wife, he wrote of the present:

I send you to keep for me the sleeve buttons and studs sent me by Mr. Pelham—they were made originally for him [Pelham] but he was killed before they were sent thereupon his friends agreed that I should have them. I enclose his letter—you remember the studs I used to wear. I wish you would give them one each to Nannie, Lizzie & Ellen or substitute Jimmie for Lizzie if you choose it would suit for chemise.

The sleeve buttons are very pretty—show them at Dundee.[28]

Jeb again penned a lengthy letter, dated April 8, to his wife in which he mentioned numerous topics. But once more his thoughts drifted to his lost gunner, and he offered the most sublime compliment in reference to his own young son: "Poor Pelham's death has created a great sensation all over the country. He was noble in every sense of the word; I want Jimmie to be just like him."

In the same letter, under a section Stuart labeled "Strictly Private," he acknowledged his wife's delicate condition and the impending birth of their next child. In particular Jeb expressed his desire to name the baby, due in six months, after his departed friend:

> An important question—What shall it be named? Let us interchange views on the subject for it involves our own happiness as well as that of the individual immediately concerned.
>
> If a boy, I wish him to be called John Pelham Stuart. I have thought of it much—it is my choice. His record is complete and it is spotless. It is noble. His family was the very best. His character was pure, his disposition as sweet and innocent as our own little Flora's. You have no idea how I feel to know that if a boy, I will have an heir named John Pelham. Think of it, my darling. If a girl, name it Maria Pelham Stuart, and thus combine two lovely natures in the name of our little one. There never can be anything to regret in either case, and she or he will be grateful while she or he lives. I do not like the name Rachel—though I have tried to. Your Ma will be very far from expecting it. You should say "Ma, you were not with us."
>
> That is certainly argument enough.
>
> I go forth on the uncertain future; my sabre will not leave my hands for months. . . . It will be gratifying to me while living to know that you have respected my wishes, and it will console me in death to feel that the birthright and heritage I leave to you and mine will be preserved as I desired.[29]

Other tributes continued for John Pelham. Stuart memorialized Pelham's name by changing the name of Camp No-Camp to Camp Pelham. In a lengthy, but fitting, editorial the *Richmond Sentinel* highlighted Pelham's accomplishments, noting "there are few who have received a prouder fame or left a more enduring record." Referring to him as a "remarkable young officer," the *Sentinel* stated that "throughout his brief but brilliant career, [Pelham] displayed an inborn genius" and predicted "that career will remain one of the most arduous, splendid and glorious which the future historians of this war will be called upon to record." Even the foreign press mentioned his demise in glowing terms. On May 6 the *London Times* stated that the piece of shell that took his life "extinguished one of the purest and bravest spirits which have yet been yielded up in this desolating war. . . . But for the accidental and irreparable loss which the Confederates have sustained in Major Pelham, there would have been little occasion to waste ten words upon so feeble and abortive an attempt to lift the curtain upon the bloody drama of 1863."[30]

Thirty-five years after Pelham's death, cannoneer Philip Preston Johnston still remembered the image of Pelham and his significance to the Army of Northern Virginia: "I can recall, with some vividness, the light eyed, fair haired, smooth faced youth whose genius made him the intimate of Lee and Jackson, as well as Stuart. All who knew him, from the most diffident private to the commanding General loved him. Under his eye, with his example, men who had merely been good soldiers became great heroes equal to the highest achievement and in the heat of conflict his superiors accepted his suggestions as orders and he became the animating guiding spirit of the battle."[31]

Those who knew him best could not resist mentioning his name with reverence. Occasionally the notation might be terse, as John Esten Cooke wrote in his journal on April 22, "Poor, poor Pelham!" or even humorous, as when Cooke noted, "I wish what poor Pelham said of me was true—that he named his horse after me because all his spurring in battle couldn't hurry him." But for the most part the remembrances were heartfelt and sorrowful. Perhaps Cooke put it best when he wrote: "Shed no tears for Pelham! His death was noble, as his life was beautiful and beneficent. Fame crowned his boyish brow with that amaranthine wreath, the words of our great chieftain Lee; and he died, as he had lived, amid hearts who loved him as the pearl of chivalry and honor."[32]

No one is fool enough to choose war instead of peace, for in peace sons bury fathers, but war violates the order of nature and fathers bury sons.

—Herodotus

Appendix

The enactment of the United States Medal of Honor became official on July 12, 1862, when President Lincoln signed the bill to honor military and naval personnel for their individual valor during the Civil War. Over two thousand such medals were handed out in the ensuing years, many given for acts less than heroic by later standards.

The Confederate Medal of Honor, officially adopted in 1977, however, was awarded to merely fifty-six recipients from the rank of general to the lowest private. All of the Confederate medals were given for unquestionable acts of gallantry. For his valiant efforts on December 13, 1862, John Pelham would be awarded the Confederate Medal of Honor, albeit posthumously.

Pelham's decoration reads as follows:

Confederate Medal of Honor
CITATION
Major John Pelham
Stuart's Horse Artillery, C.S.A.
Battle of Fredericksburg, Virginia
13 December 1862

Advancing with just two guns—a Blakely rifle and 12-pounder Napoleon— Major Pelham flanked and surprised an advancing division of enemy infantry with a furious bombardment of solid shot. Retaliation brought the concentrated fire of five enemy batteries to his position but despite losing the Blakely early in the action, Major Pelham continued his attack with the single Napoleon, skillfully maneuvering the piece to take full advantage of the terrain. Although notified that he might withdraw whenever he saw fit, Major Pelham replied, "Tell the General I can hold my ground," and again shifted his position in the midst of a storm of exploding shellfire for a better vantage on the enemy. Despite the continued bombardment, Major Pelham ignored a second advisory to seek cover and instead, joined his men in serving the gun. Only when his ammunition had nearly been exhausted and a third message to seek cover reached him, did Major Pelham order a withdrawal, his section having single-handedly halted the advance of an enemy division for more than an hour. In witnessing this gallant action, the commanding General of the Army stated, "It is glorious to see such courage in one so young!"[1]

Abbreviations

ACPL   Anniston-Calhoun County Public Library, Anniston, Alabama.
ADAH   Alabama Department of Archives and History, Montgomery, Alabama.
B&L   *Battles and Leaders of the Civil War.* 4 vols. 1884. Reprint. New York: Castle Books, 1956.
BPL   Birmingham Public Library, Fred R. Martin Scrapbook Collection, Birmingham, Alabama.
DSFP   Douglas Southall Freeman Papers, Manuscript Division, Library of Congress, Washington, D.C.
JPL   Jacksonville Public Library, John Pelham Collection, Jacksonville, Alabama.
NAB   National Archives Building, Washington, D.C.
OR   U.S. War Department, *The War of the Rebellion: A Compilation of the Official Records of the Union and Confederate Armies.* 128 vols. Washington D.C., 1880–1901.
SHSP   *Southern Historical Society Papers.* 52 vols. Carmel, IN: Guild Press of Indiana, 1998.

Notes

Introduction

1. Adams, "Reminiscences of a Childhood Spent at Hayfield Plantation."
2. Lasswell, *Rags and Hope,* 81–82.

Chapter 1

1. Certain sources evidence discrepancies as to the actual date of birth. Philip Mercer's *Gallant Pelham,* 15, lists it as September 14. Interestingly, a plaque placed at the site of the original homestead also ascribes the fourteenth as the birthdate. However, the family Bible, as well as numerous family members, places it on September 7.

2. "Genealogy" (file #11) and an undated, unidentified author in the same file, "Yester-Years: John Pelham," JPL; "Gallant Pelham," Centenary 1838–1938, *Anniston Star,* September 18, 1938, BPL. See also Sergent, *Growing Up in Alabama,* 18; Mercer, *Gallant Pelham,* 13–14; Malone, *Dictionary of American Biography,* 14:408.

3. Charles Pelham to Edwin P. Cox, November 21, 1898, DSFP; Milham, *Gallant Pelham,* 12; Sergent, *Growing Up in Alabama,* 21.

4. Charles Pelham to Edwin P. Cox, November 21, 1898. Although various letters and sources give somewhat differing dates of births and deaths, these dates were taken from the tombstones in the Pelham family plot in Jacksonville, Alabama, as well as the family Bible. It has been stated that the marriage ceremony was performed by the governor of North Carolina, David L. Swain. However, knowing Atkinson Pelham's political staunchness as a Whig, it is unlikely that Swain, a Democrat, was even invited to the occasion.

5. Although all three photographs are undated, Atkinson appears to be about sixty years of age in the earlier one, a daguerreotype. This priceless photograph was discovered by Dan Sullivan, a grandson of William Pelham, in his attic at his home in Atlanta, Georgia. On the back, it is identified as "Dr. Atkinson Pelham." There is no date, but the dress is antebellum. The second Atkinson photograph belonged to Mary Pelham Graves. No identification exists, but comparison to the earlier one clearly indicates Atkinson as an older man. The Martha Pelham pose was found by Dan Sullivan in his attic as well. It, too, is identified as "Mrs. Atkinson Pelham." Pelham files, JPL.

6. "Genealogy" (folder II), JPL; *Anniston Star,* December 4, 1938, BPL; Mercer, *Gallant Pelham,* 15.

7. Charles Pelham to Edwin P. Cox, November 21, 1898. Mahlep, the birthplace home of John Pelham, stood for many years but burned down on March 25, 1985. Vogtsberger, *The Can-*

noneer 3, no. 6 (May 1985). Today a modest plaque indicates the site of the original home, but it incorrectly dates John's birth as September 14. Ironically, a nearby marker pointing curious tourists in the direction of the spot has the correct date of September 7.

8. Some sources use the spelling "Bettie," while at least one refers to Eliza as "Betsy."

9. Besides John, his five brothers served in the Fifty-first Alabama Cavalry. Brothers Charles and Peter joined first on March 26, 1862, enlisting in nearby Talladega. William later enlisted and was captured at Shelbyville, Tennessee, on June 27, 1863, and was sent to Johnson's Island Prison on Lake Erie on July 6, 1863. Samuel and Thomas served in the same unit, Thomas entering just before his fifteenth birthday. Not to be outdone, sister Eliza married a Confederate officer. "Genealogy" (folder II) and "Genealogy" (file #11); Mrs. John Williams, "The 'Gallant' John Pelham," JPL.

10. Milham, *Gallant Pelham,* 11. A photograph from the *Anniston Star,* 75th anniversary issue (1957), shows the old house, one-and-a-half stories with a large front porch. Around the building is a picket fence with a large oak tree to the left of the porch.

11. Peter Pelham's wife to Edwin P. Cox, [1898], DSFP.

12. Brother Peter Pelham's daughter once remarked, "None of the Pelhams could ever spell." Sergent, *Growing Up in Alabama,* 13.

13. Fred R. Martin, "Gallant Pelham," *Anniston Star,* and "Pelham's Boyhood and West Point Days," in "General Articles" file, JPL; *Anniston Star,* December 11, 1938, BPL; Hassler, *Col. John Pelham,* 2–3; Milham, *Gallant Pelham,* 15.

14. Milham, *Gallant Pelham,* 14.

15. Sergent, *Growing Up in Alabama,* 42–43.

16. Hassler, *Col. John Pelham,* 2–3.

17. Sergent, *Growing Up in Alabama,* 37. Jacob and Sabina Forney had four sons who fought for the Confederacy during the Civil War. John Forney, who graduated from West Point in the Class of 1852, taught infantry tactics at the academy in 1860 while Pelham was a cadet. Resigning from the army at the outbreak of the Civil War, John Forney joined the Confederacy and rose to the rank of major general. Surviving the war, he returned to Alabama where he died on September 13, 1902, at age seventy-three. William Henry Forney, John's older brother, suffered thirteen wounds during his service and was raised in rank to a brigadier general. He survived the war, served nearly twenty years in the U.S. House of Representatives, and died at age seventy on January 16, 1894. Both brothers are buried in Jacksonville. Bergeron, "John Horace Forney"; Sommers, "William Henry Forney"; Faust, *Encyclopedia of the Civil War,* 268–69.

18. Peter Pelham to Edwin P. Cox, November 25, 1898, DSFP. The ACPL contains in its collection John Pelham's authentic book *The Student's Manual: Designed by Specific Directions to Aid in Forming and Strengthening the Intellectual and Moral Character and Habits of the Student,* published in 1848 and written by the Reverend John Todd.

19. Thomas Benton Bush later attended a military school in Marietta, Georgia, while John Pelham set out for West Point. Bush commanded a company in an Alabama regiment and died in battle in Virginia early in the war. Charles Pelham to Edwin P. Cox, November 21, 1898.

20. "Youth" files, JPL. The mulatto domestic servant Myrian is sometimes referred to as Myrum.

21. Peter Pelham's wife to Edwin P. Cox, [1898].

22. John's mother, Martha, standing 5'9" tall, taught all her children to walk erect. Once, as a young girl, Martha overheard a comment that she "would be so much prettier if only she stood up to her fullest height," words she never forgot.

23. Statement made by Captain William Morrell McGregor in McLemore, "Reminiscences of Major John Pelham," 436; Sergent, *They Lie Forgotten,* 168.

24. Charles Pelham to Edwin P. Cox, November 21, 1898.

25. Schaff, *Old West Point,* 2.

26. "West Point" (file #2), JPL; Peter Pelham to Mrs. Oscar Twitty of Camille, Georgia, January 15, 1917, published in *The History of Mitchell County, Georgia* by Spence and Fleming, JPL. Controversy exists over who actually appointed John Pelham to West Point. A few sources credit J. L. M. Curry. Harris actually selected Pelham, but Curry succeeded Harris in 1857. Thereafter, Curry labeled young John as "his cadet." "U.S. Military Academy Cadet Application Papers, 1805–1866," microfilm, M688, roll 203, NAB; Martin, "Gallant Pelham" and "Pelham's Boyhood and West Point Days."

27. Sergent, *Growing Up in Alabama,* 52, 53; Atkinson Pelham to Jefferson Davis, March 18, 1856, microfilm, M688, roll 203, NAB; the letter is also in Pelham files, JPL.

28. Article written by an unknown friend of the Pelham boys in 1884 in BPL.

Chapter 2

1. Schaff, *Old West Point,* 15–16; Sergent, *They Lie Forgotten,* 75, 77; Wert, *Custer,* 28.

2. "West Point" file, JPL; Schaff, *Old West Point,* 38.

3. Born on a farm near Charlottesville, Virginia, on October 15, 1836, Tom Rosser was one of seven children. His family moved to Panola County, Texas, alongside the Sabine River in 1849, settling onto a 640-acre ranch. A contemporary described him as "a great, swarthy-looking cadet, who seemed altogether too big for his bobtailed coat and turned-over white collar." Sergent, *They Lie Forgotten,* 177.

4. Sergent, *They Lie Forgotten,* 29–30, 38; Schaff, *Old West Point,* 49.

5. Ambrose, *Crazy Horse and Custer,* 103; Waugh, *The Class of 1846,* 16; Sergent, *They Lie Forgotten,* 24, 113; Schaff, *Old West Point,* 104.

6. Ambrose, *Crazy Horse and Custer,* 102; "West Point" file; Sergent, *They Lie Forgotten,* 47, 37. Pelham and his sidekick Rosser racked up nearly the exact amount of demerits in their tenure at West Point, 550 and 547, respectively.

7. Bushong and Bushong, *Fightin' Tom Rosser,* 5.

8. Former cadet and future writer of lasting fame Edgar Allan Poe thought Benny Havens "the only congenial soul in the entire God-forsaken place." Waugh, *Class of 1846,* 37–38; Monaghan, *Custer,* 24.

9. When Pelham resigned in 1861, he carried Elderkin's photograph in his pocket. Vogtsberger, "The West Point John Pelham Knew," 11.

10. Sources vary on the spelling of Henry's first name, using either Mathias or Mathis. The Henry family prefers Mathis.

11. Prior to his death, Kirby expressed sorrow for his widowed mother and sisters. President Abraham Lincoln, who happened to be in the hospital at the time, authorized Kirby's commission to brigadier general. This act of kindness ensured a higher pension for his family. Faust, *Encyclopedia of the Civil War,* 419.

12. A possible brain tumor caused Upton's severe headaches, sleeplessness, and irrational behavior following the war. In a state of total emotional distress, Upton shot himself in the mouth with a Colt .45 pistol on March 15, 1881. Welsh, *Medical Histories of Union Generals,* 348–49.

Material on Pelham's classmates was gathered from the following sources: Cullum, *Register of Graduates;* Vogtsberger, "The West Point John Pelham Knew," 10–14; *The Congressional Medal of Honor;* and Faust, *Encyclopedia of the Civil War.*

13. Schaff, *Old West Point,* 67; Sergent, *They Lie Forgotten,* 38; Waugh, *Class of 1846,* 4, 29.

14. Delafield's first tenure in this position lasted from September 1, 1838, until August 15, 1845. Selected superintendent again, he served from September 8, 1856, until his resignation on January 23, 1861. I'd like to thank West Point archivist Mrs. Charlyn Richardson for this information.

15. "West Point" file; Waugh, *Class of 1846*, 32–33; Sergent, *They Lie Forgotten*, 40.

16. Bushong and Bushong, *Fightin' Tom Rosser*, 5; Monaghan, *Custer*, 20–21; Milham, *Gallant Pelham*, 19; Schaff, *Old West Point*, 60, 68, 77; Sergent, *They Lie Forgotten*, 44, 46, 47.

17. Milham, *Gallant Pelham*, 21.

18. Alexander, *Fighting for the Confederacy*, 174.

19. Peter Pelham's wife to Edwin P. Cox, [1898]. Although no definitive evidence exists on the identification of Pelham's opponent, it seems he might have been Luke G. Harmon. A New Yorker, Harmon dropped out prior to graduation. Cullum, *Register of Graduates*, 249.

20. Schaff, *Old West Point*, 67; Monaghan, *Custer*, 107. The Alabama Department of Archives and History has in its collection a math book that was used and signed twice by John Pelham. My thanks are extended to chief curator Robert Bradley and senior archivist Nancy Dupree for allowing me to see, touch, and photograph this treasure.

21. "West Point" (file #2).

22. Milham, *Gallant Pelham*, 23; Randall, "Gallant Pelham."

23. "West Point" (file #2); Vogtsberger, "The West Point John Pelham Knew," 14; Sergent, *They Lie Forgotten*, 63.

Chapter 3

1. The cadets were Charles Edward Jesup and William Cushing Paine. Interestingly, Paine graduated first in the Class of 1858 while Jesup ranked last in the same class. The future military careers of Jesup and Paine are hardly noteworthy. Cullum, *Register of Graduates*, 249.

2. Ambrose, *Crazy Horse and Custer*, 99; Wert, *Custer*, 30. Morris Schaff, a friend of Custer's, remembered him as "a cadet so exuberant, one who cared so little for serious attempts to elevate and burnish. Yet we all loved him. . . . I cannot mention his name without swimming eyes." Schaff, *Old West Point*, 26; Sergent, *They Lie Forgotten*, 65.

3. Milham, *Gallant Pelham*, xiv; Randall, "Gallant Pelham," 340; Mercer, *Gallant Pelham*, 18.

4. "West Point" file; John Pelham Papers, ADAH.

5. John Pelham to Atkinson Pelham, March 29, 1858, John Pelham Papers, ADAH; Sergent, *They Lie Forgotten*, 70.

6. "West Point" file; John Pelham Collection by Fred R. Martin, ACPL; Sergent, *They Lie Forgotten*, 72, 73.

7. John Pelham to Charles Pelham, September 25, 1858, "Letters and Official Reports" file, JPL; Dolly Dalrymple, "Gallant Pelham Letters Published," *Birmingham News-Age Herald*, January 18, 1931, JPL.

8. John Pelham to Charles Pelham, October 12, 1858, "Letters and Official Reports" file; Dalrymple, "Gallant Pelham Letters Published"; Sergent, *They Lie Forgotten*, 38. All underlined words for emphasis appear in the original letters. Pelham's joy at the change in curriculum was premature. In fact, he would not graduate in June 1860. The five-year plan remained in effect.

9. No reason was given for Pelham's dislike of Delafield, but his hatred grew stronger in future letters. John Pelham to Martha Pelham, February 26, 1859, and John Pelham to Samuel Pelham, February 26, 1859, John Pelham Papers, ADAH; "Letters and Official Reports" file.

10. John Pelham to niece, March 20, 1859, John Pelham Papers, ADAH. No other source has been found that mentions a dog owned by Pelham at West Point.

11. John Pelham to Atkinson Pelham, May 29, 1859, John Pelham Papers, ADAH.

12. John Pelham to Martha Pelham, June 12, 1859, "Letters and Official Reports" file. In an earlier letter to his mother John requested: "Will you send me a razor? I need it as soon as you

can get it to me." Evidently his blond stubble had been sighted by an unamused officer. Sergent, *They Lie Forgotten,* 37, 68.

13. Pelham's class had lost two more cadets who failed their examinations, and it now numbered fifty. In general merit, Pelham stood forty-fifth. No evidence has been revealed for the bitterness that Pelham harbored for Delafield. Obviously, Pelham felt just cause for this abhorrence. John Pelham to his brother, July 13, 1859, "Letters and Official Reports" file.

14. "West Point" and "Youth" files; *Anniston Star,* December 11, 1938.

15. Martin, "Gallant Pelham"; Mercer, *Gallant Pelham,* 18; Mrs. John Williams, "The 'Gallant' John Pelham."

16. John Pelham to A. J. Walker, October 19, 1859, John Pelham Papers, ADAH.

17. Custer's bout with gonorrhea concluded with admittance to the post hospital on August 29, 1859. Wert, *Custer,* 34; Welsh, *Medical Histories of Union Generals,* 88.

18. Schaff, *Old West Point,* 137, 138.

19. Fleming, "Band of Brothers," 26. James B. Washington from the Class of 1863 would resign from the academy prior to his graduation. James Ewell Brown Stuart, better known as Jeb, would become John Pelham's close friend and commanding officer during the Civil War.

20. Bushong and Bushong, *Fightin' Tom Rosser,* 10; Sergent, *They Lie Forgotten,* 82, 168; Schaff, *Old West Point,* 142, 143.

21. Schaff, *Old West Point,* 144–48; Sergent, *They Lie Forgotten,* 82; Fleming, "Band of Brothers," 26; Kirshner, *Class of 1861,* 7; Milham, *Gallant Pelham,* 28.

22. Sergent, *They Lie Forgotten,* 168; Schaff, *Old West Point,* 84; Fleming, "Band of Brothers," 26.

23. Sergent, *They Lie Forgotten,* 85; Vogtsberger, "The West Point John Pelham Knew," 9.

24. John Pelham to Atkinson Pelham, December 29, 1859, "Letters and Official Reports" file; the letter is also in John Pelham Papers, ADAH.

25. John Pelham to Martha Pelham, January 25, 1860, John Pelham Papers, ADAH; Sergent, *They Lie Forgotten,* 49. Evidently, John's lady friend was a red-haired beauty from the nearby town of Newburgh.

26. John Pelham to Atkinson Pelham, May 13, 1860, "Letters and Official Reports" file; Sergent, *They Lie Forgotten,* 56; Schaff, *Old West Point,* 150–51. Schaff did not mention Pelham's leadership in the Dialectic Society but found little positive to say about the organization, remarking critically, "It held but two meetings when I was a cadet."

27. Gallagher, *Stephen Dodson Ramseur,* 26–27; Lewis, *Guns of Cedar Creek,* 149.

28. John Pelham to Atkinson Pelham, June 4, 1860, John Pelham Papers, ADAH. Of the proposed furlough John wrote, "I never wanted to go home so much in my life." He further added his pessimism about the possibility of receiving time off from the academy. "My Class were sadly disappointed at the destruction of their hopes for a Furlough," he wrote. "I have spoken to several of the Professors and they think the whole class will get off yet, but I don't think they will." Sergent, *They Lie Forgotten,* 73.

29. "West Point" file; Milham, *Gallant Pelham,* 24. In January 1860, Pelham received thirty demerits, the highest number in his class. In February he received none but in March he was back up to fifteen. Many of the demerits were given to him for being "inattentive to the regulations." Fred R. Martin Notes, box 26, John Pelham Collection by Fred R. Martin, ACPL.

30. Milham, *Gallant Pelham,* 24–25. Some dispute that furlough was not allowed to Pelham and his classmates that summer. However, Pelham mentioned the leave given in two separate instances. In a letter to his father, dated August 13, 1860, John wrote of being officer of the day, stating, "I have been Acting Lieutenant ever since I got back from leave." He further noted, "I am enjoying myself about as much as could be expected so soon after returning from leave." Sergent, *They Lie Forgotten,* 73, 85.

Chapter 4

1. John Pelham to Atkinson Pelham, August 13, 1860, John Pelham Papers, ADAH. The commission that Pelham referred to consisted of chairman Jefferson Davis, three other members of Congress, Major Robert Anderson of the First Artillery, and Captain Andrew A. Humphreys of the Topographical Engineers. Pelham's prediction of the non-change in the five-year course was, of course, correct. However, the commission voted to improve the conditions of the food. Critic Tully McCrea admitted the "mess hall fare . . . now presents a respectable appearance" but added, "Last night my coffee tasted so plainly of soapsuds that had not been rinsed from my cup that I could not drink it." Sergent, *They Lie Forgotten,* 84.

2. John Pelham to his brother, September 18, 1860, John Pelham Papers, ADAH; Sergent, *They Lie Forgotten,* 42.

3. Albert Edward, the eldest son of Queen Victoria and Prince Albert, was crowned Edward VII, King of England, on January 22, 1901.

4. "West Point" (file #2); Sergent, *They Lie Forgotten,* 87; Schaff, *Old West Point,* 92–93.

5. Sergent, *They Lie Forgotten,* 89; speech on Pelham (speaker unidentified), DSFP.

6. Schaff, *Old West Point,* 93; Wert, *Custer,* 35. When Prince Edward expressed that he hoped to someday visit West Point a second time, McCrea noted sarcastically, "I hope it will be after I leave, for I do not care about exhibiting myself before Royalty." Sergent, *They Lie Forgotten,* 89.

7. John Pelham to Eliza Pelham, October 18, 1860, John Pelham Papers, ADAH. The Prince of Wales, invited to the United States by President James Buchanan, arrived in Detroit on September 20. He visited Washington, D.C., on October 3, Philadelphia on the ninth, New York on the eleventh (where he was photographed in Mathew Brady's studio), and Boston on the seventeenth. Embarking at Portland, Maine, on October 20, he returned to England. The BPL includes a copy of the photograph that Brady took of the prince.

8. Sergent, *They Lie Forgotten,* 89; Bushong and Bushong, *Fightin' Tom Rosser,* 11; Mercer, *Gallant Pelham,* 35.

9. Monaghan, *Custer,* 37; Bushong and Bushong, *Fightin' Tom Rosser,* 13; Schaff, *Old West Point,* 155, 157.

10. Fleming, "Band of Brothers," 26; Vogtsberger, "The West Point John Pelham Knew," 9; Sergent, *They Lie Forgotten,* 90. Farley is credited with firing the signal shot that began the bombardment of Fort Sumter five months later.

11. Sam Houston to T. L. Rosser, November 17, 1860, Rosser Mss., DSFP. Houston continued to support the Union and was eventually deposed as governor after Texas seceded. Never faltering from his unpopular attitude, Houston died in the midst of the Civil War at age seventy on July 26, 1863. For many years his name was anathema to Texans.

12. A. J. Walker to John Pelham, early December 1860, and John Pelham to Atkinson Pelham, December 11, 1860, John Pelham Papers, ADAH.

13. John Pelham to Martha Pelham, December 18, 1860, John Pelham Papers, ADAH; Sergent, *They Lie Forgotten,* 75, 77, 78.

14. Schaff, *Old West Point,* 173, 174.

15. Charles Pelham to Edwin P. Cox, November 21, 1898; Ambrose, "War Comes to West Point," 34.

16. Schaff, *Old West Point,* 133, 192.

17. Ambrose, "War Comes to West Point," 34; A. J. Walker to Andrew B. Moore, January 16, 1861, Governor A. B. Moore Papers, ADAH.

18. Schaff, *Old West Point,* 195. Delafield returned as superintendent on a temporary basis on January 28. His permanent replacement, Colonel Alexander H. Bowman, took the superinten-

dent's post officially on March 1, 1861. My thanks go to archivist Charlyn Richardson of West Point for this information.

19. Sergent, *They Lie Forgotten,* 94.

20. Faust, *Encyclopedia of the Civil War,* 161. Davis's entire inaugural address can be found in Commager, *The Civil War Archive,* 61–63.

21. Schaff, *Old West Point,* 168, 208; Fleming, "Band of Brothers," 25; Monaghan, *Custer,* 38–39. Although Schaff mentions nearly a dozen cadets who participated in the cheering, he makes no mention of Pelham being there; undoubtedly, he was.

22. John Pelham to Jefferson Davis, February 27, 1861, Compiled Service Records of Confederate Generals & Staff Officers & Non-Regimental Enlisted Men, microfilm, M331, roll 195, NAB; John Pelham Collection by Fred R. Martin, ACPL; BPL; Sergent, *They Lie Forgotten,* 95.

23. John Pelham to his sister-in-law, March 9, 1861, "Letters and Official Reports" file; John Pelham Papers, ADAH; Sergent, *They Lie Forgotten,* 95.

24. Atkinson Pelham to Jefferson Davis, March 15, 1861, Compiled Service Records of Confederate Generals; Milham, *Gallant Pelham,* 33. It is rather doubtful that Atkinson's letter made a difference. His letter to Davis, dated March 15, must have taken some time to arrive in Montgomery. The commission as first lieutenant is dated March 16, too early for both to have been sent and received.

25. John Pelham to his cousin Marianna, March 26, 1861, Garrison Family Papers, Sophia Smith Collection, Smith College, Northampton, MA. The author expressly thanks Ms. Susan Boone, reference archivist, for obtaining permission to publish this letter.

26. Henry du Pont to his mother, March 27, 1861; John Pelham to A. J. Walker, March 31, 1861. "Miscellaneous" file, JPL; John Pelham Papers, ADAH; Lake, "A Crisis of Conscience"; "Letters and Official Reports" file; Sergent, *They Lie Forgotten,* 95, 52. It is noteworthy that during this time Pelham reread Nolan's *Cavalry—Its History and Tactics,* part of which contained a section on horse artillery. See BPL.

27. "Miscellaneous" file; Lake, "A Crisis of Conscience"; Sergent, *They Lie Forgotten,* 93–94.

28. Sergent, *They Lie Forgotten,* 94.

29. Schaff, *Old West Point,* 219, 220.

30. "Miscellaneous" file; Lake, "A Crisis of Conscience."

31. Letters of the Secretary of War, 1861–1864, M493, NAB.

32. Sergent, *They Lie Forgotten,* 168, 95.

33. "West Point" file; John Pelham Papers, ADAH.

34. In a letter from Mrs. Peter Pelham to Edwin P. Cox, she stated: "A friend of John's from Philadelphia named Cameron, who joined the Federal army wrote John during the war and told him he got his diploma for him & left it with his Sister Mary Cameron in Phila—Cameron was killed & I don't think any of the family have ever communicated with Miss Cameron." The diploma has never surfaced.

Chapter 5

1. Charles Pelham to Edwin P. Cox, November 21, 1898; Bushong and Bushong, *Fightin' Tom Rosser,* 13.

2. Some sources, such as *Fightin' Tom Rosser* by Bushong and Bushong, give the town as New Harmony, Indiana. Circuitous as their trek was, it certainly did not take them to New Harmony, which is approximately 150 miles west (near the Illinois border) of where they crossed the Ohio River.

3. Charles Pelham to Edwin P. Cox, November 21, 1898.

4. *Jacksonville Republican,* May 2, 1861; Trout, *Galloping Thunder,* 14.

5. This delightful anecdote, so insightful to John Pelham's personality, as well as his father's, is in Charles Pelham to Edwin P. Cox, November 21, 1898. All of the underlined emphases are in Charles's original letter. To its credit, the Tenth Alabama became an outstanding unit of fighting men in the Eastern Theater.

6. Peter Pelham's wife was an eyewitness to the scene. Mrs. Peter Pelham to Edwin Cox, [1898].

7. Milham, *Gallant Pelham,* 38.

8. McCoy, *Adventures of Charles L. Scott,* 153, 154.

9. Williams, *UDC Magazine* 44, no. 9, in "General Articles" file, JPL.

10. The original pay voucher is located in Compiled Service Records of Confederate Generals.

11. The two Confederate forces, the Army of the Shenandoah and the Army of the Potomac, would eventually merge and be rechristened to the more familiar Army of Northern Virginia.

12. Freeman, *Lee's Lieutenants,* vol. 1, *Manassas to Malvern Hill,* 45.

13. Vandiver, *Mighty Stonewall,* 154–55.

Chapter 6

1. W. Davis, *Battle of Bull Run,* 253.

2. Wise, *Long Arm of Lee,* 1:130.

3. Wise, *Long Arm of Lee,* 1:132.

4. Vandiver, *Mighty Stonewall,* 161.

5. Cooke, *Wearing of the Gray,* 126; B. Davis, *Jeb Stuart,* 84.

6. Eighty-year-old widow Judith Carter Henry refused to leave her farmhouse during the battle. Her son, John, daughter, Ellen, and a black servant, Lucy Griffith, remained with her. At the height of the battle shells repeatedly hit the house, splintering the wood. All survived except Judith. Shell fragments threw her to the floor with wounds in her side and neck. One foot was nearly blown off. She was later buried directly behind her house. W. Davis, *Battle of Bull Run,* 204–5.

7. Poague, *Gunner with Stonewall,* 9. Poague referred to Pelham as "afterwards the most distinguished artillery officer in the Army of Northern Virginia."

8. B. Mitchell, *Edmund Ruffin,* 194–96. Whether a man in his sixties is capable of straddling a cannon barrel with a weapon in each hand is certainly questionable. Quite possibly Ruffin carried only one weapon while riding in a much safer spot atop the carriage of the cannon. Scarborough, *The Diary of Edmund Ruffin,* vol. 2, *The Years of Hope, April 1861–June 1863,* 87–89. At war's end, the indomitable Ruffin put a rifle into his mouth and snuffed out his own life rather than be subjected to "perfidious Yankee rule."

9. Randall and Donald, *The Civil War and Reconstruction,* 199–200.

10. Wise, *Long Arm of Lee,* 1:136.

11. Peter Pelham to Mrs. Oscar Twitty, January 15, 1917; BPL; Sergent, *They Lie Forgotten,* 109.

12. Bee was shot sometime after naming Jackson "Stonewall" and died the following day. Bartow, potentially a great soldier, was Savannah born, attended Yale and the University of Georgia, and served in the Georgia legislature following his marriage. R. K. Krick, *Lee's Colonels,* 41.

13. Trout, *With Pen & Saber,* 20.

14. Kirshner, *Class of 1861*, 22; W. Davis, *Battle of Bull Run*, 219.

15. Beauregard, "The First Battle of Bull Run," *B&L*, 1:215; *OR*, series 1, 2:494.

16. *OR*, series 1, 2:494, 481.

17. In his letter Judge Walker does not identify Colonel Martin. However, it would undoubtedly be James Benson Martin of Talladega and Jacksonville, Alabama. Martin was killed at Dranesville, Virginia, five months later on December 20, 1861. R. K. Krick, *Lee's Colonels*, 244.

18. A. J. Walker to John Pelham, July 31, 1861, John Pelham Papers, ADAH; Joseph Wheeler speech, *SHSP*, 26:297.

19. Cullum, *Register of Graduates*. For an account of Adelbert Ames's heroics in winning the Medal of Honor, see Charles Griffin's report in *OR*, series 1, 2:394.

20. Pelham's numbers are, of course, highly exaggerated.

21. These were actually the two batteries of Griffin and Ricketts.

22. Pelham's information on the Fourth Alabama's losses among their officers is incorrect. Colonel Egbert J. Jones was mortally wounded, shot through both hips, and died on September 2, 1861. Major Charles Lewis Scott survived a leg wound but was forced to resign because of the unhealed wound. Lieutenant Colonel Evander M. Law suffered a severely wounded left arm but survived and eventually became a brigadier general. R. K. Krick, *Lee's Colonels*, 195, 310; Welsh, *Medical Histories of Confederate Generals*, 129; Trout, *Galloping Thunder*, 660.

23. John Pelham to Atkinson Pelham, published in the *Jacksonville Republican*, August 8, 1861, John Pelham Papers, ADAH; Trout, *Galloping Thunder*, 16–18; Sergent, *They Lie Forgotten*, 110.

Chapter 7

1. Sears, *McClellan*, 95.

2. Trout, *Galloping Thunder*, 23–24; Compiled Service Records of Confederate Generals; Compiled Service Records of Confederate Soldiers Who Served in Organizations from the State of Virginia, Pendleton microfilm, no. 324, roll #224, NAB.

3. Wise, *Long Arm of Lee*, 1:108; speech by Douglas Southall Freeman to Confederate Veterans, in "Miscellaneous" file; R. K. Krick, "Thomas Lafayette Rosser," in W. Davis, *The Confederate General*, 5:113.

4. *OR*, series 1, 5:777; Wert, "James Ewell Brown Stuart," 6:19; O'Neill, "Cavalry on the Peninsula," 8.

5. The historian Jennings Cropper Wise credits Confederate cavalryman Turner Ashby with first suggesting the creation of the horse artillery (*Long Arm of Lee*, 1:153, 162). Interestingly, Stuart at first considered a relative through marriage, John Esten Cooke, and then James W. Breathed to lead his horse artillery before selecting John Pelham. Moore, *The 1st and 2nd Stuart Horse Artillery*, 1.

6. A. Mitchell, *Letters*, 225–26, 230; "Stuart Horse Artillery" (file #6), JPL; B. Duncan, *Letters of General J. E. B. Stuart to His Wife*, 19, 23.

7. Randall, "Gallant Pelham," 345; Compiled Service Records of Confederate Generals.

8. *Jacksonville Republican*, December 19, 1861; Trout, *Galloping Thunder*, 25–26; Moore, *Stuart Horse Artillery*, 3–4.

9. Milham, *Gallant Pelham*, 64; Hassler, *Col. John Pelham*, 26. Each gun crew included a "sponger," whose duty consisted of ramming a dampened sponge—on the opposite end of the ramrod—into the barrel of the cannon to extinguish any burning residue prior to reloading the gun.

10. Moore, *Stuart Horse Artillery*, 166, 168, 8; Trout, *Galloping Thunder*, 25; Alexander, *Fighting for the Confederacy*, 76. Oddly, after the war the flamboyant Fauntleroy became a Methodist minister.

11. Moore, *Stuart Horse Artillery*, 8; Compiled Service Records of Confederate Generals.

12. Trout, "*The Hoss*," 1.

13. Naisawald, *Grape and Canister*, 37–39; Faust, *Encyclopedia of the Civil War*, 66, 373–74, 520, 755, 823. Gunpowder for cannons consisted of a combination of charcoal, saltpeter (potassium nitrate, or niter), and sulfur in the ratio of 75:15:10 or 76:14:10. Ripley, *Artillery and Ammunition of the Civil War*, 241.

14. A. Mitchell, *Letters*, 233–34, 235; Hassler, *Col. John Pelham*, 28; B. Davis, *Jeb Stuart*, 84.

15. Von Borcke, *Memoirs*, 2:13–14.

16. Breathed was praised by those who observed this "intrepid, reckless, [and] dashing" young officer. General Williams C. Wickham labeled him "the best man for the management of a battery of horse artillery I ever saw." John Esten Cooke effusively wrote, "Napoleon would have made him a marshal." Severely wounded on June 29, 1864, Breathed survived the war and once again took up the practice of medicine. He died in Hancock, Maryland, on February 14, 1870, one day after his thirty-second birthday. Matthews, "Recollections of Major James Breathed," 346–48; Trout, "*The Hoss*," 15–16; Moore, *Stuart Horse Artillery*, 164.

17. McGregor suffered an unusual fourteen wounds during the war, but his worst injury occurred on November 10, 1862, when both bones in his lower right leg were broken. Married following the war, he fathered eight children. He practiced law until his death on December 23, 1908, at age sixty-nine. Trout, "*The Hoss*," 21–23.

18. The twenty-one-year-old Ford, a former student at Virginia Military Institute, served with distinction until a rifle bullet struck him in the forehead, killing him instantly, near Hanover Court House on May 31, 1864. He became the only officer of the Stuart Horse Artillery to be killed in action while serving his guns during the war. Trout, "*The Hoss*," 126–28.

19. Compiled Service Records of Confederate Generals.

20. Private Jacob Hickle, who hailed from Rockingham County, Virginia, and enlisted in the horse artillery at age sixteen, perished from typhoid fever at Moore Hospital, Manassas Junction, on January 10, 1862. Moore, *Stuart Horse Artillery*, 171; Trout, "*The Hoss*," 81.

21. Trout, *Galloping Thunder*, 51–52.

22. Milham, *Gallant Pelham*, 82–83.

23. Moore, *Stuart Horse Artillery*, 9–10; Vogtsberger, "Needless and Oppressive Seizure," 3–5; Boatner, *Civil War Dictionary*, 577.

24. Pelham's signed promotion, in John Pelham Papers, ADAH; Compiled Service Records of Confederate Generals.

25. Becoming dissatisfied with the lack of proper rations, the raccoon eventually gnawed "in two the rope which confined him, actually deserted, and was never more seen!" Cooke, *Wearing of the Gray*, 185–87.

26. Thomas, *Bold Dragoon*, 91; Trout, *They Followed the Plume*, 50.

27. B. Davis, *Jeb Stuart*, 98. A caroming cannonball that removed fellow officer Matthew Calbraith Butler's foot also ripped off Will Farley's leg at the knee during the fighting at Brandy Station on June 9, 1863. Bravely, Farley asked that his severed leg be brought to him. He clutched it "as an old friend" until he died shortly afterward from loss of blood and shock. Redmond Burke died mysteriously on the night of November 25, 1862, in Shepherdstown, Virginia. He was shot by a party of the Second Massachusetts Infantry. Whether it happened in "cold blood" or while he was trying to escape an ambush has not been determined. Trout, *Plume*, 112, 76, 106.

28. Thomas, *Bold Dragoon*, 91; Trout, *Plume*, 163.

29. Stuart's father-in-law, General Philip St. George Cooke, fought in the Union army under McClellan. Jeb once wrote to Flora's brother of his father-in-law's decision, "He will regret it but once and that will be continually." So embarrassed by this indefensible loyalty to the Federal cause, Jeb changed the name of his son from Philip to Jimmie A. Mitchell, *Letters*, 233, 250; Thomas, *Bold Dragoon*, 94.

30. Severely wounded in the throat on June 19, 1863, Von miraculously survived, but his stint in the cavalry had ended. Returning to Prussia to recuperate, he spent twenty years outside the United States. When he returned in 1884, he had added nearly two hundred pounds to his already monstrous frame. Trout, *Plume*, 273–79.

31. A beardless photograph of Stuart taken while at West Point indicates the nickname was not negative. His chin appears strong. With his hair brushed back on a high forehead, expressive eyes, and full lips, Stuart possesses a handsome look. He sent the daguerreotype to a lady friend with the comment, "I send you a likeness of 'Beauty.' You perceive I was looking my *prettiest* when it was taken." B. Davis, *Jeb Stuart*, 29.

32. Mercer, *Gallant Pelham*, 45; Thomason, *Jeb Stuart*, 1–2.

33. John Esten Cooke, "General Stuart in Camp and Field," in *Annals of the War*, 672; B. Davis, *Jeb Stuart*, 20.

34. Cooke, *Wearing of the Gray*, 189. Handsome Sam Sweeney, in his early thirties, hailed from Appomattox County, Virginia. His older brother, Joe, reportedly invented the banjo and performed as a black-faced minstrel for Queen Victoria of England. Unfortunately, much of the music at Stuart's camp ended when Sam Sweeney died of smallpox on January 13, 1864. Cooke remembered Sweeney's passing as "a great loss" and added, "What shall we do without him? He was a gentleman in character and manners—knew his place everywhere—had the *savoir faire* which makes a man graceful in the hut or the palace. . . . Heaven rest him!" Trout, *Pen & Saber*, 223.

35. No immutable evidence exists of Stuart's infidelity to his wife. Persistent rumors were spread by his enemies, and no doubt numerous opportunities availed themselves to Stuart, but nothing more has been revealed. Strangely, one of those who accused Stuart of unfaithfulness was none other than Tom Rosser. Dissension started when Rosser became convinced that Stuart withheld his promotions. The contrary is true, as Stuart worked diligently for Rosser's increase in rank. Sadly, Rosser did not see it that way and spelled out his venom in letters to his wife. "I know the measure of his friendship only too well now to be trifled with by him longer," wrote Rosser. "Stuart Stuart Stuart! I am done with him. . . . I will never give him an opportunity of deceiving me again." He added, "[Stuart] has been as false to me as [he] has ever been to his country and his wife. I will leave him in his glory." Kirshner, *Class of 1861*, 59–60; Lewis, *Cedar Creek*, 86–87; Thomas, *Bold Dragoon*, 261.

36. Neese, *Three Years in the Confederate Horse Artillery*, 167–68.

37. *Annals of the War*, 669, 665.

38. *Annals of the War*, 675; B. Davis, *Jeb Stuart*, 264; Milham, *Gallant Pelham*, 61.

39. Mercer, *Gallant Pelham*, 48; "Monuments" file, JPL; Thomason, *Jeb Stuart*, 360.

Chapter 8

1. H. H. Matthews, "Organization of the Pelham-Breathed Battery of Stuart's Horse Artillery Operating with Stuart's Cavalry, Army of Northern Virginia, including the Battle of Williamsburg, May 5, 1862," *St. Mary's Beacon*, November 3, 1904; *OR*, series 1, 12:1, 417.

2. Waugh, *Class of 1846*, 346. Reasons for this inexplicable exaggeration vary, but certainly,

Allan Pinkerton, a Union spy, must share the blame. Hired to scout the Confederate lines, Pinkerton estimated the Rebel force as nearly 180,000.

3. O'Neill, "Cavalry on the Peninsula," 20.

4. *OR*, 11:1, 572; Moore, *Stuart Horse Artillery*, 12–13; McCoy, *Charles L. Scott*, 153.

5. Martin's personal notes, BPL; O'Neill, "Cavalry on the Peninsula," 38. Upon viewing Payne's severe wound, Jeb Stuart believed it mortal.

6. Early was actually hit twice with one wound only slight. The other, a flattened bullet, when removed, indicated a wound that could have been fatal had it not hit bone first. His horse was shot through both eyes in the charge. Bushong, *Old Jube*, 55.

7. Sears, *Gates of Richmond*, 82.

8. *OR*, 11:1, 574–75; Trout, *Galloping Thunder*, 53, 55. Pelham's information on his wounded was incorrect. Summers appears to be Private Tazewell Sumner, wounded at Williamsburg, and no record exists of a Gibson in the horse artillery at this time. Corporal Moses Alexander Febrey, on the gun crew with the Blakely, was wounded. Trout, "*The Hoss*," 78.

9. A. Mitchell, *Letters*, 253–54; Thomason, *Jeb Stuart*, 136.

10. *OR*, 11:1, 571–73.

11. *OR*, 11:1, 568.

12. *OR*, 11:1, 575; Trout, *Galloping Thunder*, 56. Colonel Averell claimed he captured "5 pieces of artillery" and "21 prisoners" that Johnston "abandoned in his hasty flight" but does not mention the skirmish with Pelham's cannon. *OR*, 11:1, 436.

13. O'Neill, "Cavalry on the Peninsula," 42; Trout, *Galloping Thunder*, 58; Matthews, "Organization of the Pelham-Breathed Battery."

14. *OR*, 11:1, 642; Trout, *Galloping Thunder*, 58–59.

15. Rosser reluctantly gave up command and was removed to Richmond, where he recuperated at the home of Dr. Charles Bell Gibson. Rosser returned to active duty to find he had been promoted to lieutenant colonel of artillery on June 10. In less than two weeks he would be transferred to Jeb Stuart's cavalry. O'Neill, "Cavalry on the Peninsula," 44, 45; Bushong and Bushong, *Fightin' Tom Rosser*, 20.

16. Records indicate that Pelham's horse artillery was hit hard by measles with a number of recruits bedridden; two, William Stump and Jacob Zowder, perished from the disease. Trout, *Galloping Thunder*, 58.

17. Sears, *Gates of Richmond*, 95–96.

18. Sears, *Gates of Richmond*, 138; Johnston, "Manassas to Seven Pines," 215.

19. Govan and Livingwood, *General Joseph E. Johnston*, 157–58.

20. Sears, *McClellan*, 180; Waugh, *Class of 1846*, 360.

21. *OR*, 11:3, 590; Mewborn, "A Wonderful Exploit"; Thomason, *Jeb Stuart*, 140; B. Davis, *Jeb Stuart*, 110.

22. For reasons not identified, John Pelham did not go along on Stuart's ride. Pelham biographers disagree as to why: William Hassler (*Colonel John Pelham*) maintains Pelham "magnanimously" chose Breathed to go in his stead, an extremely unlikely scenario; Charles Milham (*Gallant Pelham*) guesses that Pelham was suffering from measles, was away on furlough, or was busy with recruiting in Richmond. Certainly a furlough at this critical juncture seems improbable as would a recruiting mission. Since various illnesses had hit the Confederate army, it appears that Pelham possibly had been afflicted with measles or another ailment. Robert Trout (*Galloping Thunder*, 60, 666) offers concrete evidence that Milham's suggestions of a furlough or recruitment are unwarranted as theories. Perhaps Pelham's services were esteemed to be of greater service with the main army. Interestingly, Jennings Cropper Wise (*Long Arm of Lee*) incorrectly

insists that Pelham went along. More amazingly, one of Stuart's officers, William Todd Robins, who actually rode with the command around McClellan, mentions Pelham as a fellow rider.

23. Thomas, *Bold Dragoon,* 114; Mosby, "The Ride around McClellan," 249. Stuart kept their destination a "profound secret" but encouraged the thought that his troopers were headed for the Shenandoah Valley. "I purposely directed my first day's march toward Louisa, so as to favor the idea of re-enforcing Jackson." *OR,* 11:1, 1036.

24. Captain William Latané was Stuart's only fatality, killed on June 13. The captured man was Private John Jacob Schwartz, a German immigrant who, according to Mosby, "drank too much of a sutler's Rhine wine and had to be left behind." Mosby, *Mosby's Memoirs,* 118; Mosby, "The Ride around McClellan," 252; Mewborn, "A Wonderful Exploit," 49; Symonds, *Battlefield Atlas of the Civil War,* 35.

25. *OR,* 11:1, 1042; H. Bridges, *Lee's Maverick General,* 61; Thomas, *Bold Dragoon,* 125, 128; Robins, "Stuart's Ride around McClellan," 275; Mewborn, "A Wonderful Exploit," 49; Mosby, "The Ride around McClellan," 254; Allan, *Army of Northern Virginia,* 64; *Richmond Enquirer,* June 16, 1862.

26. *OR,* 11:1, 1045.

27. Freeman, *R. E. Lee,* 2:107.

Chapter 9

1. Daughter Mary Anne died on January 25 at age one. The following day four-year-old James Jr. perished. Six days later on February 1, son Augustus died at age six. Barely surviving was thirteen-year-old son Garland. Wert, *General James Longstreet,* 97.

2. Trout, *Pen & Saber,* 74. Order No. 75 is given in its entirety in *OR,* 11:2, 498–99, Allan, *Army of Northern Virginia,* 75–77, and Dowdey, *Wartime Papers of R. E. Lee,* 198–200.

3. Milham, *Gallant Pelham,* 92–93.

4. Sears, *Gates of Richmond,* 208. Confederate artillerist Edward Porter Alexander questioned Jackson's lack of temerity that day by stating, "[Jackson] marched only 14 miles over good roads & had no opposition except that a single squadron of Federal cavalry had opposed his crossing of Totopotomoy Creek" (*Fighting for the Confederacy,* 100). The historian Robert K. Krick, however, believes that Jackson on this day should be "immune to criticism" and gives compelling reasons to support his opinion. "Sleepless in the Saddle," 72–73.

5. Quite likely the McGehee family residing here in Hanover County was somehow related to John Pelham, whose ancestors settled in this part of the country. According to the historian Robert E. L. Krick, McGhee may be the correct spelling.

6. *OR,* 11:2, 836; Allan, *Army of Northern Virginia,* 88.

7. Beale added, "What had been the necessity for the long and tiresome detour we had made, we did not know" (*Lieutenant of Cavalry,* 33, 34).

8. *OR,* 11:2, 528.

9. Stuart's post-battle report states that the Federal batteries appeared with "eight pieces," but Stephen Weed pronounced the number to be twelve.

10. "Miscellaneous" file; *Anniston Star,* May 18, 1921, BPL; Trout, *Pen & Saber,* 76; Cooke, *Surry of Eagle's-Nest,* 235; Mercer, *Gallant Pelham,* 64.

11. These freshly arriving Confederate batteries were those of Captains John B. Brockenborough, James Carrington, and Alfred R. Courtney (H. B. McClellan, *I Rode with Jeb Stuart,* 76). Interestingly, Stephen Weed gave more credit to the Confederate infantry than the artillery

for his withdrawal from the field, referring to the artillery fire as a diversion they "entirely disregarded." John C. Tidball credits the artillery as well as the "sharp fire of musketry" to his retreat. Between the two Federal batteries a total of 1,600 rounds of artillery shells had been fired. *OR*, 11:2, 354, 245; Trout, *Galloping Thunder*, 63.

12. Walters's originality and quaint spelling and grammar have been retained. Vogtsberger, *The Cannoneer* 11, no. 1 (July 1992): 4; Trout, *Galloping Thunder*, 62. Walters was mortally wounded at the Battle of Chancellorsville on May 2, 1863.

13. Cooke, *Surry of Eagle's-Nest*, 64; McCoy, *Charles L. Scott*, 153.

14. *OR*, 11:2, 515.

15. *OR*, 11:2, 556.

16. Thomas, *Bold Dragoon*, 133; Douglas, *I Rode with Stonewall*, 104; Sears, *Gates of Richmond*, 241; Sword, *Embrace an Angry Wind*, 6–8. The eminent historian Douglas Southall Freeman labels Hood's breakthrough the "most brilliant single achievement in the Seven Days." *Lee's Lieutenants*, 1:653.

17. *OR*, 11:2, 758; Sears, *Gates of Richmond*, 226, 249, 251; Sears, *McClellan*, 213; Caldwell, *History of a Brigade*, 44, Library of Congress.

18. John Esten Cooke's journal, in Trout, *Pen & Saber*, 75, 77; Vandiver, *Mighty Stonewall*, 309; R. E. L. Krick, "The Men Who Carried This Position Were Soldiers Indeed," 204–5.

19. Pelham would later send the prayer book to Miss Sallie Dandridge at her beautiful home, the Bower. Inside the book he penned "Picked up on the battlefield at Cold Harbor" and initialed it simply "J. P." Milham, *Gallant Pelham*, 98.

20. Blackford, *War Years*, 75; Hassler, *Col. John Pelham*, 39–40.

21. *Anniston Star*, May 18, 1921; Milham, *Gallant Pelham*, 100; Hassler, *Col. John Pelham*, 40–41; Dasinger, "Gallant Pelham," 29.

22. *OR*, 11:2, 516–17.

23. *OR*, 11:2, 516.

24. Cooke, *Wearing of the Gray*, 457, 458; Blackford, *War Years*, 75–76.

25. G. Beale, *Lieutenant of Cavalry*, 37; Trout, *Pen & Saber*, 80; Milham, *Gallant Pelham*, 100; Hassler, *Col. John Pelham*, 44.

26. *OR*, 11:2, 517–18; G. Beale, *Lieutenant of Cavalry*, 39.

27. *OR*, 11:2, 529, 531; Trout, *Galloping Thunder*, 65–66.

28. Milham, *Gallant Pelham*, 102; Moore, *Stuart Horse Artillery*, 19.

29. Allan, *Army of Northern Virginia*, 128, 137; Sears, *Gates of Richmond*, 335; H. Bridges, *Maverick General*, 77.

30. "Miscellaneous" file. Although Pelham's note is mentioned in *OR*, 11:2, 519, the original copy along with the map exists in the Duke University Library in Durham, North Carolina. I expressly thank the Research Services librarian, Janie C. Morris, at Duke University for making these copies available to me.

31. According to Stuart's report, W. W. Blackford and a handful of men had tailed McClellan's army to Harrison's Landing the day before. Blackford avowed that he scaled the Heights and witnessed a "magnificent panorama" of the Army of the Potomac below. He further maintained that with the help of two compatriots, he climbed a tree for a better view with his field glasses: "the nearest part of their camp was not over three hundred yards distant and I could hear voices distinctly." He added, "I sketched a map of the position . . . and wrote a report, sending them off at once to General Stuart." Strangely, Blackford does not mention Pelham's part in the episode. *War Years*, 82–84.

32. *OR*, 11:2, 520; Wise, *Long Arm of Lee*, 1:233; Sears, *McClellan*, 224.

33. *OR*, 11:2, 520.

34. Blackford, *War Years*, 85; B. Davis, *Jeb Stuart*, 145; Hassler, *Col. John Pelham*, 48–49. Positioned on a seven- to nine-foot directing stick, the Congreve rocket consisted of a warhead attached to a sheet iron case filled with propellant composed of niter, sulfur, and charcoal. With a range of approximately one mile, the rockets had less than desirable accuracy, but as one contemporary stated, "they rise more or less, become deflected and rush about in a most destructive manner." McKee and Mason, *Civil War Projectiles II*, 135; Lord, *Civil War Collector's Encyclopedia*, 219; Ripley, *Artillery and Ammunition*, 345.

35. *OR*, 11:2, 520. Today a single cannon stands where John Pelham eyed the Army of the Potomac. The Evelynton House is in the background. A plaque at the spot reads: "From this site on July 2, 1862, Confederate General J. E. B. Stuart commanded his First Virginia Cavalry in the shelling of Federal soldiers encamped at Harrison's Landing and Westover Plains across Herring Creek. Known to history as the 'Battle of Evelynton Heights,' it contributed to the failure of Union General George B. McClellan's Peninsula Campaign against Richmond."

36. Jennings Cropper Wise, perhaps overly critical, cynically states, "Thus, by Stuart's horseplay, McClellan was at once apprised of his peril, and by causing the Federal general to immediately reoccupy Evelington Heights, Lee's last opportunity to force him to the offensive was sacrificed by Stuart." *Long Arm of Lee*, 1:233.

37. Sears, *Gates of Richmond*, 343. Losses in Pelham's horse artillery were slight. The only one to die was thirty-one-year-old George W. Brown. Three others were wounded and one was captured.

38. R. Dabney, *Campaigns of Jackson*, 467. For a rather complete rundown of Jackson's physical condition during the Seven Days Battles, see R. E. L. Krick, "Sleepless in the Saddle," 66–95.

39. *OR*, 11:2, 522.

40. Stuart had worked diligently to obtain Rosser's transfer from the artillery to his cavalry. On June 23, Stuart wrote to Rosser: "I pushed through your Colonelcy of 5th Virginia Cavalry. Today the commission is ordered by the Secretary. Come to me at daylight in the morning and I will give you the particulars. You are in my brigade and must play an important part in the next battle. 'Come a-runnin.'" A. Mitchell, *Letters*, 257.

41. *OR*, 11:2, 521. The rumor of Rosser scoring a hit on one of the balloons was false. During the Peninsular Campaign, young George Custer, a staff officer to McClellan, rode in one of the balloons. How tragic it might have been had Rosser's shot downed Custer, a friend of both Rosser and Pelham. Perhaps Pelham would have been pleased to know that fellow classmates and friends Lieutenant Adelbert Ames of the Fifth U.S. Artillery and Lieutenant Henry Kingsbury of the West Point Battery, Battery D, received numerous accolades for their performances at Malvern Hill, while Samuel N. Benjamin would eventually be awarded the Medal of Honor for his heroics during the Seven Days. Bohannon, "One Solid Unbroken Roar of Thunder," 238; Sergent, *They Lie Forgotten*, 120.

Chapter 10

1. Freeman, *Lee's Lieutenants*, 2:443.

2. Von Borcke, *Memoirs*, 1:82.

3. Blackford, *War Years*, 90.

4. Compiled Service Records of Confederate Generals; Milham, *Gallant Pelham*, 109.

5. Dr. Lucien Bonaparte Price was not the father of staff officer Channing Price, as is mistakenly noted in some sources. Channing's father, Thomas Randolph Price Sr., was a merchant in Richmond, and the two Price families appear to be unrelated.

6. Nannie's true name was Ann Overton Price. It is obvious that Jeb Stuart was somewhat enchanted by the wiles and beauty of his cousin Nannie. Although their relationship remained strictly platonic, he wrote her often during the war and occasionally began his correspondence with "My Dear Sweety." He once penned, "How much I have thought of you and wondered if you still cherished my memory" (A. Mitchell, *Letters*, 269). Nannie married Thomas Ballard after the war.

7. In 1864, while recovering from a severe neck wound, von Borcke returned to his native Prussia. Supposedly, he brokenheartedly tossed the engagement ring overboard into the Atlantic. Stuart-Mosby Historical Society, *Southern Cavalry Review* 2, no. 5 (March 1985), JPL.

8. Bushong and Bushong, *Fightin' Tom Rosser*, 42–43; Milham, *Gallant Pelham*, 110. Pelham, of course, died before his friend's marriage. James Dearing, who had resigned from the West Point class of 1862, stood in as best man. At least one source makes the egregious error of having Pelham present at Rosser's wedding. The Rossers produced six children, one of whom was named John Pelham Rosser.

9. Lasswell, *Rags and Hope*, 79–80.

10. Hodges, *C. B. Fleet*, 45.

11. Redwood, "Jackson's 'Foot Cavalry' at the Second Bull Run," 530; *OR*, 12:3, 474; Allan, *Army of Northern Virginia*, 156; Hennessy, *Return to Bull Run*, 82; Waugh, *Class of 1846*, 363.

12. Mosby, *Memoirs*, 123; Chamberlayne, *Ham Chamberlayne*, 91; Blackford, *War Years*, 96.

13. Hennessy, "Stuart's Revenge," 40; Hennessy, *Return to Bull Run*, 25–26.

14. *OR*, 12:2, 119; Milham, *Gallant Pelham*, 113; von Borcke, *Memoirs*, 1:96.

15. Longacre, *Lee's Cavalrymen*, 107; Thomason, *Jeb Stuart*, 216; Blackford, *War Years*, 95; Milham, *Gallant Pelham*, 115. Pelham biographer William Hassler claims that Stuart's engagement with the enemy that day netted "two hundred prisoners." This figure is well off the mark, as Stuart's official report explains. *Col. John Pelham*, 54.

16. Longacre, *Lee's Cavalrymen*, 108; *OR*, 12:2, 121. Stuart wrote a much fuller account of this engagement than what is contained in his original report of December 20, 1862. Interestingly, in neither report did he mention John Pelham's excellent work. Stuart did, however, point out the malfunctioning of the Blakely. *OR*, 12:2, 119–21.

17. Compiled Service Records of Confederate Generals; Mercer, *Gallant Pelham*, 69–70.

18. Trout, *Plume*, 84. Chew returned to the Stuart Horse Artillery in June 1863. He eventually replaced Robert Beckham, who had taken over the horse artillery after Pelham's death.

19. Hennessy, "Stuart's Revenge," 40; Thomason, *Jeb Stuart*, 220. Lee's plans are stated verbatim in Dowdey, *Wartime Papers of R. E. Lee*, 259–60.

20. Mosby, *Memoirs*, 138.

21. Mustered out of service on September 11, 1862, Rogers returned to his home in Pontiac, Michigan. He carefully preserved Stuart's hat for years. "The hat I took to California with me packed in a trunk," wrote Rogers, "and being smashed very flat, I took it to a hat store in San Francisco to be put in order, where I allowed it to remain for a long time, and when I called for it, it could not be found, having been cleared out with a lot of old second-hand hats." Robertson, *Michigan in the War*, 919; Freeman, *Lee's Lieutenants*, 2:60.

22. A. Mitchell, *Letters*, 260–61; Thomason, *Jeb Stuart*, 225. In Pope's official report, he stated: "Among the papers taken was an autograph[ed] letter of General Robert E. Lee to General Stuart, dated Gordonsville, August 13, which made manifest to me the position and force of the enemy, and their determination to overwhelm the army under my command before it could be reinforced by any portion of the Army of the Potomac.... I determined accordingly to withdraw behind the Rappahannock with all speed." *OR*, 12:2, 29; Allan, *Army of Northern Virginia*, 183–84.

23. *OR*, 12:2, 726; Longacre, *Lee's Cavalrymen*, 114; Milham, *Gallant Pelham*, 121.

24. *OR*, 12:2, 730, 316; Trout, *Galloping Thunder*, 79–80. Perhaps Milroy was unaware that Pelham often changed the position of his guns to keep the enemy from zeroing in on his exact location.

25. *OR*, 12:2, 317.

26. Trout, *Galloping Thunder*, 80–81; Moore, *Stuart Horse Artillery*, 26; Milham, *Gallant Pelham*, 123; *OR*, 12:2, 303–4.

27. *OR*, 12:2, 728, 729; Dowdey, *Wartime Papers of R. E. Lee*, 260. John Pelham did not go with Stuart on the raid behind Pope. Charles Milham (*Gallant Pelham*) speculates that Pelham "ruefully" stayed behind as Stuart assuaged the artillerist's feelings with the explanation that he was needed to help guard the Rappahannock. More likely Pelham was left behind because of the losses he incurred that morning and the fact that he and his men needed rest.

28. B. Davis, *Jeb Stuart*, 167.

29. Mason, "Marching on Manassas," 528.

30. Hennessy, "Stuart's Revenge," 45; B. Davis, *Jeb Stuart*, 171; Blackford, *War Years*, 107.

31. One of the shoulder straps, showing the two stars of a Federal major general, is privately owned by a gentleman from Marietta, Georgia.

32. *OR*, 12:2, 732–33; A. Mitchell, *Letters*, 262.

33. *OR*, 12:3, 941; Dowdey, *Wartime Papers of R. E. Lee*, 262.

Chapter 11

1. Milham, *Gallant Pelham*, 126–27. Pope had knowledge of Jackson's beginning movement, but he soon lost track of the Rebels when his cavalry tired out and lost their enthusiasm for patrol. Pope naïvely believed the Confederate forces were off to the Shenandoah Valley. Esposito, *West Point Atlas of American Wars*, vol. 1, map 58.

2. Redwood, "Jackson's 'Foot-Cavalry' at the Second Bull Run," 530–31; Caldwell, *History of a Brigade*, 57; R. Dabney, *Campaigns of Jackson*, 517; Robertson, *Jackson*, 550.

3. Milham, *Gallant Pelham*, 135; Hennessy, *Return to Bull Run*, 139.

4. Trimble and Stuart captured 300 prisoners, 200 blacks, 8 cannons, and nearly 250 horses. They also seized an estimated 50,000 pounds of bacon, 1,000 barrels of corned beef, 2,000 barrels of salt pork, 2,000 barrels of flour, and huge amounts of ordnance and medical supplies. Trimble lost only fifteen men wounded. *OR*, 12:2, 644; Allan, *Army of Northern Virginia*, 215.

5. Sorrel, *Recollections*, 96; Blackford, *War Years*, 111.

6. Hennessy, *Return to Bull Run*, 127. Three of Pelham's biographers (Hassler, *Col. John Pelham*, 59; Milham, *Gallant Pelham*, 131; and Mercer, *Gallant Pelham*, 74–75) have him participating in the fighting against Taylor's men; however, he would not arrive until later in the day. Neither Jackson nor Stuart mentioned Pelham as part of this action in their post-battle reports, but Jackson did specify the batteries of William Poague and Joseph Carpenter. *OR*, 12:2, 643–44, 734–35. Also see Trout, *Galloping Thunder*, 669–70n43.

7. *OR*, 12:2, 735.

8. Edward McCrady speech, August 21, 1884, *SHSP*, 1:312; Worsham, *One of Jackson's Foot Cavalry*, 120–21.

9. Caldwell, *History of a Brigade*, 58; T. Jones, *Lee's Tigers*, 118; Chamberlayne, *Ham Chamberlayne*, 100.

10. Von Borcke, *Memoirs*, 1:138; Milham, *Gallant Pelham*, 132; Hassler, *Col. John Pelham*, 59.

11. *OR*, 12:2, 753. Written battle reports from Pelham are rare thus treasured. In the case of

Second Manassas, however, Pelham wrote two upon the urging of Jeb Stuart: January 10 and March 7, 1863. Since the reports are lengthy and cover the entire battle, I have deemed it best to segment them for each part of the fighting.

12. Blackford, *War Years*, 116–19.

13. Robertson, *The Stonewall Brigade*, 146–47. Botts, a kinsman of W. W. Blackford, won much publicity as the defense counsel for John Brown during his trial in 1859. Botts died from his wound fourteen days later on September 11.

14. Ewell, who had served Jackson so competently since early in the war, would be lost from the Army of Northern Virginia for nine months, returning in May 1863. At that time he replaced Jackson, who died on May 10 as the result of a wound. For further details on Ewell's wounding and amputation, see Welsh, *Medical Histories of Confederate Generals*, 63–64, and Pfanz, *Richard S. Ewell*, 257–59.

15. *OR*, 12:2, 754; Hennessy, *Return to Bull Run*, 185; Trout, *Galloping Thunder*, 84.

16. *Anniston Star*, May 18, 1921; Milham, *Gallant Pelham*, 137–38; *OR*, 12:2, 754.

17. Hennessy, *Return to Bull Run*, 187–88; Dawes, *The Sixth Wisconsin Volunteers*, 68.

18. *OR*, 12:2, 645, 735. The confusion in Pelham's rank is justified. His promotion to major had been announced but was yet unconfirmed.

19. *OR*, 12:2, 753–55.

20. McGuire, "Characteristics of Jackson," 307; Caldwell, *History of a Brigade*, 32; Robertson, *Jackson*, 563.

Chapter 12

1. *OR*, 12:2, 735, 740.

2. *OR*, 12:2, 735–36; Chambers, *Stonewall Jackson*, 2:160; von Borcke, *Memoirs*, 1:146–47.

3. Hennessy, *Return to Bull Run*, 220; *OR*, 12:2, 646, 736; H. B. McClellan, *I Rode with Stuart*, 105.

4. As previously mentioned, Pelham filed two reports of his actions at Second Manassas. In his first report, written on January 10, 1863, Pelham stated that Jackson "gave me discretionary orders to engage my battery where fitting opportunity should occur." In his second report, dated March 7, 1863, Pelham stated that Jackson "gave me discretionary orders to act as the occasion might require." *OR*, 12:2, 755; Milham, *Gallant Pelham*, 140.

5. *OR*, 12:2, 755.

6. *OR*, 12:2, 646, 559.

7. *Anniston Star*, May 18, 1921; Hassler, *Col. John Pelham*, 67; Trout, *Galloping Thunder*, 85; von Borcke, *Memoirs*, 1:149.

8. *OR*, 12:2, 754–55. Besides the death of Wilson Turner, the members of the horse artillery suffered five wounded: Charles A. Evans, whose arm was amputated at the shoulder (he survived but was granted permanent disability); Sergeant William Hoxton, who was later promoted to lieutenant and was twice more wounded in the war; Sergeant J. Henry Thomas, so severely wounded he remained behind Union lines until mid-December; and Privates W. W. Mangum and James Mann. Sergeant Robert P. P. Burwell, whom Pelham praised as R. T. Burwell, received a mortal wound at Brandy Station on August 1, 1863, dying on August 31 at age nineteen. Trout, "*The Hoss*," 69–70, 78, 132–33; Moore, *Stuart Horse Artillery*, 165.

9. Hennessy, *Return to Bull Run*, 225; Sorrel, *Recollections*, 96.

10. Casler, *Four Years in the Stonewall Brigade*, 112, Library of Congress.

11. Sorrel, *Recollections*, 97; Longstreet, *Manassas to Appomattox*, 181–82; Longstreet, "Our March against Pope," 519; Wert, *Longstreet*, 169.

12. Wert, *Longstreet*, 169; J. I. Robertson, *Jackson*, 566; Longstreet, *Manassas to Appomattox*, 182–84.

13. Randall, "Gallant Pelham," 342; Hassler, *Col. John Pelham*, 68.

14. Hennessy, *Return to Bull Run*, 242. William Woods Hassler states that John Pelham shouted: "Don't shoot him! Capture him!" This story may, in effect, be true, but numerous Confederates were shouting to save Major Barney. The same author has Pelham's gunners opening up at close range and firing "twelve shells per minute on a thicket behind which enemy reinforcements were gathering" and tearing "holes in the supporting lines with each puff of gunsmoke" (Hassler, *Col. John Pelham*, 70–71). In fact, it appears that Pelham and his guns remained rather dormant on August 30. In Pelham's post-battle report, dated March 7, 1863, he stated: "I held my battery in readiness on the field for action during the 30th, but it being the only battery of horse artillery, would be very much needed in case of a retreat or pursuit. General Jackson ordered me to reserve my ammunition for any emergency." *OR*, 12:2, 755; Milham, *Gallant Pelham*, 144; Mercer, *Gallant Pelham*, 80.

15. T. Jones, *Lee's Tigers*, 124; *OR*, 12:2, 669; Blackford, *War Years*, 132; S. D. Lee, "The Second Battle of Manassas," 66; Allan, *Army of Northern Virginia*, 281–82.

16. H. B. McClellan, *I Rode with Stuart*, 106; von Borcke, *Memoirs*, 1:157; *OR*, 12:2, 737.

17. T. Jones, *Lee's Tigers*, 125; Lasswell, *Rags and Hope*, 130; Allan, *Army of Northern Virginia*, 308.

18. Milham, *Gallant Pelham*, 144; Lasswell, *Rags and Hope*, 130.

19. Mercer, *Gallant Pelham*, 81. Mercer cites the source for his quote as John Esten Cooke, *Life of Stonewall Jackson*, 305. Interestingly, Cooke's biography of Jackson, published in New York by Charles B. Richardson in 1863, has no such quote by Cooke concerning the Battle of Chantilly. Another source that puts Pelham in the middle of the action on this day is R. Beale, *History of the 9th Virginia Cavalry*, 36. The reports of neither Stonewall Jackson nor Jeb Stuart, however, mention Pelham as a participant in the action. Furthermore, Stapleton Crutchfield, one of Jackson's artillerists, reported "no artillery engaged" on this day. "The character of the ground," stated Crutchfield, "was such that it [artillery] could not be brought into action. Several batteries were posted so as to check any success of the enemy, but none became engaged." *OR*, 12:2, 654.

20. Von Borcke, *Memoirs*, 1:173–74; Trout, *Galloping Thunder*, 87.

21. *OR*, 12:2, 744; Longacre, *Lee's Cavalrymen*, 127; Moore, *Stuart Horse Artillery*, 31.

22. G. McClellan, *McClellan's Own Story*, 535; Murfin, *The Gleam of Bayonets*, 71.

23. Hennessy, *Return to Bull Run*, 453–54; Pope, "The Second Battle of Bull Run," 490; G. McClellan, "From the Peninsula to Antietam," 551.

24. A. Mitchell, *Letters*, 263–64; Thomason, *Jeb Stuart*, 257–58. According to Norman Dasinger, young men enamored with Pelham's heroics signed a waiting list to become a part of his horse artillery when vacancies occurred. Dasinger, "Gallant Pelham," 29.

25. J. I. Robertson, *General A. P. Hill*, 128; Quaife, *From the Cannon's Mouth*, 111; Hennessy, *Return to Bull Run*, 471; J. I. Robertson, *Jackson*, 575.

26. Pope, "Second Battle of Bull Run," 494; Hennessy, *Return to Bull Run*, 471. Pope recorded another memorable comment pertaining to an oft-quoted statement from his past: "A good deal of cheap wit has been expended upon a fanciful story that I published an order or wrote a letter or made a remark that my 'headquarters would be in the saddle.' . . . Certainly I never used this expression or wrote or dictated it, nor does any such expression occur in any order of mine; and as it has perhaps served its time and effected its purpose, it ought to be retired" ("Second Battle of Bull Run," 493–94). Pope resigned in 1866. He died at age seventy on September 23, 1892, at the Old Soldiers' and Sailors' Home in Sandusky, Ohio.

27. Chamberlayne, *Ham Chamberlayne*, 102. For all his elation Pender does not conceal his contempt for some: "Jackson added new laurels to his brow—not that I like to be under [him],

for he forgets that one ever gets tired, hungry, or sleepy." Pender later added: "Jackson would kill up any army the way he marches and the bad management in the subsistence Dept" (William Hassler, *One of Lee's Best Men,* 171, 173).

28. Milham, *Gallant Pelham,* 147.

Chapter 13

1. *OR,* 19:2, 597.

2. Hassler, *Col. John Pelham,* 77.

3. Douglas, "Stonewall Jackson in Maryland," 620–21.

4. Murfin, *Gleam of Bayonets,* 93, 94; Hunter, "Four Years in the Ranks," 507. Artillerist Edward Porter Alexander admitted a few years later that "in the matter of shoes, clothing, and food" the army was "upon the whole, probably worse off than it had ever been before or ever was again." Bohannon, "Dirty, Ragged, and Ill-Provided For," 101.

5. Caldwell, *History of a Brigade,* 72.

6. Milham, *Gallant Pelham,* 150; speech on Pelham (speaker unidentified), DSFP; Shreve, "Reminiscences." Reproduced with kind permission of the Jefferson County Museum, Charles Town, West Virginia. I would like to thank Susan M. Collins, curator of the Jefferson County Museum, for permission to cite from Shreve's "Reminiscences."

7. Hassler, *Col. John Pelham,* 79–80.

8. Von Borcke, *Memoirs,* 1:192–93.

9. R. E. Lee, "Proclamation to the People of Maryland," September 8, 1862, (copy transcribed directly from an original for distribution at Antietam National Battlefield). Lee undoubtedly was referring to the Lincoln administration's forceful role in maintaining Maryland's statehood for the Union and his expressed desire for Maryland to reconsider secession. The entire text of Lee's proclamation can be found in *OR,* 19:2, 601–2, Dowdey, *Wartime Papers of R. E. Lee,* 299–300, and Longstreet, *Manassas to Appomattox,* 280–81. Of the delicate wording of this document, John Esten Cooke noted: "When a great cause has such leaders, it is already won." *Life of Stonewall Jackson,* 202.

10. The renovated Female Academy at Urbana, utilized as a silk mill at its beginning in 1754, is today privately owned and called the Landon House. Tours are given on the six-acre estate and throughout the building where the proprietors show the graffiti drawn on the walls by various Confederates and the 155th Pennsylvania Infantry. The ballroom where Stuart headed the dance measures approximately twenty-five feet by twenty-five feet and remains the highlight of the tour. See www.LandonHouse.com.

11. Blackford, *War Years,* 141; von Borcke, *Memoirs,* 1:194.

12. Von Borcke, *Memoirs,* 1:196; Trout, *Galloping Thunder,* 91. Von Borcke's flair for the dramatic may have tainted his perception of the skirmish. He claims that "many [were] killed and wounded, and a considerable number of prisoners [taken]." These statements appear highly exaggerated. Furthermore, von Borcke's assertion concerning Pelham's role in firing cannon at the Federals is questionable. Charles Milham's statement that Pelham used two of Hart's guns in the fray is also certainly debatable (*Gallant Pelham,* 152; Trout, *Galloping Thunder,* 672). Perhaps Blackford put it best when he mentioned "we hastened back 'covered with glory,' at least in the ladies' eyes" (*War Years,* 141).

13. Blackford, *War Years,* 141–42; Longacre, *Lee's Cavalrymen,* 130.

14. Sears, *Landscape Turned Red,* 90–91; Freeman, *Lee's Lieutenants,* 2:160–61. The entire text of Special Orders No. 191 can be found in *OR,* 19:2, 603–4, Dowdey, *Wartime Papers of R. E. Lee,* 301–3, Longstreet, *Manassas to Appomattox,* 203, and Allan, *Army of Northern Virginia,* 332.

15. Sears, *Landscape Turned Red*, 96; Freeman, *Lee's Lieutenants*, 2:721.

16. Walker, "Jackson's Capture of Harper's Ferry," 607.

17. Sears, *Landscape Turned Red*, 105.

18. Trout, *Galloping Thunder*, 92.

19. Von Borcke, *Memoirs*, 1:212–13; Trout, *Galloping Thunder*, 94, 98; Moore, *Stuart Horse Artillery*, 33. Only von Borcke refers to this intriguing tale of Pelham's disappearance; no other details exist. From von Borcke's jumbled and puzzling account of the entire South Mountain episode, it is quite easy to confuse the date of this occurrence. Pelham may have become separated from the others following the fighting at South Mountain on September 14 when the disorder of the retreat with a host of men missing and lines virtually nonexistent prevailed.

20. Regrettably, the name of the stranger, who had much to do with saving Lee's army in Maryland, has been lost to history.

21. H. Bridges, *Lee's Maverick General*, 104; Sears, *Landscape Turned Red*, 126.

22. *OR*, 19:2, 281; Grattan, "The Battle of Boonsboro Gap or South Mountain," 32; Longstreet, *Manassas to Appomattox*, 214; Sears, *McClellan*, 281–82; Murfin, *Gleam of Bayonets*, 133; Sorrel, *Recollections*, 106.

23. *OR*, 19:2, 281; Longstreet, *Manassas to Appomattox*, 215; G. McClellan, "From the Peninsula to Antietam," 555.

24. Blackford, *War Years*, 143; D. H. Hill, "The Battle of South Mountain, or Boonsboro.' " For further information on the Lost Orders, see the appendixes of Sears, *Landscape Turned Red*, 349–52, and Murfin, *Gleam of Bayonets*, 328–38. Appreciation for Hill's lack of duplicity can be garnered in H. Bridges, *Lee's Maverick General*, 94–98. Jackson's original, handwritten copy sent to D. H. Hill is in the collection of the Hill Papers at the North Carolina Department of Archives and History in Raleigh, North Carolina. The copy that made its way into Federal hands is in the Manuscript Division of the George B. McClellan Papers, Library of Congress. My thanks are extended to the staff members who allowed me to make a copy of the Orders. Microfilm, reel #31, container 78.

25. *OR*, 19:1, 1019; Freeman, *Lee's Lieutenants*, 2:167. The town of Boonsboro is often referred to as Boonsborough.

26. *OR*, 19:1, 1032; Trout, *Galloping Thunder*, 99; Freeman, *Lee's Lieutenants*, 2:180; Hassler, *Col. John Pelham*, 86; Pierro, *Maryland Campaign of September 1862*, 174.

27. Basler, *Collected Works of Abraham Lincoln*, 5:426; Murfin, *Gleam of Bayonets*, 189; *OR*, 19:1, 951; Freeman, *Lee's Lieutenants*, 2:199; Freeman, *Lee*, 2:379.

28. Nanzig, *3rd Virginia Cavalry*, 20–21; G. Beale, *Lieutenant of Cavalry*, 45; Milham, *Gallant Pelham*, 156–57; Trout, *Galloping Thunder*, 101.

29. Murfin, *Gleam of Bayonets*, 139.

30. Caldwell, *History of a Brigade*, 72; Freeman, *Lee's Lieutenants*, 2:200.

31. "McClellan's failure to attack Lee on the 15th was a serious mistake," noted William Allan; "his failure to do so on the 16th was fatal." *Army of Northern Virginia*, 371.

32. Walker, "Sharpsburg," 675.

33. This property belonged to the Nicodemus family whose son, Joseph Leonard Nicodemus, graduated from West Point in 1858, one year after Pelham entered the academy. The undistinguished Class of 1858 listed twenty-seven seniors, of which Nicodemus ranked number twenty-three. After graduation he participated in the Utah Expedition against the Mormons. During the Civil War, he fought at the Battle of Valverde, New Mexico, and later served as a signal officer. Following the war, he was a professor at the University of Wisconsin until his death on January 6, 1879. Cullum, *Register of Graduates*, 249.

34. *OR*, 19:1, 223, 243; G. Beale, *Lieutenant of Cavalry*, 47. Some uncertainty appears as to which unit actually fired the shots for the Confederate artillery. Allan claimed that William

Poague's Rockbridge Battery probably did so. Beale, however, believed, without firm conviction, that Pelham's guns should receive credit. Wrote Beale, "I have come to the conclusion that the gun, or guns, opposing [Hooker] must have been one or more of Pelham's, but I cannot verify my conclusion."

35. *OR,* 19:1, 218. Robert E. L. Krick seriously challenges Hooker's "appreciation of the situation," stating, "There is no evident explanation why Hooker did not take the elevation . . . apart from the disorientation normally felt by commanders when they encounter new terrain." Krick concludes, "General Hooker's indifference to the advantages of Nicodemus Heights remains one of the battle's mysteries" ("Defending Lee's Flank," 196, 198, 215).

36. Channing Price to his mother, September 18, 1862, in Trout, *Pen & Saber,* 100; R. E. L. Krick, "Defending Lee's Flank," 198.

37. R. E. L. Krick, "Defending Lee's Flank," 198–99; Moore, *Stuart Horse Artillery,* 33–34; Sears, *Landscape Turned Red,* 177–78; *OR,* 19:1, 819. Both Pelham biographers, Charles G. Milham (*Gallant Pelham,* 198) and William W. Hassler (*Col. John Pelham,* 127), incorrectly place this incident over seven weeks later during the Ten Days Battles on November 2, 1862.

Seventeen-year-old Robert M. Mackall, a color-bearer, first enlisted in the Thirteenth Virginia Infantry in 1861 before transferring to Pelham's battery in May 1862. He contracted gonorrhea in March 1864. In August of that year he transferred to the First Virginia Cavalry. Following the war he lived well into the twentieth century, dying on June 21, 1934, at age ninety. Moore, *Stuart Horse Artillery,* 173; Trout, "*The Hoss,*" 84–85.

38. Dawes, *Sixth Wisconsin,* 87; Quaife, *From the Cannon's Mouth,* 125.

Chapter 14

1. Sears, *McClellan,* 301.

2. R. E. L. Krick, "Defending Lee's Flank," 200, 196.

3. A rather full weather report for the day is given in Murfin, *Gleam of Bayonets,* 212.

4. R. E. L. Krick, "Defending Lee's Flank," 200–201; *OR,* 19:1, 236, 226. The historian Dennis Frye states that "Nicodemus Heights was the key not only to the opening phase of the battle but to the entire battle. . . . Lee's entire line is untenable if Nicodemus is lost." Frye labels Nicodemus Heights the "Little Round Top of Antietam," an obvious reference to the Federal stronghold at Gettysburg. Frye, interview by the author, October, 30, 1999.

5. R. E. L. Krick, "Defending Lee's Flank," 201; Pierro, *Maryland Campaign of September 1862,* 220; Chiles, "Artillery Hell!" 16; G. Beale, *Lieutenant of Cavalry,* 48. Heros von Borcke claimed that he "was exchanging some friendly words" with Thornton when the horrible incident occurred. However, since von Borcke mentions that it took place at "midday," his involvement must be seriously challenged (*Memoirs,* 1:232). At the close of the war, on April 7, 1865, Robert E. Lee visited the widow of Thornton in Farmville, Virginia, on Beech Street. After offering his condolences the commanding general surrendered two days later at Appomattox Court House. Calkins, *The Appomattox Campaign,* 117.

6. Officially known as the German Baptist Brethren Church, the name Dunker originated from locals who witnessed the baptismal ceremony of completely immersing an individual three times in a stream. See *The Dunker Church.*

7. Contrary to the notion of some writers, Henry Jackson Hunt was not one of Pelham's artillery instructors at West Point.

8. Blackford, *War Years,* 151; Mrs. John Williams, "The 'Gallant' John Pelham"; Hassler, *Col. John Pelham,* 90. R. E. L. Krick states that the Nicodemus family escaped into Federal lines the

night before and suggests that perhaps Blackford's narrative pertains to the family of Alfred Pof-fenberger. "Defending Lee's Flank," 200, 217.

9. The following day Channing Price wrote his mother that "The artillery firing yesterday was the most terrific of the war, exceeding all imagination." Trout, *Pen & Saber*, 101.

10. *OR*, 19:1, 254; Naisawald, *Grape and Canister*, 192; Pierro, *Maryland Campaign of September 1862*, 220; R. E. L. Krick, "Defending Lee's Flank," 202; Dawes, *Sixth Wisconsin*, 87.

11. Dawes, *Sixth Wisconsin*, 90–91; Milham, *Gallant Pelham*, 162; Hassler, *Col. John Pelham*, 91; Cooke, *Surry of Eagle's-Nest*, 333.

12. *OR*, 19:1, 967, 969; R. E. L. Krick, "Defending Lee's Flank," 203; Sears, *McClellan*, 305.

13. Pierro, *Maryland Campaign of September 1862*, 226; Bohannon, "Dirty, Ragged and Ill-Provided For," 117; Freeman, *Lee's Lieutenants*, 2:208; Hood, *Advance and Retreat*, 44; Chiles, "Artillery Hell!" 25; Naisawald, *Grape and Canister*, 197.

14. Nolan, *The Iron Brigade*, 142; McMurry, *John Bell Hood*, 59; Freeman, *Lee's Lieutenants*, 2:209.

15. Wise, *Long Arm of Lee*, 1:301–2; Allan, *Army of Northern Virginia*, 393; Pierro, *Maryland Campaign of September 1862*, 246–47; Moore, *Stuart Horse Artillery*, 34.

16. Driver, *The Staunton Artillery*, 25; Trout, *Galloping Thunder*, 103.

17. *OR*, 19:1, 820, 245; Sears, *Landscape Turned Red*, 206.

18. Wise, *Long Arm of Lee*, 1:302. Thorough study of the advance of the Twelfth Corps has given the historian R. E. L. Krick an opposing view of Pelham's heroics against Mansfield's at-tackers. Krick claims that the thick West Woods hindered Pelham's vantage point against the Twelfth Corps. Furthermore, Pelham again had to avoid hitting Jackson's infantrymen with his blasts. "Defending Lee's Flank," 205–6.

19. Pierro, *Maryland Campaign of September 1862*, 260; Sears, *Landscape Turned Red*, 223. The historian L. Van Loan Naisawald pulls no punches, labeling Sumner's attack "gallant but stupid," since the lack of reconnaissance and absence of Federal artillery to support the advance literally doomed it. *Grape and Canister*, 204.

20. Moore, *Stuart Horse Artillery*, 34; R. E. L. Krick, "Defending Lee's Flank," 209.

21. Moe, *The Last Full Measure*, 181.

22. The first bullet hit Sedgwick in the leg, the next struck his wrist, and the third hit his shoulder. He recovered from his wounds and continued his fine career in the Army of the Po-tomac. Winslow, *General John Sedgwick*, 47.

23. *OR*, 19:1, 820.

24. Dawes, *Sixth Wisconsin*, 93.

25. Fred R. Martin, "Gallant Pelham Was Our Top War Hero," *Anniston Star*, 75th anniver-sary issue. Jennings Cropper Wise adds, "Pelham, greatly outmatched in the number of pieces as well as the weight of his metal, had with unsurpassed courage and skill done all of which his men and material were capable. . . . Without Pelham's guns, to deny the approach, never could Jackson have withstood the shock of those dense masses . . . ominously banked against his left" (*Long Arm of Lee*, 1:304, 310).

26. *OR*, 19:1, 821. In his report the normally meticulous Stuart mistakenly included the bat-tery of Willie Pegram with those of Poague and Carrington as those who fought under Pelham that day.

27. Article (author unknown), John Pelham Scrapbook, ADAH; Adams, "Reminiscences of a Childhood Spent at Hayfield Plantation"; Cooke, *Surry of Eagle's-Nest*, 332; Dasinger, "Gallant Pelham," 29.

28. Gordon, *Reminiscences*, 87. Gordon, seemingly a magnet for Yankee bullets that day, would eventually take his fifth wound "which struck me squarely in the face, and passed out, barely

missing the jugular vein. I fell forward and lay unconscious with my face in my cap." Bleeding profusely into the hat, Gordon might have suffocated in his own blood had not a bullet hole in his cap from a previous shot allowed the blood to escape. Prior to this injury, he had taken wounds in the right calf, right thigh, left arm, "tearing asunder the tendons and mangling the flesh," and the shoulder. He was out of the war for seven months; his convalescence was slow. Upon his return to the Army of Northern Virginia, Gordon received a promotion to brigadier general and fought with Lee's army the remainder of the war. *Reminiscences,* 89–90.

29. Hard-fighting Edward Cross was killed on July 2, 1863, at Gettysburg when a rifle ball struck him in the abdomen.

30. J. Robertson, *Michigan in the War,* 915; Murfin, *Gleam of Bayonets,* 262.

31. Longstreet, "The Invasion of Maryland," 669.

32. Antietam Creek averages twenty to twenty-five yards in width. Some argue that the depth of the stream hindered any attempt to wade across. However, Kyd Douglas, a resident of the area, argued otherwise: "Go look at it and tell me if you don't think Burnside and his corps might have executed a hop, skip, and jump and landed on the other side. One thing is certain, they might have waded it that day without getting their waist belts wet in any place." Douglas further added that years later a U.S. Army officer said to him: "What puzzles me, is how did Burnside keep his troops from breaking over" (*I Rode with Stonewall,* 172).

33. Cullum, *Register of Graduates,* 251; Sears, *Landscape Turned Red,* 262–63. The first bullet to hit Kingsbury broke his leg; a second struck his foot. As his men lifted him onto a stretcher, a third penetrated his shoulder. The last bullet ripped open his abdomen. His near lifeless body was carried to the Rohrbach house. Kingsbury was the beloved brother-in-law of David "Neighbor" Jones, whose forces gunned Kingsbury down. Some speculate that Jones's heart attack a few weeks later was caused by this knowledge. Three months after Kingsbury's death, his wife, Eva Taylor, bore him a son, Henry Walter Kingsbury Jr., in December. Sergent, *They Lie Forgotten,* 155–56; Kirshner, *Class of 1861,* 33; Simpson, "General McClellan's Bodyguard," 45.

34. Walker, "Sharpsburg," 679; Sears, *Landscape Turned Red,* 274–75; R. E. L. Krick, "Defending Lee's Flank," 212, 221.

35. For a detailed description of A. P. Hill's ailment, see J. I. Robertson, *A. P. Hill.* Hill's best friend and roommate at West Point was George McClellan. Hill reportedly attended McClellan's wedding to Ellen Marcy, Hill's former love, in New York City on May 22, 1860. Next to McClellan, Hill's best friend had been Ambrose Burnside. They graduated from the academy in 1847.

36. *OR,* 19:2, 643; Freeman, *Lee's Lieutenants,* 2:247.

37. Waugh, *Class of 1846,* 389; *OR,* 19:1, 981; Douglas, "Stonewall Jackson in Maryland," 629.

38. Poague, *Gunner with Stonewall,* 47; Pierro, *Maryland Campaign of September 1862,* 311; R. E. L. Krick, "Defending Lee's Flank," 212.

39. R. E. L. Krick, "Defending Lee's Flank," 212–13; Poague, *Gunner with Stonewall,* 47; *OR,* 19:1, 1010, 228, 306.

40. *OR,* 19:1, 1010; Poague, *Gunner with Stonewall,* 47–48.

41. Ezra Carman, author of Pierro's edited *Maryland Campaign of September 1862,* criticized Jeb Stuart for not having better reconnaissance at Nicodemus Heights, thus being unaware of the enemy strength facing them (311–12).

42. Cooke, *Wearing of the Gray,* 121; Cooke, *Surry of Eagle's-Nest,* 332, 339.

43. No other mention of why Pelham singled out Private Dudley is available. A native Virginian, Dudley had entered Virginia Military Institute at age fifteen in the summer of 1861. He left school and joined the Stuart Horse Artillery on July 26, 1862. Dudley later transferred to the Fifth Virginia Cavalry. He was severely wounded in the leg at Trevilian Station on June 11, 1864.

Following an amputation, he lingered on for nearly a month, but died on July 9 at the age of eighteen. Moore, *Stuart Horse Artillery,* 35, 167–68; Trout, " *The Hoss,* " 77.

44. Sears, *McClellan,* 318–19; Murfin, *Gleam of Bayonets,* 312. McClellan's bloated self-appraisal has come under intense scrutiny from participants in the battle as well as modern historians.

45. Von Borcke, *Memoirs,* 1:240–41; Walker, "Sharpsburg," 682; B. Davis, *Jeb Stuart,* 208.

Chapter 15

1. Dawes, *Sixth Wisconsin,* 95.

2. Caldwell, *History of a Brigade,* 86–87.

3. Hassler, *Col. John Pelham,* 98. Unfortunately, the young lady's name has been forgotten to history. Von Borcke simply refers to her as the "Maid of Sargossa," from George Byron's *Childe Harold.*

4. Mercer, *Gallant Pelham,* 95–96; von Borcke, *Memoirs,* 1:250–51; Trout, *Galloping Thunder,* 106.

5. Von Borcke, *Memoirs,* 1:255–56; Mercer, *Gallant Pelham,* 96–97; *OR,* 19:1, 821; Thomason, *Jeb Stuart,* 288.

6. Milham, *Gallant Pelham,* 170; Mercer, *Gallant Pelham,* 97. Milham had the pleasure of interviewing Alburtis's daughter in 1933. She still resided at that time in the same Alburtis homestead, and undoubtedly the quotes attributed to her father were derived from that interview. Since Milham's interview was conducted seventy-one years after the dinner Pelham attended, it is possible that Miss Alburtis was present and remembered the actual conversation.

7. Von Borcke, *Memoirs,* 1:258; Milham, *Gallant Pelham,* 170.

8. Second in command to Marcellus Moorman was Captain John J. "Bird" Shoemaker, who flatly stated that the transfer of their battery to Pelham's command "was regarded as a promotion and distinction any battery in the army would have been proud of." Shoemaker would later state that "although we had been under his [Pelham's] command but a short time, we had learned to love him for his own sake and to respect him for his invincible courage and gallantry in battle, and to this day we mourn his death." Young, "Shoemaker's Battery"; Shoemaker, *Shoemaker's Battery.*

9. Although this story may be apocryphal, Hassler mentions it on page 101 of his book. The reorganization of the horse artillery is taken from "Miscellaneous" file; Milham, *Gallant Pelham,* 171–72; and Hassler, *Col. John Pelham,* 101.

10. Artillerist Ham Chamberlayne described Pendleton best. Referring to the artillery chieftain as "an absurd humbug" and "Lee's weakness," Chamberlayne further stated that Pendleton "is like the elephant, we have him & we don't know what on earth to do with him, and it costs a devil of a sight to feed him" (*Ham Chamberlayne,* 118, 134).

11. Breathed survived the war, went back to his medical practice, and died on February 14, 1870, one day past his thirty-second birthday. Copy of H. H. Matthews's letter, John Pelham Collection by Fred R. Martin, ACPL; Trout, " *The Hoss,* " 13–16; Moore, *Stuart Horse Artillery,* 37; Trout, *Galloping Thunder,* 470, 547–48.

12. Henry's outstanding performance at Fredericksburg in December 1862 would earn him a major's commission and a transfer to John Hood's division as chief of artillery. Going to the Western Theater with Hood in 1863, Henry fought at Atlanta and on through the Carolinas. Captured at Salisbury, North Carolina, on April 12, 1865, Henry was held as a prisoner of war at Johnson's Island until his release on July 25, 1865. Following the war he made his way to Mexico

and served briefly under Maximilian. Henry was living in Brooklyn, New York, when paralysis struck him severely. He died two weeks later on November 28, 1877, the exact date of his thirty-ninth birthday. Sergent, *They Lie Forgotten,* 141–43; Trout, "*The Hoss,*"119–21.

13. Brzustowicz, "The Bower"; Milham, *Gallant Pelham,* 172. Originally built on 2,100 acres, the Bower was occupied by the Dandridge family until December 1919. At that time only 328 acres of land remained in their ownership. Today the Bower stands unoccupied. My two visits there, both made in October, rendered an aesthetic quality that time has not diminished. One must see the Bower to appreciate its haunting romanticism.

14. Unfortunately, Stuart's Oak died several years ago. Brzustowicz, "The Bower."

15. Blackford, *War Years,* 155; Longacre, *Lee's Cavalrymen,* 139.

16. Von Borcke, *Memoirs,* 1:270; Blackford, *War Years,* 154–56. Jeb Stuart added his own compliments of the magnificent mansion in a letter to his cousin Nannie Price on October 22, 1862: " 'The Bower' is a charming place, full of pretty girls, all dear friends of mine but none, no not one, can usurp the place of Nannie" (A. Mitchell, *Letters,* 270). According to H. H. Matthews, "Stuart and Pelham were in clover" with the "very beautiful bevy of girls," and referred to the general and his number one artillerist as "the lions of the day" ("Pelham-Breathed Battery: The Chambersburg Raid," *St. Mary's Beacon,* February 2, 1905).

17. Undoubtedly, Belle was mistaken in placing a middle initial "S" in John's name. Found among John Pelham's possessions after his death, the Bible was given to his brother Samuel. It was later donated to the Alabama Department of Archives and History in Montgomery by Samuel's son and remains one of the few John Pelham treasures in existence. The Bible and Belle Boyd's message are still clearly on display. Milham, *Gallant Pelham,* 57–58; Hooper, "John Pelham and Belle Boyd," JPL; "Miscellaneous" file.

18. Blackford, *War Years,* 163–64; "Homes" file, JPL. In the Pelham files of the Jacksonville Public Library there is a photograph of Sallie Dandridge taken in 1861 or 1862. It shows her, with stately bearing, standing with her arms crossed on a pedestal. It reveals an attractive face with a firm chin and full lips. Her hair is parted in the middle and pulled back on both sides. It also gives her year of birth as 1839 and her date of death as 1879.

19. Hassler, *Col. John Pelham,* 101.

20. Cooke, *Wearing of the Gray,* 121; Brzustowicz, "The Bower." Interestingly, at no time does Cooke mention Sallie Dandridge by name.

21. Martin, "Our Top War Hero," in "General Articles" file, JPL; Milham, *Gallant Pelham,* 173. One handwritten statement, appearing in the "Miscellaneous" file of the JPL, states that an aunt, Mary Pelham Graves, claims she actually read letters between Atkinson Pelham and Stephen Dandridge concerning the engagement and that Mr. Dandridge expressed his happiness over the intended marriage.

22. Matthews, "Pelham-Breathed Battery"; Trout, *Galloping Thunder,* 114.

23. Sergent, *They Lie Forgotten,* 142; Trout, "*The Hoss,*"123. Robert Burwell suffered wounds during the Seven Days fighting and again at Chancellorsville. At Brandy Station on August 1, 1863, he was once more wounded in the arm. Infection set in and Robert died on August 31 at age nineteen. His older brother George survived the war but was killed on December 21, 1866, while fighting for Maximilian in Mexico. Trout, "*The Hoss,*"123–25; Moore, *Stuart Horse Artillery,* 165.

The closeness of Carter Hall and Glenvin, one owned by Major George H. Burwell and the other by Nathaniel Burwell, has prompted a common error made by at least two writers. Charles Milham records the two Burwell boys as sons of George (*Gallant Pelham,* 171). Artillerist George Shreve made the same mistake (Moore, *Stuart Horse Artillery,* 38).

24. Following the war, Henry traveled to Nevada and became superintendent of a quicksilver mine. In 1875 he ventured back to Virginia and apparently renewed his acquaintance with Susan.

Following their marriage, which produced two daughters, the Henrys moved back to Nevada and later to Brooklyn, New York.

25. Von Borcke, *Memoirs,* 1:289–90, 292; Longacre, *Mounted Raids of the Civil War,* 22.

26. Von Borcke, *Memoirs,* 1:271–72. Strangely, von Borcke constantly refers to his hunting companion and noted musician, Sam Sweeney, as Bob. A far worse error is made by the historians Millard and Dean Bushong, who refer to Sam Sweeney as a "Negro banjo player." Bushong and Bushong, *Fightin' Tom Rosser,* 31.

27. Von Borcke, *Memoirs,* 1:272; Blackford, *War Years,* 159–61. Blackford further stated that von Borcke pushed Stuart to confer the title chief of staff on him so he could boast about it in his book. Blackford also maintained that few of Von's black servants could tolerate the Prussian's boorish behavior and soon left him.

28. Von Borcke, *Memoirs,* 1:273–75; Blackford, *War Years,* 162–63; Milham, *Gallant Pelham,* 175; Hassler, *Col. John Pelham,* 102. According to von Borcke, "[Stuart] had been with General Pleasonton at West Point, and they had there been bitter enemies. Pleasonton had annoyed Stuart greatly in the olden days by his foppish vanity, and in the latter days by his dash and enterprise" (*Memoirs,* 1:275). Stuart certainly had a strong dislike for Pleasonton, but von Borcke is obviously mistaken concerning its origin. Pleasonton graduated in the Class of 1844, a full ten years ahead of Stuart's class. It is also engaging that Stuart would find his own qualities annoying in someone else.

29. Von Borcke, *Memoirs,* 1:277; Blackford, *War Years,* 163; Milham, *Gallant Pelham,* 175.

30. Von Borcke, *Memoirs,* 1:293; Blackford, *War Years,* 156. Born in Urbana, Maryland, on December 27, 1827, Brien graduated from Georgetown College in 1846. After the war in 1882 he returned to Urbana and purchased Tyrone, a beautiful mansion that had been part of a military school prior to the war and had become Shirley Female Institute, the same academy where Stuart held his "Sabers and Roses Ball" on September 8, 1862. In his postwar career Brien worked for the Illinois Central Railroad. He died on November 25, 1912, at age eighty-four of tuberculosis and bronchitis. Trout, *Plume,* 72–75; R. K. Krick, *Lee's Colonels,* 59.

31. Blackford, *War Years,* 156–58; Hassler, *Col. John Pelham,* 102–3; Longacre, *Lee's Cavalrymen,* 140. For all his boasting, von Borcke does not mention "The Operation" in his memoirs.

32. Von Borcke, *Memoirs,* 1:293–94; Blackford, *War Years,* 158–59; Milham, *Gallant Pelham,* 175; Hassler, *Col. John Pelham,* 104; Longacre, *Lee's Cavalrymen,* 140–41.

33. Many of the cavalry horses had suffered severe hoof problems from the macadamized roads of Maryland. Also afflicting the mounts was improper nourishment. Digesting green corn stalks had caused numerous cases of diarrhea. Daughtry, *Gray Cavalier,* 95.

34. *OR,* 19:2, 55; Freeman, *Lee's Lieutenants,* 2:285; B. Davis, *Jeb Stuart,* 214.

35. B. Davis, *Jeb Stuart,* 214; Trout, *Pen & Saber,* 105; Hassler, *Col. John Pelham,* 105–6; Longacre, *Lee's Cavalrymen,* 143.

36. *OR,* 19:2, 55–56; Mercer, *Gallant Pelham,* 100–101; Freeman, *Lee's Lieutenants,* 2:286; Longacre, *Mounted Raids,* 29.

37. *OR,* 19:2, 56; H. B. McClellan, *I Rode with Stuart,* 137; Thomason, *Jeb Stuart,* 298; Daughtry, *Gray Cavalier,* 98; Matthews, "Pelham-Breathed Battery."

38. *OR,* 19:2, 57.

Chapter 16

1. Blackford, *War Years,* 166.
2. H. B. McClellan, *I Rode with Stuart,* 140.

3. Blackford, *War Years,* 166–67.

4. H. B. McClellan, *I Rode with Stuart,* 140; Matthews, "Pelham-Breathed Battery"; Trout, *Galloping Thunder,* 115.

5. Matthews, "Pelham-Breathed Battery"; Trout, *Galloping Thunder,* 117.

6. Price, "Chambersburg Raid," 10; *OR,* 19:2, 57; Longacre, *Mounted Raids,* 32–34.

7. *OR,* 19:2, 65, 59; Freeman, *Lee's Lieutenants,* 2:305–6; Milham, *Gallant Pelham,* 179.

8. Longacre, *Lee's Cavalrymen,* 147; H. B. McClellan, *I Rode with Stuart,* 144–46; B. Davis, *Jeb Stuart,* 220–21.

9. *OR,* 19:2, 53.

10. Milham, *Gallant Pelham,* 180–81.

11. Channing Price estimated the damage of the remaining Federal equipment, including the five thousand rifles, to be $1,000,000. Ironically, much of the ammunition destroyed came from James Longstreet's ordnance train that escaping Federals had captured from Harpers Ferry the previous month. Price, "Chambersburg Raid," 11; Trout, *Pen & Saber,* 107; Sears, *Landscape Turned Red,* 328. Sears's estimate of the value of goods destroyed was far lower than that of Price—$250,000.

12. *OR,* 19:2, 66; Thomas, *Bold Dragoon,* 179; B. Davis, *Jeb Stuart,* 225.

13. Blackford, *War Years,* 172; *OR,* 19:2, 53; Matthews, "Pelham-Breathed Battery"; Trout, *Galloping Thunder,* 118.

14. Blackford, *War Years,* 173; Hassler, *Col. John Pelham,* 112. Blackford mentions two riders chasing her down but fails to identify either of them.

15. B. Davis, *Jeb Stuart,* 227.

16. Blackford, *War Years,* 173–74; Hassler, *Col. John Pelham,* 114.

17. Blackford, *War Years,* 179; Longacre, *Lee's Cavalrymen,* 148; B. Davis, *Jeb Stuart,* 229; Thomas, *Bold Dragoon,* 177.

18. Blackford, *War Years,* 179–80; Freeman, *Lee's Lieutenants,* 2:292; B. Davis, *Jeb Stuart,* 229. Stuart was often accused of infidelity, but Blackford strongly defended him: "On the contrary, though he dearly loved . . . to kiss a pretty girl, and the pretty girls dearly loved to kiss him, he was as pure as they. . . . all this I know to be true, for it would have been impossible for it to have been otherwise and I not to have known it" (*War Years,* 155). Jeb apparently saw no need to mention his side trip to the Cockey house in his official report.

Although Stuart never again saw the "New York Rebel," Blackford spent some time with her and Heros von Borcke in Baltimore in 1884. "We had many pleasant memories to recall," wrote Blackford, "but it was hard to realize that the middle-aged, matronly looking lady and the huge gentleman weighing between four and five hundred pounds were those who danced so gracefully then [at Urbana in 1862]. . . . [Von Borcke] was immense—his neck as large as his head, and all his manly beauty gone" (*War Years,* 220).

19. H. B. McClellan, *I Rode with Stuart,* 153; Matthews, "Pelham-Breathed Battery"; Trout, *Galloping Thunder,* 119.

20. Milham, *Gallant Pelham,* 185.

21. *OR,* 19:1, 73; H. B. McClellan, *I Rode with Stuart,* 154; Freeman, *Lee's Lieutenants,* 2:306.

22. *OR,* 19:2, 53; "Chambersburg Raid" file, JPL; von Borcke, *Memoirs,* 1:306.

23. H. B. McClellan, *I Rode with Stuart,* 156–57.

24. *OR,* 19:2, 50; Blackford, *War Years,* 175–76.

25. H. B. McClellan, *I Rode with Stuart,* 157–58; Moore, *Stuart Horse Artillery,* 42; Daughtry, *Gray Cavalier,* 102; Allan, *Army of Northern Virginia,* 453; Freeman, *Lee's Lieutenants,* 2:299–300, 308; Milham, *Gallant Pelham,* 187. Biles estimated Rooney Lee's force at over 1,500 men and

made no mention of Lee's ultimatum note. Pleasonton remained convinced that if Biles had held the elevation, the "capture of Stuart's whole force would have been certain and inevitable," but Stoneman labeled this thought as "simply ridiculous." *OR,* 19:2, 40, 44; "Miscellaneous" file.

26. Nye, "How Stuart Re-crossed the Potomac," 46; Blackford, *War Years,* 176.

27. *OR,* 19:2, 53; Moore, *Stuart Horse Artillery,* 42; Blackford, *War Years,* 176; Hassler, *Col. John Pelham,* 117–18; H. B. McClellan, *I Rode with Stuart,* 158. Blackford maintains that Pelham used two guns, pointed in opposite directions, to withstand the Federal advance. Other sources, including Stuart's official report, mention his use of only one cannon: "The enemy's loss is not known, but Pelham's one gun compelled the enemy's battery to change its position three times" (*OR,* 19:2, 54).

28. Blackford, *War Years,* 176–77; Freeman, *Lee's Lieutenants,* 2:300–301; H. B. McClellan, *I Rode with Stuart,* 158–59; Trout, *Galloping Thunder,* 120. Blackford's horse, Magic, was as much a hero in the rescue of Butler's men as was Blackford himself. The proud owner mentions the horse on numerous occasions in his book, often referring to the mare's "tremendous powers of endurance."

29. Blackford, *War Years,* 178; Hassler, *Col. John Pelham,* 118; Longacre, *Mounted Raids,* 44; Price, "Chambersburg Raid," 13; Trout, *Pen & Saber,* 108; Trout, *Galloping Thunder,* 121. Stuart judiciously did not mention the near loss of his rearguard in his official report.

A discrepancy occurs in the writings of W. W. Blackford and Channing Price regarding the crossing of White's Ford. When Blackford approached to cross the ford, he clearly identified Pelham fighting off the Federals: "There stood Pelham with his piece and there the enemy, just as I had left them." Price, however, with equal clarity stated: "The Genl [Stuart] sent me to bring off Capt Breathed & his gun . . . as he was the last to leave." In the heat of the moment either of the two could have been mistaken. Since both reporters were known for their accuracy, it is entirely possible that Pelham and Breathed were with the gun in question when it crossed the ford.

30. *OR,* 19:2, 39, 45; B. Davis, *Jeb Stuart,* 234–35; H. B. McClellan, *I Rode with Stuart,* 160.

31. Trout, *Galloping Thunder,* 121; Blackford, *War Years,* 178.

32. *OR,* 19:2, 54; H. B. McClellan, *I Rode with Stuart,* 160, 161; Trout, *Pen & Saber,* 109; Longacre, *Lee's Cavalrymen,* 151; Mercer, *Gallant Pelham,* 110; Freeman, *Lee's Lieutenants,* 2:302. The only wounded man on the venture was Frederick W. Arnholter of Hart's battery.

Channing Price wrote his mother on December 1 concerning the return of "Mulatto Bob": "The General's boy Bob has just arrived. . . . He gives a very strange and interesting account of his adventures: the horses he left at the house of a good Southern man near Hyattstown, Md. and they will be brought to Leesburg as soon as possible." "Mulatto Bob" bravely returned to Stuart's camp where, reportedly, Jeb forgave him. Trout, *Pen & Saber,* 117; Thomason, *Jeb Stuart,* 317.

33. Blackford, *War Years,* 164; Douglas, *I Rode with Stonewall,* 194.

34. Starr, *The Union Cavalry in the Civil War,* 1:319–20; *OR,* 19:2, 39–40.

35. Trout, *Galloping Thunder,* 121.

36. *OR,* 19:2, 52–54; von Borcke, *Memoirs,* 1:307–9; "Chambersburg Raid" file; Freeman, *Lee's Lieutenants,* 2:303.

37. Thomas, *Bold Dragoon,* 180; Esposito, *West Point Atlas,* vol. 1, map 70; Hassler, *One of Lee's Best Men,* 184; Wellman, *Giant in Gray,* 99.

38. *OR,* 19:2, 54; Price, "Chambersburg Raid," 15, 42; Thomas, *Bold Dragoon,* 180; Esposito, *West Point Atlas,* vol. 1, map 70; Freeman, *Lee's Lieutenants,* 2:309. Interestingly, nowhere in Lee's report did he mention the failure to destroy the bridge.

39. *OR,* 19:2, 485; "Miscellaneous" file; Basler, *Works of Abraham Lincoln,* 5:474, 477; H. B.

McClellan, *I Rode with Stuart,* 161–62; Sears, *McClellan,* 334; Murfin, *Gleam of Bayonets,* 318; Mercer, *Gallant Pelham,* 111.

40. Chambers, *Jackson,* 2:249; Daughtry, *Gray Cavalier,* 103; Foote, *The Civil War,* 1:751; B. Davis, *Jeb Stuart,* 235.

41. Sears, *Landscape Turned Red,* 328; *OR,* 19:2, 421; R. Duncan, *Blue-Eyed Child of Fortune,* 253; Thomas, *Bold Dragoon,* 183; *New York Times,* October 16, 1862.

42. A. Mitchell, *Letters,* 267–68.

Chapter 17

1. H. B. McClellan, *I Rode with Stuart,* 167; von Borcke, *Memoirs,* 1:311; Milham, *Gallant Pelham,* 190.

2. Blackford, *War Years,* 182–83; Sorrel, *Recollections,* 123. Vizetelly sailed for England in 1864 but returned to the Confederacy within months to continue his pursuit of recording the war via his writings and drawings. He even joined President Jefferson Davis's flight from Richmond in April 1865. In 1883, while reporting the war in Egypt, he was killed at the battle of Kashgil in the Sudan. Unfortunately, only some of his original drawings remain today in the Harvard College Library collection. Most of the originals were destroyed in the bombings of London in the Battle of Britain during World War II. Douglas, *I Rode with Stonewall,* 370; Faust, *Encyclopedia of the Civil War,* 789–90.

3. A. Mitchell, *Letters,* 270–71, 274–76, 271–72. Pelham's promotion would not come until it was awarded posthumously in March 1863. Although Stuart preferred Thomas Munford over the acerbic "Grumble" Jones, the unwanted promotion stood. Rosser would have to wait eleven months before he received his commission as a brigadier, and his bitterness toward Stuart, although unwarranted, remained. Munford was never officially recognized as a brigadier. Interestingly, a bitter feud occurred between Munford and Rosser during the war that did not end until the latter's death on March 29, 1910.

4. *OR,* 19:2, 414; H. B. McClellan, *I Rode with Stuart,* 169; Thomas, *Bold Dragoon,* 187. Fortunately for Stuart, many Federal horses were also troubled by this ailment, known as "rotten-hoof" to Pleasonton, which may have been contracted in the recent Pennsylvania raid. *OR,* 19:2, 112; Milham, *Gallant Pelham,* 197.

5. These words are most likely apocryphal but are quoted in Hassler, *Col. John Pelham,* 122. Pelham's prediction was, of course, inaccurate. The next time Sallie saw him, she was dressed in black, as she stood before his lifeless body in Richmond in March 1863.

6. Von Borcke, *Memoirs,* 1:323; Blackford, *War Years,* 183. Nine months later, following the defeat at Gettysburg, some of Stuart's cavalry, including Blackford, returned to the Bower. Although the Dandridge family welcomed the troopers, the joy of their previous stay in the autumn of 1862 had long since ceased. "A shade of sadness hung over our meeting," wrote Blackford, "when we thought how many who were with us during our former visit were dead or absent from wounds" (*War Years,* 235).

7. *OR,* 19:2, 141; G. Beale, *Lieutenant of Cavalry,* 53.

8. Cooke, *Wearing of the Gray,* 279–80.

9. Cooke, *Wearing of the Gray,* 121, 280; *Anniston Star,* May 18, 1921; Milham, *Gallant Pelham,* 194–95; Trout, *Galloping Thunder,* 126; von Borcke, *Memoirs,* 2:13. Stuart may not have been as excited by Pelham's overdue appearance as he noted, "Our pursuit had been too rapid for the artillery to keep pace, but it finally came up" (*OR,* 19:2, 141).

10. Cooke, *Wearing of the Gray*, 281–82; von Borcke, *Memoirs*, 2:15–16; Thomas, *Bold Dragoon*, 182. Burke Davis describes the same scene but mistakenly places the incident in Upperville. *Jeb Stuart*, 241.

11. Some sources use the spelling Philemont or Philomount.

12. Wise, *Long Arm of Lee*, 1:348; Milham, *Gallant Pelham*, 195.

13. G. Beale, *Lieutenant of Cavalry*, 54–55.

14. *OR*, 19:2, 142; H. B. McClellan, *I Rode with Stuart*, 175–76; Mercer, *Gallant Pelham*, 115. Stuart did not write his report of the Ten Days Battles until more than a year later on February 27, 1864.

15. Trout, *Galloping Thunder*, 127; Moore, *Stuart Horse Artillery*, 43. Costigan's first name is sometimes referred to as Cosgrove or Charley, rather than Christian.

16. "Roll and Roster of Pelham's," 350–51; Trout, *Galloping Thunder*, 127; *OR*, 19:2, 113.

17. *OR*, 19:2, 142; Milham, *Gallant Pelham*, 196–97; Hassler, *Col. John Pelham*, 125–26; B. Davis, *Jeb Stuart*, 242. Jennings Cropper Wise proclaims: "Pelham performed a feat of arms second only to that which he was soon destined to accomplish at Fredericksburg" (*Long Arm of Lee*, 1:350). G. W. Beale saw the episode in a slightly different light: "[Pelham] dashed forward with two of his guns at a gallop far beyond our line and through an open field, and delivered his fire close to the enemy's line. We were in deepest concern lest a sudden charge by the Federal cavalry might capture his pieces before we could reach him, but they only seemed dazed and disconcerted by the unwonted boldness of his action" (*Lieutenant of Cavalry*, 55).

18. *OR*, 19:2, 142; H. B. McClellan, *I Rode with Stuart*, 176; Mercer, *Gallant Pelham*, 115; von Borcke, *Memoirs*, 2:18–19. Although von Borcke correctly depicts this episode, his descriptions of the fighting on November 1–3 are often overlapping, confused, and jumbled.

19. Von Borcke, *Memoirs*, 2:22–23.

20. Rather than Seaton's Hill, as most sources indicate, Pelham may have actually been positioned on Venus Hill. Vogtsberger, "The Ten Days."

21. *OR*, 19:2, 142; H. B. McClellan, *I Rode with Stuart*, 176; Mercer, *Gallant Pelham*, 116; G. Beale, *Lieutenant of Cavalry*, 55; Trout, *Galloping Thunder*, 127.

22. Milham, *Gallant Pelham*, 197; Hassler, *Col. John Pelham*, 126. Artillery expert Ken Baumann assures me that such a precise shot "could be made by an expert artillerist with exceptional reflexes, most notably a keen eye." It should also be noted that von Borcke all but credits himself for the amazing shot and "driving our contemptuous adversaries into headlong flight" (*Memoirs*, 2:24–25).

23. *OR*, 19:2, 132; H. B. McClellan, *I Rode with Stuart*, 175.

24. Milham, *Gallant Pelham*, 197–98.

25. A. Mitchell, *Letters*, 278; "Stuart's Correspondence to His Wife," 454; B. Davis, *Jeb Stuart*, 242–43.

26. Von Borcke, *Memoirs*, 2:28–29; Cooke, *Wearing of the Gray*, 18; B. Davis, *Jeb Stuart*, 243.

27. Von Borcke, *Memoirs*, 2:30; Mercer, *Gallant Pelham*, 116–17.

28. Von Borcke, *Memoirs*, 2:31; Hassler, *Col. John Pelham*, 128–29.

29. *OR*, 19:2, 143; H. B. McClellan, *I Rode with Stuart*, 177–78; Wise, *Long Arm of Lee*, 1:350; Milham, *Gallant Pelham*, 199; Moore, *Stuart Horse Artillery*, 44; Trout, *Galloping Thunder*, 681.

30. Milham, *Gallant Pelham*, 200; Hassler, *Col. John Pelham*, 130; Mercer, *Gallant Pelham*, 118.

31. Cooke, *Surry of Eagle's-Nest*, 348–49; Mercer, *Gallant Pelham*, 119, 120, 125; Hassler, *Col. John Pelham*, 132.

32. Cooke, *Surry of Eagle's-Nest*, 350; Mercer, *Gallant Pelham*, 127.

33. Mercer, *Gallant Pelham*, 121. Pleasonton's report for the day stated: "Averell sends me word

he had two guns and 300 prisoners of Stuart's at one time, and then lost them." This supposed capture, of course, was grossly misleading. Pleasonton further stated that "it is more important to us just now to gain information than gain glory by thrashing Stuart" (*OR*, 19:2, 116).

34. Von Borcke, *Memoirs*, 2:40–43; B. Davis, *Jeb Stuart*, 244.

35. Von Borcke, *Memoirs*, 2:45; *OR*, 19:2, 144. Von Borcke described the imported cannon as 15-pounders, but he may have been mistaken.

36. *Anniston Star*, May 18, 1921; Starr, *Union Cavalry*, 1:321; *OR*, 19:2, 144, 126; Trout, *Galloping Thunder*, 130–31. Stuart later reported: "In this engagement, Captain [Mathis Winston] Henry's battery, of the Stuart Horse Artillery, behaved with the most signal gallantry" (*OR*, 19:2, 144).

37. *OR*, 19:2, 146; H. B. McClellan, *I Rode with Stuart*, 183–84; Starr, *Union Cavalry*, 1:322; Longacre, *Lee's Cavalrymen*, 155–56. Pleasonton further stated, "The rebels acknowledge themselves badly whipped at Barbee. . . . Give us ten days more good weather, and [we'll] wind up the campaign in a blaze of glory" (*OR*, 19:2, 118, 120, 123).

38. A. Mitchell, *Letters*, 279; "Stuart's Correspondence to His Wife," 454–55; von Borcke, *Memoirs*, 2:48–49; Thomas, *Bold Dragoon*, 188–89; B. Davis, *Jeb Stuart*, 245. Flora died eleven days before her fifth birthday.

39. A. Mitchell, *Letters*, 280–81; B. Davis, *Jeb Stuart*, 245–46; Thomas, *Bold Dragoon*, 189; Cooke, *Wearing of the Gray*, 16. Von Borcke later recalled, "[Stuart] thought of her even on his deathbed, when, drawing me towards him, he whispered, 'My dear friend, I shall soon be with little Flora again'" (*Memoirs*, 2:49).

40. Cooke, *Wearing of the Gray*, 125. On November 8 Pleasonton reported: "I have found another gun abandoned by Stuart's cavalry. The carriage they burnt up, but the caisson is all right. This makes the third gun taken this morning. The caisson is full of 6-pounder ammunition, and the gun is a 12-pounder iron. I hear that Stuart's command is about played out" (*OR*, 19:2, 118). Confederate sources and surviving officers of the horse artillery strongly refute this, claiming none of Pelham's guns was taken at any time during the war. (See H. B. McClellan, *I Rode with Stuart*, 184.) It is possible that the buried guns might have been the two brought over from Europe by Wade Hampton. Admittedly "too heavy for flying artillery," the bulky cannons would have slowed Stuart's withdrawal. It is conceivable that these guns would have been the most logical to abandon. Even so, Pleasonton's claim is certainly embellished.

41. Blackford, *War Years*, 183.

42. *OR*, 19:2, 145, 127; H. B. McClellan, *I Rode with Stuart*, 185; von Borcke, *Memoirs*, 2:57–58.

43. Von Borcke, *Memoirs*, 2:58; Trout, *Galloping Thunder*, 132–33. McGregor, who took a total of fourteen wounds during the war, survived this horrific injury and was ultimately sent back to Alabama to recuperate. Attempting to return to the horse artillery too quickly, he often was forced to return home for care. He finally recovered sufficiently to make his way back to the army and was promoted to the rank of major. Trout, "*The Hoss*," 22.

44. Von Borcke, *Memoirs*, 2:60; Thomas, *Bold Dragoon*, 188; Milham, *Gallant Pelham*, 202–3; Thomason, *Jeb Stuart*, 334–35; Hassler, *Col. John Pelham*, 134. There are some discrepancies as to the exact date that Stuart lost his facial hair. Various historians place the occurrence on November 9, 10, or 11, but the most logical date appears to be November 10. Needless to say, Stuart found no reason to mention the embarrassing episode in his report.

45. Mercer, *Gallant Pelham*, 129–30.

46. Von Borcke, *Memoirs*, 2:61.

47. *OR*, 19:145; "Miscellaneous" file; Trout, *Galloping Thunder*, 133; Moore, *Stuart Horse Artillery*, 45.

48. Cooke, *Wearing of the Gray*, 121–22; H. B. McClellan, *I Rode with Stuart*, 173, 186; Wise,

Long Arm of Lee, 1:349; Driver, *First & Second Maryland Infantry C.S.A.,* 140; U. R. Brooks, *Stories of the Confederacy,* 134.

Chapter 18

1. Monaghan, *Custer,* 106.

2. McClellan's day in the sun as head of the Army of the Potomac had ended. As a Democrat he ran against Lincoln in 1864 but suffered a resounding defeat. However, he was elected governor of New Jersey in 1878. After an acute attack of angina pectoris, McClellan died at age fifty-eight on October 29, 1885.

3. Jeb Stuart to Samuel Cooper, November 11, 1862, in "Field Letters from Stuart's Headquarters," 191–92.

4. Rosser's long-awaited promotion to brigadier general finally arrived on October 10, 1863.

5. Trout, *Galloping Thunder,* 135; Thomas, *Bold Dragoon,* 191; Milham, *Gallant Pelham,* 205.

6. Henderson, *Stonewall Jackson,* 2:301; Wise, *Long Arm of Lee,* 1:361–62.

7. J. I. Robertson, *Jackson,* 647; Henderson, *Stonewall Jackson,* 2:303.

8. Milham, *Gallant Pelham,* 206.

9. Blackford, *War Years,* 94; Milham, *Gallant Pelham,* 205–6.

10. Light, *War at Our Doors,* 51; Diary of Helen Struan Bernard Robb, November 30, 1862, "Homes" file, JPL.

11. Light, *War at Our Doors,* 52; Bernard Diary, December 2, 1862.

12. Light, *War at Our Doors,* 52–54; Bernard Diary, December 2–3, 1862.

13. Light, *War at Our Doors,* 54–55; Bernard Diary, December 4, 1862. D. H. Hill later wrote: "The ruffians commenced shelling the town, full of women and children," but reported that the only damages done included a dog that was killed and a black man wounded. *OR,* 21:642.

14. *OR,* 21:36–37; Longacre, *Lee's Cavalrymen,* 160.

15. *OR,* 21:642, 37; Trout, *Galloping Thunder,* 139. The seriously injured gunner, Private William A. S. Clopton from Moorman's Lynchburg Battery, was wounded below the knee and died an hour after midnight while undergoing an operation. Rooney Lee reported, "He behaved with marked gallantry and coolness" (Trout, "*The Hoss,*" 155).

16. Von Borcke, *Memoirs,* 2:82. D. H. Hill further reported: "From Yankee sources, we learned that the pirates lost 6 killed and 20 wounded. Whether they overestimated or underestimated their loss I do not know," but he added in his typically sardonic manner, "They sometimes lie on one side and sometimes on another" (*OR,* 21:643).

17. Hill further praised his own artillery captain, Hardaway, for his excellence: "I make this report to call the attention of the War Department to the extraordinary merit of the Whitworth gun in the hands of such a man as Hardaway—the best practical artillerist I have seen in service. He still remains a captain, while officers never engaged have been promoted over him" (*OR,* 21:37).

18. *OR,* 21:37–38, 28.

19. Von Borcke, *Memoirs,* 2:82–85; B. Davis, *Jeb Stuart,* 250.

20. "Extracts from T. R. R. Cobb's Letters to His Wife," 299; Freeman, *Lee's Lieutenants,* 2:330.

21. Stackpole, *Drama on the Rappahannock,* 127; Freeman, *Lee's Lieutenants,* 2:395; Sorrel, *Recollections,* 131.

22. Longstreet, "The Battle of Fredericksburg," 71; *OR,* 21:551; Wise, *Long Arm of Lee,* 1:363.

23. Alexander, *Fighting for the Confederacy,* 170. The colorful Barksdale would suffer a mortal

wound on July 2, 1863, while advancing his men toward Little Round Top at Gettysburg. A bullet severed his breast while others struck his legs. He died at age forty-one the following day.

24. Von Borcke, *Memoirs*, 2:86; Light, *War at Our Doors*, 56–57; Bernard Diary, December 6, 7, and 8, 1862. Charles Milham mentions the dinner although he gives the date as Monday, December 7, when Monday actually fell on the eighth. Milham further states that Blackford attended the dinner. This seems highly unlikely since neither Blackford nor his wife's cousin Helen Bernard mentions his being there. Milham also writes that just as the meal had been finished, a courier arrived to report that Burnside was attacking at Fredericksburg and that the party of officers frantically rode back to find the report false. In no other source could this information be found. Furthermore, von Borcke has no word of it and says they "reluctantly" left Gay Mont the following day "on a reconnaissance up the river." Milham, *Gallant Pelham*, 206–7.

25. Blackford, *War Years*, 187; von Borcke, *Memoirs*, 2:112; Almond, "Captain Lewis Guy Phillips" (1992), 6–7; Milham, *Gallant Pelham*, 207. Blackford was further impressed by Phillips's bravery once the battle began: "[Phillips] was so desirous to see everything that he went under fire freely and showed perfect coolness, though it was his first experience." The thirty-one-year-old Phillips was London born and educated at Eton and Christchurch College Oxford. He joined the First Battalion Grenadier Guards Regiment on June 15, 1855. Almond, "Captain Lewis Guy Phillips" (2006), 4.

26. Von Borcke, *Memoirs*, 2:89–92; Blackford, *War Years*, 187–88; Milham, *Gallant Pelham*, 207; Hassler, *Col. John Pelham*, 138–39. Private Thomas Frazer Chancellor, the courier who extended the invitation to the dance, later died of a mortal wound on July 15, 1863. Trout, *Plume*, 303.

27. Longacre, *Man behind the Guns*, 131–32; Blackford, *War Years*, 191; Hennessy, "For All Anguish for Some Freedom," 16; Foote, *Civil War*, 2:28.

28. Longacre, *Man behind the Guns*, 132; Foote, *Civil War*, 2:28. G. Moxley Sorrel claimed Barksdale's bravery "stands as one of the finest acts of heroism and stubborn resistance in our military annals." *Recollections*, 139.

29. O'Reilly, *Fredericksburg Campaign: Winter War*, 125.

30. Von Borcke, *Memoirs*, 2:113; Milham, *Gallant Pelham*, 210; Hassler, *Col. John Pelham*, 142–43.

Chapter 19

1. O'Reilly, *Fredericksburg Campaign: "Stonewall" Jackson*, 27–28; Dabney, *Campaigns of Jackson*, 610; Allan, *Army of Northern Virginia*, 478; O'Reilly, "Pennsylvania Reserves,'" 9.

2. Von Borcke, *Memoirs*, 2:114.

3. Longstreet, "The Battle of Fredericksburg," 79; Klein, *Edward Porter Alexander*, 51; O'Reilly, *Fredericksburg Campaign: Winter War*, 267; Mertz, "Stonewall Jackson's Artillerists," 94. Jennings Cropper Wise noted that "never in the history of war, perhaps, was an army on the defense more willing to be attacked by overwhelming numbers" (*Long Arm of Lee*, 1:399).

4. B. Davis, *Jeb Stuart*, 254; Freeman, *Lee's Lieutenants*, 2:349; J. I. Robertson, *Jackson*, 655.

5. Although some sources refer to this road as Massaponax Road, the historian Frank O'Reilly claims it to be nameless on most maps of that time. *Fredericksburg Campaign: "Stonewall" Jackson*, 40.

6. Von Borcke, *Memoirs*, 2:118; O'Reilly, *Fredericksburg Campaign: Winter War*, 143; Freeman, *Lee's Lieutenants*, 2:349; B. Davis, *Jeb Stuart*, 255. Discrepancies exist among eyewitnesses, contemporaries, biographers, and scholars as to whether Pelham took two guns, the Napoleon and a Blakely, to open fire on the advancing Federals or merely one. Certainly, a Blakely would

eventually be used by Pelham's gunners, but possibly not at the onset. Others dispute this. Among the contemporaries and eyewitnesses, John Esten Cooke, Channing Price, a notorious stickler for detail, William Allan, G. W. Beale, and Henry B. McClellan (quoting Price) maintain that Pelham had only one cannon in the beginning. Heros von Borcke and Edward Porter Alexander, however, clearly mention two guns brought forward by Pelham, while Sergeant George W. Shreve, an actual participant, used the word "guns" to describe the opening bombardment. Historians have also disagreed on the subject. Frank A. O'Reilly, a renowned scholar on the Fredericksburg Campaign, clearly opts for the single gun notion, as does Robert H. Moore II. Jennings Cropper Wise, an early twentieth-century expert on Lee's artillery, stated that two guns were brought forward but mistakenly labels them both Napoleons, and Robert J. Trout, in his exceptional book on the Stuart Horse Artillery, makes the strong case for two guns as well. Even Pelham biographers enter the dispute: Charles G. Milham and William Woods Hassler mention the immediate use of two guns while Philip Mercer maintains a single cannon initiated the attack. Nowhere in the *Official Records* does anyone's report clear up the dispute (neither Stuart nor Pelham describes the incident), although Pelham's exploit is mentioned several times by various eyewitnesses. Taking all circumstances and descriptions into account and admittedly wavering from one side to the other, I am satisfied that Pelham took a single Napoleon with him that morning.

7. Alexander, *Fighting for the Confederacy,* 173–74; O'Reilly, *Fredericksburg Campaign: "Stonewall" Jackson,* 40; Shreve, "Reminiscences"; Trout, *Galloping Thunder,* 146; O'Reilly, *Fredericksburg Campaign: Winter War,* 143–44; Mertz, "Stonewall Jackson's Artillerists," 77.

8. O'Reilly, *Fredericksburg Campaign: "Stonewall" Jackson,* 42; Shreve, "Reminiscences"; Trout, *Galloping Thunder,* 146; O'Reilly, *Fredericksburg Campaign: Winter War,* 145; Mertz, "Stonewall Jackson's Artillerists," 77.

9. Shreve, "Reminiscences"; Trout, *Galloping Thunder,* 146; Mertz, "Stonewall Jackson's Artillerists," 77; Moore, *Stuart Horse Artillery,* 47. Private Hammond is mentioned in the rosters of Trout, "*The Hoss*" (135), and Moore, *Stuart Horse Artillery* (170), but neither a first name nor any further information is given.

10. *OR,* 21:514, 511, 483, 484; Naisawald, *Grape and Canister,* 249; Freeman, *Lee's Lieutenants,* 2:350.

11. *OR,* 21:91; Stackpole, *Drama on the Rappahannock,* 180; Milham, *Gallant Pelham,* 212.

12. Various sources, including eyewitness accounts, place the number of Federal batteries facing Pelham as four, five, or six. These same sources total up the guns as "sixteen," "fifteen or twenty," "thirty-two," or even "one hundred." E. P. Alexander maintained that Pelham faced "six 6 gun batteries" (*Fighting for the Confederacy,* 174). In Robert E. Lee's report he wrote that Pelham had "four batteries immediately turned upon him, but he sustained their fire with the unflinching courage that ever distinguished him" (*OR,* 21:553; Dowdey, *Papers of R. E. Lee,* 370; Freeman, *Lee's Lieutenants,* 2:350). Part of the reason for the discrepancy in numbers obviously lies in the fact that the Federal batteries were not brought in at the same time, thus, Pelham faced different numbers at various times.

13. Milham, *Gallant Pelham,* 211; Cooke, *Wearing of the Gray,* 127; Shreve, "Reminiscences"; Trout, *Galloping Thunder,* 146–47; Moore, *Stuart Horse Artillery,* 47; Mertz, "Stonewall Jackson's Artillerists," 80. The identity of the decapitated gunner is unknown but might have been David R. Barton, who is noted in Moore, *Stuart Horse Artillery,* 163, as killed at Fredericksburg and was a member in the battery that also included Shreve. Robert J. Trout ("*The Hoss*") does not list Barton on the roster of this battery.

14. Alexander, *Fighting for the Confederacy,* 173–74; Caldwell, *History of a Brigade,* 91; H. B. McClellan, *I Rode with Stuart,* 193; Trout, *Pen & Saber,* 121; "'The Gallant Pelham' and His Gun at Fredericksburg," 468; Longstreet, "The Battle of Fredericksburg," 78.

15. H. B. McClellan, *I Rode with Stuart,* 193; Thomason, *Jeb Stuart,* 341; O'Reilly, *Fredericksburg Campaign: "Stonewall" Jackson,* 45; J. I. Robertson, *Jackson,* 656; Mertz, "Stonewall Jackson's Artillerists," 81; O'Reilly, *Fredericksburg Campaign: Winter War,* 148.

16. G. Beale, *Lieutenant of Cavalry,* 64; O'Reilly, *Fredericksburg Campaign: "Stonewall" Jackson,* 41–42.

17. John Esten Cooke, *Philadelphia Weekly Times,* April 26, 1879; *OR,* 21:458; O'Reilly, *Fredericksburg Campaign: Winter War,* 147–48; Trout, *Galloping Thunder,* 145; Naisawald, *Grape and Canister,* 250; Moore, *Stuart Horse Artillery,* 47.

18. Milham, *Gallant Pelham,* 212; Cardwell, "A Horse Battery," 6; G. Beale, *Lieutenant of Cavalry,* 65; O'Reilly, "Pennsylvania Reserves," 12; O'Reilly, *Fredericksburg Campaign: Winter War,* 147; Moore, *Stuart Horse Artillery,* 48. Pelham had lost two men, as the Blakely explosion had earlier killed Private Hammond.

19. Von Borcke, *Memoirs,* 2:118; Trout, *Galloping Thunder,* 145; Hassler, *Col. John Pelham,* 147–48; Freeman, *Lee's Lieutenants,* 2:350; Mertz, "Stonewall Jackson's Artillerists," 80.

20. Mercer, *Gallant Pelham,* 138; Milham, *Gallant Pelham,* 213. On August 6, 1903, Smith dedicated a granite marker, inscribed with "Stuart and Pelham, Battle of Fredericksburg, Dec. 13, 1862," on the battle site. It is the oldest monument to John Pelham.

21. Article (author unknown), John Pelham Scrapbook, ADAH. Lee's familiar quote commending Pelham's bravery appears in virtually all sources from the contemporary Cooke, *Wearing of the Gray,* 122, to the modern O'Reilly, *Fredericksburg Campaign: "Stonewall" Jackson,* 41.

22. Trout, *Galloping Thunder,* 147. Phlegar, age twenty-two, had his arm amputated just below the elbow from a wound to the wrist but survived the war. Two marriages produced nine children. He died at age eighty-two on January 19, 1923. Fifteen-year-old Samuel Evans's medical record indicated a "bombshell contusion of all internal organs over stomach. Greatly prostrated on admittance—Afterwards daily improving." He later served as a courier to Robert E. Lee. Evans became a doctor after the war and died at approximately age forty-three on January 9, 1890. The records on Henderson Boothe are, unfortunately, incomplete. Moore, *Stuart Horse Artillery,* 175, 168, 163; Trout, "*The Hoss,*"138–39, 134, 131.

23. Oddly, little agreement can be derived from officers on either side as to the exact amount of time that Pelham battled with the Federals on the Confederate right. Robert E. Lee said "about two hours," Jackson "about an hour," A. P. Hill "for an hour or more," William B. Franklin "two hours or more," Captain James H. Cooper of Battery B, First Pennsylvania Light Artillery, "about one hour" (see *OR,* 21:516, 547, 631, 645). Modern writers, too, offer differing amounts of time from "thirty minutes," "forty-five minutes," "an hour," to "fully two hours." Considering the time that Pelham began his barrage (and even that is disputed) to the time the fighting recommenced after he pulled back, a full hour, possibly a bit longer, seems about right.

24. Casualties for the full day of fighting verify the fact that Doubleday's division was held in reserve. His division lost a total of 214 (31 killed, 161 wounded, 22 missing). Gibbon's division lost six times more men with 1,266 casualties (141 killed, 1,023 wounded, 102 missing). Meade's division suffered the heaviest count, totaling 1,853 (175 killed, 1,241 wounded, 437 missing), or more than eight and a half times those lost by Doubleday. "The Opposing Forces at Fredericksburg," 145.

25. *OR,* 21:547, 553, 631; Dowdey, *Papers of R. E. Lee,* 361; Alexander, *Fighting for the Confederacy,* 174; Freeman, *R. E. Lee,* 2:457; Mertz, "Stonewall Jackson's Artillerists," 80; Milham, *Gallant Pelham,* 218; Haskell, *The Haskell Memoirs,* 46; Sergent, *They Lie Forgotten,* 142; Moore, *Stuart Horse Artillery,* 48. Both A. P. Hill and Jubal Early referred to Pelham in their official reports, but William Pendleton, the Army of Northern Virginia's chief of artillery, did not de-

scribe or even mention Pelham's act. Perhaps more surprising is that Stuart, who usually lauded Pelham's every move, did not find cause to detail it.

26. Cooke, *Wearing of the Gray,* 122, 127; Douglas, *I Rode with Stonewall,* 204.

27. Article (author unknown), John Pelham Scrapbook, ADAH; "West Point" file; Schaff, *Old West Point,* 132–33; Monaghan, *Custer,* 104. Schaff credits George Custer with sending the note, but Monaghan flatly states that Custer was on furlough in Monroe, Michigan, during December 1862. It still could have been from Custer, who did not have to be at the Battle of Fredericksburg to have written the note. It probably was Custer. The note was found folded in Pelham's purse after his death. John Esten Cooke claimed that Pelham kept the note in his belongings until his death, but Cooke cited the wording a bit differently: "After long silence, I write. God bless you, dear Pelham; I am proud of your success." Cooke further mentions that Pelham never spoke of or "even alluded to the paper. . . . He never exhibited the least trait of self-love, remaining what he had always been, as modest, unassuming, and simple as a child" (*Wearing of the Gray,* 124).

28. O'Reilly, *Fredericksburg Campaign: "Stonewall" Jackson,* 52.

29. G. Beale, *Lieutenant of Cavalry,* 65; *OR,* 21:631, 638; Mertz, "Stonewall Jackson's Artillerists," 83.

30. *The Civil War. Rebels Resurgent,* 65; O'Reilly, "Pennsylvania Reserves," 13; *OR,* 21:669.

31. Driver, *The 1st and 2nd Rockbridge Artillery,* 36; Wise, *Long Arm of Lee,* 1:385; Poague, *Gunner with Stonewall,* 54; O'Reilly, *Fredericksburg Campaign: "Stonewall" Jackson,* 60; Moore, *Stuart Horse Artillery,* 48; O'Reilly, *Fredericksburg Campaign: Winter War,* 160. Private Thomas M. Wade of the Rockbridge Artillery is credited with the description of Pelham "playing ball."

32. Trout, *Pen & Saber,* 122; O'Reilly, *Fredericksburg Campaign: "Stonewall" Jackson,* 60; H. B. McClellan, *I Rode with Stuart,* 194. The Richmond Howitzers suffered not only the loss of Utz but eventually nine of fourteen men and eleven of twelve horses, as well as a limber chest destroyed.

33. Mertz, "Stonewall Jackson's Artillerists," 91.

34. Poague, *Gunner with Stonewall,* 54–55; O'Reilly, *Fredericksburg Campaign: Winter War,* 161. Charles G. Milham words Pelham's statement a bit differently: "Well, you men stand killing better than any I ever saw" (*Gallant Pelham,* 217).

35. "Fredericksburg" file, JPL. The story told by Willis Lee is most likely true, including the statistical losses of men and horses. Caution, however, is advised: some modern-day historians use these figures and Willis Lee's description of the fighting for the initial contact made by Pelham on Meade's infantry. In fact, the two fights are separate parts of the battle, occurring more than an hour apart. The Richmond Howitzers had absolutely nothing to do with Pelham's first duel, conducted with his Napoleon and Blakely. Furthermore, Willis possibly exaggerated the size of the enemy cannon, which may have been 20-pounders.

36. *OR,* 21:649; Carmichael, *Lee's Young Artillerist,* 78. The distinguished British historian G. F. R. Henderson states that "even Pelham could do but little" to stem the Federal tide in perhaps an overstatement on John Pelham's power. *Stonewall Jackson,* 2:316; Milham, *Gallant Pelham,* 215.

37. O'Reilly, *Fredericksburg Campaign: "Stonewall" Jackson,* 64–65, 57; O'Reilly, *Fredericksburg Campaign: Winter War,* 165. Dead were Captain Louis E. D'Aquin, Lieutenant James S. Utz, and Lieutenant James D. Ellett. Captain George W. Wooding lay mortally wounded. Captain John B. Brockenborough suffered a crippling injury when a jagged piece of shrapnel mangled his arm as he was sighting a gun. Lieutenant Valentine J. Clutter was wounded and Captain Asher W. Garber had been knocked senseless in a fall from his horse.

38. O'Reilly, *Fredericksburg Campaign: "Stonewall" Jackson*, 86; R. K. Krick, "Maxcy Gregg," 21–22; Allan, *Army of Northern Virginia*, 487; O'Reilly, *Fredericksburg Campaign: Winter War*, 175, 177. Maxcy Gregg was carried a few miles south of Fredericksburg to the Thomas Yerby house, Belvoir, where he died at 5:00 A.M. on December 15.

39. Trout, *Pen & Saber*, 122.

40. "The Opposing Forces at Fredericksburg," 145, 147; O'Reilly, *Fredericksburg Campaign: Winter War*, 243; O'Reilly, "Pennsylvania Reserves," 22.

41. Carmichael, *Lee's Young Artillerist*, 78, 106; Maxwell, "Willie Pegram," 135. Willie Pegram continued his heroics throughout the war and rose to the rank of colonel before being mortally wounded at the Battle of Five Forks on April 1, 1865.

42. McIntosh became one of Willie Pegram's closest friends and eventually married Virginia (Jennie) Pegram, Willie's sister. Maxwell, "Willie Pegram," 134.

43. O'Reilly, *Fredericksburg Campaign: "Stonewall" Jackson*, 117. Latimer, who had been a sophomore at Virginia Military Institute when the war broke out, fell mortally wounded at Gettysburg on July 2, 1863.

44. Couch, "Sumner's 'Right Grand Division,'" 113. Of Couch's three divisions, Hancock's bore the largest losses with 219 killed, 1,581 wounded, and 229 missing, totaling 2,029, or nearly half of the corps' entire loss of 4,102.

45. Longstreet, *Manassas to Appomattox*, 312, 313, 315; *OR*, 21:432; "The Opposing Forces at Fredericksburg," 144.

46. *OR*, 21:634; Henderson, *Stonewall Jackson*, 2:322.

47. Von Borcke, *Memoirs*, 2:129; Milham, *Gallant Pelham*, 217; Henderson, *Stonewall Jackson*, 2:323.

48. Silliker, *Rebel Yell & the Yankee Hurrah*, 59. If Private Haley's description is accurate, the losses Pelham sustained have not been identified.

49. Thomason, *Jeb Stuart*, 342; A. Mitchell, *Letters*, 284; Thomas, *Bold Dragoon*, 193–94.

50. *OR*, 21:634; Allan, *Army of Northern Virginia*, 511; Stackpole, *Drama on the Rappahannock*, 194; Henderson, *Stonewall Jackson*, 2:324; O'Reilly, *Fredericksburg Campaign: "Stonewall" Jackson*, 178.

51. G. Beale, *Lieutenant of Cavalry*, 67; Henderson, *Stonewall Jackson*, 2:324; J. I. Robertson, *Jackson*, 660, 905–6; Chambers, *Jackson*, 2:300. Von Borcke relates that two days later, on December 15, with Burnside's army still on the Confederate side of the Rappahannock, Jackson continued to favor a night attack and "proposed that our men should be stripped naked to the waist, so that they might easily recognize each other in the darkness and confusion of the conflict" (*Memoirs*, 2:139).

52. "The Opposing Forces at Fredericksburg," 145, 147; Wise, *Long Arm of Lee*, 1:407–8. See *OR*, 21:129–42, for detailed Federal losses in each unit.

53. Couch, "Sumner's 'Right Grand Division,'" 116.

54. *OR*, 21:95; Stackpole, *Drama on the Rappahannock*, 230–31; Couch, "Sumner's 'Right Grand Division,'" 117.

55. Hassler, *Col. John Pelham*, 150. John Esten Cooke offers a more detailed and heartfelt rendition of Jean Bacigalupo's death on pages 370–72 of *Surry of Eagle's-Nest*. Philip Mercer in *Gallant Pelham* submits a nearly verbatim version of the same on pages 142–46. Although the story told is most compelling, the reader must be cautioned of Cooke's penchant for mixing fact and fiction.

56. Cooke, *Wearing of the Gray*, 127; H. B. McClellan, *I Rode with Stuart*, 195; Cooke, *Surry of Eagle's-Nest*, 373; Dasinger, "Gallant Pelham," 31; Milham, *Gallant Pelham*, 218; Hassler, *Col. John Pelham*, 151.

57. Von Borcke, *Memoirs,* 2:133; Mercer, *Gallant Pelham,* 141. Exactly what Phillips did with the colorful ribbon is unknown and its whereabouts remain a mystery. Phillips left the Army of Northern Virginia on December 17 and returned to Canada. He later went back to England, where he continued to serve in the Grenadier Guards. He retired on July 18, 1885, with the honorary rank of brevet major general and died two years later at age fifty-six. Almond, "Captain Lewis Guy Phillips" (2006), 4–5.

Chapter 20

1. Von Borcke, *Memoirs,* 2:136.
2. Poague, *Gunner with Stonewall,* 61; O'Reilly, *Fredericksburg Campaign: Winter War,* 441.
3. Blackford, *War Years,* 194. The Blackford family moved from the house to Lynchburg sometime in the 1840s, but the original building still stands in Fredericksburg on Caroline Street. Hennessy, "For All Anguish for Some Freedom," 63–64.
4. Von Borcke, *Memoirs,* 2:142.
5. Von Borcke, *Memoirs,* 2:143; B. Davis, *Jeb Stuart,* 259.
6. Bernard Diary, December 16, 1862; Light, *War at Our Doors,* 61. Rooney Lee was certainly the favorite of the ladies at Gay Mont. Further evidence of this is supplied from William Poague's memoirs: "Once Colonel [J. Thompson] Brown came to see me and after supper took me with him to call on the Gay Mont people. Here we found Pelham and we were just beginning to have a pleasant time—there being two young ladies among the inmates—when in steps General 'Rooney' Lee and a couple of his staff. At once it seemed as if an iceberg had floated into the room. Such frigid dignity I never encountered and so it was not long before Colonel Brown, Pelham and myself took our leave, having been completely frozen out" (*Gunner with Stonewall,* 62).
7. Eighty-four buildings, almost 10 percent of the town, had been destroyed. Hennessy, "For All Anguish for Some Freedom," 6.
8. Sorrel, *Recollections,* 145–46; Wise, *Long Arm of Lee,* 2:409–10.
9. O'Reilly, *Fredericksburg Campaign: "Stonewall" Jackson,* 193–94; Naisawald, *Grape and Canister,* 269.
10. Chamberlayne, *Ham Chamberlayne,* 146; O'Reilly, *Fredericksburg Campaign: "Stonewall" Jackson,* 195; *OR,* 21:644; Lasswell, *Rags and Hope,* 148–49, 156.
11. Compiled Service Records of Confederate Generals; Cox, "Presentation of a Portrait of 'The Gallant Pelham,'" 293; *Anniston Star,* May 18, 1921; Hassler, *Col. John Pelham,* 151; Milham, *Gallant Pelham,* 218.
12. Mertz, "Stonewall Jackson's Artillerists," 93.
13. Cooke, *Wearing of the Gray,* 124.
14. Cooke, *Surry of Eagle's-Nest,* 378.
15. J. I. Robertson, *Jackson,* 667. Although Jackson officially kept his headquarters in the small building, he spent much time as a dinner guest in Moss Neck, where he became a favorite of the Corbin family. Moss Neck was the property of Richard Corbin, a member of the Ninth Virginia Cavalry, and his wife, Roberta. The Corbins' daughter, five-year-old Janie, was a sparkling child who took an immediate liking to Jackson. The feeling was mutual, as he obviously missed his own infant daughter, and Janie became his "pet" and constant friend. Unfortunately, Janie contracted scarlet fever in March 1863. She died on the seventeenth of the month, and Jackson wept uncontrollably. Ironically, her death date was the same day as Pelham's mortal wounding.

16. Von Borcke, *Memoirs*, 2:153.

17. Unfortunately, Pelham's wartime correspondence has been lost. We can thus only assume that his relationship with Sallie remained the same since no letters penned by either one of them exist. Furthermore, none of his friends mentions the love affair during the many weeks spent away from the Bower.

18. Hassler, *Col. John Pelham*, 153.

19. O'Reilly, *Fredericksburg Campaign: Winter War*, 464. Interestingly, Price has them leaving at noon on Christmas Day. Price to his sister, Ellen, January 2, 1863, cited in Trout, *Pen & Saber*, 135. This lengthy and wonderful letter will hereafter be referred to as simply "Price letter," with the page numbers from Trout's outstanding work.

20. *OR*, 21:731.

21. *OR*, 21:723, 730–31, 731–32; Price letter, 135–36; *Anniston Star*, May 18, 1921; Trout, *Galloping Thunder*, 150; Daughtry, *Gray Cavalier*, 107.

22. *OR*, 21:732, 738; H. B. McClellan, *I Rode with Stuart*, 198.

23. Channing Price noted that Bullock's wound was so frightful, he had to be left behind at a house near Dumfries (Price letter, 136). Bullock's immediate commander, Fitz Lee, mentioned that Bullock had been hit twice by enemy fire while Rosser stated he had been "pierced by several wounds" and labeled his loss "a sad calamity" (*OR*, 21:739).

24. *OR*, 21:732; Price letter, 136. In his report Stuart chose not to mention either of the two lost regiments or his angst over their disappearance. Pelham, however, would be exceedingly proud of Captain James Breathed, who, with his two rifled pieces, according to Fitz Lee's report, "did excellent service" (*OR*, 21:739).

25. Price letter, 136; H. B. McClellan, *I Rode with Stuart*, 198; *OR*, 21:732.

26. *OR*, 21:733; Price letter, 136; Thomason, *Jeb Stuart*, 350; Trout, *Galloping Thunder*, 151; O'Reilly, *Fredericksburg Campaign: Winter War*, 465.

27. Price letter, 136. Stuart makes no mention of this in his report, nor does Price add any further details as to the mystery man's identity or what information he brought. More than likely this stranger will forever be nameless.

28. *OR*, 21:733, 739; Driver, *5th Virginia Cavalry*, 43–44; Longacre, *Lee's Cavalrymen*, 165; Trout, *Galloping Thunder*, 151; O'Reilly, *Fredericksburg Campaign: Winter War*, 465.

29. *OR*, 21:739, 733; H. B. McClellan, *I Rode with Stuart*, 200–201; *Anniston Star*, May 18, 1921; Freeman, *Lee's Lieutenants*, 2:403–4; Trout, *Galloping Thunder*, 151; Longacre, *Lee's Cavalrymen*, 165.

30. *OR*, 21:734, 739; Price letter, 137.

31. *OR*, 21:734; H. B. McClellan, *I Rode with Stuart*, 201; Milham, *Gallant Pelham*, 220; Thomason, *Jeb Stuart*, 350–51. The original draft sent by Stuart undoubtedly embarrassed Federal officials and possibly for that reason has disappeared. Thus, the exact wording is not known. Many sources, however, perhaps to add flavor to the text, quote the telegraphed message verbatim.

32. Price letter, 138; *OR*, 21:718, 734; O'Reilly, *Fredericksburg Campaign: Winter War*, 466; Longacre, *Lee's Cavalrymen*, 166; Freeman, *Lee's Lieutenants*, 2:406.

33. *OR*, 21:734; Price letter, 138–39; O'Reilly, *Fredericksburg Campaign: Winter War*, 466.

34. Price letter, 139. McGregor would take nearly a year to recover and resume his duties. He would later rank as a major in the horse artillery. After the war he owned a newspaper and worked as an attorney in Texas. He died at age sixty-six (Trout, *Pen & Saber*, 311). Although the meticulous Channing Price neglected to mention Dr. Herndon's first name, Robert Trout identifies him as Dr. William A. Herndon, who would be at Pelham's bedside in less than three months attending to his fatal wounds. *Galloping Thunder*, 685.

35. Price letter, 135, 139.

36. *OR,* 21:735; Price letter, 139.

37. *OR,* 21:735; Mercer, *Gallant Pelham,* 149; Milham, *Gallant Pelham,* 220. In summing up the positive outcomes of his raid, Stuart did not mention the burning of the Accotink bridge. This is noticeably absent since on so many other occasions he had failed to destroy critically important bridges. Robert E. Lee, however, in his report praised the successful destruction of the bridge. See *OR,* 21:1114–15.

38. Price letter, 139–40.

Chapter 21

1. O'Reilly, *Fredericksburg Campaign: "Stonewall" Jackson,* 195.

2. Cooke, *Wearing of the Gray,* 120.

3. Haskell, *Memoirs,* 81; Vogtsberger, "How Artillerists Rated Pelham."

4. Pelham was not mentioned again in the letter. Trout, *Pen & Saber,* 141.

5. Von Borcke, *Memoirs,* 2:171–73; Poague, *Gunner with Stonewall,* 62–63.

6. Foote, *Civil War,* 2:128–29; Catton, *The Army of the Potomac,* 89; O'Reilly, *Fredericksburg Campaign: Winter War,* 478, 480.

7. A. Mitchell, *Letters,* 288–89. Part of Stuart's motive to promote Rosser was undeniably based on his desire to rid his cavalry of William "Grumble" Jones, an officer of considerable skill who openly disliked Jeb and was not afraid to show his disdain. Despite Stuart's negative stance, Jones remained with his cavalry for many months. Had Rosser known how hard Jeb pushed for his promotion, perhaps he would have written kinder words on Stuart.

8. Compiled Service Records of Confederate Generals; A. Mitchell, *Letters,* 293–94; Milham, *Gallant Pelham,* 222–23.

9. Compiled Service Records of Confederate Generals; *OR,* 25:2, 640; Trout, *Galloping Thunder,* 158–59; Wise, *Long Arm of Lee,* 1:424; Trout, *Plume,* 258; Milham, *Gallant Pelham,* 223; Hassler, *Col. John Pelham,* 156.

10. Compiled Service Records of Confederate Generals; *OR,* 25:2, 651; Wise, *Long Arm of Lee,* 1:424; Milham, *Gallant Pelham,* 223–24; B. Davis, *Jeb Stuart,* 267.

11. Milham, *Gallant Pelham,* 224, 222; Hassler, *Col. John Pelham,* 156. Pelham's youth, in fact, may have hindered his advancement in rank, but promotions among Confederate artillerymen were amazingly slow compared to those in the other branches of the service.

12. Blackford, *War Years,* 200; Freeman, *Lee's Lieutenants,* 2:455. Blackford and his wife, Mary, had seven children. Three-year-old Landon Carter Blackford died four days after the Battle of Fredericksburg on December 17, 1862. One of their sons was named Pelham. A year after the war, on May 22, 1866, Mary died from complications following the birth of a daughter, who died shortly before her mother (Trout, *Pen & Saber,* 312). Writers commonly refer to the source simply as Napier's *Peninsula Campaign* or *Peninsula War,* evidently avoiding the haughtier but exact title, *History of the War in the Peninsula and in the South of France: From the Year 1807 to the Year 1814,* by the equally imposing Sir William Francis Patrick Napier. My thanks are extended to the Historical Research Department of the Detroit Public Library for this information.

13. Sergent, *They Lie Forgotten,* 144–45; Trout, *Galloping Thunder,* 155–56. Lou Hoxton survived the war and returned to Virginia where he taught mathematics in the Episcopal High School of Virginia near Alexandria. He lived until February 12, 1891, dying at the age of fifty-three. Oft-wounded William Hoxton also survived the war but died at the early age of thirty-two on May 31, 1876.

14. This unpublished letter is rare since nearly all of Pelham's wartime correspondence has disappeared. My gratitude is extended to Ms. Wallace Johnston Jamerman, the great-granddaughter of Philip Preston Johnston and the owner of the letter, for her permission to publish it in its entirety.

Philip Preston Johnston, a native Virginian, achieved the rank of major and was twice wounded during the war. He earned a law degree from Transylvania University in 1868. His marriage to Sallie Chiles produced seven children; one was named John Pelham. Johnston enjoyed a successful career as a politician and newspaperman. He died near Lexington, Kentucky, on February 12, 1925, at age eighty-four. Trout, "*The Hoss*," 18–21.

15. Von Borcke, *Memoirs*, 2:179. Since von Borcke was the only one who reported this incident and he referred to Tom Price as only "Lieutenant Price," numerous sources mistakenly credit Channing Price as the third party with Pelham and von Borcke. One brief entry from von Borcke's description of Price, however, identified him as Tom rather than Channing: "being lately from Europe." Tom, of course, had recently arrived from Europe while Channing had not. In the winter of 1862 Tom returned to Virginia, where his connections landed him among Stuart's staff officers. While keeping a diary, Tom occasionally wrote disparaging comments about Stuart, viewing the general as an overgrown, boastful bore. Although not meant for prying eyes, the diary unfortunately found its way into the hands of Yankee cavalry in April 1863. From there the diary was sent to the *New York Times* where published excerpts, especially those ridiculing Stuart, embarrassed the Price family and the overly sensitive Stuart. Not surprisingly, Tom Price was forced to leave Stuart's staff. Trout, *Plume*, 224–32; Trout, *Pen & Saber*, 158.

16. Von Borcke, *Memoirs*, 2:179–82; Trout, *Plume*, 227; Trout, *Pen & Saber*, 161; Milham, *Gallant Pelham*, 224; Hassler, *Col. John Pelham*, 157–58; Mercer, *Gallant Pelham*, 151–54.

17. Von Borcke, *Memoirs*, 2:182–83; Hassler, *Col. John Pelham*, 158; Mercer, *Gallant Pelham*, 154.

18. Milham, *Gallant Pelham*, 221–22. Muscoe Livingston Shackelford, a graduate of West Point in the Class of 1836, was mortally wounded on September 8, 1847, during the Mexican War at Molino del Rey. He died more than a month later in Mexico City on October 12, 1847, at age thirty-four. "U.S. Military Academy Cadet Application Papers, 1805–1866,"NAB.

19. Upon meeting Bessie for the first time in April 1863, John Esten Cooke referred to her "as that gay young lady, Miss Bessie." John Pelham file AN71, F-#330, ACPL.

20. B. Davis, *Jeb Stuart*, 267; Hassler, *Col. John Pelham*, 158; Milham, *Gallant Pelham*, 221. Without knowing which of the stories is true, I do not believe that Pelham had met Bessie Shackelford earlier. If he had met her after the Christmas raid, it seems logical that one of his friends would have mentioned her in their writings. Also, if Pelham had known Bessie previously, and if he were so struck by her, he certainly would have ventured to Culpeper more than merely one snowy night a month and a half later.

21. Von Borcke, *Memoirs*, 2:183; Milham, *Gallant Pelham*, 224–25; Mercer, *Gallant Pelham*, 154; Hassler, *Col. John Pelham*, 159.

22. Milham, *Gallant Pelham*, 225. Bessie Shackelford later married Charles Harris Lester, a captain in the Federal cavalry, whom she had met late in the war. Lester, born in Connecticut, graduated number 22 of 25 in the West Point class of 1863. He died in New York City on October 27, 1899, at age fifty-six (Cullum, *Register of Graduates*, 254). For all the time spent at the Shackelford home, it is most unusual that von Borcke, who fancied himself a ladies' man, never mentioned in his writings any of the Shackelford women by name. Interestingly, he stated nothing of Pelham's relationship with Bessie. He did recall the "frequent visits" to see "Mr. S[hackelford]" and that they "were treated with great kindness, and our time passed pleasantly away." *Memoirs*, 2:183–84.

23. Harrison, *Recollections Grave and Gay*, 65.

24. Von Borcke, *Memoirs,* 2:184.

25. John Pelham to Miss Moore, March 9, 1863, John Pelham Papers, ADAH; Milham, *Gallant Pelham,* 226; Hassler, *Col. John Pelham,* 159–60. The crudely written note was later found among John Pelham's possessions. Although Miss Moore is not further identified, Charles G. Milham suggests she may have been the daughter of Alabama's first wartime governor, Andrew Barry Moore, who served from 1857 to 1861.

Pelham offered no further explanation as to the identities of "Col. O'Neal" or "Sam." Undoubtedly, the O'Neal he referred to was Edward Asbury O'Neal, who hailed from Madison County in northern Alabama. At the time that Pelham sat with him in March 1863, O'Neal was in temporary command of a brigade consisting of all Alabama regiments, the Third, Fifth, Sixth, Twelfth, and Twenty-sixth. Later his poor performance at Gettysburg evidently caused Robert E. Lee to literally cancel O'Neal's promotion to brigadier general. After the war he returned to his law practice and was twice elected governor of Alabama in the 1880s. O'Neal died at age seventy-two on November 7, 1890. W. Davis, "Edward Asbury O'Neal," in *Confederate General,* 4:204–5; Warner, *Generals in Gray,* 226.

The "Sam" referred to in Pelham's note remains unidentified. Both Milham and Hassler refer to him as John's seventeen-year-old brother Samuel, maintaining that Samuel's regiment was encamped nearby so John decided to visit him. I strongly doubt that it was Pelham's younger brother Samuel, who belonged to the Fifty-first Alabama Cavalry. This regiment stayed in the Western Theater and was never a part of Lee's Army of Northern Virginia. Also, Colonel O'Neal's Alabamians were all in the infantry with no cavalry among them. Furthermore, John had four other brothers (Charles, Peter, William, and Thomas) who served in the Fifty-first Alabama Cavalry with Samuel. It seems most unusual that John would have mentioned only one of them. It remains possible that his brother Samuel visited John while on furlough, but this, too, seems highly unlikely. If it were true, it would only be logical that Samuel would have gone to John's bivouac rather than the other way around.

26. Thomason, *Jeb Stuart,* 354; Milham, *Gallant Pelham,* 226–27; Hassler, *Col. John Pelham,* 160; Freeman, *Lee's Lieutenants,* 2:455; B. Davis, *Jeb Stuart,* 269. "Miss Brill" is identified no further, but her first name most likely was Lucinda. Scheel, *Culpeper,* 193; Vogtsberger, "The Mysteries of Kelly's Ford."

27. Blackford, *War Years,* 201; Milham, *Gallant Pelham,* 227; B. Davis, *Jeb Stuart,* 268; Freeman, *Lee's Lieutenants,* 2:456. Pelham's planned venture to see the ladies who sent him the sweets seems to indicate that his relationship with Bessie Shackelford was platonic. If he had been in love with Bessie, Pelham would most assuredly have been heading to Culpeper to see her.

28. Blackford, *War Years;* Hassler, *Col. John Pelham,* 160–61; Milham, *Gallant Pelham,* 227; Freeman, *Lee's Lieutenants,* 2:456; B. Davis, *Jeb Stuart,* 268.

29. Blackford, *War Years,* 201.

Chapter 22

1. Numerous discrepancies, all of which are confusing to the reader, occur in a variety of sources pertaining to John Pelham's journey to Culpeper. Eyewitnesses have Pelham learning of the Federal approach on the afternoon of Monday, March 16, yet Hassler (*Col. John Pelham,* 161) has Pelham obtaining this information the night before as he "strolled the streets of Orange with Miss Brill" on his arm. This certainly could not be true since Fitz Lee himself admitted that he first received news of the Federal approach at 11:00 A.M. on March 16 (*OR,* 25:1, 61). Milham (*Gallant Pelham,* 228) has Pelham at the railroad station waiting to head back to Camp

No-Camp when word arrived from Fitz Lee's men. This, too, is erroneous because no railroad line existed at the time between Orange Court House and Fredericksburg. The normally reliable W. W. Blackford has Pelham returning to Culpeper on the morning of March 17, when undoubtedly he arrived on the afternoon of March 16 (*War Years*, 201). Heros von Borcke (*Memoirs*, 2:184) mistakenly has Pelham traveling with Stuart by train to Culpeper so that he might visit his lady friend, Bessie Shackelford. Both Mercer (*Gallant Pelham*, 156) and Thomason (*Jeb Stuart*, 353–54) follow von Borcke's lead and have Pelham accompanying Stuart by train, an obvious error. Thomason and Milham even have their calendars mixed up by referring to March 16 as a Saturday, when, in fact, it fell on a Monday.

2. It is even mistakenly conjectured by some that Pelham testified at the court-martial in Culpeper. The court-martial involved Lieutenant Colonel Henry Clay Pate of the Fifth Virginia Cavalry, a Virginian who had made Stuart's acquaintance in the mid-1850s.

3. *OR*, 25:1, 47–48. Averell, a New Yorker, graduated from West Point in the Class of 1855. While at the academy, he had befriended Virginian Fitz Lee, who graduated the following year. Afterward they remained friends and their career paths often crossed. Both fought against the Indians and each suffered a near debilitating wound. Only a few weeks before Averell's movement at Kelly's Ford, Fitz Lee raided his old friend's outpost at Hartwood Church and captured 150 bluecoats. Adding insult to Averell's embarrassment, Fitz left a note behind admonishing Averell to visit him soon and to bring along some coffee. Faust, *Encyclopedia of the Civil War*, 31–32, 411; Warner, *Generals in Blue*, 12–13.

4. *OR*, 25:1, 61; Milham, *Gallant Pelham*, 228.

5. Hassler, *Col. John Pelham*, 162; Milham, *Gallant Pelham*, 228.

6. Gilmor, *Four Years in the Saddle*, 64–65; R. K. Krick, *Lee's Colonels*, 75, 371, 286, 110; Cullum, *Register of Graduates*, 249; *OR*, 25:1, 59, 62, 63.

Twenty-six-year-old Richard Welby Carter attended Virginia Military Institute prior to the war and now served in the First Virginia Cavalry. He was later captured at Upperville on December 17, 1863, and held by the Federals until his release on July 19, 1865. He died at age fifty-one on December 18, 1888.

Solomon Williams, a twenty-seven-year-old North Carolinian, graduated in the West Point Class of 1858. He served as a colonel in the Twelfth and later the Second North Carolina cavalry regiments. He was killed at Brandy Station on June 9, 1863, merely two weeks after his marriage to Maggie Pegram. This Maggie Pegram was not a sister of the famous Pegram brothers, John and Willie, from the Army of Northern Virginia as has sometimes been mistakenly indicated.

John Puller, a native of Gloucester County, Virginia, had ranked as a major of the Fifth Virginia Cavalry since December 18, 1862. Following Puller's death at Kelly's Ford, Fitz Lee acknowledged him as "gallant and highly efficient" and his demise "a heavy loss."

James Drake, a forty-year-old from Frederick County, Virginia, served as a colonel in the First Virginia Cavalry. Both Stuart and Fitz Lee praised Drake in their post-battle reports of Kelly's Ford. His life ended exactly four months to the day from the meeting in the Virginia Hotel near Shepherdstown, West Virginia, on July 16, 1863.

Certainly one of the most intriguing of the ten men in the hotel room was Harry Gilmor himself. Born in Baltimore, Maryland, on January 24, 1838, his life, both in and out of the army, resembled that of a nomad. Prior to the war he lived in Wisconsin and Nebraska. At the war's outbreak he enlisted as a private in Turner Ashby's cavalry and rose to the rank of captain. Later he served as a scout in John Mosby's partisan force. Twice he was captured and paroled by Federal forces. His service as a volunteer aide-de-camp to Jeb Stuart began and ended rather abruptly with no explanation for the brief tenure. Yet he was promoted to major on May 27, 1863. Handsome, dashing, and glib, Gilmor appeared to have the ability to talk himself into and out of danger. Wounded twice during the war, he was once spared from death by a deck of cards that he carried. Supposedly a bullet smashed into the deck and penetrated all the cards with the exception of the ace of spades. Following the war he married Mentoria Strong and fathered three children. He served as police commissioner in Baltimore for six years. While in his mid-forties, he developed a large tumor in the back of his head, which caused paralysis. He died at age forty-five on March 4, 1883. Trout, *Plume,* 140–45; V. Jones, *Gray Ghosts and Rebel Raiders,* 215; R. K. Krick, *Lee's Colonels,* 141–42; Faust, *Encyclopedia of the Civil War,* 311–12; Gilmor, *Four Years in the Saddle.*

7. Holland, *Pierce M. B. Young,* 71; *Atlanta Constitution,* March 12, 1893, 5. Both of these sources (the biography on Young and Young's eyewitness account of Pelham sleeping on his couch) have inaccuracies. The biography incorrectly states that Pelham and Young met in Culpeper on "Saturday, March 16" (this date fell on a Monday) to "celebrate Pelham's recent promotion to lieutenant colonel" (Pelham's promotion occurred posthumously, dated April 4). In the article from the *Atlanta Constitution,* written thirty years after Pelham's death, Young stated that after partying at the Shackelford house, "Pelham was in fine spirits, and I am sure that night his dreams were tinged with roseate hues. But when morning broke we were awakened by the thunder of artillery." (The sound of artillery certainly did not awaken them.) The only truthful statement Young made was: "[Pelham] was as brave as Caesar and gentle as a girl. . . . I never knew a better friend, a braver soldier. His name is immortal." Why Young dealt in apparent falsehoods concerning Pelham is anybody's guess, but Young's roguish post–Civil War career merely adds to his questionable character.

Interestingly, another source erroneously claims that John Pelham spent his last evening at Redwood, a plantation just down the road from Kelly's Ford. It further states that Pelham had breakfast at Redwood with the family before departing for the battle. "Historic Culpeper" (Bicentennial Edition), "Homes" file, JPL.

8. *OR,* 25:1, 48; H. B. McClellan, *I Rode with Stuart,* 208–9; Milham, *Gallant Pelham,* 228–29; Naisawald, *Grape and Canister,* 293. Although most sources credit Lieutenant George Browne Jr. as the commander of the six pieces of Federal artillery, the guns, according to Federal artillery expert L. Van Loan Naisawald, belonged to Captain Joseph W. Martin.

Averell's report of "80 sharpshooters" appears to be somewhat exaggerated, but Fitz Lee concurred in his report that twenty-five of his men had been captured. More than likely, however, he exaggerated the losses of Averell's men at "30 or 40 of them" killed or wounded. *OR,* 25:1, 61.

9. Sergent, *They Lie Forgotten,* 170–71; Milham, *Gallant Pelham,* 229.

10. Milham, *Gallant Pelham,* 229; Gilmor, *Four Years in the Saddle,* 65–66; Mercer, *Gallant Pelham,* 156–57; Hassler, *Col. John Pelham,* 162; B. Davis, *Jeb Stuart,* 270.

11. Gilmor, *Four Years in the Saddle,* 66; B. Davis, *Jeb Stuart,* 270.

12. H. B. McClellan, *I Rode with Stuart,* 209–10; Wise, *Long Arm of Lee,* 1:433.

13. Gilmor, *Four Years in the Saddle,* 66; B. Davis, *Jeb Stuart,* 270; Hassler, *Col. John Pelham,* 163. Gilmor remarked that "take the bulge" was Fitz Lee's "favorite expression."

14. Gilmor, *Four Years in the Saddle,* 66–67; Thomas, *Bold Dragoon,* 206; B. Davis, *Jeb Stuart,* 270–71. The losses stated are those given by Gilmor, who further mentioned that Captain Bailey's horse was killed in the attack.

15. Gilmor, *Four Years in the Saddle,* 67–68; H. B. McClellan, *I Rode with Stuart,* 210; *OR,* 25:1, 59; Nanzig, *3rd Virginia Cavalry,* 30; Longacre, *Lee's Cavalrymen,* 173; B. Davis, *Jeb Stuart,* 270–71.

16. Gilmor, *Four Years in the Saddle,* 68, 69, 70. Fitz Lee later reported on the deaths of Puller and Lieutenant [C. S.] Harris: "both gallant and highly efficient officers [were] a heavy loss to their regiments and country." *OR,* 25:1, 63.

17. In his post-battle report Fitz Lee stated that he "particularly noticed" Rosser, whom he praised for "his habitual coolness and daring, charging at the head of his regiment." Stuart added that he "cordially concur[red]" with Fitz Lee's assessment of Rosser, "who, though severely wounded at 2 P.M., remained in command at the head of his regiment until the day was won" (*OR,* 25:1, 62, 59). Curiously, none of the battle reports nor the commonly cited books on Confederate generals detail Rosser's wound. Even Bushong and Bushong's biography (*Fightin' Tom Rosser*) fails to explain the circumstances, whereabouts, or extent of the "severe" wound. Fortunately, Channing Price sent word of Rosser's wound in a letter to his mother written four days after the battle. Noting that surgeon John Fontaine requested a sixty-day leave of absence for Rosser, Price stated that Rosser was "very badly & painfully wounded in the foot, the ball having lodged among the small bones . . . and has not been extracted." Price further added, "Rosser's loss would be felt as much as any man's I know of in the Division" (Trout, *Pen & Saber,* 182–83).

18. Some insist the Federals used mostly sabers in the close quarters struggle while the Rebels employed a preponderance of pistols as the weapon of choice. At one spot where the Confederates were forced to pull back, a Pennsylvanian claimed he heard a Virginian shout, "Draw your pistols, you Yanks, and fight like gentlemen" (Starr, *Union Cavalry,* 1:347).

19. H. H. Matthews, "Death of John Pelham," *St. Mary's Beacon,* February 16, 1905; Trout, *Galloping Thunder,* 178; Matthews, "General Lee Called Him 'The Gallant Pelham,'" 382. Matthews, who wrote this article on March 10, 1908, claimed to have heard Pelham's statement to Breathed, noting, "These were the last words I ever heard him utter."

20. Gilmor claimed that he and Pelham were on the right of the Second Virginia Cavalry, but he was undoubtedly mistaken.

21. Gilmor, *Four Years in the Saddle,* 70.

22. Even Heros von Borcke, who remained back at Camp No-Camp, maintained that he had a premonition of Pelham's death. While listening to the rumblings of cannon during the battle, von Borcke stated he was "completely overcome, my thoughts constantly reverting to my dear friend Pelham, with an obstinate foreboding that some dreadful fate must have befallen him" (*Memoirs,* 2:186).

23. Wise, *Long Arm of Lee,* 1:433; Cooke, *Wearing of the Gray,* 116; Milham, *Gallant Pelham,* 231; Freeman, *Lee's Lieutenants,* 2:463; Hassler, *Col. John Pelham,* 164; Thomason, *Jeb Stuart,* 357; Mercer, *Gallant Pelham,* 160. Some of these sources have Pelham waving his hat, not a sword. Others quote his words of encouragement to the Confederate horsemen: "Give it to 'em, boys! There they are! Give it to 'em!" (Milham, *Gallant Pelham,* 231), and "Forward! Let's get 'em!" (Hassler, *Col. John Pelham,* 164). Heros von Borcke, again not in attendance, stated that "[Pelham] rushed forward into the thickest of the fight, cheering on our men and animating them by example." Then when one of the regiments wavered, Pelham shouted, "Forward, boys! forward to victory and glory!" (*Memoirs,* 2:187). Although all these phrases are similar in wording and tone, Pelham's exact words must be considered purely conjectural.

24. *Richmond Daily Dispatch,* March 26, 1863; article (author unknown), John Pelham Scrapbook, ADAH. If Pelham were mortally wounded at the gate of the stone fence, as so many have indicated, then a piece of Hotchkiss shell surely hit him. Many years ago when the Kelly's Ford battleground was still unmarked and pristine, metal detectors were used all around the area and pieces of Hotchkiss shell were found at the gate. No other projectile pieces were discovered. A few of those Hotchkiss chunks and slivers are in my possession.

A standard-sized Hotchkiss shell, used mostly by Federal artillerists, was three inches by six and three-quarters inches. The heavy shell contained three basic parts: the base or cup section, a hollow nose for a timing fuse, and a heavy lead sabot in the middle. Inside the hollow shell was case shot, irregular balls roughly a half inch in diameter—hence a gigantic shotgun shell flying through the air. Fired by a rifled field piece, the Hotchkiss was extremely accurate, although the fuse occasionally dislodged or burned out, rendering the shell a dud. Some claim that while in the air, the Hotchkiss made a screaming noise that demoralized the enemy. McKee and Mason, *Civil War Projectiles II,* 105; Faust, *Encyclopedia of the Civil War,* 371.

25. H. B. McClellan, *I Rode with Stuart,* 210–11, 217. McClellan's commentary seems altogether too brief and stilted. He neglected to mention the name of the trooper who placed Pelham's body over the saddle, and he stated that Pelham's "life was extinct" when, in fact, Pelham lived nearly twelve more hours. Douglas Southall Freeman (*Lee's Lieutenants,* 2:463) allows for differing versions of Pelham's wounding but seems to favor the description given by Henry McClellan.

Another story pertaining to Pelham's mortal wounding mentions that Willie Hoxton—Llewellyn's brother to whom Pelham had written a letter a month earlier—assisted in putting out a brush fire that might have consumed Pelham's body. The tale further indicates that Willie assisted in removing Pelham's body from the field. Sergent, *They Lie Forgotten,* 145.

26. Matthews, "General Lee Called Him 'The Gallant Pelham,'" 382. Although H. H. Matthews credited Henry McClellan with this report, it should be noted that the overly dramatized description with its almost poetic wording does not fit McClellan's often terse writing style. Curiously, John Esten Cooke's *Surry of Eagle's-Nest,* 387, contains a nearly verbatim narrative of McClellan's alleged account of Pelham's wounding. It is so identical that only *one* person—not two—could have written it without plagiarizing.

27. Blackford, *War Years,* 202. This unsubstantiated and somewhat unclear information is unlike Blackford. Furthermore, he seems almost too eager to change the story again without support to a more romanticized cavalry charge.

28. Both letters were sent to Edwin P. Cox, DSFP. The Freeman Collection also includes a thirty-six-page unsigned, handwritten note of some mystery. Although at times difficult to decipher, it contains superb information on Pelham's wounding and death. It mentions (on page 17) Pelham's "clear voice" in leading his men, "when a shell burst over his head & one fragment went hissing through his brow." Another undated article, again with no author's name affixed, appears in the same collection and mentions—as did Mrs. Pelham's letter—Major J. M. Ryals being at Pelham's side. Strangely, no other source names Ryals in this capacity. Major J. M. Ryals undoubtedly was G. M. [Garland Mitchell] Ryals, actually a lieutenant at the time of Pelham's wounding, serving as an ordnance officer and provost marshal under Fitz Lee. Ryals, a native Virginian, was born on May 27, 1839. After joining the Confederate Army his varied career took him from the Eastern Theater to the Western Theater and back again (Trout, *Plume,* 241–47; Trout, *Pen & Saber,* 327; *OR,* 25:1, 62). Exactly why Ryals is mentioned twice as being with Pelham at the time of his wounding is not known, but it appears significant that the diligent research of Robert J. Trout does not mention him.

29. Gilmor, *Four Years in the Saddle,* 71. Gilmor's account differs considerably from Henry McClellan's except for the fact that they agree Pelham was struck by a piece of shell fragment. If Gilmor's description is to be believed, then Pelham was not leading a charge, waving his sword aloft, or cheering on the men of the Third Virginia near the stone fence—all popular versions of the Pelham legacy. Instead, Pelham would have been an observer and not an active participant at the precise time of his wounding. Certainly Pelham's war record needs no further embellishment, but if Gilmor's account is true, then others have flavored the story to enhance Pelham's heroism one last time. It is of great interest that Gilmor never referred to the Wheatley house nor the stone fence in his descriptions, two landmarks that have become central parts of the Pelham death story. Furthermore, Henry McClellan, who claimed he rode directly to Pelham's fallen body, is never mentioned by Gilmor. In either case it must be remembered that certain historians remain

skeptical of Gilmor's honesty, yet his account, mythical or factual, contains the most detail and could, in fact, be correct. (Robert Trout broaches the subject of Pelham's mortal wounding in *Galloping Thunder*, appendix 1, 649–53. Trout even adds to the mystery by asking if there were possibly two stone fences, a notion I would seriously question, and if Breathed's low fire might have been responsible for Pelham's wounding, an intriguing thought but most likely doubtful.)

30. The two men dispatched by Gilmor to take Pelham's body off the field of battle have not been identified. Minnigerode, the seventeen-year-old aide to Fitz Lee, is mentioned in some sources as assisting with Pelham's removal from the battlefield while in others his name does not appear in this capacity. After the war Minnigerode became a merchant but for unestablished reasons he committed suicide on January 25, 1888, at age forty-two (R. E. L. Krick, *Staff Officers in Gray*, 222). The identities of those who carried Pelham off the battlefield are in dispute. H. H. Matthews claimed that Henry McClellan, John Esten Cooke, and two horsemen of the Third Virginia Cavalry "placed [Pelham] on a horse, tenderly conveying him to the battery" where he was placed in the care of Dr. William Murray, the battery surgeon (*St. Mary's Beacon,* February 16, 1905). John Esten Cooke, so devoted and admiring of Pelham, does not mention his involvement in carrying Pelham off the field; therefore, it must be assumed that Matthews's information is false.

31. Gilmor, *Four Years in the Saddle,* 71–72. Burke Davis (*Jeb Stuart,* 272–73), Charles Milham (*Gallant Pelham,* 231), and Philip Mercer (*Gallant Pelham,* 160–61) follow Gilmor's description almost to the letter. Some modern scholars, however, noticeably wince at Gilmor's frequent lack of accuracy and unreliability. They further discredit his penchant for "tooting his own horn" by blatantly taking credit for things he simply did not do. Yet, his story of Pelham's wounding and death is loaded with detail that other eyewitness accounts lack, possibly giving his version more validity and credence. Whether his account of Pelham's wounding is totally accurate or not, it is to Gilmor's credit that both Jeb Stuart and Fitz Lee praise him for his service at Kelly's Ford. Lee especially lauded him "for his marked bravery and cool courage" (*OR,* 25:1, 58, 63). The mysterious thirty-six-page document in the Freeman Collection states of Gilmor's recollection concerning Pelham's demise: "It's the best of the close of this fine, good life" (17).

One of the most unusual commentaries on Pelham's mortal wounding appears in a letter (found in the John Pelham Papers, ADAH) from a magazine article titled "The Gallant Pelham: True Details of the Great Cannoneer's Death, now first told, in words of his tentmate, Captain James Louis Clark." An aide-de-camp to Stuart for approximately six months, Captain Clark alleged that he and Pelham were "bosom friends and tentmates" at the time of Pelham's death. Clark also claimed that because the staff officers were "not entirely harmonious," he and Pelham stayed mostly together in their tent. He further asserted that on the morning that Pelham left Stuart's campsite he took with him a "handsome plush lap robe" that he had borrowed from Clark to use as a poncho. The robe, as Clark described it, had "a yellow tiger on one side and black on the other that I had brought from Baltimore." Clark also professed that Gilmor found the robe at the spot where Pelham fell mortally wounded and that Gilmor took a small piece of Pelham's skull for a souvenir—"hardly the size of a three-cent piece." All or any part of Clark's claims could be true. It is interesting to note that none of those who were intimate with Pelham at the time mentions Clark. Furthermore, some of Clark's detail in the letter appears to be spurious. Photographs of Clark reveal the dashing good looks of a man in his early twenties: handsome, almost rakish, with light, penetrating eyes, slicked-back hair, and a thin, neatly trimmed moustache. He appears to have been a friend of Gilmor, yet Gilmor mentions none of this. Whether Clark's statements in the letter are true, or whether he is no more than a charlatan, will probably never be known. For biographical information on James L. Clark, see Trout, *Plume,* 86–89, 345.

32. *OR,* 25:1, 49; H. B. McClellan, *I Rode with Stuart,* 211–12. Averell insisted that "300 to 500 prisoners might have been captured," but he claimed that "the distance was too great . . . the

ground was very heavy, and the charge was made three minutes too soon, and without any prearranged support." Henry McClellan saw it differently, offering that Fitz Lee's skillful withdrawal kept Averell from gaining any advantage.

33. *OR*, 25:1, 50; Trout, *Galloping Thunder*, 180. According to Gilmor, the Rebel guns were more than "annoying" with a "terrible effect" on the enemy (*Four Years in the Saddle*, 72).

34. Henry McClellan stated that Fitz Lee's rash order was no doubt precipitated by what Fitz "knew personally of [Averell's] *character*." (*I Rode with Stuart*, 213).

35. H. B. McClellan, *I Rode with Stuart*, 213–15; Thomason, *Jeb Stuart*, 358; Wise, *Long Arm of Lee*, 1:434; Milham, *Gallant Pelham*, 231; Longacre, *Lee's Cavalrymen*, 174. The First Rhode Island Cavalry suffered more than half of the Federal reported losses in the battle (41 of 80). Henry McClellan noted, "This regiment fairly carried off the honors of the day on the Federal side." *I Rode with Stuart*, 217; *OR*, 25:1, 53.

36. *Richmond Daily Dispatch*, March 26, 1863; *OR*, 25:1, 50; H. B. McClellan, *I Rode with Stuart*, 215–16; Trout, *Galloping Thunder*, 180. McClellan scorned Averell's decision based on a "phantom" infantry "conjured up" in the Federal general's fertile "imagination." McClellan contemptuously emphasized that "there was no Confederate infantry nearer to Fitz Lee's brigade than the camps of the army in the vicinity of Fredericksburg." He closed: "We cannot excuse General Averell's conduct. He ought to have gone to Culpeper Court House."

37. *OR*, 25:1, 52, 63; H. B. McClellan, *I Rode with Stuart*, 217; Thomason, *Jeb Stuart*, 359. Fitz Lee's report cited fifty-nine individual horsemen by name for acts of gallantry. But he seemed especially proud of Sergeant W. J. Kimborough of Company G, Fifth Virginia, who, "wounded early in the day . . . refused to leave the field. In the last charge he was the first to spring to the ground to open the fence, then dashing on at the head of the column, he was twice sabered over the head, his arm shattered by a bullet, captured and carried over the river, when he escaped, and walked back 12 miles to his camp."

Harry Gilmor stated that the Third Virginia rode against a "fearful fire of canister" from a Federal battery that cost the Rebel regiment the loss of 39 men and numerous horses. He further insisted that Breathed's battery fired 20 to 30 shells, one of which "knocked off" the head of a Federal officer, another disabling an enemy gun. He summed up: "This was one of the hardest-fought cavalry battles up to that time; and, indeed, I doubt if there has been a severer one since. . . . [The Confederates] lost that day over three hundred men in killed, wounded, and prisoners" (*Four Years in the Saddle*, 72–73). Although Gilmor's overall tally is too high, his figures on the losses of the Third Virginia could be correct, as Fitz Lee noted 44 men and 51 horses as casualties for this regiment. See *OR*, 25:1, 63.

38. *OR*, 25:1, 58–59.

39. *OR*, 25:1, 64. The historian Stephen Starr regards Fitz Lee's General Orders No. 10 as "grandiloquent" and "absurd" (*Union Cavalry*, 1:348, 349). It appears that Fitz Lee's condemnation of Averell's intentions of carrying out the war in an uncivilized manner to the Southern civilians is highly exaggerated. Furthermore, his reference to "certain sneerers in our army" should also be of interest to those who implicitly believe the Army of Northern Virginia was above such petty backbiting.

40. *OR*, 25:1, 50, 53, 1073; Starr, *Union Cavalry*, 1:348–49. Starr, an expert on Union cavalry, sees the battle as a Federal victory although he, too, condemns Averell's generalship as woeful: "The Federal horse had gained the upper hand in an engagement that their commander lacked the nerve or killer instinct to fight to a finish. . . . Averell must nevertheless be given credit for a competent conduct of the fight . . . up to the moment when his imagination got the better of him and he ordered a retreat." Starr further questions the belief that a metamorphosis occurred in the morale of the Union cavalry. *Union Cavalry*, 1:349, 350.

41. Gilmor, *Four Years in the Saddle*, 73; B. Davis, *Jeb Stuart*, 273–74; Freeman, *Lee's Lieuten-

ants, 2:465. What caused the rather cold unconcern of the two nameless men who transported Pelham's body is subject to conjecture. Perhaps the most logical answer is that they both thought he was dead. Gilmor, who described himself as "overwhelmed with horror" at their actions, contended that their slovenly disregard for orders led to Pelham's death. "I firmly believe," maintained Gilmor, "that, had surgical aid been called [immediately] to remove the compression on the brain, his life might have been spared."

Although no official medical reports have been unearthed concerning Pelham's fatal wounding, it is possible to establish certain assumptions relating to his demise. In doing so, I consulted with Dr. L. J. Dragovic, the chief medical examiner of Oakland County, Michigan, who graciously offered his expertise. Since none of the surgeons attending to Pelham put into writing their observations of the wound, Dr. Dragovic could merely render his opinions based on his many years studying gunshot wounds and head injuries. He believes, based on the scanty evidence available, that Pelham's initial injury was a fatal one, and that instant attention by surgeons would probably not have spared Pelham's life. "An open head injury of the type described, especially if the brain were exposed," cites Dr. Dragovic, would have left Pelham "no chance for survival," especially with nineteenth-century technology. He further concludes that the thought among Pelham's contemporaries, particularly Harry Gilmor and Tom Rosser, that immediate care by surgeons might have avoided Pelham's death was most likely "wishful thinking."

42. Channing Price to his mother, March 21, 1863, in Trout, *Pen & Saber,* 183; Vogtsberger, "The Mysteries of Kelly's Ford," 2–4; Trout, *Galloping Thunder,* 688. Twenty-six-year-old Joseph Lee Minghini was a member of Company D, Twelfth Virginia Cavalry. After the war he lived in Martinsburg, West Virginia, where he died at age eighty-one on January 14, 1919 (Trout, *Pen & Saber,* 319; Trout, *Plume,* 316). Minghini claimed that when he approached Pelham, "some surgeons [were] attending him," yet neither Gilmor nor any others mention surgeons being on hand.

Contrary to this version of Gilmor conducting Pelham's body back to Culpeper, H. H. Matthews stated that he was "conveyed by Lieutenant McClellan . . . and some men to the house of Judge Shackelford" ('General Lee Called Him 'The Gallant Pelham,'" 382). Matthews further stated that sometime that night Captain James Breathed, Dan Shanks, "and the men of the battery who were close to [Pelham], visited the house of Dr. Herndon to pay their last respects to their dead commander the incomparable Pelham" (Matthews, *St. Mary's Beacon,* February 16, 1905). It must be noted that Pelham's body was at the Shackelford house, not Dr. Herndon's, thus making the statement entirely false.

43. Gilmor, *Four Years in the Saddle,* 73–74; article (author unknown), John Pelham Scrapbook, ADAH. Not all agree as to exactly where the piece of shell hit, nor its size or shape. Milham states that the section of shell was "possibly a quarter-inch in diameter" and further indicates that the doctors removed the piece of shell from the wound. This removal seems incorrect based on what others have written. Milham adds that the wound itself did not take Pelham's life, but, according to the doctors, the constant "manhandling, [and] the congestion for so long a time" caused his death. Thomason describes the piece of shell as a "splinter, a long, narrow sliver of steel." Minghini, a supposed eyewitness, contends that Pelham "was struck on the top of the head with a piece of shell, which went out about 2 inches from where it entered, crushing the skull." Adding to the ambiguity of the so-called facts, Jedediah Hotchkiss, the talented topographical engineer, stated that he spent "several hours with General Stuart, conversing about the late battle of Kellysville," merely seven days after the battle. Hotchkiss recalled that Stuart "laments the loss of Pelham, who was hit in the head by a musket ball while cheering on the cavalry, through a gap in the fence, to a charge, he waiting for them to pass that he might get through to go to General Stuart, having been to order in all his artillery." Milham, *Gallant Pelham,* 232–33;

Thomason, *Jeb Stuart,* 358; Trout, *Pen & Saber,* 183; Channing Price to his mother, March 21, 1863; supplement to *OR,* 4:1, 504; Trout, *Galloping Thunder,* 753.

44. One of the most endearing items found years later among Pelham's possessions is believed to be an unfinished, bloodstained bookmark with the cross-stitched words: "To My Dear Mama." Today it is in the ADAH. Again my gratitude is extended to chief curator Robert Bradley and senior archivist Nancy Dupree for allowing me to view and photograph this priceless memento.

45. Gilmor, *Four Years in the Saddle,* 74; Hassler, *Col. John Pelham,* 166; Mercer, *Gallant Pelham,* 162–63; Matthews, "General Lee Called Him 'The Gallant Pelham,'" 383; Trout, *Galloping Thunder,* 180. Both Gilmor and Douglas Southall Freeman (*Lee's Lieutenants,* 2:465) have Pelham dying at 1:00 in the afternoon, an obvious error. Gilmor also listed Pelham at "just twenty-one years old"; Pelham was twenty-four. Joseph Minghini told Channing Price that "Stuart came into town about 2 o'clock, expecting somewhat that [Pelham] was still alive & was dreadfully shocked to see his dead body" (Channing Price to his mother, March 21, 1863, Trout, *Pen & Saber,* 183). Price added, "Thus passed away a man, who with faults certainly, was one of the noblest specimens I ever had the pleasure of meeting with." Then young Price noted pragmatically, "How his place can be supplied is hard to say but I hope the General [Stuart] will be able to get some one worthy to succeed him."

Chapter 23

1. Although no one in camp identified the courier, it appears to have been Private Joseph Lee Minghini.

2. Captain W. Gordon McCabe's tribute, "A Sketch of the Heroic Boy Artillerist," John Pelham Scrapbook, ADAH; Shreve, "Reminiscences."

3. Von Borcke, *Memoirs,* 2:187, 188. The Prussian mistakenly bemoaned: "Poor Pelham! He had but just received his promotion to the rank of Lieutenant-Colonel." Pelham's promotion was still pending before the Confederate Senate and would not be formally announced until Saturday, April 4.

4. Trout, *Pen & Saber,* 180, 183.

5. Channing Price to his mother, March 20, 1863, Trout, *Pen & Saber,* 182; Blackford, *War Years,* 202.

6. A. Mitchell, *Letters,* 299; *Richmond Whig,* March 21, 1863; "Miscellaneous" file. Virtually all other sources, including Matthews, "General Lee Called Him 'The Gallant Pelham,'" 383, and Cooke, *Wearing of the Gray,* 117, quote the last sentence as, "His loss is irreparable." Why so many, including Pelham's contemporaries, remove the words "to the country" is a matter of speculation. Most likely they are omitted because his loss was to the Confederacy and not the nation as a whole. Disagreement also exists as to the use of the word "chivalric" versus "chivalrous."

7. Von Borcke, *Memoirs,* 2:188–89.

8. Von Borcke, *Memoirs,* 2:189–90; Cooke, *Wearing of the Gray,* 117; Mercer, *Gallant Pelham,* 169–70; B. Davis, *Jeb Stuart,* 275.

9. Mercer, *Gallant Pelham,* 170–71; Hooper, "The Gallant Pelham Goes Home," 4, JPL. It has been strongly suggested that "Evelyn" was not a woman but a pen name for one of Pelham's or Stuart's staff officers. One source claims that Evelyn was actually Dr. William G. Shepardson, but this appears to be unsubstantiated. Andrews, *The South Reports the Civil War;* "'Evelyn's' Report on Pelham's Death."

10. The quote comes from a Richmond correspondent for the *Atlanta Confederacy.* "Account of John Pelham's Funeral"; Hassler, *Col. John Pelham,* 166; Milham, *Gallant Pelham,* 233; von Borcke, *Memoirs,* 2:190; Hooper, "John Pelham and Belle Boyd," in "Miscellaneous" file. Interestingly, on March 19, 1984, John Pelham's one-hundred-year-old niece, Emma Pelham Hank, flatly stated that no engagement existed between Sallie and John and that the much-believed story of the romance was "entirely false." Interviews from the *Richmond Times-Dispatch* and one conducted by Peggy Vogtsberger and Laura Perkinson, "Reminiscences of Emma Pelham Hank."

11. A. Mitchell, *Letters,* 299–300.

12. Stuart-Mosby Historical Society, *Southern Cavalry Review* 2, no. 5 (March 1985).

13. Compiled Service Records of Confederate Generals; *OR,* 25:2, 675; Milham, *Gallant Pelham,* 234; Mercer, *Gallant Pelham,* 168; Hassler, *Col. John Pelham,* 167. Pelham's posthumous promotion to lieutenant colonel was granted on April 4, 1863 (to date from March 2). It was signed by the Confederate secretary of war, James Seddon. The original copy is housed in the Confederate Museum in Richmond, Virginia.

On the same day Lee penned his thoughts to President Davis, the commanding general also wrote his wife, Mary, with similar feelings: "I grieve over the loss of Major Pelham. He had been stricken down in the midst of his career of usefulness & honour, which in its progress I had hoped would have expanded in brightness" (Dowdey, *Papers of R. E. Lee,* 414).

14. Von Borcke, *Memoirs,* 2:190; Wright, *A Southern Girl in '61,* 125–26. A letter from Philip Preston Johnston, a first lieutenant in Breathed's battery, to Edwin P. Cox, December 2, 1898, offers a strangely different version of the procession and its destination. Johnston claimed the body was carried from the Capitol to Richmond's Hollywood Cemetery as a "war horse fully equiped [*sic*] following the hearse with empty saddle, and the bowed heads of the stern warriors who had fought at his side on so many desperate fields was a picture full of agony to all who witnessed it." Johnston further related that "the piece of shell that killed Pelham struck him on the back of the head making an apparently slight wound. While adjusting the body as it lay in the coffin," insisted Johnston, "I discovered that it had cut off some of the hair. I removed a lock and gave it to Miss Jane Randolph who then lived in the Allen mansion, corner of Sixth and Main. I think that had been the home of Edgar A[llen] Poe. If she is still in Richmond, she can tell you much about the personal appearance of Maj. Pelham and of his bearing in social life and of how he impressed those who met him when off duty." No evidence exists as to whether Mr. Cox communicated with Jane Randolph. Johnston's letter is in the Virginia Historical Society manuscripts collection and my gratitude is extended to E. Lee Shepard, the director of Manuscripts and Archives, for allowing me to reproduce it. A copy also remains in "Stuart Horse Artillery" (file #6), JPL.

The relative who traveled with the coffin was George Terry, a "second or third cousin of Pelham's." James V. Garrison, a native of Talladega and member of the Stuart Horse Artillery, to Thomas M. Owen, July 13, 1909, Alabama Artillery Battery file, ADAH.

15. The route of the funeral trains and the estimated distances between stations were taken from Hooper, "The Gallant Pelham Goes Home," and from a hand-drawn map in the Pelham files, JPL.

16. Mercer, *Gallant Pelham,* 173; von Borcke, *Memoirs,* 2:190.

17. *Richmond Daily Dispatch,* April 2, 1863; Pelham biography and John Pelham Scrapbook, ADAH; *OR,* 25:1, 60; "Letters and Documents" file, JPL; A. Mitchell, *Letters,* 300–301; Trout, *Pen & Saber,* 181–82; Mercer, *Gallant Pelham,* 166–67; Wise, *Long Arm of Lee,* 1:434–35. (The original General Orders No. 9 is located at the University of North Carolina library in Chapel Hill.) Jennings Cropper Wise has noted that "The written records of the American conflict fail to disclose another such tribute from so great a commander as Stuart." Wise further avowed that Pelham "was far more than a skilled and dashing soldier. . . . Modern formulae have by no means

rendered impossible the deeds of another Pelham. . . . [His] brilliant career was but a phase of the Confederate artillery service. In the final analysis of his deeds, it was not so much what he actually did as what his name stood for among his comrades. . . . It is easy to place limits upon his actual accomplishments in a tactical sense—it is impossible to define the extent of his moral ascendancy" (*Long Arm of Lee,* 1:435, 440).

18. *OR,* 25:1, 60; Vogtsberger, *The Cannoneer,* special ed. (May 1999).

19. Von Borcke, *Memoirs,* 2:90; *OR,* 25:2, 858 (March 25, 1863). Forty-one years later, on January 22, 1904, seventy-year-old John Mosby wrote a letter to Joseph Bryan stating, "[A] few days ago I was at Jacksonville, Ala—where John Pelham is buried. I went to his grave—I knew him well. It brought vividly to my mind the last time I saw him at Culpeper C. H. (March '63) a few days before he was killed. . . . I never saw John Pelham again." Mosby further explained that a monument would soon be erected for Pelham at the grave site, and the Confederate daughters of Jacksonville had suggested the inscription, "Dear Son of memory—great heir of fame, what neediest thou such weak witness of thy name" (from John Milton's lines on a monument to William Shakespeare). "Letters and Official Reports" file.

20. Mrs. Peter Pelham to Edwin P. Cox, [1898]; Freeman, *Lee's Lieutenants,* 2:466. Union officer Morris Schaff, who had known John Pelham at West Point, remembered his friend admiringly: "In the winter of 1863–64, while with the Army of the Potomac, more than once I traveled the road to Kelly's Ford, where [Pelham] was killed, little dreaming of the height of his present fame. I have always thought of the circumstances connected with the coming home of his body to his widowed mother [*sic*] in Alabama, as uniting all the beauty and mystery of night. The moon was full; and her still light lay white upon the way by the cotton-fields he knew so well, and white on the roof and in the dooryard of his home. His mother . . . stood waiting for him on the doorstep, and, as they bore him up to her, she whispered through falling tears, 'washed in the blood of the Lamb that was slain' " (Schaff, *Old West Point,* 133–34).

21. *Jacksonville Republican,* April 2, 1863; John Pelham Scrapbook, ADAH; letter collection, DSFP; Hooper, "The Gallant Pelham Goes Home." In her interviews in 1984, Emma Pelham Hank claimed that all the pallbearers were women, including her own mother, Emma McAuley, who married John's brother, Peter, in 1869.

22. Mrs. Peter Pelham to Edwin Cox, [1898]; Charles Pelham to Edwin Cox, November 21, 1898; "Jacksonville" file, JPL. Today a ten-foot marble shaft with an image of John Pelham can easily be sighted near the entrance of the cemetery. At the foot of Pelham's grave is a simple rectangular marker that reads:

JOHN PELHAM
LIEUT. COL. STUART'S VA. ARTY.
CONFEDERATE STATES ARMY
SEP. 7, 1838 MARCH 17, 1863

Around him are the graves of his brother Samuel Clay Pelham, who died on February 12, 1870, at age twenty-five; his mother, Martha, who died at age sixty-eight on August 16, 1876; his father, Atkinson, who died on July 7, 1880, at age eighty-two; and two other family members, Annie E. McGehee and Sallie A. Pelham.

23. Journal entries, March 26 and 29, 1863, in Trout, *Pen & Saber,* 187–88. Cooke further noted that "[Pelham's] passions were strong, and when he was aroused fire darted from the flint, but this was seldom. During all my acquaintance with him . . . I never had a word addressed to me that was unfriendly, and never saw him angry but twice." Cooke added that Stuart had said of Pelham, "Poor boy! He was angry with me <u>once</u>" (*Wearing of the Gray,* 128).

24. Mrs. William Herndon to Martha Pelham, March 1863, John Pelham Papers, ADAH.

25. The Alabama Department of Archives and History has the original Stuart letter. Copies can also be found in the John Pelham Collection at the ACPL. Trout, *Plume*, 211–13; "Letters and Documents" file; Vogtsberger, *The Cannoneer* 2, no. 3 (November 1983); Milham, *Gallant Pelham*, 235–37.

26. Trout, *Pen & Saber*, 189. Robert Franklin Beckham, Stuart's choice to replace Pelham, was a twenty-five-year-old native of Culpeper, Virginia. A graduate of West Point in the somewhat undistinguished Class of 1859 (he stood number 6 of 22), Beckham began his professional career in the elite Corps of Topographical Engineers. Prior to the war, he served in this capacity under George Meade in Detroit, Michigan, at Fort Wayne. Although Beckham expressed he did "not wish to be put in the Infantry or Artillery," the Confederate War Department placed him in the artillery. Somewhat disgruntled, the handsome officer proved his ability at First Manassas where his skills caught the eye of Jeb Stuart. Beckham assumed command of Stuart's Horse Artillery on April 8, 1863, and was personally congratulated for his fine service at Chancellorsville by Stonewall Jackson. Stuart pushed hard for Beckham's promotion to lieutenant colonel, but the War Department at first declined. Eventually his promotion to colonel on February 16, 1864, brought a transfer as well to John Bell Hood's army in Tennessee. On November 29, 1864, near Columbia, Tennessee, Beckham was mortally wounded when an exploding shell struck a boulder, sending a piece of fragmented rock into the back of his head. He died on December 5 at age twenty-seven and is buried in Ashwood Cemetery at St. John's Episcopal Church near Columbia, Tennessee. Trout, *Plume*, 56–62; R. K. Krick, *Lee's Colonels*, 44.

27. Atkinson Pelham to J. E. B. Stuart, April 4, 1863, John Pelham Papers, ADAH; Vogtsberger, *The Cannoneer* 2, no. 3 (November 1983).

28. J. E. B. Stuart to Flora Stuart, 1863, manuscript collection from the Virginia Historical Society of Richmond, JPL; Vogtsberger, *The Cannoneer* 2, no. 3 (November 1983). In the same letter Stuart mentioned that Tom Rosser's wedding would be held "next Wednesday." Of course, Pelham was to have been the best man. (Stuart also playfully stated, "I send Nannie her commission as A.D.C.")

29. A. Mitchell, *Letters*, 308–10. Stuart's firm notation of "*Strictly Private*" undoubtedly stemmed from his anger when he found that his mother-in-law had read, either deliberately or otherwise, an earlier letter to Flora. In the same April 8 letter he declared: "I don't know when I have been so vexed as when I heard Ma had mistaken your letter for hers and read it. I don't know what I wrote, but I certainly did not write for her to see."

Flora gave birth to a daughter on October 9, 1863. Neither Rachel nor Maria Pelham, Jeb's earlier choice of name, was given. Instead, the child was christened Virginia Pelham Stuart.

30. Letter collection, DSFP.

31. P. P. Johnston to Edwin P. Cox, December 2, 1898, Virginia Historical Society Manuscripts, Richmond.

32. Trout, *Pen & Saber*, 197; Hubbell, "The War Diary of John Esten Cooke," "Stuart Horse Artillery" (file #6), JPL; Cooke, *Surry of Eagle's-Nest*, 391; Mercer, *Gallant Pelham*, 164–65.

Appendix

1. Clemmer, *Valor in Gray*, 125.

Bibliography

Manuscript Sources and Special Collections

Alabama Department of Archives and History, Montgomery, Alabama

Cumming, Kate. Papers. Box 1, folder 23, LPR 164.

James V. Garrison to Thomas M. Owen, July 13, 1909, Alabama Artillery Battery, Pelham, F6-7, SG024917.

Jeb Stuart to Dr. Atkinson Pelham, March 29, 1863.

Moore, Governor A. B. Papers. Microfilm, SG24882.

Mrs. Herndon to Martha Pelham, March 22, 1863.

Pelham, John. Papers. LPR82.

Pelham, John. Scrapbook. Microfilm, M1998.0457.

Pelham, Major John. Biography. Loc. #SG011128, folder #15.

Allen County Library, Genealogy Department, Fort Wayne, Indiana

Driver, Robert J., Jr. *First & Second Maryland Infantry C.S.A.* Bowie, MD: Heritage Books, 2003.

McCoy, Kathy, ed. *Adventures of Charles L. Scott, Esq.* Monroeville, AL: Bolton Newspapers, 1997.

Anniston-Calhoun County Public Library, Anniston, Alabama

Hanson, Joseph Mills. "Thomas Lafayette Rosser." *Cavalry Journal* (March–April 1934).

John Pelham, boxes 241 and 242.

John Pelham Collection by Fred R. Martin, boxes 26 and 27.

John Pelham file AN71, F-#330.

Birmingham Public Library, Birmingham, Alabama

Fred R. Martin Scrapbook Collection, vol. 26.

Detroit Public Library, Detroit, Michigan

Burton Collection

Historical Research Department

Duke University Library and Archives, Durham, North Carolina

Pelham note to J. E. B. Stuart, July 3, 1862

Special Collections Library, Dalton-Brand Research Room

Jacksonville Public Library, Jacksonville, Alabama

JOHN PELHAM COLLECTION

Files: "Chambersburg Raid" (file #11), "Fredericksburg," "Genealogy" (file #11), "Genealogy" (folder II), "General Articles," "Generals/Battles" (file #4), "Homes," "Jacksonville," "Letters and Documents," "Letters and Official Reports," "Miscellaneous," "Monuments," "Pelham," "Poetry & Art" (file #9), "Stuart Horse Artillery" (file #6), "West Point" (file #2), "West Point," "Youth."

Adams, Fannie Lewis Gwathmey. "Reminiscences of a Childhood Spent at Hayfield Plantation near Fredericksburg, Virginia during the Civil War." *William and Mary Quarterly,* 2nd ser., 23, no. 3 (July 1943): 292–97.

Bashinsky, Mrs. L. M. *The Southern Magazine* (January 1937).

Brzustowicz, John. "The Bower."

Duncan, Bingham, ed. *Letters of General J. E. B. Stuart to His Wife.* Atlanta: Emory University, 1943.

Hooper, Charles H. "The Gallant Pelham Goes Home." *The Cannoneer* 22, no. 6 (May 2004).

———. "John Pelham and Belle Boyd." *Berkeley County Historical Association Bulletin,* September/October 1980.

Hubbell, Jay B. "The War Diary of John Esten Cooke." *Journal of Southern History* 7 (February–November 1941): 526–40.

Lake, Virginia T., ed. "A Crisis of Conscience: West Point Letters of Henry A. du Pont, October 1860–June 1861." *Civil War History* 25, no. 1 (1979).

Martin, Fred R. "Pelham of Alabama." *Confederate Veteran,* January 1921.

Peter Pelham to Mrs. Oscar Twitty, January 15, 1917.

Stuart, Kenneth P. "John Pelham, Lt. Col., Stuart Horse Artillery, C.S.A." Master's thesis, Pennsylvania State University, 1960.

Stuart-Mosby Historical Society. *Southern Cavalry Review* 2, no. 5 (March 1985).

Ward, John M. "The Gallant Pelham." *Alabama Bible Society Quarterly* 16, no. 2 (April 1960).

William Hoxton to his sister Sallie, February 17, 1863.

Williams, Mrs. John G. "The 'Gallant' John Pelham." *United Daughters of the Confederacy Magazine* 44, no. 9 (n.d.).

Jefferson County Museum, Charles Town, West Virginia

Shreve, George W. "Reminiscences in the History of the Stuart Horse Artillery, C.S.A." Roger Preston Chew Papers. No. 53.

Library of Congress, Washington, D.C.

Caldwell, James F. J. *The History of a Brigade of South Carolinians, Known as "Gregg's," and Subsequently "McGowan's" Brigade.* Philadelphia: King and Baird Printers, 1866. Microfilm, 43209 E.

Casler, John. *Four Years in the Stonewall Brigade.* Girard, KS: Appeal Publishing, 1906. Microfilm, 79491 E.

Freeman, Douglas Southall. Papers. Manuscripts Division, file numbers 171–74.

JOHN PELHAM COLLECTION

Charles Pelham to Edwin P. Cox, November 21, 1898.
John Pelham to Jefferson Davis, February 27, 1861.
Mrs. Peter Pelham to Edwin P. Cox [1898].
Peter Pelham to Edwin P. Cox, November 25, 1898.

Sam Houston to Tom Rosser, November 17, 1860.

W. E. Pelham to Edwin P. Cox, November 22, 1898.

Unauthored, undated speech on Pelham

Unsigned, undated, handwritten note on John Pelham's wounding and death (thirty-six pages)

McClellan, George B. Papers. Manuscript Division. Special Orders No. 191. Reel 31, container 78.

Neese, George M. *Three Years in the Confederate Horse Artillery*. New York: Neale Publishing, 1911. Microfilm, vol. 47218.

Worsham, John. *One of Jackson's Foot Cavalry: His Experience and What He Saw during the War, 1861–1865*. New York: Neale Publishing, 1912. E581.5 21st.

National Archives Building, Washington, D.C.

Compiled Service Records of Confederate Generals and Staff Officers and Non-regimental Enlisted Men. Microcopy, no. 331, roll #195.

Compiled Service Records of Confederate Soldiers Who Served in Organizations from the State of Virginia. Pendleton microfilm, microcopy, no. 324, roll #224.

Preliminary Inventory of the War Department Collection of Confederate Records, RG 109.

Letters of the Secretary of War, 1861–1864, M493

Records of the Adjutant and Inspector General's Office

Correspondence, Reports, and Other Records Relating to Department Functions

Index to Letters Received, 1861–1865, M410

Letters and Telegrams Sent, 1861–1865, M627

Letters Received, 1861–1865, M474

Records of the Army of Northern Virginia, Battle Reports, Army of Northern Virginia, 1863, RG 109, entry #67

Records Related to Military Personnel: Miscellaneous Records Relating to Officers and Cadets, 1861–1864, RG 109, entry #20

Records of United States Military Academy, M91

"Unfiled Papers and Slips" (Records Relating to Virginia), Papers of and Relating to Military and Civilian Personnel, 1861–1865, RG 109, entry #181, M347, rolls 310, 382

"U.S. Military Academy Cadet Application Papers, 1805–1866." Microfilm, M688, roll #203.

Private Collection

John Pelham to Philip Preston Johnston, February 13, 1863 (owned by Johnston's great-granddaughter, Wallace Johnston Jamerman, Riverton, Wyoming).

Smith College, Northampton, Massachusetts

Garrison Family Papers, Sophia Smith Collection.

John Pelham to his cousin Marianna, March 26, 1861.

St. Mary's County, Maryland

St. Mary's College of Maryland Library, *St. Mary's Beacon*, microfilm cabinet.

St. Mary's County Library, Lexington Park, Maryland, *St. Mary's Beacon*, microfilm collection.

United States Military Academy Archives, West Point, New York

Special Collections and Archives Division of Military Records. National Archives Microfilm Publication 688, U.S. Military Academy Cadet Application Papers, 1805–1866: Register of the Officers and Cadets of the U.S. Military Academy; Biographical Register of Officers and Graduates of the U.S. Military Academy.

Virginia Historical Society, Richmond, Virginia

Philip Preston Johnston to Edwin P. Cox, December 2, 1898, Mss2J6462a1.

Primary Sources

Alexander, Edward Porter. *Fighting for the Confederacy: The Personal Recollections of General Edward Porter Alexander.* Chapel Hill: University of North Carolina Press, 1989.

Allan, William. *Stonewall Jackson, Robert E. Lee, and the Army of Northern Virginia, 1862.* New York: Da Capo Press, 1995.

The Annals of the War, Written by the Leading Participants North and South. Philadelphia: Times Publishing Company, 1879.

Beale, G. W. *A Lieutenant of Cavalry in Lee's Army.* Boston: Gorham Press, 1918.

Beale, R. L. T. *History of the 9th Virginia Cavalry in the War between the States.* Amissville, PA: American Fundamentalist, 1981.

Blackford, W. W. *War Years with Jeb Stuart.* New York: Charles Scribner's Sons, 1945.

Brooks, U. R., ed. *Stories of the Confederacy.* Columbia, SC: The State Company, 1912.

Chamberlayne, John Hampden. *Ham Chamberlayne—Virginian: Letters and Papers of an Artillery Officer in the War for Southern Independence, 1861–1865.* Wilmington, NC: Broadfoot Publishing, 1992.

Cooke, John Esten. *The Life of Stonewall Jackson.* New York: Charles B. Richardson, 1863.

———. *Surry of Eagle's-Nest: The Memoirs of a Staff Officer Serving in Virginia.* Ridgewood, NJ: Gregg Press, 1866.

———. *Wearing of the Gray: Personal Portraits, Scenes and Adventures of the War.* New York: E. B. Trent and Company, 1867.

Dabney, Robert L. *Life and Campaigns of General T. J. (Stonewall) Jackson.* Harrisonburg, VA: Sprinkle Publications, 1977.

Dawes, Rufus R. *The Sixth Wisconsin Volunteers.* Dayton, OH: Morningside Bookshop, 1984.

Douglas, Henry Kyd. *I Rode with Stonewall: The War Experiences of the Youngest Member of Jackson's Staff.* Chapel Hill: University of North Carolina Press, 1940.

Dowdey, Clifford, ed. *The Wartime Papers of R. E. Lee.* Boston: Little, Brown and Company, 1961.

Duncan, Russell, ed. *Blue-Eyed Child of Fortune: The Civil War Letters of Colonel Robert Gould Shaw.* Athens: University of Georgia Press, 1999.

Galway, Thomas Francis. *The Valiant Hours.* Harrisburg, PA: Stackpole, 1961.

Gilmor, Harry. *Four Years in the Saddle.* Introduction by Daniel Carroll Toomey. New York: Harper and Brothers, 1866.

Gordon, John Brown. *Reminiscences of the Civil War.* Dayton, OH: Morningside Bookshop, 1981.

Harrison, Mrs. Burton. *Recollections Grave and Gay.* New York: Charles Scribner's Sons, 1911. Property of the University of North Carolina at Chapel Hill, Academic Affairs Library, www.docsouth.unc.edu/.

Haskell, John Cheves. *The Haskell Memoirs.* New York: Putnam's Sons, 1960.

Hassler, William W., ed. *One of Lee's Best Men: The Civil War Letters of General William Dorsey Pender.* Chapel Hill: University of North Carolina Press, 1965.

Holden, Walter, William E. Ross, and Elizabeth Slomba, eds. *Stand Firm and Fire Low: The Civil War Writings of Colonel Edward E. Cross.* Lebanon, NH: University Press of New England, 2003.

Hood, John Bell. *Advance and Retreat: Personal Experiences of the United States and Confederate States Armies.* Reprint. Lincoln: University of Nebraska Press, 1996.

Jackson, Mary Anna. *Memoirs of Stonewall Jackson.* Reprint. Dayton, OH: Morningside Bookshop, 1976.

Keller, S. Roger, ed. *Riding with Rosser.* Shippensburg, PA: Burd Street Press, 1997.

Lasswell, Mary, ed. *Rags and Hope: The Recollections of Val C. Giles, Four Years with Hood's Brigade, Fourth Texas Infantry, 1861–1865.* New York: Coward-McCann, 1961.

Lee, Robert E. "Proclamation to the People of Maryland." September 8, 1862. Copy transcribed from an original for distribution at Antietam National Battlefield Park.

Light, Rebecca Campbell. *War at Our Doors: The Civil War Diaries and Letters of the Bernard Sisters of Virginia.* Fredericksburg, VA: American History Company, 1998.

Long, Armistead Lindsay. *Memoirs of Robert E. Lee: His Military and Personal History.* New York: J. M. Stoddart and Company, 1886.

Longstreet, James. *From Manassas to Appomattox: Memoirs of the Civil War in America.* Secaucus, NJ: Blue and Gray Press, 1984.

McClellan, George B. *McClellan's Own Story.* New York: Charles L. Webster and Company, 1887.

McClellan, H. B. *I Rode with Jeb Stuart: The Life and Campaigns of Major General J. E. B. Stuart.* Bloomington: Indiana University Press, 1958.

Mitchell, Adele H., ed. *The Letters of Major General James E. B. Stuart.* Stuart-Mosby Historical Society, 1990.

Mosby, John S. *The Memoirs of Colonel John S. Mosby.* Boston: Little, Brown and Company, 1917.

Nanzig, Thomas P., ed. *The Civil War Memoirs of a Virginia Cavalryman: Lt. Robert E. Hubard, Jr.* Tuscaloosa: University of Alabama Press, 2007.

Nevins, Allan, ed. *A Diary of Battle: The Personal Journals of Colonel Charles S. Wainwright, 1861–1865.* New York: Harcourt, Brace and World, 1962.

Pierro, Joseph, ed. *The Maryland Campaign of September 1862: Ezra A. Carman's Definitive Study of the Union and Confederate Armies at Antietam.* New York: Routledge, Taylor and Francis Group, 2008.

Poague, William Thomas. *Gunner with Stonewall.* Wilmington, NC: Broadfoot Publishing, 1987.

Quaife, Milo M., ed. *From the Cannon's Mouth: The Civil War Letters of General Alpheus S. Williams.* Lincoln: University of Nebraska Press, 1995.

Robertson, John. *Michigan in the War.* Lansing, MI: W. S. George and Company, 1882.

Scarborough, William Kauffman, ed. *The Diary of Edmund Ruffin.* Vol. 2, *The Years of Hope, April 1861–June 1863.* Baton Rouge: Louisiana State University Press, 1976.

Schaff, Morris. *The Spirit of Old West Point, 1858–1862.* Boston: Houghton Mifflin, 1907.

Shoemaker, John J. *Shoemaker's Battery, Stuart Horse Artillery, Pelham's Battalion.* Reprint. Gaithersburg, MD: Butternut Press, 1983.

Silliker, Ruth L., ed. *The Rebel Yell & the Yankee Hurrah: The Civil War Journal of a Maine Volunteer.* Camden, ME: Down East Books, 1985.

Sorrel, G. Moxley. *Recollections of a Confederate Staff Officer.* New York: Neale Publishing, 1905.

Supplement to the Official Records of the Union and Confederate Armies. Wilmington, NC: Broadfoot Publishing, 1994.

Taylor, Richard. *Destruction and Reconstruction: Personal Experiences of the Late War.* New York: Longmans, Green and Company, 1955.

Tower, R. Lockwood, ed. *Lee's Adjutant: The Wartime Letters of Colonel Walter Herron Taylor, 1862–1865.* Columbia: University of South Carolina Press, 1995.

Truxall, Aida Craig, ed. *"Respects to All": Letters of Two Pennsylvania Boys in the War of the Rebellion.* Pittsburgh: University of Pittsburgh Press, 1962.

von Borcke, Heros. *Memoirs of the Confederate War for Independence.* 2 vols. New York: Peter Smith, 1938.

War of the Rebellion: A Compilation of the Official Records of the Union and Confederate Armies. 128 vols. Washington, DC, 1880–1901.

Wright, Mrs. D. Giraud. *A Southern Girl in '61: The War-Time Memories of a Confederate Senator's Daughter.* New York: Doubleday, Page, 1905. Property of the University of North Carolina at Chapel Hill, Academic Affairs Library, www.docsouth.unc.edu/.

Secondary Sources

Ackinclose, Timothy. *Sabres & Pistols: The Civil War Career of Colonel Harry Gilmor, C.S.A.* Gettysburg, PA: Stan Clark Military Books, 1997.

Albaugh, William A., III, and Edward N. Simmons. *Confederate Arms.* New York: Bonanza Books, 1957.

Ambrose, Stephen E. *Crazy Horse and Custer: The Parallel Lives of Two American Warriors.* Garden City, NY: Doubleday, 1975.

Andrews, J. Cutler. *The South Reports the Civil War.* Princeton: Princeton University Press, 1970.

Basler, Roy P., ed. *The Collected Works of Abraham Lincoln.* 9 vols. New Brunswick, NJ: Rutgers University Press, 1953.

Bergeron, Arthur W., Jr. "John Horace Forney." In *The Confederate General,* ed. William C. Davis, 2:134–35. National Historical Society Publications, 1991.

Blair, William A. "The Seven Days and the Radical Persuasion: Convincing Moderates in the North of the Need for a Hard War." In *The Richmond Campaign of 1862: The Peninsula & the Seven Days,* ed. Gary W. Gallagher, 153–80. Chapel Hill: University of North Carolina Press, 2000.

Boatner, Mark M., III. *The Civil War Dictionary.* New York: David McKay Company, 1959.

Bohannon, Keith S. "Dirty, Ragged, and Ill-Provided For: Confederate Logistical Problems in the 1862 Maryland Campaign and Their Solutions." In *The Antietam Campaign,* ed. Gary W. Gallagher, 101–42. Chapel Hill: University of North Carolina Press, 1999.

———. "One Solid Unbroken Roar of Thunder: Union and Confederate Artillery at the Battle of Malvern Hill." In *The Richmond Campaign of 1862: The Peninsula & the Seven Days,* ed. Gary W. Gallagher, 217–49. Chapel Hill: University of North Carolina Press, 2000.

Bridges, David P. *Fighting with Jeb Stuart: Major James Breathed and the Confederate Horse Artillery.* Arlington, VA: Breathed Bridges Best, Inc., 2006.

Bridges, Hal. *Lee's Maverick General: Daniel Harvey Hill.* Lincoln: University of Nebraska Press, 1961.

Bushong, Millard K. *Old Jube: A Biography of General Jubal A. Early.* Boyce, VA: Carr Publishing, 1955.

Bushong, Millard Kessler, and Dean McKuin Bushong. *Fightin' Tom Rosser, C.S.A.* Shippensburg, PA: Beidel Printing House, 1983.

Calkins, Chris M. *The Appomattox Campaign, March 29–April 9, 1865.* Conshohocken, PA: Combined Books, 1997.

Carmichael, Peter S. *Lee's Young Artillerist: William R. J. Pegram.* Charlottesville: University Press of Virginia, 1995.

———. *The Purcell, Crenshaw and Letcher Artillery.* Lynchburg, VA: H. E. Howard, 1990.

Catton, Bruce. *The Army of the Potomac: Glory Road.* Garden City, NY: Doubleday, 1952.

Chambers, Lenoir. *Stonewall Jackson.* 2 vols. New York: William Morrow, 1959.

The Civil War. Lee Takes Command: From Seven Days to Second Bull Run. Alexandria, VA: Time-Life Books, 1984.

The Civil War. Rebels Resurgent: Fredericksburg to Chancellorsville. Alexandria, VA: Time-Life Books, 1984.

Cleaves, Freeman. *Meade of Gettysburg.* Norman: University of Oklahoma Press, 1960.

Clemmer, Gregg S. *Valor in Gray: The Recipients of the Confederate Medal of Honor.* Staunton, VA: Hearthside Publishing, 1998.

Coco, Gregory A. *A Vast Sea of Misery: A History and Guide to the Union and Confederate Field Hospitals at Gettysburg, July 1–November 20, 1863.* Gettysburg, PA: Thomas Publications, 1988.

Commager, Henry Steele, ed. *The Civil War Archive: The History of the Civil War in Documents.* New York: Black Dog and Leventhal, 2000.

The Congressional Medal of Honor: The Names, the Deeds. Forest Ranch, CA: Sharp and Dunnigan, 1984.

Cowley, Robert, and Thomas Guinzburg, eds. *West Point: Two Centuries of Honor and Tradition.* New York: Warner Books, 2002.

Cullum, George W. *Biographical Register of the Officers and Graduates of the U.S. Military Academy at West Point, New York since Its Establishment in 1802.* New York: J. F. Trow, Printer.

Daughtry, Mary Bandy. *Gray Cavalier: The Life and Wars of General W. H. F. "Rooney" Lee.* Cambridge, MD: Da Capo Press, 2002.

Davis, Burke. *Jeb Stuart: The Last Cavalier.* New York: Bonanza Books, 1957.

Davis, William C. *Battle of Bull Run: A History of the First Major Campaign of the Civil War.* Garden City, NY: Doubleday, 1977.

———, ed. *The Confederate General.* 6 vols. National Historical Society Publications, 1991.

Driver, Robert J., Jr. *The 1st and 2nd Rockbridge Artillery.* Lynchburg, VA: H. E. Howard, 1987.

———. *5th Virginia Cavalry.* Lynchburg, VA: H. E. Howard, 1997.

———. *The Staunton Artillery—McClanahan's Battery.* Lynchburg, VA: H. E. Howard, 1988.

Dufour, Charles L. *Gentle Tiger: The Gallant Life of Roberdeau Wheat.* Baton Rouge: Louisiana State University Press, 1957.

Eisenhower, John S. D. *Agent of Destiny: The Life and Times of General Winfield Scott.* Norman: University of Oklahoma Press, 1997.

Esposito, Vincent J., ed. *The West Point Atlas of American Wars.* 2 vols. New York: Praeger, 1959.

Faust, Patricia L., ed. *Historical Times Illustrated Encyclopedia of the Civil War.* New York: Harper and Row, 1986.

Foote, Shelby. *The Civil War: A Narrative.* 3 vols. New York: Random House, 1958.

Freeman, Douglas Southall. *Lee's Lieutenants: A Study in Command.* 3 vols. New York: Charles Scribner's Sons, 1944.

———. *R. E. Lee: A Biography.* 4 vols. New York: Charles Scribner's Sons, 1934.

Gallagher, Gary W., ed. *The Antietam Campaign.* Chapel Hill: University of North Carolina Press, 1999.

———. *The Fredericksburg Campaign: Decision on the Rappahannock.* Chapel Hill: University of North Carolina Press, 1995.

———. *The Richmond Campaign of 1862: The Peninsula & the Seven Days.* Chapel Hill: University of North Carolina Press, 2000.

———. *Stephen Dodson Ramseur: Lee's Gallant General.* Chapel Hill: University of North Carolina Press, 1985.

Govan, Gilbert E., and James W. Livingwood. *General Joseph E. Johnston, C.S.A.: A Different Valor.* New York: Bobbs-Merrill, 1956.

Hassler, Warren W., Jr. *Commanders of the Army of the Potomac.* Baton Rouge: Louisiana State University Press, 1962.

Hassler, William Woods. *Colonel John Pelham: Lee's Boy Artillerist.* Richmond, VA: Garrett and Massie, 1960.

Hatch, Thom. *Clashes of Cavalry: The Civil War Careers of George Armstrong Custer and Jeb Stuart.* Mechanicsville, PA: Stackpole Books, 2001.

Henderson, G. F. R. *Stonewall Jackson and the American Civil War.* 2 vols. 1898. Reprint. Secaucus, NJ: Blue and Grey Press.

Hennessy, John J. *Return to Bull Run: The Campaign and Battle of Second Manassas.* New York: Simon and Schuster, 1993.

Hodges, Elizabeth M. *C. B. Fleet: The Man and the Company.* Lynchburg, VA: Lynchburg Bicentennial, 1986.

Holland, Lynwood M. *Pierce M. B. Young: The Warwick of the South.* Athens: University of Georgia Press, 1964.

Johnson, Clint. *In the Footsteps of J. E. B. Stuart.* Winston-Salem, NC: John F. Blair, 2003.

Johnson, Curt, and Richard C. Anderson Jr. *Artillery Hell: The Employment of Artillery at Antietam.* With the 1940 report by Joseph Mills Hanson. College Station: Texas A & M University Press, 1995.

Jones, Terry L. *Lee's Tigers: The Louisiana Infantry in the Army of Northern Virginia.* Baton Rouge: Louisiana State University Press, 1987.

Jones, Virgil Carrington. *Gray Ghosts and Rebel Raiders.* New York: Henry Holt and Company, 1956.

———. *Ranger Mosby.* Chapel Hill: University of North Carolina Press, 1944.

Kirshner, Ralph. *The Class of 1861: Custer, Ames, and Their Classmates after West Point.* Carbondale: Southern Illinois University Press, 1999.

Klein, Maury. *Edward Porter Alexander.* Athens: University of Georgia Press, 1971.

Krick, Robert E. L. "Defending Lee's Flank: J. E. B. Stuart, John Pelham, and Confederate Artillery on Nicodemus Heights." In *The Antietam Campaign,* ed. Gary W. Gallagher, 192–222. Chapel Hill: University of North Carolina Press, 1999.

———. "The Men Who Carried This Position Were Soldiers Indeed: The Decisive Charge of Whiting's Division at Gaines's Mill." In *The Richmond Campaign of 1862: The Peninsula & the Seven Days,* ed. Gary W. Gallagher, 181–216. Chapel Hill: University of North Carolina Press, 2000.

———. "Sleepless in the Saddle: Stonewall Jackson in the Seven Days." In *The Richmond Campaign of 1862: The Peninsula & the Seven Days,* ed. Gary W. Gallagher, 66–95. Chapel Hill: University of North Carolina Press, 2000.

———. *Staff Officers in Gray: A Biographical Register of the Staff Officers in the Army of Northern Virginia.* Chapel Hill: University of North Carolina Press, 2003.

Krick, Robert K. *Lee's Colonels: A Biographical Register of the Field Officers of the Army of Northern Virginia.* Dayton, OH: Morningside Press, 1979.

———. "Thomas Lafayette Rosser." In *The Confederate General,* ed. William C. Davis, 5:112–15. National Historical Society Publications, 1991.

Lewis, Thomas A. *The Guns of Cedar Creek.* New York: Harper and Row, 1988.

Longacre, Edward G. *Fitz Lee: A Military Biography of Major General Fitzhugh Lee, C.S.A.* Cambridge, MD: Da Capo Press, 2005.

———. *Lee's Cavalrymen: A History of the Mounted Forces of the Army of Northern Virginia.* Mechanicsburg, PA: Stackpole Books, 2002.

———. *The Man behind the Guns: A Biography of General Henry Jackson Hunt, Chief of Artillery, Army of the Potomac.* New York: A. S. Barnes and Company, 1977.

———. *Mounted Raids of the Civil War.* New York: A. S. Barnes and Company, 1975.

Lord, Francis A. *Civil War Collector's Encyclopedia: Arms, Uniforms, and Equipment of the Union and Confederacy.* Harrisburg, PA: The Stackpole Company, 1963.

Malone, Dumas, ed. *Dictionary of American Biography.* New York: Charles Scribner's Sons, 1934.

McKee, W. Reid, and M. E. Mason Jr. *Civil War Projectiles II: Small Arms and Field Artillery.* Moss Publications, 1980.

McMurry, Richard M. *John Bell Hood and the War for Southern Independence.* Lincoln: University of Nebraska Press, 1982.

Mercer, Philip. *The Gallant Pelham.* Macon, GA: J. W. Burke Company, 1929.

Milham, Charles G. *Gallant Pelham: American Extraordinary.* Washington, DC: Public Affairs Press, 1959.

Mitchell, Betty L. *Edmund Ruffin: A Biography.* Bloomington: Indiana University Press, 1981.

Moe, Richard. *The Last Full Measure: The Life and Death of the First Minnesota Volunteers.* New York: Henry Holt and Company, 1993.

Monaghan, Jay. *Custer: The Life of General George Armstrong Custer.* Lincoln: University of Nebraska Press, 1959.

Moore, Robert H., II. *The 1st and 2nd Stuart Horse Artillery.* Lynchburg, VA: H. E. Howard, 1985.

Murfin, James V. *The Gleam of Bayonets: The Battle of Antietam and the Maryland Campaign of 1862.* New York: Bonanza Books, 1965.

Naisawald, L. Van Loan. *Grape and Canister: The Story of the Field Artillery of the Army of the Potomac, 1861–1865.* Washington, DC: Zenger Publishing, 1960.

Nanzig, Thomas P. *3rd Virginia Cavalry.* Lynchburg, VA: H. E. Howard, 1989.

Nolan, Alan T. *The Iron Brigade: A Military History.* Berrien Springs, MI: Hardscrabble Books, 1983.

O'Reilly, Francis Augustin. *The Fredericksburg Campaign: "Stonewall" Jackson at Fredericksburg, The Battle of Prospect Hill, December 13, 1862.* Lynchburg, VA: H. E. Howard, 1993.

———. *The Fredericksburg Campaign: Winter War on the Rappahannock.* Baton Rouge: Louisiana State University Press, 2003.

Pfanz, Donald C. *Richard S. Ewell: A Soldier's Life.* Chapel Hill: University of North Carolina Press, 1998.

Pfanz, Harry W. *Gettysburg: The Second Day.* Chapel Hill: University of North Carolina Press, 1987.

Priest, John M. *Antietam: The Soldiers' Battle.* New York: Oxford University Press, 1989.

Rable, George C. *Fredericksburg! Fredericksburg!* Chapel Hill: University of North Carolina Press, 2002.

———. "'It Is Well That War Is So Terrible': The Carnage of Fredericksburg." In *The Fredericksburg Campaign: Decision on the Rappahannock,* ed. Gary W. Gallagher, 48–79. Chapel Hill: University of North Carolina Press, 1995.

Randall, J. G., and David Donald. *The Civil War and Reconstruction.* Boston: C. C. Heath and Company, 1961.

Ripley, Warren. *Artillery and Ammunition of the Civil War.* New York: Van Nostrand Reinhold Company, 1970.

Robertson, James I., Jr. *General A. P. Hill: The Story of a Confederate Warrior.* New York: Random House, 1987.

———. *The Stonewall Brigade.* Baton Rouge: Louisiana State University Press, 1963.

———. *Stonewall Jackson: The Man, the Soldier, the Legend.* New York: MacMillan, 1997.

Scheel, Eugene M. *Culpeper: A Virginia County's History through 1920.* Orange, VA: Green Publishing, 1982.

Sears, Stephen W. *George B. McClellan: The Young Napoleon.* New York: Ticknor and Fields, 1988.

——. *Landscape Turned Red: The Battle of Antietam.* New York: Ticknor and Fields, 1983.

——. *To the Gates of Richmond: The Peninsula Campaign.* New York: Ticknor and Fields, 1992.

Sergent, Mary Elizabeth. *Growing Up in Alabama.* Middletown, NY: Prior King Press, 1988.

——. *They Lie Forgotten: The United States Military Academy, 1856–1861, Together with a Class Album for the Class of May, 1861.* Middletown, NY: Prior King Press, 1986.

Simpson, Brooks D. "General McClellan's Bodyguard: The Army of the Potomac after Antietam." In *The Antietam Campaign,* ed. Gary W. Gallagher, 44–73. Chapel Hill: University of North Carolina Press, 1999.

Sommers, Richard J. "William Henry Forney." In *The Confederate General,* ed. William C. Davis, 2:136–37. National Historical Society Publications, 1991.

Stackpole, Edward J. *Drama on the Rappahannock: The Fredericksburg Campaign.* New York: Bonanza Books, 1957.

Starr, Stephen Z. *The Union Cavalry in the Civil War.* 3 vols. Baton Rouge: Louisiana State University Press, 1979.

Sword, Wiley. *Embrace an Angry Wind; The Confederacy's Last Hurrah: Spring Hill, Franklin, and Nashville.* New York: Harper Collins, 1992.

Symonds, Craig L. *A Battlefield Atlas of the Civil War.* Baltimore: Nautical and Aviation Publishing Company of America, 1983.

Thomas, Emory M. *Bold Dragoon: The Life of J. E. B. Stuart.* New York: Harper and Row, 1986.

Thomason, John W., Jr. *Jeb Stuart.* New York: Charles Scribner's Sons, 1930.

Trout, Robert J. *Galloping Thunder: The Stuart Horse Artillery Battalion.* Mechanicsville, PA: Stackpole Books, 2002.

——. *"The Hoss": Officer Biographies and Rosters of the Stuart Horse Artillery Battalion.* Jebflo Press, 2003.

——. *They Followed the Plume: The Story of J. E. B. Stuart and His Staff.* Mechanicsburg, PA: Stackpole Books, 1993.

——. *With Pen & Saber: The Letters and Diaries of J. E. B. Stuart's Staff Officers.* Mechanicsburg, PA: Stackpole Books, 1995.

Tucker, Glenn. *High Tide at Gettysburg.* Dayton, OH: Morningside Bookshop, 1973.

Vandiver, Frank E. *Mighty Stonewall.* New York: McGraw-Hill, 1957.

Warner, Ezra J. *Generals in Blue: Lives of the Union Commanders.* Baton Rouge: Louisiana State University Press, 1964.

——. *Generals in Gray: Lives of the Confederate Commanders.* Baton Rouge: Louisiana State University Press, 1959.

Waugh, John C. *The Class of 1846: From West Point to Appomattox, Stonewall Jackson, George McClellan and Their Brothers.* New York: Warner Books, 1994.

Wellman, Manley Wade. *Giant in Gray: A Biography of Wade Hampton of South Carolina.* New York: Charles Scribner's Sons, 1949.

Welsh, Jack D., MD. *Medical Histories of Confederate Generals.* Kent, OH: Kent State University Press, 1995.

——. *Medical Histories of Union Generals.* Kent, OH: Kent State University Press, 1996.

Wert, Jeffry D. *Cavalryman of the Lost Cause: A Biography of J. E. B. Stuart.* New York: Simon and Schuster, 2008.

——. *Custer: The Controversial Life of George Armstrong Custer.* New York: Simon and Schuster, 1996.

——. *General James Longstreet: The Confederacy's Most Controversial Soldier, a Biography.* New York: Simon and Schuster, 1993.

———. "James Ewell Brown Stuart." In *The Confederate General,* ed. William C. Davis, 6:18–23. National Historical Society Publications, 1991.

Wiley, Bell Irvin. *The Life of Johnny Reb: The Common Soldier of the Confederacy.* Indianapolis: Bobbs-Merrill, 1943.

Williams, Kenneth P. *Lincoln Finds a General: A Military Study of the Civil War.* 5 vols. New York: MacMillan, 1949–59.

Williams, T. Harry. *Lincoln and His Generals.* New York: Alfred A. Knopf, 1952.

Winslow, Richard Elliott, III. *General John Sedgwick: The Story of a Union Corps Commander.* Novato, CA: Presidio Press, 1982.

Wise, Jennings Cropper. *The Long Arm of Lee: The History of the Artillery of the Army of Northern Virginia.* 2 vols. Lynchburg, VA: J. P. Bell Company, 1915.

Periodicals and Other Materials

"Account of John Pelham's Funeral." *The Cannoneer* 8, no. 5 (n.d). www.gallantpelham.org/.

"Address of Major H. B. McClellan, of Lexington, Ky., on the Life, Campaigns, and Character of Gen. J. E. B. Stuart." *Southern Historical Society Papers* 8 (October 27, 1880): 433–56.

Aimone, Alan, and Barbara Aimone. "Much to Sadden—and Little to Cheer: The Civil War Years at West Point." *Blue & Gray Magazine* 9, no. 2 (1991): 12–28, 48–64.

Almond, Col. Barrie. "Captain Lewis Guy Phillips." *The Cannoneer* 11, no. 3 (November 1992).

———. "Captain Guy Lewis Phillips." *The Cannoneer* 25, no. 11 (Summer 2006).

Ambrose, Stephen E. "The War Comes to West Point." *Civil War Times Illustrated* 4, no. 5 (August 1965): 32–38.

Averell, William W. "With the Cavalry on the Peninsula." In *Battles and Leaders of the Civil War,* 2:429–33. New York: Castle Books, 1956.

"The Battle of Fredericksburg" (papers of Gen. E. P. Alexander). *Southern Historical Society Papers* 10 (n.d.): 382–92.

Beauregard, P. G. T. "The First Battle of Bull Run." In *Battles and Leaders of the Civil War,* 1:196–227. New York: Castle Books, 1956.

Brooksher, William R., and David K. Snider. "Around McClellan Again." *Civil War Times Illustrated* 13, no. 5 (August 1974): 5–8, 39–48.

———. "Stuart's Ride: The Great Circuit around McClellan." *Civil War Times Illustrated* 12, no. 1 (April 1973): 4–10, 40–47.

Cardwell, David. "A Horse Battery." *Confederate Veteran* (November–December 1988): 6–7.

"Characteristics of Jackson as Described by his Chief Surgeon, Dr. Hunter McGuire." *Southern Historical Society Papers* 19 (n.d.): 298–318.

Chiles, Paul. "Artillery Hell! The Guns of Antietam." *Blue & Gray Magazine* 16, no. 2 (1999): 6–25, 41, 43–59.

Coffin, Charles Carleton. "Antietam Scenes." In *Battles and Leaders of the Civil War,* 2:682–85. New York: Castle Books, 1956.

Colgrove, Silas. "The Finding of Lee's Lost Orders." In *Battles and Leaders of the Civil War,* 2:603. New York: Castle Books, 1956.

Couch, Darius N. "Sumner's 'Right Grand Division.'" In *Battles and Leaders of the Civil War,* 3:105–20. New York: Castle Books, 1956.

Cox, Edwin P. "On the Occasion of the Presentation of a Portrait of 'The Gallant Pelham,' to R. E. Lee Camp Confederate Veterans." *Southern Historical Society Papers* 26 (December 16, 1899): 293–95.

Custer, George Armstrong. "War Memoirs: Was the Battle of Bull Run a National Disaster?" *Galaxy* (May 1876): 627–28.

Dabney, F. Y. "General Johnston to the Rescue." In *Battles and Leaders of the Civil War,* 2:275–76. New York: Castle Books, 1956.

Dasinger, Norman Roy, Jr. "The Gallant Pelham." *Confederate Veteran* (November–December 1988).

"Death of James B. Gordon." From the Charlotte *Observer,* January 8, 1902. *Southern Historical Society Papers* 29: 139–44.

Douglas, Henry Kyd. "Stonewall Jackson in Maryland." In *Battles and Leaders of the Civil War,* 2:620–29. New York: Castle Books, 1956.

The Dunker Church: Antietam National Battle Site. Department of the Interior, National Park Service.

"'Evelyn's' Report on Pelham's Death." *The Cannoneer* 11, no. 5 (n.d). *www.gallantpelham.org/.*

"Extracts from T. R. R. Cobb's Letters to His Wife (Feb. 3, 1861–Dec. 10, 1862)." *Southern Historical Society Papers* 27: 280–303.

"Field Letters from Stuart's Headquarters." *Southern Historical Society Papers* 3 (n.d.): 191–93.

Fleming, Thomas. "Band of Brothers." *MHQ: The Quarterly Journal of Military History* (The Civil War: A Special Issue, 1994): 24–33.

Frayser, Richard E. "Stuart's Raid in Rear of the Army of the Potomac." *Southern Historical Society Papers* 11 (November 1883): 505–17.

"'The Gallant Pelham' and His Gun at Fredericksburg." Letter from Maj. H. B. McClellan. *Southern Historical Society Papers* 12 (n.d.): 466–70.

Goss, Warren Lee. "Campaigning to No Purpose: Recollections of a Private." In *Battles and Leaders of the Civil War,* 2:153–59. New York: Castle Books, 1956.

Grattan, George D. "The Battle of Boonsboro Gap or South Mountain." *Southern Historical Society Papers* 39 (n.d.): 31–44.

Hanson, Joseph Mills. "John Pelham." *Field Artillery Magazine* (1932): 161–77.

Hennessy, John J. "For All Anguish for Some Freedom: Fredericksburg in the War." *Blue & Gray Magazine* 22, no. 1 (Winter 2005): 6–20, 47–50.

———. "Stuart's Revenge." *Civil War Times Illustrated* 34, no. 2 (May/June 1995): 38–45.

Hill, Daniel H. "The Battle of South Mountain, or Boonsboro.'" In *Battles and Leaders of the Civil War,* 2:559–81. New York: Castle Books, 1956.

———. "Lee Attacks North of the Chickahominy." In *Battles and Leaders of the Civil War,* 2:347–62. New York: Castle Books, 1956.

———. "McClellan's Change of Base and Malvern Hill." In *Battles and Leaders of the Civil War,* 2:383–95. New York: Castle Books, 1956.

Horstman, James A. "The Brief But Legendary Career of Confederate Colonel John Pelham." *Military History* 24, no. 1 (March 2007): 13–14.

Hunter, Alexander. "Four Years in the Ranks." *Southern Historical Society Papers* 10 (n.d.): 503–12.

Irwin, Lt. Col. Richard B. "The Removal of McClellan." In *Battles and Leaders of the Civil War,* 3:102–4. New York: Castle Books, 1956.

Johnston, Joseph E. "Manassas to Seven Pines." In *Battles and Leaders of the Civil War,* 2:202–18. New York: Castle Books, 1956.

Jones, Wilbur D. "Ego, Carelessness, and Three Cigars: How Lee's Special Orders No. 191 Was Lost." *Journal of America's Military Past* 24, no. 1 (Spring 1997).

Krick, Robert K. "Maxcy Gregg, Political Extremist and Confederate General." *Civil War History* 19, no. 4 (1973): 3–23.

Lee, Stephen Dill. "The Second Battle of Manassas: A Reply to General Longstreet." *Southern Historical Society Papers* 6 (n.d.): 59–70.

Leese, Captain Douglas G. "John Pelham Operated by Tenets of Modern Military Operations." *The Artilleryman* 23, no. 1 (2001). www.artillerymanmagazine.com/.

"Letter from Major General [Henry] Heth." *Southern Historical Society Papers* 4 (June 1877): 151–60.

Longacre, Edward G. "All the Way Around." *Civil War Times Illustrated* 41, no. 3 (June 2002): 22–29, 59.

Longstreet, James. "The Battle of Fredericksburg." In *Battles and Leaders of the Civil War,* 3:70–85. New York: Castle Books, 1956.

———. "The Invasion of Maryland." In *Battles and Leaders of the Civil War,* 2:663–74. New York: Castle Books, 1956.

———. "Our March against Pope." In *Battles and Leaders of the Civil War,* 2:512–26. New York: Castle Books, 1956.

———. "The Seven Days Including Frayser's Farm." In *Battles and Leaders of the Civil War,* 2:396–405. New York: Castle Books, 1956.

Mason, W. Roy. "Marching on Manassas." In *Battles and Leaders of the Civil War,* 2:528–29. New York: Castle Books, 1956.

Matthews, Henry H. "General Lee Called Him 'The Gallant Pelham'—Records Prove His Bravery." From Richmond, Va., *Times-Dispatch,* March 29, 1908. *Southern Historical Society Papers* 38: 379–84.

———. "Recollections of Major James Breathed." *Southern Historical Society Papers* 30 (January 17, 1903): 346–54.

Maxwell, Jerry H. "A Knight and His Scoundrels: Rob Wheat and the Louisiana Tigers." *Lincoln Herald* 84, no. 2 (Summer 1981): 631–40.

———. "Willie Pegram: 'That Damned Little Man with the Specs.'" *Lincoln Herald* 90, no. 4 (1988): 134–39.

McClellan, George B. "From the Peninsula to Antietam." In *Battles and Leaders of the Civil War,* 2:545–55. New York: Castle Books, 1956.

———. "The Peninsular Campaign." In *Battles and Leaders of the Civil War,* 2:160–87. New York: Castle Books, 1956.

McGuire, Hunter. "Characteristics of Jackson as Described by His Chief Surgeon, Dr. Hunter McGuire." *Southern Historical Society Papers* 19 (n.d.): 298–317.

———. "Jackson's Career and Character." *Southern Historical Society Papers* 25 (n.d.): 91–112.

McLaws, Lafayette. "The Confederate Left at Fredericksburg." In *Battles and Leaders of the Civil War,* 3:86–94. New York: Castle Books, 1956.

McLemore, Jeff. "Reminiscences of Major John Pelham." *Confederate Veteran* 6 (September 1898).

Mertz, Gregory A. "'A Severe Day on All the Artillery': Stonewall Jackson's Artillerists and the Defense of the Confederate Right." *Regiments: A Journal of the American Civil War* 4, no 4 (1995): 70–99

Mewborn, Horace. "A Wonderful Exploit: Jeb Stuart's Ride around the Army of the Potomac, June 12–15, 1862." *Blue & Gray Magazine* 15, no. 6 (August 1998): 6–21, 46–54.

Moore, J. H. "With Jackson at Hamilton's Crossing." In *Battles and Leaders of the Civil War,* 3:139–41. New York: Castle Books, 1956.

Mosby, John S. "The Ride around McClellan." *Southern Historical Society Papers* 26 (May 22, 1898): 246–54.

Nye, Wilbur S. "How Stuart Re-crossed the Potomac." *Civil War Times Illustrated* 4, no. 9 (January 1966): 45–48.

O'Neill, Robert F. "Cavalry on the Peninsula: Fort Monroe to the Gates of Richmond, March to May, 1862." *Blue & Gray Magazine* 19, no. 5, special issue (2002): 6–22, 38–51.

"The Opposing Forces at Fredericksburg, Va." In *Battles and Leaders of the Civil War,* 3:143–47. New York: Castle Books, 1956.

O'Reilly, Frank A. "'Busted Up and Gone to Hell': The Assault of the Pennsylvania Reserves at Fredericksburg." *Civil War Regiments: A Journal of the American Civil War* 4, no. 4 (1995): 1–27.

O'Reilly, Frank A. "The Real Battle of Fredericksburg: Stonewall Jackson, Prospect Hill, and the Slaughter Pen." *Blue & Gray Magazine* 25, no. 5 (2008): 6–29, 44–50.

Pope, John. "The Second Battle of Bull Run." In *Battles and Leaders of the Civil War,* 2:449–94. New York: Castle Books, 1956.

Preston, David L. "'The Glorious Light Went Out Forever': The Death of Brig. Gen. Thomas R. R. Cobb." *Civil War Regiments: A Journal of the American Civil War* 4, no. 4 (1995): 28–46

Price, Channing. "Stuart's Chambersburg Raid: An Eyewitness Account." *Civil War Times Illustrated* 4, no. 9 (January 1966): 8–15, 42–48.

Randall, James R. "The Gallant Pelham: Jeb Stuart's 'Boy Artillerist from Alabama.'" *Southern Historical Society Papers* 30 (May 20, 1898): 338–45.

Redwood, Allen C. "Jackson's 'Foot Cavalry' at the Second Bull Run." In *Battles and Leaders of the Civil War,* 2:530–38. New York: Castle Books, 1956.

"Reminiscences of the Famous Leader by Dr. Hunter McGuire, Chief Surgeon of the Second Corps of the Army of Northern Virginia." *Southern Historical Society Papers* 19 (n.d.): 298–318.

Robins, Col. W. T. "Stuart's Ride around McClellan." In *Battles and Leaders of the Civil War,* 2:271–75. New York: Castle Books, 1956.

"Roll and Roster of Pelham's." *Southern Historical Society Papers* 30 (n.d.): 348–54.

Stackpole, Edward A. *The Battle of Fredericksburg.* Harrisburg, PA: Historical Times, 1965.

"Stuart's Correspondence to His Wife." *Southern Historical Society Papers* 8 (November 2, 1862): 433–56.

Sword, Wiley. "Cavalry on Trial at Kelly's Ford." *Civil War Times Illustrated* 13, no. 1 (1974): 32–40.

Thompson, David L. "In the Ranks to the Antietam." In *Battles and Leaders of the Civil War,* 2:556–58. New York: Castle Books, 1956.

Vogtsberger, Peggy. *The Cannoneer* 2, no. 3 (November 1983).

———. *The Cannoneer* 3, no. 6 (May 1985).

———. *The Cannoneer* 11, no. 1 (July 1992): 4.

———. *The Cannoneer,* special ed. (May 1999).

———. "How Artillerists Rated Pelham." *The Cannoneer* 4, no. 4 (n.d). www.gallantpelham.org/.

———. "The Mysteries of Kelly's Ford." *The Cannoneer* 5, no. 5 (July 1985): 2–4.

———. "Needless and Oppressive Seizure." *The Cannoneer* 10, no. 3 (n.d). www.gallantpelham.org/.

———. "Reminiscences of Emma Pelham Hank." *The Cannoneer* 2, no. 6 (n.d). www.gallantpelham.org/.

———. "The Ten Days." *The Cannoneer* 1, nos. 4 and 5 (n.d). www.gallantpelham.org/.

———. "The West Point John Pelham Knew." *The Cannoneer* 4, no. 3 (November 1985): 9–14.

Walker, John G. "Jackson's Capture of Harper's Ferry." In *Battles and Leaders of the Civil War,* 2:604–11. New York: Castle Books, 1956.

———. "Sharpsburg." In *Battles and Leaders of the Civil War,* 2:675–82. New York: Castle Books, 1956.

White, Julius. "The Capitulation of Harper's Ferry." In *Battles and Leaders of the Civil War,* 2:612–15. New York: Castle Books, 1956.

"With Stonewall Jackson—Chapter 5—Fredericksburg." *Southern Historical Society Papers* 43 (n.d.): 27–43.

Young, Jennifer. "Shoemaker's Battery, Stuart Horse Artillery, Pelham's Battalion." *The Cannoneer* 2, no. 3 (n.d.). www.gallantpelham.org/.

Newspapers

Alabama Christian Advocate
Anniston Evening Star
Anniston Hot Blast
Anniston Republican
Anniston Star
Anniston Star, 75th anniversary edition (1957)
Arkansas Gazette
Atlanta Confederacy
Atlanta Constitution
Atlanta, Georgia News
Birmingham News
Birmingham News-Age Herald
Birmingham Post-Herald
Daily Tribune News (Cartersville, GA)
Houston, Texas Journal
Jacksonville Republican
London Times
Mobile Advertiser and Register
Montgomery Advertiser
New York Times
Philadelphia Inquirer
Philadelphia Weekly Times
Piedmont Inquirer
Richmond Daily Dispatch
Richmond Daily Examiner
Richmond Enquirer
Richmond Sentinel
Richmondthenandnow.com/Newspaper
Richmond Times-Dispatch
Richmond Whig
St. Mary's Beacon
Sunny South, Atlanta, GA, 1896

Index